Expert C++

Become a proficient programmer by learning coding best practices with C++17 and C++20's latest features

Vardan Grigoryan
Shunguang Wu

BIRMINGHAM - MUMBAI

Expert C++

Commissioning Editor: Richa Tripathi
Acquisition Editor: Denim Pinto
Content Development Editor: Pathikrit Roy
Senior Editor: Rohit Singh
Technical Editor: Romy Dias
Copy Editor: Safis Editing
Project Coordinator: Francy Puthiry
Proofreader: Safis Editing
Indexer: Tejal Daruwale Soni
Production Designer: Alishon Mendonsa

First published: April 2020

Production reference: 1100420

Published by Packt Publishing Ltd.
Livery Place
35 Livery Street
Birmingham
B3 2PB, UK.

ISBN 978-1-83855-265-7

www.packt.com

To my mother, Karine, and to my little princess, Leia, for their encouragement and support.

–

Vardan Grigoryan

To my wife, Wen, and to my sons, Justin and Zachary.

- Shunguang Wu

Packt.com

Subscribe to our online digital library for full access to over 7,000 books and videos, as well as industry leading tools to help you plan your personal development and advance your career. For more information, please visit our website.

Why subscribe?

- Spend less time learning and more time coding with practical eBooks and Videos from over 4,000 industry professionals
- Improve your learning with Skill Plans built especially for you
- Get a free eBook or video every month
- Fully searchable for easy access to vital information
- Copy and paste, print, and bookmark content

Did you know that Packt offers eBook versions of every book published, with PDF and ePub files available? You can upgrade to the eBook version at `www.packt.com` and as a print book customer, you are entitled to a discount on the eBook copy. Get in touch with us at `customercare@packtpub.com` for more details.

At `www.packt.com`, you can also read a collection of free technical articles, sign up for a range of free newsletters, and receive exclusive discounts and offers on Packt books and eBooks.

Contributors

About the authors

Vardan Grigoryan is a senior backend engineer and C++ developer with more than 9 years of experience. Vardan started his career as a C++ developer and then moved to the world of server-side backend development. While being involved in designing scalable backend architectures, he always tries to incorporate the use of C++ in critical sections that require the fastest execution time. Vardan loves tackling computer systems and program structures on a deeper level. He believes that true excellence in programming can be achieved by means of a detailed analysis of existing solutions and by designing complex systems.

Shunguang Wu is a senior professional staff at Johns Hopkins University Applied Physics Laboratory, and received his PhDs in theoretical physics and electrical engineering from Northwestern University (China) and Wright State University (USA), respectively. He published about 50 reviewed journal papers in the area of nonlinear dynamics, statistical signal processing and computer vision in his early career. His professional C++ experience started with teaching undergraduate courses in the late 1990s. Since then he has been designing and developing lots of R&D and end-user application software using C++ in world-class academic and industrial laboratories. These projects span both the Windows and Linux platforms.

About the reviewers

Lou Mauget learned to program long ago at Michigan State University as a physics major, learning to use software in designing a cyclotron. Afterward, he worked for 34 years at IBM. He is currently consulting for Keyhole Software of Leawood, Kansas. Lou has coded in C++, Java, JavaScript, Python, and newer languages, as each was conceived. Current interests include reactive functional programming, containers, Node.js, NoSQL, geospatial systems, mobile, and any new language or framework. He has coauthored three computer books. He has written two IBM DeveloperWorks XML tutorials and co-written several J2EE certification tests for IBM. He has been a reviewer for Packt Publishing and others.

Scott Hutchinson leads a team of C++ and F# developers in Oxnard, California. After a few years as a VB/VBA developer, he started developing with .NET Framework immediately after its launch in 2002. Since 2016, he has done most of his development in C++. He is a mentor for the F# track on Exercism, and teaches functional programming in F# to his team at work. His main professional interests are functional programming and machine learning. When he's not learning some new software development skill, he's usually hiking in the mountains of Southern California.

Packt is searching for authors like you

If you're interested in becoming an author for Packt, please visit `authors.packtpub.com` and apply today. We have worked with thousands of developers and tech professionals, just like you, to help them share their insight with the global tech community. You can make a general application, apply for a specific hot topic that we are recruiting an author for, or submit your own idea.

Table of Contents

Preface

This book will provide readers with details of C++ programs with regard to the C++17 and C++20 standards, and how they are compiled, linked, and executed. It will also cover how memory management works, what the best practices are as regards memory management problems, what classes are and how they are implemented, how a compiler optimizes code, and what the compiler's approach is in terms of supporting class inheritance, virtual functions, and templates.

The book will also tell readers how to apply memory management, object-oriented programming, concurrency, and design patterns to create world-ready production applications.

Readers will learn the inner details of efficient data structures and algorithms, and will understand how to measure and compare them to choose what fits best for a specific problem.

This book will help readers to incorporate system design skills with essential design patterns into C++ applications.

By way of a bonus, the book also provides an introduction into the AI world, including machine learning basics using the C++ programming language.

By the end of this book, readers should be confident enough to design and architect real-world, scalable C++ applications using efficient data structures and algorithms.

Who this book is for

C++ developers seeking to find details relating to the language and program structure, or who are trying to advance their expertise by digging into the essence of programs to design reusable, scalable architectures, will benefit from this book. Those developers who are intending to design efficient data structures and algorithms using the new features of C++17 and C++20 will also benefit.

What this book covers

`Chapter 1`, *Introduction to Building C++ Applications*, contains an introduction to the C++ world, its applications, and recent updates to the language standard. This chapter also includes a good overview of the topics covered by C++ and an introduction to the code compilation, linking, and execution phases.

`Chapter 2`, *Low-Level Programming with C++*, focuses on a discussion of C++ data types, arrays, pointers, and addressing and manipulation with pointers, along with low-level details of conditionals, loops, functions, function pointers, and structs. This chapter also includes an introduction to structures (structs).

`Chapter 3`, *Details of Object-Oriented Programming*, dives into the structure of classes and objects, and how a compiler implements object lifetimes. By the end of this chapter, the reader will understand the implementation details of inheritance and virtual functions, as well as the essential inner details of OOP in C++.

`Chapter 4`, *Understanding and Designing Templates*, introduces C++ templates, examples of template functions, template classes, template specialization, and template meta-programming in general. Traits and meta-programming will incorporate the magic in C++ applications.

`Chapter 5`, *Memory Management and Smart Pointers*, dives into the details of memory sections, allocation, and management in general, including the use of smart pointers to avoid potential memory leaks.

`Chapter 6`, *Digging into Data Structures and Algorithms in STL*, introduces data structures and their STL implementation. This chapter also includes a comparison of data structures and a discussion of proper applications with real-world examples.

`Chapter 7`, *Functional Programming*, focuses on functional programming, which is a different programming paradigm, allowing readers to concentrate on the "functional" rather than the "physical" structure of the code. Mastering functional programming provides developers with a new skill that helps to offer even better solutions to problems.

`Chapter 8`, *Concurrency and Multithreading*, focuses on how to make your programs run faster by leveraging concurrency. When an efficient data structure with efficient algorithms hits the limits of program performance, concurrency comes to the rescue.

`Chapter 9`, *Designing Concurrent Data Structures*, focuses on leveraging data structures and concurrency to design lock-based and lock-free concurrent data structures.

`Chapter 10`, *Designing World-Ready Applications*, focuses on incorporating the knowledge acquired from previous chapters into designing robust real-world applications by using design patterns. This chapter also includes understanding and applying domain-driven design by designing an Amazon clone.

`Chapter 11`, *Designing a Strategy Game Using Design Patterns*, deals with incorporating the knowledge acquired from previous chapters into designing a strategy game by using design patterns and best practices.

`Chapter 12`, *Networking and Security*, introduces network programming in C++ and how to build a dropbox backend clone by leveraging network programming skills. This chapters also includes a discussion of how to ensure coding best practices.

`Chapter 13`, *Debugging and Testing*, focuses on debugging C++ applications and best practices to avoid bugs in code, applying static code analysis in order to reduce issues in the program, introduction, and application of test-driven development and behavior-driven development. This chapter also includes a discussion of the difference between behavior-driven development and TDD as well as use cases.

`Chapter 14`, *Graphical User Interface with Qt*, introduces the Qt library and its main components. This chapter also includes an understanding of the cross-platform nature of the Qt, continuing the dropbox example by building a simple desktop client.

`Chapter 15`, *Using C++ in Machine Learning Tasks*, deals with a brief introduction to the AI concepts and recent developments in the field. This chapter also includes an introduction to machine learning and tasks such as regression analysis and clustering, as well as how to build a simple neural network.

`Chapter 16`, *Implementing a Dialog-Based Search Engine*, deals with applying the knowledge of all previous chapters to design an efficient search engine described as *dialog-based* because it finds the right document by asking (and learning) the corresponding questions of the user.

To get the most out of this book

Basic C++ experience, including a familiarity with memory management, object-oriented programming, and basic data structures and algorithms, will be a big plus. If you have a yearning to learn how this complex program works under the hood, as well as a desire to understand the details of the programming concepts and best practices of C++ application design, then you should definitely proceed further with this book.

Software/hardware covered in the book	OS requirements
g++ compiler	Ubuntu Linux is a plus, but not a requirement

You will also need the Qt framework to be installed on your computer. Details are covered in the relevant chapter.

At the time of writing this book, not all C++ compilers were supporting all the new C++20 features, consider using the latest version of your compiler in order to test out more features introduced in the chapter.

Download the example code files

You can download the example code files for this book from your account at `www.packt.com`. If you purchased this book elsewhere, you can visit `www.packt.com/support` and register to have the files emailed directly to you.

You can download the code files by following these steps:

1. Log in or register at `www.packt.com`.
2. Select the **SUPPORT** tab.
3. Click on **Code Downloads & Errata**.
4. Enter the name of the book in the **Search** box and follow the onscreen instructions.

Once the file is downloaded, please make sure that you unzip or extract the folder using the latest version of:

- WinRAR/7-Zip for Windows
- Zipeg/iZip/UnRarX for Mac
- 7-Zip/PeaZip for Linux

The code bundle for the book is also hosted on GitHub at `https://github.com/PacktPublishing/Expert-CPP`. In case there's an update to the code, it will be updated on the existing GitHub repository.

We also have other code bundles from our rich catalog of books and videos available at `https://github.com/PacktPublishing/`. Check them out!

Download the color images

We also provide a PDF file that has color images of the screenshots/diagrams used in this book. You can download it here: `https://static.packt-cdn.com/downloads/9781838552657_ColorImages.pdf`

Conventions used

There are a number of text conventions used throughout this book.

`CodeInText`: Indicates code words in text, database table names, folder names, filenames, file extensions, pathnames, dummy URLs, user input, and Twitter handles. Here is an example: "The preceding code declares two `readonly` properties with preassigned values."

A block of code is set as follows:

```
Range book = 1..4;
var res = Books[book] ;
Console.WriteLine($"\tElement of array using Range: Books[{book}] =>
{Books[book]}");
```

When we wish to draw your attention to a particular part of a code block, the relevant lines or items are set in bold:

```
private static readonly int num1=5;
private static readonly int num2=6;
```

Any command-line input or output is written as follows:

```
dotnet --info
```

Bold: Indicates a new term, an important word, or words that you see on screen. For example, words in menus or dialog boxes appear in the text like this. Here is an example: "Select **System info** from the **Administration** panel."

Warnings or important notes appear like this.

Tips and tricks appear like this.

Get in touch

Feedback from our readers is always welcome.

General feedback: If you have questions about any aspect of this book, mention the book title in the subject of your message and email us at customercare@packtpub.com.

Errata: Although we have taken every care to ensure the accuracy of our content, mistakes do happen. If you have found a mistake in this book, we would be grateful if you would report this to us. Please visit www.packt.com/submit-errata, selecting your book, clicking on the Errata Submission Form link, and entering the details.

Piracy: If you come across any illegal copies of our works in any form on the internet, we would be grateful if you would provide us with the location address or website name. Please contact us at copyright@packt.com with a link to the material.

If you are interested in becoming an author: If there is a topic that you have expertise in, and you are interested in either writing or contributing to a book, please visit authors.packtpub.com.

Reviews

Please leave a review. Once you have read and used this book, why not leave a review on the site that you purchased it from? Potential readers can then see and use your unbiased opinion to make purchase decisions, we at Packt can understand what you think about our products, and our authors can see your feedback on their book. Thank you!

For more information about Packt, please visit packt.com.

1
Section 1: Under the Hood of C++ Programming

In this section, the reader will learn the details of C++ program compilation and linking, and dive into the details of **Object-Oriented Programming (OOP)**, templates, and memory management.

This section comprises the following chapters:

1
Introduction to Building C++ Applications

Programming languages differ by their program execution model; the most common are interpreted and compiled languages. Compilers translate source code into machine code, which a computer can run without intermediary support systems. Interpreted language code, on the other hand, requires support systems, interpreters, and the virtual environment to work.

C++ is a compiled language, which makes programs run faster than their interpreted counterparts. While C++ programs should be compiled for each platform, interpreted programs can operate cross-platform.

We are going to discuss the details of a program-building process, starting with the phases of processing the source code – done by the compiler- and ending with the details of the executable file (the compiler's output). We will also learn why a program built for one platform won't run on another one.

The following topics will be covered in this chapter:

- Introduction to C++20
- Details of the C++ preprocessor
- Under the hood of the source code compilation
- Understanding the linker and its functionality
- The process of loading and running an executable file

Technical requirements

The g++ compiler with the option `-std=c++2a` is used to compile the examples throughout the chapter. You can find the source files used in this chapter at `https://github.com/PacktPublishing/Expert-CPP`.

Introduction to C++20

C++ has evolved over the years and now it has a brand-new version, C++20. Since C++11, the C++ standard has grown the language feature set tremendously. Let's look at notable features in the new C++20 standard.

Concepts

Concepts are a major feature in C++20 that provides a set of requirements for types. The basic idea behind concepts is the compile-time validation of template arguments. For example, to specify that the template argument must have a default constructor, we use the `default_constructible` concept in the following way:

```
template <default_constructible T>
void make_T() { return T(); }
```

In the preceding code, we missed the `typename` keyword. Instead, we set a concept that describes the `T` parameter of the `template` function.

We can say that concepts are types that describe other types – meta-types, so to speak. They allow the compile-time validation of template parameters along with a function invocation based on type properties. We will discuss concepts in detail in `Chapter 3`, *Details of Object-Oriented Programming,* and `Chapter 4`, *Understanding and Designing Templates.*

Coroutines

Coroutines are special functions able to stop at any defined point of execution and resume later. Coroutines extend the language with the following new keywords:

- `co_await` suspends the execution of the coroutine.
- `co_yield` suspends the execution of the coroutine while also returning a value.

- `co_return` is similar to the regular `return` keyword; it finishes the coroutine and returns a value. Take a look at the following classic example:

```
generator<int> step_by_step(int n = 0) {
  while (true) {
    co_yield n++;
  }
}
```

A coroutine is associated with a `promise` object. The `promise` object stores and alerts the *state* of the coroutine. We will dive deeper into coroutines in `Chapter 8`, *Concurrency and Multithreading*.

Ranges

The `ranges` library provides a new way of working with ranges of elements. To use them, you should include the `<ranges>` header file. Let's look at `ranges` with an example. A range is a sequence of elements having a beginning and an end. It provides a `begin` iterator and an `end` sentinel. Consider the following vector of integers:

```
import <vector>

int main()
{
  std::vector<int> elements{0, 1, 2, 3, 4, 5, 6};
}
```

Ranges accompanied by range adapters (the `|` operator) provide powerful functionality to deal with a range of elements. For example, examine the following code:

```
import <vector>
import <ranges>

int main()
{
  std::vector<int> elements{0, 1, 2, 3, 4, 5, 6};
  for (int current : elements | ranges::view::filter([](int e) { return
   e % 2 == 0; }))
  {
    std::cout << current << " ";
  }
}
```

In the preceding code, we filtered the range for even integers using `ranges::view::filter()`. Pay attention to the range adapter `|` applied to the elements vector. We will discuss ranges and their powerful features in `Chapter 7`, *Functional Programming*.

More C++20 features

C++20 is a new big release of the C++ language. It contains many features that make the language more complex and flexible. **Concepts**, **ranges**, and **coroutines** are some of the many features that will be discussed throughout the book.

One of the most anticipated features is **modules**, which provide the ability to declare modules and export types and values within those modules. You can consider modules an improved version of header files with the now redundant include-guards. We'll cover C++20 modules in this chapter.

Besides notable features added in C++20, there is a list of other features that we will discuss throughout the book:

- The spaceship operator: `operator<=>()`. The verbosity of operator overloading can now be controlled by leveraging `operator<=>()`.
- `constexpr` conquers more and more space in the language. C++20 now has the `consteval` function, `constexpr std::vector` and `std::string`, and many more.
- Math constants, such as `std::number::pi` and `std::number::log2e`.
- Major updates to the Thread library, including stop tokens and joining threads.
- The iterator concepts.
- Move-only views and other features.

To better understand some new features and also dive into the essence of the language, we will introduce the language's core starting from previous versions. This will help us to find better uses for new features compared to older ones, and will also help in supporting legacy C++ code. Let's now start by gaining an understanding of the C++ application building-process.

Building and running programs

You can use any text editor to write code, because, ultimately, code is just text. To write code, you are free to choose between simple text editors such as *Vim*, or an advanced **integrated development environment** (**IDE**) such as *MS Visual Studio*. The only difference between a love letter and source code is that the latter might be interpreted by a special program called a **compiler** (while the love letter cannot be compiled into a program, it might give you butterflies in your stomach).

To mark the difference between a plain text file and source code, a special file extension is used. C++ operates with the `.cpp` and `.h` extensions (you may also occasionally encounter `.cxx` and `.hpp` as well). Before getting into the details, think of the compiler as a tool that translates the source code into a runnable program, known as an executable file or just an **executable**. The process of making an executable from the source code is called **compilation**. Compiling a C++ program is a sequence of complex tasks that results in machine code generation. **Machine code** is the native language of the computer— that's why it's called machine code.

Typically, a C++ compiler parses and analyzes the source code, then generates intermediate code, optimizes it, and finally, generates machine code in a file called an **object file**. You may have already encountered object files; they have individual extensions – `.o` in Linux and `.obj` in Windows. The created object file contains more than just machine code that can be run by the computer. Compilation usually involves several source files, and compiling each source file produces a separate object file. These object files are then linked together by a tool called the **linker** to form a single executable file. The linker uses additional information stored in object files to link them properly (linking will be discussed later in this chapter).

The following diagram depicts the program-building phases:

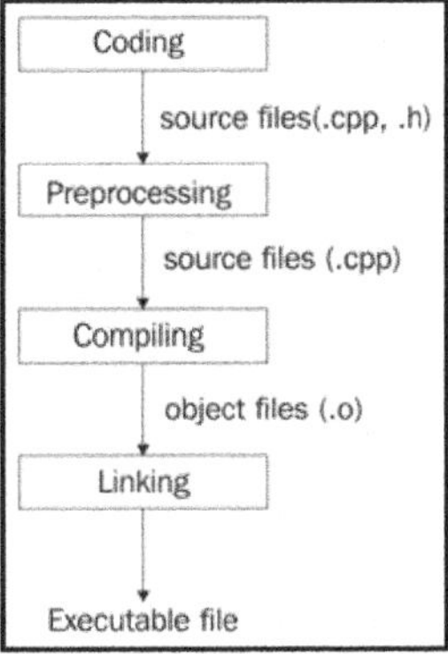

The C++ application-building process consists of three major steps: **preprocessing**, **compiling**, and **linking**. All of these steps are done using different tools, but modern compilers encapsulate them in a single tool, thereby providing a single and more straightforward interface for programmers.

The generated executable file persists on the hard drive of the computer. In order to run it, it should be copied to the main memory, the RAM. The copying is done by another tool, named the **loader**. The loader is a part of the operating system that knows what and where should be copied from the contents of the executable file. After loading the executable file to the main memory, the original executable file won't be deleted from the hard drive.

The loading and running of a program is done by the **operating system** (**OS**). The OS manages the execution of the program, prioritizes it over other programs, unloads it when it's done, and so on. The running copy of the program is called a **process**. A process is an instance of an executable file.

Understanding preprocessing

A **preprocessor** is intended to process source files to make them ready for compilation. A preprocessor works with preprocessor **directives**, such as `#define`, `#include`, and so on. Directives don't represent program statements, but they are commands for the preprocessor, telling it what to do with the text of the source file. The compiler cannot recognize those directives, so whenever you use preprocessor directives in your code, the preprocessor resolves them accordingly before the actual compilation of the code begins. For example, the following code will be changed before the compiler starts to compile it:

```
#define NUMBER 41
int main() {
  int a = NUMBER + 1;
  return 0;
}
```

Everything that is defined using the `#define` directive is called a **macro**. After preprocessing, the compiler gets the transformed source in this form:

```
int main() {
  int a = 41 + 1;
  return 0;
}
```

As already mentioned, the preprocessor is just processing the text and does not care about language rules or its syntax. Using preprocessor directives, especially macro definitions, as in the previous example, `#define NUMBER 41` is error-prone, unless you realize that the preprocessor simply replaces any occurrence of `NUMBER` with `41` without interpreting `41` as an integer. For the preprocessor, the following lines are both valid:

```
int b = NUMBER + 1;
struct T {}; // user-defined type
T t = NUMBER; // preprocessed successfully, but compile error
```

This produces the following code:

```
int b = 41 + 1
struct T {};
T t = 41; // error line
```

When the compiler starts compilation, it finds the assignment `t = 41` erroneous because there is `no viable conversion from 'int' to 'T'`.

It is even dangerous to use macros that are correct syntactically but have logical errors:

```
#define DOUBLE_IT(arg) (arg * arg)
```

The preprocessor will replace any occurrence of `DOUBLE_IT(arg)` with `(arg * arg)`, therefore the following code will output `16`:

```
int st = DOUBLE_IT(4);
std::cout << st;
```

The compiler will receive this code as follows:

```
int st = (4 * 4);
std::cout << st;
```

Problems arise when we use complex expressions as a macro argument:

```
int bad_result = DOUBLE_IT(4 + 1);
std::cout << bad_result;
```

Intuitively, this code will produce `25`, but the truth is that the preprocessor doesn't do anything but text processing, and in this case, it replaces the macro like this:

```
int bad_result = (4 + 1 * 4 + 1);
std::cout << bad_result;
```

This outputs `9`, and `9` is obviously not `25`.

To fix the macro definition, surround the macro argument with additional parentheses:

```
#define DOUBLE_IT(arg) ((arg) * (arg))
```

Now the expression will take this form:

```
int bad_result = ((4 + 1) * (4 + 1));
```

It is strongly suggested to use `const` declarations instead of macro definitions wherever applicable.

As a rule of thumb, avoid using macro definitions. Macros are error-prone and C++ provides a set of constructs that make the use of macros obsolete.

The same preceding example would be type-checked and processed at compile time if we used a `constexpr` function:

```
constexpr int double_it(int arg) { return arg * arg; }
int bad_result = double_it(4 + 1);
```

Use the `constexpr` specifier to make it possible to evaluate the return value of the function (or the value of a variable) at compile time. The example with the `NUMBER` definition would be better rewritten using a `const` variable:

```
const int NUMBER = 41;
```

Header files

The most common use of the preprocessor is the `#include` directive, intended to include header files in the source code. Header files contain definitions for functions, classes, and so on:

```
// file: main.cpp
#include <iostream>
#include "rect.h"
int main() {
  Rect r(3.1, 4.05)
  std::cout << r.get_area() << std::endl;
}
```

Let's suppose the header file `rect.h` is defined as follows:

```
// file: rect.h
struct Rect
{
private:
  double side1_;
  double side2_;
public:
  Rect(double s1, double s2);
  const double get_area() const;
};
```

The implementation is contained in `rect.cpp`:

```
// file: rect.cpp
#include "rect.h"

Rect::Rect(double s1, double s2)
  : side1_(s1), side2_(s2)
{}

const double Rect::get_area() const {
  return side1_ * side2_;
}
```

After the preprocessor examines `main.cpp` and `rect.cpp`, it replaces the `#include` directives with corresponding contents of `iostream` and `rect.h` for `main.cpp` and `rect.h` for `rect.cpp`. C++17 introduces the `__has_include` preprocessor constant expression. `__has_include` evaluates to `1` if the file with the specified name is found and `0` if not:

```
#if __has_include("custom_io_stream.h")
#include "custom_io_stream.h"
#else
#include <iostream>
#endif
```

When declaring header files, it's strongly advised to use so-called *include-guards* (`#ifndef, #define, #endif`) to avoid double declaration errors. We are going to introduce the technique shortly. Those are, again, preprocessor directives that allow us to avoid the following scenario: type `Square` is defined in `square.h`, which includes `rect.h` in order to derive `Square` from `Rect`:

```
// file: square.h
#include "rect.h"
struct Square : Rect {
```

```
  Square(double s);
};
```

Including both `square.h` and `rect.h` in `main.cpp` leads to including `rect.h` twice:

```
// file: main.cpp
#include <iostream>
#include "rect.h"
#include "square.h"
/*
  preprocessor replaces the following with the contents of square.h
*/
// code omitted for brevity
```

After preprocessing, the compiler will receive `main.cpp` in the following form:

```
// contents of the iostream file omitted for brevity
struct Rect {
  // code omitted for brevity
};
struct Rect {
  // code omitted for brevity
};
struct Square : Rect {
  // code omitted for brevity
};
int main() {
  // code omitted for brevity
}
```

The compiler will then produce an error because it encounters two declarations of type `Rect`. A header file should be guarded against multiple inclusions by using include-guards in the following way:

```
#ifndef RECT_H
#define RECT_H
struct Rect { ... }; // code omitted for brevity
#endif // RECT_H
```

When the preprocessor meets the header for the first time, `RECT_H` is not defined and everything between `#ifndef` and `#endif` will be processed accordingly, including the `RECT_H` definition. The second time the preprocessor includes the same header file in the same source file, it will omit the contents because `RECT_H` has already been defined.

These include-guards are part of directives that control the compilation of parts of the source file. All of the conditional compilation directives are `#if`, `#ifdef`, `#ifndef`, `#else`, `#elif`, and `#endif`.

Conditional compilation is useful in many cases; one of them is logging function calls in so-called **debug** mode. Before releasing the program, it is advised to debug your program and test against logical flaws. You might want to see what happens in the code after invoking a certain function, for example:

```
void foo() {
  log("foo() called");
  // do some useful job
}
void start() {
  log("start() called");
  foo();
  // do some useful job
}
```

Each function calls the `log()` function, which is implemented as follows:

```
void log(const std::string& msg) {
#if DEBUG
  std::cout << msg << std::endl;
#endif
}
```

The `log()` function will print the `msg` if `DEBUG` is defined. If you compile the project enabling `DEBUG` (using compiler flags, such as `-D` in g++), then the `log()` function will print the string passed to it; otherwise, it will do nothing.

Using modules in C++20

Modules fix header files with annoying include-guard issues. We can now get rid of preprocessor macros. Modules incorporate two keywords, `import` and `export`. To use a module, we `import` it. To declare a module with its exported properties, we use `export`. Before listing the benefits of using modules, let's look at a simple usage example. The following code declares a module:

```
export module test;

export int twice(int a) { return a * a; }
```

The first line declares the module named `test`. Next, we declared the `twice()` function and set it to `export`. This means that we can have functions and other entities that are not exported, thus, they will be private outside of the module. By exporting an entity, we set it `public` to `module` users. To use `module`, we import it as done in the following code:

```
import test;

int main()
{
  twice(21);
}
```

Modules are a long-awaited feature of C++ that provides better performance in terms of compilation and maintenance. The following features make modules better in the competition with regular header files:

- A module is imported only once, similar to precompiled headers supported by custom language implementations. This reduces the compile time drastically. Non-exported entities have no effect on the translation unit that imports the module.
- Modules allow expressing the logical structure of code by allowing you to select which units should be exported and which should not. Modules can be bundled together into bigger modules.
- Getting rid of workarounds such as include-guards, described earlier. We can import modules in any order. There are no more concerns for macro redefinitions.

Modules can be used together with header files. We can both import and include headers in the same file, as demonstrated in the following example:

```
import <iostream>;
#include <vector>

int main()
{
  std::vector<int> vec{1, 2, 3};
  for (int elem : vec) std::cout << elem;
}
```

When creating modules, you are free to export entities in the interface file of the module and move the implementations to other files. The logic is the same as in managing `.h` and `.cpp` files.

Understanding Compiling

The C++ compilation process consists of several phases. Some of the phases are intended to analyze the source code, and others generate and optimize the target machine code. The following diagram shows the phases of compilation:

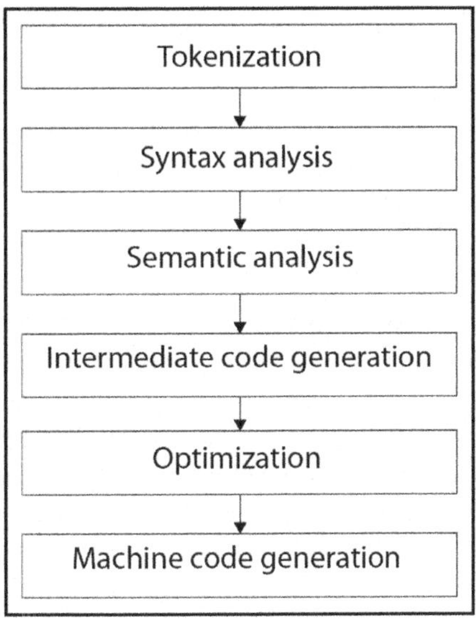

Let's look at each of these phases in detail.

Tokenization

The analysis phase of the compiler aims to split the source code into small units called tokens. A **token** may be a word or just a single symbol, such as = (the equals sign). A token is the *smallest unit* of the source code that carries meaningful value for the compiler. For example, the expression `int a = 42;` will be divided into the tokens `int`, `a`, `=`, `42`, and `;`. The expression isn't just split by spaces, because the following expression is being split into the same tokens (though it is advisable not to forget the spaces between operands):

```
int a=42;
```

The splitting of the source code into tokens is done using sophisticated methods using regular expressions. It is known as **lexical analysis**, or **tokenization** (dividing into tokens). For compilers, using a tokenized input presents a better way to construct internal data structures used to analyze the syntax of the code. Let's see how.

Syntax analysis

When speaking about programming language compilation, we usually differentiate two terms: syntax and semantics. The syntax is the structure of the code; it defines the rules by which tokens combined make structural sense. For example, *day nice* is a syntactically correct phrase in English because it doesn't contain errors in either of the tokens. **Semantics**, on the other hand, concerns the actual meaning of the code. That is, *day nice* is semantically incorrect and should be corrected as *a nice day*.

Syntax analysis is a crucial part of source analysis, because tokens will be analyzed syntactically and semantically, that is, as to whether they bear any meaning that conforms to the general grammar rules. Take the following, for example:

```
int b = a + 0;
```

It may not make sense for us, because adding zero to the variable won't change its value, but the compiler doesn't look on logical meaning here—it looks for the *syntactic correctness* of the code (a missing semicolon, a missing closing parenthesis, and more). Checking the syntactic correctness of the code is done in the syntax analysis phase of compilation. The lexical analysis divides the code into tokens; **syntax analysis** checks for syntactic correctness, which means that the aforementioned expression will produce a syntax error if we have missed a semicolon:

```
int b = a + 0
```

g++ will complain with the `expected ';' at end of declaration` error.

Semantic analysis

If the previous expression was something like `it b = a + 0;` , the compiler would divide it into the tokens `it`, `b`, `=`, and others. We already see that `it` is something unknown, but for the compiler, it is fine at this point. This would lead to the compilation error `unknown type name "it"` in g++. Finding the meaning behind expressions is the task of **semantic analysis** (parsing).

Intermediate code generation

After all the analysis is completed, the compiler generates intermediate code that is a light version of C++ mostly C. A simple example would be the following:

```
class A {
public:
  int get_member() { return mem_; }
private:
  int mem_;
};
```

After analyzing the code, *intermediate code* will be generated (this is an abstract example meant to show the idea of the intermediate code generation; compilers may differ in implementation):

```
struct A {
  int mem_;
};
int A_get_member(A* this) { return this->mem_; }
```

Optimization

Generating intermediate code helps the compiler to make optimizations in the code. Compilers try to optimize code a lot. Optimizations are done in more than one pass. For example, take the following code:

```
int a = 41;
int b = a + 1;
```

This will be optimized into this during compilation:

```
int a = 41;
int b = 41 + 1;
```

This again will be optimized into the following:

```
int a = 41;
int b = 42;
```

Some programmers have no doubt that, nowadays, compilers code better than programmers.

Machine code generation

Compiler optimizations are done in both intermediate code and generated machine code. So what is it like when we compile the project? Earlier in the chapter, when we discussed the preprocessing of the source code, we looked at a simple structure containing several source files, including two headers, `rect.h` and `square.h`, each with its `.cpp` files, and `main.cpp`, which contained the program entry point (the `main()` function). After the preprocessing, the following units are left as input for the compiler: `main.cpp`, `rect.cpp`, and `square.cpp`, as depicted in the following diagram:

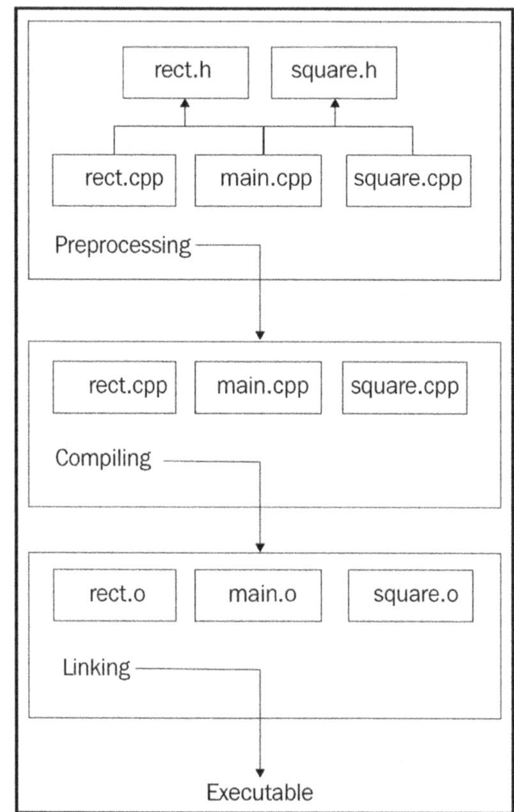

The compiler will compile each separately. Compilation units, also known as source files, are *independent* of each other in some way. When the compiler compiles `main.cpp`, which has a call to the `get_area()` function in `Rect`, it does not include the `get_area()` implementation in `main.cpp`. Instead, it is just sure that the function is implemented somewhere in the project. When the compiler gets to `rect.cpp`, it does not know that the `get_area()` function is used somewhere.

Here's what the compiler gets after `main.cpp` passes the preprocessing phase:

```
// contents of the iostream
struct Rect {
private:
  double side1_;
  double side2_;
public:
  Rect(double s1, double s2);
  const double get_area() const;
};

struct Square : Rect {
  Square(double s);
};

int main() {
  Rect r(3.1, 4.05);
  std::cout << r.get_area() << std::endl;
  return 0;
}
```

After analyzing `main.cpp`, the compiler generates the following intermediate code (many details are omitted to simply express the idea behind compilation):

```
struct Rect {
  double side1_;
  double side2_;
};
void _Rect_init_(Rect* this, double s1, double s2);
double _Rect_get_area_(Rect* this);

struct Square {
  Rect _subobject_;
};
void _Square_init_(Square* this, double s);

int main() {
  Rect r;
  _Rect_init_(&r, 3.1, 4.05);
  printf("%d\n", _Rect_get_area(&r));
  // we've intentionally replace cout with printf for brevity and
  // supposing the compiler generates a C intermediate code
  return 0;
}
```

The compiler will remove the `Square` struct with its constructor function (we named it `_Square_init_`) while optimizing the code because it was never used in the source code.

At this point, the compiler operates with `main.cpp` only, so it sees that we called the `_Rect_init_` and `_Rect_get_area_` functions but did not provide their implementation in the same file. However, as we did provide their declarations beforehand, the compiler trusts us and believes that those functions are implemented in other compilation units. Based on this trust and the minimum information regarding the function signature (its return type, name, and the number and types of its parameters), the compiler generates an object file that contains the working code in `main.cpp` and somehow marks the functions that have no implementation but are trusted to be resolved later. The resolving is done by the linker.

In the following example, we have the simplified variant of the generated object file, which contains two sections—code and information. The code section has addresses for each instruction (the hexadecimal values):

```
code:
0x00 main
  0x01 Rect r;
  0x02 _Rect_init_(&r, 3.1, 4.05);
  0x03 printf("%d\n", _Rect_get_area(&r));
information:
  main: 0x00
  _Rect_init_: ????
  printf: ????
  _Rect_get_area_: ????
```

Take a look at the `information` section. The compiler marks all the functions used in the code section that were not found in the same compilation unit with `????`. These question marks will be replaced by the actual addresses of the functions found in other units by the linker. Finishing with `main.cpp`, the compiler starts to compile the `rect.cpp` file:

```
// file: rect.cpp
struct Rect {
  // #include "rect.h" replaced with the contents
  // of the rect.h file in the preprocessing phase
  // code omitted for brevity
};
Rect::Rect(double s1, double s2)
  : side1_(s1), side2_(s2)
{}
const double Rect::get_area() const {
  return side1_ * side2_;
}
```

Following the same logic here, the compilation of this unit produces the following output (don't forget, we're still providing abstract examples):

```
code:
  0x00 _Rect_init_
  0x01 side1_ = s1
  0x02 side2_ = s2
  0x03 return
  0x04 _Rect_get_area_
  0x05 register = side1_
  0x06 reg_multiply side2_
  0x07 return
information:
  _Rect_init_: 0x00
  _Rect_get_area_: 0x04
```

This output has all the addresses of the functions in it, so there is no need to wait for some functions to be resolved later.

Platforms and object files

The abstract output that we just saw is somewhat similar to the actual object file structure that the compiler produces after the compilation of a unit. The structure of an object file depends on the platform; for example, in *Linux,* it is represented in *ELF* format (*ELF* stands for *Executable and Linkable Format*). A **platform** is an environment in which a program is executed. In this context, by platform, we mean the combination of the computer architecture (more specifically, the *instruction set architecture*) and operating system. Hardware and operating systems are designed and created by different teams and companies. Each of them has different solutions to design problems, which leads to major differences between platforms. Platforms differ in many ways, and those differences are projected onto the executable file format and structure as well. For example, the executable file format in Windows systems is **Portable Executable** (**PE**), which has a different structure, number, and sequence of sections than the ELF format in Linux.

An object file is divided into **sections**. Most important for us are the code sections (marked as `.text`) and the data section (`.data`). The `.text` section holds the program instructions and the `.data` section holds the data used by instructions. Data itself may be split into several sections, such as *initialized, uninitialized,* and *read-only* data.

An important part of the object files in addition to the `.text` and `.data` sections is the **symbol table**. The symbol table stores the mappings of strings (symbols) to locations in the object file. In the preceding example, the compiler-generated output had two portions, the second portion of which was marked as `information:`, which holds the names of the functions used in the code and their relative addresses. This `information:` is the abstract version of the actual symbol table of the object file. The symbol table holds both symbols defined in the code and symbols used in the code that need to be resolved. This information is then used by the linker in order to link the object files together to form the final executable file.

Introducing Linking

The compiler outputs an object file for each compilation unit. In the previous example, we had three `.cpp` files and the compiler produced three object files. The task of the linker is to combine these object files together into a single object file. Combining files together results in relative address changes; for example, if the linker puts the `rect.o` file after `main.o`, the starting address of `rect.o` becomes `0x04` instead of the previous value of `0x00`:

```
code:
  0x00 main
  0x01 Rect r;
  0x02 _Rect_init_(&r, 3.1, 4.05);
  0x03 printf("%d\n", _Rect_get_area(&r));
  0x04 _Rect_init_
  0x05 side1_ = s1
  0x06 side2_ = s2
  0x07 return
  0x08 _Rect_get_area_
  0x09 register = side1_
  0x0A reg_multiply side2_
  0x0B return
information (symbol table):
  main: 0x00
  _Rect_init_: 0x04
  printf: ????
  _Rect_get_area_: 0x08
  _Rect_init_: 0x04
  _Rect_get_area_: 0x08
```

The linker correspondingly updates the symbol table addresses (the `information:` section in our example). As mentioned previously, each object file has its symbol table, which maps the string name of the symbol to its relative location (address) in the file. The next step of linking is to resolve all the unresolved symbols in the object file.

Now that the linker has combined `main.o` and `rect.o` together, it knows the relative location of unresolved symbols because they are now located in the same file. The `printf` symbol will be resolved the same way, except this time it will link the object files with the standard library. After all the object files are combined together (we omitted the linking of `square.o` for brevity), all addresses are updated, and all the symbols are resolved, the linker outputs the one final object file that can be executed by the operating system. As discussed earlier in the chapter, the OS uses a tool called the loader to load the contents of the executable file into the memory.

Linking libraries

A library is similar to an executable file, with one major difference: it does not have a `main()` function, which means that it cannot be invoked as a regular program. Libraries are used to combine code that might be reused with more than one program. You already linked your programs with the standard library by including the `<iostream>` header, for example.

Libraries can be linked with the executable file either as **static** or **dynamic** libraries. When you link them as a static library, they become a part of the final executable file. A dynamically linked library should also be loaded into memory by the OS to provide your program with the ability to call its functions. Let's suppose we want to find the square root of a function:

```
int main() {
  double result = sqrt(49.0);
}
```

The C++ standard library provides the `sqrt()` function, which returns the square root of its argument. If you compile the preceding example, it will produce an error insisting that the `sqrt` function has not been declared. We know that to use the standard library function, we should include the corresponding `<cmath>` header. But the header file does not contain the implementation of the function; it just declares the function (in the `std` namespace), which is then included in our source file:

```
#include <cmath>
int main() {
  double result = std::sqrt(49.0);
}
```

The compiler marks the address of the `sqrt` symbol as unknown, and the linker should resolve it in the linking stage. The linker will fail to resolve it if the source file is not linked with the standard library implementation (the object file containing the library functions).

The final executable file generated by the linker will consist of both our program and the standard library if the linking was static. On the other hand, if the linking is dynamic, the linker marks the `sqrt` symbol to be found at runtime.

Now when we run the program, the loader also loads the library that was dynamically linked to our program. It loads the contents of the standard library into the memory as well and then resolves the actual location of the `sqrt()` function in memory. The same library that is already loaded into the memory can be used by other programs as well.

Summary

In this chapter, we touched on a few of the many new features of C++20 and are now ready to dive deeper into the language. We discussed the process of building a C++ application and its compilation phases. This includes analyzing the code to detect syntactical and grammatical errors, generating intermediate code to make optimizations, and finally, generating the object file that will be linked together with other generated object files to form the final executable file.

In the next chapter, we will learn about C++ data types, arrays, and pointers. We will also gain an understanding of what pointers are and look at low-level details of conditionals.

Questions

1. What is the difference between a compiler and an interpreter?
2. List the program compilation phases.
3. What does the preprocessor do?
4. What are the tasks of the linker?
5. What is the difference between statically and dynamically linked libraries?

Further reading

For more information, refer to *Advanced C and C++ Compiling* at `https://www.amazon.com/Advanced-C-Compiling-Milan-Stevanovic/dp/1430266678/`

LLVM Essentials, https://www.packtpub.com/application-development/llvm-essentials

2
Low-Level Programming with C++

Initially, C++ was perceived as the successor of the C language; however, since then it has evolved into something big, sometimes scary, and even untamable. With recent language updates, it now represents a complex beast that requires time and patience to tame. We will start this chapter with the basic constructs that almost every language supports, such as data types, conditional and loop statements, pointers, structs, and functions. We will look at those constructs from the perspective of a low-level systems programmer, curious how even a simple instruction can be executed by the computer. A deep understanding of these basic constructs is mandatory in building a solid base for more advanced and abstract topics such as object-oriented programming.

In this chapter, we will learn more about the following:

- The details of program execution and its entry point
- Special properties of the `main()` function
- Intricacies behind the function call and recursion
- Memory segments and addressing fundamentals
- Data types and how variables reside in memory
- Pointers and arrays
- The low-level details of conditionals and loops

Technical requirements

The g++ compiler with the option `--std=c++2a` is used to compile the examples throughout the chapter.

You can find the source files used in this chapter at `https://github.com/PacktPublishing/Expert-CPP`.

Program execution

In `Chapter 1`, *Building C++ Applications*, we learned that the compiler generates an executable file after compiling the source code. The executable file contains machine code that can be copied to the memory of the computer to be run by the **Central Processing Unit (CPU)**. The copying is done by an internal tool of the OS called a loader. So the **operating system (OS)** copies the contents of the program to the memory and starts executing the program by passing its first instruction to the CPU.

main()

Program execution starts with the `main()` function, the *designated start of the program* as stated in the standard. A simple program outputting the `Hello, World!` message will look like this:

```
#include <iostream>
int main() {
  std::cout << "Hello, World!" << std::endl;
  return 0;
}
```

You may have encountered or used in your programs the arguments of the `main()` function. It has two arguments, `argc` and `argv`, allowing strings to be passed from the environment, usually referred to as the **command-line arguments**.

The names `argc` and `argv` are conventional and can be replaced with anything you want. The `argc` argument holds the number of command-line arguments passed to the `main()` function; the `argv` argument holds the arguments:

```
#include <iostream>
int main(int argc, char* argv[]) {
 std::cout << "The number of passed arguments is: " << argc << std::endl;
 std::cout << "Arguments are: " << std::endl;
```

```
  for (int ix = 1; ix < argc; ++ix) {
    std::cout << argv[ix] << std::endl;
  }
  return 0;
}
```

For example, we can compile and run the preceding example with the following arguments:

```
$ my-program argument1 hello world --some-option
```

This will output the following to the screen:

```
The number of passed arguments is: 5
Arguments are:
argument1
hello
world
--some-option
```

When you look at the number of arguments, you'll notice that it is `5`. The first argument is always the name of the program; that's why we skipped it in the example by starting the loop from number `1`.

Rarely, you can see a widely supported but not standardized third argument, most commonly named `envp`. The type of `envp` is an array of `char` pointers and it holds the environment variables of the system.

The program can contain lots of functions, but the execution of the program always starts with the `main()` function, at least from the programmer's perspective. Let's try to compile the following code:

```
#include <iostream>

void foo() {
  std::cout << "Risky foo" << std::endl;
}

// trying to call the foo() outside of the main() function
foo();

int main() {
  std::cout << "Calling main" << std::endl;
  return 0;
}
```

g++ raises an error on the `foo();` call `C++ requires a type specifier for all declarations`. The call was parsed as a declaration rather than an instruction to execute. The way we tried to call a function before `main()` might seem silly for seasoned developers, so let's try another way. What if we declare something that calls a function during its initialization? In the following example, we define a `BeforeMain` struct with a constructor printing a message, and then we declare an object of type `BeforeMain` in the global scope:

```
#include <iostream>

struct BeforeMain {
  BeforeMain() {
    std::cout << "Constructing BeforeMain" << std::endl;
  }
};

BeforeMain b;

int main() {
  std::cout << "Calling main()" << std::endl;
  return 0;
}
```

The example successfully compiles and the program outputs the following:

```
Constructing BeforeMain
Calling main()
```

What if we add a member function to `BeforeMain` and try to call it? See the following code to understand this:

```
struct BeforeMain {
  // constructor code omitted for brevity
  void test() {
    std::cout << "test function" << std::endl;
  }
};

BeforeMain b;
b.test(); // compiler error

int main() {
  // code omitted for brevity
}
```

The call to test() won't be successful. So we cannot call a function before main(), but we can declare variables- objects that would be initialized by default. So there is definitely something that does an *initialization* before main() is actually called. It turns out that the main() function is not the true starting point of a program. The actual starting function of the program prepares the environment, that is, collects the arguments passed to the program, and then calls the main() function. This is required because C++ supports global and static objects that need to be initialized before the program begins, which means before the main() function is called. In the Linux world, this function is referred to as __libc_start_main. The compiler augments the generated code with the call of __libc_start_main, which in turn may or may not call other initialization functions before the main() function gets called. Going abstract, just imagine that the preceding code will be altered to something similar to the following:

```
void __libc_start_main() {
  BeforeMain b;
  main();
}
__libc_start_main(); // call the entry point
```

We will examine the entry point in more detail in the upcoming chapters.

Special properties of main()

We concluded that main() is not actually the entry point of the program, though the standard states that it is the designated start. The compiler pays special attention to main(). It behaves like a regular C++ function, but besides being the first function to be called, it has other special properties. First of all, it is the only function that could omit the return statement:

```
int main() {
  // works fine without a return statement
}
```

The returned value indicates the success of the execution. By returning 0, we aim to tell the control that main() ended successfully, so if the control reaches the end without encountering a corresponding return statement, it will consider the call successful and the effect is the same as return 0;.

Another interesting property of the `main()` function is that its return type cannot be deduced automatically. It is not allowed to use the `auto` placeholder type specifier, which indicates that the return type will be deduced from function's `return` statement. Here's how it works for regular functions:

```
// C++11
auto foo() -> int {
  std::cout << "foo in alternative function syntax" << std::endl;
  return 0;
}

// C++14
auto foo() {
  std::cout << "In C++14 syntax" << std::endl;
  return 0;
}
```

By placing the `auto` specifier, we tell the compiler to automatically deduce the `return` type. With C++11, we also placed the type name after the arrow (->) although the second syntax is shorter. Consider the `get_ratio()` function, which returns the standard ratio as an integer:

```
auto get_ratio(bool minimum) {
  if (minimum) {
    return 12; // deduces return type int
  }
  return 18; // fine: get_ratio's return type is already deduced to int
}
```

To successfully compile C++ code containing new features specified in C++11, C++14, C++17, or C++20, you should use proper compiler flags. When compiling with g++, use the `--std` flag and specify the standard version. The recommended value is `--std=c++2a`.

The example compiles successfully, but look at what happens when we try the same trick with the `main()` function:

```
auto main() {
  std::cout << get_ratio(true);
  return 0;
}
```

The compiler will produce the following errors:

- `cannot initialize return object of type 'auto' with an rvalue of type 'int'`
- `'main' must return 'int'.`

Something strange is going on with the `main()` function. This is because the `main()` function allows omitting the `return` statement, but for the compiler, the `return` statement must exist to support automatic `return` type deduction.

It's important to remember that if there are multiple `return` statements, they must all deduce to the same type. Let's suppose we need an updated version of the function, which returns an integer value (as shown in the previous example), and if specified, returns a more precise `float` value:

```
auto get_ratio(bool precise = false) {
  if (precise) {
    // returns a float value
    return 4.114f;
  }
  return 4; // returns an int value
}
```

The preceding code won't compile successfully because there are two `return` statements with different deduced types.

constexpr

The `constexpr` specifier declares that the value of the function is possible to evaluate at compile time. The same definition applies to variables as well. The name itself consists of `const` and `expression`. This is a useful feature because it allows optimizing your code to the fullest. Let's take a look at the following example:

```
int double_it(int number) {
  return number * 2;
}

constexpr int triple_it(int number) {
  return number * 3;
}

int main() {
  int doubled = double_it(42);
  int tripled = triple_it(42);
```

```
    int test{0};
    std::cin >> test;
    int another_tripled = triple_it(test);
  }
```

Let's see how the compiler modifies the `main()` function in the preceding example. Supposing the compiler won't optimize the `double_it()` function on its own (for example, making it an *inline* function), the `main()` function will take the following form:

```
  int main() {
    int doubled = double_it(42);
    int tripled = 126; // 42 * 3
    int test = 0;
    std::cin >> test;
    int another_tripled = triple_it(test);
  }
```

`constexpr` is not a guarantee that the function value will be computed at compile time; however, the compiler is able to do so if the input of the `constexpr` function is known at compile time. That's why the preceding example transformed directly to a computed value of `126` for the `tripled` variable and had no effect on the `another_tripled` variable as the input is not known to the compiler (and nor us).

C++20 introduces the `consteval` specifier, allowing you to insist on the compile-time evaluation of the function result. In other words, a `consteval` function produces a constant expression at compile time. The specifier makes the function an *immediate* one, which will produce an error if the function call cannot lead to a constant expression. The `main()` function cannot be declared as `constexpr`.

C++20 also introduces the `constinit` specifier. We use `constinit` to declare a variable with static or thread storage duration. We will discuss thread storage duration in `Chapter 8`, *Concurrency and Multithreading*. The most notable difference with `constinit` is that we can use it with objects that have no `constexpr` destructor. This is because `constexpr` requires the object to have static initialization and constant destruction. Furthermore, `constexpr` makes the object const-qualified while `constinit` does not. However, `constinit` requires the object to have static initialization.

Recursion

Another special property of `main()` is that it cannot be called recursively. From the perspective of the OS, the `main()` function is the entry point of the program, so calling it again would mean starting everything over; therefore, it is prohibited. However, calling a function recursive just because it calls itself is partially correct. For example, the `print_number()` function calls itself and never stops:

```
void print_number(int num) {
 std::cout << num << std::endl;
 print_number(num + 1); // recursive call
}
```

Calling the `print_number(1)` function will output numbers `1`, `2`, `3`, and so on. This is more like a function that calls itself infinitely rather than a correct recursive function. We should add a couple more properties to make the `print_number()` function a useful recursive one. First of all, the recursive function must have a base case, a scenario when further function calls stop, which means the recursion stops propagating. We can make such a scenario for the `print_number()` function if, for example, we want to print numbers up to 100:

```
void print_number(int num) {
  if (num > 100) return; // base case
  std::cout << num << std::endl;
  print_number(num + 1); // recursive call
}
```

There is one more property for a function to be recursive: solving smaller problems that will eventually lead to the base case. In the preceding example, we already had it by solving a smaller problem for the function, that is, by printing one number. After printing one number, we move to the next small problem: printing the next number. Finally, we get to the base case and we are done. There isn't any magic in a function calling itself; think of it as a function calling a different function with the same implementation. What's really interesting is how a recursive function affects the program execution overall. Let's take a look at a simple example of calling a function from an other function:

```
int sum(int n, int m) { return n + m; }
int max(int x, int y) {
  int res = x > y ? x : y;
  return res;
}
int calculate(int a, int b) {
  return sum(a, b) + max(a, b);
}
```

```
int main() {
  auto result = calculate(11, 22);
  std::cout << result; // outputs 55
}
```

When a function is called, memory space is allocated for its arguments and local variables. The program starts with the `main()` function, which in this example simply calls the `calculate()` function by passing literal values `11` and `22`. The control *jumps* to the `calculate()` function and the `main()` function is kind of *on hold*; it waits until the `calculate()` function returns to continue its execution. The `calculate()` function has two arguments, `a` and `b`; although we named parameters of the `sum()`, `max()`, and `calculate()` differently, we could use the same names in all the functions. Memory space is allocated for these two arguments. Let's suppose that an int takes 4 bytes of memory, therefore a minimum of 8 bytes are required for the `calculate()` function to be executed successfully. After allocating 8 bytes, the values `11` and `22` should be copied to the corresponding locations (see the following diagram for details):

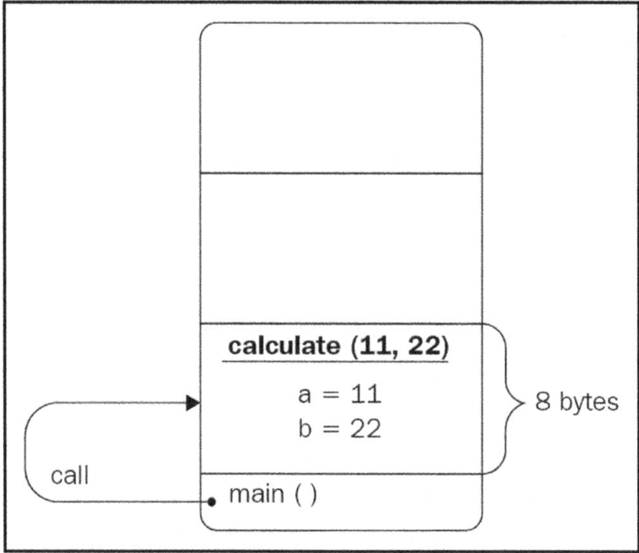

The `calculate()` function calls the functions `sum()` and `max()` and passes its argument values to them. Correspondingly, it waits for both functions to be executed sequentially in order to form the value to return to the `main()`. The `sum()` and `max()` functions are not called simultaneously. First, `sum()` is called, which leads to a copy of the values of variables `a` and `b` to the locations allocated for the arguments of `sum()`, named `n` and `m`, which again take eight bytes in total. Take a look at the following diagram to understand this better:

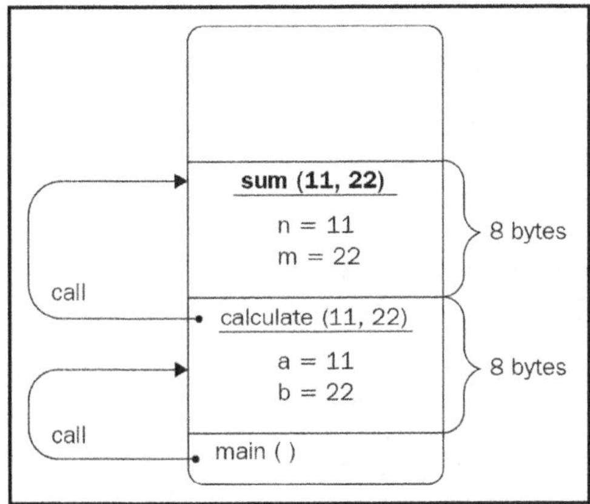

Their sum is calculated and returned. After the function is done and it returns a value, the memory space is freed. This means that variables `n` and `m` are not accessible anymore and their locations can be reused.

We don't consider temporary variables at this point. We will revisit this example later to show the hidden details of function execution, including temporary variables and how to avoid them as much as possible.

After `sum()` has returned a value, the `max()` function is called. It follows the same logic: memory is allocated to the arguments `x` and `y`, and to the `res` variable. We intentionally store the result of the ternary operator `(?:)` in the `res` variable to make the `max()` function allocate more space for this example. So, 12 bytes are allocated to the `max()` function in total. At this point, the x `main()` function is still on hold and waits for `calculate()`, which in turn, is on hold and waits for the `max()` function to complete (see the following diagram for details):

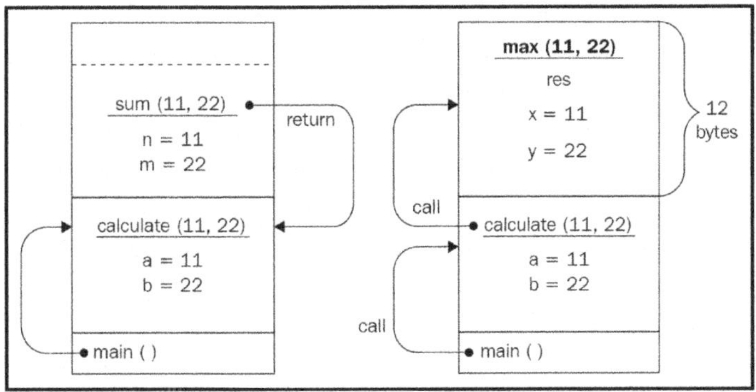

When `max()` is done, the memory allocated to it is freed and its return value is used by `calculate()` to form a value to return. Similarly, when `calculate()` returns, the memory is freed and the `main()` function's local variable result will contain the value returned by `calculate()`.

The `main()` function then finishes its work and the program exits, that is, the OS frees the memory allocated for the program and can reuse it later for other programs. The described process of allocating and freeing memory (deallocating it) for functions is done using a concept called a stack.

A stack is a data structure *adapter*, which has its rules to insert and access the data inside of it. In the context of function calls, the stack usually means a memory segment provided to the program that automatically manages itself following the rules of the stack data structure adapter. We will discuss this in more detail later in this chapter.

Going back to recursion, when the function calls itself, memory should be allocated to the newly called function's arguments and local variables (if any). The function calls itself again, which means the stack will continue to grow (to provide space for the new functions). It doesn't matter that we call the same function; from the stack perspective, each new call is a call to a completely different function, so it allocates space for it with a serious look on its face while whistling its favorite song. Take the look at the following diagram:

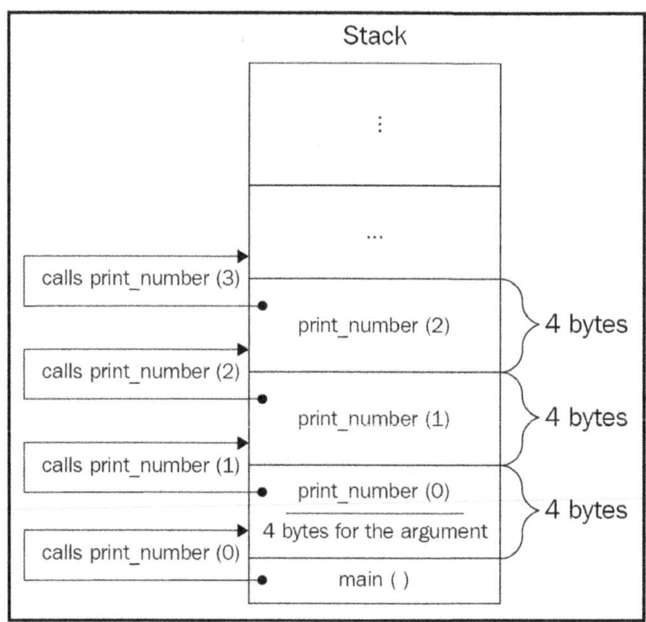

The first call of the recursive function is on hold and waits for the second call of the same function, which in turn is on hold and waits for the third call to finish and return a value, which is in turn on hold, and so on. If there is a bug in the function or the recursion base is difficult to reach, the stack will sooner or later overgrow, which will lead to a program crash with the reason known as **stack overflow**.

Though recursion provides more elegant solutions to a problem, try to avoid recursion in your programs and use the iterative approach (loops). In mission-critical system development guidelines such as the navigation system of a Mars rover, using recursion is completely prohibited.

In `chapter 1`, *Building C++ Applications*, we mentioned coroutines. Although we will discuss them in detail later in the book, you should note that the main function cannot be a coroutine.

Working with data

When we refer to computer memory, we consider the **Random Access Memory** (**RAM**) by default, and also the RAM is a general term for either SRAM or DRAM; we will mean DRAM by default unless otherwise stated. To clear things out, let's take a look at the following diagram, which illustrates the memory hierarchy:

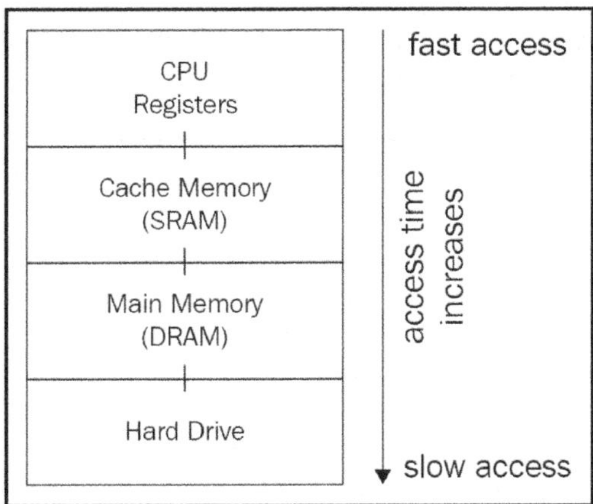

When we compile a program, the compiler stores the final executable file in the hard drive. To run the executable file, its instructions are loaded into the RAM and are then executed by the CPU one by one. This leads us to the conclusion that any instruction required to be executed should be in the RAM. This is partially true. The environment that is responsible for running and monitoring programs plays the main role.

Programs we write are executed in the hosted environment, which is in the OS. The OS loads the contents of the program (its instructions and data, that is, the process) not directly into the RAM, but the **virtual memory**, a mechanism that makes it possible both to handle processes conveniently and to share resources between processes. Whenever we refer to the memory that a process is loaded to, we mean the virtual memory, which in turn *maps* its contents to the RAM.

Most of the time, we use the terms RAM, DRAM, virtual memory, and memory interchangeably, considering virtual memory as an abstraction around the physical memory (the DRAM).

Let's begin with an introduction to the memory structure and then investigate data types within the memory.

Virtual memory

The memory consists of lots of boxes, each of which is able to store a specified amount of data. We will refer to these boxes as *memory cells*, considering that each cell can store 1 byte representing 8 bits. Each memory cell is unique even if they store the same value. The uniqueness is achieved by addressing the cells so that each cell has its unique address in the memory. The first cell has the address **0**, the second cell **1**, and so on.

The following diagram illustrates an excerpt of the memory, each cell with its unique address and ability to store 1 byte of data:

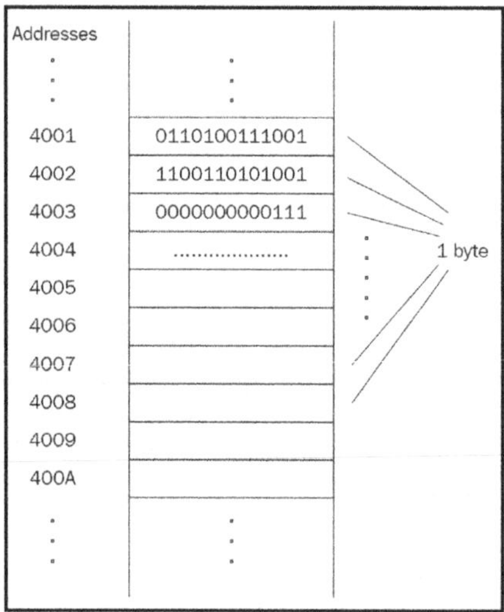

The preceding diagram can be used to abstractly represent both physical and virtual memories. The point of having an additional layer of abstraction is the ease of managing processes and providing more functionality than with physical memory. For example, OSes can execute programs greater than physical memory. Take a computer game as an example of a program taking almost 2 GB of space and a computer with a physical memory of 512 MB. Virtual memory allows the OS to load the program portion by portion by unloading old parts from the physical memory and mapping new parts.

Virtual memory also better supports having more than one program in memory, thus supporting parallel (or pseudo-parallel) execution of multiple programs. This also provides efficient use of shared code and data, such as dynamic libraries. Whenever two different programs require the same library to work with, the single instance of the library could exist in memory and be used by both programs without them knowing about each other. Take a look at the following diagram, which depicts three programs loaded into memory:

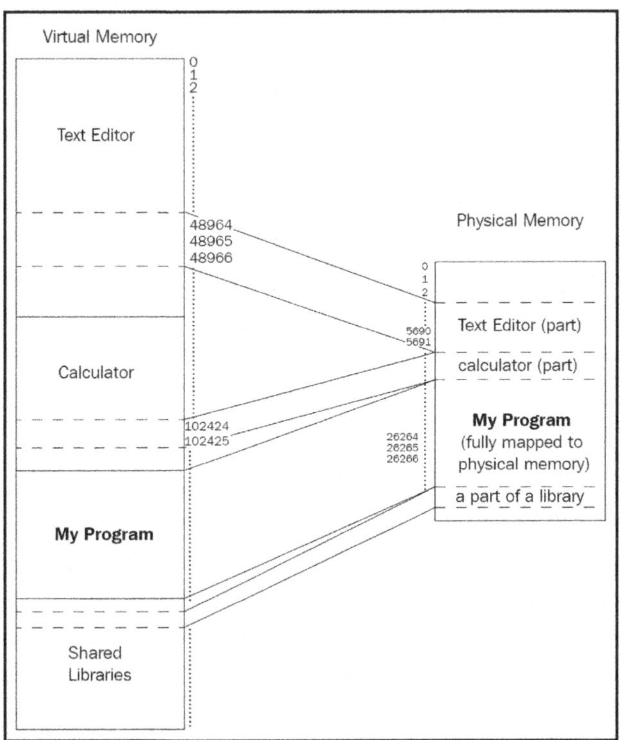

There are three running programs in the preceding diagram; each of the programs takes up some space in virtual memory. **My Program** is fully contained in the physical memory while the **Calculator** and **Text Editor** are partially mapped to it.

Addressing

As mentioned earlier, each memory cell has its unique **address**, which is the guarantee of the uniqueness of each cell. An address is usually represented in a *hexadecimal* form because it's shorter and it's faster to convert to **binary** rather than decimal numbers. A program that is loaded into virtual memory operates and sees *logical* addresses. These addresses, also called virtual addresses, are *fake* and provided by the OS, which *translates* them to physical addresses when needed. To optimize the translation, the CPU provides **Translation Lookaside Buffer**, a part of its **Memory Management Unit** (**MMU**). Translation Lookaside Buffer caches recent translations of virtual addresses to physical addresses. So the efficient address translation is a software/hardware task. We will dive into the address structure and translation details in `Chapter 5`, *Memory Management and Smart Pointers*.

The length of the address defines the size of total the memory that can be operated by the system. When you encounter statements such as a 32 bits system or a 64 bits system, it actually means the length of the address, that is, the address is 32 bits or 64 bits long. The longer the address, the bigger the memory. To make things clear, let's compare an 8 bits long address with a 32 bits long one. As agreed earlier, each memory cell is able to store 1 byte of data and has a unique address. If the address length is 8 bits, the address of the first memory cell is all zeros— **0000 0000**. The address of the next cell is greater by one, that is, it's **0000 0001**, and so on.

The biggest value that can be represented by 8 bits is **1111 1111**. So, how many memory cells can be represented with an address length of 8 bits? This question is worth answering in more detail. How many different values can be represented by 1 bit? Two! Why so? Because 1 bit can represent either **1** or **0**. How many different values can be represented by 2 bits? Well, **00** is one value, **01** is another value, **10**, and finally, **11**. So, four different values in total can be represented by 2 bits. Let's make a table:

number of bits	number of values	values
1 bit	2	0, 1
2 bit	4	00, 01, 10, 11
3 bit	8	000, 001, 010, 100, ...
4 bit	16	0000, 0001, 0010, ...
......	......	......

We can see a pattern here. Each position (each bit) in a number can have two values, so we can calculate the number of different values represented by N bits by finding 2^N; therefore, the number of different values represented by 8 bits is $2^8 = 256$. This means that an 8 bits system can address up to 256 memory cells. On the other hand, a 32-bit system is able to address $2^{32} = 4\ 294\ 967\ 296$ memory cells, each storing 1 byte of data, that is, storing $4294967296 * 1\ byte = 4\ GB$ of data.

Data types

What's the point of having data types at all? Why can't we program in C++ using some `var` keyword to declare variables and forget about variables such as `short`, `long`, `int`, `char`, `wchar`, and so on? Well, C++ does support a similar construct, the `auto` keyword that we have already used previously in this chapter, a so-called *placeholder type specifier*. It's named a placeholder because it is, indeed, a placeholder. We cannot (and we must not ever be able to) declare a variable and then change its type during runtime. The following code might be valid JavaScript code, but it is definitely not valid C++ code:

```
var a = 12;
a = "Hello, World!";
a = 3.14;
```

Imagine the C++ compiler could compile this code. How many bytes of memory should be allocated for the `a` variable? When declaring `var a = 12;`, the compiler could deduce its type to `int` and specify 4 bytes of memory space, but when the variable changes its value to `Hello, World!`, the compiler has to reallocate the space, or invent a new hidden variable named `a1` of type `std::string`. Then the compiler tries to find every access to the variable in the code that accesses it as a string and not as an integer or a double and replace the variable with the hidden `a1`. The compiler might just quit and start to ask itself the meaning of life.

We can declare something similar to the preceding code in C++ as follows:

```
auto a = 12;
auto b = "Hello, World!";
auto c = 3.14;
```

The difference between the previous two examples is that the second example declares three different variables of three different types. The previous non-C++ code declared just one variable and then assigned values of different types to it. You can't change the type of a variable in C++, but the compiler allows you to use the `auto` placeholder and deduces the type of the variable by the value assigned to it.

It is crucial to understand that the type is deduced at compile time, while languages such as JavaScript allow you to deduce the type at runtime. The latter is possible because such programs are run in environments such as virtual machines, while the only environment that runs the C++ program is the OS. The C++ compiler must generate a valid executable file that could be copied into the memory and run without a support system. This forces the compiler to know beforehand the actual size of the variable. Knowing the size is important to generate the final machine code because accessing a variable requires its address and size, allocating memory space to a variable requires the number of bytes that it should take.

The C++ type system classifies types into two major categories:

- **Fundamental types** (`int`, `double`, `char`, `void`)
- **Compound types** (pointers, arrays, classes)

The language even supports special type traits, `std::is_fundamental` and `std::is_compound`, to find out the category of a type, for example:

```
#include <iostream>
#include <type_traits>

struct Point {
  float x;
  float y;
};

int main() {
  std::cout << std::is_fundamental_v<Point> << " "
            << std::is_fundamental_v<int> << " "
            << std::is_compound_v<Point> << " "
            << std::is_compound_v<int> << std::endl;
}
```

We used `std::is_fundamental_v` and `std::is_compound_v` helper variable templates, defined as follows:

```
template <class T>
inline constexpr bool is_fundamental_v = is_fundamental<T>::value;
template <class T>
inline constexpr bool is_compound_v = is_compound<T>::value;
```

The program outputs: `0 1 1 0`.

You can use the `std::boolalpha` I/O manipulator before printing the type categories to print `true` or `false` instead of `1` or `0`.

Most of the fundamental types are arithmetic types such as `int` or `double`; even the `char` type is arithmetic. It actually holds a number rather than a character, for example:

```
char ch = 65;
std::cout << ch; // prints A
```

A `char` variable holds 1 byte of data, which means it can represent 256 different values (because 1 byte is 8 bits, and 8 bits can be used in 2^8 ways to represent a number). What if we use one of the bits as a *sign* bit, for example, allowing the type to support negative values as well? That leaves us with 7 bits for representing the actual value, and following the same logic, it allows us to represent 27 different values, that is, 128 (including 0) different values of positive numbers and the same amount of negative values. Excluding 0 gives us the range -127 to +127 for the signed `char`. This signed versus unsigned representation applies to almost all integral types.

So whenever you encounter that, for example, the size of an int is 4 bytes, which is 32 bits, you should already know that it is possible to represent the numbers 0 to 2^{32} in an unsigned representation, and the values -2^{31} to $+2^{31}$ in a signed representation.

Pointers

C++ is a unique language in the way that it provides access to low-level details such as addresses of variables. We can take the address of any variable declared in the program using the `&` operator as shown:

```
int answer = 42;
std::cout << &answer;
```

This code will output something similar to this:

```
0x7ffee1bd2adc
```

Notice the hexadecimal representation of the address. Although this value is just an integer, it is used to store in a special variable called a pointer. A pointer is just a variable that is able to store address values and supports the `*` operator (dereferencing), allowing us to find the actual value stored at the address.

For example, to store the address of the variable answer in the preceding example, we can declare a pointer and assign the address to it:

```
int* ptr = &answer;
```

The variable answer is declared as an `int`, which usually takes 4 bytes of memory space. We already agreed that each byte has its own unique address. Can we conclude that the answer variable has four unique addresses? Well, yes and no. It does acquire four distinct but contiguous memory bytes, but when the address operator is used against the variable, it returns the address of its first byte. Let's take a look at a portion of code that declares a couple of variables and then illustrate how they are placed in the memory:

```
int ivar = 26;
char ch = 't';
double d = 3.14;
```

The size of a data type is implementation-defined, though the C++ standard states the minimum supported range of values for each type. Let's suppose the implementation provides 4 bytes for an `int`, 8 bytes for a double, and 1 byte for `char`. The memory layout for the preceding code should look like this:

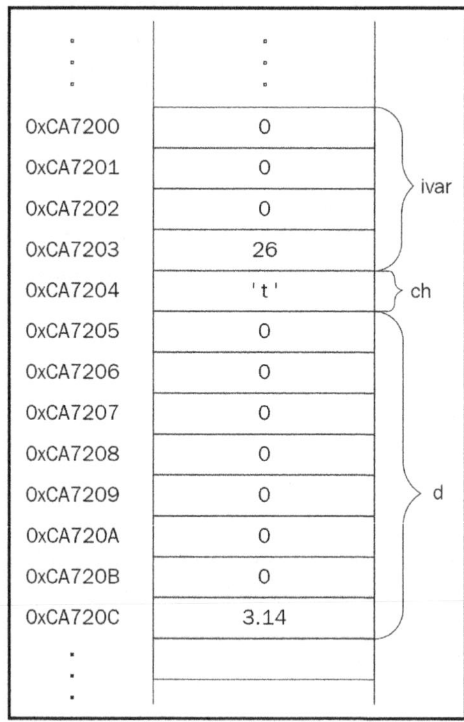

Pay attention to `ivar` in the memory layout; it resides in four contiguous bytes.

Whenever we take the address of a variable, whether it resides in a single byte or more than one byte, we get the address of the first byte of the variable. If the size doesn't affect the logic behind the address operator, then why do we have to declare the type of the pointer? In order to store the address of `ivar` in the preceding example, we should declare the pointer as an `int*`:

```
int* ptr = &ivar;
char* pch = &ch;
double* pd = &d;
```

The preceding code is depicted in the following diagram:

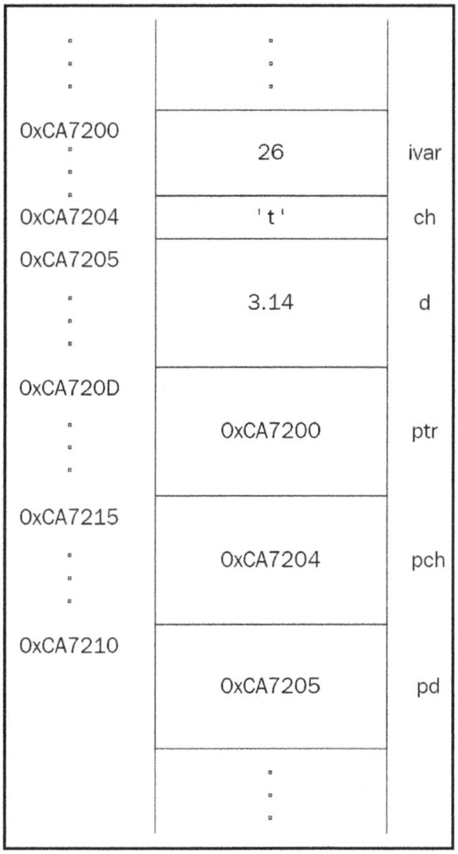

OxCA7200 26 ivar
OxCA7204 't' ch
OxCA7205 3.14 d
OxCA720D OxCA7200 ptr
OxCA7215 OxCA7204 pch
OxCA7210 OxCA7205 pd

Turns out, the type of the pointer is crucial in accessing the variable using that very pointer. C++ provides the dereferencing operator (the `*` symbol before the pointer name):

```
std::cout << *ptr; // prints 26
```

It basically works like this:

1. Reads the contents of the pointer
2. Finds the address of the memory cell that is equal to the address in the pointer
3. Returns the value that is stored in that memory cell

The question is, what if the pointer points to the data that resides in more than one memory cell? That's where the type of the pointer comes in. When dereferencing the pointer, its type is used to determine how many bytes it should read and return starting from the memory cell that it points to.

Now that we know that a pointer stores the address of the first byte of the variable, we can actually read any byte of the variable by moving the pointer forward. We should remember that the address is just a number, so adding or subtracting another number from it will produce another address. What if we point to an integer variable with a `char` pointer?

```
int ivar = 26;
char* p = (char*)&ivar;
```

When we try to dereference the `p` pointer, it will return only the first byte of `ivar`.

Now, if we want to move to the next byte of `ivar`, we add `1` to the `char` pointer:

```
// the first byte
*p;
// the second byte
*(p + 1);
// the third byte
*(p + 2);

// dangerous stuff, the previous byte
*(p - 1);
```

Take a look at the following diagram; it clearly shows how we access bytes of the `ivar` integer:

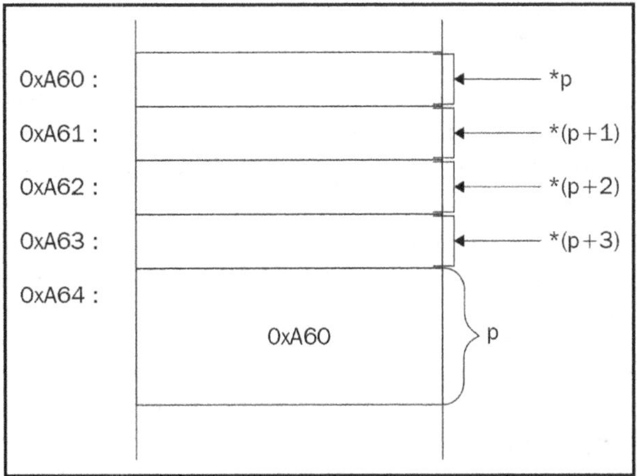

If you want to read the first or the last two bytes, you can use a short pointer:

```
short* sh = (short*)&ivar;
std::cout << *sh; // print the value in the first two bytes of ivar
std::cout << *(sh + 1); // print the value in the last two bytes of ivar
```

You should be careful with pointer arithmetics, as adding or subtracting a number will actually move the pointer by the defined size of the data type. Adding 1 to an `int` pointer will add `sizeof(int) * 1` to the actual address.

What about the size of a pointer? As mentioned previously, a pointer is just a variable that is special in the way that it can store a memory address and provide a dereferencing operator that returns the data located at that address. So if the pointer is just a variable, it should reside in memory as well. We might consider that the size of a `char` pointer is less than the size of an `int` pointer just because the size of a `char` is less than the size of an `int`.

Here's the catch: the data that is stored in the pointer has nothing to do with the type of data the pointer points to. Both `char` and `int` pointers store the address of the variable, so to define the size of the pointer, we should consider the size of the address. The size of the address is defined by the system we work in. For example, in a 32-bit system, the address size is 32 bits long, and in a 64-bit system, the address size is 64 bits long. This leads us to a logical conclusion: the size of the pointer is the same regardless of the type of data it points to:

```
std::cout << sizeof(ptr) << " = " << sizeof(pch) << " = " << sizeof(pd);
```

It will output `4 = 4 = 4` in a 32-bit system, and `8 = 8 = 8` in a 64-bit system.

Memory segments

The memory consists of segments and the program segments are distributed through these memory segments during the loading. These are artificially divided ranges of memory addresses that make it easier to manage the program by the OS. A binary file is also divided into segments, such as code and data. We previously mentioned code and data as sections. Sections are the division of a binary file needed for the linker, which uses the sections that are meant for the proper work of the linker and combines the sections that are meant for the loader into segments.

Basically, when we discuss a binary file from the runtime perspective, we mean segments. The data segment contains all the data required and used by the program, and the code segment contains the actual instructions that process the very same data. However, when we mention data, we don't mean every single piece of data used in the program. Let's take a look at this example:

```
#include <iostream>
int max(int a, int b) { return a > b ? a : b; }
int main() {
  std::cout << "The maximum of 11 and 22 is: " << max(11, 22);
}
```

The code segment of the preceding program consists of the instructions of the `main()` and `max()` functions, where `main()` prints the message using the `operator<<` of the `cout` object and then calls the `max()` function. What data actually resides in the data segment? Does it contain `a` and `b` arguments of the `max()` function? As it turns out, the only data that is contained in the data segment is the string `The maximum of 11 and 22 is:`, along with other static, global, or constant data. We didn't declare any global or static variables, so the only data is the mentioned message.

The interesting thing comes with values the `11` and `22`. These are literal values, which means they have no address; therefore they are not located anywhere in the memory. If they are not located anywhere, the only logical explanation of how they are located within the program is that they reside in the code segment. They are a part of the `max()` call instruction.

What about the a and b arguments of the max() function? And here comes the segment in the virtual memory that is responsible for storing variables that have automatic storage duration— the stack. As already mentioned previously, the stack automatically handles the allocation/deallocation of memory space for local variables and function arguments. The arguments a and b will be located in the stack when the max() function is called. In general, if an object is said to have automatic storage duration, the memory space will be allocated at the beginning of the enclosing block. So when the function is called, its arguments are pushed into the stack:

```
int max(int a, int b) {
  // allocate space for the "a" argument
  // allocate space for the "b" argument
  return a > b ? a : b;
  // deallocate the space for the "b" argument
  // deallocate the space for the "a" argument
}
```

When the function is done, the automatically allocated space will be freed at the end of the enclosing code block.

The enclosing code block represents not only the function body but also the block of the conditional statements and loops.

It's said that the arguments (or local variables) are popped out of the stack. **Push** and **pop** are terms used within the context of the stack. You insert data into the stack by *pushing* it, and you retrieve (and remove) data out of the stack by *popping* it. You might have encountered the **LIFO** term, which stands for **last in, first out**. That perfectly describes the push and pop operations of the stack.

When the program is run, the OS provides the fixed size of the stack. The stack is able to grow in size and if it grows to the extent that no more space is left, it crashes because of the stack overflow.

The heap

We described the stack as a manager of variables with *automatic storage duration*. The word *automatic* suggests that programmers shouldn't care about the actual memory allocation and deallocation. Automatic storage duration could be achieved only if the size of data or a collection of the data is known beforehand. This way, the compiler is aware of the number and type of function arguments and local variables. At this point, it seems more than fine, but programs tend to work with dynamic data— data of an unknown size. We will study dynamic memory management in detail in `Chapter 5`, *Memory Management and Smart Pointers;* for now, let's look at a simplified diagram of memory segments and find out what the heap is used for:

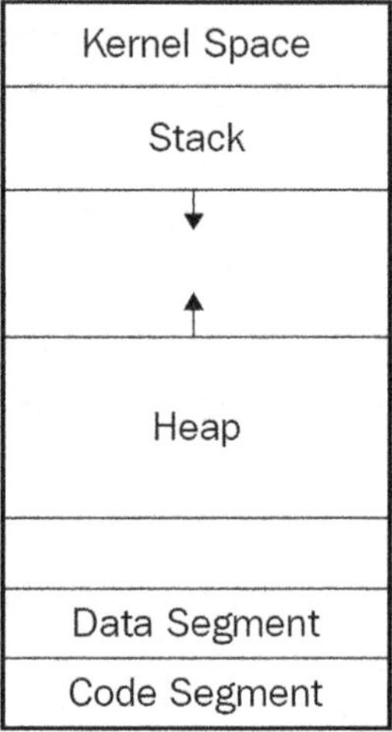

The program uses the heap segment in order to request more memory space than has been required before. This is done at runtime, which means the memory is being allocated dynamically during the program execution. The program requests the OS for new memory space whenever required. The OS doesn't actually know whether the memory is required for an integer, or for a user-defined `Point`, or even for an array of user-defined `Point`. The program requests the memory by passing the actual size of bytes that it requires. For example, to request a space for an object of type `Point`, the `malloc()` function can be used as follows:

```
#include <cstdlib>
struct Point {
  float x;
  float y;
};
```

```
int main() {
  std::malloc(sizeof(Point));
}
```

The `malloc()` function came from the C language and to use it we need to include the `<cstdlib>` header file.

The `malloc()` function allocates a contiguous memory space of `sizeof(Point)` bytes—let's say 8 bytes. It then returns the address of the first byte of that memory as it is the only way to provide access to space. And the thing is, `malloc()` doesn't actually know whether we requested memory space for a `Point` object or an `int`, and it simply returns `void*`. `void*` stores the address of the first byte of allocated memory, but it definitely cannot be used to fetch the actual data by dereferencing the pointer simply because `void` does not define the size of the data. Take a look at the following diagram; it shows that `malloc` allocates memory on the heap:

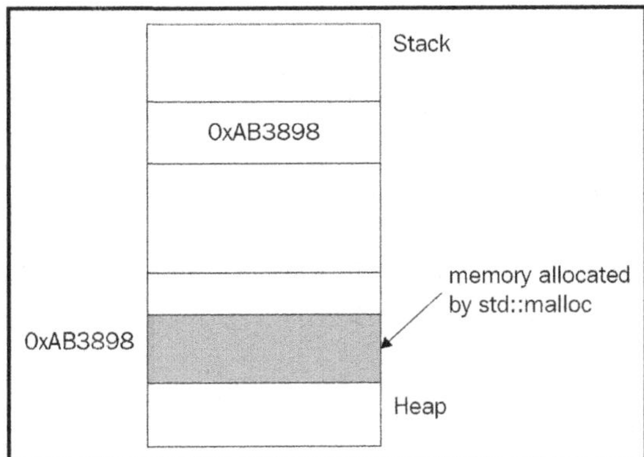

To actually use the memory space, we need to cast the `void` pointer to the desired type:

```
void* raw = std::malloc(sizeof(Point));
Point* p = static_cast<Point*>(raw);
```

Or, simply declare and initialize the pointer with a cast result:

```
Point* p = static_cast<Point*>(std::malloc(sizeof(Point)));
```

C++ solves this headache by introducing the `new` operator, which automatically fetches the size of the memory space to be allocated and converts the result to the desired type:

```
Point* p = new Point;
```

Dynamic memory management is a manual process; there is no similar construct to the stack that automatically deallocates the memory space if it is not required anymore. To manage the memory resource correctly, we should use the `delete` operator when we want to deallocate the space. We will find out the details in `Chapter 5` *Memory Management and Smart Pointers*.

What happens when we access the members of the `Point` object pointed to by `p`? Dereferencing `p` returns the full `Point` object, so to change the value of member `x`, we should do the following:

```
(*p).x = 0.24;
```

Or, better still, access it with the arrow operator:

```
p->x = 0.24;
```

We will dive into the user-defined types and structs in particular in `Chapter 3`, *Details of Object-Oriented Programming*.

Arrays

An array is the basic data structure that provides a collection of data contiguously stored in memory. Many adapters, such as the stack, are implemented using arrays. Their uniqueness is that array elements are all of the same type, which plays a key role in accessing array elements. For example, the following declaration creates an array of 10 integers:

```
int arr[]{0, 1, 2, 3, 4, 5, 6, 7, 8, 9};
```

The name of the array decays to a pointer to its first element. Considering the fact that array elements have the same type, we can access any element of the array by advancing the pointer to its first element. For example, the following code prints the third element of the array:

```
std::cout << *(arr + 2);
```

The same goes with the first element; the following three lines of code are doing the same thing:

```
std::cout << *(arr + 0);
std::cout << *arr;
std::cout << arr[0];
```

To make sure that `arr[2]` and `*(arr + 2)` do the exact same thing, we can do the following:

```
std::cout << *(2 + arr);
```

Moving the `2` behind the `+` won't affect the result, so the following code is valid as well:

```
std::cout << 2[arr];
```

And it prints the third element of the array.

An array element is accessed in constant time, which means accessing the first and the last elements of the array takes the same amount of time. It's because every time we access an array element, we do the following:

1. Advance the pointer by adding the corresponding numeric value
2. Read the contents of memory cells placed at the result pointer

The type of the array indicates how many memory cells should be read (or written). The following diagram illustrates the access:

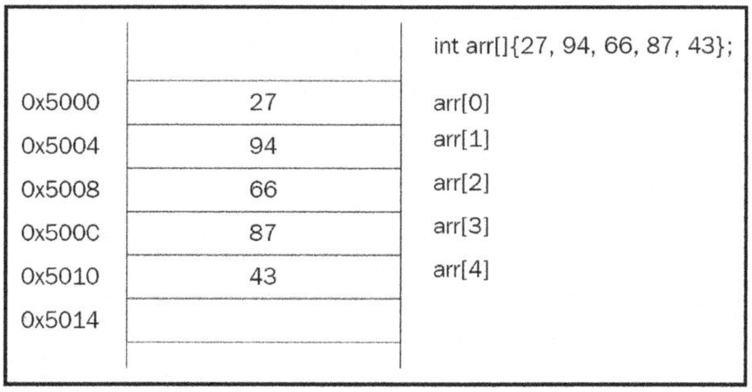

		int arr[]{27, 94, 66, 87, 43};
0x5000	27	arr[0]
0x5004	94	arr[1]
0x5008	66	arr[2]
0x500C	87	arr[3]
0x5010	43	arr[4]
0x5014		

This idea is crucial when creating dynamic arrays, which are arrays that are located in the heap rather than the stack. As we already know, allocating memory from the heap gives the address of its first byte, so the only chance to access elements other than the first one, is by using pointer arithmetic:

```
int* arr = new int[10];
arr[4] = 2; // the same as *(arr + 4) = 2
```

We will discuss more about the structure of arrays and other data structures in `Chapter 6`, *Digging into Data Structures and Algorithms in STL*.

Control flow

The most basic concepts of almost any programming language are conditional statements and loops. We are going to explore them in detail.

Conditionals

It's hard to imagine a program that doesn't contain a conditional statement. It's almost a habit to check the input arguments of functions securing their safe execution. For example, the `divide()` function takes two arguments, divides one by the other, and returns the result. It's pretty clear that we need to make sure that the divisor is not zero:

```
int divide(int a, int b) {
  if (b == 0) {
    throw std::invalid_argument("The divisor is zero");
  }
  return a / b;
}
```

Conditionals are at the core of programming languages; after all, a program is a collection of actions and decisions. For example, the following code uses conditional statements to find the maximum value out of two input arguments:

```
int max(int a, int b) {
  int max;
  if (a > b) {
    // the if block
    max = a;
  } else {
    // the else block
    max = b;
  }
  return max;
}
```

The preceding example is oversimplified on purpose to express the usage of the `if-else` statement as is. However, what interests us the most is the implementation of such a conditional statement. What does the compiler generate when it encounters an `if` statement? The CPU executes instructions sequentially one by one, and instructions are simple commands doing exactly one thing. We can use complex expressions in a single line in a high-level programming language such as C++, while the assembly instructions are simple commands that can do only one simple operation in one cycle: `move`, `add`, `subtract`, and so on.

The CPU fetches the instruction from the code memory segment, decodes it to find out what it should exactly do (move data, add numbers, subtract them), and executes the command.

To run at its fastest, the CPU stores the operands and the result of the execution in storage units called **registers**. You can think of registers as temporary variables of the CPU. Registers are physical memory units that are located within the CPU so the access is much faster compared to the RAM. To access the registers from an assembly language program, we use their specified names, such as `rax`, `rbx`, `rdx`, and so on. The CPU commands operate on registers rather than the RAM cells; that's why the CPU has to copy the contents of the variable from the memory to registers, execute operations and store the results in a register, and then copy the value of the register back to the memory cell.

For example, the following C++ expression takes just a single line of code:

```
a = b + 2 * c - 1;
```

It would look similar to the following assembly representation (comments are added after semicolons):

```
mov rax, b; copy the contents of "b"
          ; located in the memory to the register rax
mov rbx, c; the same for the "c" to be able to calculate 2 * c
mul rbx, 2; multiply the value of the rbx register with
          ; immediate value 2 (2 * c)
add rax, rbx; add rax (b) with rbx (2*c) and store back in the rax
sub rax, 1; subtract 1 from rax
mov a, rax; copy the contents of rax to the "a" located in the memory
```

A conditional statement suggests that a portion of the code should be skipped. For example, calling `max(11, 22)` means the `if` block will be omitted. To express this in the assembly language, the idea of jumps is used. We compare two values and, based on the result, we jump to a specified portion of the code. We label the portion to make it possible to find the set of instructions. For example, to skip adding `42` to the register `rbx`, we can *jump* to the portion labeled `UNANSWERED` using the unconditional jump instruction `jpm` as shown:

```
mov rax, 2
mov rbx, 0
jmp UNANSWERED
add rbx, 42; will be skipped
UNANSWERED:
  add rax, 1
  ; ...
```

The jmp instruction performs an unconditional jump; that means it starts the execution of the first instruction at a specified label without any condition check. The good news is that the CPU provides conditional jumps as well. The body of the max() function will translate into the following assembly code (simplified), where the jg and jle commands are interpreted as *jump if greater than* and *jump if less than or equal*, respectively (based on the results of the comparison using the cmp instruction):

```
mov rax, max; copy the "max" into the rax register
mov rbx, a
mov rdx, b
cmp rbx, rdx; compare the values of rbx and rdx (a and b)
jg GREATER; jump if rbx is greater than rdx (a > b)
jl LESSOREQUAL; jump if rbx is lesser than
GREATER:
  mov rax, rbx; max = a
LESSOREQUAL:
  mov rax, rdx; max = b
```

In the preceding code, the labels GREATER and LESSOREQUAL represent the if and else clauses of the max() function implemented earlier.

The switch statement

Conditionals such as the switch statement use the same logic as shown:

```
switch (age) {
case 18:
  can_drink = false;
  can_code = true;
  break;
case 21:
  can_drink = true;
  can_code = true;
  break;
default:
  can_drink = false;
}
```

Let's suppose rax represents the age, rbx represents can_drink, and rdx represents can_code. The preceding example will translate into the following assembly instructions (simplified to express the basic idea):

```
cmp rax, 18
je CASE_18
cmp rax, 21
```

```
je CASE_21
je CASE_DEFAULT
CASE_18:
  mov rbx, 0; cannot drink
  mov rdx, 1; can code
  jmp BEYOND_SWITCH; break
CASE_21:
  mov rbx, 1
  mov rdx, 1
  jmp BEYOND_SWITCH
CASE_DEFAULT:
  mov rbx, 0
BEYOND_SWITCH:
  ; ....
```

Each `break` statement translates into jumping to the `BEYOND_SWITCH` label, so if we forget the `break` keyword, for example, in the case where `age` is `18`, the execution will reach through `CASE_21` as well. That's why you should not forget the `break` statement.

Let's find a way to avoid using conditionals in the source, both to make the code shorter and possibly faster. We will use function pointers.

Replacing conditionals with function pointers

Previously, we looked at memory segments, and one of the most important segments is the code segment (also called a text segment). This segment contains the program image, which is the instructions of the program that should be executed. Instructions are usually grouped into functions, which provide a unique name allowing us to call them from other functions. Functions reside in the code segment of the executable file.

A function has its address. We can declare a pointer that takes the address of the function and then use it later to call that function:

```
int get_answer() { return 42; }
int (*fp)() = &get_answer;
// int (*fp)() = get_answer; same as &get_answer
```

The function pointer can be called the same way as the original function:

```
get_answer(); // returns 42
fp(); // returns 42
```

Let's suppose we are writing a program that takes two numbers and a character from the input and executes an arithmetic operation on the numbers. The operation is specified by the character, whether it's `+`, `-`, `*`, or `/`. We implement four functions, `add()`, `subtract()`, `multiply()`, and `divide()`, and call one of them based on the value of the character input.

Instead of checking the value of the character in a bunch of `if` statements or a `switch` statement, we will map the type of the operation to the specified function using a hash table:

```
#include <unordered_map>
int add(int a, int b) { return a + b; }
int subtract(int a, int b) { return a - b; }
int multiply(int a, int b) { return a * b; }
int divide(int a, int b) { return (b == 0) ? 0 : a / b; }

int main() {
  std::unordered_map<char, int (*)(int, int)> operations;
  operations['+'] = &add;
  operations['-'] = &subtract;
  operations['*'] = &multiply;
  operations['/'] = &divide;
  // read the input
  char op;
  int num1, num2;
  std::cin >> num1 >> num2 >> op;
  // perform the operation, as follows
  operations[op](num1, num2);
}
```

As you can see, `std::unordered_map` maps `char` to a function pointer defined as `(*)(int, int)`. That is, it can point to any function that takes two integers and returns an integer.

The hash table is represented by `std::unordered_map`, defined in the `<unordered_map>` header. We will discuss it in detail in `Chapter 6`, *Digging into Data Structures and Algorithms in STL*

Now we don't need to write the following:

```
if (op == '+') {
  add(num1, num2);
} else if (op == '-') {
  subtract(num1, num2);
} else if (op == '*') {
  ...
```

Instead, we simply call the function mapped by the character:

```
operations[op](num1, num2);
```

Though the use of a hash table is much prettier and looks more professional, you should take care of unexpected cases, such as invalid user input.

Functions as types

The second argument for `unordered_map` is `int (*)(int, int)`, which literally means a pointer to a function taking two integers and returning an integer. C++ supports the class template `std::function` as a general-purpose function wrapper allowing us to store callable objects including ordinary functions, lambda expressions, functions objects, and so on. The stored object is referred to as the target of `std::function` and if it doesn't have a target, it will throw the `std::bad_function_call` exception if invoked. This helps us both to make the `operations` hash table accept any callable object as its second parameter and to handle exceptional cases such as invalid character input, mentioned earlier.

The following code block illustrates this:

```
#include <functional>
#include <unordered_map>
// add, subtract, multiply and divide declarations omitted for brevity
int main() {
  std::unordered_map<char, std::function<int(int, int)> > operations;
  operations['+'] = &add;
  // ...
}
```

Notice the argument for `std::function`; it has the form `int(int, int)` rather than `int(*)(int, int)`. Using `std::function` helps us to handle exceptional situations. For example, calling `operations['x'](num1, num2);` will lead to, creation of the empty `std::function` mapped to the character `x`.

And calling it will throw an exception, so we can ensure the safety of the code by properly handling the call:

```
// code omitted for brevity
std::cin >> num1 >> num2 >> op;
try {
  operations[op](num1, num2);
} catch (std::bad_function_call e) {
  // handle the exception
  std::cout << "Invalid operation";
}
```

Finally, we can use *lambda expressions*— unnamed functions constructed in place and able to capture variables in scope. For example, instead of declaring the preceding functions and then inserting them into the hash table, we can create a lambda expression right before inserting it into the hash table:

```
std::unordered_map<char, std::function<int(int, int)> > operations;
operations['+'] = [](int a, int b) { return a + b; }
operations['-'] = [](int a, int b) { return a * b; }
// ...
std::cin >> num1 >> num2 >> op;
try {
  operations[op](num1, num2);
} catch (std::bad_functional_call e) {
  // ...
}
```

Lambda expressions will be covered throughout the book.

Loops

Loops may be perceived as repeatable `if` statements, which again should be translated into CPU comparison and jump instructions. For example, we can calculate the sum of numbers from 0 to 10 using the `while` loop:

```
auto num = 0;
auto sum = 0;
while (num <= 10) {
  sum += num;
  ++num;
}
```

This will translate to the following assembly code (simplified):

```
mov rax, 0; the sum
mov rcx, 0; the num
LOOP:
  cmp rbx, 10
  jg END; jump to the END if num is greater than 10
  add rax, rcx; add to sum
  inc rcx; increment num
  jmp LOOP; repeat
END:
  ...
```

C++17 introduced init statements that can be used in conditionals and loops. The `num` variable declared outside of the `while` loop may now be moved into the loop:

```
auto sum = 0;
while (auto num = 0; num <= 10) {
  sum += num;
  ++num;
}
```

The same rule applies to the `if` statement, for example:

```
int get_absolute(int num) {
  if (int neg = -num; neg < 0) {
    return -neg;
  }
  return num;
}
```

C++11 introduced the range-based `for` loop, which makes the syntax much clearer. For example, let's call all the arithmetic operations we defined earlier using the new `for` loop:

```
for (auto& op: operations) {
  std::cout << op.second(num1, num2);
}
```

Iterating `unordered_map` returns a pair with the first and second members, the first being the key, and the second being the value mapped to that key. C++17 moved us even further, allowing us to write the same loop as follows:

```
for (auto& [op, func]: operations) {
  std::cout << func(num1, num2);
}
```

Knowing what the compiler actually generates is key in designing and implementing efficient software. We touched on the low-level details of conditionals and loops, which are at the base of almost every program.

Summary

In this chapter, we introduced the details of program execution. We discussed functions and the `main()` function with some of its special properties. We found out how the recursion works and that the `main()` function cannot be called recursively.

As C++ is one of the few high-level languages that supports low-level programming concepts such as accessing memory bytes by their address, we studied how data resides in the memory and how can we incorporate pointers in accessing that data. Understanding these details is a must for a professional C++ programmer.

Lastly, we touched on the topic of conditionals and loops from the perspective of an assembly language. Throughout the chapter, we introduced C++20 features.

In the next chapter, we will learn more about **object-oriented programming (OOP)**, including the inner details of the language object model. We will dive into the details of virtual functions and see how to use polymorphism.

Questions

1. How many parameters does the `main()` function have?
2. What is the `constexpr` specifier used for?
3. Why is it advised to use iteration over recursion?
4. What's the difference between the stack and the heap?

5. What is the size of the `ptr` if it is declared as `int*`?
6. Why is access to an array element considered a constant time operation?
7. What will happen if we forget the `break` keyword in any case of the `switch` statement?
8. How would you implement the `multiply()` and `divide()` functions from the arithmetic operations example as lambda expressions?

Further reading

You can refer to the following book for more information on the topics covered in this chapter: *C++ High Performance,* by Viktor Sehr and Bjorn Andrist (`https://www.amazon.com/gp/product/1787120953`).

3
Details of Object-Oriented Programming

The difficulty of designing, implementing, and maintaining a software project arises with respect to the complexity of the project. A simple calculator could be written using the procedural approach (that is, the procedural programming paradigm), while a bank account management system would be too complex to implement using the same approach.

C++ supports **Object-Oriented programming (OOP)**, a paradigm that is built upon dissecting entities into objects that exist in a web of close intercommunication. Imagine a simple scenario in the real world when you take the remote to change the TV channel. At least three different objects take part in this action: the remote, the TV, and, most importantly, you. To express the real-world objects and their relationship using a programming language, we aren't forced to use classes, class inheritance, abstract classes, interfaces, virtual functions, and so on. The mentioned features and concepts make the process of designing and coding a lot easier as they allow us to express and share ideas in an elegant manner, but they are not mandatory. As the creator of C++, Bjarne Stroustrup, says, "Not every program should be object-oriented." To understand high-level concepts and features of the OOP paradigm, we will try to look behind the scenes. Throughout this book, we will dive into the design of object-oriented programs. Understanding the essence of objects and their relationship, and then using them to design object-oriented programs, is one of the goals of this book.

In this chapter, we'll learn about the following topics in detail:

- Introduction to OOP
- The C++ object model
- Class relationships, including inheritance
- Polymorphism
- Useful design patterns

Technical requirements

The g++ compiler with the `-std=c++2a` option is used to compile the examples throughout this chapter.

You can find the source files for this chapter at `https://github.com/PacktPublishing/Expert-CPP` .

Understanding objects

Most of the time, we operate with a collection of data grouped under a certain name, thus making an **abstraction**. Variables such as `is_military`, `speed`, and `seats` don't make much sense if they're perceived separately. Grouping them under the name with `spaceship` changes the way we perceive the data stored in the variables. We now refer to the many variables packed as one single object. To do so, we use abstraction; that is, we collect the individual properties of a real-world object from the perspective of the observer. An abstraction is a key tool in the programmer's toolchain as it allows them to deal with complexity. The C language introduced the `struct` as a way to aggregate data, as shown in the following code:

```
struct spaceship {
  bool is_military;
  int speed;
  int seats;
};
```

Grouping data is somewhat necessary for object-oriented programming. Each group of data is referred to as an object.

Low-level details of objects

C++ does its best to support compatibility with the C language. While C structs are just a tool that allows us to aggregate data, C++ makes them equal to classes, allowing them to have constructors, virtual functions, inherit others structs, and so on. The only difference between a `struct` and a `class` is the default visibility modifier: `public` for structs and `private` for classes. There is usually no difference in using structs over classes or vice versa. OOP requires more than just a data aggregation. To fully understand OOP, let's find out how we would we incorporate the OOP paradigm if we have only simple structs providing data aggregation and nothing more.

A central entity of an e-commerce marketplace such as Amazon or Alibaba is the `Product`, which we represent in the following way:

```
struct Product {
  std::string name;
  double price;
  int rating;
  bool available;
};
```

We will add more members to the `Product` if necessary. The memory layout of an object of the `Product` type can be pictured like this:

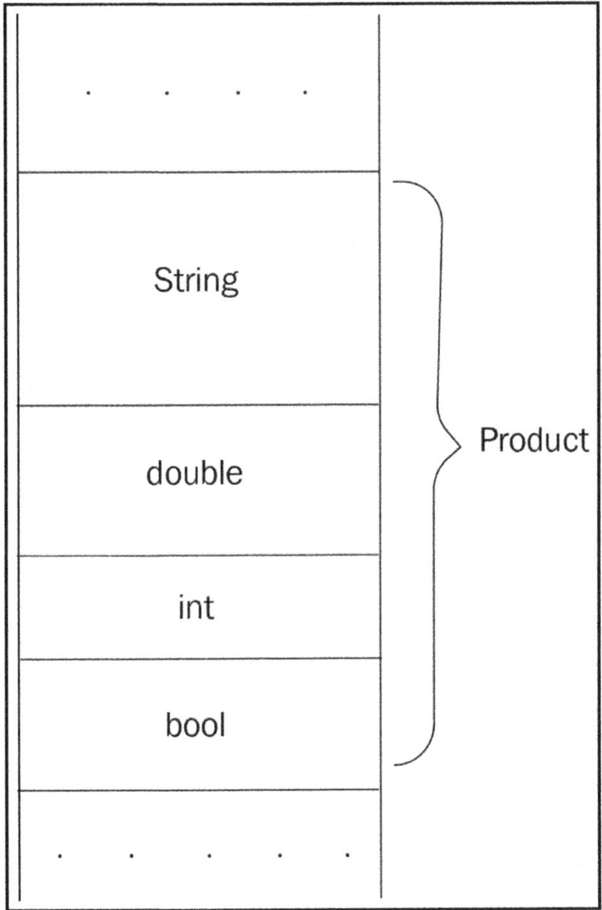

Declaring a `Product` object takes `sizeof(Product)` space in memory, while declaring a pointer or a reference to the object takes the space required to store the address (usually 4 or 8 bytes). See the following code block:

```
Product book;
Product tshirt;
Product* ptr = &book;
Product& ref = tshirt;
```

We can picture the preceding code as follows:

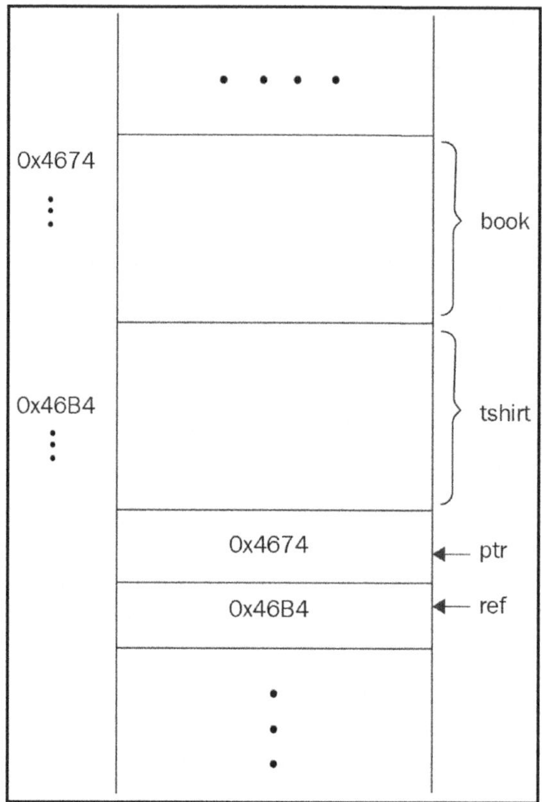

Let's start with the space the `Product` object takes in memory. We can calculate the size of the `Product` object summing up the sizes of its member variables. The size of a `boolean` variable is 1 byte. The exact size of the `double` or the `int` is not specified in the C++ standard. In 64-bit machines, a `double` variable usually takes 8 bytes and an `int` variable takes 4 bytes.

The implementation of `std::string` is not specified in the standard, so its size depends on the library implementation. `string` stores a pointer to a character array, but it also might store the number of allocated characters to efficiently return it when `size()` is called. Some implementations of `std::string` take 8, 24, or 32 bytes of memory, but we will stick to 24 bytes in our example. By summing it up, the size of the `Product` will be as follows:

```
24 (std::string) + 8 (double) + 4 (int) + 1 (bool) = 37 bytes.
```

Printing the size of the `Product` outputs a different value:

```
std::cout << sizeof(Product);
```

It outputs `40` instead of the calculated 37 bytes. The reason behind the redundant bytes is the padding of the struct, a technique practiced by the compiler to optimize the access to individual members of the object. The **Central Processing Unit (CPU)** reads the memory in fixed-size words. The size of the word is defined by the CPU (usually, it's 32 or 64 bits long). The CPU is able to access the data at once if it's starting from a word-aligned address. For example, the `boolean` data member of the `Product` requires 1 byte of memory and can be placed right after the rating member. As it turns out, the compiler aligns the data for faster access. Let's suppose the word size is 4 bytes. This means that the CPU will access a variable without redundant steps if the variable starts from an address that's divisible by 4. The compiler augments the struct earlier with additional bytes to align the members to word-boundary addresses.

High-level details of objects

We deal with objects as entities representing the result of abstraction. We have already mentioned the role of the observer, that is, the programmer who defines the object based on the problem domain. The way the programmer defines this represents the process of abstraction. Let's take an example of an e-commerce marketplace and its products. Two different teams of programmers might have different views of the same product. The team that implements the website cares about the properties of the object that are essential to website visitors: buyers. The properties that we showed earlier in the `Product` struct are mostly meant for website visitors, such as the selling price, the rating of the product, and so on. Programmers that implement the website touch the problem domain and verify the properties that are essential to defining a `Product` object.

The team that implements the online tools that help manage the products in the warehouse cares about the properties of the object that are essential in terms of product placement, quality control, and shipment. This team shouldn't actually care about the **rating** of the product or even its **price**. This team mostly cares about the **weight**, **dimensions**, and **conditions** of the product. The following illustration shows the properties of interest:

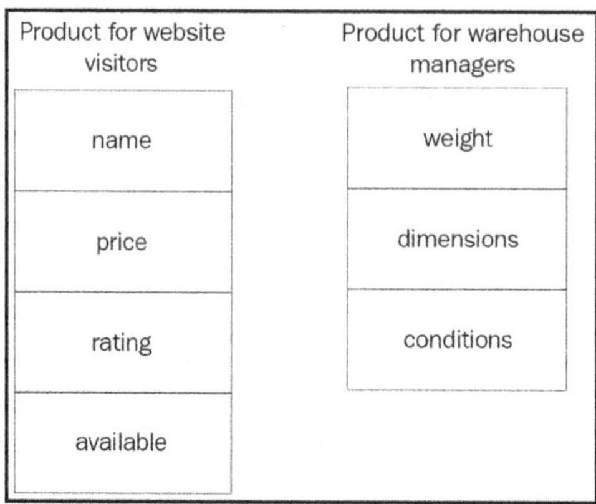

The first thing that programmers should do when starting the project is to analyze the problem and gather the requirements. In other words, they should get familiar with the *problem domain* and define the *project requirements*. The process of analyzing leads to defining objects and their types, such as the `Product` we discussed earlier. To get proper results from analyzing, we should think in objects, and, by thinking in objects, we mean considering the three main properties of objects: **state**, **behavior**, and **identity**.

State

Each object has a state that may or may not differ from the state of other objects. We've already introduced the `Product` struct, which represents an abstraction of a physical (or digital) product. All the members of a `product` object collectively represent the state of the object. For example, the `Product` contains members such as `available`, which is a Boolean; it equals `true` if the product is in stock. The values of the member variables define the state of the object. If you assign new values to the object member, its state will change:

```
Product cpp_book; // declaring the object
...
// changing the state of the object cpp_book
cpp_book.available = true;
cpp_book.rating = 5;
```

The state of the object is the combination of all of its properties and values.

Identity

Identity is what differentiates one object from another. Even if we try to declare two physically indistinguishable objects, they will still have different names for their variables, that is, different identities:

```
Product book1;
book1.rating = 4;
book1.name = "Book";
Product book2;
book2.rating = 4;
book2.name = "Book";
```

The objects in the preceding example have the same state, but they differ by the names we refer to them by, that is, `book1` and `book2`. Let's say we had the ability to somehow create objects with the same name, as shown in the following code:

```
Product prod;
Product prod; // won't compile, but still "what if?"
```

If this was the case, they would still have different addresses in memory:

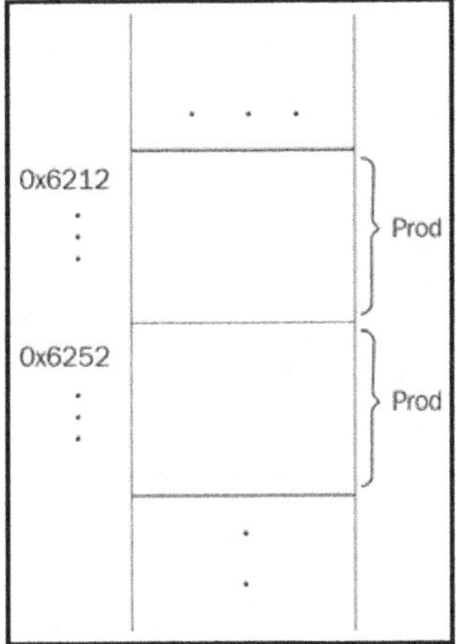

Identity is a fundamental property of the object and is one of the reasons why we can't create *empty* objects, such as the following:

```
struct Empty {};

int main() {
  Empty e;
  std::cout << sizeof(e);
}
```

The preceding code will not output 0 as expected. The size of an empty object is not specified in the standard; compiler developers tend to allocate 1 byte for such objects, though you might encounter 4 or 8 as well. Two or more instances of Empty should have different addresses in memory, so the compiler must make sure objects will take up at least 1 byte of memory.

Behavior

In previous examples, we assigned 5 and then 4 to the rating member variable. We can easily make things unexpectedly wrong by assigning invalid values to the object, like so:

```
cpp_book.rating = -12;
```

-12 is invalid in terms of the rating of a product and will confuse users, if allowed to. We can control the behavior of the changes made to the object by providing **setter** functions:

```
void set_rating(Product* p, int r) {
  if (r >= 1 && r <= 5) {
    p->rating = r;
  }
  // otherwise ignore
}
...
set_rating(&cpp_book, -12); // won't change the state
```

An object acts and reacts to the requests from other objects. The requests are performed via function calls, which otherwise are called **messages**: an object passes a message to another. In the preceding example, the object that passed the corresponding set_rating message to the cpp_book object represents the object that we call the set_rating() function in. In this case, we suppose that we call the function from main(), which doesn't actually represent any object at all. We could say it's the global object, the one that operates the main() function, though there is not an entity like that in C++.

We distinguish the objects conceptually rather than physically. That's the main point of thinking in objects. The physical implementation of some concepts of object-oriented programming is not standardized, so we can name the Product struct as a class and claim that cpp_book is an **instance** of the Product ,and that it has a member function called set_rating(). The C++ implementation almost does the same: it provides syntactically convenient structures (classes, visibility modifiers, inheritance, and so on) and translates them into simple structs with global functions such as set_rating() in the preceding example. Now, let's dive into the details of the C++ object model.

Mimicking a class

A struct allows us to group variables, name them, and create objects. The idea of a class is to include the corresponding operations in the object, grouping both data and operations that are applicable to that particular data. For example, for the object of the `Product` type, it will be natural to call the `set_rating()` function on the object directly, rather than having a separate global function that takes a `Product` object via a pointer and modifies it. However, as we agreed to use structs in the C manner, we can't afford it to have member functions. To mimic a class using a C struct, we have to declare functions that work with the `Product` object as global functions, as shown in the following code:

```
struct Product {
  std::string name;
  double price;
  int rating;
  bool available;
};

void initialize(Product* p) {
  p->price = 0.0;
  p->rating = 0;
  p->available = false;
}

void set_name(Product* p, const std::string& name) {
  p->name = name;
}

std::string get_name(Product* p) {
  return p->name;
}

void set_price(Product* p, double price) {
  if (price < 0 || price > 9999.42) return;
  p->price = price;
}

double get_price(Product* p) {
  return p->price;
}

// code omitted for brevity
```

To use the struct as a class, we should manually call the functions in the proper order. For example, to use the object with properly initialized default values, we have to call the `initialize()` function first:

```
int main() {
  Product cpp_book;
  initialize(&cpp_book);
  set_name(&cpp_book, "Mastering C++ Programming");
  std::cout << "Book title is: " << get_name(&cpp_book);
  // ...
}
```

This seems doable, but the preceding code will quickly turn into an unorganized mess if new types are added. For example, consider the `Warehouse` struct that keeps track of products:

```
struct Warehouse {
  Product* products;
  int capacity;
  int size;
};

void initialize_warehouse(Warehouse* w) {
  w->capacity = 1000;
  w->size = 0;
  w->products = new Product[w->capacity];
  for (int ix = 0; ix < w->capacity; ++ix) {
    initialize(&w->products[ix]); // initialize each Product object
  }
}

void set_size(int size) { ... }
// code omitted for brevity
```

The first obvious issue is the naming of functions. We had to name the initializer function of the `Warehouse` `initialize_warehouse` to avoid conflict with the already declared `initialize()` function for the `Product`. We might consider renaming the functions for the `Product` type to avoid possible conflicts in the future. Next comes the mess with functions. Now, we have a bunch of global functions, which will increase in number as we add new types. It will be even more unmanageable if we add some hierarchy of types.

Though compilers tend to translate classes into structs with global functions, as we showed earlier, C++ and other high-level programming languages solve these and other issues that had not been mentioned by, introducing classes with smooth mechanisms of organizing them into hierarchies. Conceptually, keywords (`class`, `public`, or `private`) and mechanisms (inheritance and polymorphism) are there for developers to conveniently organize their code, but won't make the life of the compiler any easier.

Working with classes

Classes make things a lot easier when dealing with objects. They do the simplest necessary thing in OOP: they combine data with functions for manipulating data. Let's rewrite the example of the `Product` struct using a class and its powerful features:

```
class Product {
public:
  Product() = default; // default constructor
  Product(const Product&); // copy constructor
  Product(Product&&); // move constructor

  Product& operator=(const Product&) = default;
  Product& operator=(Product&&) = default;
  // destructor is not declared, should be generated by the compiler
public:
  void set_name(const std::string&);
  std::string name() const;
  void set_availability(bool);
  bool available() const;
  // code omitted for brevity

private:
  std::string name_;
  double price_;
  int rating_;
  bool available_;
};

std::ostream& operator<<(std::ostream&, const Product&);
std::istream& operator>>(std::istream&, Product&);
```

The class declaration seems more organized, even though it exposes more functions than we use to define a similar struct. Here's how we should illustrate the class:

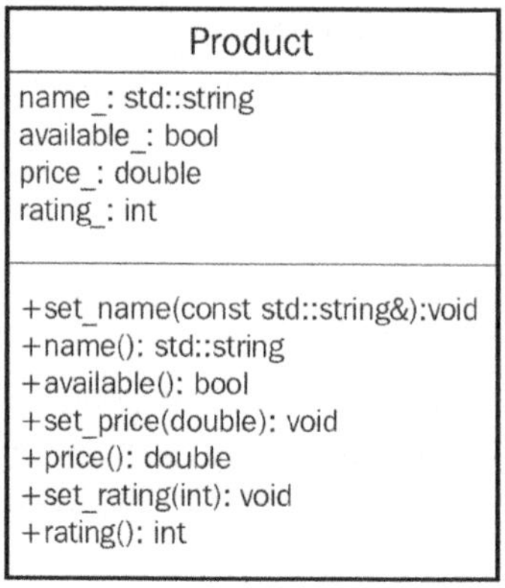

Product

name_: std::string
available_: bool
price_: double
rating_: int

+set_name(const std::string&):void
+name(): std::string
+available(): bool
+set_price(double): void
+price(): double
+set_rating(int): void
+rating(): int

The preceding image is somewhat special. As you can see, it has organized sections, signs before the names of functions, and so on. This type of diagram is called a **Unified Modeling Language (UML)** class diagram. UML is a way to standardize the process of illustrating classes and their relationship. The first section is the name of the class (in bold), next comes the section for member variables, and then the section for member functions. The + (plus) sign in front of a function name means that the function is public. Member variables are usually private, but, if you need to emphasize this, you can use the - (minus) sign. We can omit all the details by simply illustrating the class, as shown in the following UML diagram:

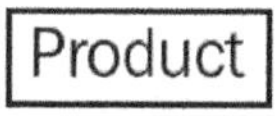

Product

We will use UML diagrams throughout this book and will introduce new types of diagrams as needed. Before dealing with initializing, copying, moving, default and deleted functions, and, of course, operator overloading, let's clear a couple of things up.

Classes from the compiler perspective

First of all, no matter how monstrous the class from earlier may seem in comparison to the previously introduced struct, the compiler will translate it into the following code (we slightly modified it for the sake of simplicity):

```
struct Product {
  std::string name_;
  bool available_;
```

```
  double price_;
  int rating_;
};

// we forced the compiler to generate the default constructor
void Product_constructor(Product&);
void Product_copy_constructor(Product& this, const Product&);
void Product_move_constructor(Product& this, Product&&);
// default implementation
Product& operator=(Product& this, const Product&);
// default implementation
Product& operator=(Product& this, Product&&);

void Product_set_name(const std::string&);
// takes const because the method was declared as const
std::string Product_name(const Product& this);
void Product_set_availability(Product& this, bool b);
bool Product_availability(const Product& this);

std::ostream& operator<<(std::ostream&, const Product&);
std::istream& operator>>(std::istream&, Product&);
```

Basically, the compiler generates the same code that we introduced earlier as a way to mimic class behavior using a simple struct. Though compilers vary in techniques and methods of implementing the C++ object model, the preceding example is one of the popular approaches practiced by compiler developers. It balances the space and time efficiency in accessing object members (including member functions).

Next, we should consider that the compiler edits our code by augmenting and modifying it. The following code declares the global `create_apple()` function, which creates and returns a `Product` object with values specific to an apple. It also declares a book object in the `main()` function:

```
Product create_apple() {
  Product apple;
  apple.set_name("Red apple");
  apple.set_price("0.2");
  apple.set_rating(5);
  apple.set_available(true);
  return apple;
}

int main() {
  Product red_apple = create_apple();
  Product book;
  Product* ptr = &book;
  ptr->set_name("Alice in Wonderland");
```

```
    ptr->set_price(6.80);
    std::cout << "I'm reading " << book.name()
              << " and I bought an apple for " << red_apple.price()
              << std::endl;
}
```

We already know that the compiler modifies the class to translate it into a struct and moves member functions to the global scope, each of which takes the reference (or a pointer) to the class as its first parameter. To support those modifications in the client code, it should also modify all access to the objects.

A line or lines of code that declare or use already declared class objects are referred to as **client code**.

Here's how we will assume the compiler modifies the preceding code (we used the word *assume* because we're trying to introduce a compiler-abstract rather than a compiler-specific approach):

```
void create_apple(Product& apple) {
  Product_set_name(apple, "Red apple");
  Product_set_price(apple, 0.2);
  Product_set_rating(apple, 5);
  Product_set_available(apple, true);
  return;
}

int main() {
  Product red_apple;
  Product_constructor(red_apple);
  create_apple(red_apple);
  Product book;
  Product* ptr;
  Product_constructor(book);
  Product_set_name(*ptr, "Alice in Wonderland");
  Product_set_price(*ptr, 6.80);
  std::ostream os = operator<<(std::cout, "I'm reading ");
  os = operator<<(os, Product_name(book));
  os = operator<<(os, " and I bought an apple for ");
  os = operator<<(os, Product_price(red_apple));
  operator<<(os, std::endl);
  // destructor calls are skipped because the compiler
  // will remove them as empty functions to optimize the code
  // Product_destructor(book);
  // Product_destructor(red_apple);
}
```

The compiler also optimized the call to the `create_apple()` function to avoid temporary object creation. We will discuss the invisible temporaries that were generated by the compiler later in this chapter.

Initialization and destruction

As shown previously, the creation of an object is a two-step process: memory allocation and initialization. Memory allocation is a result of an object declaration. C++ doesn't care about the initialization of variables; it allocates the memory (whether it is automatic or manual) and it's done. The actual initialization should be done by the programmer, which is why we have a constructor in the first place.

The same logic follows for the destructor. If we skip the declarations of the default constructor or destructor, the compiler should generate them implicitly, which it would also remove in case they are empty (to eliminate redundant calls to empty functions). The default constructor will not be generated by the compiler if any constructor with parameters is declared, including the copy constructor. We can force the compiler to implicitly generate the default constructor:

```
class Product {
public:
  Product() = default;
  // ...
};
```

We also can force it not to generate the compiler by using the `delete` specifier, as shown here:

```
class Product {
public:
  Product() = delete;
  // ...
};
```

This will prohibit default-initialized object declarations, that is, `Product p;` won't compile.

Destructors are called in the order opposite to object declarations because the automatic memory allocation is managed by a stack and the stack, is a data structure adapter that follows the **last in, first out (LIFO)** rule.

Object initialization happens on its creation. Destruction usually happens when the object is no longer accessible. The latter may be tricky when the object is allocated on the heap. Take a look at the following code; it declares four `Product` objects in different scopes and segments of memory:

```
static Product global_prod; // #1

Product* foo() {
  Product* heap_prod = new Product(); // #4
  heap_prod->name = "Sample";
  return heap_prod;
}

int main() {
  Product stack_prod; // #2
  if (true) {
    Product tmp; // #3
    tmp.rating = 3;
  }
  stack_prod.price = 4.2;
  foo();
}
```

`global_prod` has a static storage duration and is placed in the global/static section of the program; it is initialized before `main()` is called. When `main()` starts, `stack_prod` is allocated on the stack and will be destroyed when `main()` ends (the closing curly brace of the function is considered as its end). Though the conditional expression looks weird and too artificial, it's a good way to express the block scope.

The `tmp` object will also be allocated on the stack, but its storage duration is limited to the scope it has been declared in: it will be automatically destroyed when the execution leaves the `if` block. That's why variables on the stack have *automatic storage duration*. Finally, when the `foo()` function is called, it declares the `heap_prod` pointer, which points to the address of the `Product` object allocated on the heap.

The preceding code contains a memory leak because the `heap_prod` pointer (which itself has an automatic storage duration) will be destroyed when the execution reaches the end of `foo()`, while the object allocated on the heap won't be affected. Don't mix the pointer and the actual object it points to: the pointer just contains the value of the object, but it doesn't represent the object.

Don't forget to deallocate the memory that's dynamically allocated on the heap, either by manually calling the delete operator or using smart pointers. Smart pointers will be discussed in `Chapter 5`, *Memory Management and Smart Pointers.*

When the function ends, the memory for its arguments and local variables allocated on the stack will be freed, but `global_prod` will be destroyed when the program ends, that is, after the `main()` function finishes. The destructor will be called when the object is about to be destroyed.

Copying objects

There are two kinds of copying: a *deep* copy and a *shallow* copy of objects. The language allows us to manage copy-initialization and the assignment of objects with the **copy constructor** and the **assignment operator**. This is a necessary feature for programmers because we can control the semantics of copying. Take a look at the following example:

```
Product p1;
Product p2;
p2.set_price(4.2);
p1 = p2; // p1 now has the same price
Product p3 = p2; // p3 has the same price
```

The line `p1 = p2;` is a call to the assignment operator, while the last line is a call to the copy constructor. The equals sign shouldn't confuse you regarding whether it's an assignment or a copy constructor call. Each time you see a declaration followed by an assignment, consider it a copy construction. The same applies to the new initializer syntax (`Product p3{p2};`).

The compiler will generate the following code:

```
Product p1;
Product p2;
Product_set_price(p2, 4.2);
operator=(p1, p2);
Product p3;
Product_copy_constructor(p3, p2);
```

The default implementation of the copy constructor (and assignment operator) performs a member-wise copy of objects, as shown in the following diagram:

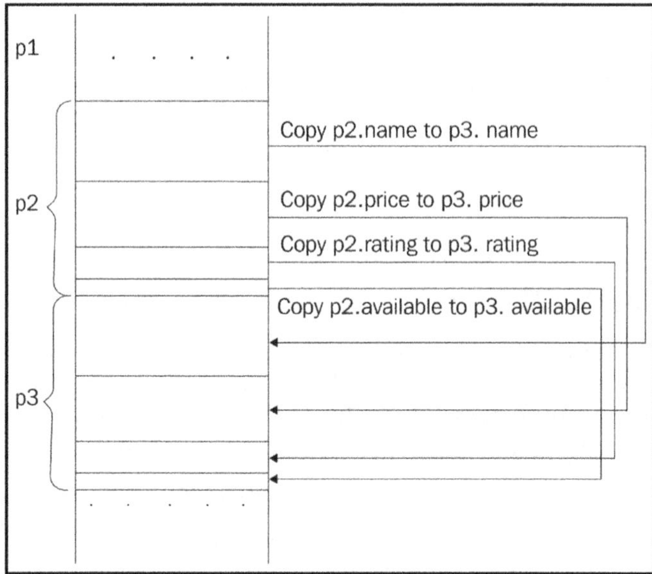

Custom implementation is required in case the member-wise copy produces invalid copies. For example, consider the following copy of `Warehouse` objects:

```
class Warehouse {
public:
  Warehouse()
    : size_{0}, capacity_{1000}, products_{nullptr}
  {
    products_ = new Products[capacity_];
  }

  ~Warehouse() {
    delete [] products_;
  }

public:
  void add_product(const Product& p) {
    if (size_ == capacity_) { /* resize */ }
    products_[size_++] = p;
  }
  // other functions omitted for brevity

private:
```

```
  int size_;
  int capacity_;
  Product* products_;
};

int main() {
  Warehouse w1;
  Product book;
  Product apple;
  // ...assign values to products (omitted for brevity)
  w1.add_product(book);
  Warehouse w2 = w1; // copy
  w2.add_product(apple);
  // something somewhere went wrong...
}
```

The preceding code declares two `Warehouse` objects, and two different products are then added to the warehouses. Though this example is somewhat unnatural, it shows the dangers of the default implementation of copying. The following illustration shows us what went wrong in the code:

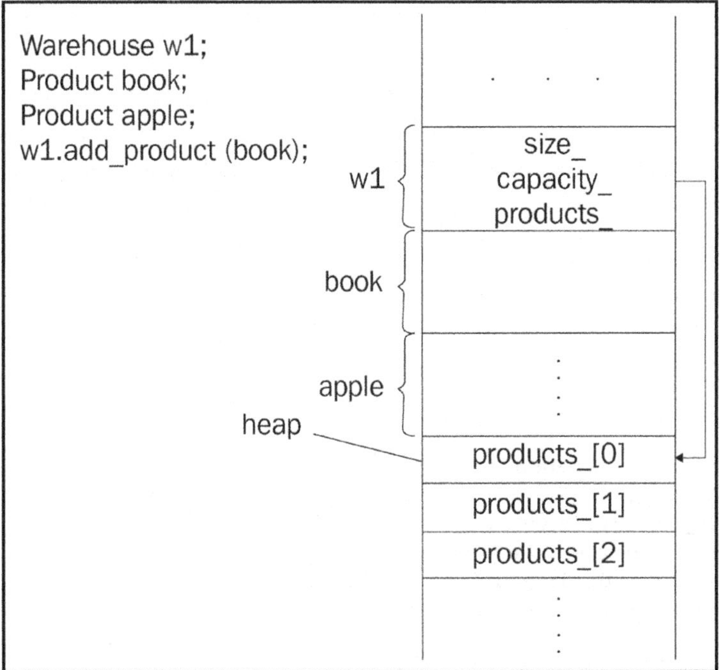

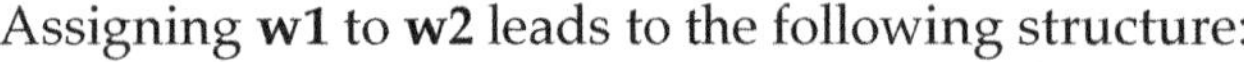

Assigning **w1** to **w2** leads to the following structure:

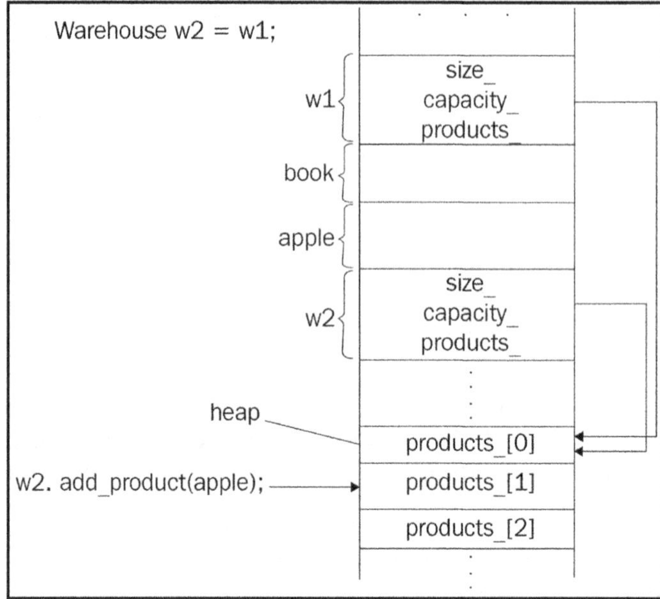

The default implementation simply copies each member of `w1` to `w2`. After copying, both `products_` members of `w1` and `w2` point to the same location on the heap. When we add a new product to `w2`, the array pointed to by `w1` is affected. It's a logical error that could lead to undefined behavior in the program. We need a *deep* rather than a *shallow* copy; that is, we need to actually create a new array of products that has a copy of w1's array.

A custom implementation of the copy constructor and the assignment operator solves this issue of *shallow* copying:

```
class Warehouse {
public:
  // ...
  Warehouse(const Warehouse& rhs) {
    size_ = rhs.size_;
    capacity_ = rhs.capacity_;
    products_ = new Product[capacity_];
    for (int ix = 0; ix < size_; ++ix) {
      products_[ix] = rhs.products_[ix];
    }
  }
  // code omitted for brevity
};
```

The custom implementation of the copy constructor creates a new array. Then, it copies the source objects' array elements one by one, this way eliminating the `product_` pointer from pointing to a wrong memory address. In other words, we implemented a deep copy of `Warehouse` objects by creating a new array.

Moving objects

Temporary objects are everywhere in code. Most of the time, they are required to make the code work as expected. For example, when we add two objects together, a temporary object is created to hold the return value of `operator+`:

```
Warehouse small;
Warehouse mid;
// ... some data inserted into the small and mid objects
Warehouse large{small + mid}; // operator+(small, mid)
```

Let's take a look at the implementation of the global `operator+()` for `Warehouse` objects:

```
// considering declared as friend in the Warehouse class
Warehouse operator+(const Warehouse& a, const Warehouse& b) {
  Warehouse sum; // temporary
  sum.size_ = a.size_ + b.size_;
  sum.capacity_ = a.capacity_ + b.capacity_;
  sum.products_ = new Product[sum.capacity_];
  for (int ix = 0; ix < a.size_; ++ix) { sum.products_[ix] =
a.products_[ix]; }
  for (int ix = 0; ix < b.size_; ++ix) { sum.products_[a.size_ + ix] =
b.products_[ix]; }
  return sum;
}
```

The preceding implementation declares a temporary object and returns it after filling it with necessary data. The call in the previous example could be translated into the following:

```
Warehouse small;
Warehouse mid;
// ... some data inserted into the small and mid objects
Warehouse tmp{operator+(small, mid)};
Warehouse large;
Warehouse_copy_constructor(large, tmp);
__destroy_temporary(tmp);
```

The *move semantics,* which was introduced in C++11, allows us to skip the temporary creation by *moving* the return value into the `Warehouse` object. To do so, we should declare a **move constructor** for the `Warehouse`, which can *distinguish* between temporaries and treat them efficiently:

```
class Warehouse {
public:
  Warehouse(); // default constructor
  Warehouse(const Warehouse&); // copy constructor
  Warehouse(Warehouse&&); // move constructor
  // code omitted for brevity
};
```

The parameter of the move constructor is an **rvalue reference** (&&).

Lvalue references

Before understanding why rvalue references were introduced in the first place, let's clear things up regarding `lvalues`, `references`, and `lvalue-references`. When a variable is an lvalue, it can be addressed, it can be pointed to, and it has a scoped storage duration:

```
double pi{3.14}; // lvalue
int x{42}; // lvalue
int y{x}; // lvalue
int& ref{x}; // lvalue-reference
```

`ref` is an `lvalue reference`, a synonym for a variable that can be treated as a `const` pointer:

```
int * const ref = &x;
```

Besides the ability to modify the objects by a reference, we pass heavy objects to functions by reference in order to optimize and avoid redundant object copies. For example, the `operator+` for the `Warehouse` takes two objects *by reference,* thus making it copy addresses of objects rather than full objects.

`Lvalue` references optimize the code in terms of function calls, but, to optimize temporaries, we should move on to rvalue references.

Rvalue references

We cannot bind `lvalue` references to temporaries. The following code won't compile:

```
int get_it() {
  int it{42};
  return it;
}
...
int& impossible{get_it()}; // compile error
```

We need to declare an `rvalue` reference to be able to bind to temporaries (including literal values):

```
int&& possible{get_it()};
```

`Rvalue` references allow us to skip the generation of temporaries as much as possible. For example, a function that takes the result as an rvalue reference runs faster by eliminating temporary objects:

```
void do_something(int&& val) {
  // do something with the val
}
// the return value of the get_it is moved to do_something rather than
copied
do_something(get_it());
```

To imagine the effect of moving, imagine that the preceding code will be translated into the following (just to get the full idea of moving):

```
int val;
void get_it() {
  val = 42;
}
void do_something() {
  // do something with the val
}
do_something();
```

Before moving was introduced, the preceding code would look like this (with some compiler optimization):

```
int tmp;
void get_it() {
  tmp = 42;
}
void do_something(int val) {
  // do something with the val
```

```
}
do_something(tmp);
```

The move constructor, along with the move operator, `=()`, has the effect of copying without actually carrying out a copy operation when the input argument represents an `rvalue`. That's why we should also implement these new functions in the class: so that we can optimize the code wherever it makes sense. The move constructor can grab the source object instead of copying it, as shown here:

```
class Warehouse {
public:
  // constructors omitted for brevity
  Warehouse(Warehouse&& src)
    : size_{src.size_},
      capacity_{src.capacity_},
      products_{src.products_}
  {
    src.size_ = 0;
    src.capacity_ = 0;
    src.products_ = nullptr;
  }
};
```

Instead of creating a new array of `capacity_` size and then copying each element of the `products_` array, we just grabbed the pointer to the array. We know that the `src` object is an rvalue and that it will soon be destroyed, which means the destructor will be called and the destructor will delete the allocated array. Now, we point to the allocated array from the newly created `Warehouse` object, which is why we cannot let the destructor delete the source array. Due to this, we assign `nullptr` to it to make sure the destructor will miss the allocated object. So, the following code will be optimized because of the move constructor:

```
Warehouse large = small + mid;
```

The result of `+` operator will be moved rather than copied. Take a look at the following diagram:

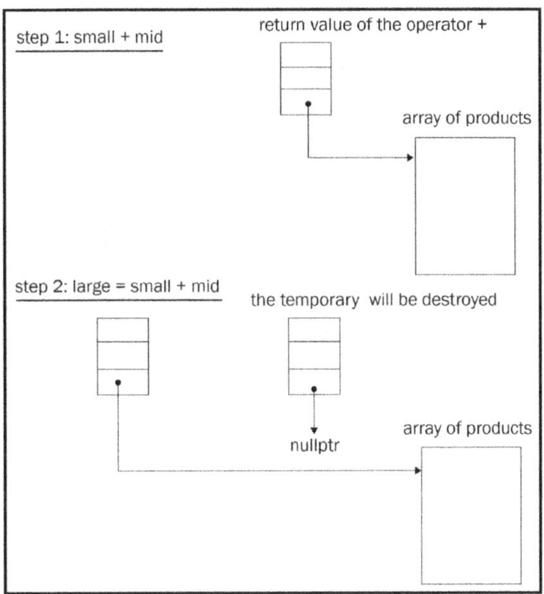

The preceding diagram demonstrates how the temporary is being moved to the large object.

Notes on operator overloading

C++ provides a powerful mechanism for overloading operators for custom types. It's much better to calculate the sum of two objects using the + operator, rather than calling a member function. Calling a member function also involves remembering its name before calling it. It might be `add`, `calculateSum`, `calculate_sum`, or something else. Operator overloading allows for a consistent approach in class design. On the other hand, overloading operators increases unnecessary verbosity in the code. The following snippet represents a list of comparison operators being overloaded, along with addition and subtraction for the `Money` class:

```
constexpr bool operator<(const Money& a, const Money& b) {
  return a.value_ < b.value_;
}
constexpr bool operator==(const Money& a, const Money& b) {
  return a.value_ == b.value_;
}
constexpr bool operator<=(const Money& a, const Money& b) {
  return a.value_ <= b.value_;
}
constexpr bool operator!=(const Money& a, const Money& b) {
```

```
  return !(a == b);
}
constexpr bool operator>(const Money& a, const Money& b) {
  return !(a <= b);
}
constexpr bool operator>=(const Money& a, const Money& b) {
  return !(a < b);
}
constexpr Money operator+(const Money& a, const Money& b) {
  return Money{a.value_ + b.value_};
}
constexpr Money operator-(const Money& a, const Money& b) {
  return Money{a.value_ - b.value_};
}
```

As you can see, most of the preceding functions directly access the value member of the `Money` instance. To make it work, we should declare them as friends for `Money`. Here's what `Money` will look like:

```
class Money
{
public:
  Money() {}
  explicit Money(double v) : value_{v} {}
  // construction/destruction functions omitted for brevity

public:
  friend constexpr bool operator<(const Money&, const Money&);
  friend constexpr bool operator==(const Money&, const Money&);
  friend constexpr bool operator<=(const Money&, const Money&);
  friend constexpr bool operator!=(const Money&, const Money&);
  friend constexpr bool operator>(const Money&, const Money&);
  friend constexpr bool operator>=(const Money&, const Money&);
  friend constexpr bool operator+(const Money&, const Money&);
  friend constexpr bool operator-(const Money&, const Money&);

private:
  double value_;
};
```

The class looks monstrous. C++20 introduces the spaceship operator, which allows us to skip the definition of comparison operators. `operator<=>()`, also known as the three-way comparison operator, requests the compiler to generate relational operators. For the `Money` class, we can use the default `operator<=>()`, as shown here:

```
class Money
{
```

```
    // code omitted for brevity
    friend auto operator<=>(const Money&, const Money&) = default;
};
```

The compiler will generate the `==`, `!=`, `<`, `>`, `<=`, `>=` operators. The `spaceship` operator reduces the redundant definitions for operators and also provides a way to implement a generic behavior for all the generated operators. When implementing a custom behavior for the `spaceship` operator, we should note the return value type of the operator. It can be one of the following:

- `std::strong_ordering`
- `std::weak_ordering`
- `std::partial_ordering`
- `std::strong_equality`
- `std::weak_equality`

All of them are defined in the `<compare>` header. The compiler generates operators based on the return type of the three-way operator.

Encapsulation and the public interface

Encapsulation is a key concept in object-oriented programming. It allows us to hide the implementation details of objects from the client code. Take, for example, a computer keyboard; it has keys for letters, numbers, and symbols, each of which acts if we press on them. Its usage is simple and intuitive, and it hides a lot of low-level details that only a person familiar with electronics would be able to handle. Imagine a keyboard without keys— one that has a bare board with unlabeled pins. You would have to guess which one to press to achieve the desired key combination or text input. Now, imagine a keyboard without pins— you have to send proper signals to the corresponding sockets to get the key *pressed* event of a particular symbol. Users could be confused by the absence of labels and they also could use it incorrectly by pressing or sending signals to invalid sockets. The keyboard as we know it solves this issue by encapsulating the implementation details – the same way programmers encapsulate objects so that they don't load the user with redundant members and to make sure users won't use the object in the wrong way.

Visibility modifiers serve that purpose in the class by allowing us to define the accessibility level of any member. The `private` modifier prohibits any use of the `private` member from the client code. This allows us to control the modification of the `private` member by providing corresponding member functions. A `mutator` function, familiar to many as a setter function, modifies the value of a `private` member after testing the value against specified rules for that particular class. An example of this can be seen in the following code:

```
class Warehouse {
public:
  // rather naive implementation
  void set_size(int sz) {
    if (sz < 1) throw std::invalid_argument("Invalid size");
    size_ = sz;
  }
  // code omitted for brevity
private:
  int size_;
};
```

Modifying a data member through a `mutator` function allows us to control its value. The actual data member is private, which makes it inaccessible from the client code, while the class itself provides public functions to update or read the contents of its private members. These functions, along with the constructors, are often referred to as the *public interface* of the class. Programmers strive to make the class' public interface user-friendly.

Take a look at the following class, which represents a quadratic equation solver: an equation of the form $ax^2 + bx + c = 0$. One of the solutions is finding a discriminant using the formula `D = b2 - 4ac` and then calculating the value of `x` based on the value of the discriminant (D). The following class provides five functions, that is, for setting the values of `a`, `b`, and `c`, respectively, to find the discriminant, and to solve and return the value of `x`:

```
class QuadraticSolver {
public:
  QuadraticSolver() = default;
  void set_a(double a);
  void set_b(double b);
  void set_c(double c);
  void find_discriminant();
  double solve(); // solve and return the x
private:
  double a_;
  double b_;
  double c_;
```

```
    double discriminant_;
};
```

The public interface includes the previously mentioned four functions and the default constructor. To solve the equation $2x^2 + 5x - 8 = 0$, we should use `QuadraticSolver` like so:

```
QuadraticSolver solver;
solver.set_a(2);
solver.set_b(5);
solver.set_c(-8);
solver.find_discriminant();
std::cout << "x is: " << solver.solve() << std::endl;
```

The public interface of the class should be designed wisely; the preceding example shows signs of bad design. The user must know the protocol, that is, the exact order to call the functions in. If the user misses the call to `find_discriminant()`, the result will be undefined or invalid. The public interface forces the user to learn the protocol and to call functions in the proper order, that is, setting values of `a`, `b`, and `c`, then calling the `find_discriminant()` function, and, finally, calling the `solve()` function to get the desired value of `x`. A good design should provide an intuitively easy public interface. We can overwrite `QuadraticSolver` so that it only has one function that takes all the necessary input values, calculates the discriminant itself, and returns the solution:

```
class QuadtraticSolver {
public:
  QuadraticSolver() = default;
  double solve(double a, double b, double c);
};
```

The preceding design is more intuitive than the previous one. The following code demonstrates the usage of `QuadraticSolver` to find the solution to the equation, $2x2 + 5x - 8 = 0$:

```
QuadraticSolver solver;
std::cout << solver.solve(2, 5, -8) << std::endl;
```

The last thing to consider here is the idea that a quadratic equation can be solved in more than one way. The one we introduced is done by finding the discriminant. We should consider that, in the future, we could add further implementation methods to the class. Changing the name of the function may increase the readability of the public interface and secure the future updates to the class. We should also note that the `solve()` function in the preceding example takes `a`, `b`, and `c` as arguments, and we don't need to store them in the class since the solution is calculated directly in the function.

It's obvious that declaring an object of the `QuadraticSolver` just to be able to access the `solve()` function seems to be a redundant step. The final design of the class will look like this:

```
class QuadraticSolver {
public:
  QuadraticSolver() = delete;

  static double solve_by_discriminant(double a, double b, double c);
  // other solution methods' implementations can be prefixed by "solve_by_"
};
```

We renamed the `solve()` function to `solve_by_discriminant()`, which also exposes the underneath method of the solution. We also made the function *static,* thus making it available to the user without declaring an instance of the class. However, we also marked the default constructor *deleted,* which, again, forces the user not to declare an object:

```
std::cout << QuadraticSolver::solve_by_discriminant(2, 5, -8) << std::endl;
```

The client code now spends less effort using the class.

Structs in C++

Structs are almost the same as classes in C++. They have all the features of classes, and you can inherit a class from a structure and vice versa. The only difference between a `class` and a `struct` is the default visibility. For structs, the default visibility modifier is public. It relates to inheritance as well. For example, when you inherit a class from another class without using a modifier, it inherits privately. The following class inherits from `Base` privately:

```
class Base
{
public:
  void foo() {}
};

class Derived : Base
{
  // can access foo() while clients of Derived can't
};
```

Following the same logic, the following struct inherits the `Base` publicly:

```
struct Base
{
```

```
  // no need to specify the public section
  void foo() {}
};

struct Derived : Base
{
  // both Derived and clients of Derived can access foo()
};
```

The same relates to the class that inherits from a struct. For example, the `Derived` class inherits from `Base` privately if not specified directly:

```
struct Base
{
  void foo() {}
};

// Derived inherits Base privately
class Derived: Base
{
  // clients of Derived can't access foo()
};
```

In C++, structs and classes are interchangeable, but most programmers prefer to use structs for simple types. The C++ standard gives a better definition of simple types and calls them **aggregates**. A class (struct) is an aggregate if it conforms to the following rules:

- No private or protected non-static data members
- No user-declared or inherited constructors
- No virtual, private, or protected base classes
- No virtual member functions

Most of these rules will be a lot clearer after you finish this chapter. The following struct is an example of an aggregate:

```
struct Person
{
  std::string name;
  int age;
  std::string profession;
};
```

Before diving into inheritance and virtual functions, let's see what benefits aggregates bring when initializing. We can initialize `Person` objects in the following way:

```
Person john{"John Smith", 22, "programmer"};
```

C++20 provides even more fancy ways to initialize aggregates:

```
Person mary{.name = "Mary Moss", .age{22}, .profession{"writer"}};
```

Note how we mixed the initialization of members by designators.

Structured binding allows us to declare variables bound to aggregate members, as shown in the following code:

```
const auto [p_name, p_age, p_profession] = mary;
std::cout << "Profession is: " << p_profession << std::endl;
```

Structured binding is also applicable to arrays.

Class relationships

Object intercommunication is at the heart of object-oriented systems. The relationship is the logical link between objects. The way we can distinguish or set up a proper relationship between classes of objects defines both the performance and quality of the system design overall. Consider the `Product` and `Warehouse` classes; they are in a relationship called aggregation because the `Warehouse` contains `Products`, that is, the `Warehouse` aggregates `Products`:

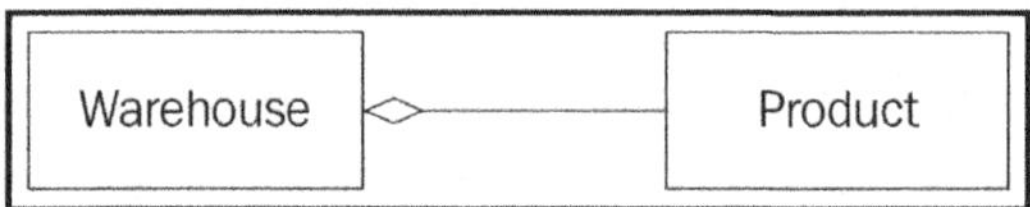

There are several kinds of relationships in terms of pure OOP, such as association, aggregation, composition, instantiation, generalization, and others.

Aggregation and composition

We encountered aggregation in the example of the `Warehouse` class. The `Warehouse` class stores an array of Products. In more general terms, it can be called an *association*, but to strongly emphasize the exact containment, we use the term *aggregation* or *composition*. In the case of aggregation, the class that contains an instance or instances of other classes could be instantiated without the aggregate. This means that we can create and use a `Warehouse` object without necessarily creating `Product` objects contained in the `Warehouse`.

Another example of aggregation is the `Car` and the `Person`. A `Car` can contain a `Person` object (as a driver or passenger) since they are associated with each other, but the containment is not strong. We can create a `Car` object without a `Driver` in it, as follows:

```
class Person; // forward declaration
class Engine { /* code omitted for brevity */ };
class Car {
public:
  Car();
  // ...
private:
  Person* driver_; // aggregation
  std::vector<Person*> passengers_; // aggregation
  Engine engine_; // composition
  // ...
};
```

The strong containment is expressed by **composition**. For the `Car` example, an object of the `Engine` class is required to make a complete `Car` object. In this physical representation, the `Engine` member is automatically created when a `Car` is created.

The following is the UML representation of aggregation and composition:

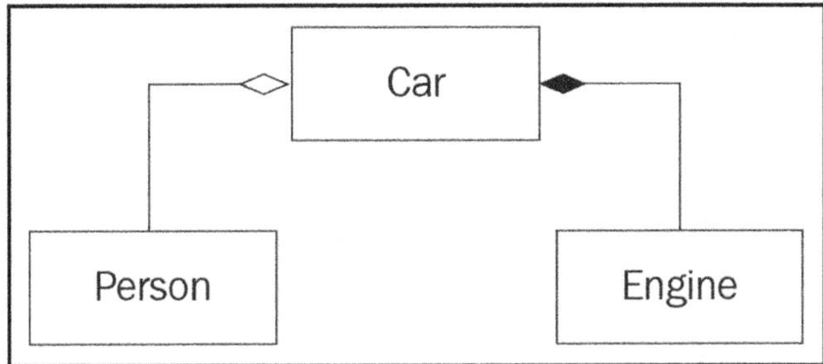

When designing classes, we have to decide on their relationship. The best way to define the composition between the two classes is the *has-a* relationship test. A `Car` has-a `Engine`, because a car has an engine. Any time you can't decide whether the relationship should be expressed in terms of composition, ask the *has-a* question. Aggregation and composition are somewhat similar; they just describe the strength of the connection. For aggregation, the proper question would be *can have a*; for example, a `Car` can have a driver (of the `Person` type); that is, the containment is weak.

Inheritance

Inheritance is a programming concept that allows us to reuse classes. Programming languages provide different implementations of inheritance, but the general rule always stands: the class relationship should answer the *is-a* question. For example, a `Car` is-a `Vehicle`, which allows us to inherit the `Car` from the `Vehicle`:

```
class Vehicle {
public:
  void move();
};

class Car : public Vehicle {
public:
  Car();
  // ...
};
```

The `Car` now has the `move()` member function derived from the `Vehicle`. Inheritance itself represents a generalization/specialization relationship, where the parent class (`Vehicle`) is the generalization and the child class (`Car`) is the specialization.

The parent class could be referred to as the base class or the superclass, while the child class could be referred to as the derived class or the subclass, respectively.

You should only consider using inheritance if it is absolutely necessary. As we mentioned earlier, classes should satisfy the *is-a* relationship, and sometimes, this is a bit tricky. Consider the `Square` and `Rectangle` classes. The following code declares the `Rectangle` class in its simplest possible form:

```
class Rectangle {
public:
  // argument checks omitted for brevity
  void set_width(int w) { width_ = w; }
  void set_height(int h) { height_ = h; }
  int area() const { return width_ * height_; }
private:
  int width_;
  int height_;
};
```

The Square *is-a* Rectangle, so we could easily inherit it from the Rectangle:

```
class Square : public Rectangle {
public:
  void set_side(int side) {
    set_width(side);
    set_height(side);
  }

  int area() {
    area_ = Rectangle::area();
    return area_;
  }
private:
  int area_;
};
```

The Square extends the Rectangle by adding a new data member, area_, and overwriting the area() member function with its own implementation. In practice, the area_ and the way we calculate its value are redundant; we did this to demonstrate a bad class design and to make the Square extend its parent to some extent. Soon, we will conclude that the inheritance, in this case, is a bad design choice. Square is a Rectangle, so it should be used as a Rectangle wherever the Rectangle is used, as shown here:

```
void make_big_rectangle(Rectangle& ref) {
  ref->set_width(870);
  ref->set_height(940);
}

int main() {
  Rectangle rect;
  make_big_rectangle(rect);
  Square sq;
  // Square is a Rectangle
  make_big_rectangle(sq);
}
```

The make_big_rectangle() function takes a reference to the Rectangle and the Square inherits it, so it's totally fine to send a Square object to the make_big_rectangle() function; the Square *is-a* a Rectangle. This example of the successful substitution of a type with its subtype is known as the **Liskov Substitution Principle**. Let's find out why this substitution works in practice and then decide if we made a design mistake by inheriting the Square from the Rectangle (yes, we did).

Inheritance from the compiler perspective

We can picture the Rectangle class we declared earlier in the following way:

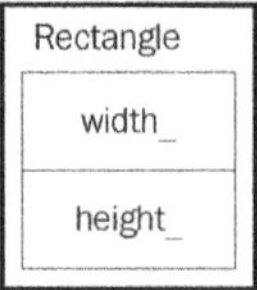

When we declare the rect object in the main() function, the space that's required for the local objects of the function is allocated in the stack. The same logic follows for the make_big_rectangle() function when it's called. It doesn't have local arguments; instead, it has an argument of the Rectangle& type, which behaves in a similar fashion to a pointer: it takes the memory space required to store a memory address (4 or 8 bytes in 32- and 64-bit systems, respectively). The rect object is passed to make_big_rectangle() by reference, which means the ref argument refers to the local object in main():

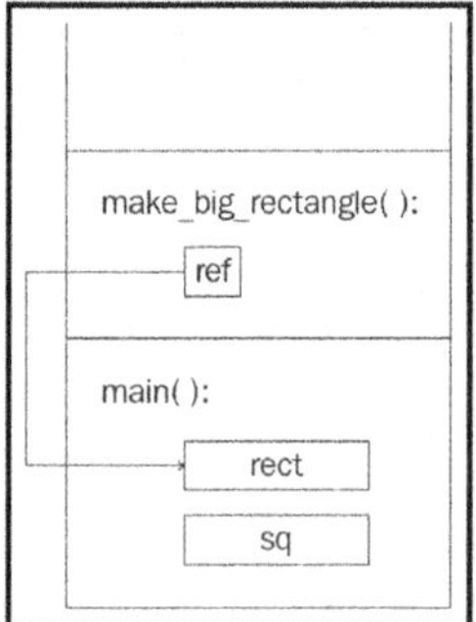

Here is an illustration of the Square class:

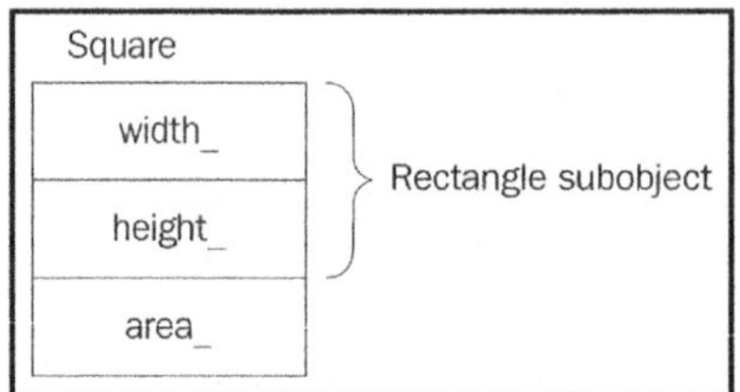

As shown in the preceding diagram, the Square object contains a **subobject** of Rectangle; it partially represents a Rectangle. In this particular example, the Square class doesn't extend the rectangle with new data members.

The Square object is passed to make_big_rectangle(), though the latter takes an argument of the Rectangle& type. We know that the type of the pointer (reference) is required when accessing the underlying object. The type defines how many bytes should be read from the starting address pointed to by the pointer. In this case, ref stores the copy of the starting address of the local rect object declared in main(). When make_big_rectangle() accesses the member functions via ref, it actually calls global functions that take a Rectangle reference as its first parameter. The function is translated into the following (again, we slightly modified it for the sake of simplicity):

```
void make_big_rectangle(Rectangle * const ref) {
  Rectangle_set_width(*ref, 870);
  Rectangle_set_height(*ref, 940);
}
```

Dereferencing ref implies reading sizeof(Rectangle) bytes, starting from the memory location pointed to by ref. When we pass a Square object to make_big_rectangle(), we assign the starting address of sq (the Square object) to ref. This will work fine because the Square object actually contains a Rectangle subobject. When the make_big_rectangle() function dereferences ref, it is only able to access the sizeof(Rectangle) bytes of the object and doesn't *see* the additional bytes of the actual Square object. The following diagram illustrates the part of the subobject ref points to:

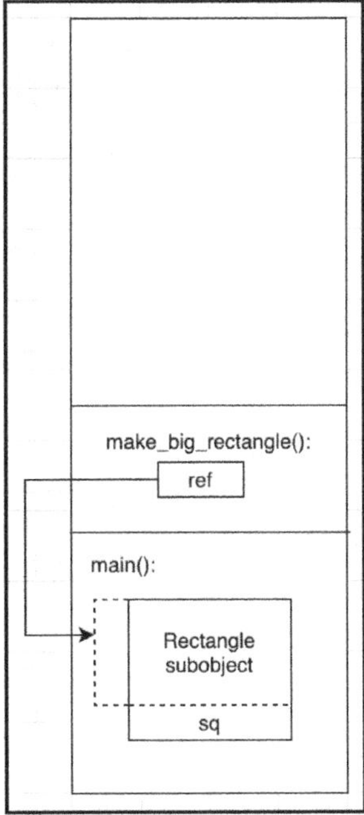

Inheriting the `Square` from the `Rectangle` is almost the same as declaring two structs, one of which (the child) contains the other (the parent):

```
struct Rectangle {
  int width_;
  int height_;
};

void Rectangle_set_width(Rectangle& this, int w) {
  this.width_ = w;
}

void Rectangle_set_height(Rectangle& this, int h) {
  this.height_ = h;
}

int Rectangle_area(const Rectangle& this) {
  return this.width_ * this.height_;
}

struct Square {
  Rectangle _parent_subobject_;
  int area_;
};

void Square_set_side(Square& this, int side) {
  // Rectangle_set_width(static_cast<Rectangle&>(this), side);
  Rectangle_set_width(this._parent_subobject_, side);
  // Rectangle_set_height(static_cast<Rectangle&>(this), side);
  Rectangle_set_height(this._parent_subobject_, side);
}

int Square_area(Square& this) {
  // this.area_ = Rectangle_area(static_cast<Rectangle&>(this));
  this.area_ = Rectangle_area(this._parent_subobject_);
  return this.area_;
}
```

The preceding code demonstrates the compiler's way of supporting inheritance. Take a look at the commented lines of code for the `Square_set_side` and `Square_area` functions. We don't actually insist on this implementation, but it expresses the full idea of how the compiler processes OOP code.

Composition versus inheritance

The C++ language provides us with convenient and OOP-friendly syntax so that we can express the inheritance relationship, but the way the compiler processes it resembles composition rather than inheritance. It's actually even better to use composition instead of inheritance wherever it is applicable. The `Square` class and its relationship with the `Rectangle` was claimed to be a bad design choice. One of the reasons was the subtype substitution principle, which allowed us to use the `Square` the wrong way: pass it to a function that modifies it as a `Rectangle` rather than a `Square`. This tells us that the *is-a* relationship is not correct because the `Square` is not a `Rectangle` after all. It is an adaptation of a `Rectangle` rather than a `Rectangle` itself, which means it doesn't actually represent a `Rectangle`; it uses it to provide limited functionality to class users.

Users of the `Square` shouldn't know that it can be used as a `Rectangle`; otherwise, at some point, they would send invalid or unsupported messages to `Square` instances. Examples of invalid messages are the calls to the `set_width` or `set_height` function. The `Square` shouldn't actually support two different member functions to modify its sides separately, but it can't hide this because it announced that it's inherited from the `Rectangle`:

```
class Square : public Rectangle {
  // code omitted for brevity
};
```

What if we change the modifier from public to private? Well, C++ supports both public and private inheritance types. It also supports protected inheritance as well. When inheriting privately from a class, the subclass intends to use the parent class and has access to its public interface. However, the client code is not aware that it deals with a derived class. Furthermore, the public interface that's inherited from the parent class becomes private for users of the child class. It seems like the `Square` transforms inheritance into a composition:

```
class Square : private Rectangle {
public:
  void set_side(int side) {
    // Rectangle's public interface is accessible to the Square
    set_width(side);
 set_height(side);
  }
  int area() {
    area_ = Rectangle::area();
    return area_;
  }
private:
  int area_;
};
```

The client code cannot access members inherited from the `Rectangle`:

```
Square sq;
sq.set_width(14); // compile error, the Square has no such public member
make_big_rectangle(sq); // compile error, can't cast Square to Rectangle
```

The same can be achieved by declaring a `Rectangle` member in the private section of the `Square`:

```
class Square {
public:
  void set_side(int side) {
    rectangle_.set_width(side);
    rectangle_.set_height(side);
  }
  int area() {
    area_ = rectangle_.area();
    return area_;
  }
private:
  Rectangle rectangle_;
  int area_;
};
```

You should carefully analyze usage scenarios and completely answer the *is-a* question in order to use inheritance without a doubt. Every time you encounter a choice between composition and inheritance, choose composition.

We can omit the modifier when inheriting privately. The default access modifier for classes is private, so `class Square : private Rectangle {};` is the same as `class Square : Rectangle {};`. On the contrary, the default modifier for structs is public.

Protected inheritance

Finally, we have the **protected** access modifier. It specifies the access level of the class members if they're used in the class body. Protected members are private to the class users, but are public to derived classes. If the modifier is used to specify the type of inheritance, it behaves similarly to the private inheritance for derived class users. While private inheritance hides the public interface of the base class from all the derived class users, protected inheritance makes it accessible to descendants of the derived class.

It's hard to imagine a scenario where you would need protected inheritance, but you should consider it as a tool that might be useful in unexpectedly obvious designs. Let's suppose we need to design a stack data structure adapter. The stack is usually implemented based on a vector (one-dimensional array), a linked list, or a dequeue.

The stack conforms to the LIFO rule, which states that the last element inserted into the stack will be accessed first. Similarly, the first element inserted into the stack will be accessed last. We will discuss data structures and data structure adapters in more detail in `Chapter 6`, *Digging into Data Structures and Algorithms in STL*

The stack itself doesn't represent a data structure; it *sits* on top of a data structure and adapts its usage by limiting, modifying, or extending its functions. The following is a simple declaration of the `Vector` class representing a one-dimensional array of integers:

```
class Vector {
public:
  Vector();
  Vector(const Vector&);
  Vector(Vector&&);
  Vector& operator=(const Vector&);
  Vector& operator=(Vector&&);
  ~Vector();

public:
  void push_back(int value);
  void insert(int index, int value);
  void remove(int index);
  int operator[](int index);
  int size() const;
  int capacity() const;

private:
  int size_;
  int capacity_;
  int* array_;
};
```

The preceding `Vector` is not an STL-compatible container with random access iterator support; it contains the bare minimum for a dynamically increasing array. It can be declared and used in the following way:

```
Vector v;
v.push_back(4);
v.push_back(5);
v[1] = 2;
```

While the `Vector` class provides `operator[]`, which allows us to access any of its items randomly, the `Stack` prohibits random accesses. The `Stack` provides `push` and `pop` operations so that we can insert a value into its underlying data structure and fetch the value, respectively:

```
class Stack : private Vector {
public:
  // constructors, assignment operators and the destructor are omitted for
brevity
  void push(int value) {
    push_back(value);
  }
  int pop() {
    int value{this[size() - 1]};
    remove(size() - 1);
    return value;
  }
};
```

The `Stack` can be used in the following way:

```
Stack s;
s.push(5);
s.push(6);
s.push(3);
std::cout << s.pop(); // outputs 3
std::cout << s.pop(); // outputs 6
s[2] = 42; // compile error, the Stack has no publicly available operator[]
defined
```

The stack *adapts* the `Vector` and provides two member functions so that we can access it. Private inheritance allows us to use the full capabilities of the `Vector` and hide the inheritance information from the `Stack` users. What if we want to inherit the `Stack` to create an advanced version of it? Let's say the `AdvancedStack` class provides the `min()` function, which returns the minimum value contained in the stack in constant time.

The private inheritance prohibits the `AdvancedStack` so that it uses the public interface of the `Vector`, so we need a way to allow the `Stack` subclasses to use its base class, but hide the base class' existence from class users. Protected inheritance serves that goal, as shown in the following coe:

```
class Stack : protected Vector {
  // code omitted for brevity
};

class AdvancedStack : public Stack {
  // can use the Vector
};
```

By inheriting the `Stack` from the `Vector`, we allow the subclass of the `Stack` to use the `Vector` public interface. But the users of both the `Stack` and `AdvancedStack` won't be able to access them as a `Vector`.

Polymorphism

Polymorphism is another key concept in object-oriented programming. It allows subclasses to have their own implementation for the functions that are derived from the base class. Let's suppose we have the `Musician` class, which has the `play()` member function:

```
class Musician {
public:
  void play() { std::cout << "Play an instrument"; }
};
```

Now, let's declare the `Guitarist` class, which has the `play_guitar()` function:

```
class Guitarist {
public:
  void play_guitar() { std::cout << "Play a guitar"; }
};
```

This is the obvious case of using inheritance because the `Guitarist` just screams that it *is-a* `Musician`. It would be natural for the `Guitarist` to not extend the `Musician` by adding a new function (such as `play_guitar()`); instead, it should provide its own implementation of the `play()` function derived from the `Musician`. To accomplish this, we use **virtual functions**:

```
class Musician {
public:
  virtual void play() { std::cout << "Play an instrument"; }
```

```
};

class Guitarist : public Musician {
public:
  void play() override { std::cout << "Play a guitar"; }
};
```

Now, it's obviously simple that the `Guitarist` class provides its own implementation to the `play()` function and that the client code can access it by just using the pointer to the base class:

```
Musician armstrong;
Guitarist steve;
Musician* m = &armstrong;
m->play();
m = &steve;
m->play();
```

The preceding example shows polymorphism in action. While the use of virtual functions comes naturally, it actually doesn't make much sense unless we use it properly. First of all, the `play()` function of the `Musician` should not have any implementation at all. The reason for this is simple: a musician should be able to play on a concrete instrument as they cannot play on more than one instrument simultaneously. To get rid of the implementation, we set the function as a **pure virtual function** by assigning `0` to it:

```
class Musician {
public:
  virtual void play() = 0;
};
```

This leads to a compile error when the client code tries to declare an instance of the `Musician`. And, of course, it must lead to a compile error, because you shouldn't be able to create an object that has an *undefined* function. The `Musician` serves a single purpose: it must only be inherited by other classes. The class that exists to be inherited is called an **abstract class**. Actually, the `Musician` is called an **interface** rather than an abstract class. An abstract class is a semi-interface semi-class that can have both types of functions: with and without implementation.

Getting back to our example, let's add the `Pianist` class, which also implements the `Musician` interface:

```
class Pianist : public Musician {
public:
  void play() override { std::cout << "Play a piano"; }
};
```

To express the full power of polymorphism, let's suppose that we have a function declared somewhere that returns a collection of musicians, either guitarist or pianists:

```
std::vector<Musician*> get_musicians();
```

From the perspective of the client code, it will be hard to dissect the return value of the `get_musicians()` function and find out what the actual subtype of the object is. It could be either `Guitarist` or `Pianist`, or even a pure `Musician`. The point is that the client shouldn't really care about the actual type of objects as it knows that the collection contains Musicians and a `Musician` object has the `play()` function. So, to get them in action, the client can just iterate through the collection and make each musician play its instrument (each object calls its implementation):

```
auto all_musicians = get_musicians();
for (const auto& m: all_musicians) {
  m->play();
}
```

The preceding code expresses the full power of polymorphism. Now, let's understand how the language supports polymorphism at a low level.

Virtual functions under the hood

Although polymorphism is not limited to virtual functions, we will discuss them in more detail because dynamic polymorphism is the most popular form of polymorphism in C++. And again, the best way to better understand a concept or technology is by implementing it on your own. Whether we declare a virtual member function in a class or it has a base class with virtual functions, the compiler augments the class with an additional pointer. The pointer points to a table that's usually referred to as a virtual functions table, or simply a *virtual table*. We also refer to the pointer as the *virtual table pointer*.

Let's suppose we are implementing a class subsystem for a bank customer account management. Let's say that the bank asks us to implement cashing out based on the account type. For example, a savings account allows cashing out money once a year, while the checking account allows cashing out money whenever the customer wants. Without diving into any unnecessary details about the `Account` class, let's declare the bare minimum that will help us understand virtual member functions. Let's look at the `Account` class definition:

```
class Account
{
public:
  virtual void cash_out() {
```

```
    // the default implementation for cashing out
  }

  virtual ~Account() {}
private:
  double balance_;
};
```

The compiler transforms the `Account` class into a structure that has a pointer to the virtual functions table. The following code represents pseudocode, explaining what happens when we declare virtual functions in the class. As always, note that we provide a general explanation rather than a compiler-specific implementation (the name mangling is also in a generic form; for example, we rename `cash_out` `Account_cash_out`):

```
struct Account
{
  VTable* __vptr;
  double balance_;
};

void Account_constructor(Account* this) {
  this->__vptr = &Account_VTable;
}

void Account_cash_out(Account* this) {
  // the default implementation for cashing out
}

void Account_destructor(Account* this) {}
```

Take a good look at the preceding pseudocode. The `Account` struct has `__vptr` as its first member. Since the previously declared `Account` class has two virtual functions, we can imagine the virtual table as an array with two pointers to virtual member functions. See the following representation:

```
VTable Account_VTable[] = {
  &Account_cash_out,
  &Account_destructor
};
```

With our previous presumptions at hand, let's find out what code the compiler will generate when we call a virtual function on an object:

```
// consider the get_account() function as already implemented and returning
an Account*
Account* ptr = get_account();
ptr->cash_out();
```

Here's what we can imagine the compiler's generated code to be like for the preceding code:

```
Account* ptr = get_account();
ptr->__vptr[0]();
```

Virtual functions show their power when they're used in hierarchies. `SavingsAccount` inherits from the `Account` class like so:

```
class SavingsAccount : public Account
{
public:
  void cash_out() override {
    // an implementation specific to SavingsAccount
  }
  virtual ~SavingsAccount() {}
};
```

When we call `cash_out()` via a pointer (or a reference), the virtual function is invoked based on the target object that the pointer points to. For example, suppose `get_savings_account()` returns a `SavingsAccount` as `Account*`. The following code will call the `SavingsAccount` implementation of `cash_out()`:

```
Account* p = get_savings_account();
p->cash_out(); // calls SavingsAccount version of the cash_out
```

Here's what the compiler generates for `SavingsClass`:

```
struct SavingsAccount
{
  Account _parent_subobject_;
  VTable* __vptr;
};

VTable* SavingsAccount_VTable[] = {
  &SavingsAccount_cash_out,
  &SavingsAccount_destructor,
};

void SavingsAccount_constructor(SavingsAccount* this) {
  this->__vptr = &SavingsAccount_VTable;
}

void SavingsAccount_cash_out(SavingsAccount* this) {
  // an implementation specific to SavingsAccount
}

void SavingsAccount_destructor(SavingsAccount* this) {}
```

So, we have two different tables of virtual functions. When we create an object of the `Account` type, its `__vptr` points to `Account_VTable`, while the object of the `SavingsAccount` type has its `__vptr` pointing to `SavingsAccount_VTable`. Let's take a look at the following code:

```
p->cash_out();
```

The preceding code translates into this:

```
p->__vptr[0]();
```

Now, it's obvious that `__vptr[0]` resolves to the correct function because it is read via the `p` pointer.

What if `SavingsAccount` doesn't override the `cash_out()` function? In that case, the compiler just places the address of the base class implementation in the same slot as `SavingsAccount_VTable`, as shown here:

```
VTable* SavingsAccount_VTable[] = {
  // the slot contains the base class version
  // if the derived class doesn't have an implementation
  &Account_cash_out,
  &SavingsAccount_destructor
};
```

Compilers implement the virtual functions' representation and management differently. Some implementations use even different models, rather than the one we introduced earlier. We brought a popular approach and represented it in a generic way for the sake of simplicity. Now, we will take a look at what is going on under the hood of the code that incorporates dynamic polymorphism.

Design patterns

Design patterns are one of the most expressive tools for programmers. They allow us to solve design problems in an elegant and well-tested way. When you are struggling to provide the best possible design of your classes and their relationship, a well-known design pattern may come to the rescue.

The simplest example of a design pattern is a **Singleton**. It provides us with a way to declare and use only one instance of the class. For example, suppose that the e-commerce platform has only one `Warehouse`. To access the `Warehouse` class, the project may require that we include and use it in many source files. To keep things in sync, we should make the `Warehouse` a Singleton:

```
class Warehouse {
public:
  static create_instance() {
    if (instance_ == nullptr) {
      instance_ = new Warehouse();
    }
    return instance_;
  }

  static remove_instance() {
    delete instance_;
    instance_ = nullptr;
  }

private:
  Warehouse() = default;

private:
  static Warehouse* instance_ = nullptr;
};
```

We declared a static `Warehouse` object and two static functions for creating and destroying the corresponding instance. The private constructor leads to a compile error each time the user tries to declare a `Warehouse` object in the old way. To be able to use the `Warehouse`, the client code has to call the `create_instance()` function:

```
Warehouse* w = Warehouse::create_instance();
Product book;
w->add_product(book);
Warehouse::remove_instance();
```

The singleton implementation of the `Warehouse` is not complete and is just an example to introduce design patterns. We will introduce more design patterns throughout this book.

Summary

In this chapter, we discussed the fundamental concepts of object-oriented programming. We touched on the low-level details of classes and the compiler implementation of the C++ object model. Knowing how to design and implement classes without actually having classes helps a lot in using the classes the right way.

We also discussed the need for inheritance and tried to employ composition instead of inheritance wherever it might be applicable. C++ supports three types of inheritance: public, private, and protected. All of these types have their applications in particular class designs. Finally, we understood the use and power of polymorphism by bringing an example that drastically increases the convenience of the client code.

In the next chapter, we will learn more about templates and template metaprogramming, which we will use as the basis to dive into a new C++20 feature called concepts.

Questions

1. What are the three properties of objects?
2. What's the advantage of moving objects instead of copying them?
3. What's the difference between structs and classes in C++?
4. What's the difference between aggregation and composition relations?
5. What's the difference between private and protected inheritance?
6. How is the size of the class affected if we define a virtual function in it?
7. What's the point of using the Singleton design pattern?

Further reading

For more information, refer to:

- Grady Booch, *Object-Oriented Analysis and Design* (`https://www.amazon.com/Object-Oriented-Analysis-Design-Applications-3rd/dp/020189551X/`)
- Stanley Lippman, *Inside the C++ Object Model* (`https://www.amazon.com/Inside-Object-Model-Stanley-Lippman/dp/0201834545/`)

4
Understanding and Designing Templates

Templates are a unique feature of C++ by which functions and classes have the ability to support generic data types – in other words, we can implement a function or class independent of a particular data type; for example, a client may request a `max()` function to handle different data types. Instead of implementing and maintaining many similar functions by using function overloading, we can just implement one `max()` and pass the data type as a parameter. Moreover, templates can work together with multiple inheritance and operator overloading to create powerful generic data structures and algorithms in C++ such as the **Standard Template Library** (**STL**). Additionally, templates can also be applied to compile-time computation, compile-time and runtime code optimization, and more.

In this chapter, we will learn about the syntax of function and class templates, their instantiations, and their specializations. Then, we will introduce *variadic* templates and their applications. Next, we will discuss template parameters and the corresponding arguments that are used for instantiating them. After that, we'll learn how to implement a type *trait* and how to use this type of information to optimize algorithms. Finally, we will present techniques that we can use to speed up programs when they're executed, which includes compile-time computation, compile-time code optimization, and static polymorphism.

This chapter will cover the following topics:

- Exploring function and class templates
- Understanding variadic templates
- Understanding template parameters and arguments
- What are traits?
- Template meta-programming and its applications

Technical requirements

The code for this chapter can be found in this book's GitHub repository: `https://github.com/PacktPublishing/Expert-CPP` .

Exploring function and class templates

We will start this section by introducing the syntax of function templates and their instantiations, deductions, and specializations. Then, we will move on to class templates and look at similar concepts, as well as examples.

Motivation

So far,when we have defined a function or a class, we have had to provide input, output, and intermediate parameters. For example, let's say we have a function to performs the addition of two int type integers. How do we extend this so that it handles all the other basic data types, such as float, double, char, and so on? One way is to use function overloading by manually copying, pasting, and slightly modifying each function. Another way is to define a macro to do the addition operation. Both approaches have their own side effects.

Moreover, what happens if we fix a bug or add a new feature for one type, and this update needs to be done for all the other overloading functions and classes later? Instead of using this silly copy-paste-and-replacement method, do we have a better way of handling this kind of situation?

In fact, this is a generic problem that any computer language can face. Pioneered by the general-purpose functional programming **Meta Language** (**ML**) in 1973, ML permits writing common functions or types that differ only in the set of types that they operate on when used, thus reducing duplication. Later inspired by the parameterized modules provided in the **chartered life underwriter** (**CLU**) and the generics provided by Ada, C++ adopted the template concept, which allows functions and classes to operate with generic types. In other words, it allows a function or class to work on different data types without them needing to be rewritten.

Actually, from an abstract point of view, C++ functions or class templates (such as cookie cutters) serve as a pattern for creating other similar functions or classes. The basic idea behind this is to create a function or class template without having to specify the exact type(s) of some or all variables. Instead, we define a function or class template using placeholder types, called **template type parameters**. Once we have a function or class template, we can automatically generate functions or classes by using an algorithm that has been implemented in other compilers.

There are three kinds of templates in C++: *function* templates, *class* templates, and *variadic* templates. We'll take a look at these next.

Function templates

A function template defines how a family of functions can be generated. A family here means a group of functions that behave similarly. As shown in the following diagram, this includes two phases:

- Creating a function template; that is, the rules on how to write it.
- Template instantiation; that is, the rules that are used to generate functions from their template:

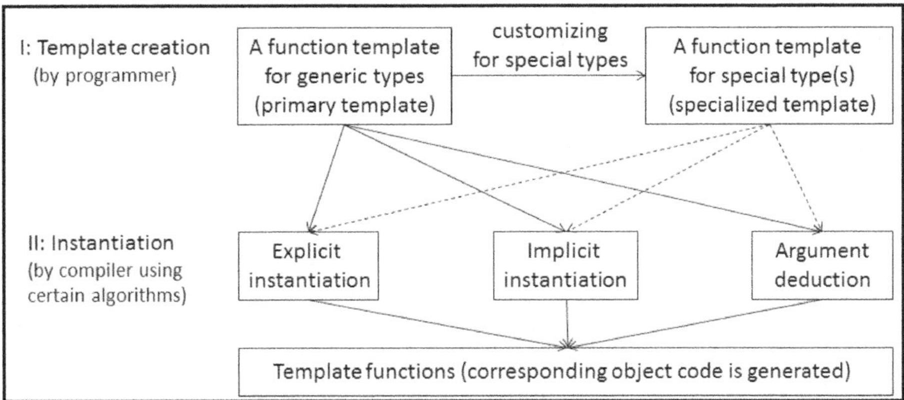

Function template format

In **part I** of the preceding diagram, we discuss the format that will be used to create a function template for generic types, but with respect to the **specialized template**, which we also refer to as the **primary template**. Then, in **part II**, we introduce the three ways to generate functions from the template. Lastly, the specialization *and* overloading subsection tells us how to customize the **primary template** (by changing its behavior) for special types.

Syntax

There are two ways to define function templates, as shown in the following code:

```
template <typename identifier_1, …, typename identifier_n >
function_declaration;

template <class identifier_1,…, class identifier_n>
function_declaration;
```

Here, `identifier_i (i=1,…,n)` is the type or class parameter and `function_declaration` declares the function body part. The only difference in the preceding two declarations is the keywords –one uses `class` while the other uses `typename`, but both have the same meaning and behavior. Since a type (such as the basic types – int, float, double,enum, struct, union, and so on) is not a class, the `typename` keyword method was introduced to avoid confusion.

For example, the classic find maximum value function template, `app_max()`, can be declared as follows:

```
template <class T>
T app_max (T a, T b) {
  return (a>b?a:b);    //note: we use ((a)>(b) ? (a):(b)) in macros
}                      //it is safe to replace (a) by a, and (b) by b now
```

This function template can work for many data types or classes, as long as there's a copy-constructible type where the *a>b* expression is valid. For user-defined classes, this means that the greater-than operator (>) must be defined.

Note that the function template and template function are different things. Function template refers to a kind of template that's used to generate functions by a compiler, so the compiler does not generate any object code for it. On the other hand,template function means an instance from a function template. Since it is a function, the corresponding object code is generated by the compiler. However, the latest C++ standard documents suggest avoiding using the imprecision term template function. Therefore, we will use function templates and member function templates in this book.

Instantiation

Since we may potentially have an infinite number of types and classes, the concept of function templates not only saves space in the source code file but also makes code easier to read and maintain. However, compared to writing separate functions or classes for the different data types that are used in our applications, it does not produce smaller object code. For instance, consider a program using a float and int version of `app_max()`:

```
cout << app_max<int>(3,5) << endl;
cout << app_max<float>(3.0f,5.0f) << endl;
```

The compiler will generate two new functions in the object file, as follows:

```
int app_max<int> ( int a, int b) {
  return (a>b?a:b);
}

float app_max<float> (float a, float b) {
  return (a>b?a:b);
}
```

This process of creating a new definition of a function from a function template declaration is called **template instantiation**. During this instantiation process, the compiler determines the template arguments and generates actual functional code on demand for your application. Typically, there are three forms: *explicit instantiations, implicit instantiations,* and *template deductions.* In the next sections, let's discuss each form.

Explicit instantiations

A lot of very useful C++ function templates can be written and consumed without ever using explicit instantiation, but we will describe them here just so you know that they do exist if you ever need them. First, let's have a look at the syntax of explicit instantiations before C++11. There are two forms, as shown in the following code:

```
template return-type
function_name < template_argument_list > ( function_parameter-list ) ;

template return-type
function_name ( function_parameter_list ) ;
```

An explicit instantiation definition, also known as a **directive**, forces the instantiation of a function template for certain type(s), regardless of the template function that will be called in the **future**. The location of the explicit instantiations can be anywhere after the definition of the function template, and it is only allowed to appear once for a given argument list in the source code.

The syntax for explicit instantiation directives, since C++11, is as follows. Here, we can see that the `extern` keyword is added before the `template` keyword:

```
extern template return-type
function_name < template_argument_list > (function_parameter_list );
(since C++11)

extern template return-type
function_name ( function_parameter_list ); (since C++11)
```

Using the `extern` keyword prevents implicit instantiations of that function template (see the next section for more details).

Regarding the previously declared `app_max()` function template, it can be explicitly instantiated using the following code:

```
template double app_max<double>(double, double);
template int app_max<int>(int, int);
```

It can also be explicitly instantiated using the following code:

```
extern template double app_max<double>(double, double);//(since c++11)
extren template int app_max<int>(int, int);            //(since c++11)
```

This can also be done in a template argument deduced way:

```
template double f(double, double);
template int f(int, int);
```

Finally, this can also be done like so:

```
extern template double f(double, double); //(since c++11)
extern template int f(int, int);          //(since c++11)
```

Moreover, there are some other rules for explicit instantiation. If you want to find out more, please refer to the *Further reading* section [10] for more details.

Implicit instantiations

When a function is called, the definition of that function needs to exist. If this function has not been explicitly instantiated, an implicit instantiation approach is reached, in which the list of template arguments need to be either explicitly supplied or deduced from the context. `Part A` of the following program provides some examples of the implicit instantiation of `app_max()` in this catalog:

```
//ch4_2_func_template_implicit_inst.cpp
#include <iostream>
```

```
template <class T>
T app_max (T a, T b) { return (a>b?a:b); }
using namespace std;
int main(){
 //Part A: implicit instantiation in an explicit way
 cout << app_max<int>(5, 8) << endl;        //line A
 cout << app_max<float>(5.0, 8.0) << endl; //line B
 cout << app_max<int>(5.0, 8) << endl;      //Line C
 cout << app_max<double>(5.0, 8) << endl;   //Line D

 //Part B: implicit instantiation in an argument deduction way
 cout << app_max(5, 8) << endl;            //line E
 cout << app_max(5.0f, 8.0f) << endl;      //line F

 //Part C: implicit instantiation in a confuse way
 //cout<<app_max(5, 8.0)<<endl;           //line G
 return 0;
}
```

The implicit instantiations of lines `A`, `B`, `C`, and `D` are `int app_max<int>(int,int)`, `float app_max<float>(float, float>)`, `int app_max<int>(int,int)`, and `double app_max<double>(double, double)`, respectively.

Deduction

When you call a template function, the compiler needs to figure out the template arguments first, even if not every template argument is specified. Most of the time, it will deduce the missing template arguments from the function arguments. For example, in part B of the preceding function, when you call `app_max(5, 8)` in line `E`, the compiler deduces the template argument as an int type, `(int app_max<int>(int,int))`, because the input parameters, `5` and `8`, are integers. Similarly, line `F` will be deduced as a float type, that is, `float app_max<float>(float,float)`.

However, what happens if there is confusion during instantiation? For instance, in the commented out line for `G` of the previous program, depending on the compiler, it might call `app_max<double>(double, double)`, `app_max<int>(int, int)`, or just give a compile error message. The best way to help the compiler deduce the type is to call the function template by giving a template argument explicitly. In this case, if we call `app_max<double>(5, 8.0)`, any confusion will be resolved.

From the compiler's point of view, there are several ways to do template argument deduction – deduction from a function call, deduction from a type, auto type deduction, and non-deduced contexts [4]. However, from a programmer's point of view, you should never write fancy code to ill-use the concept of function template deduction to confuse other programmers such as line G in the previous example.

Specialization and overloading

Specialization allows us to customize the template code for a given set of template arguments. It allows us to define a special behavior for specific template arguments. A specialization is still a template; you still need an instantiation to get the real code (automatically by the compiler).

In the following sample code, the primary function template, `T app_max(T a, T b)`, will return `a` or `b` based on the return of operator *a>b*, but we can specialize it for `T = std::string` so that we only compare the 0-*th* elements of `a` and `b`; that is, `a[0] >b[0]`:

```
//ch4_3_func_template_specialization.cpp
#include <iostream>
#include <string>

//Part A: define a  primary template
template <class T> T app_max (T a, T b) { return (a>b?a:b); }

//Part B: explicit specialization for T=std::string,
template <>
std::string app_max<std::string> (std::string a, std::string b){
    return (a[0]>b[0]?a:b);
}

//part C: test function
using namespace std;
void main(){
 string a = "abc", b="efg";
 cout << app_max(5, 6) << endl; //line A
 cout << app_max(a, b) << endl; //line B

 //question: what's the output if un-comment lines C and D?
 //char *x = "abc", *y="efg";     //Line C
 //cout << app_max(x, y) << endl; //line D
}
```

The preceding code defines a primary template first, and then it explicitly specializes `T` as `std::string`; that is, instead of comparing the values of `a` and `b`, we only care about `a[0]` and `b[0]` (the behavior of `app_max()` is specialized). In the test function, `line A` calls `app_max<int>(int,int)` and `line B` calls the specialized version because there is no ambiguity at the deduction time. If we uncomment lines `C` and `D`, the primary function template, `char* app_max<char > (char*, char*)`, will be called, since `char*` and `std::string` are different data types.

Essentially, specialization somewhat conflicts with function overload resolution: the compiler needs an algorithm to resolve this conflict by finding the right match among the template and overloading functions. The algorithm for selecting the right function involves the following two steps:

1. Perform overload resolution among regular functions and non-specialized templates.
2. If a non-specialized template is selected, check if a specialization exists that would be a better match for it.

For example, in the following code block, we're declaring the primary (`line 0`) and specialized function templates (`lines 1-4`), as well as the overload functions (`lines 5-6`) of `f()`):

```
template<typename T1, typename T2> void f( T1, T2 );// line 0
template<typename T> void f( T );                   // line 1
template<typename T> void f( T, T );                // line 2
template<typename T> void f( int, T* );             // line 3
template<> void f<int>( int );                      // line 4
void f( int, double );                              // line 5
void f( int );                                      // line 6
```

`f()` will be called several times in the following code block. Based on the preceding two-step rule, we can show which function is chosen in the comments. We'll explain the reason for doing this after:

```
int i=0;
double d=0;
float x=0;
complex<double> c;
f(i);      //line A: choose f() defined in line 6
f(i,d);    //line B: choose f() defined in line 5
f<int>(i); //line C: choose f() defined in line 4
f(c);      //line D: choose f() defined in line 1
f(i,i);    //line E: choose f() defined in line 2
f(i,x);    //line F: choose f() defined in line 0
f(i, &d);  //line G: choose f() defined in line 3
```

For `lines A` and `line B`, since `f()` defined in `lines 5` and `line 6` are regular functions, they have the highest priority to be chosen, so `f(i)` and `f(i,d)` will choose them, respectively. For `line C`, because the specialized template exists, the `f()` generated from `line 4` is a better match than what was created from `line 1`. For `line D`, since `c` is a `complex<double>` type, only the primary function template defined in `line 1` matches it. `Line E` will choose `f()` that was created by `line 2` because the two input variables are the same type. Finally, `lines F` and `line G` will pick up the functions created from the templates in lines `0` and `3`, respectively.

Having learned about the functional templates, we will now move on to class templates.

Class templates

A class template defines a family of classes, and it is often used to implement a container. For example, the C++ Standard Library contains many class templates, such as `std::vector`, `std::map`, `std::deque`, and so on. In *OpenCV*, `cv::Mat` is a very powerful class template and it can handle 1D, 2D, and 3D matrices or images with built-in data types such as `int8_t`, `uint8_t`, `int16_t`, `uint16_t`, `int32_t`, `uint32_t`, `float`, `double`, and so on.

Similar to function templates, as shown in the following diagram, the concept of class templates contains a template creation syntax, its specialization, and its implicit and explicit instantiations:

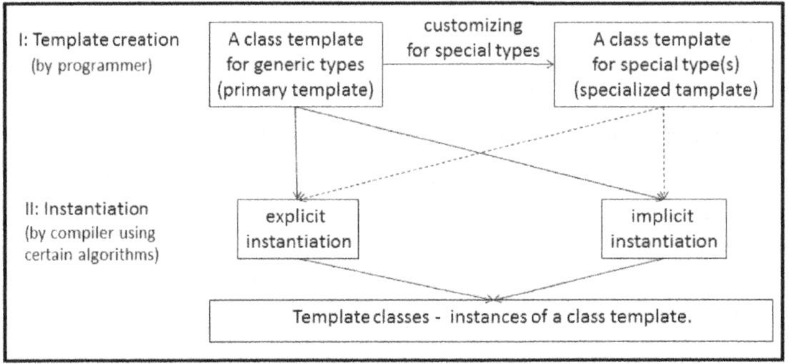

In **part I** of the preceding diagram, with a certain syntax format, we can create a class template for generic types, also known as a primary template, and it can be customized for special types with different member functions and/or variables. Once we have a class template, in **part II**, the compiler will instantiate it to template classes either explicitly or implicitly based on the application's demand.

Now, let's look at the syntax for creating a class template.

Syntax

The syntax for creating a class template is as follows:

```
[export] template <template_parameter_list> class-declaration
```

Here, we have the following:

- `template_parameter-list` (see the link in *further reading* context [10]) is a non-empty comma-separated list of the template parameters, each of which is either a non-type parameter, a type parameter, a template parameter, or a parameter pack of any of those.
- `class-declaration` is the part that's used to declare a class that contains a class name and its body in curly brackets. By doing so, the declared class name also becomes a template name.

For example, we can define a class template, `V`, so that it contains all kinds of 1D data types:

```
template <class T>
class V {
public:
  V( int n = 0) : m_nEle(n), m_buf(0) { creatBuf();}
  ~V(){  deleteBuf();  }
  V& operator = (const V &rhs) { /* ... */}
  V& operator = (const V &rhs) { /* ... */}
  T getMax(){ /* ... */ }
protected:
  void creatBuf() { /* ... */}
  void deleteBuf(){ /* ... */}

public:
  int m_nEle;
  T * m_buf;
};
```

Once we have this class template, the compiler can generate classes during the instantiation process. For the reason we mentioned in the *Function template* subsection, we will avoid using the imprecise term `template` class in this book. Instead, we will use the class template.

Instantiation

Considering the class template, `V`, we defined in the previous section, we'll assume the following declarations appear later:

```
V<char> cV;
V<int>  iV(10);
V<float> fV(5);
```

Then, the compiler will create three instances of the `V` class, as follows:

```
class V<char>{
public:
  V(int n=0);
 // ...
public:
  int  m_nEle;
  char *m_buf;
};

class V<int>{
public:
  V(int n=0);
 // ...
public:
  int  m_nEle;
  int *m_buf;
};

class V<float>{
public:
  V(int n = 0);
  // ...
public:
  int   m_nEle;
  float *m_buf;
};
```

Similar to function template instantiation, there are two forms of class template instantiation – explicit instantiation and implicit instantiation. Let's take a look at them.

Explicit instantiation

The syntax for explicit instantiation is as follows:

```
template class template_name < argument_list >;
extern template class template_name < argument_list >;//(since C++11)
```

An explicit instantiation definition forces instantiation of the class, struct, or union they refer to. In the C++0x standard, the implicit instantiation of a template specialization or its members is suppressed. Similar to the explicit instantiation of function templates, the location of this explicit instantiation can be anywhere after its template definition, and it is only permitted to be defined once in the entire program in one file.

Moreover, since C++11, an implicit instantiation step will be bypassed by an explicit instantiation declaration (extern template). This can be used to reduce compilation times.

Going back to the template class, `V`, we can explicitly instantiate it as follows:

```
template class V<int>;
template class V<double>;
```

Alternatively, we can do the following (since C++11):

```
extern template class V<int>;
extern template class V<double>;
```

The compiler will present us with an error message if we explicitly instantiate a function or class template but there is no corresponding definition in the program, as shown here:

```
//ch4_4_class_template_explicit.cpp
#include <iostream>
using namespace std;
template <typename T>       //line A
struct A {
  A(T init) : val(init) {}
  virtual T foo();
  T val;
};                         //line B
                           //line C
template <class T> //T in this line is template parameter
T A<T>::foo() {    //the 1st T refers to function return type,
                   //the T in <> specifies that this function's template
                   //parameter is also the class template parameter
  return val;
}                         //line D

extern template struct A<int>;  //line E
#if 0                           //line F
int A<int>::foo() {
    return val+1;
}
#endif                         //line G

int main(void) {
```

```
    A<double> x(5);
    A<int> y(5);
    cout<<"fD="<<x.foo()<<",fI="<<y.foo()<< endl;
    return 0;          //output: fD=5,fI=6
}
```

In the preceding code block, we defined a class template between lines A and B, and then we implemented its member function, `foo()`, from `lines C` to `line D`. Next, we explicitly instantiated it for the `int` type at `line E`. Since the code block between `lines F` and `line G` is commented out (which means that there is no corresponding definition of `foo()` for this explicit `int` type instantiation), we have a linkage error. To fix this, we need to replace `#if 0` with `#if 1` at `line F`.

Finally, there are some additional restrictions for explicit instantiation declarations, as follows:

- **Static**: A static class member can be named, but a static function cannot be allowed in an explicit instantiation declaration.
- **Inline**: There is no effect for inline functions in explicit instantiation declarations, and inline functions are implicitly instantiated.
- **Class and its members**: It is no equivalent for explicitly instantiating a class and all its members.

Implicit instantiation

When referring to a template class, the compiler will only generate code from its template on-demand if it has not been explicitly instantiated or explicitly specialized. This is called **implicit instantiation**, and its syntax is as follows:

```
class_name<argument list> object_name; //for non-pointer object
class_name<argument list> *p_object_name; //for pointer object
```

For a non-pointer object, a template class is instantiated and its object is created, but only the member functions used by this object are generated. For a pointer object, unless a member is used in the program, it is not instantiated.

Consider the following example, where we define a class template, `X` ,in the `ch4_5_class_template_implicit_inst.h` file:

```
//file ch4_5_class_template_implicit_inst.h
#ifndef __CH4_5_H__
#define __CH4_5_H__
#include <iostream>
template <class T>
```

```
class X {
public:
    X() = default;
    ~X() = default;
    void f() { std::cout << "X::f()" << std::endl; };
    void g() { std::cout << "X::g()" << std::endl; };
};
#endif
```

Then, it is included by the following four `cpp` files, which has `ain()` in each:

```
//file ch4_5_class_template_implicit_inst_A.cpp
#include "ch4_5_class_template_implicit_inst.h"
void main()
{
    //implicit instantiation generates class X<int>, then create object xi
    X<int>   xi ;
    //implicit instantiation generates class X<float>, then create object
xf
    X<float> xf;
    return 0;
}
```

In `ch4_5_class_template_implicit_inst_A.cpp`, the compiler will implicitly instantiate the `X<int>` and `X<float>` classes, and then create the `xi` and `xf` objects. But since `X::f()` and `X::g()` are not used, they are not instantiated.

Now, let's look at `ch4_5_class_template_implicit_inst_B.cpp`:

```
//file ch4_5_class_template_implicit_inst_B.cpp
#include "ch4_5_class_template_implicit_inst.h"
void main()
{
    //implicit instantiation generates class X<int>, then create object xi
    X<int> xi;
    xi.f();      //and generates function X<int>::f(), but not X<int>::g()

    //implicit instantiation generates class X<float>, then create object
    //xf and generates function X<float>::g(), but not X<float>::f()
    X<float> xf;
    xf.g() ;
}
```

Here, the compiler will implicitly instantiate the `X<int>` class, create the `xi` object, and then generate the `X<int>::f()` function, but not `X<int>::g()`. Similarly, it will instantiate the `X<float>` class, create the `xf` object, and generate the `X<float>::g()` function, but not `X<float>::f()`.

Then, we have `ch4_5_class_template_implicit_inst_C.cpp`:

```
//file ch4_5_class_template_implicit_inst_C.cpp
#include "ch4_5_class_template_implicit_inst.h"
void main()
{
   //inst. of class X<int> is not required, since p_xi is pointer object
   X<int> *p_xi ;
   //inst. of class X<float> is not required, since p_xf is pointer object
   X<float> *p_xf ;
}
```

Since `p_xi` and `p_xf` are pointer objects, there is no need to instantiate their corresponding template classes through the compiler.

Finally, we have `ch4_5_class_template_implicit_inst_D.cpp`:

```
//file ch4_5_class_template_implicit_inst_D.cpp
#include "ch4_5_class_template_implicit_inst.h"
void main()
{
//inst. of class X<int> is not required, since p_xi is pointer object
 X<int> *p_xi;

 //implicit inst. of X<int> and X<int>::f(), but not X<int>::g()
 p_xi = new X<int>();
 p_xi->f();

//inst. of class X<float> is not required, since p_xf is pointer object
 X<float> *p_xf;
 p_xf = new X<float>();//implicit inst. of X<float> occurs here
 p_xf->f();            //implicit inst. X<float>::f() occurs here
 p_xf->g();            //implicit inst. of X<float>::g() occurs here

 delete p_xi;
 delete p_xf;
}
```

This will implicitly instantiate `X<int>` and `X<int>::f()`, but not `X<int>::g()`; similarly, for `X<float>`, `X<float>::f()` and `X<float>::g()` will be instantiated.

Specialization

Similar to function specialization, the explicit specialization of a class template defines a different implementation for a primary template when a specific type is passed as a template parameter. However, it is still a class template and you need to get the real code by instantiation.

For example, let's suppose that we have a `struct X` template that can store one element of any data type, and it has just one member function named `increase()`. But for the char type data, we want a different implementation of `increase()` and need to add a new member function called `toUpperCase()` to it. Therefore, we decide to declare a class template specialization for that type. We do this as follows:

1. Declare a primary class template:

```
template <typename T>
struct X {
  X(T init) : m(init) {}
  T increase() { return ++m; }
  T m;
};
```

   This step declares a primary class template in which its constructor initializes the `m` member variable and `increase()` adds one to `m` and returns its value.

2. Next, we need to perform specialization for the char type data:

```
template <>   //Note: no parameters inside <>, it tells compiler
              //"hi i am a fully specialized template"
struct X<char> { //Note: <char> after X, tells compiler
                 // "Hi, this is specialized only for type char"
  X(char init) : m(init) {}
  char increase() { return (m<127) ? ++m : (m=-128); }
  char toUpperCase() {
    if ((m >= 'a') && (m <= 'z')) m += 'A' - 'a';
    return m;
  }
  char m;
};
```

   This step creates a specialized (with respect to the primary class template) class template with an additional member function, `toUpperCase()`, for the char type data only.

3. Now, we run a test:

```
int main() {
 X<int> x1(5);          //line A
 std::cout << x1.increase() << std::endl;

 X<char> x2('b');      //line B
 std::cout << x2.toUpperCase() << std::endl;
 return 0;
}
```

Finally, we have a `main()` function to test it. In line A, `x1` is an object that has been implicitly instantiated from the primary template, `X<T>`. Since the initial value of `x1.m` is `5`, `6` will be returned from `x1.increase()`. In `line B`, `x2` is an object instantiated from the specialization template, `X<char>`, and the value of `x2.m` is `b` when it is executed. After calling `x2.toUpperCase()`, `B` will be the return value.

The complete code for this example can be found at `ch4_6_class_template_specialization.cpp`.

In summary, the syntax that's used in the class template's explicit specialization is as follows:

```
template <> class[struct] class_name<template argument list> { ... };
```

Here, the empty template parameter list, `template <>`, is used to explicitly declare it as a template specialization and `<template argument list>` is the type parameter(s) to be specialized. For example, in `ex4_6_class_template_specialization.cpp`, we use the following:

```
template <> struct X<char> { ... };
```

Here, `<char>` after `X` identifies the type we are going to declare a template class specialization for.

Additionally, when we do specializations for a template class, all its members – even those that are identical in the primary template – must be defined because there is no inheritance concept for the primary template during template specializations.

Next, we'll take a look at partial specialization. This is a general statement of explicit specialization. Compared to the format of explicit specialization, which only has a template argument list, both the template parameter list and argument list are required for a partial specialization. For a template instantiation, the partial specialization template will be selected by the compiler if a user's template argument list matches a subset of the template arguments. Then, a new class definition from the partial specialization template will be generated by the compiler.

In the following example, for the primary class template `A`, we can partially specialize it for const `T` in the argument list. Note that both of them have the same parameter list, which is `<typename T>`:

```
//primary class template A
template <typename T>  class A{ /* ... */ };

//partial specialization for const T
template <typename T>  class A<const T>{ /* ... */ };
```

In the following example, the primary class template `B` has two parameters: `<typename T1` and `typename T2 >`. We partially specialize it by `T1=int`, keeping `T2` unchanged:

```
//primary class template B
template <typename T1, typename T2> class B{ /* ... */ };

//partial specialization for T1 = int
template <typename T2> class B<int, T2>{ /* ... */};
```

Finally, in the following example, we can see that the number of template parameters in a partial specialization does not have to match the parameter numbers that appeared in the original primary template. However, the number of template arguments (appearing after the class name in angle brackets) must match the number and type of the parameters in the primary template:

```
//primary class template C: template one parameter
template <typename T> struct C { T type; };

//specialization: two parameters in parameter list
//but still one argument (<T[N]>) in argument list
template <typename T, int N> struct C<T[N]>
{T type; };
```

Again, a class template partial specialization is still a class template. You must provide definitions for its member functions and number variables separately.

To end this section, let's summarize what we've learned so far. In the following table, you can see a comparison between function and class templates, their instantiation, and specialization:

	Function Templates	Class Templates	Comments
Declaration	`template <class T1, class T2> void f(T1 a, T2 b) { ... }`	`template <class T1, class T2> class X { ... };`	The declaration defines a function/class template, `<class T1, class T2>` called template parameters.
Explicit Instantiation	`template void f <int, int >( int, int);` or extern template `void f <int, int >( int, int);` (since C++11)	`template class X<int, float>;` or `extern template class X<int,float>;` (since C++11)	After instantiation there are now functions/classes, but they are called template functions/classes.
Implicit Instantiation	{ ... `f(3, 4.5); f<char, float>(120, 3.14);` }	{ ... `X<int,float> obj; X<char, char> *p;` }	When a function call or a class object/pointer is declared, if it has not been explicitly instantiated, the implicit instantiation approach used.
Specialization	`template <> void f<int,float>(int a, float b) { ... }`	`template <> class X <int, float>{ ... };`	A fully customized version (no parameter list) of the primary template still needs to be instantiated.
Partial Specialization	`template <class T> void f<T,T>(T a, T b) { ... }`	`template <class T> class X <T, T>{ ... };`	A partial customized version (has a parameter list) of the primary template still needs to be instantiated.

Five concepts need to be emphasized here:

- **Declaration**: We need to follow the syntax that's used to define a function or class template. At this point, a function or class template by itself is not a type, a function, or any other entity. In other words, there are only template definitions in the source file and no code, which can be complied to an object file, is generated.

- **Implicit Instantiation**: For any code to appear, a template must be instantiated. During this process, it becomes imperative to determine the template arguments so that the compiler can generate an actual function or class. In other words, they are compiled on-demand, which means that compiling the code of a template function or class does not happen until an instantiation with specific template arguments is given.
- **Explicit Instantiation**: Tells the compiler to instantiate the template with the given types, regardless of whether they are used. Typically, it is used for providing libraries.
- **Full Specialization**: This has no parameter list (fully customized); it only has an argument list. The most useful thing about template specialization is that you can create special templates for particular type arguments.
- **Partial Specialization**: This is similar to fully specialization, but is part parameter list (partially customized) and part argument list.

Understanding variadic templates

In the previous section, we learned how to write function or class templates with a fixed number of type parameters. But since C++11, standard generic functions and class templates can accept a variable number of type parameters. This is called **variadic templates**, which is an extension of C++ in *Further reading* context [6]. We will learn about the syntax and usage of variadic templates by looking at examples.

Syntax

If a function or class template takes zero or more parameters, it can be defined as follows:

```
//a class template with zero or more type parameters
template <typename... Args> class X { ... };

//a function template with zero or more type parameters
template <typename... Args> void foo( function param list) { ...}
```

Here, `<typename ... Args>` declares a parameter pack. Note that here, `Args` is not a keyword; you can use any valid variable names. The preceding class/function template can take any number of `typename` as its arguments need to be instantiated, as shown here:

```
X<> x0;                          //with 0 template type argument
X<int, std::vector<int> > x1;   //with 2 template type arguments
```

```
//with 4 template type arguments
X<int, std::vector<int>, std::map<std::string, std::vector<int>>> x2;

//with 2 template type arguments
foo<float, double>( function argument list );

//with 3 template type arguments
foo<float, double, std::vector<int>>( function argument list );
```

If a variadic template needs at least one type parameter, then the following definition is used:

```
template <typename A, typename... Rest> class Y { ... };

template <typename A, typename... Rest>
void goo( const int a, const float b) { ....};
```

Similarly, we can instantiate them by using the following code:

```
Y<int > y1;
Y<int, std::vector<int>, std::map<std::string, std::vector<int>>> y2;
goo<int, float>(  const int a, const float b );
goo<int,float, double, std::vector<int>>(  const int a, const float b );
```

In the preceding code, we created the `y1` and `y2` objects from the instantiations of the variadic class template, `Y`, with one and three template arguments, respectively. For the variadic function `goo` template, we instantiate it as two template functions with two and three template arguments, respectively.

Examples

The following is probably the simplest example that shows a variadic template being used to find the minimum values of any input argument list. This example is using the concept of recursion until it reaches `my_min(double n)` to exit:

```
//ch4_7_variadic_my_min.cpp
//Only tested on g++ (Ubuntu/Linaro 7.3.0-27 ubuntu1~18.04)
//It may have compile errors for other platforms
#include <iostream>
#include <math.h>
double my_min(double n){
  return n;
}
template<typename... Args>
double my_min(double n, Args... args){
  return fmin(n, my_min(args...));
```

```
}
int main() {
  double x1 = my_min(2);
  double x2 = my_min(2, 3);
  double x3 = my_min(2, 3, 4, 5, 4.7,5.6, 9.9, 0.1);
  std::cout << "x1="<<x1<<", x2="<<x2<<", x3="<<x3<<std::endl;
  return 0;
}
```

The `printf()` variadic function is probably one of the most useful and powerful functions in C or C++; however, it's not type-safe. In the following code block, we're adopting the classic type-safe `printf()` example to demonstrate the usefulness of variadic template. As always, first, we need to define a base function, `void printf_vt(const char *s)`, which ends the recursion:

```
//ch4_8_variadic_printf.cpp part A: base function - recursive end
void printf_vt(const char *s)
{
  while (*s){
    if (*s == '%' && *(++s) != '%')
      throw std::runtime_error("invalid format string: missing arguments");
     std::cout << *s++;
  }
}
```

Then, in its variadic template function, `printf_vt()`, whenever `%` is hit, the value is printed, and the rest is passed to its recursion until the base function is reached:

```
//ch4_8_variadic_printf.cpp part B: recursive function
template<typename T, typename... Rest>
void printf_vt(const char *s, T value, Rest... rest)
{
  while (*s) {
    if (*s == '%' && *(++s) != '%') {
      std::cout << value;
      printf_vt(s, rest...); //called even when *s is 0,
      return;                //but does nothing in that case
    }
    std::cout << *s++;
  }
}
```

Finally, we can test and compare it with the traditional `printf()` using the following code:

```
//ch4_8_variadic_printf.cpp Part C: testing
int main() {
  int x = 10;
  float y = 3.6;
  std::string s = std::string("Variadic templates");
  const char* msg1 = "%s can accept %i parameters (or %s), x=%d, y=%f\n";
  printf(msg1, s, 100, "more",x,y);  //replace 's' by 's.c_str()'
                                     //to prevent the output bug
  const char* msg2 = "% can accept % parameters (or %); x=%,y=%\n";
  printf_vt(msg2, s, 100, "more",x,y);
  return 0;
}
```

The output of the preceding code is as follows:

```
p.]ï¿½U can accept 100 parameters (or more), x=10, y=3.600000
Variadic templates can accept 100 parameters (or more); x=10,y=3.6
```

At the beginning of the first line, we can see some ASCII characters from `printf()` because the corresponding variable type of `%s` should be a pointer to chars, but we give it a type of `std::string`. To fix this, we need to pass `s.c_str()`. However, with the variadic template version function, we do not have this issue. Moreover, we only need to provide `%`, which is even better – at least, it is for this implementation.

In summary, this section briefly introduced variadic templates and their applications. Variadic templates provide the following benefits (since C++11):

- It is a lightweight extension to the template family.
- It demonstrates the ability to implement numerous template libraries without the use of ugly templates and preprocessor macros. Thus, the implementation code is capable of being understood and debugged, and it saves compile time as well.
- It enables type-safe implementations of `printf()` variadic functions.

Next, we will explore template parameters and arguments.

Exploring template parameters and arguments

We learned about function and class templates and their instantiations in previous two sections. We know that, when defining a template, its parameter list need to be given. While we instantiate it, the corresponding argument list must be provided. In this section, we will further study the classifications and details of these two lists.

Template parameters

Recall the following syntax, which is used to define a class/function template. There is a <> symbol after the `template` keyword, in which one or more template parameters must be given:

```
//class template declaration
template <parameter-list> class-declaration

//function template declaration
template <parameter-list> function-declaration
```

A parameter inside the parameter list could be one of the following three types:

- `Non-type template parameter`: Refers to the compile-time constant values, such as integers and pointers, that reference static entities. These are often referred to as non-type parameters.
- `Type template parameter`: This refers to either built-in type names or user-defined classes.
- `Template template parameter`: This indicates the parameters are other templates.

We'll discuss these in more detail in the following subsections.

Non-type template parameter

The syntax of the non-type template parameter is as follows:

```
//for a non-type template parameter with an optional name
type name(optional)

//for a non-type template parameter with an optional name
//and a default value
```

```
type name(optional)=default

//For a non-type template parameter pack with an optional name
type ... name(optional) (since C++11)
```

Here, `type` is one of the following types – integral type, enumeration, pointer to object or to function, `lvalue` reference to an object or to a function, pointer to member object or to member function, and `std::nullptr_t` (since C++11). Additionally, we may put arrays and/or function types in template declarations, but they are automatically replaced with data and/or function pointer(s).

The following example shows a class template that uses a non-type template parameter, `int N`. In `main()`, we instantiate and create an object, `x`, and thus `x.a` has five elements with initial values of `1`. After setting its fourth element value as `10`, we print the output:

```
//ch4_9_none_type_template_param1.cpp
#include <iostream>
template<int N>
class V {
public:
  V(int init) {
    for (int i = 0; i<N; ++i) { a[i] = init; }
  }
  int a[N];
};

int main()
{
  V<5> x(1); //x.a is an array of 5 int, initialized as all 1's
  x.a[4] = 10;
  for( auto &e : x.a) {
    std::cout << e << std::endl;
  }
}
```

The following is an example of a function template that uses `const char*` as a non-type template parameter:

```
//ch4_10_none_type_template_param2.cpp
#include <iostream>
template<const char* msg>
void foo() {
  std::cout << msg << std::endl;
}

// need to have external linkage
extern const char str1[] = "Test 1";
```

```
constexpr char str2[] = "Test 2";
extern const char* str3 = "Test 3";
int main()
{
  foo<str1>();                    //line 1
  foo<str2>();                    //line 2
  //foo<str3>();                  //line 3
  const char str4[] = "Test 4";
  constexpr char str5[] = "Test 5";
  //foo<str4>();                  //line 4
  //foo<str5>();                  //line 5
  return 0;
}
```

In `main()`, we successfully instantiate `foo()` with `str1` and `str2` since they are both compile-time constant values and have external linkages. Then, if we uncomment lines 3-5, the compiler will report error messages. The reasons for getting these compiler errors are as follows:

- **Line 3**: `str3` is not a const variable, so the value being pointed to by `str3` cannot be changed. However, the value of `str3` can be changed.
- **Line 4**: `str4` is not a valid template argument of the `const char*` type because it has no linkage.
- **Line 5**: `str5` is not a valid template argument of the `const char*` type because it has no linkage.

Another of the most common usages of non-type parameters is the size of an array. If you want to find out more, please go to `https://stackoverflow.com/questions/33234979`.

Type template parameter

The syntax of the type template parameter is as follows:

```
//A type Template Parameter (TP) with an optional name
typename |class name(optional)

//A type TP with an optional name and a default
typename[class] name(optional) = default

//A type TP pack with an optional name
typename[class] ... name(optional) (since C++11)
```

Note: Here, we use the `typename` and `class` keywords interchangeably. Inside the body of the template declaration, the name of a type parameter is a `typedef-name`. When the template is instantiated, it aliases the type supplied.

Now, let's look at some examples:

- A type template parameter without the default:

```
Template<class T>                //with name
class X { /* ... */ };

Template<class >                 //without name
class Y { /* ... */ };
```

- A type template parameter with the default:

```
Template<class T = void>    //with name
class X { /* ... */ };

Template<class = void >     //without name
class Y { /* ... */ };
```

- A type template parameter pack:

```
template<typename... Ts>   //with name
class X { /* ... */ };

template<typename... >   //without name
class Y { /* ... */ };
```

This template parameter pack can accept zero or more template arguments, and it only works on C++11 onward.

Template template parameter

The syntax of the template template parameter is as follows:

```
//A template template parameter with an optional name
template <parameter-list> class name(optional)

//A template template parameter with an optional name and a default
template <parameter-list> class name(optional) = default

//A template template parameter pack with an optional name
template <parameter-list> class ... name(optional) (since C++11)
```

Note: In template template parameter declaration, only the `class` keyword can be used; `typename` is not allowed. In the body of the template declaration, the name of a parameter is a `template-name`, and we need arguments to instantiate it.

Now, suppose you have a function that acts as a stream output operator for a list of objects:

```
template<typename T>
static inline std::ostream &operator << ( std::ostream &out,
    std::list<T> const& v)
{
    /*...*/
}
```

From the preceding code, you can see that for sequence containers such as vectors, double end queues, and a multitude of map types, they are the same. Hence, using the concept of the template template parameter, it would be possible to have a single operator, <<, to rule them all. An example of this can be found in `exch4_tp_c.cpp`:

```
/ch4_11_template_template_param.cpp (courtesy: https://stackoverflow.com/
questions/213761)
#include <iostream>
#include <vector>
#include <deque>
#include <list>
using namespace std;
template<class T, template<class, class...> class X, class... Args>
std::ostream& operator <<(std::ostream& os, const X<T, Args...>& objs) {
  os << __PRETTY_FUNCTION__ << ":" << endl;
  for (auto const& obj : objs)
    os << obj << ' ';
  return os;
}

int main() {
  vector<float> x{ 3.14f, 4.2f, 7.9f, 8.08f };
  cout << x << endl;

  list<char> y{ 'E', 'F', 'G', 'H', 'I' };
  cout << y << endl;

  deque<int> z{ 10, 11, 303, 404 };
  cout << z << endl;
  return 0;
}
```

The output of the preceding program is as follows:

```
class std::basic_ostream<char,struct std::char_traits<char> > &__cdecl
operator
<<<float,class std::vector,class std::allocator<float>>(class
std::basic_ostream
<char,struct std::char_traits<char> > &,const class std::vector<float,class
std:
:allocator<float> > &):
3.14 4.2 7.9 8.08
class std::basic_ostream<char,struct std::char_traits<char> > &__cdecl
operator
<<<char,class std::list,class std::allocator<char>>(class
std::basic_ostream<cha
r,struct std::char_traits<char> > &,const class std::list<char,class
std::alloca
tor<char> > &):
E F G H I
class std::basic_ostream<char,struct std::char_traits<char> > &__cdecl
operator
<<<int,class std::deque,class std::allocator<int>>(class
std::basic_ostream<char
,struct std::char_traits<char> > &,const class std::deque<int,class
std::allocat
or<int> > &):
10 11 303 404
```

As expected, the first part of the output for each call is the template function name in a `pretty` format, while the second part outputs the element values of each container.

Template arguments

To instantiate a template, all the template parameters must be replaced with their corresponding template arguments. The arguments are either explicitly provided, deduced from the initializer (for class templates), deduced from the context (for function templates), or defaulted. Since there are three categories of template parameters, we will have three corresponding template arguments as well. These are template non-type arguments, template type arguments, and template template arguments. Besides these, we will also discuss the default template arguments.

Template non-type arguments

Recall that non-type template parameters refer to compile-time constant values such as integers, pointers, and references to static entities. A non-type template argument provided in the template argument list must match with one of these values. Typically, non-type template arguments are used for class initialization or the class container's size specifications.

Although a discussion of the detailed rules for each type (integral and arithmetic types, pointers to objects/functions/members, `lvalue` reference parameters, and so on) of non-type argument is beyond the scope of this book, the overall general rule is that the template non-type arguments should be converted into constant expressions of the corresponding template parameters.

Now, let's take a look at the following example:

```
//part 1: define template with non-type template parameters
template<const float* p> struct U {}; //float pointer non-type parameter
template<const Y& b> struct V {};     //L-value non-type parameter
template<void (*pf)(int)> struct W {};//function pointer parameter

//part 2: define other related stuff
void g(int,float);   //declare function g()
void g(int);         //declare an overload function of g()
struct Y {           //declare structure Y
    float m1;
    static float m2;
};
float a[10];
Y y; //line a: create a object of Y

//part 3: instantiation template with template non-type arguments
U<a> u1;       //line b: ok: array to pointer conversion
U<&y> u2;      //line c: error: address of Y
U<&y.m1> u3;   //line d: error: address of non-static member
U<&y.m2> u4;   //line e: ok: address of static member
V<y> v;        //line f: ok: no conversion needed
W<&g> w;       //line g: ok: overload resolution selects g(int)
```

In the preceding code, in `part 1`, we defined three template structs with different non-type template parameters. Then, in `part 2`, we declared two overload functions and `struct Y`. Finally, in `part 3`, we looked at the correct way to instantiate them by different non-type arguments.

Template type arguments

Compared to the template non-type arguments, the rule of a template type argument (for a type template parameter) is simple and requires that it must be a `typeid`. Here, a `typeid` is a standard C++ operator that returns type identification information at runtime. It basically returns a `type_info` object that can be compared with other `type_info` objects.

Now, let's look at the following example:

```
//ch4_12_template_type_argument.cpp
#include <iostream>
#include <typeinfo>
using namespace std;

//part 1: define templates
template<class T> class C  {};
template<class T> void f() { cout << "T" << endl; };
template<int i>   void f() { cout << i << endl; };

//part 2: define structures
struct A{};            // incomplete type
typedef struct {} B; // type alias to an unnamed type

//part 3: main() to test
int main() {
  cout << "Tid1=" << typeid(A).name() << "; ";
  cout << "Tid2=" << typeid(A*).name() << "; ";
  cout << "Tid3=" << typeid(B).name()  << "; ";
  cout << "Tid4=" << typeid(int()).name() << endl;

  C<A> x1;    //line A: ok,'A' names a type
  C<A*> x2;   //line B: ok, 'A*' names a type
  C<B> x3;    //line C: ok, 'B' names a type
  f<int()>(); //line D: ok, since int() is considered as a type,
              //thus calls type template parameter f()
  f<5>();     //line E: ok, this calls non-type template parameter f()
  return 0;
}
```

In this example, in `part 1`, we defined three classes and function templates: the class template C with its type template parameter, two function templates with a type template parameter, and a non-type template parameter, respectively. In `part 2`, we have an incomplete `struct A` and an unnamed type, `struct B`. Finally, in `part 3`, we tested them. The outputs of the four `typeid()` in Ubuntu 18.04 are as follows:

```
Tid1=A; Tid2=P1A; Tid3=1B; Tid4=FivE
```

From x86 MSVC v19.24, we have the following:

```
Tid1=struct A; Tid2=struct A; Tid3=struct B; Tid4=int __cdecl(void)
```

Additionally, since `A`, A*, `B`, and `int()` have typeids, the code segment from lines A to D is linked with the template type classes or functions. Only line E is instantiated from the non-type template parameter function template, that is, `f()`.

Template template arguments

For a template template parameter, its corresponding template argument is the name of a class template or a template alias. While finding a template to match the template template argument, only primary class templates are considered.

Here, a primary template refers to the template that is being specialized. Even though their parameter lists might match, the compiler will not consider any partial specialization with that of the template template parameter.

Here is an example of a template template argument:

```
//ch4_13_template_template_argument.cpp
#include <iostream>
#include <typeinfo>
using namespace std;

//primary class template X with template type parameters
template<class T, class U>
class X {
public:
    T a;
    U b;
};

//partially specialization of class template X
template<class U>
class X<int, U> {
public:
    int a;  //customized a
    U b;
};

//class template Y with template template parameter
template<template<class T, class U> class V>
class Y {
public:
    V<int, char> i;
```

```
    V<char, char> j;
};

Y<X> c;
int main() {
    cout << typeid(c.i.a).name() << endl; //int
    cout << typeid(c.i.b).name() << endl; //char
    cout << typeid(c.j.a).name() << endl; //char
    cout << typeid(c.j.b).name() << endl; //char
    return 0;
}
```

In this example, we're defining a primary class template, `X`, and its specialization, then a class template, `Y`, with a template template parameter. Next, we implicitly instantiate `Y` with template template argument `X` and create an object, `c`. Finally, `main()` outputs the names of the four `typeid()`, and the results are `int`, `char`, `char`, and `char`, respectively.

Default template arguments

In C++, a function is called by passing arguments, and the arguments are used by the function. If, while invoking a function, the arguments are not passed, the default values are used. Similar to the function parameter default values, template parameters can have default arguments. When we define a template, we can set its default arguments, like so:

```
/ch4_14_default_template_arguments.cpp       //line 0
#include <iostream>                          //line 1
#include <typeinfo>                          //line 2
template<class T1, class T2 = int> class X;  //line 3
template<class T1 = float, class T2> class X;//line 4
template<class T1, class T2> class X {       //line 5
public:                                      //line 6
 T1 a;                                       //line 7
 T2 b;                                       //line 8
};                                           //line 9
using namespace std;
int main() {
 X<int> x1;          //<int,int>
 X<float>x2;         //<float,int>
 X<>x3;              //<float,int>
 X<double, char> x4; //<double, char>
 cout << typeid(x1.a).name() << ", " << typeid(x1.b).name() << endl;
 cout << typeid(x2.a).name() << ", " << typeid(x2.b).name() << endl;
 cout << typeid(x3.a).name() << ", " << typeid(x3.b).name() << endl;
 cout << typeid(x4.a).name() << ", " << typeid(x4.b).name() << endl;
 return 0
}
```

There are certain rules that need to be followed when we set the default arguments for template parameters:

- The declaration order matters – the declaration of the default template arguments must be on the top of the primary template declaration. For instance, in the preceding example, you cannot move the code at lines 3 and 4 after line 9.
- If one parameter has a default argument, then all the parameters after it must also have default arguments. For example, the following code is incorrect:

```
template<class U = char, class V, class W = int> class X { };  //Error
template<class V, class U = char,  class W = int> class X { }; //OK
```

- You cannot give the same parameter default arguments twice in the same scope. For example, you will get an error message if you use the following code:

```
template<class T = int> class Y;

//compiling error, to fix it, replace "<class T = int>" by "<class T>"
template<class T = int> class Y {
    public: T a;
};
```

Here, we have discussed two lists: `template_parameter_list` and `template_argument_list`. These are used in function or class template creation and instantiation, respectively.

We also learned about two other important rules:

- When we define a class or function template, we need to give its `template_parameter_list`:

```
template <template_parameter_list>
class X { ... }

template <template_parameter_list>
void foo( function_argument_list ) { ... } //assume return type is void
```

- When we instantiate them, we must provide the corresponding `argument_list`:

```
class X<template_argument_list> x
void foo<template_argument_list>( function_argument_list )
```

The parameter or argument types in these two lists can be classified into three categories, as shown in the following table. Note that although the top row is for class templates, these properties also apply to function templates:

	When defining a template **template <template_parameter_list> class X { ... }**	**When instantiating a template** **class X<template_argument_list> x**
non-type	An entity in this parameter list can be one of the following: • Integral or enumeration • Pointer to object or pointer to function • `lvalue` reference to an object or `lvalue` reference to a function • Pointer to member • C++11 std `::nullptr_t` C++11 ends	• Non-type arguments in this list are expressions whose value can be determined at compile time. • Such arguments must be constant expressions, addresses of functions or objects with external linkage, or addresses of static class members. • Non-type arguments are normally used to initialize a class or to specify the sizes of class members.
type	An entity in this parameter list can be one of the following: • Must start with typename or class. • Inside the body of the template declaration, the name of a type parameter is a `typedef-name`. When the template is instantiated, it aliases the type supplied.	• The type of argument must have a `typeid`. • It cannot be a local type, a type with no linkage, an unnamed type, or a type compounded from any of these types.
template	An entity in this parameter list can be one of the following: • `template <parameter-list>` class name • `template <parameter-list>` class ... name (optional) (since C++11)	A template argument in this list is the name of a class template.

In the upcoming section, we will explore how to implement traits in C++ and optimize algorithms using them.

Exploring traits

Generic programming means writing code that works with any data type under certain requirements. It is the most efficient way of delivering reusable high-quality code in the software engineering industry. However, there are times in generic programming where being generic just isn't good enough. Whenever the differences between types are too complex, it is very hard for an efficient generic to optimize a common implement. For example, while implementing a sort function template, if we know the argument type is a linked list but not an array, a different strategy will be implemented to optimize the performance.

Although template specialization is one approach to overcome this problem, it doesn't provide type-related information in a broad way. A type trait is a technique that's used to collect information about the type. With its help, we can make more intelligent decisions to develop high-quality optimized algorithms in generic programming.

In this section, we will introduce how to implement a type trait, and then show you how to use type information to optimize algorithms.

Type trait implementation

To understand type traits, we'll look at the classic implementations of boost::is_void and boost::is_pointer.

boost::is_void

First, let's look at one of the simplest traits classes, the is_void trait, which was created by boost. It defines a generic template that's used to implement the default behavior; that is, accept a void type, but anything else is void. Hence, we have is_void::value = false:

```
//primary class template is_void
template< typename T >
struct is_void{
    static const bool value = false;  //default value=false
};
```

Then, we fully specialize it for the void type:

```
//"<>" means a full specialization of template class is_void
template<>
struct is_void< void >{              //fully specialization for void
    static const bool value = true; //only true for void type
};
```

Thus, we have a complete traits type that can be used to detect if any given type, T, is_void by checking the following expression:

```
is_void<T>::value
```

Next, let's learn how to use partial specialization in boost::is_pointer traits.

boost::is_pointer

Similar to the boost::avoid traits, a primary class template is defined as follows:

```
//primary class template is_pointer
template< typename T >
struct is_pointer{
    static const bool value = false;
};
```

Then, it is partially specialized for all pointer types:

```
//"typename T" in "<>" means partial specialization
template< typename T >
struct is_pointer< T* >{ //<T*> means partial specialization only for type
T*
  static const bool value = true;  //set value as true
};
```

Now, we have a complete traits type that can be used to detect if any given type, `T`, `is_pointer` by checking the following expression:

```
is_pointer<T>::value
```

Since the boost type traits feature has already been formally introduced to the C++ 11 Standard Library, we can show the usage of `std::is_void` and `std::is_pointer` without including the preceding source code in the following example:

```
//ch4_15_traits_boost.cpp
#include <iostream>
#include <type_traits>  //since C++11
using namespace std;
struct X {};
int main()
{
 cout << boolalpha; //set the boolalpha format flag for str stream.
 cout << is_void<void>::value << endl;          //true
 cout << is_void<int>::value << endl;           //false
 cout << is_pointer<X *>::value << endl;        //true
 cout << is_pointer<X>::value << endl;          //false
 cout << is_pointer<X &>::value << endl;        //false
 cout << is_pointer<int *>::value << endl;      //true
 cout << is_pointer<int **>::value << endl;     //true
 cout << is_pointer<int[10]>::value << endl;    //false
 cout << is_pointer< nullptr_t>::value << endl; //false
}
```

The preceding code sets the `boolalpha` format flag for the string stream at the beginning. By doing so, all the bool values are extracted by their text representation, which is either true or false. Then, we use several `std::cout` to print the values of `is_void<T>::value` and `is_pointer<T>::value`. The output of each value is displayed at the end of the corresponding commented-out line.

Optimizing algorithms using traits

Instead of talking about this topic in a generic abstract way, we will use a classic optimized copy example to show the usage of type traits. Consider the standard library algorithm known as `copy`:

```
template<typename It1, typename It2>
It2 copy(It1 first, It1 last, It2 out);
```

Obviously, we can write a generic version of `copy()` for any iterator types, that is, `It1` and `It2` here. However, as explained by the authors of the boost library, there are some circumstances where the copy operation can be performed by `memcpy()`. We can use `memcpy()` if all of the following conditions are satisfied:

- Both types of iterator, `It1` and `It2`, are pointers.
- `It1` and `It2` must point to the same type, except for const and volatile qualifiers
- A trivial assignment operator must be provided by the type that `It1` points to.

Here, the trivial assignment operator means that the type is either a scalar type or one of the following:

- There is no user-defined assignment operator for the type.
- There is no reference type of data members inside the type.
- Trivial assignment operators must be defined in all the base classes and data member objects.

Here, a scalar type includes an arithmetic type, enumeration type, pointer, pointer to member, or const- or volatile-qualified version of one of these types.

Now, let's take a look at the original implementation. It includes two parts – the copier class template and the user interface function, that is, `copy()`:

```
namespace detail{
//1. Declare primary class template with a static function template
template <bool b>
struct copier {
    template<typename I1, typename I2>
    static I2 do_copy(I1 first, I1 last, I2 out);
};
//2. Implementation of the static function template
template <bool b>
template<typename I1, typename I2>
I2 copier<b>::do_copy(I1 first, I1 last, I2 out) {
    while(first != last) {
```

```
        *out = *first;
         ++out;
         ++first;
    }
    return out;
};
//3. a full specialization of the primary function template
template <>
struct copier<true> {
    template<typename I1, typename I2>
    static I2* do_copy(I1* first, I1* last, I2* out){
        memcpy(out, first, (last-first)*sizeof(I2));
        return out+(last-first);
    }
};
}  //end namespace detail
```

As mentioned in the comment lines, the preceding copier class template has two static function templates – one is the primary and the other is fully specialized. The primary does an element-by-element hard copy, while the full specialization one copies all the elements at once via `memcpy()`:

```
//copy() user interface
template<typename I1, typename I2>
inline I2 copy(I1 first, I1 last, I2 out) {
    typedef typename boost::remove_cv
    <typename std::iterator_traits<I1>::value_type>::type v1_t;

    typedef typename boost::remove_cv
    <typename std::iterator_traits<I2>::value_type>::type v2_t;

    enum{ can_opt = boost::is_same<v1_t, v2_t>::value
                    && boost::is_pointer<I1>::value
                    && boost::is_pointer<I2>::value
                    && boost::has_trivial_assign<v1_t>::value
   };
   //if can_opt= true, using memcpy() to copy whole block by one
   //call(optimized); otherwise, using assignment operator to
   //do item-by-item copy
   return detail::copier<can_opt>::do_copy(first, last, out);
}
```

To optimize the copy operation, the preceding user interface function defines two `remove_cv` template objects, `v1_t` and `v2_t`, and then evaluates whether `can_opt` is true. After that, the `do_copy()` template function is called. By using the test code posted in the boost utility library (`algo_opt_ examples.cpp`), we can see that there is a significant improvement in using the optimized implementation; that is, it could be 8 or 3 times faster for copying char or int types of data.

Finally, let's conclude this section with the following highlights:

- A trait gives additional information other than just the type. It is implemented through template specializations.
- By convention, traits are always implemented as structs. The structs that are used to implement traits are known as trait classes.
- Bjarne Stroustrup said that we should think of a trait as a small object whose main purpose is to carry information that's used by another object or algorithm to determine policy or implementation details. *Further reading* context [4]
- Scott Meyers also summarized that we should use traits classes to gather information about types *Further reading* context [5].
- Traits can help us implement generic algorithms in an efficient/optimized way.

Next, we will explore template metaprogramming in C++.

Exploring template metaprogramming

A programming technique in which computer programs have the ability to treat other programs as their data is known as **metaprogramming**. This means that a program can be designed to read, generate, analyze, or transform other programs, and even modify itself while running. One kind of metaprogramming is a compiler, which takes a text format program as an input language (C, Fortran, Java, and so on) and produces another binary machine code format program in an output language.

C++ **template metaprogramming** (**TMP**) means producing metaprograms in C++ using templates. It has two components – a template must be defined, and a defined template must be instantiated. TMP is Turing-complete, which means it has the capability to compute anything that is computable, at least in principle. Also, because variables are all immutable (variables are constants) in TMP, recursion rather than iteration is used to process the elements of a set.

Why do we need TMP? Because it can speed up our programs during execution time! But since there is no free lunch in the optimization world, the prices we paid for TMP are longer compile-time and/or larger binary code sizes. Additionally, not every problem can be solved with TMP; it only works when we're computing something that is constant during compile time; for example, finding out all the primary numbers that are smaller than a constant integer, the factorial of a constant integer, unrolling a constant number of loops or iterations, and so on.

From a practical point of view, template metaprogramming has the ability to solve problems in the following three categories: compile-time computation, compile-time optimization, and replacing dynamic polymorphism with static polymorphism by avoiding virtual table lookup during runtime. In the following subsections, we will provide examples from each category to demonstrate how metaprogramming works.

Compile-time computation

Typically, if the inputs and outputs of a task are known at compile-time, we can use template metaprogramming to do the computation during compilation and thus save any runtime overhead and the memory footprint. This is really useful in real-time intense CPU utilization projects.

Let's take a look at the factorial function, which calculates `n!`. This is the product of all positive integers less than or equal to *n*, with 0!=1 by definition. Thanks to the concept of recursion, we can implement this using a simple function, as follows:

```
//ch4_17_factorial_recursion.cpp
#include <iostream>
uint32_t f1(const uint32_t n) {
  return (n<=1) ? 1 : n * f1(n - 1);
}

constexpr uint32_t f2(const uint32_t n) {
  return ( n<=1 )? 1 : n * f2(n - 1);
}

int main() {
  uint32_t a1 = f1(10);          //run-time computation
  uint32_t a2 = f2(10);          //run-time computation
  const uint32_t a3 = f2(10);    //compile-time computation
  std::cout << "a1=" << a1 << ", a2=" << a2 << std::endl;
}
```

`f1()` does the computation at runtime, while `f2()` can do it either at runtime or compile-time, depending on its usage.

Similarly, by using a template with a non-type parameter, its specialization, and the recursion concept, the template metaprogramming version of this problem is as follows:

```
//ch4_18_factorial_metaprogramming.cpp
#include <iostream>
//define a primary template with non-type parameters
template <uint32_t n>
struct fact {
  const static uint32_t value = n * fact<n - 1>::value;
  //use next line if your compiler does not support declare and initialize
  //a constant static int type member inside the class declaration
  //enum { value = n * fact<n - 1>::value };
};

//fully specialized template for n as 0
template <>
struct fact<0> {
    const static uint32_t value = 1;
    //enum { value = 1 };
};
using namespace std;
int main() {
    cout << "fact<0>=" << fact<0>::value << endl;   //fact<0>=1
    cout << "fact<10>=" << fact<10>::value << endl; //fact<10>=3628800

    //Lab: uncomments the following two lines, build and run
    //     this program, what are you expecting?
    //uint32_t m=5;
    //std::cout << fact<m>::value << std::endl;
}
```

Here, we created a class template with a non-type parameter, and like other const expressions, values of `const static uint32_t` or enumeration constants are evaluated at compile time. This compile-time evaluation constraint means only const variables make sense. Also, since we are working with classes only, static objects make sense.

When the compiler sees a new argument for a template, it creates a new instance of the template. For instance, when the compiler sees `fact<10>::value` and it tries to create an instance of `fact` with the argument as 10, it turns out that `fact<9>` must also be created. For `fact<9>`, it needs `fact<8>` and so on. Finally, the compiler uses `fact<0>::value` (which is 1), and the recursion during compile time terminates. This process can be seen in the following code block:

```
fact<10>::value = 10* fact<9>::value;
fact<10>::value = 10* 9 * fact<8>::value;
fact<10>::value = 10* 9 * 8 * fact<7>::value;
```

```
.
.
.
fact<10>::value = 10* 9 * 8 *7*6*5*4*3*2*fact<1>::value;
fact<10>::value = 10* 9 * 8 *7*6*5*4*3*2*1*fact<0>::value;
...
fact<10>::value = 10* 9 * 8 *7*6*5*4*3*2*1*1;
```

Note that to be able to use templates in this way, we must provide a constant argument in template argument list. That's why if you uncomment the last two lines of code, you will get a complaint from the compiler: `fact:template parameter n: m: a variable with non-static storage duration cannot be used as a non-type argument.`

Finally, let's end this subsection by briefly comparing the **constexpr functions** (**CF**) and TMP:

- **Computation time**: CF executes at either compile-time or runtime, depending on its usage, but TMP only executes at compile time.
- **Argument lists**: CF can only take values, but TMP can take both value and type parameters.
- **Control structure**: CF can use recursion, conditions, and loops, but TMP only uses recursion.

Compile-time code optimization

Although the previous example can calculate the factorial of a constant integer at compile-time, we can use a runtime loop to unroll the dot-products of two -*n* vectors (where *n* is known at compile time). The benefit of a more traditional length-*n* vector is that unrolling the loops is feasible, which results in very optimized code.

As an example, the traditional dot-product function template can be implemented in the following way:

```
//ch4_19_loop_unoolling_traditional.cpp
#include <iostream>
using namespace std;
template<typename T>
T dotp(int n, const T* a, const T* b)
{
  T ret = 0;
  for (int i = 0; i < n; ++i) {
      ret += a[i] * b[i];
  }
```

```
  return ret;
}

int main()
{
  float a[5] = { 1, 2, 3, 4, 5 };
  float b[5] = { 6, 7, 8, 9, 10 };
  cout<<"dot_product(5,a,b)=" << dotp<float>(5, a, b) << '\n'; //130
  cout<<"dot_product(5,a,a)=" << dotp<float>(5, a, a) << '\n'; //55
}
```

Loop unrolling means that if we can optimize the for loop inside the `dotp()` function as `a[0]*b[0] + a[1]*b[1] + a[2]*b[2] + a[3]*b[3] + a[4]*b[4]`, then it will save more runtime computations. That is exactly what metaprogramming does in the following code block:

```
//ch4_20_loop_unroolling_metaprogramming.cpp
#include <iostream>

//primary template declaration
template <int N, typename T>
class dotp {
public:
  static T result(T* a, T* b) {
    return (*a) * (*b) + dotp<N - 1, T>::result(a + 1, b + 1);
  }
};

//partial specialization for end condition
template <typename T>
class dotp<1, T> {
public:
  static T result(T* a, T* b) {
    return (*a) * (*b);
  }
};

int main()
{
  float a[5] = { 1, 2, 3, 4, 5 };
  float b[5] = { 6, 7, 8, 9, 10 };
  std::cout << "dot_product(5,a,b) = "
            << dotp<5, float>::result( a, b) << '\n'; //130
  std::cout << "dot_product(5,a,a) = "
            << dotp<5,float>::result( a, a) << '\n'; //55
}
```

Similar to the factorial metaprogramming example, in the `dotp<5, float>::result( a, b)` statement, the instantiation process recursively does the following computing:

```
dotp<5, float>::result( a, b)
= *a * *b + dotp<4,float>::result(a+1,b+1)
= *a * *b + *(a+1) * *(b+1) + dotp<3,float>::result(a+2,b+2)
= *a * *b + *(a+1) * *(b+1) + *(a+2) * *(b+2)
  + dotp<2,float>::result(a+3,b+3)
= *a * *b + *(a+1) * *(b+1) + *(a+2) * *(b+2) + *(a+3) * *(b+3)
  + dotp<1,float>::result(a+4,b+4)
= *a * *b + *(a+1) * *(b+1) + *(a+2) * *(b+2) + *(a+3) * *(b+3)
  + *(a+4) * *(b+4)
```

Since *N* is 5, it recursively calls the `dotp<n, float>::results()` template function four times until `dotp<1, float>::results()` is reached. The final expression that's evaluated by `dotp<5, float>::result( a, b)` is displayed in the last two lines of the preceding block.

Static polymorphism

Polymorphism means multiple functions have the same name. Dynamic polymorphism allows users to determine the actual function method to be executed at runtime (see `chapter 3`, *Details of Object-Oriented Programming,* for more details), while *static* polymorphism means that the actual function to call (or, in general, the actual code to run) is known at compile time. By default, C++ matches a function call with the correct function definition at compile time by checking the types and/or the number of arguments. This process is also called **static binding** or **overloading**. However, by using a virtual function, the compiler also does dynamic binding or overriding in runtime.

For example, in the following code, a virtual function, `alg()`, is defined in both base `class B` and derived `class D`. When we use the derived object pointer `p` as an instance pointer of the base class, the `p->alg()` function call will invoke the derived `alg()` defined in the derived class:

```
//ch4_21_polymorphism_traditional.cpp
#include <iostream>
class B{
public:
    B() = default;
    virtual void alg() {
        std::cout << "alg() in B";
    }
};
```

```
class D : public B{
public:
    D() = default;
    virtual void alg(){
        std::cout << "alg() in D";
    }
};

int main()
{
    //derived object pointer p as an instance pointer of the base class
    B *p = new D();
    p->alg();       //outputs "alg() in D"
    delete p;
    return 0;
}
```

However, in cases where the polymorphism behavior is invariant and can be determined at compile-time, the **Curiously Recurring Template Pattern** (**CRTP**) can be used to achieve static polymorphism, which imitates static polymorphism and resolves the binding at compile time. Thus, the program will get out of checking `virtual-lookup-table` at runtime. The following code implements the previous example in a static polymorphism way:

```
//ch4_22_polymorphism_metaprogramming.cpp
#include <iostream>
template <class D> struct B {
    void ui() {
        static_cast<D*>(this)->alg();
    }
};

struct D : B<D> {
    void alg() {
        cout << "D::alg()" << endl;
     }
};

int main(){
    B<D> b;
    b.ui();
    return 0;
}
```

In summary, the general idea of template metaprogramming is to let the compiler do some computation during compilation time. In this way, the runtime overhead can be resolved to a certain degree. The reason we can compute something during compilation time is that something is constant before runtime.

As mentioned in further reading context [14],C++ TMP is a very powerful method for performing computational tasks at compilation time. The first approach is not easy, and we must be very careful regarding compile errors because the templates tree is unrolled. From a practical point of view, the boost **Metaprogramming Library** (**MPL**) is a good reference to start. It provides a compile-time TMP framework for algorithms, sequences, and metafunctions in a general-purpose way. Moreover, the new `std::variant` and `std::visit` features in C++17 can also be used for static polymorphism for scenarios where there are no related types sharing the inheritance kind of an interface.

Summary

In this chapter, we discussed generic programming-related topics in C++. Starting by reviewing C macros and function overloading, we introduced the development motivations of C++ templates. Then, we presented the syntax of class and function templates with a fixed number of parameters, as well as their specializations and instantiations. Since C++11, variadic templates are accepted by the standard generic function and class templates. Based on this, we further classified the template parameters and arguments into three categories: non-type template parameters/arguments, type template parameters/arguments, and template template parameters/arguments.

We also learned about traits and template metaprogramming. As a byproduct of template specialization, traits classes can provide us with more information about types. With the help of type information, eventually, the optimizations of implementing generic algorithms become possible. Another application of class and/or function templates is to compute some constant tasks during compile time via recursion, which is called template metaprogramming. It has the ability to perform compile-time computation and/or optimization, as well as avoid virtual table lookup during runtime.

Now, you should have a deep understanding of templates. You should be able to create your own function and class templates in applications, as well as practice using traits to optimize your algorithm and use template metaprogramming to do compile-time computation for additional optimization

In the next chapter, we will learn about memory and management-related topics, such as the concept of memory access, allocation and de-allocation techniques, and garbage collection basics. This is the most unique feature of C++, and thus it must be understood by every C++ developer.

Questions

1. What are the side effects of macros?
2. What is a class/function template? What is a template class/function?
3. What is a template parameter list? What is a template argument list? Once we have a class template, we can instantiate it either explicitly or implicitly. In what kind of scenario is explicit instantiation necessary?
4. What does polymorphism mean in C++? What is the difference between function overloading and function overriding?
5. What are type traits? How do we implement a type trait?
6. In the `ch4_5_class_template_implicit_inst_B.cpp` file, we said implicit instantiation generates the `X<int>` class, and then creates the `xi` object and generates the `X<int>::f()` function, but not `X<int>::g()`. How can you verify that `X<int>::g()` is not generated?
7. Using template metaprogramming, solve the problem of *f(x,n) = x^n*, where *n* is a const and *x* is a variable.
8. Extend `ch4_17_loop_unrolling_metaprogramming.cpp` to values of n=10,100,10^3,10^4,10^6, ..., until you reach your system memory limits. Compare the compile time, object file size, and running CPU time.

Further reading

As referenced throughout this chapter, have a look at the following sources to find out more regarding what was covered in this chapter:

- Milner, R., Morris, L., Newey, M. (1975). *A Logic for Computable Functions with Reflexive and Polymorphic Types.* Proceedings of the Conference on Proving and Improving Programs.
  `https://www.research.ed.ac.uk/portal/en/publications/a-logic-for-computable-functions-with-reflexive-and-polymorphic-types(9a69331e-b562-4061-8882-2a89a3c473bb).html`
- *Curtis, Dorothy (2009-11-06). CLU home page.*Programming Methodology Group, Computer Science and Artificial Intelligence Laboratory. Massachusetts Institute of Technology.
  `http://www.pmg.csail.mit.edu/CLU.html`
- *Technical Corrigendum for Ada 2012,* published by ISO. Ada Resource Association. 2016-01-29.
  https://www.adaic.org/2016/01/technical-corrigendum-for-ada-2012-published-by-iso/
- B. Stroustrup, C++.
  `https://dl.acm.org/doi/10.5555/1074100.1074189`
- *S. Meyers, Effective C++ 55 Specific Ways to Improve Your Programs and Designs (3rd Edition), Chapter 7.*
  `https://www.oreilly.com/library/view/effective-c-55/0321334876/`
- D. Gregor and J. Järvi (February 2008). *Variadic Templates for C++0x.*Journal of Object Technology. pp. 31–51
  `http://www.jot.fm/issues/issue_2008_02/article2.pdf`
- `https://www.boost.org/` for type traits, unit testing etc.
- `https://www.ibm.com/support/knowledgecenter/ssw_ibm_i_72/rzarg/templates.htm` for generic templates discussions.
- `https://stackoverflow.com/questions/546669/c-code-analysis-tool` for code analysis tools.
- `https://en.cppreference.com` for template explicit instantiations.

- `http://www.cplusplus.com` for library references and usage examples.
- `http://www.drdobbs.com/cpp/c-type-traits/184404270` for type-traits.
- `https://accu.org/index.php/journals/424` for template metaprogramming.
- `https://en.wikipedia.org/wiki/Template_metaprogramming` for template metaprogramming.
- K. Czarnecki, U. W. Eisenecker, *Generative Programming: Methods, Tools, and Applications*, Chapter 10.
- N. Josuttis; D. Gregor and D. Vandevoorde, *C++ Templates: The Complete Guide (2nd Edition)*, Addison-Wesley Professional 2017.

5 Memory Management and Smart Pointers

Memory management comes at a price in C++. Concerned programmers often complain about C++ because of its manual memory management requirements. While languages like C# and Java use automatic memory management, it makes the programs run slower than their C++ counterparts. Manual memory management is often error-prone and unsafe. As we have already seen in the previous chapters, a program represents data and instructions. Almost every program uses computer memory to some extent. It's hard to imagine a useful program that doesn't require memory allocation.

Memory allocation and deallocation starts with the simplest call of a function. Calling a function usually implies passing arguments to it. The function needs space to store those arguments. To make life easier, it's handled automatically. The same automatic allocation happens when we declare objects in the code. Their lifetime depends on the scope they have declared. Whenever they go out of scope, they will be deallocated automatically. Most programming languages provide similar automatic deallocation functionality for dynamic memory. The dynamically allocated memory – as opposed to automatic allocation – is a term used by programmers to identify code portions that request new memory upon requirements. For example, this would be used in a program storing the list of customers' requests for new memory space upon the increase of the number of customers. To somehow differentiate between *types* of memory management, whether it's automatic or manual, programmers use memory segmentation. A program operates with several segments of memory, the stack, the heap, the read-only segment, and so on, although all of them have the same structure and are part of the same virtual memory.

Most languages provide simplified methods for accessing dynamic memory without being concerned with its deallocation strategies, leaving the hard work up to the runtime support environment. C++ programmers have to deal with the low-level details of memory management. Whether it's due to the philosophy, structure, or age of the language, C++ doesn't provide high-level memory management functionality. Therefore, a deep understanding of memory structure and its management is a must for every C++ programmer. Let's now illuminate the mystery behind memory and proper memory management techniques in this chapter.

In this chapter, we will cover the following topics:

- What is memory and how do we access it in C++?
- Memory allocation in detail
- Memory management techniques and idioms
- Garbage collection basics

Technical requirements

The `g++` compiler with the option `-std=c++2a` is used to compile the examples throughout the chapter.

You can find the source files used in this chapter at `https://github.com/PacktPublishing/Expert-CPP`.

Understanding computer memory

At the lowest level of representation, the memory is a device that stores the state of a bit. Let's say we are inventing a device that can store a single bit of information. Nowadays, it seems both meaningless and magical at the same time. It's meaningless to invent something that has already been invented, a long time ago. It's magical because programmers nowadays have the luxury of stable multifunctional environments providing tons of libraries, frameworks, and tools to create programs without even understanding them under the hood. It has become ridiculously easy to declare a variable or allocate a dynamic memory, as shown in the following code snippet:

```
int var;
double* pd = new double(4.2);
```

It's hard to describe how the device stores these variables. To somehow shed some light on that magical process, let's try to design a device that stores a bit of information.

Designing a memory storage device

We will use electrical circuits, relays, and logic gates to design a simple device able to store a bit. The purpose of this section is to understand the structure of the memory at its lowest level.

Here's a simple illustration of an electric circuit that would be familiar to you from physics classes:

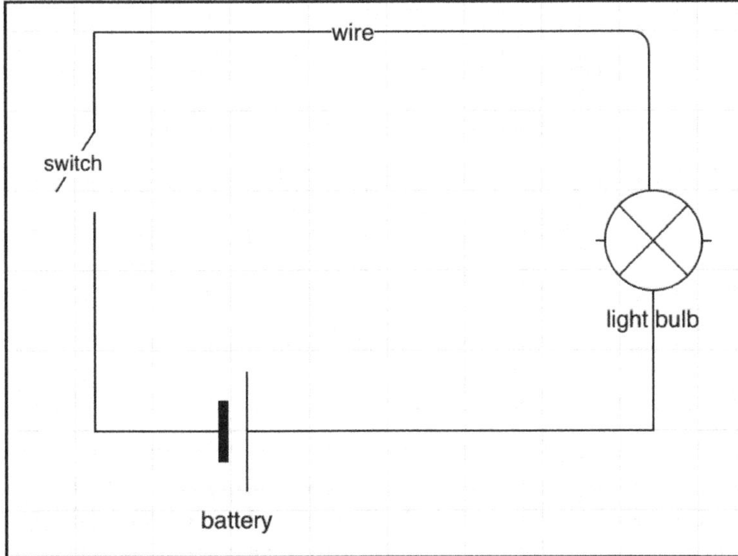

It consists of a **wire** connecting the battery to the **light bulb**. The **wire** has a **switch** that controls the state of the light bulb. The **light bulb** is on when the switch is closed, otherwise, it's off. We will add to this circuit two NOR logical elements. The NOR is short for Not OR. It's usually represented the following way:

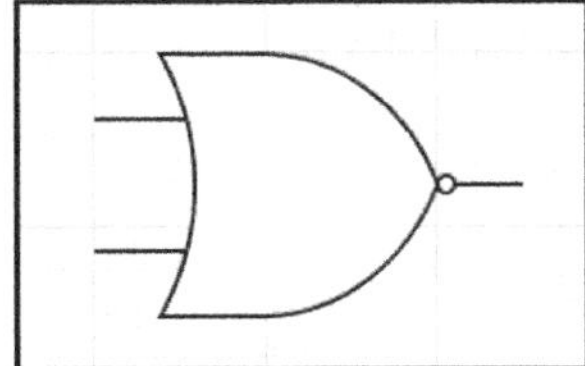

It has two inputs (the wires leading into the element), each of which represents an electrical signal. We say that the output (the wire coming out from the element) is 1 if both inputs are 0. That's why we call it *Not OR* because the OR element outputs 1 if any of its inputs are 1. The preceding NOR element is simply constructed using two relays. A relay is a switch that uses an electromagnet to close and open the contacts. Look at the following diagram:

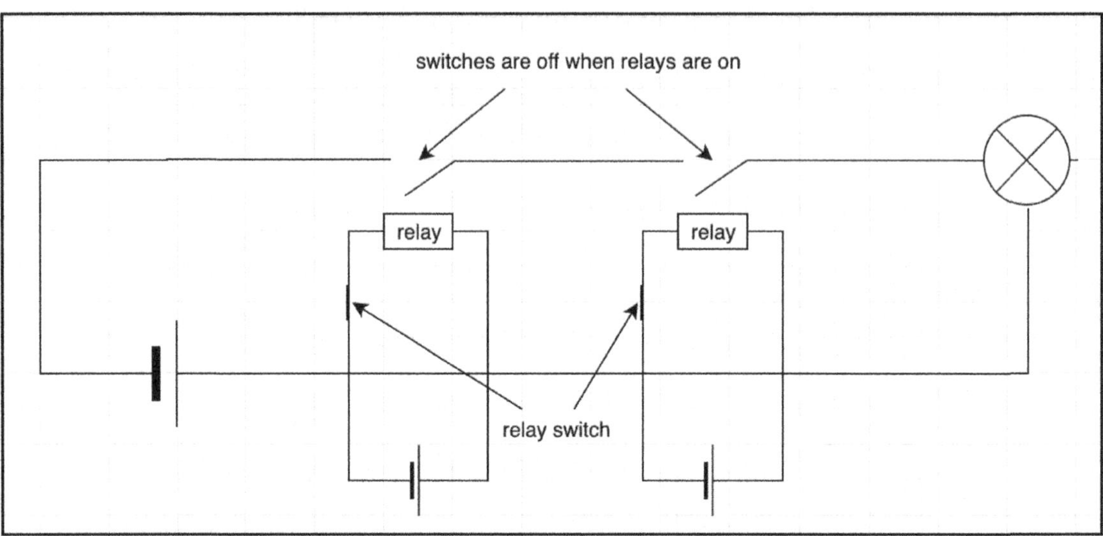

When both **switches** of **relays** are closed (meaning the **relays** are working and pulling down the **switches** of the circuit), the light bulb is *off*. When we move the **switch** to the open position of both **relays**, the light bulb turns *on*. The preceding diagram is one of the ways to depict a NOR gate. At this point, we can create a logic element using electric wires, light bulbs, batteries, and relays. Now let's see a strange combination of two NOR elements leading to an interesting discovery:

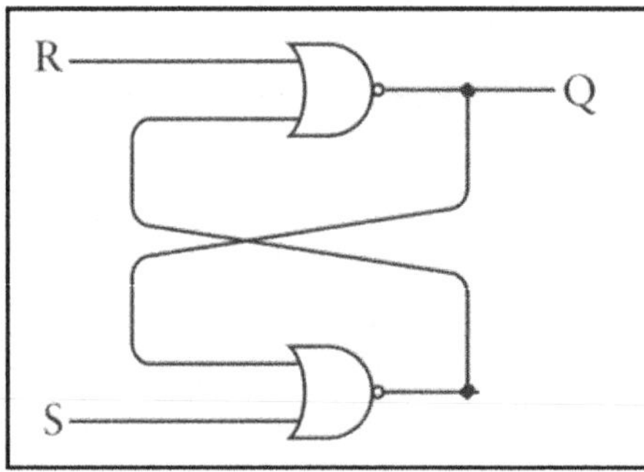

The preceding diagram is the typical representation of an **R-S flip-flop**. **R** is for *reset*, **S** is for *set*. The device built by the preceding scheme can store one bit. The output **Q** is the wire from which we can read the contents of the device. If we set the flip-flop to store the bit, the output will be 1. You should carefully examine the diagram and imagine passing signals to its inputs one by one or both at the same time and see the output at **Q**. When the input **S** is 1, **Q** becomes 1. When **R** is 1, **Q** becomes 0. This way we *set* or *reset* the bit. It will store the bit as long as we supply current to the device.

Now imagine having a lot of devices as designed earlier interconnected together so that we will store more than one bit of information. This way, we can construct complex memory devices storing bytes or even **kilobytes** (**KB**), of data.

The preceding device is similar to those used in computers before the invention of transistors. A transistor is a much smaller device capable of storing bits. Transistors differ in types. Modern devices don't use relays; instead, they incorporate millions of transistors to store and manipulate data. A **Central Processing Unit** (**CPU**) register is an example of a device that leverages transistors to store a specified amount of bits. Usually, a general-purpose register stores up to 64 bits of data. However, you can't store all your programs and data using only registers. The organization of computer memory is much more sophisticated. Let's now move on to examining the hierarchy of computer memory from a higher-level perspective.

Understanding computer memory from a higher-level perspective

Knowing the details of computer memory and data storage is crucial in writing professional programs. When programmers refer to the term *memory*, most of the time they mean the virtual memory. Virtual memory is an abstraction supported by the **Operating System** (**OS**) that controls and provides memory space for processes. Each process has its address space represented as a collection of several segments. We discussed what memory segments there are and how a given program uses each in `Chapter 2`, *Low-Level Programming with C++*. From the programmer's perspective, accessing a memory space is mostly limited to an object declaration and use. Whether we declare an object on the stack, heap, or static memory, we access the same memory abstraction – the virtual memory. Although complicated, virtual memory makes life a lot easier. Working directly with physical memory is harder, although it is a great advancement in a programmer's skills. You should at least know what memory storage units there are and how you can leverage that knowledge to write better code.

In this section, we have discussed the physical memory hierarchy. We call it a *hierarchy* because each memory unit at a lower level provides faster access but a smaller space. Each consecutively higher level of memory provides more space in exchange for slower access.

We discuss the physical memory hierarchy because it will help us design better code. Knowing how memory works at each level improves us as programmers and allows us to organize data manipulation better. The following diagram illustrates the memory hierarchy:

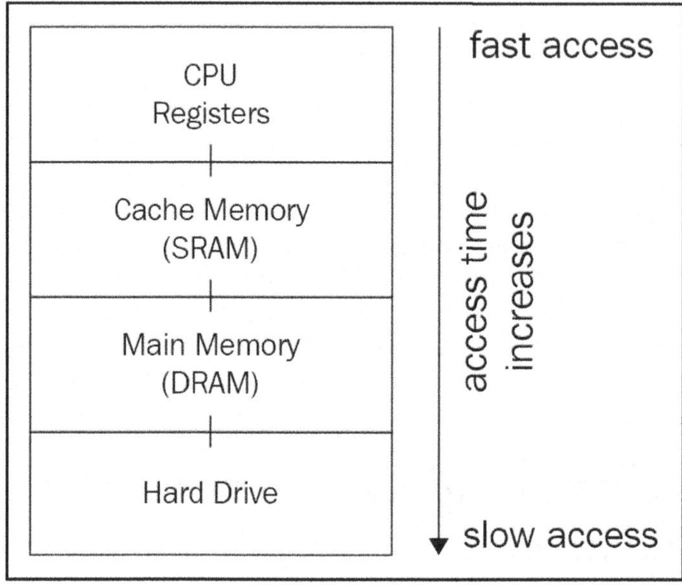

Registers are the fastest accessible memory units placed in the CPU. The number of registers is limited so we can't keep all the program data in them. On the other hand, **Dynamic RAM (DRAM)** is able to store a wide range of data for the program. It takes much longer to access data from the DRAM because of its physical structure and distance from the CPU. The CPU accesses DRAM via the data bus, which is a set of wires transferring data between the CPU and DRAM. To signal to the DRAM controller whether it will read or write data, the CPU uses the control bus. We will refer to DRAM as the *main memory*. Let's look at the memory hierarchy in detail.

Registers

Registers hold a fixed amount of data. The CPU word size is usually defined by the maximum length of a register, for example, eight bytes or four bytes. We can't directly access a register from a C++ program.

C++ supports embedding assembly code using the `asm` declaration, for example, `asm("mov edx, 4")`. It's a platform-specific and artificial augmentation to the code, so we don't suggest using it.

In older versions of the language, we could use the `register` keyword when declaring a variable:

```
register int num = 14;
```

The modifier specified the compiler to store the variable in the register. This way, it gave programmers a fake sense of code optimization.

Compilers are sophisticated tools translating higher-level C++ code into machine code. In the translation process, the code takes several transformations, including code optimizations. When programmers apply *tricks* to force the compiler to optimize a portion of the code, the compiler takes them as suggestions rather than commands.

For example, accessing a variable in a loop will be faster if that variable is placed in a register rather than in the DRAM. For example, the following loop accesses objects one million times:

```
auto number{42};
for (int ix = 0; ix < 10000000; ++ix) {
  int res{number + ix};
  // do something with res
}
```

As we know, the `number` has an automatic storage duration (it has nothing to do with the `auto` keyword) and is placed on the stack. The stack is a segment in the virtual memory, and the virtual memory is an abstraction over the physical DRAM. It's way faster to access the object in a register than in DRAM. Let's suppose reading the value of `number` from the DRAM is five times slower than from a `register`. It might seem obvious to optimize the preceding loop using the `register` keyword, as shown:

```
register auto number{42};
// the loop omitted for code brevity
```

However, compilers make better optimizations nowadays, so the need for the modifier has faded over time and it is now a deprecated language feature. A better optimization would be getting rid of the `number` object altogether.

For example, the following code represents the compile-optimized version that uses the actual value rather than accessing it via the variable that resides in the DRAM:

```
for (int ix = 0; ix < 1000000; ++ix) {
  int res{42 + ix};
  // do something with res
}
```

Although the preceding example is arguably simple, we should consider compiler optimizations that take place during compilation.

Discovering the registers improves our understanding of program execution details. The point is that everything the CPU performs happens via the registers, including the instructions that the CPU should decode and execute are accessed using a specific register, commonly referred to as the **instruction pointer**. When we run the program, the CPU accesses its instructions and decodes and executes them. Reading data from the main memory and writing data to the memory is performed by copying it from and to the registers. Usually, general-purpose registers are used to temporarily hold data while the CPU performs operations on it. The following diagram depicts an abstract view of the **CPU** and its interaction with the main memory via buses:

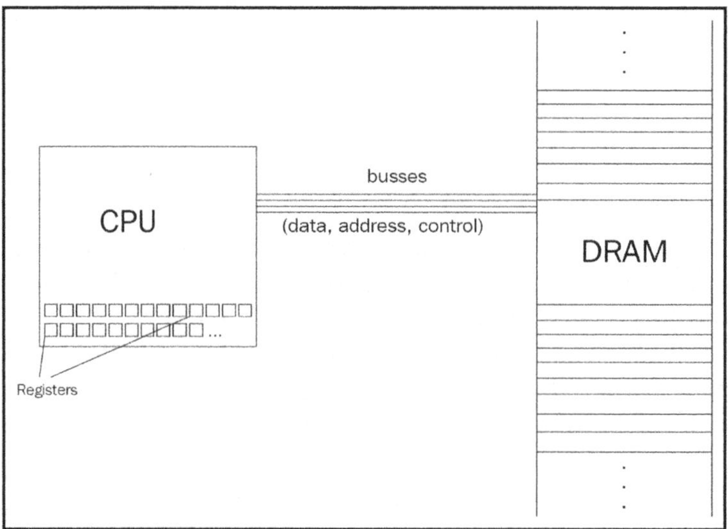

As you can see, the communication between the CPU and DRAM happens via various buses. In `Chapter 2`, *Low-Level Programming with C++*, we discussed the low-level representation of C++ programs – you should take a quick look at that to better understand the following example.

Now, let's see registers in action. The following C++ code declares two variables and stores their sum in the third variable:

```
int a{40}, b{2};
int c{a + b};
```

To execute the sum instruction, the CPU moves values of variables `a` and `b` into its registers. After calculating the sum, it then moves the result into another register. An assembler pseudo-code representation of the program looks similar to the following:

```
mov eax, a
mov ebx, b
add eax, ebx
```

It's not mandatory for the compiler to generate code that maps each variable to one register – the number of registers is limited. You just need to remember that you should keep regularly accessed variables small enough to fit into one of the registers. For larger objects, the cache memory comes to the rescue. Let's see how.

Cache memory

The idea of caching is common in programming and computer systems. Images loaded in the browser are cached to avoid further requests to the web server to download it in case the user visits the website again in the future. Caching makes programs run faster. The concept can be leveraged in many forms, including in single functions. For example, the following recursive function calculates the factorial of a number:

```
long factorial(long n) {
  if (n <= 1) { return 1; }
  return n * factorial(n - 1);
}
```

The function doesn't remember its previously calculated values, so the following calls lead to five and six recursive calls, respectively:

```
factorial(5); // calls factorial(4), which calls factorial(3), and so on
factorial(6); // calls factorial(5), which calls factorial(4), and so on
```

We can cache already calculated values at each step by storing them in a globally accessible variable, as shown:

```
std::unordered_map<long, long> cache;

long factorial(long n) {
  if (n <= 1) return 1;
```

```
    if (cache.contains(n)) return cache[n];
    cache[n] = n * factorial(n - 1);
    return cache[n];
}
```

The modifications optimize further calls to the function:

```
factorial(4);
// the next line calls factorial(4), stores the result in cache[5], which
then calls factorial(3)
// and stores the result in cache[4] and so on
factorial(5);
factorial(6); // calls the factorial(5) which returns already calculated
value in cache[5]
```

The same way the concept of caching makes the factorial function run faster, an actual memory device named the **cache** is placed inside the CPU. This device stores recently accessed data in order to make further access to that data faster. The following diagram depicts **registers** and **cache memory** inside the CPU:

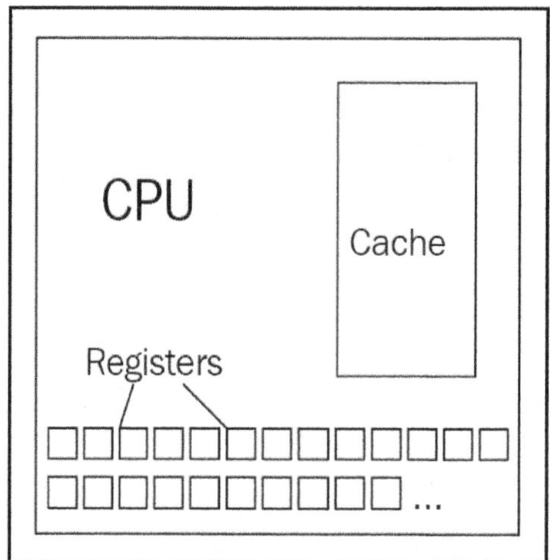

The cache size usually ranges from 2 KB to 64 KB (and, rarely, 128 KB). While it doesn't seem big enough for applications such as Photoshop, where the image data size can be way bigger than the cache size itself, it really does help in many scenarios. For example, suppose we store more than 1,000 numbers in a vector:

```
std::vector<int> vec;
vec.push_back(1);
...
vec.push_back(9999);
```

The following code prints the vector items:

```
for (auto it: vec) {
  std::cout << it;
}
// 1
// 2
// 3
// ...
// 9999
```

Suppose that to print the item, the **CPU** copies it from memory to the rax register, then calls the operator <<, which prints the value of the rax to the screen. On each iteration of the loop, the **CPU** copies the next item of the vector into the rax register and calls the function to print its value. Each copy operation requires the **CPU** to place the address of the item on the **address bus** and set the **control bus** to a read mode. The **DRAM** microcontroller accesses the data by the address received by the address bus and copies its value to the data bus, thereby sending the data to the **CPU**. The **CPU** directs the value to the rax register and then executes instructions to print its value. The following diagram shows this interaction between the **CPU** and **DRAM**:

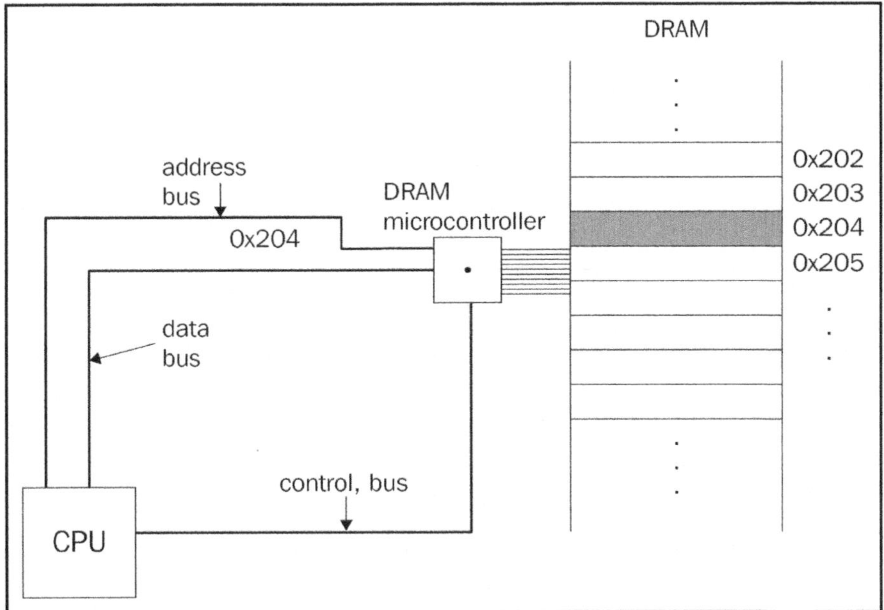

To optimize the loop, the CPU maintains an idea of data locality, that is, it copies the whole vector into the cache and accesses vector items from the cache, omitting the unnecessary requests to DRAM. In the following diagram, you can see that the data received from the DRAM via the data bus is then stored in the **cache memory**:

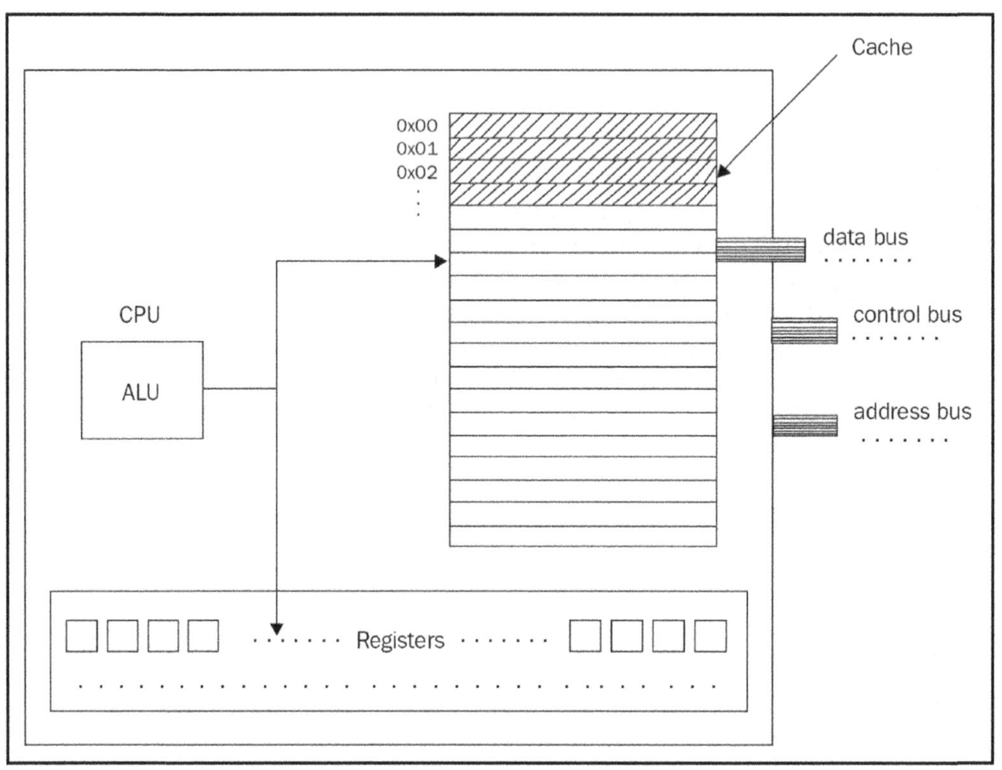

The cache residing in the CPU is known as **level 1 (L1) cache**. This is the smallest in capacity and resides inside the CPU. Many architectures have **level 2 (L2) cache**, which resides outside the CPU (though closer than the main memory) and is accessed the same way as the DRAM. The difference between the L2 Cache and DRAM is the physical structure and data access patterns. The L2 Cache represents **Static RAM (SRAM)**, which is faster than DRAM but also is much more expensive.

Some runtime environments leverage the idea of caching when implementing garbage collection. They separate the objects into categories based on their lifetime with objects that have the smallest lifetime, such as the ones allocated in the local scope of the code, being placed in the cache both to be accessed and deallocated faster.

New levels of cache memories serve as caches for the lower level. For example, the L2 Cache serves as a cache memory for the L1 Cache. When the CPU encounters a cache miss, it requests the L2 Cache, and so on.

Main memory

The physical structure of the DRAM forces it to refresh its charge to keep the data stable, while the SRAM doesn't need to be refreshed like DRAM. We call DRAM the main memory mostly because programs are loaded into it; the OS maintains virtual memory and maps it to DRAM. All the actual work happens through the main memory first.

As we already discussed, the main memory represents a sequence of addressable bytes of data. Each byte has its own unique address and is accessed using that address. We mentioned earlier how the CPU places the address of the data on the address bus, thereby letting the DRAM microcontroller fetch the requested data and send it via the data bus.

As we know, the OS introduces virtual memory as an abstraction over the physical memory. It maps the contents of the virtual memory to the physical memory, which involves the CPU's **Translation Lookaside Buffer** (**TLB**). The TLB is another form of cache memory: it stores the recent translations of **virtual memory** to **physical memory**, thereby caching it for future requests. As shown in the following diagram, the **CPU** coordinates with the **TLB** in order to properly translate virtual addresses to physical addresses:

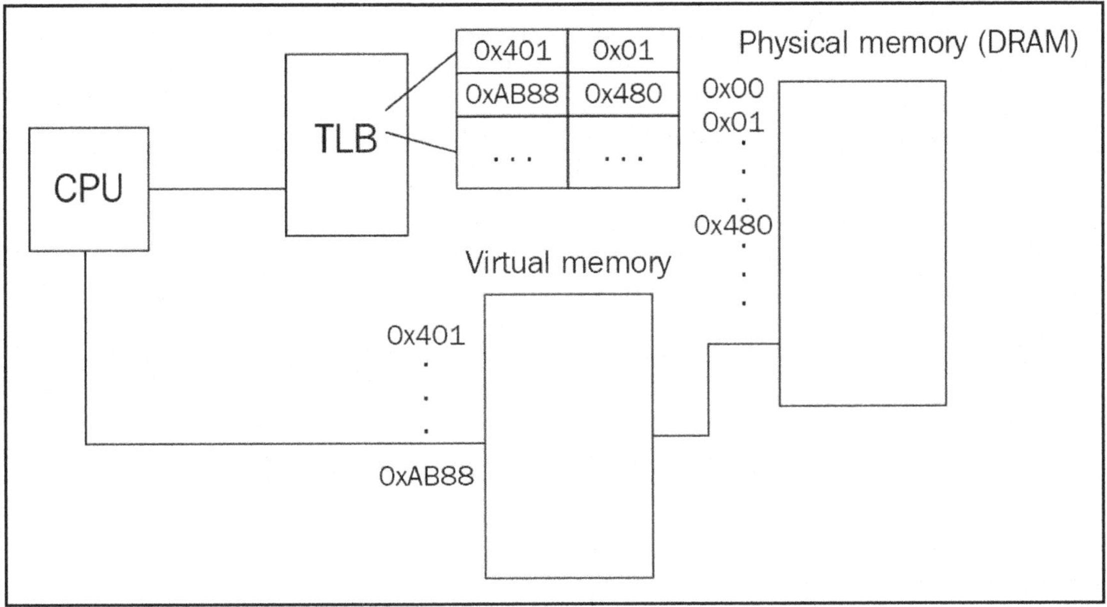

Though memory management is sophisticated, the OS provides us a simple enough abstraction to manage memory required for our programs. We have the ability to allocate it either automatically using the stack, or dynamically on the heap. The automatic memory allocation actually doesn't involve many concerns and difficulties; we just declare objects and they are placed on the stack and then automatically removed whenever the execution leaves the scope. In the case of dynamic memory (not to be confused with the hardware DRAM mentioned earlier), both the allocation and deallocation should be done manually, which creates possibilities for making errors leading to memory leaks.

Permanent storage

When we turn off the computer, the contents of the main memory are erased (because the charge is not refreshed anymore). To store the data permanently even when the power is off, computers are equipped with a **Hard Disk Drive** (**HDD**) or a **Solid-State Drive** (**SSD**). From the perspective of programmers, permanent storage is used to store programs with their necessary data. We already know that in order to run a program, it should be loaded into the main memory, that is, copied from the HDD to the DRAM. The OS handles it using the loader and creates a program image in memory, commonly referred to as a process. When the program is done or the user closes it, the OS marks the address range of the process as free to use.

Let's suppose we use a text editor to write notes while learning C++. The text typed into the editor resides in the main memory unless we save it on the HDD. This is important to note because most programs keep track of recent user activity and also allow the user to modify program settings. To keep these settings the way the user modified them even after the program is relaunched, the program stores them as a separate *settings* file on the HDD. The next time the program runs, it first reads the corresponding settings file or files from the HDD and updates itself to apply the recent modifications of settings.

Usually, permanent storage has a much bigger capacity compared to the main memory, which makes it possible to use the HDD as a backup for virtual memory. The OS can maintain the virtual memory and fake its size, making it bigger than the physical DRAM. For example, the DRAM's two GB maximum capacity could be quickly exhausted by launching several heavyweight applications. However, the OS still can maintain a larger virtual memory by backing up its additional space with the HDD. When the user switches between applications, the OS copies the exceeding bytes of virtual memory to the HDD and maps the currently running application to the physical memory.

This makes programs and the OS run slower but allows us to keep them open without caring about the limited size of the main memory. Let's now dive a little deeper into memory management in C++.

The basics of memory management

Most of the time, issues arising during memory management happen when programmers forget about deallocating memory space. This results in memory leaks. A memory leak is a widespread issue in almost every program. When the program requests a new memory space for its data, the OS marks the provided space as **busy**. That is, no other instruction of the program or any other program can request that busy memory space. When the portion of the program is done with the memory space, ideally, it must notify the OS to remove the busy label to make the space available for others. Some languages provide automatic control over dynamically allocated memory, leaving the programmer to worry about the logic of the application rather than constantly being concerned with deallocating memory resources. However, C++ assumes that the programmer is responsible and smart (which is not always the case). Dynamically allocated memory management is the programmer's responsibility. That's why the language provides both "new" and "delete" operators to deal with memory space, where the new operator allocates memory space and the delete operator deallocates it. In other words, the ideal code dealing with dynamically allocated memory looks like the following:

```
T* p = new T(); // allocate memory space
p->do_something(); // use the space to do something useful
delete p; // deallocate memory space
```

Forgetting to call the delete operator makes the allocated memory space *busy forever*. By *forever*, we mean as long as the program is running. Now imagine a web browser that is always open on the user computer. Memory leaks here and there might lead to memory starvation over time, and sooner or later the user has to restart the program or, even worse, the OS.

This issue is applicable to any resource that we work with, whether it's a file or a socket we forget to close (more about sockets in `Chapter 12`, *Networking and Security*). To solve this issue, C++ programmers use the **Resource Acquisition Is Initialization** (**RAII**) idiom, stating that a resource should be acquired on its initialization, which allows it to be properly released later. Let's see it in action.

An example of memory management

Consider the following function that dynamically allocates an array of 420 `shorts`, reads their values from the user input, prints them in ascending order, and deallocates the array:

```
void print_sorted() {
  short* arr{new short[420]};
  for (int ix = 0; ix < 420; ++ix) {
```

```
    std::cin >> arr[ix];
  }
  std::sort(arr, arr + 420);
  for (int ix = 0; ix < 420; ++ix) {
    std::cout << arr[ix];
  }
  delete arr; // very bad!
}
```

We already made a mistake in the preceding code by using the wrong `delete` operator to deallocate the memory. To deallocate an array, we must use the `delete[]` operator, otherwise, the code leads to memory leaks. Here's how we illustrate the allocation of the array:

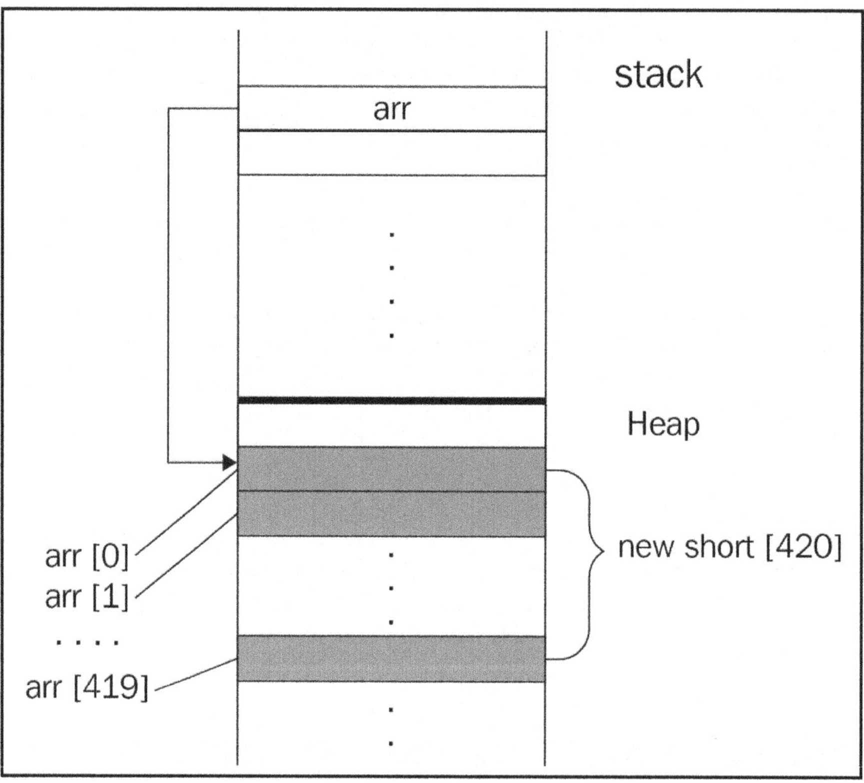

Let's say we release the space using `delete` instead of `delete[]`. It will treat the `arr` as a short pointer, and therefore will remove the first two bytes starting at the address contained in the `arr` pointer, as shown in the following diagram:

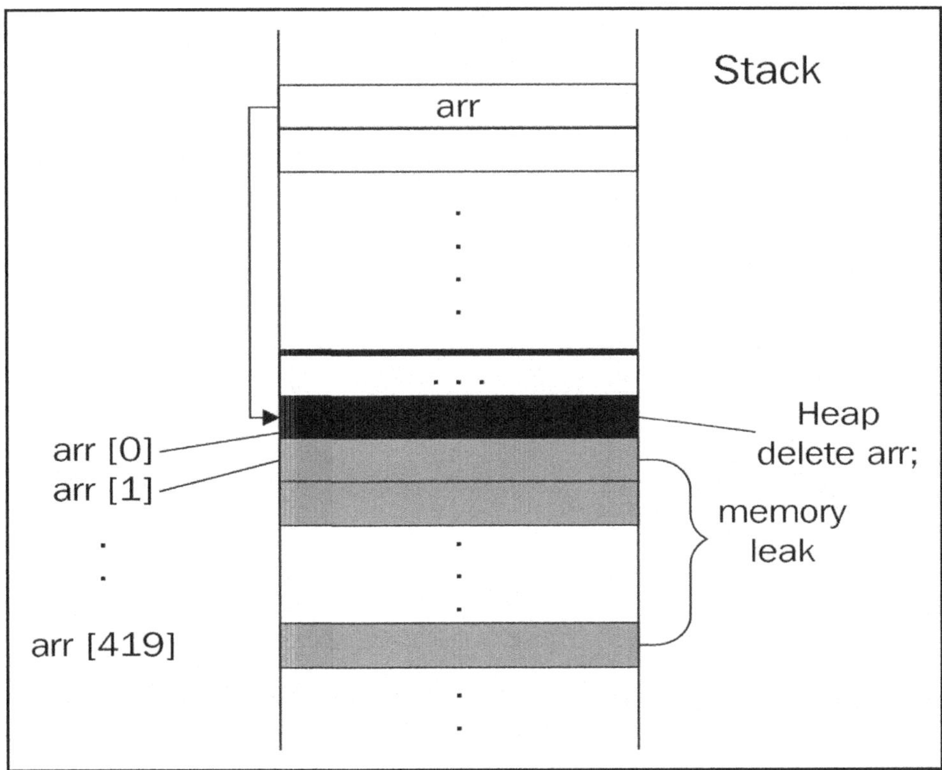

So now we removed the first item out of 420 items and left the 419 `shorts` untouched on the heap. Whenever we need new space on the heap, that small section containing the 419 **untouchables** won't be ever reused again. Though the family of new and delete operators is implementation-defined, we shouldn't really hope for the best implementation that avoids memory leaks.

Let's modify the preceding code to properly release the allocated memory for the array and let's make sure we eliminate the possibility of inputting negative numbers:

```
void print_sorted() {
  short* arr{new short[420]};
  for (int ix = 0; ix < 420; ++ix) {
    std::cin >> arr[ix];
    if (arr[ix] < 0) return;
  }
  std::sort(arr, arr + 420);
  // print the sorted array, code omitted for brevity
  delete[] arr;
}
```

The preceding modifications are another example of a possible memory leak, though we clearly wrote ugly code for the sake of simplicity. The point is, whenever the user inputs a negative number, the function returns. This leaves us with 420 orphan `shorts` that should be released somehow. However, the only access to the allocated memory was the `arr` pointer, which is declared on the stack, therefore it will be automatically deleted (the pointer variable, not the memory space pointed to it) when the function returns. To eliminate the possibility of a memory leak, we should simply call the `delete[]` operator before the function exits:

```
void print_sorted() {
  short* arr{new short[420]};
  for(int ix = 0; ix < 420; ++ix) {
    std::cin >> arr[ix];
    if (arr[ix] < 0) {
      delete[] arr;
      return;
    }
  }
  // sort and print the sorted array, code omitted for brevity
  delete[] arr;
}
```

The code gets somewhat ugly but it fixes the memory leak. What if we modify the function further and use a third-party library function to sort the array:

```
import <strange_sort.h>;

void print_sorted() {
  short* arr{new short[420]};
  for (...) { /* code omitted for brevity */ }
  strange_sort::sort(arr, arr + 420);
  // print the sorted array, code omitted for brevity
  delete[] arr;
}
```

Turns out that the `strange_sort::sort` throws an exception when the value of the array item exceeds 420 (that's why it's a strange sort, after all). If the exception is left uncaught, it will bubble up to the caller function unless it is caught somewhere or the program crashes. The uncaught exception leads to stack unwinding, which leads to automatic destruction of the `arr` variable (the pointer), so we face another possibility of a memory leak. To fix it, we could wrap the `strange_sort::sort` in a try-catch block:

```
try {
  strange_sort::sort(arr, arr + 420);
} catch (ex) { delete[] arr; }
```

C++ programmers constantly seek ways to deal with memory leaks, such as the RAII idiom and smart pointers, which we will discuss in the next sections.

Using smart pointers

There are many languages supporting automated garbage collection. For example, memory acquired for an object is tracked by the runtime environment. It will deallocate the memory space after the object with a reference to it goes out of the scope. Consider the following, for example:

```
// a code sample of the language (not-C++) supporting automated garbage
collection
void foo(int age) {
  Person p = new Person("John", 35);
  if (age <= 0) { return; }
  if (age > 18) {
   p.setAge(18);
  }
  // do something useful with the "p"
}
// no need to deallocate memory manually
```

In the preceding code block, the `p` reference (usually, references in garbage-collected languages are similar to pointers in C++) refers to the memory location returned by the `new` operator. The automatic garbage collector manages the lifetime of the object created by the `new` operator. It also tracks references to that object. Whenever the object has no references on it, the garbage collector deallocates its space. Something similar to that might be achieved by using the RAII idiom in C++. Let's see it in action.

Leveraging the RAII idiom

As already mentioned, the RAII idiom suggests acquiring the resource on its initialization. Look at the following class:

```
template <typename T>
class ArrayManager {
public:
  ArrayManager(T* arr) : arr_{arr} {}
  ~ArrayManager() { delete[] arr_; }

  T& operator[](int ix) { return arr_[ix]; }
```

```
  T* raw() { return arr_; }
};
```

The `print_sorted` function can now use the `ArrayManager` to properly release the allocated array:

```
void print_sorted() {
  ArrayManager<short> arr{new short[420]};
  for (int ix = 0; ix < 420; ++ix) {
    std::cin >> arr[ix];
  }
  strange_sort::sort(arr.raw(), arr.raw() + 420);
  for (int ix = 0; ix < 420; ++ix) {
    std::cout << arr[ix];
  }
}
```

We suggest using standard containers such as `std::vector` rather than `ArrayManager`, though it's a good example of the RAII application: acquiring the resource on initialization. We created an instance of `ArrayManager` and initialized it with the memory resource. From that point, we can forget about its release because the actual release happens in the destructor of `ArrayManager`. And as we declared the `ArrayManager` instance on the stack, it will be automatically destroyed when the function returns or an uncaught exception occurs, and the destructor will be called.

Using a standard container is preferred in this scenario, so let's implement the RAII idiom for single pointers. The following code dynamically allocates memory for a `Product` instance:

```
Product* apple{new Product};
apple->set_name("Red apple");
apple->set_price(0.42);
apple->set_available(true);
// use the apple
// don't forget to release the resource
delete apple;
```

If we apply the RAII idiom to the preceding code, it will release the resource at the proper point of code execution:

```
ResourceManager<Product> res{new Product};
res->set_name("Red apple");
res->set_price(0.42);
res->set_available(true);
// use the res the way we use a Product
// no need to delete the res, it will automatically delete when gets out of
the scope
```

The `ResourceManager` class should also overload operators `*` and `->` because it has to behave like a pointer in order to properly acquire and manage a pointer:

```
template <typename T>
class ResourceManager {
public:
  ResourceManager(T* ptr) : ptr_{ptr} {}
  ~ResourceManager() { delete ptr_; }

  T& operator*() { return *ptr_; }
  T* operator->() { return ptr_; }
};
```

The `ResourceManager` class cares about the idea of the smart pointer in C++. C++11 introduced several types of smart pointers. We name them *smart* because they wrap around the resource and manage its automatic deallocation. It happens solely because of the fact that the destructor of an object will be called when the object is set to destroy. That said, we operate with the dynamically allocated space through the object with an automatic storage duration. When the handler object goes out of scope, its destructor executes the necessary actions to deallocate the underlying resource.

However, smart pointers might bring additional issues. The simple smart pointer discussed in the preceding paragraph has several issues that would arise eventually. For example, we didn't take care of the `ResourceManager` copying:

```
void print_name(ResourceManager<Product> apple) {
  std::cout << apple->name();
}

ResourceManager<Product> res{new Product};
res->set_name("Red apple");
print_name(res);
res->set_price(0.42);
// ...
```

The preceding code leads to undefined behavior. The following diagram shows the disguised problem:

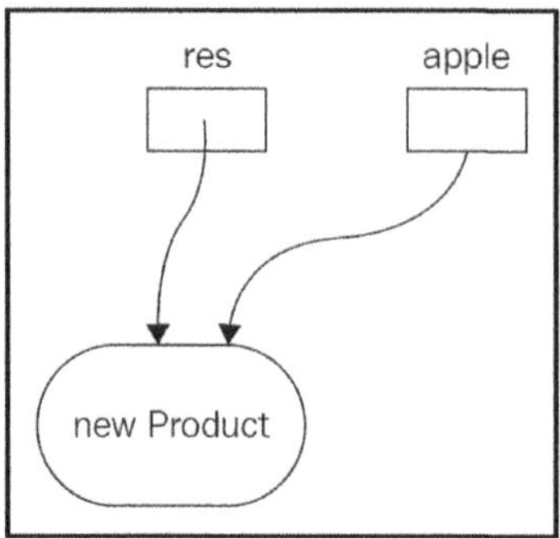

Both **res** and **apple** acquire the same resource. Whenever one of them goes out of scope (**apple**), the underlying resource is released, which leaves the other `ResourceManager` instance with a dangling pointer. When the other `ResourceManager` instance goes out of scope, it will try to delete the pointer twice. Usually, programmers are aware of the *kind* of smart pointer they need in a specific case. That's why C++ provides several types of smart pointers that, which we will discuss further. To use them in your programs, you should import the `<memory>` header.

std::unique_ptr

Similar to the `ResourceManager` instance we implemented earlier, `std::unique_ptr` represents a basic smart pointer. For example, to manage the `Product` object using this smart pointer, we do the following:

```
std::unique_ptr<Product> res{new Product};
res->set_name("Red apple");
// res will delete its acquired resource when goes out of scope
```

Note how we access the `Product` member function `set_name`. We treat the `res` object as something that has the type `Pointer*`.

`unique_ptr` is named unique because it provides a semantics of strict ownership— it is obligated to destroy the acquired object. More interestingly, `unique_ptr` can't be copied. It doesn't have a copy constructor or assignment operator. That's why its **ownership** is *strict*. Of course, that doesn't mean that we can't move a `unique_ptr` class. In that case, we completely pass the ownership to the other instance of the unique pointer.

One of the main requirements for smart pointers is keeping them lightweight. We can surely agree on that. While `unique_ptr` is a full class with several member functions, it doesn't *pollute* with additional data members. It's just a wrapper around the raw pointer to the allocated object. We can access that raw pointer by calling the `release()` member function of `unique_ptr`, as shown:

```
Product* p = res.release();
// now we should delete p manually to deallocate memory
```

Note that the `release()` function doesn't call the delete operator. It only gives back ownership. After calling the `release()` function, the `unique_ptr` no longer owns the resource. To reuse a `unique_ptr` that already owns a resource, you should use the `reset()` member function. It calls the delete operator for the underlying pointer and *resets* the unique pointer for further use. On the other hand, if you want to get the underlying object without releasing the ownership, you should call the `get()` member function:

```
std::unique_ptr<Product> up{new Product()};
Product* p = res.get();
// now p also points to the object managed by up
```

We can't use a `unique_ptr` class in the following scenario because it can't be copied:

```
// Don't do this
void print_name(std::unique_ptr<Product> apple) {
  std::cout << apple->name();
}
std::unique_ptr<Product> res{new Product};
res->set_name("Red apple");
print_name(res); // bad code
res->set_price(0.42);
// ...
```

However, it's not what we look for in the preceding code. You can consider the preceding code a bad design, because it confuses the ownership details. Let's move on to the next smart pointer in C++ that, which solves the issue of passing `unique_ptr` to functions.

std::shared_ptr and std::weak_ptr

We need a smart pointer providing *shared ownership*. What we need was introduced back in C++11 as `std::shared_ptr`. It's harder to implement a smart pointer with shared ownership, because you should take care of the correct deallocation of the resource. For example, when the `print_name()` function in the preceding code block finishes its work, its arguments and local objects will be destroyed. Destroying a smart pointer leads to the proper deallocation of the resource it owns. How would the smart pointer know if that resource is still owned by another smart pointer? One of the popular solutions is keeping the count of references to the resource. The `shared_ptr` class does the same: it keeps the number of pointers pointing to the underlying object and deletes it when the use count becomes 0. Therefore, several shared pointers can own the same object.

Now, the example we just discussed should be rewritten like this:

```
void print_name(std::shared_ptr<Product> apple) {
  std::cout << apple->name();
}
std::shared_ptr<Product> res{new Product};
res->set_name("Red apple");
print_name(res);
res->set_price(0.42);
// ...
```

After calling the `print_name()` function, the use count of the shared pointer increases by 1. It will decrease by 1 when the function finishes its work but the managed object won't be deallocated. It's because the `res` object is not yet out of the scope. Let's slightly modify the example to print the count of references to the shared object:

```
void print_name(std::shared_ptr<Product> apple) {
  std::cout << apple.use_count() << " eyes on the " << apple->name();
}

std::shared_ptr<Product> res{new Product};
res->set_name("Red apple");
std::cout << res.use_count() << std::endl;
print_name(res);
std::cout << res.use_count() << std::endl;
res->set_price(0.42);
// ...
```

The preceding code will print the following to the screen:

```
1
2 eyes on the Red apple
1
```

When the last shared_ptr goes out of scope, it also destroys the underlying object. However, you should be careful when sharing an object between shared pointers. The following code shows an obvious issue with shared ownership:

```
std::shared_ptr<Product> ptr1{new Product()};
Product* temp = ptr1.get();
if (true) {
  std::shared_ptr<Product> ptr2{temp};
  ptr2->set_name("Apple of truth");
}
ptr1->set_name("Peach"); // danger!
```

Both ptr1 and ptr2 point to the same object, but they are not aware of each other. So when we modify the Product object via ptr2, it will affect ptr1. When ptr2 goes out of scope (after the if statement), it will destroy the underlying object, which is still owned by ptr1. It happens because we make ptr2 own the object by passing the raw temp pointer to it. ptr1 can't track that.

The ownership can be shared only using the copy constructor or the assignment operator of std::shared_ptr. This way, we avoid deleting the object if it's in use by another shared_ptr instance. Shared pointers implement shared ownership using control blocks. Each shared pointer holds two pointers, one to the object it manages, and a pointer to the control block. The control block represents a dynamically allocated space containing the use count of the resource. It also contains several other things crucial for shared_ptr, for example, the allocator and the deleter of the resource. We will introduce allocators in the next section. The deleter usually is the regular delete operator.

The control block also contains the number of weak references. It's done because the owned resource might be pointed to a weak pointer, too. std::weak_ptr is the smaller brother of std::shared_ptr. It refers to an object managed by a shared_ptr instance, but doesn't own it. weak_ptr is a way to access and use the resource owned by shared_ptr without owning it. However, there is a way to convert a weak_ptr instance to shared_ptr using the lock() member function.

Both unique_ptr and shared_ptr can be used for managing dynamically allocated arrays. The template parameter must be specified correctly:

```
std::shared_ptr<int[]> sh_arr{new int[42]};
sh_arr[11] = 44;
```

To access an element of the underlying array, we use the `[]` operator of the shared pointer. Also, note that using a smart pointer won't have drawbacks when used in dynamic polymorphism. For example, let's suppose we have the following class hierarchy:

```
struct Base
{
  virtual void test() { std::cout << "Base::test()" << std::endl; }
};

struct Derived : Base
{
  void test() override { std::cout << "Derived::test()" << std::endl; }
};
```

The following code works as expected and outputs `Derived::test()` to the screen:

```
std::unique_ptr<Base> ptr = std::make_unique_default_init<Derived>();
ptr->test();
```

Although the use of smart pointers might seem to spoil the beauty of pointers, it is suggested to intensively use smart pointers to avoid memory leaks. However, it's worth noting that replacing all pointers with smart pointers, whether it's a `unique_ptr` or a `shared_ptr` pointer, will not solve all the memory leak problems. They have their disadvantages, too. Consider a balanced approach, or better, thoroughly understand both the problem and the smart pointers themselves in detail before applying them to the problem.

Managing memory in C++ programs comes at a price. The most important thing that we've discussed is the proper deallocation of memory space. The language doesn't support automatic memory deallocation, but it's worth mentioning garbage collectors. However, to have a complete garbage collector, we need language-level support. C++ doesn't provide any of that. Let's try to imitate a garbage collector in C++.

Garbage collection

A garbage collector is a separate module usually incorporated in the runtime environments of interpretable languages. For example, C# and Java both have garbage collectors, which makes the life of programmers a lot easier. The garbage collector tracks all the object allocations in the code and deallocates once they are not in use anymore. It's called a **garbage collector** because it deletes the memory resource after it's been used: it collects the garbage left by programmers.

It's said that C++ programmers don't leave garbage after them, that's why the language doesn't have support for a garbage collector. Though programmers tend to defend the language stating that it doesn't have a garbage collector because it's a fast language, the truth is that it can survive without one.

Languages like C# compile the program into intermediate byte-code representation, which is then interpreted and executed by the runtime environment. The garbage collector is a part of the environment and is actively tracking all object allocations. It is a sophisticated beast that tries its best to manage the memory in a reasonable time. The following diagram depicts a typical runtime environment that allocates memory supervised by the garbage collector:

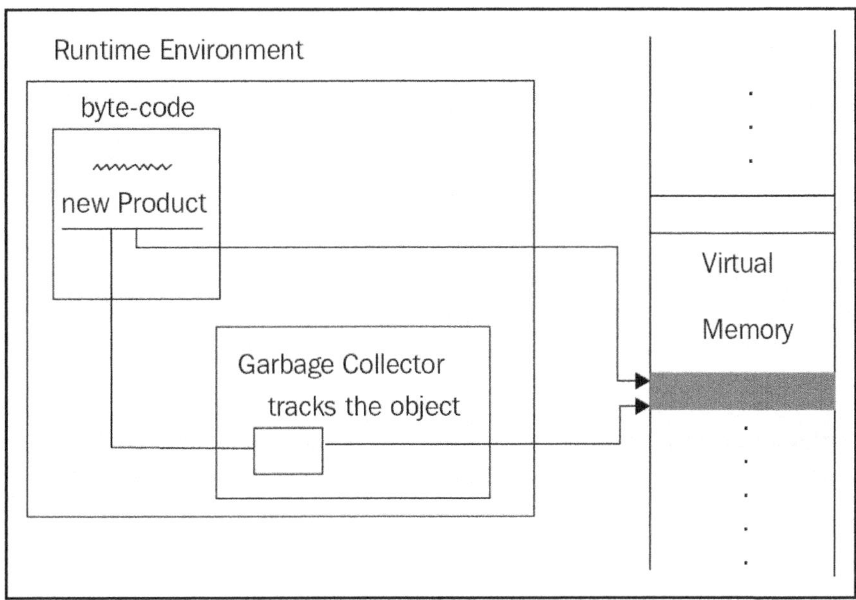

We manually call the `delete` operator to release the memory space in C++ even when using smart pointers. Smart pointers just acquire the object and delete the object when it goes out of scope. The key point is that even though smart pointers introduce some semi-automatic behavior, they still act as if the programmer didn't forget to release the resource at a specified point of the code. The garbage collector does that automatically and usually uses separate execution threads. It tries its best not to slow down the actual program execution speed.

Some of the garbage collection implementation techniques include classifying objects by their lifetime duration. Classification makes the garbage collector visit the objects and release the memory space if objects aren't in use anymore. To make this process faster, objects with short lifetime duration should be visited more often than objects with longer duration. Take, for example, the following code:

```
struct Garbage {
  char ch;
  int i;
};

void foo() {
  Garbage* g1 = new Garbage();
  if (true) {
    Garbage* g2 = new Garbage();
  }
}

int main() {
  static Garbage* g3 = new Garbage();
}
```

If C++ had a garbage collector, then the objects `g1`, `g2`, and `g3` would be deleted in different time slots of the program execution. If the garbage collector classifies them by their lifetime duration, then `g2` would have the shortest lifetime and should be visited first in order to release it.

To really implement a garbage collector in C++, we should make it a part of the program. The garbage collector should first take care of allocating memory to track and remove it:

```
class GarbageCollector {
public:
 template <typename T>
 static T* allocate() {
   T* ptr{new T()};
   objects_[ptr] = true;
   return ptr;
 }

 static void deallocate(T* p) {
   if (objects_[p]) {
     objects_[p] = false;
     delete p;
   }
 }

private:
```

```
    std::unordered_map<T*, bool> objects_;
};
```

The preceding class keeps track of objects allocated through the static `allocate()` function. If the object is in use, it deletes it through the `deallocate()` function. Here's how `GarbageCollector` can be used:

```
int* ptr = GarbageCollector::allocate<int>();
*ptr = 42;
GarbageCollector::deallocate(ptr);
```

Actually, this class makes memory management a little bit harder than smart pointers. Basically, there is no need to implement a garbage collector in C++ because smart pointers provide handling almost any scenario regarding *automatic* memory deallocation.

However, let's see one of the tricks that will allow the garbage collector to properly deallocate the space pointed to by some pointer. In our simplest possible preceding implementation, we kept track of all the pointers that we provided to users. Each pointer points to some space on the heap that should be freed at some point in the program execution. In `GarbageCollector`, we would use the standard `delete` operator. The question is, how does it know how many bytes should be freed? Take a look at the following example:

```
Student* ptr = new Student;
int* ip = new int{42};
// do something with ptr and ip
delete ptr;
delete ip;
```

Let's suppose that a `Student` instance takes 40 bytes of memory and an integer takes four bytes. We should somehow pass that information to the delete operator. In the preceding code, we delete both `ptr` and `ip`, each of which points to memory space of different sizes. So how does it know that 40 bytes should be marked as free in the case of `ptr` and four bytes should be marked as free in the case of `ip`? There is more than one solution to this problem, so let's look at one of them.

Whenever we allocate memory, the new operator puts the size of the allocated space just before the actual memory space, as shown in the following diagram:

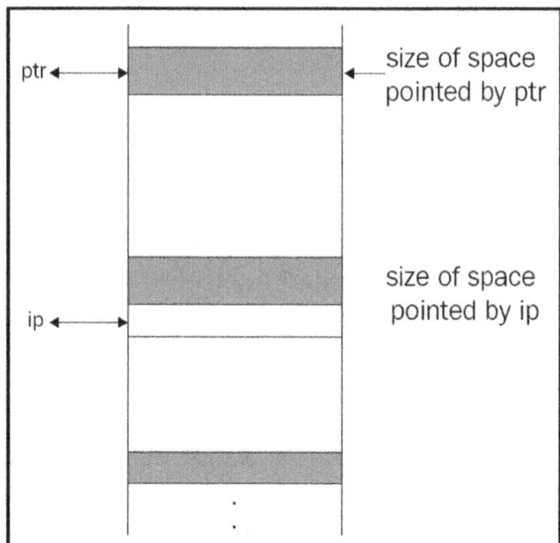

This information is then used by the `delete` operator, which reads the size of the memory space by reading the corresponding bytes placed before the memory space. One of the top concerns of C++ is managing memory for collections of data. STL containers, such as `std::vector` and `std::list`, described in `Chapter 6`, *Digging into Data Structures and Algorithms in STL*, have different models for working with memory. By default, a container has a specified memory allocator that handles the memory allocation and deallocation for container elements. Let's tackle an allocator in more detail.

Using allocators

The idea behind an allocator is to provide control to container memory management. In simpler words, an allocator is an advanced garbage collector for C++ containers. Although we discuss allocators in the scope of container memory management, you can surely expand the idea to a generic garbage collector. At the beginning of this section, we implemented a badly designed garbage collector. When examining allocators, you will find a lot of similarities between the poorly designed `GarbageCollector` class and the default allocator in C++. Defined in the `<memory>`, the default allocator has two basic functions – `allocate()` and `deallocate()`. The `allocate()` function is defined as follows:

```
[[nodiscard]] constexpr T* allocate(std::size_t num);
```

The `allocate()` function acquires space for `num` objects of type `T`. Pay attention to the `[[nodiscard]]` attribute – it means that the return value should not be discarded by the caller. The compiler will print a warning message otherwise.

Let's use the allocator to acquire space for five integers:

```
import <memory>;

int main()
{
  std::allocator<int> IntAlloc;
  int* ptr = IntAlloc.allocate(5);
  // construct an integer at the second position
  std::allocator_traits<IntAlloc>::construct(IntAlloc, ptr + 1, 42);
  IntAlloc.deallocate(ptr, 5); // deallocate all
}
```

Note how we used `std::allocator_traits` to construct objects in the allocated space. The following illustration shows

The `deallocate()` function is defined as follows:

```
constexpr void deallocate(T* p, std::size_t n)
```

In the previous code snippet, we used the `deallocate()` function by passing the pointer returned by the `allocate()` function.

You might not use allocators in your project directly, however, whenever you need a custom behavior for memory management, using existing or introducing new allocators can be helpful. STL containers use allocators mostly because they are different in structure and behavior, which leads to the need to have specialized behavior for memory allocation and deallocation. We will discuss STL containers in more detail in the next chapter.

Summary

Garbage collectors in languages like C# are provided by the environment. They work in parallel with the user program and try to clean up after the program whenever it seems efficient. We cannot do the same in C++; all we can achieve is the implementation of a garbage collector directly in the program, providing a semi-automatic way of freeing the used memory resource. This mechanism is properly covered by the smart pointers introduced in the language since C++11.

Memory management is one of the key components of every computer program. A program should be able to request memory dynamically during its execution. Good programmers understand the inner details of memory management. That helps them to design and implement more performant applications. While manual memory management is considered an advantage, it tends to become painful in larger applications. We have learned in this chapter how we can avoid errors and handle memory deallocation using smart pointers. Having this basic understanding, you should grow your confidence in designing programs that avoid memory leaks.

In the next chapter, we will learn about STL, focusing on data structures and algorithms, and will dive into their STL implementation. Besides comparing data structures and algorithms, we will introduce one of the notable new features in C++20: concepts.

Questions

1. Explain computer memory.
2. What is virtual memory?
3. Which are the operators used for memory allocation and deallocation?
4. What is the difference between `delete` and `delete[]`?
5. What is a garbage collector and why doesn't C++ support one?

Further reading

For more information, refer to the following links:

- What every programmer should know about memory, by Ulrich Drepper, at `https://people.freebsd.org/~lstewart/articles/cpumemory.pdf`
- Code: The hidden language of computer hardware and software, by Charles Petzold, at `https://www.amazon.com/Code-Language-Computer-Hardware-Software/dp/0735611319/`

2

Section 2: Designing Robust and Efficient Applications

This section will concentrate on the efficiency of data processing using data structures, algorithms, and concurrency tools. We will also introduce essential design patterns and best practices.

This section comprises the following chapters:

- `Chapter 6`, *Digging into Data Structures and Algorithms in STL*
- `Chapter 7`, *Functional Programming*
- `Chapter 8`, *Concurrency and Multithreading*
- `Chapter 9`, *Designing Concurrent Data Structures*
- `Chapter 10`, *Designing World-Ready Applications*
- `Chapter 11`, *Designing a Strategy Game Using Design Patterns*
- `Chapter 12`, *Networking and Security*
- `Chapter 13`, *Debugging and Testing*
- `Chapter 14`, *Graphical User Interface with Qt*

6
Digging into Data Structures and Algorithms in STL

Mastering data structures is essential for programmers. The way you store your data most of the time defines the overall efficiency of the application. Consider an email client, for example. You can design an email client that shows the 10 latest emails and it could have the best UI out there; displaying 10 recent emails will work smoothly on almost any device. The user of your email application will receive hundreds of thousands of emails, say, in two years of using your application. When the user needs to search for an email, that's where your data structure knowledge will play a significant role. The way you store the hundreds of thousands of emails and the methods (algorithms) you use to sort and search them will be what differentiates your program from all the others out there.

Programmers strive to find the best solutions to daily problems while working on projects. Using proven data structures and algorithms can drastically improve the work of the programmer. One of the most important features of a good program is its speed, which we gain by devising new algorithms or using existing ones.

Finally, C++20 introduces **concepts** for defining **metatypes**—types describing other types. This powerful feature of the language makes the data architecting complete.

There are plenty of data structures and algorithms covered in the C++ **Standard Template Library** (**STL**). We will explore the ways to organize data efficiently using data structures by leveraging STL containers. And then we will dive into algorithm implementations provided by the STL. It's crucial to understand and use concepts in STL containers, because C++20 introduces big improvements in iterators by introducing iterator concepts.

The following topics will be covered in this chapter:

- Data structures
- STL containers
- Concepts and iterators
- Mastering algorithms
- Exploring trees and graphs

Technical requirements

The g++ compiler with the option `-std=c++2a` is used to compile the examples throughout the chapter. You can find the source files used in this chapter in the GitHub repository for this book at `https://github.com/PacktPublishing/Expert-CPP` .

Data structures

As a programmer, you are probably familiar with using an array for storing and ordering a collection of data. Programmers intensively use data structures other than arrays in their projects. Knowing and applying proper data structures may play a significant role in program performance. To choose the right data structure, you need to get to know them better. An obvious question might arise of whether we need to study the zoo of data structures— vectors, linked lists, hash tables, graphs, trees, and so on. To answer this question, let's have an imaginary scenario where the necessity for a better data structure will become apparent naturally.

In the introductory content, we mentioned designing an email client. Let's get a general understanding of the basic tasks during its design and implementation.

An email client is an application that lists emails received from various senders. We can install it on desktop computers or smartphones, or use a browser version. The main tasks of an email client application involve sending and receiving emails. Now let's suppose that we are designing a simple-enough email client. As usually happens in programming books, let's suppose that we use some library that encapsulates the job of sending and receiving emails. We'd rather concentrate on designing mechanisms specifically for storing and retrieving emails. An email client user should be able to view a list of emails that reside in the **Inbox** section of the app. We should also take into account the operations that the user might want to perform on emails. They can delete them one by one, or many at once. They can choose any email selected at random and reply to its sender or forward the email to someone else.

We discuss the software design process and best practices in `Chapter 10`, *Designing Real-World Applications*. For now, let's sketch a simple struct that describes an email object, as follows:

```
struct Email
{
  std::string subject;
  std::string body;
  std::string from;
  std::chrono::time_point datetime;
};
```

The first thing that should bother us is storing a collection of emails in an easily accessible structure. An array might sound fine. Let's suppose we store all the incoming emails in an array, as shown in the following code block:

```
// let's suppose a million emails is the max for anyone
const int MAX_EMAILS = 1'000'000;
Email inbox[MAX_EMAILS];
```

We can store 10 emails in any form – it won't affect the application's performance. However, it's obvious that, over time, the number of emails will grow. For each newly received email, we push an `Email` object with the corresponding fields into the `inbox` array. The last element of the array represents the most recently received email. So, to show the list of ten recent emails, we need to read and return the last ten elements of the array.

Issues arise when we try to manipulate the thousands of emails stored in the `inbox` array. What if we want to search for the word `friend` in all the emails? We have to scan all the emails in the array and collect the ones containing the word `friend` in a separate array. Look at the following pseudocode:

```
std::vector<Email> search(const std::string& word) {
  std::vector<Email> search_results;
  for (all-million-emails) {
    if (inbox[i].subject.contains(word)) {
      search_results.push_back(inbox[i]);
    }
  }
  return search_results;
}
```

Using an array to store all the data is more than enough for small collections. The situation changes drastically in real-world applications dealing with bigger sets of data. The point of using a specific data structure is to make the application run more smoothly. The preceding example shows a simple problem: searching through a list of emails to match a particular value. Finding that value in one email takes a reasonable amount of time.

If we suppose that the subject field of an email might consist of up to ten words, then searching for a particular word in an email subject requires comparing the word against all the words in the subject. In the *worst case*, there is no match. We emphasize the worst case because it's the only case when the lookup will require checking each word in the subject. Doing the same for thousands or hundreds of thousands of emails will make the user wait unreasonably long.

Choosing the right data structure for the specific problem is crucial in terms of application efficiency. For example, let's suppose we use a hash table to map words to email objects. Each word will be mapped to a list of email objects that contain that word. This approach will increase the efficiency of the searching operation, as shown in the following diagram:

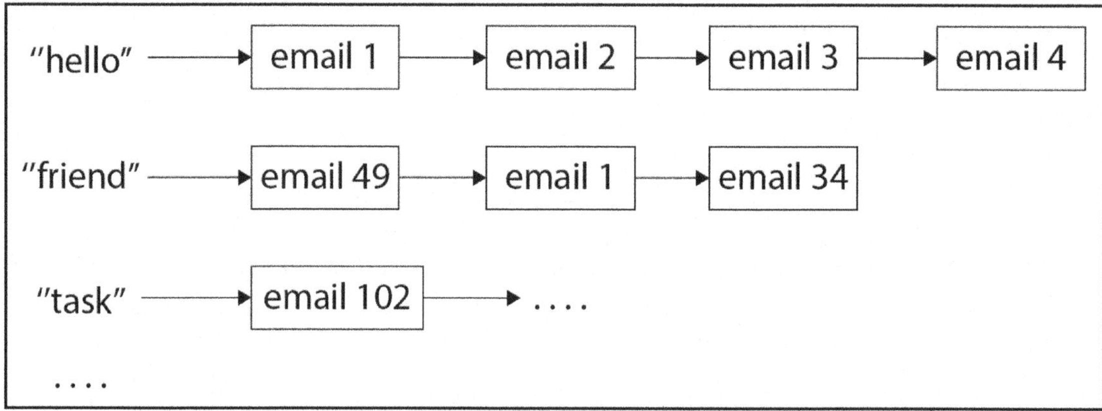

The `search()` function will just return the list referred to by the hash table key:

```
std::vector<Email> search(const std::string& word) {
  return table[word];
}
```

This approach will just require processing each received email to split it into words and update the hash table.

For the sake of simplicity, we use `Email` objects as values rather than references. Note that it would be better to store pointers to `Email` in the vector.

Let's now take a look at different data structures and their applications.

Sequential data structures

One of the most common data structures that developers use is the dynamically growing one-dimensional array, usually referred to as a vector. The STL provides a container with the same name: `std::vector`. The key idea behind the vector is that it contains items of the same type placed sequentially in memory. For example, a vector consisting of 4 byte integers would have the following memory layout. Each box represents a four byte space. The indexes of the vector are on the right-hand side of the following diagram:

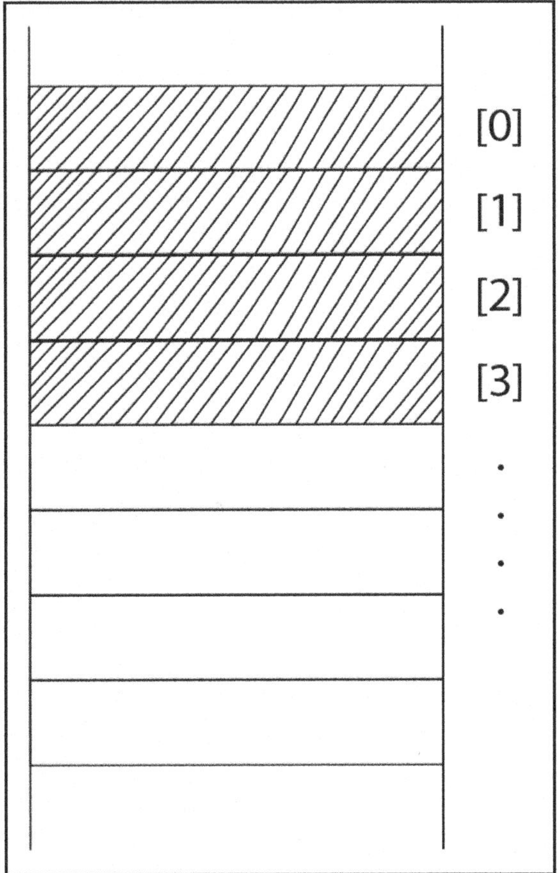

The physical structure of the vector allows any of its elements to be accessed in real time.

We should differentiate containers with their operations in order to apply them properly in specific problems. To do so we usually define the complexity of running time of their operations in relation to the number of elements in the container. For example, the vector's element access is defined as a constant time operation, which means that it takes the same number of instructions to fetch a vector item regardless of the vector length.

Accessing the first element of the vector and accessing the 100th element of the vector take the same amount of work, therefore, we call it a constant time operation, also known as ***O(1)* operation**.

While the element access is fast in vector, adding new elements is somewhat tricky. Whenever we insert a new item at the end of the vector, we should also consider the capacity of the vector. It should dynamically grow in size when there is no more space allocated for the vector. Take a look at the following `Vector` class with its `push_back()` function:

```
template <typename T>
class Vector
{
public:
  Vector() : buffer_{nullptr}, capacity_{2}, size_{0}
  {
    buffer_ = new T[capacity_]; // initializing an empty array
  }
  ~Vector() { delete [] buffer_; }
  // code omitted for brevity

public:
  void push_back(const T& item)
  {
    if (size_ == capacity_) {
      // resize
    }
    buffer_[size_++] = item;
  }
  // code omitted for brevity
};
```

Before diving into the implementation of the `push_back()` function, let's take a look at the following diagram:

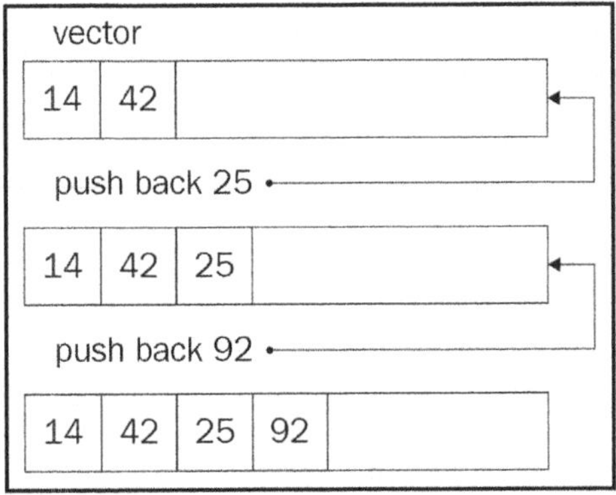

We should allocate a brand-new array, copy all the elements of the old one into the new array, and then add the newly inserted element at the next free slot at the end of the new array. This is shown in the following code snippet:

```
template <typename T>
class Vector
{
public:
  // code omitted for brevity
  void push_back(const T& item)
  {
    if (size_ == capacity_) {
      capacity_ *= 2; // increase the capacity of the vector twice
      T* temp_buffer = new T[capacity_];
      // copy elements of the old into the new
      for (int ix = 0; ix < size_; ++ix) {
        temp_buffer[ix] = buffer_[ix];
      }
      delete [] buffer_; // free the old array
      buffer_ = temp_buffer; // point the buffer_ to the new array
    }
    buffer_[size_++] = item;
  }
  // code omitted for brevity
};
```

The resizing factor can be chosen differently – we set it to `2`, which makes the vector grow twice of its size whenever it's full. So we could insist that, most of the time, inserting a new item at the end of the vector takes constant time. It just adds the item at the free slot and increases its `private size_` variable. From time to time, adding a new element will require allocating a new, bigger vector and copying the old one into the new one. For cases like this, the operation is said to take **amortized** constant time to complete.

We can't say the same when we add an element at the front of the vector. The point is, all the other elements should be moved by one slot to the right in order to free up a slot for the new element, as shown in the following diagram:

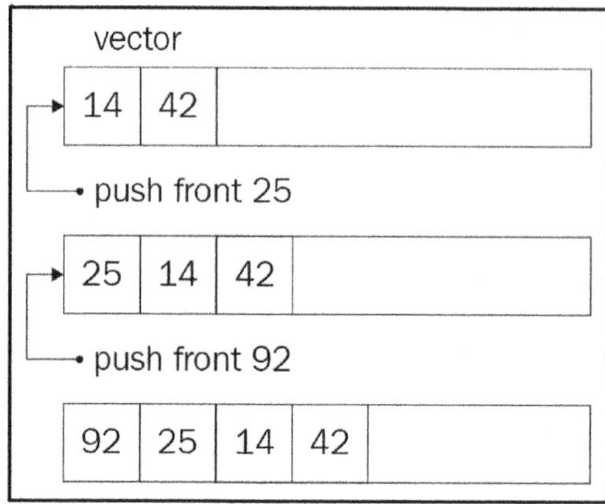

Here's how we would implement it in our `Vector` class:

```
// code omitted for brevity
void push_front(const T& item)
{
  if (size_ == capacity_) {
    // resizing code omitted for brevity
  }
  // shifting all the elements to the right
  for (int ix = size_ - 1; ix > 0; --ix) {
    buffer_[ix] = buffer[ix - 1];
  }
  // adding item at the front
  buffer_[0] = item;
  size_++;
}
```

In cases where you need to insert new elements only at the front of the container, choosing a vector is not a good option. That's one of the examples where other containers should be considered.

Node-based data structures

Node-based data structures don't take contiguous blocks of memory. A node-based data structure allocates nodes for its elements without any order – they might be spread randomly in memory. We express each item as a node linked to the other nodes.

The most popular and introductory node-based data structure is the linked list. The following diagram shows the visual structure of a doubly linked list:

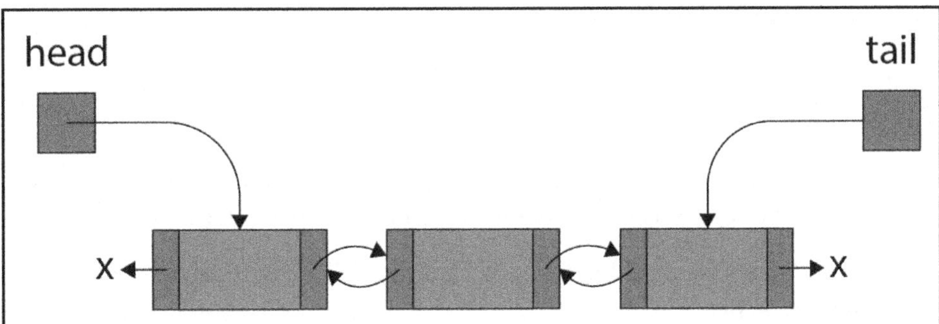

A linked list is very different from a vector. Some of its operations are faster, though it lacks the compactness of a vector.

To keep it short, let's implement the element insertion at the front of the list. We will keep each node as a struct:

```
template <typename T>
struct node
{
  node(const T& it) : item{it}, next{nullptr}, prev{nullptr} {}
  T item;
  node<T>* next;
  node<T>* prev;
};
```

Pay attention to the `next` member – it points to the same struct, this way allowing the chaining of nodes together, as shown in the preceding illustration.

To implement a linked list, all we need is to keep a pointer to its first node, usually called the head of the list. Inserting an element at the front of the list is simple:

```
template <typename T>
class LinkedList
{
  // code omitted for brevity
```

```
public:
  void push_front(const T& item)
  {
    node<T>* new_node = new node<T>{item};
    if (head_ != nullptr) {
      new_node->next = head_->next;
      if (head_->next != nullptr) {
        head_->next->prev = new_node;
      }
    }
    new_node->next = head_;
    head_ = new_node;
  }
private:
  node<T>* head_;
};
```

There are three cases that we should consider when inserting an element into a list:

- Inserting an element at the front of the list, as discussed earlier, takes the following steps:

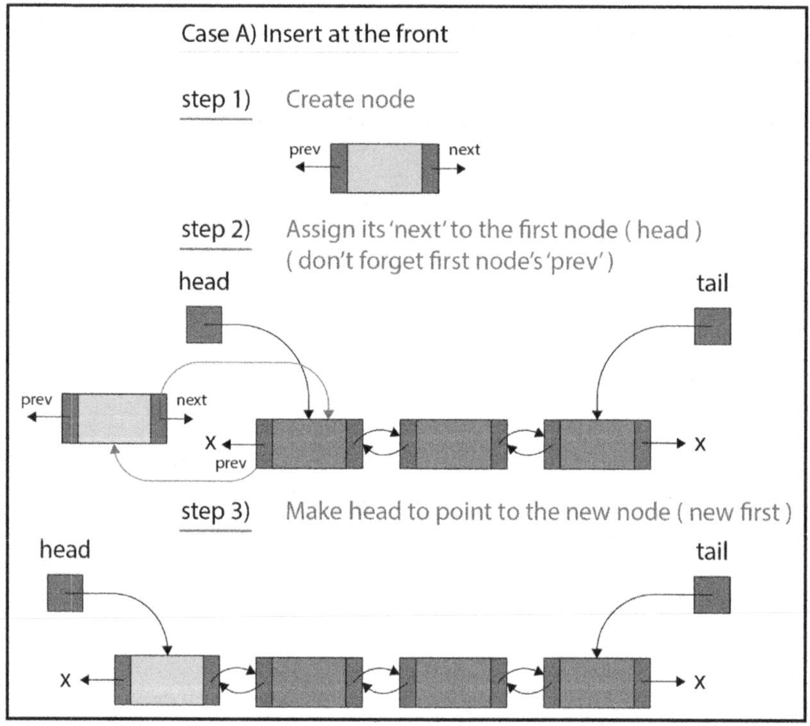

* Inserting an element at the end of the list is shown in the following diagram:

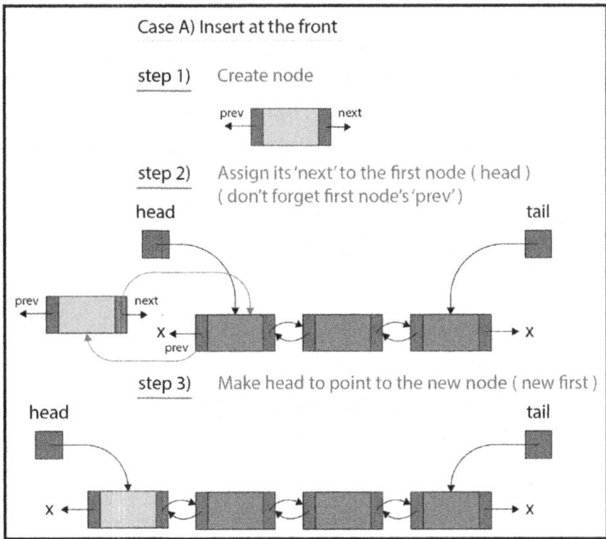

* Finally, inserting an element in the middle of the list is done as follows:

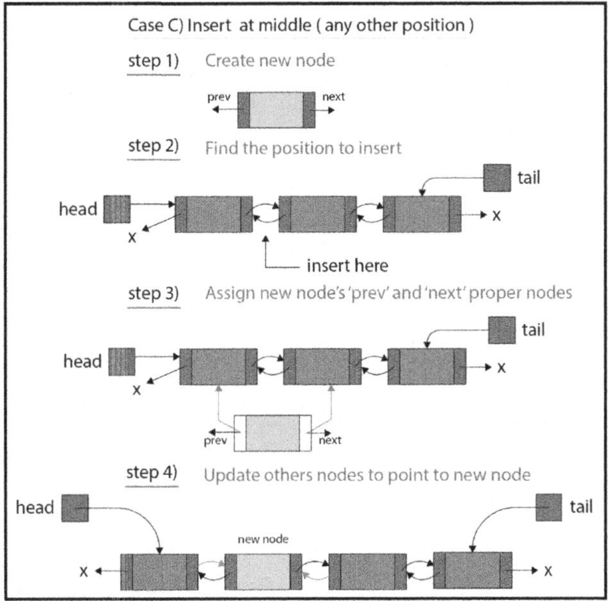

In the preceding diagrams, inserting an element into a vector is obviously different from inserting an element into the list. How would you choose between a vector and a list? You should concentrate on the operations and their speed. For example, reading any element from the vector takes constant time. We can store a one million emails in a vector, and retrieve the one at position 834,000 without any additional effort. For linked lists, the operation is linear. So, if you need to store a collection of data that will be mostly read, but not written, then using a vector is obviously a reasonable choice.

Inserting an element at any position in the list takes a constant-time operation, while the vector will strive to insert an element at a random position. Therefore, when you need a collection of objects to/from which data can be intensively added/removed, the better choice would be a linked list.

We should also take into account the cache memory. Vectors have good data locality. Reading the first element of a vector involves copying the first *N* elements into the cache. Further reads of vector elements will be even faster. We can't say the same for linked lists. To find out the reason, let's move ahead to compare the memory layouts of a vector and a linked list.

Containers in memory

As you already know from the previous chapters, an object takes memory space on one of the memory segments provided to the process. Most of the time, we are interested in the stack or heap memory. An automatic object takes space on the stack. The following two declarations both reside on the stack:

```
struct Email
{
  // code omitted for brevity
};

int main() {
  Email obj;
  Email* ptr;
}
```

Although `ptr` represents a pointer to an `Email` object, it takes space on the stack. It can point to a memory location allocated on the heap, but the pointer itself (the variable storing the address of a memory location) resides on the stack. This is crucial to understand and remember before going further with vectors and lists.

As we saw earlier in the chapter, implementing a vector involves encapsulating a pointer to an inner buffer that represents an array of elements of the specified type. When we declare a `Vector` object, it takes the necessary amount of stack memory to store its member data. The `Vector` class has the following three members:

```
template <typename T>
class Vector
{
public:
  // code omitted for brevity

private:
  int capacity_;
  int size_;
  T* buffer_;
};
```

Supposing that an integer takes 4 bytes and a pointer takes 8 bytes, the following `Vector` object declaration will take at least 16 bytes of stack memory:

```
int main()
{
  Vector<int> v;
}
```

Here's how we picture the memory layout for the preceding code:

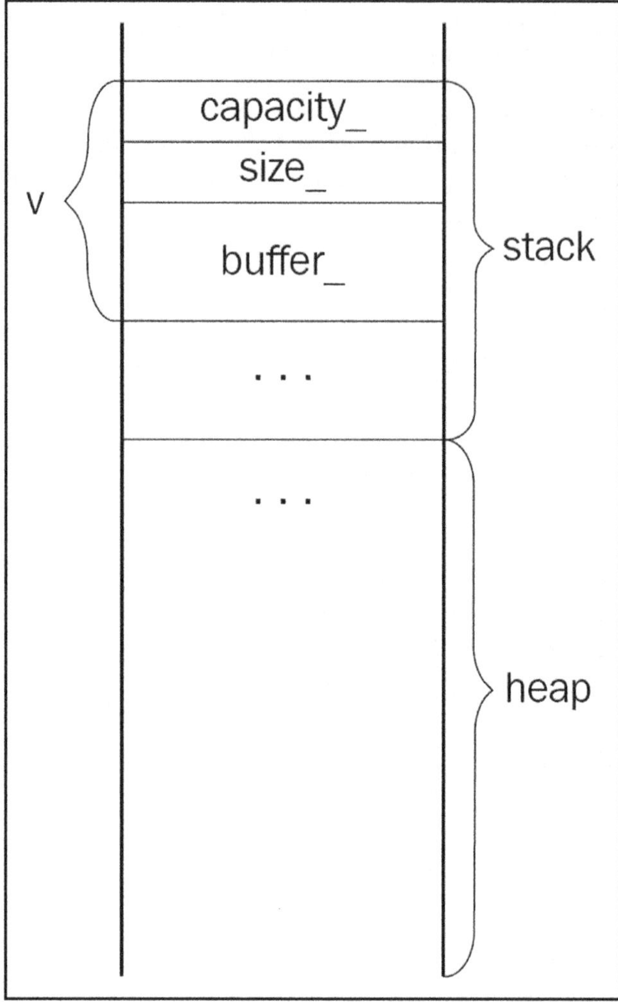

After inserting elements, the size of the vector on the stack will stay the same. The heap comes to the scene. The `buffer_` array points to a memory location allocated using the `new[]` operator. For example, look at the following code:

```
// we continue the code from previous listing
v.push_back(17);
v.push_back(21);
v.push_back(74);
```

Each new element that we push to the vector will take space on the heap, as shown in the following diagram:

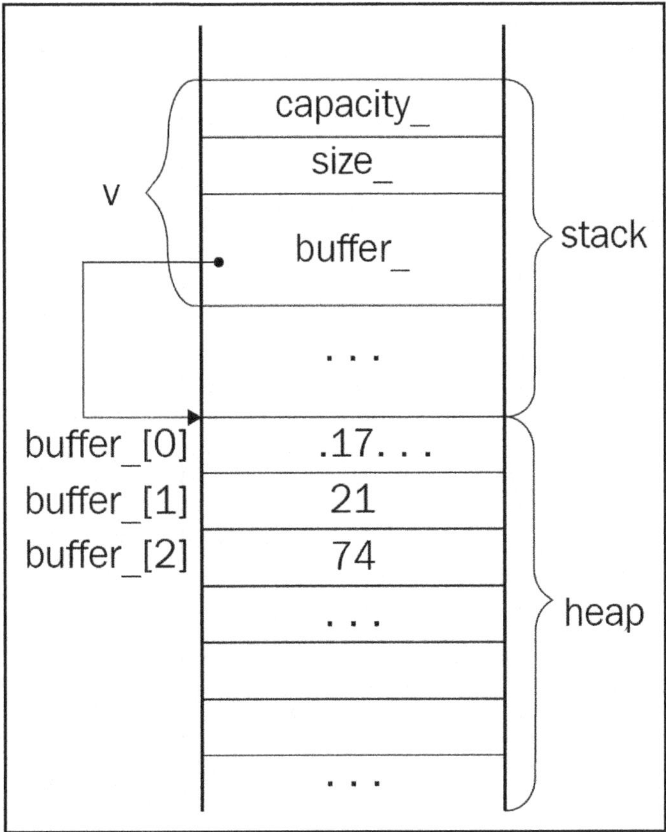

Each newly inserted element resides right after the last element of the `buffer_` array. That's why we can say the vector is a cache-friendly container.

Declaring a linked-list object also takes memory space on the stack for its data members. If we discuss the simple implementation that stores only the `head_` pointer, the following list object declaration will take at least 8 bytes of memory (for the `head_` pointer only):

```
int main()
{
  LinkedList<int> list;
}
```

The following illustration depicts the memory layout for the preceding code:

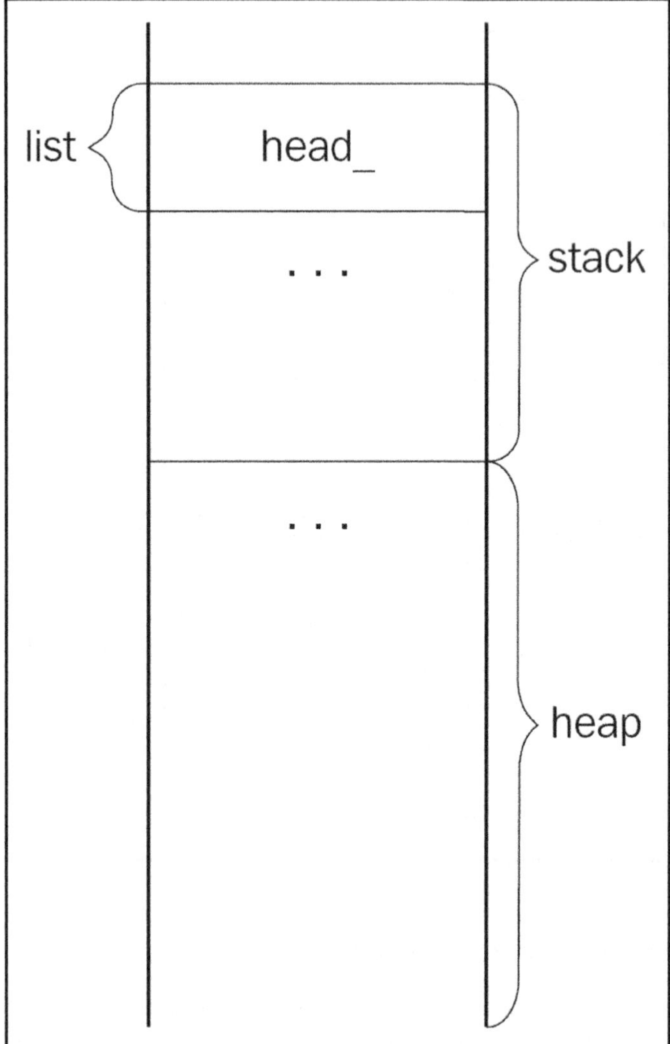

Inserting a new element creates an object of type `node` on the heap. Take a look at the following line:

```
list.push_back(19);
```

Here's how the memory illustration will change after inserting a new element:

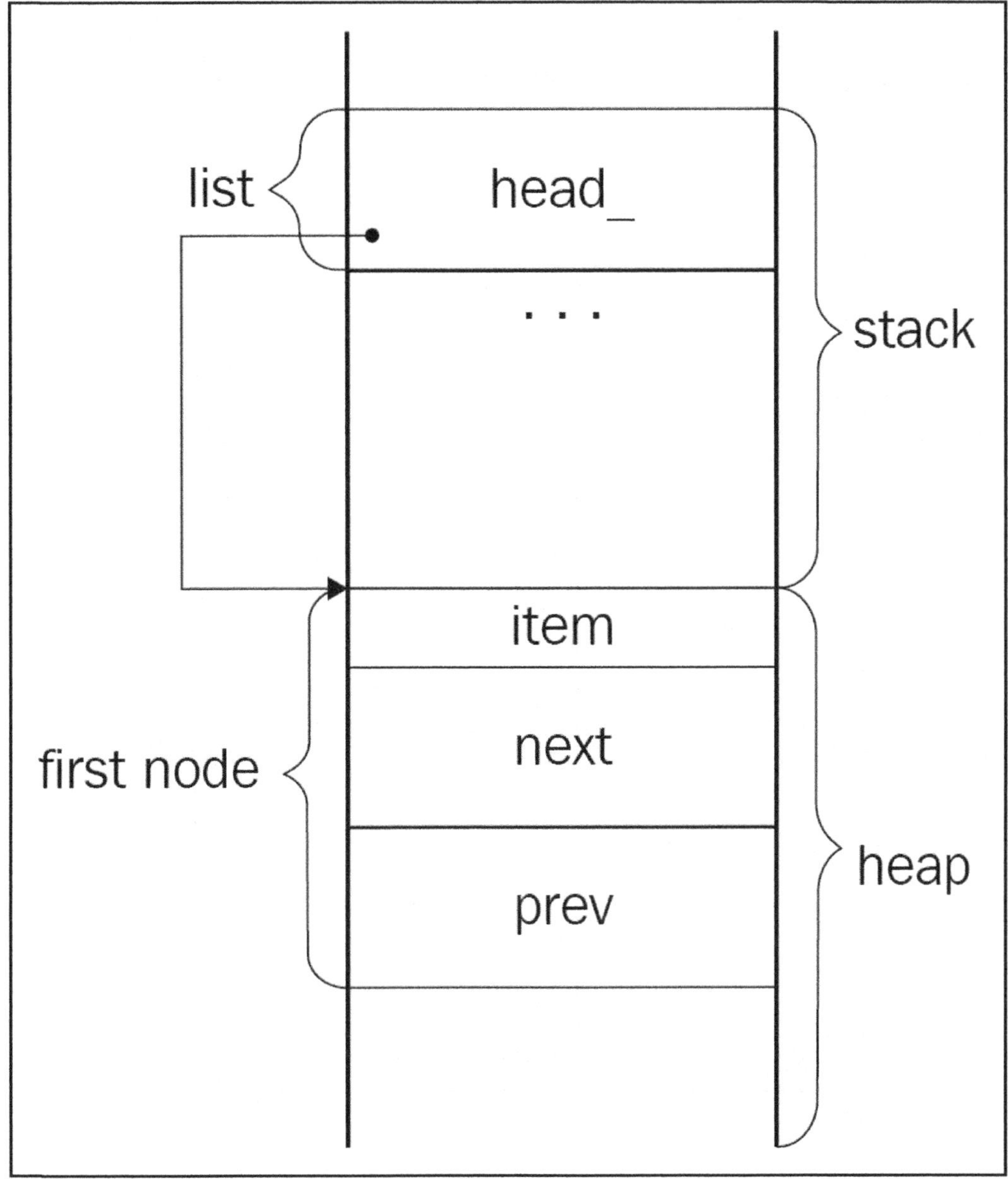

Take care that the node with all its data members resides on the heap. The item stores the value that we have inserted. When we insert another element, again a new node will be created. This time, the next pointer of the first node will point to the newly inserted element. And the newly inserted node's prev pointer will point to the previous node of the list. The following illustration depicts the linked list's memory layout after inserting the second element:

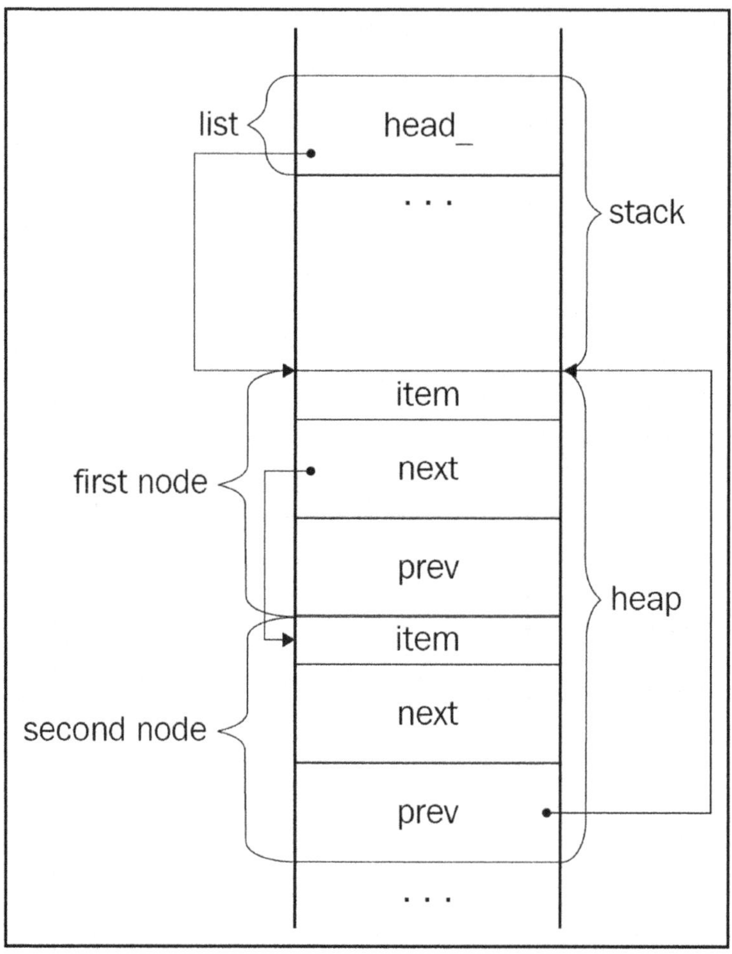

An interesting thing happens when we allocate some random objects on the heap in between inserting elements into the list. For example, the following code inserts a node into the list, then allocates space for an integer (not related to the list). Finally, it again inserts an element into the list:

```
int main()
{
  LinkedList<int> list;
  list.push_back(19);
  int* random = new int(129);
  list.push_back(22);
}
```

This intermediate random object declaration spoils the order of list elements, as shown in the following diagram:

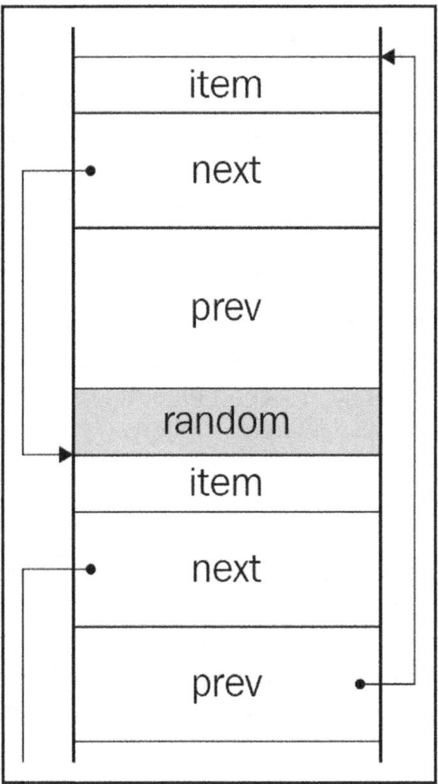

The preceding diagram gives us a hint that the list is not a cache-friendly container, because of its structure and the allocation of its elements.

Pay attention to the memory overhead created by incorporating each new node into the code. We pay an additional 16 bytes (considering the pointer takes 8 bytes of memory) for one element. Thus, lists lose the game of optimal memory use to vectors.

We can try to fix the situation by introducing a preallocated buffer in the list. Each new node creation will then pass via the **placement new** operator. However, it's wiser to choose a data structure that better fits the problem of interest.

In real-world application development, programmers rarely implement their own vectors or linked lists. They usually use tested and stable library versions. C++ provides standard containers for both vectors and linked lists. Moreover, it provides two separate containers for singly and doubly linked lists.

STL containers

The STL is a powerful collection of algorithms and containers. Although understanding and implementing data structures is a great skill for programmers, you don't have to implement them each time you need one in the project. The library providers take care of implementing stable and tested data structures and algorithms for us. By understanding the inner details of data structures and algorithms, we are making better choices of STL containers and algorithms while solving problems.

The vectors and linked lists discussed previously are implemented in the STL as `std::vector<T>` and `std::list<T>`, where `T` is the type of each element of the collection. Besides the type, containers also take a second default `template` parameter as an allocator. The `std::vector`, for example, is declared as follows:

```
template <typename T, typename Allocator = std::allocator<T> >
class vector;
```

As introduced in the previous chapter, an allocator handles the efficient allocation/deallocation of container elements. The `std::allocator` is the default allocator for all standard containers in the STL. A more sophisticated allocator that behaves differently based on the memory resource is the `std::pmr::polymorphic_allocator`. The STL provides `std::pmr::vector` as an alias template that uses a polymorphic allocator, defined as follows:

```
namespace pmr {
  template <typename T>
  using vector = std::vector<T, std::pmr::polymorphic_allocator<T>>;
}
```

Let's now take a closer look at `std::vector` and `std::list`.

Using std::vector and std::list

The `std::vector` is defined in the `<vector>` header. Here's the simplest usage example:

```
#include <vector>

int main()
{
  std::vector<int> vec;
  vec.push_back(4);
  vec.push_back(2);
  for (const auto& elem : vec) {
    std::cout << elem;
  }
}
```

The `std::vector` grows dynamically. We should consider the growth factor. When declaring a vector, it has some default capacity, which will then grow upon element insertion. Each time the number of elements exceeds the capacity of the vector, it increases its capacity by a given factor (usually, it doubles its capacity). If we know the approximate number of elements that we will need in the vector, we can optimize its use by initially allocating that capacity for the vector using the `reserve()` method. For example, the following code reserves a 10,000-element capacity:

```
std::vector<int> vec;
vec.reserve(10000);
```

It forces the vector to allocate space for 10,000 elements, thereby avoiding resizing during element insertion (unless we reach the 10,000-element threshold).

On the other hand, if we encounter a scenario where the capacity is much bigger than the actual number of elements in the vector, we can shrink the vector to free the unused memory. We need to call the `shrink_to_fit()` function, as shown in the following example:

```
vec.shrink_to_fit();
```

This reduces the capacity to fit the size of the vector.

Accessing vector elements is done the same way we access a regular array, using the `operator[]`. However, the `std::vector` provides two options for accessing its elements. One of them is considered a safe approach and is done via the `at()` function, as follows:

```
std::cout << vec.at(2);
// is the same as
std::cout << vec[2];
// which is the same as
std::cout << vec.data()[2];
```

The difference between `at()` and `operator[]` is that `at()` accesses the specified element with bounds checking; that is, the following line throws an `std::out_of_range` exception:

```
try {
  vec.at(999999);
} catch (std::out_of_range& e) { }
```

We use the `std::list` almost the same way. These lists mostly have a similar public interface. Later in the chapter, we will discuss iterators that allow abstracting from specific containers so that we can replace a list with a vector without much of a penalty. Before that, let's see the difference between the list's and vector's public interfaces.

Besides the standard set of functions that both containers support, such as `size()`, `resize()`, `empty()`, `clear()`, `erase()`, and others, the list has the `push_front()` function that inserts an element at the front of the list. This is done efficiently because the `std::list` represents a doubly linked list. As shown in the following code, the `std::list` supports `push_back()` as well:

```
std::list<double> lst;
lst.push_back(4.2);
lst.push_front(3.14);
// the list contains: "3.14 -> 4.2"
```

The list supports additional operations that come in handy in many situations. For example, to merge two sorted lists, we use the `merge()` method. It takes another list as its argument and moves all of its elements to the current list. The list passed as an argument to the `merge()` method becomes empty after the operation.

The STL also provides a singly linked list, represented by `std::forward_list`. To use it, you should include the `<forward_list>` header. As the singly linked list node has only one pointer, it's cheaper in terms of memory than the doubly linked list.

The `splice()` method is somewhat similar to `merge()`, except that it moves a portion of the list provided as an argument. By moving, we mean re-pointing internal pointers to proper list nodes. This is true for both `merge()` and `splice()`.

When we use containers for storing and manipulating complex objects, the price of copying elements plays a big role in the program's performance. Consider the following struct representing a three-dimensional point:

```
struct Point
{
  float x;
  float y;
  float z;

  Point(float px, float py, float pz)
    : x(px), y(py), z(pz)
  {}

  Point(Point&& p)
    : x(p.x), y(p.y), z(p.z)
  {}
};
```

Now, look at the following code, which inserts a `Point` object into a vector:

```
std::vector<Point> points;
points.push_back(Point(1.1, 2.2, 3.3));
```

A temporary object is constructed and then moved to the vector's corresponding slot. We can represent it visually as follows:

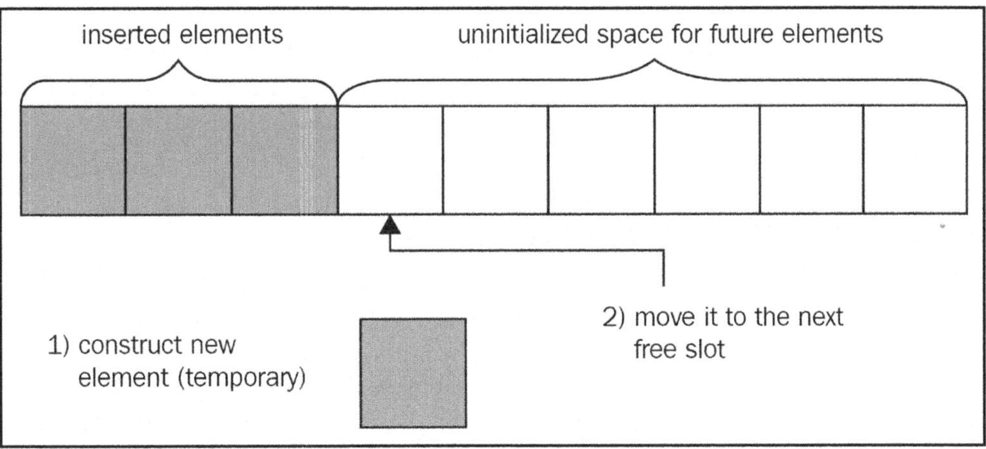

Obviously, the vector occupies more space beforehand to delay resize operations for as long as possible. When we insert a new element, the vector copies it to the next available slot (and will reallocate more space if it's full). We can use that uninitialized space for creating a new element in place. The vector provides the `emplace_back()` function for that purpose. Here's how we can use it:

```
points.emplace_back(1.1, 2.2, 3.3);
```

Pay attention to the arguments we passed directly to the function. The following illustration depicts the use of `emplace_back()`:

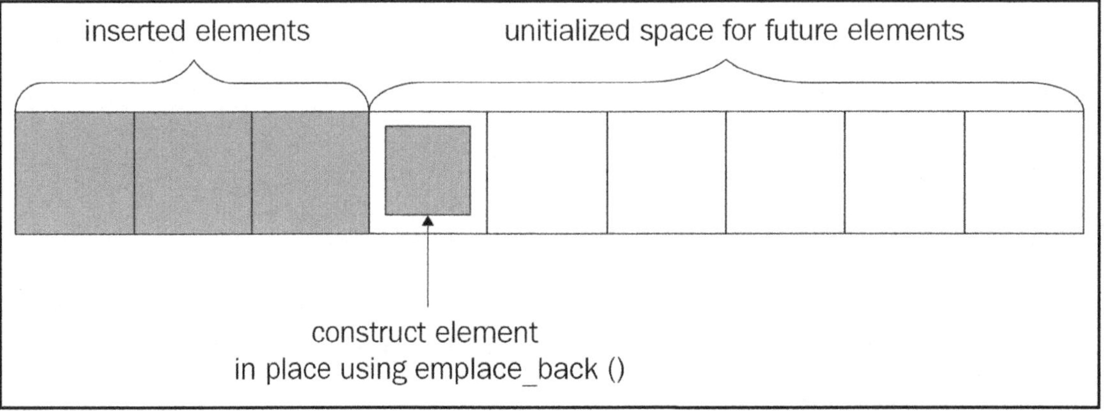

The `emplace_back()` constructs the element through `std::allocator_traits::construct()`. The latter typically uses the placement of new operator to construct the element at already allocated uninitialized space.

The `std::list` also provides an `emplace_front()` method. Both functions return a reference to the inserted element. The only requirement is for the type of element to be `EmplaceConstructible`. For vectors, the type should also be `MoveInsertable`.

Using container adapters

You might have encountered descriptions of the stack and the queue as data structures (or *containers*, in terms of C++). Technically, they are not data structures, but data structure adapters. In STL, `std::stack` and `std::queue` adapt containers by providing a special interface to access them. The term *stack* is almost everywhere. So far, we have used it to describe a memory segment for objects with automatic storage duration. The segment takes the name *stack* because of its allocation/deallocation strategy.

We say that objects are pushed to the stack each time we declare them, and popped out on destruction. The objects are popped in the reverse order in which they have been pushed. That's the reason for calling the memory segment the stack. The same **last-in, first-out (LIFO)** method applies to the stack adapter. The crucial functions provided by `std::stack` are as follows:

```
void push(const value_type& value);
void push(value_type&& value);
```

The `push()` function effectively calls the `push_back()` of the underlying container. Usually, the stack is implemented using a vector. We've already discussed such a scenario in `Chapter 3`, *Details of Object-Oriented Programming*, when we introduced protected inheritance. `std::stack` has two template parameters; one of them is the container. It doesn't matter what you choose, but it must have a `push_back()` member function. The default container for `std::stack` and `std::queue` is `std::deque`.

`std::deque` allows fast insertion at its beginning and its end. It is an indexed sequential container similar to `std::vector`. The name deque stands for *double-ended queue*.

Let's see stack in action:

```
#include <stack>

int main()
{
  std::stack<int> st;
  st.push(1); // stack contains: 1
  st.push(2); // stack contains: 2 1
  st.push(3); // stack contains: 3 2 1
}
```

A better alternative to the `push()` function is the `emplace()`. It calls the `emplace_back()` of the underlying container, therefore, constructs element in place.

To pull the element out, we call the `pop()` function. It doesn't take any arguments and doesn't return anything, it just removes the top element from the stack. To access the top element of the stack, we call the `top()` function. Let's modify the previous example to print all the stack elements before popping them out:

```
#include <stack>

int main()
{
  std::stack<int> st;
  st.push(1);
```

```
    st.push(2);
    st.push(3);
    std::cout << st.top(); // prints 3
    st.pop();
    std::cout << st.top(); // prints 2
    st.pop();
    std::cout << st.top(); // prints 1
    st.pop();
    std::cout << st.top(); // crashes application
}
```

The `top()` function returns a reference to the top element. It calls the `back()` function of the underlying container. Pay attention to the last `top()` function that we called on the empty stack. We suggest you check the size of the stack using `size()` before calling `top()` on the empty one.

`queue` is another adapter with slightly different behavior from the stack. The logic behind the queue is that it returns the first inserted element first: it maintains the **first-in, first-out (FIFO)** principle. Look at the following diagram:

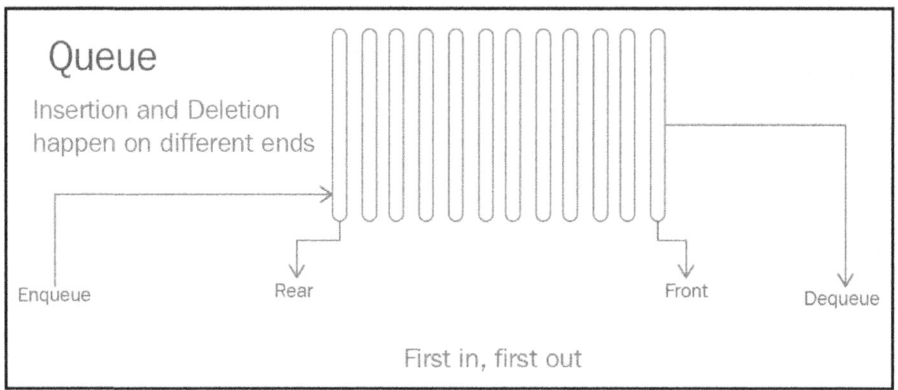

The formal names for inserting and retrieving operations in a queue are **enqeue** and **dequeue**. `std::queue` keeps a consistent approach and provides the `push()` and `pop()` functions. To access the first and last elements of the queue, you should use `front()` and `back()`. Both return references to elements. Here's a simple usage example:

```
#include <queue>

int main()
{
    std::queue<char> q;
    q.push('a');
    q.push('b');
```

```
  q.push('c');
  std::cout << q.front(); // prints 'a'
  std::cout << q.back(); // prints 'c'
  q.pop();
  std::cout << q.front(); // prints 'b'
}
```

Knowing various containers and adapters is useful when you apply them correctly. There isn't a silver bullet in choosing the right container for all kinds of problems. Many compilers use the stack to parse code expressions. For example, it's easy to validate the parentheses in the following expression using the stack:

```
int r = (a + b) + (((x * y) - (a / b)) / 4);
```

Try it for practice. Write a small program that validates the preceding expression using a stack.

The applications of queues are even wider. We will see one of them in `Chapter 11`, *Designing a Strategy Game using Design Patterns*, where we design a strategy game.

Another container adapter is `std::priority_queue`. A priority queue usually adapts a balanced, node-based data structure, such as max- or min-heap. We will examine trees and graphs toward the end of this chapter and see how the priority queue works under the hood.

Iterating containers

The idea of a container that is not iterable is like a car that cannot be driven. After all, a container is a collection of items. One of the common ways to iterate over container elements is to use the plain old `for` loop:

```
std::vector<int> vec{1, 2, 3, 4, 5};
for (int ix = 0; ix < vec.size(); ++ix) {
  std::cout << vec[ix];
}
```

Containers provide a different set of operations for element access. For example, the vector provides the `operator[]`, whereas the list does not. The `std::list` has the `front()` and `back()` methods, which return the first and last elements, respectively. The `std::vector`, as already discussed, additionally provides `at()` and `operator[]`.

This means that we can't use the preceding loop for iterating list elements. But we can loop over a list (and vector) with a range-based `for` loop as follows:

```
std::list<double> lst{1.1, 2.2, 3.3, 4.2};
for (auto& elem : lst) {
  std::cout << elem;
}
```

It might seem confusing, but the trick is hidden in the range-based `for` implementation. It retrieves an iterator pointing to the first element of the container using the `std::begin()` function.

An **iterator** is an object that points to the container element and can be advanced to the next element based on the physical structure of the container. The following code declares a `vector` iterator and initializes it with an iterator pointing to the beginning of the `vector`:

```
std::vector<int> vec{1, 2, 3, 4};
std::vector<int>::iterator it{vec.begin()};
```

Containers provide two member functions, `begin()` and `end()`, returning iterators to the beginning and the end of the container, respectively. The following diagram shows how we treat the beginning and the end of the container:

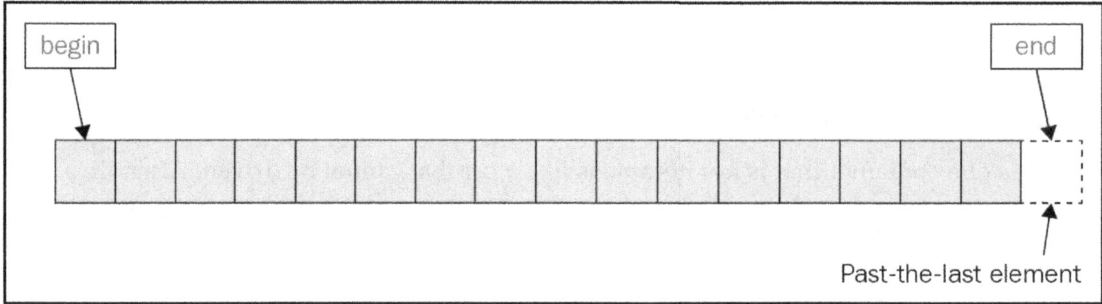

The previous code that iterated over the list elements using a range-based `for` can be considered something like the following:

```
auto it_begin = std::begin(lst);
auto it_end = std::end(lst);
for ( ; it_begin != it_end; ++it_begin) {
  std::cout << *it_begin;
}
```

Pay attention to the `*` operator that we used in the previous code to access the underlying element by an iterator. We consider an iterator a *clever* pointer to the container element.

The `std::begin()` and `std::end()` functions typically call the containers' `begin()` and `end()` methods, respectively. However, they are also applicable to regular arrays.

The container iterator knows exactly how to work with the container elements. For example, advancing a vector iterator moves it to the next slot of the array, while advancing a list iterator moves it to the next node using the corresponding pointer, as illustrated in the following code:

```
std::vector<int> vec;
vec.push_back(4);
vec.push_back(2);
std::vector<int>::iterator it = vec.begin();
std::cout << *it; // 4
it++;
std::cout << *it; // 2

std::list<int> lst;
lst.push_back(4);
lst.push_back(2);
std::list<int>::iterator lit = lst.begin();
std::cout << *lit; // 4
lit++;
std::cout << *lit; // 2
```

Each container has its own iterator implementation; that's why list and vector iterators have the same interface but behave differently. The behavior of the iterator is defined by its *category*. For example, a vector's iterator is a random-access iterator, which means we can randomly access any element using the iterator. The following code accesses the fourth element of the vector via its iterator by adding `3` to it, as follows:

```
auto it = vec.begin();
std::cout << *(it + 3);
```

There are six iterator categories in STL:

- Input
- Output (the same as input, but supporting write access)
- Forward
- Bidirectional
- Random access
- Contiguous

The **input iterator** provides read access (by calling the `*` operator) and enables forwarding the iterator position using prefix and postfix increment operators. An input iterator doesn't support multiple passes, that is, we can use an iterator to iterate over the container only once. The **forward iterator**, on the other hand, supports multiple passes. Multiple-pass support means we can read the value of the element through the iterator more than once.

The **output iterator** doesn't provide access to the element, but it allows assigning new values to it. A combination of an input iterator and output iterator with the multiple passes feature comprises the forward iterator. However, the forward iterator supports only increment operations, whereas the **bidirectional iterators** support moving the iterator to any position. They support decrementing operations. For example, the `std::list` supports bidirectional iterators.

Finally, the **random access iterator** allows *jumping* through elements by adding/subtracting a number to/from the iterator. The iterator will jump to the position specified by the arithmetic operation. The `std::vector` provides random access iterators.

Each of the categories defines the set of operations that can be applied to the iterator. For example, the input iterator can be used to read the value of the element and advance to the next element by incrementing the iterator. On the other hand, the random access iterator allows incrementing and decrementing the iterator with arbitrary values, reading and writing the value of the element, and so on.

A combination of all of the features described thus far in this section falls into the **contiguous iterator** category, which also expects the container to be a contiguous one. This means that container elements are guaranteed to reside right next to the other. An example of a contiguous container is the `std::array`.

Functions such as `distance()` use the information about the iterator to achieve the fastest result in execution. For example, the `distance()` function between two bidirectional iterators takes a linear time of execution, while the same function for random access iterators runs in constant time.

The following pseudocode demonstrates a sample implementation:

```
template <typename Iter>
std::size_type distance(Iter first, Iter second) {
  if (Iter is a random_access_iterator) {
    return second - first;
  }
  std::size_type count = 0;
  for ( ; first != last; ++count, first++) {}
  return count;
}
```

Although the pseudocode shown in the preceding example works fine, we should consider that checking the category of an iterator at runtime is not an option. It is defined at compile time, so we need to use template specialization in order to generate the `distance()` function for random access iterators. A better solution would be using the `std::is_same` type trait, defined in `<type_traits>`:

```
#include <iterator>
#include <type_traits>

template <typename Iter>
typename std::iterator_traits<Iter>::difference_type distance(Iter first,
Iter last)
{
  using category = std::iterator_traits<Iter>::iterator_category;
  if constexpr (std::is_same_v<category, std::random_access_iterator_tag>)
{
    return last - first;
  }
  typename std::iterator_traits<Iter>::difference_type count;
  for (; first != last; ++count, first++) {}
  return count;
}
```

`std::is_same_v` is a helper template for the `std::is_same`, defined as follows:

```
template <class T, class U>
inline constexpr bool is_same_v = is_same<T, U>::value;
```

The most important quality of iterators is providing loose coupling between containers and algorithms:

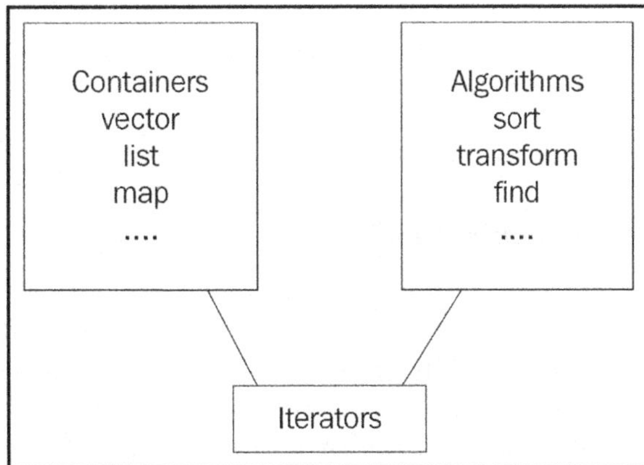

STL is based upon those three concepts: containers, algorithms, and iterators. While a vector, a list, or any other container is different, they serve the same purpose: storing data.

On the other hand, algorithms are functions that work with data; most of the time they work with collections of data. An algorithm definition usually represents a generic way of specifying the steps that should be taken to handle container elements. For example, a sorting algorithm sorts container elements in ascending or descending order.

Vectors are contiguous containers, while lists are node-based containers. Sorting them will require a deeper understanding of the particular container's physical structure. To properly sort a vector, a separate sort function should be implemented for it. The same logic applies to lists.

Iterators take this multiplicity of implementations to a generic level. They provide the library designers the ability to implement just one sorting function, which will deal only with iterators, abstracting from the container type. In the STL, the `sort()` algorithm (defined in `<algorithm>`) deals with iterators, and we can sort both vectors and lists with the same function:

```
#include <algorithm>
#include <vector>
#include <list>
...
std::vector<int> vec;
// insert elements into the vector
std::list<int> lst;
// insert elements into the list

std::sort(vec.begin(), vec.end());
std::sort(lst.begin(), lst.end());
```

The iterators described in this section are now considered legacy features. C++20 introduces a new system of iterators based on **concepts**.

Concepts and iterators

C++20 introduces **concepts** as one of its major features. Along with concepts, C++20 has new iterators based on concepts. Although the iterators discussed in this chapter up to here are now considered legacy features, lots of lines of code have already been written using them. That's why we introduced them first before continuing with the new iterator concepts. Now, let's find out what concepts are and how to use them.

Understanding concepts

Abstraction is essential in computer programming. We introduced classes in `Chapter 3`, *Details of Object-Oriented Programming,* as a way to represent data and operations as an abstract entity. After that, in `Chapter 4`, *Understanding and Designing Templates,* we dove into templates and saw how we can make classes even more flexible by reusing them for various aggregate types. Templates not only provide abstraction from the specific type, but also incorporate loose coupling between the entity and aggregate types. Take, for example, `std::vector`. It provides a generic interface to store and manipulate collections of objects. We can easily declare three different vectors that will contain three different types of objects, as follows:

```
std::vector<int> ivec;
std::vector<Person> persons;
std::vector<std::vector<double>> float_matrix;
```

If not templates, we would have to do something like the following for the preceding code:

```
std::int_vector ivec;
std::custom_vector persons; // supposing the custom_vector stores void*
std::double_vector_vector float_matrix;
```

Although the preceding code is ridiculously unacceptable, we should agree on the fact that templates are the basis of generic programming. Concepts introduce even more flexibility to generic programming. Now it is possible to set restrictions on template parameters, check for constraints, and discover inconsistent behavior at compile time. A template class declaration has the following form:

```
template <typename T>
class Wallet
{
  // the body of the class using the T type
};
```

Pay attention to the `typename` keyword in the preceding code block. Concepts go even further: they allow replacing it with a type description that describes the template parameter. Let's say we want the `Wallet` to work with types that can be added together, that is, they should be *addable*. Here's how using a concept will help us achieve that in the code:

```
template <addable T>
class Wallet
{
  // the body of the class using addable T's
};
```

So, now we can create `Wallet` instances by providing types that are addable. Whenever the type doesn't satisfy the constraint, the compiler will throw an error. It looks a bit supernatural. The following snippet declares two `Wallet` objects:

```
class Book
{
  // doesn't have an operator+
  // the body is omitted for brevity
};

constexpr bool operator+(const Money& a, const Money& b) {
  return Money{a.value_ + b.value_};
}

class Money
{
  friend constexpr bool operator+(const Money&, const Money&);
  // code omitted for brevity
private:
  double value_;
};

Wallet<Money> w; // works fine
Wallet<Book> g; // compile error
```

The `Book` class has no `+` operator, so the construction of `g` will fail because of the `template` parameter type restriction.

The declaration of a concept is done using the `concept` keyword and has the following form:

```
template <parameter-list>
concept name-of-the-concept = constraint-expression;
```

As you can see, a concept is also declared using templates. We can refer to them as types that describe other types. Concepts rely heavily on **constraints**. A constraint is a way to specify requirements for template arguments, and, as follows, a concept is a set of constraints. Here's how we can implement the preceding addable concept:

```
template <typename T>
concept addable = requires (T obj) { obj + obj; }
```

Standard concepts are defined in the `<concepts>` header.

We can also combine several concepts into one by requiring the new concept to support the others. To achieve that we use the `&&` operator. Let's see how iterators leverage concepts and bring an example of an `incrementable` iterator concept that combines other concepts.

Using iterators in C++20

After the introduction to concepts, it is obvious that iterators are first to leverage them to the fullest. Iterators and their categories are now considered legacy because, starting from C++20, we use iterator concepts such as `readable` (which specifies that the type is readable by applying the `*` operator) and `writable` (which specifies that a value can be written to an object referenced by the iterator). As promised, let's see how `incrementable` is defined in the `<iterator>` header:

```
template <typename T>
concept incrementable = std::regular<T> && std::weakly_incrementable<T>
            && requires (T t) { {t++} -> std::same_as<T>; };
```

So, the `incrementable` concept requires the type to be `std::regular`. That means it should be constructible by default and have a copy constructor and `operator==()`. Besides that, the `incrementable` concept requires the type to be `weakly_incrementable`, which means the type supports pre- and post-increment operators, except that the type is not required to be equality-comparable. That's why the `incrementable` joins `std::regular` to require the type to be equality-comparable. Finally, the addition `requires` constraint points to the fact that the type should not change after an increment, that is, it should be the same type as before. Although `std::same_as` is represented as a concept (defined in `<concepts>`), in previous versions we used to use `std::is_same` defined in `<type_traits>`. They basically do the same thing, but the C++17 version – `std::is_same_v` – was verbose, with additional suffixes.

So, instead of iterator categories, we now refer to iterator concepts. Besides the ones we introduced earlier, the following concepts should also be taken into consideration:

- `input_iterator` specifies that the type allows its referenced values to be read and is both pre- and post-**incrementable**.
- `output_iterator` specifies that values of the type can be written to and the type is both pre- and post-**incrementable**.
- `input_or_output_iterator`, the unnecessarily long name aside, specifies that the type is **incrementable** and can be dereferenced.
- `forward_iterator` specifies that the type is an `input_iterator` that additionally supports equality comparison and multi-pass.

- `bidirectional_iterator` specifies that the type supports `forward_iterator` and additionally supports the backward movement.
- `random_access_iterator` specifies that the type as a `bidirectional_iterator`, supporting advancement in constant time and subscripting.
- `contiguous_iterator` specifies that the type is a `random_access_iterator`, referring to elements that are contiguous in memory.

They almost repeat the legacy iterators that we discussed earlier, but now they can be used when declaring template parameters so that the compiler will take care of the rest.

Mastering algorithms

As already mentioned, algorithms are functions taking some input, processing it, and returning an output. Usually, an algorithm in the context of the STL implies a function processing a collection of data. Collections of data are presented in the form of containers, such as `std::vector`, `std::list`, and others.

Choosing an efficient algorithm is a common task in a programmer's routine. For example, searching a sorted vector using the binary search algorithm will be much more efficient than using sequential searching. To compare the efficiency of algorithms, a so-called **asymptotic analysis** is performed, which takes into consideration the speed of the algorithm with regard to the input data size. This means that we shouldn't actually compare two algorithms by applying them to a container with ten or a 100 elements.

The actual difference of algorithms shows itself when applied to *big enough* containers, having a one million or even a one billion records. Measuring the efficiency of an algorithm is also known as verifying its complexity. You might've encountered *O(n)* algorithms or *O(log N)* algorithms. The *O()* function (pronounced *big-oh*) defines the complexity of an algorithm.

Let's take a look at the searching algorithms and compare their complexity along the way.

Searching

Searching an element in the container is a common task. Let's implement sequential searching of an element in a vector:

```
template <typename T>
int search(const std::vector<T>& vec, const T& item)
{
  for (int ix = 0; ix < vec.size(); ++ix) {
    if (vec[ix] == item) {
      return ix;
    }
  }
  return -1; // not found
}
```

This is a simple algorithm that iterates through a vector and returns the index at which the element is equal to the value passed as the search key. We name it sequential searching because it sequentially scans the vector elements. Its complexity is linear: $O(n)$. To measure it, we should somehow define the number of operations that the algorithm takes to find the result. Supposing the vector contains n elements, the following code contains a comment on each line of the search function about its operations:

```
template <typename T>
int search(const std::vector<T>& vec, const T& item)
{
  for (int ix = 0;           // 1 copy
       ix < vec.size;        // n + 1 comparisons
       ++ix)                 // n + 1 increments
  {
    if (vec[ix] == item) {   // n comparisons
      return ix;             // 1 copy
    }
  }
  return -1;                 // 1 copy
}
```

We have three copy operations, $n + 1$ and n (that is, $2n + 1$) comparisons, and $n + 1$ increment operations. What if the desired element is in the first position of the vector? Well, in that case, we would scan only the first element of the vector and return from the function.

However, it doesn't mean that our algorithm is so efficient that it takes just one step to perform its task. In order to measure the complexity of an algorithm, we should take into consideration the worst-case scenario: the desired element either doesn't exist in the vector or resides in the last position of the vector. The following diagram shows the three scenarios for the element that we are about to find:

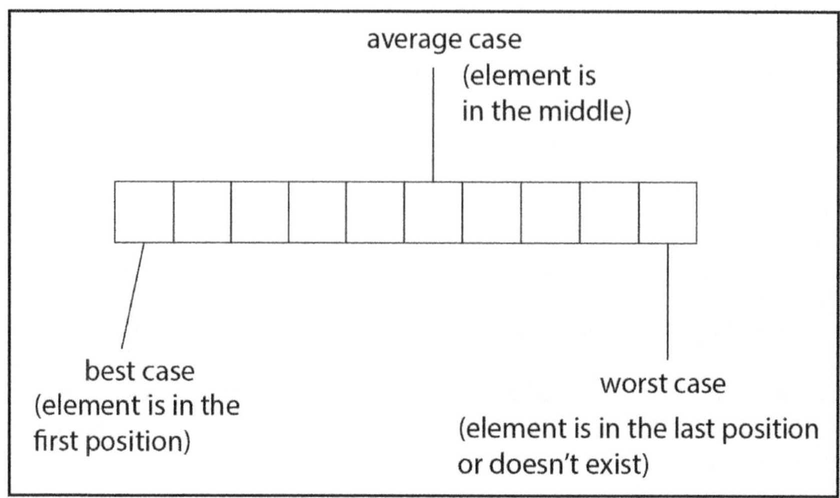

We should consider the worst-case scenario only because it covers all the other cases as well. If we define the complexity of an algorithm for the worst case, we can be sure it won't ever work slower than that.

To find out the complexity of an algorithm, we should find the connection between the number of operations and the size of the input. In this case, the size of the input is the length of the container. Let's denote copies as A, comparisons as C, and increment operations as I, so that we have 3A + (2n + 1)C + (n + 1)I operations. The complexity of the algorithm will be defined as follows:

$$O(3A + (2n + 1)C + (n + 1)I)$$

This then can be simplified in the following way:

- $O(3A + (2n + 1)C + (n + 1)I) =$
- $O(3A + 2nC + C + nI + I) =$
- $O(n(2C + I) + (3A + C + I)) =$
- $O(n(2C + I))$

Finally, the *O()'s* properties allow us to get rid of the constant coefficients and smaller members, because the actual algorithm complexity is related only to the size of the input, which is *n*, and we get the final complexity equal to *O(n)*. In other words, the sequential searching algorithm has linear time complexity.

As already mentioned, the essence of the STL is to connect containers and algorithms via iterators. That's why the sequential search implementation is not considered STL-compatible: because it has strict restrictions on input parameters. To make it generic, we should consider implementing it using iterators only. To cover a wide range of container types, use forward iterators. The following code uses operators on the type `Iter`, assuming it's a forward iterator:

```
template <typename Iter, typename T>
int search(Iter first, Iter last, const T& elem)
{
  for (std::size_t count = 0; first != last; first++, ++count) {
    if (*first == elem) return count;
  }
  return -1;
}
...
std::vector<int> vec{4, 5, 6, 7, 8};
std::list<double> lst{1.1, 2.2, 3.3, 4.4};

std::cout << search(vec.begin(), vec.end(), 5);
std::cout << search(lst.begin(), lst.end(), 5.5);
```

Actually, any type of iterators can be passed to the `search()` function. We ensure that we use forward iterators just by applied operations on iterators themselves. We use only the increment (move forward), reading (the `*` operator), and strict comparisons (`==` and `!=`), which are supported by forward iterators.

Binary search

On the other hand is the binary search algorithm, which is simple to explain. At first, it looks for the middle element of the vector and compares the search key with it, and if it is equal, then the algorithm is done: it returns the index. Otherwise, if the search key is less than the middle element, it proceeds to the left of the vector. If the search key is greater than the middle element, the algorithm proceeds to the right-hand subvector.

In order to get the binary search to work correctly for a vector, it should be sorted. The very essence of the binary search implies comparing the search key with vector elements and proceeding to the left- or right-hand subvectors, each of which contains a smaller or greater element compared to the middle element of the vector. Take a look at the following diagram, which depicts the binary search algorithm in action:

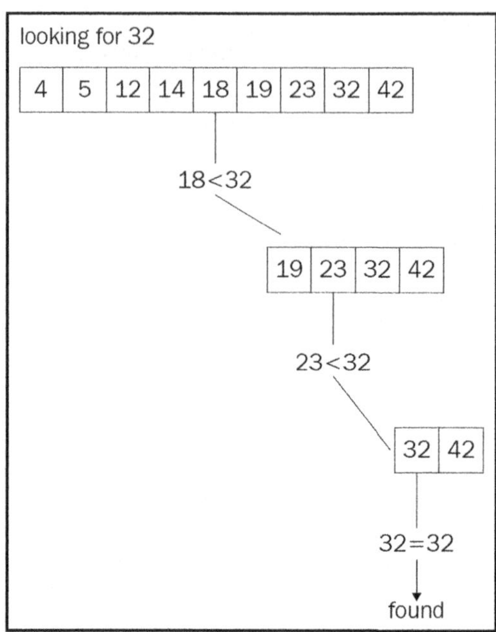

The binary search algorithm has an elegant recursive implementation (though it's better to use an iterative implementation) – take a look at it in the following code:

```
template <typename T>
std::size_t binsearch(const std::vector<T>& vec, const T& item, int start,
int end)
{
  if (start > end) return -1;
  int mid = start + (end - start) / 2;
  if (vec[mid] == item) {
    return mid; // found
  }
  if (vec[mid] > item) {
    return binsearch(vec, item, start, mid - 1);
  }
  return binsearch(vec, item, mid + 1, end);
}
```

Pay attention to the middle element calculation. Instead of the `(start + end) / 2;`, we used the `start + (end - start) / 2;` technique just to avoid the famous bug in binary search implementations (assuming we didn't leave other bugs). The point is that for big values of start and end, their sum (*start* + *end*) will produce an integer overflow, which will make the program crash at some point.

Now let's find the complexity of the binary search. It's obvious that on each step of the execution, the source array gets halved so that we deal with the smaller or greater half of it in the next step. This means that the worst-case scenario is the case when we divide the vector until there is one or no element left. To find the number of steps in the algorithm, we should find the number of divisions with regard to the size of the vector. If the vector has 10 elements, then we divide it and get a subvector of five elements; by dividing it again, we get two-element subvector, and finally, dividing it again will bring us to a single element. So, for the 10-element vector, the number of divisions is 3. For the *n*-element vector, the number of divisions is *log(n)*, because, on each step, *n* becomes *n/2*, which then becomes *n/4*, and so on. The complexity of the binary search is *O(logn)* (that is, logarithmic).

STL algorithms are defined in the `<algorithm>` header file; where the implementation of the binary search resides. The STL implementation returns true if the element exists in the container. Take a look at its prototype:

```
template <typename Iter, typename T>
bool binary_search(Iter start, Iter end, const T& elem);
```

STL algorithms don't work directly with containers, instead, they work with iterators. This allows us to abstract from the specific container and to use the `binary_search()` with all the containers supporting a forward iterator. The following example calls the `binary_search()` function for both vectors and lists:

```
#include <vector>
#include <list>
#include <algorithm>
...
std::vector<int> vec{1, 2, 3, 4, 5};
std::list<int> lst{1, 2, 3, 4};
binary_search(vec.begin(), vec.end(), 8);
binary_search(lst.begin(), lst.end(), 3);
```

The `binary_search()` checks the category of the iterator, and in the case of a random access iterator, it uses the full power of the binary search algorithm (otherwise, it falls back to sequential search).

Sorting

The binary search algorithm is applicable only to sorted containers. Sorting is a known and old task for computer programmers, who nowadays rarely write their own implementation of a sorting algorithm. You might've used `std::sort()` many times without even caring about its implementation. Basically, a sorting algorithm takes a collection as an input and returns a new sorted collection (in the order defined by the algorithm user).

Of the many sorting algorithms out there, the most popular (or even the fastest one) is **quicksort**. The basic idea of any sorting algorithm is to find smaller (or greater) elements and exchange them with greater (or smaller) elements until the whole collection is sorted. For example, the selection sort logically divides the collection into two parts, sorted and unsorted, where the sorted subarray is initially empty like so:

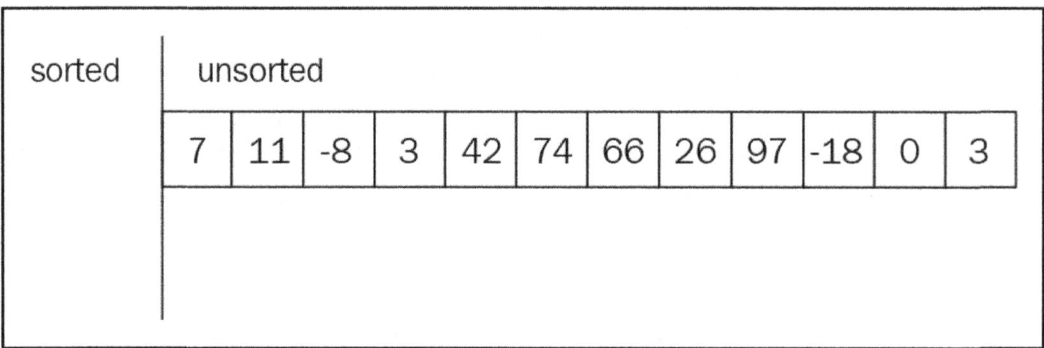

The algorithm starts to look for the smallest element in the unsorted subarray and put it to the sorted subarray by exchanging it with the first element of the unsorted subarray. After the each step, the length of the sorted subarray increases by one, whereas the length of the unsorted subarray decreases like so:

The process continues until the unsorted subarray becomes empty.

The STL provides the `std::sort()` function, taking two random-access iterators:

```
#include <vector>
#include <algorithm>
...
std::vector<int> vec{4, 7, -1, 2, 0, 5};
std::sort(vec.begin(), vec.end());
// -1, 0, 2, 4, 5, 7
```

The sort function can't be applied to `std::list` because it doesn't support random access iterators. Instead, you should call the `sort()` member function of the list. Though this contradicts the idea of the STL having generic functions, it is done for efficiency.

The `sort()` function has a third parameter: a comparing function that can be used to compare container elements. Let's suppose we store `Product` objects in our vector:

```
struct Product
{
  int price;
  bool available;
  std::string title;
};

std::vector<Product> products;
products.push_back({5, false, "Product 1"});
products.push_back({12, true, "Product 2"});
```

To sort the container properly, its elements must support the less-than operator, or <. We should define the corresponding operator for our custom type. However, we can omit the operator definition if we create a separate comparator function for our custom type, as shown in the following block:

```
class ProductComparator
{
public:
  bool operator()(const Product& a, const Product& b) {
    return a.price > b.price;
  }
};
```

Passing `ProductComparator` to the `std::sort()` function allows it to compare the vector elements without diving into details of the type of its elements, as follows:

```
std::sort(products.begin(), products.end(), ProductComparator{});
```

While this is a good technique, it would be more elegant to use lambda functions instead, which are anonymous functions just perfect for scenarios like the preceding one. Here's how we can overwrite it:

```
std::sort(products.begin(), products.end(),
  [](const Product& a, const Product& b) { return a.price > b.price; })
```

The preceding code allows omitting the declaration of `ProductComparator`.

Exploring trees and graphs

The binary search algorithm and sorting algorithms combined together lead to the idea of having a container that keeps items sorted by default. One such container is the `std::set`, based on a balanced tree. Before discussing the balanced tree itself, let's take a look at the binary search tree, a perfect candidate for fast lookups.

The idea of the binary search tree is that the values of the left-hand subtree of a node are less than the node's value. By contrast, the values of the right-hand subtree of a node are greater than the node's value. Here's an example of a binary search tree:

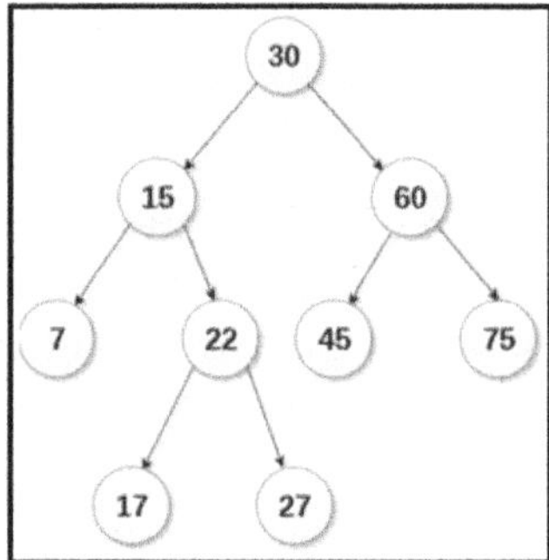

As you can see in the preceding diagram, the element with the value 15 resides in the left-hand subtree because it's less than 30 (the root element). On the other hand, the element with the value 60 resides in the right-hand subtree because it's greater than the root element. The same logic applies to the rest of the tree elements.

A binary tree node is represented as a struct containing the item and two pointers to each child. Here's a sample code representation of a tree node:

```
template <typename T>
struct tree_node
{
```

```
  T item;
  tree_node<T>* left;
  tree_node<T>* right;
};
```

Searching, inserting, or removing an element takes *O(logn)* in a fully balanced binary search tree. The STL doesn't provide a separate container for trees, but it has similar ones that are based on a tree implementation. For example, the `std::set` container is based on a balanced tree that uniquely stores elements in sorted order:

```
#include <set>
...
std::set<int> s{1, 5, 2, 4, 4, 4, 3};
// s has {1, 2, 3, 4, 5}
```

The `std::map` is also based on a balanced tree, but this one provides a container that maps a key to some value, as follows, for example:

```
#include <map>
...
std::map<int, std::string> numbers;
numbers[3] = "three";
numbers[4] = "four";
...
```

As shown in the preceding code, the function `map numbers` maps integers to strings. So when we tell the map to store the value of `3` as a key and the string `three` as a value, it adds a new node to its inner tree with the key equal to `3` and the value equal to `three`.

`set` and `map` operations are logarithmic, which makes it a very efficient data structure in most cases. However, a more efficient data structure comes next.

Hash tables

The hash table is the fastest data structure out there. It is based on the simple idea of a vector indexing. Imagine a big vector that contains pointers to lists:

```
std::vector<std::list<T> > hash_table;
```

Access to vector elements takes constant time. That's the main superpower of vectors. The hash table allows us to use any type as the key of the container. The basic idea of the hash table is to use a well-curated hash function that will generate a unique index for the input key. For example, when we use a string as a hash table key, the hash table uses a hash function to generate the hash as the index value for the underlying vector:

```
template <typename T>
int hash(const T& key)
{
  // generate and return and efficient
  // hash value from key based on the key's type
}

template <typename T, typename U>
void insert_into_hashtable(const T& key, const U& value)
{
  int index = hash(key);
  hash_table[index].push_back(value); // insert into the list
}
```

Here's how we can illustrate a hash table:

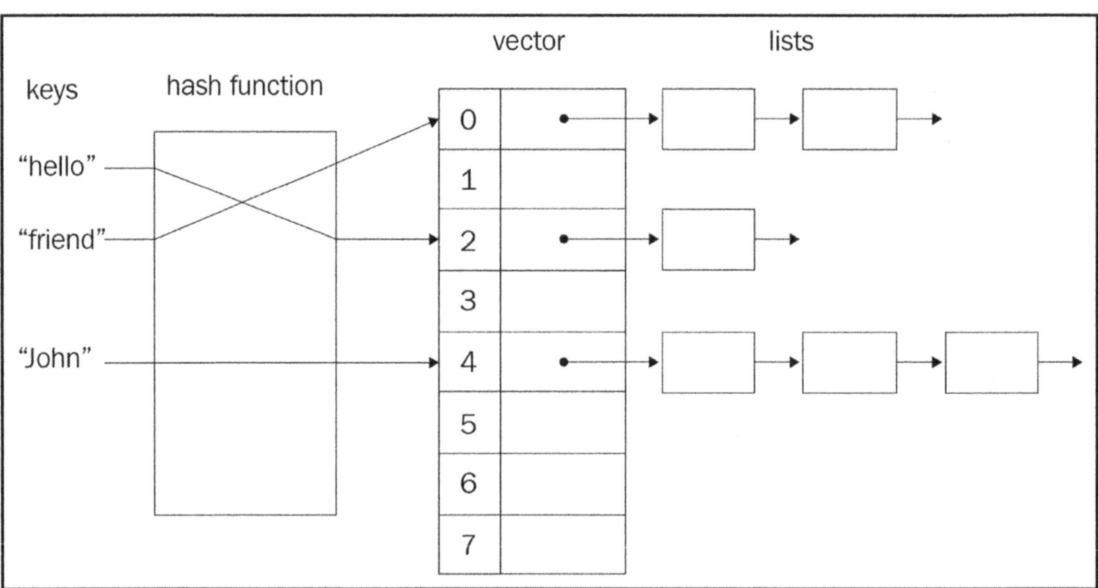

Accessing a hash table takes constant time because it operates based on the vector. Though there could be different keys that will result in the same hash value, these collisions are fixed by using a list of values as the vector element (as shown in the preceding diagram).

The STL supports a hash table named `std::unordered_map`:

```
#include <unordered_map>
...
std::unordered_map<std::string, std::string> hashtable;
hashtable["key1"] = "value 1";
hashtable["key2"] = "value 2";
...
```

To generate the hash value for provided keys, the function `std::unordered_map` uses the `std::hash()` function defined in the `<functional>` header. You can specify a custom implementation for the hash function. The third `template` parameter of the `std::unordered_map` is the hash function, which defaults to `std::hash`.

Graphs

The balancing nature of the binary search tree is based upon many search index implementations. For example, database systems use a balanced tree called a B-tree for table indexing. The B-tree is not a *binary* tree, but it follows the same balancing logic, as shown in the following diagram:

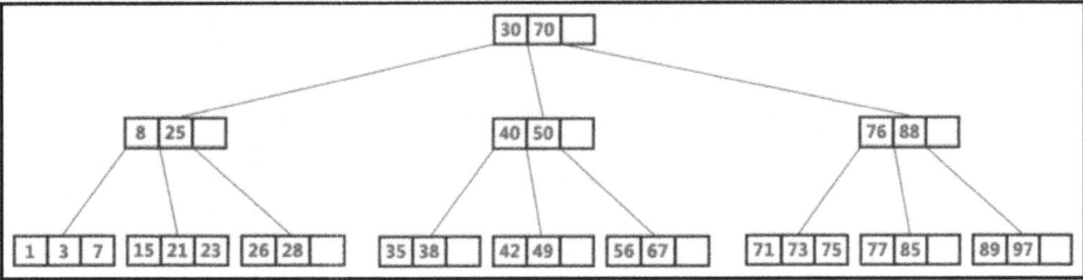

Graphs, on the other hand, represent connected nodes with no proper order:

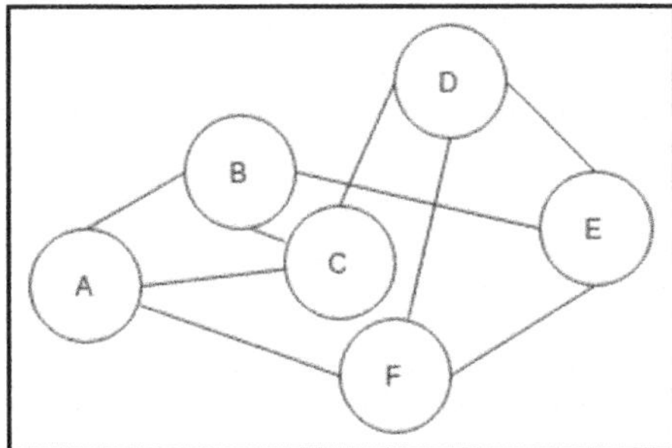

Let's suppose we are building a social network that will eventually beat Facebook off the market. The users in the social network can follow each other, which can be represented as a graph. For example, if A follows B, B follows C, and C both follows B back and follows A at the same time, then we can represent the relationships as the following graph:

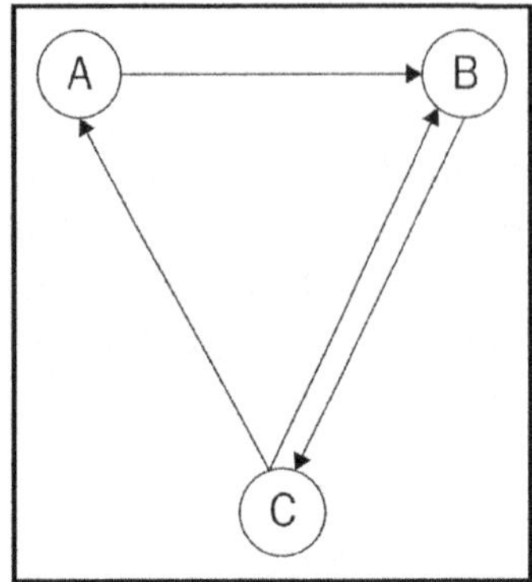

A node is called a **vertex** in the graph. The link between two nodes is called an **edge**. There isn't actually a fixed graph representation, so we should choose from several. Let's think of our social network – how would we represent the information that user A follows user B?

One of the best options here is using a hash table. We can map each user to all of the users they follow:

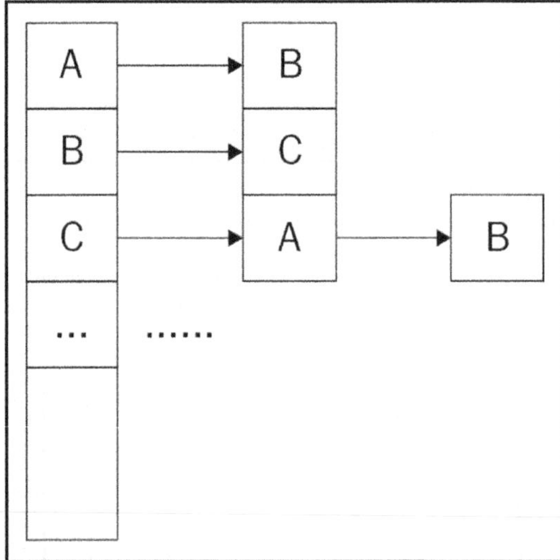

The graph implementation becomes a hybrid container:

```
#include <list>
#include <unordered_map>

template <typename T>
class Graph
{
public:
  Graph();
  ~Graph();
  // copy, move constructors and assignment operators omitted for brevity

public:
  void insert_edge(const T& source, const T& target);
  void remove_edge(const T& source, const T& target);

  bool connected(const T& source, const T& target);

private:
  std::unordered_map<T, std::list<T> > hashtable_;
};
```

To make an STL-compatible container, let's add an iterator for the graph. Though iterating a graph is not a good idea, adding an iterator is not a bad idea.

Strings

Strings are similar to vectors: they store characters, they expose iterators, and they are containers. However, they are somewhat different because they specifically express one kind of data: strings. The following diagram depicts the string **hello, C++** as an array of characters ending with a special **\0** character:

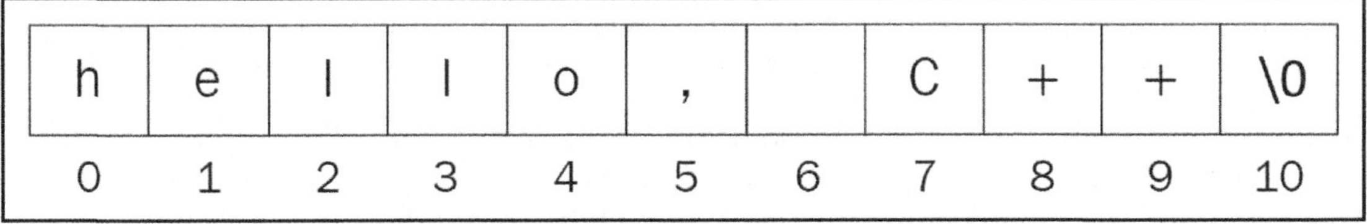

The special **\0** character (also known as the null character) serves as a string termination. The compiler reads characters one after the other until it encounters the null character.

A string is implemented the same way we implemented a vector at the beginning of the chapter:

```
class my_string
{
public:
 my_string();
 // code omitted for brevity

public:
 void insert(char ch);
 // code omitted for brevity

private:
 char* buffer_;
 int size_;
 int capacity_;
};
```

C++ has its powerful `std::string` class, which provides a bunch of functions to work with. Besides `std::string` member functions, algorithms defined in <algorithm> are also applicable to strings.

Summary

Data structures and algorithms are crucial in developing efficient software. By understanding and leveraging the data structures discussed in this chapter, you will have the full power of C++20 to make your programs run faster. It's not a secret that a programmer with strong problem-solving skills is more desired in the market. Problem-solving skills are gained first of all by deeply understanding the fundamental algorithms and data structures. As you've seen already in this chapter, leveraging a binary search algorithm in searching tasks makes the code run much faster compared to its sequential alternative. Efficient software saves time and provides a better user experience, which eventually makes your software an outstanding alternative to existing ones.

In this chapter, we have discussed fundamental data structures and their differences. We learned to use them based on problem analysis. For example, applying a linked list in problems requiring random lookups is considered time-consuming because of the complexity of the linked-list element access operations. In such scenarios, using a dynamically growing vector is more appropriate due to its constant-time element access. On the contrary, using a vector in problems requiring fast insertions at the front of the container is more expensive compared to, for example, the list.

The chapter also introduced algorithms and ways to measure their efficiency. We compared several problems to apply better algorithms to solve them more efficiently.

In the next chapter, we are going to discuss functional programming in C++. Having studied the essentials of the STL, we are now going to apply functional programming techniques on containers.

Questions

1. Describe the insertion of an element into a dynamically growing vector.
2. What's the difference between inserting an element at the front of a linked list and at the front of a vector?
3. Implement a hybrid data structure that will store its elements in both a vector and a list. For each operation, choose the underlying data structure with the fastest implementation of the operation.
4. How would a binary search tree look if we insert 100 elements in increasing order?
5. What is the difference between the selection sort and insertion sort algorithms?
6. Implement the sorting algorithm described in the chapter, known as the counting sort.

Further reading

For more information, refer to the following resources:

- *Programming Pearls* by Jon Bentley, available from `https://www.amazon.com/Programming-Pearls-2nd-Jon-Bentley/dp/0201657880/`
- *Data Abstraction and Problem Solving Using C++: Walls and Mirrors* by Frank Carrano,and Timothy Henry, available from `https://www.amazon.com/Data-Abstraction-Problem-Solving-Mirrors/dp/0134463978/`
- *Introduction to Algorithms* by Cormen, Leiserson, Rivest, and Stein, available from `https://www.amazon.com/Introduction-Algorithms-3rd-MIT-Press/dp/0262033844/`
- *C++ Data Structures and Algorithms* by Wisnu Anggoro, available from `https://www.packtpub.com/application-development/c-data-structures-and-algorithms`

7
Functional Programming

Object-Oriented Programming (**OOP**) provides us with a way of thinking about objects, thus expressing the real world in terms of classes and their relationships. Functional programming is a completely different programming paradigm as it allows us to concentrate on the *functional* structure rather than the *physical* structure of code. Learning and using functional programming are useful in two ways. First, it is a new paradigm that forces you to think very differently. Solving problems requires having flexible thinking. People that are attached to a single paradigm tend to provide similar solutions to any problem, while most elegant solutions require a wider approach. Mastering functional programming provides developers with a new skill that helps them provide even better solutions to problems. Secondly, using functional programming reduces the number of bugs in software. One of the biggest reasons for that functional programming's unique approach: it decomposes programs into functions, each of which doesn't modify the state of the data.

We will discuss the fundamental blocks of functional programming in this chapter, along with ranges. Introduced in C++20, ranges provide us with a great way to compose algorithms so that they work with collections of data. Composing algorithms so that we can apply them to this collection of data sequentially is at the heart of functional programming. That's why we'll also discuss ranges in this chapter.

The following topics will be covered in this chapter:

- Introduction to functional programming
- Introduction to the ranges library
- Pure functions
- Higher-order functions
- Delving more deeply into recursion
- Metaprogramming in functional C++

Technical requirements

The g++ compiler, along with the `-std=c++2a` option, will be used to compile the examples in this chapter.

You can find the source files for this chapter at `https://github.com/PacktPublishing/Expert-CPP`.

Unveiling functional programming

As we mentioned earlier, functional programming is a programming paradigm. You can think of a paradigm as a way of thinking when constructing programs. C++ is a multi-paradigm language. We can use it to develop programs in a procedural paradigm, that is, by executing statements one after one another. In Chapter 3, *Details of Object-Oriented Programming*, we discussed the object-oriented approach, which involves decomposing a complex system into intercommunicating objects. Functional programming, on the other hand, encourages us to decompose the system into functions rather than objects. It operates with expressions rather than statements. Basically, you take something as input and pass it to a function that produces an output. This can then be used as input for another function. This might seem simple at first, but functional programming incorporates several rules and practices that feel hard to grasp initially. However, when you manage this, your brain will unlock a new way of thinking – the functional way.

To make this a bit clearer, let's start with an example that will demonstrate the essence of functional programming. Let's suppose we have been given a list of integers and need to count the number of even numbers in it. The only catch is that there are several such vectors. We should count the even numbers in all vectors separately and produce a result as a new vector containing the results of the calculation for each input vector.

The input is provided as a matrix, that is, a vector of vectors. The simplest way to express this in C++ is by using the following type:

```
std::vector<std::vector<int>>
```

We can simplify the preceding code even more by using type aliases, as follows:

```
using IntMatrix = std::vector<std::vector<int>>;
```

The following is an illustration of this problem. We have a bunch of vectors containing integers, and as a result we should get a vector containing a count of even numbers:

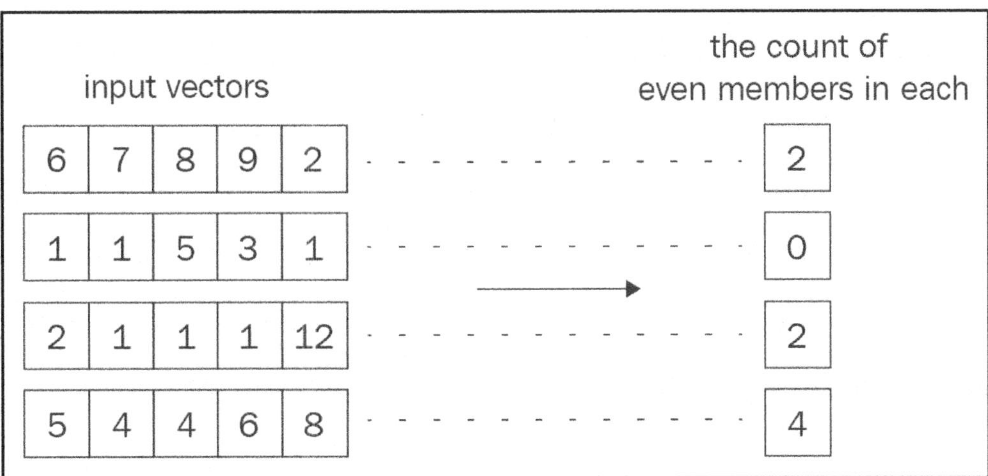

Look at the following function. It takes a vector of integer vectors (also known as a matrix) as its argument. The function counts the number of even numbers:

```
std::vector<int> count_all_evens(const IntMatrix& numbers)
{
  std::vector<int> even_numbers_count;
  for (const auto& number_line: numbers) {
    int even{0};
    for (const auto& number: number_line) {
      if (number % 2 == 0) {
        ++even;
      }
    }
    even_numbers_count.push_back(even);
  }
  return even_numbers_count;
}
```

The preceding function keeps a separate vector to store the count of even numbers for each vector. The input is provided as a vector of vectors, which is why the function loops over the first vector to retrieve the inner vectors. For each retrieved vector, it loops over it and increments a counter each time it encounters an even number in the vector. After completing the loop for each vector, the final result is pushed to the vector containing the list of numbers. While you might wish to go back to the preceding example and make the code better, we'll move on for now and decompose it into smaller functions. First, we move the portion of the code responsible for counting the even numbers into a separate function.

Let's name it `count_evens`, as follows:

```
int count_evens(const std::vector<int>& number_line) {
  return std::count_if(number_line.begin(),
       number_line.end(), [](int num){return num % 2 == 0;});
}
```

Note how we applied the `count_if()` algorithm. It takes two iterators and puts them at the beginning and the end of the container, respectively. It also takes a third parameter, a *unary predicate*, which is called for each element of the collection. We passed a lambda as a unary predicate. You can use any other callable entity too, such as a function pointer, an `std::` function, and so on.

Now that we have a separate counting function, we can call it in the original `count_all_evens()` function. The following implementation of `count_all_evens()` expresses functional programming in C++:

```
std::vector<int> count_all_evens(const std::vector<std::vector<int>>&
numbers) {
  return numbers | std::ranges::views::transform(count_evens);
}
```

Before delving into the preceding code, let's agree on the first thing that catches our eye – not the weird use of the `|` operator, but the conciseness of the code. Compare it to the version of the code we introduced at the beginning of this section. They both do the same job, but the second one – the functional one – does it more concisely. Also, note that the function doesn't keep or change any state. It has no side-effects. This is crucial in functional programming because a function must be a *pure* function. It takes an argument, then processes it without modifying it, and returns a new value (usually based on the input). The first challenge in functional programming is decomposing a task into smaller independent functions that are easily composed.

Although we came to the functional solution from an imperative one, it's not the right way to use it when leveraging the functional programming paradigm. Instead of writing the imperative code first and modifying it to get the functional version, you should change the way you think and how you approach the problem. You should tame the process of thinking functionally. The problem of counting all the even numbers leads to our solving the problem for one vector. If we can find a way to solve the problem for a single vector, we can solve the problem for all the vectors. The `count_evens()` function takes a vector and produces a single value, as shown in the following screenshot:

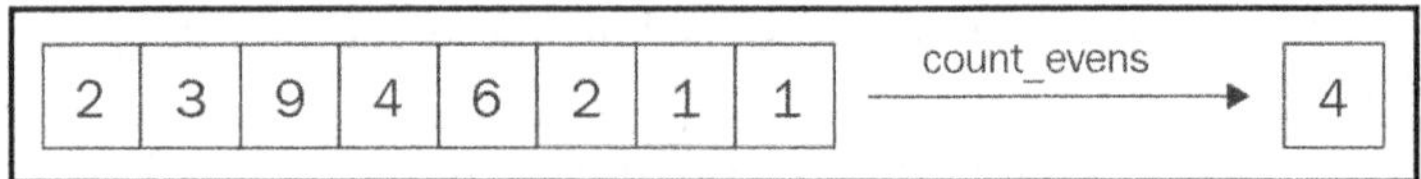

After solving the problem for one vector, we should move on to the original problem by applying the solution to all the vectors. The `std::transform()` function essentially does what we need: it takes a function that can be applied to a single value and transforms it in order to process a collection. The following image illustrates how we use it to implement a function (`count_all_evens`) that can process a collection of items from functions (`count_evens`) that process only one item at a time:

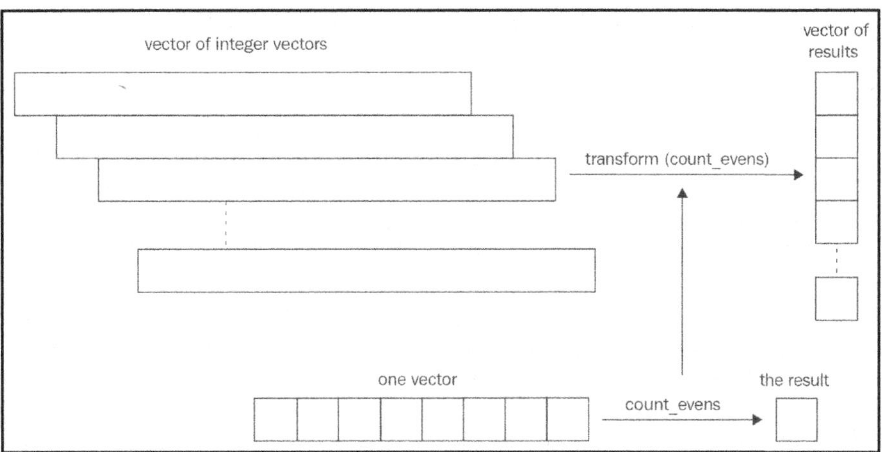

Splitting bigger problems into smaller, independent tasks is at the heart of functional programming. Each function is specialized to do one simple enough task without realizing the original problem. Functions are then composed together to generate a collection of transformed items from the raw initial input.

Now, the final version of the `count_all_evens()` function leverages ranges. Let's find out what they are and how to use them because we will need them in further examples.

Using ranges

Ranges are tied to views. We will examine them both in this section. We discussed STL containers and algorithms in `Chapter 6`, *Digging into Data Structures and Algorithms in STL*. They provide us with a generic approach to composing and working with collections of objects. As you already know, we use iterators a lot to loop over containers and work with their elements. Iterators are tools that allow us to have loose coupling between algorithms and containers.

For example, earlier, we applied `count_if()` to the vector, but `count_if()` is not aware of what container it is was applied to. Take a look at the following declaration of `count_if()`:

```
template <typename InputIterator, typename UnaryPredicate>
constexpr typename iterator_traits<InputIterator>::difference_type
  count_if(InputIterator first, InputIterator last, UnaryPredicate p);
```

As you can see, besides its verbose declaration, which is specific to C++, `count_if()` doesn't take a container as an argument. Instead, it operates with iterators – specifically, input iterators.

An input iterator supports iterating forward using the `++` operator and accessing each element using the `*` operator. We also can compare input iterators using the `==` and `!=` relationships.

Algorithms iterate over containers without actually knowing the exact type of the container. We can use `count_if()` on any entity that has a beginning and an end, as follows:

```
#include <array>
#include <iostream>
#include <algorithm>

int main()
{
  std::array<int, 4> arr{1, 2, 3, 4};
  auto res = std::count_if(arr.cbegin(), arr.cend(),
    [](int x){ return x == 3; });
  std::cout << "There are " << res << " number of elements equal to 3";
}
```

Besides their generic nature, algorithms don't compose well. Usually, we apply an algorithm to a collection and store the result of the algorithm as another collection that we can apply to more algorithms in the same manner at a later date. We use `std::transform()` to put the results into another container. For example, the following code defines a vector of Products:

```
// consider the Product is already declared and has a "name", "price", and
"weight"
// also consider the get_products() is defined
// and returns a vector of Product instances

using ProductList = std::vector<std::shared_ptr<Product>>;
ProductList vec{get_products()};
```

Suppose that the project has been developed by a different team of programmers and they chose to keep the name of a product as any number; for example, 1 is for an apple, 2 is for a peach, and so on. This means that `vec` will contain `Product` instances, each of which will have a number character in its `name` field (whereas the name's type is `std::string` – this is why we keep the number as a character instead of its integer value). Now, our task is to transform the names of Products from numbers into full strings (`apple`, `peach`, and so on). We can use `std::transform` for this:

```
ProductList full_named_products; // type alias has been defined above
using ProductPtr = std::shared_ptr<Product>;
std::transform(vec.cbegin(), vec.cend(),
  std::back_inserter(full_named_products),
  [](ProductPtr p){ /* modify the name and return */ });
```

After executing the preceding code, the `full_named_products` vector will contain Products with full product names. Now, to filter out all the apples and copy them to a vector of apples, we need to use `std::copy_if`:

```
ProductList apples;
std::copy_if(full_named_products.cbegin(), full_named_products.cend(),
  std::back_inserter(apples),
  [](ProductPtr p){ return p->name() == "apple"; });
```

One of the biggest disadvantages of the preceding code examples is the lack of nice composition until the introduction of ranges. Ranges provide us with an elegant way to work with container elements and compose algorithms.

Simply put, a range is a traversable entity; that is, a range has a `begin()` and an `end()`, much like the containers we've worked with so far. In these terms, every STL container can be treated as a range. STL algorithms are redefined to take ranges as direct arguments. By doing this, they allow us to pass a result from one algorithm directly to the other instead of storing intermediary results in local variables. For instance, `std::transform`, which we used earlier with a `begin()` and an `end()`, has the following form if applied to a range (the following code is pseudocode). By using ranges, we can rewrite the previous example in the following way:

```
ProductList apples = filter(
  transform(vec, [](ProductPtr p){/* normalize the name */}),
  [](ProductPtr p){return p->name() == "apple";}
);
```

Don't forget to import the `<ranges>` header. The transform function will return a range containing `Product` pointers whose names are normalized; that is, the numeric value is replaced with a string value.The filter function will then take the result and return the range of products that have `apple` as their name.

Note that we simplified these code examples by omitting `std::ranges::views` from in front of the `filter` and `transform` functions. Use them as `std::ranges::views::filter` and `std::ranges::views::transform`, accordingly.

Finally, the overloaded operator, `|`, which we used in the example at the beginning of this chapter, allows us to pipe ranges together. This way, we can compose algorithms to produce a final result, as follows:

```
ProductList apples = vec | transform([](ProductPtr p){/* normalize the name
*/})
                         | filter([](ProductPtr p){return p->name() ==
"apple";});
```

We used piping instead of nesting function calls. This might be confusing at first because we used to use the `|` operator as a bitwise OR. Whenever you see it applied to a collection, it refers to piping ranges.

The `|` operator is inspired by the Unix shell pipe operator. In Unix, we can pipe the results of several processes together; for example, `ls -l | grep cpp | less` will find `cpp` in the result of the `ls` command and show the final result one screen at a time using the `less` program.

As we already stated, a range is an abstraction over a collection. This doesn't mean it's a collection. That's why the previous example doesn't carry any overhead – it just passes a range from a function to function, where the range just provides the beginning and the end of a collection. Also, it allows us to access the underlying collection elements. The following diagram illuminates this idea:

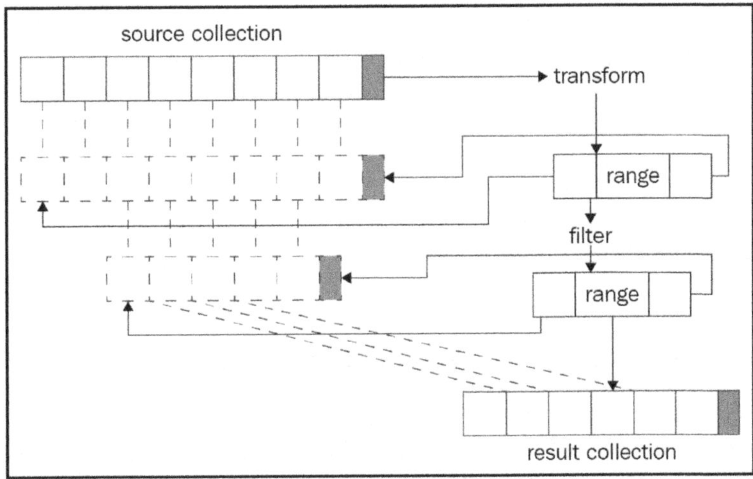

The function (either **transform** or **filter**) returns a range structure instead of a collection. The `begin()` iterator of the range will point to the element in the source collection that satisfies the predicate. The range's iterator is a proxy object: it differs from a regular iterator in that it points to an element that satisfies the given predicate. We sometimes refer to them as **smart iterators** because, every time we advance it (by incrementing, for example), it finds the next element in the collection that satisfies the predicate. What's more interesting is that the "smartness" of the iterator depends on the kind of function we apply to the collection. For example, the `filter()` function returns a range that has smart iterators for their increment operator. This is mostly because the result of a filter might contain fewer elements than the original collection. Transform, on the other hand, doesn't return a result with a reduced number of elements – it just transforms the elements. This means that a range that's returned by transform has the same functionality for increment/decrement operations, but the element access will differ. For each access, the smart iterator of the range will return the transformed element from the original collection. In other words, it simply implements the `*()` operator for the iterator, similar to what can be seen in the following code snippet:

```
auto operator*()
{
  return predicate(*current_position);
}
```

This way, we are creating a new *view* of the collection rather than a new collection of transformed elements. The same applies to `filter` and other functions. More interestingly, range views leverage *lazy evaluation*. For our preceding example, even if we have two range transformations, the result is produced by evaluating them in a single pass.

In the example with `transform` and `filter`, each of the functions defines a view, but they don't modify or evaluate anything. When we assign the result to the result collection, the vector is constructed from the view by accessing each element. That's where the evaluation happens.

It's as simple as that – ranges provide us with function composition with lazy evaluation. We briefly touched on the toolset that's used in functional programming earlier. Now, let's find out about the benefits of the paradigm.

Why use functional programming?

First of all, functional programming introduces conciseness. The code is much shorter compared to its imperative counterparts. It provides simple but highly expressive tools. When there's less code, fewer bugs will crop up.

Functions don't mutate anything, which makes it much easier to parallelize them. This is one of the main concerns in concurrent programs because concurrent tasks need to share mutable data between them. Most of the time, you have to explicitly synchronize threads using primitives such as mutexes. Functional programming frees us from explicit synchronization and we can run the code on multiple threads without adapting it. In `chapter 8`, *Digging into Data Structures*, we will discuss data races in detail.

The functional paradigm considers all functions as *pure*; that is, functions that do not mutate the program state. They simply take input, transform it in a user-defined manner, and provide an output. A pure function generates the same result for the same input, independent of how many times it has been invoked. Whenever we speak about functional programming, we should take all pure functions into account by default.

The following function takes a `double` as its input and returns its square:

```
double square(double num) { return num * num; }
```

Writing solely pure functions might feel like intentionally making the program run slower.

Some compilers, such as GCC, provide attributes that help the compiler optimize the code. For example, the `[[gnu::pure]]` attribute tells the compiler that the function can be considered a pure function. This will reassure the compiler that the function doesn't access any global variable and that the function's result depends solely on its input.

There are numerous scenarios where a *regular* function could bring a faster solution. However, in order to adapt to the paradigm, you should force yourself to think functionally. For example, the following program declares a vector and calculates the square roots of its elements:

```
void calc_square_roots(std::vector<double>& vec)
{
  for (auto& elem : vec) {
    elem = std::sqrt(elem);
  }
}

int main()
{
  std::vector<double> vec{1.1, 2.2, 4.3, 5.6, 2.4};
  calc_square_roots(vec);
}
```

Here, we're passing the vector by reference. This means that, if we change it in the function, we change the original collection. This obviously isn't a pure function because it mutates the input vector. A functional alternative would return the transformed elements in a new vector, leaving the input untouched:

```
std::vector<double> pure_calc_square_roots(const std::vector<double>& vec)
{
  std::vector<double> new_vector;
  for (const auto& elem : vec) {
    new_vector.push_back(std::sqrt(elem));
  }
  return new_vector;
}
```

An even better example of functional thinking is to solve a smaller problem and apply it to the collection. The smaller problem, in this case, is calculating the square root of a single number, which is already implemented as `std::sqrt`. Applying it to the collection is done with `std::ranges::views::transform`, as follows:

```
#include <ranges>
#include <vector>

int main()
{
 std::vector<double> vec{1.1, 2.2, 4.3, 5.6, 2.4};
 auto result = vec | std::ranges::views::transform(std::sqrt);
}
```

As we already know, by using ranges we can avoid storing intermediary objects. In the previous example, we applied `transform` directly to the vector. `transform` returns a view, but not a full collection consisting of the transformed elements of the source vector. The actual transformed copies of elements are made when we construct the `result` vector. Also, note that `std::sqrt` is considered to be a pure function.

The example that we solved at the beginning of this chapter gave us the necessary perspective for functional programming. To get a better grasp of this paradigm, we should become familiar with its principles. In the next section, we will delve into the principles of functional programming so that you have an even better idea of how and when to use the paradigm.

Principles of functional programming

Although the functional paradigm is old (it was born in the 1950s), it didn't take the world of programming by storm. Most of the dominant paradigms these days include imperative and object-oriented languages. As we've stated many times in this and many other books, C++ is a **multi-paradigm language**. That's the beauty of studying C++; we can tune it to fit almost every environment. Grasping the paradigm is not an easy task. You have to feel it and apply it until you finally start thinking in terms of the paradigm. After that, you will see solutions to regular tasks in a matter of seconds.

If you can remember when you first time learned about object-oriented programming, you might recall the principles that made you struggle a bit before you could unlock the true potential of OOP. The same is true for functional programming. In this section, we are going to discuss the basic concepts of functional programming that will be the base for further development. You can apply (or have already done so) some of these concepts without actually using the functional paradigm. However, try to put some effort into understanding and applying each of the following principles.

Pure functions

As we mentioned previously, a *function is pure if it doesn't mutate the state*. Pure functions can be treated as less performant compared to their non-pure counterparts; however, they are great as they avoid most of the bugs that can arise in code due to state modifications. The bugs are related to the program state in some way. Obviously, programs work with data, so they compose state-modifying functionality that leads to some expected results for the end user.

In object-oriented programming, we decompose the program into objects, each of which has a list of special features. One of the fundamental features of an object in OOP is its *state*. Modifying an object's state by sending messages to it (in other words, calling its methods) is crucial in OOP. Usually, a member function invocation leads to the object state's modification. In functional programming, we organize code into a collection of pure functions, each of which has its own purpose and is independent of the others.

Let's take a look at a simple example, just to make this concept clear. Let's say we're dealing with user objects in a program and each user object contains the age associated with the user. The `User` type is described as a `struct` in the following code block:

```
struct User
{
  int age;
  string name;
  string phone_number;
  string email;
};
```

There is a need to update users' ages on a yearly basis. Let's suppose we have a function that is being invoked for each `User` object once a year. The following function takes a `User` object as input and increases its `age` by `1`:

```
void update_age(User& u)
{
  u.age = u.age + 1;
}
```

The `update_age()` function takes the input by reference and updates the original object. This is not the case in functional programming. Instead of taking the original object by reference and mutating its value, the following pure function returns a totally different `user` object with the same properties, except for the updated `age` property:

```
User pure_update_age(const User& u) // cannot modify the input argument
{
  User tmp{u};
  tmp.age = tmp.age + 1;
  return tmp;
}
```

Though it seems inefficient compared to `update_age()`, one of the pros of this approach is that it makes operations crystal clear (this is really useful when we're debugging code). Now, it's guaranteed that `pure_update_age()` won't modify the original object. We can modify the preceding code so that it will take the object by value. This way, we will skip creating the `tmp` object as the argument itself represents a copy:

```
User pure_update_age(User u) // u is the copy of the passed object
{
  u.age = u.age + 1;
  return u;
}
```

If a pure function is called multiple times with the same arguments, it must return the same result every time. The following code demonstrates that our `pure_update_age()` function returns the same value when it's given the same input:

```
User john{.age{21}, .name{"John"}};

auto updated{pure_update_age(john)};
std::cout << updated.age; // prints 22

updated = pure_update_age(john);
std::cout << updated.age; // prints 22
```

It is a great benefit for a function to behave the same way each time it is called for the same input data. This means we can design the logic of the application by decomposing it into smaller functions, each of which has an exact and clear purpose. However, there is overhead for the pure function in terms of the additional temporary object. A regular design involves having a centralized store that contains the program state, which is updated indirectly by pure functions. After each pure function invocation, the function returns the modified object as a new object that can be stored if necessary. You can think of it as tweaking the code to omit passing the entire object.

Higher-order functions

In functional programming, functions are considered *first-class* objects (you might encounter first-class citizens as well). This means we should treat them as objects rather than a set of instructions. What difference does this make to us? Well, the only thing that is important at this point for a function to be treated as an object is the ability to pass it to other functions. Functions that take other functions as arguments are called **higher-order functions**.

It's not uncommon for C++ programmers to pass one function into another. Here's how this can be done the old-school way:

```
typedef  void (*PF)(int);
void foo(int arg)
{
  // do something with arg
}

int bar(int arg, PF f)
{
  f(arg);
  return arg;
}

bar(42, foo);
```

In the preceding code, we declared a pointer to a function. `PF` represents a type definition for the function, takes one integer parameter, and doesn't return any value. The previous example is a popular way of passing pointers functions to other functions as arguments. We treat the function as an object. However, this depends on what we understand by an *object*.

In the previous chapters, we defined an object as something that has a state. This means that, if we treat a function as an object, we should also be able to somehow change its state if needed. For function pointers, this isn't the case. Here's a better way to pass a function to another function:

```
class Function
{
public:
  void modify_state(int a) {
    state_ = a;
  }

  int get_state() {
    return state_;
  }

  void operator()() {
    // do something that a function would do
  }
private:
  int state_;
};

void foo(Function f)
```

```
{
  f();
  // some other useful code
}
```

Take a good look at the preceding code . It declares a class that has an overloaded `operator()`. Whenever we overload the operator of a class, we make it *callable*. And as obvious as it may sound, anything that is callable is treated as a function. So, an object of a class that has an overloaded `operator()` could be considered a function (sometimes. it's referred to as a *functor*). This is like a trick in a way because instead of making a function an object, we made an object callable. However, this allowed us to achieve what we were looking for: a function that has a state. The following client code demonstrates that a `Function` object has a state:

```
void foo(Function f)
{
  f();
  f.modify_state(11);
  cout << f.get_state(); // get the state
  f(); // call the "function"
}
```

By doing this, we can, for example, track how many times the function has been called. Here's a simple example that tracks the number of calls:

```
class Function
{
public:
  void operator()() {
    // some useful stuff
    ++called_;
  }

private:
  int called_ = 0;
};
```

Finally, `std::function`, which is defined in the `<functional>` header in the following code, demonstrates another way of defining a higher-order function:

```
#include <functional>

void print_it(int a) {
  cout << a;
}

std::function<void(int)> function_object = print_it;
```

When `function_object` is called (using `operator()`), it delegates the call to the `print_it` function. `std::function` encapsulates any function and allows it to work with it as an object (and pass it to other functions as well).

The functions in the preceding examples that took other functions as arguments are all examples of higher-order functions. A function that returns a function is also called a higher-order function. To sum this up, a higher-order function is a function that takes or returns another function or functions. Take a look at the following example:

```
#include <functional>
#include <iostream>

std::function<int (int, int)> get_multiplier()
{
  return [](int a, int b) { return a * b; };
}

int main()
{
  auto multiply = get_multiplier();
  std::cout << multiply(3, 5) << std::endl; // outputs 15
}
```

`get_multiplier()` returns a lambda wrapped in `std::function`. Then, we call the result, just like we would call a regular function. The `get_multiplier()` function is a higher-order function. We can implement **currying** using a higher-order function, similar to what we did in the preceding example. In functional programming, currying is where we make a function take several arguments into several functions, each of which takes a single argument; for example, making `multiply(3, 5)` into `multiply(3)(5)`. Here's how we can achieve this:

```
std::function<int(int)> multiply(int a)
{
  return [a](int b) { return a * b; };
}

int main()
{
  std::cout << multiply(3)(5) << std::endl;
}
```

`multiply()` takes one argument and returns a function that also takes a single argument. Pay attention to the lambda capture: it captures the value of `a` so that it can multiply it by `b` in its body.

Currying is a reference to logician Haskell Curry. The Haskell, Brook, and Curry programming languages are also named after him.

One of the most useful features of currying is having abstract functions that we can compose together. We can create specialized versions of `multiply()` and pass them to other functions, or use them wherever they're applicable. This can be seen in the following code:

```
auto multiplyBy22 = multiply(22);
auto fiveTimes = multiply(5);

std::cout << multiplyBy22(10); // outputs 220
std::cout << fiveTimes(4); // outputs 20
```

You must've used a higher-order function when working with the STL. Many STL algorithms take predicates to filter out or process collections of objects. For example, the `std::find_if` function finds the element that satisfies the passed predicate object, as shown in the following example:

```
std::vector<int> elems{1, 2, 3, 4, 5, 6};
std::find_if(elems.begin(), elems.end(), [](int el) {return el % 3 == 0;});
```

`std::find_if` takes a lambda as its predicate and calls it for all the elements in the vector. Whichever element satisfies the condition is returned as the requested one.

Another example of a higher-order function would be `std::transform`, which we introduced at the beginning of this chapter (not to be confused with `ranges::view::transform`). Let's use it to transform a string into uppercase letters:

```
std::string str = "lowercase";
std::transform(str.begin(), str.end(), str.begin(),
  [](unsigned char c) { return std::toupper(c); });
std::cout << str; // "LOWERCASE"
```

The third parameter is the beginning of the container and is where the `std::transform` function inserts its current results.

Folding

Folding (or reduction) is the process of combining a collection of values together to generate a reduced number of results. Most of the time, we're speaking about a single result. Folding abstracts the process of iterating over structures that are recursive in nature. For example, a linked list or a vector has a recursive nature in terms of element access. While the recursive nature of the vector is arguable, we will consider it recursive since it allows us to access its elements by repeatedly incrementing the index. To work with such structures, we usually keep track of the result at each step and process the next item to be combined with the previous result later. Folding is called *left* or *right* folding based on the direction we process the collection elements in.

For example, the `std::accumulate` function (another example of a higher-order function) is a perfect example of folding functionality because it combines values in the collection. Take a look at the following simple example:

```
std::vector<double> elems{1.1, 2.2, 3.3, 4.4, 5.5};
auto sum = std::accumulate(elems.begin(), elems.end(), 0);
```

The last argument to the function is the accumulator. This is the initial value that should be used as the previous value for the first element of the collection. The preceding code calculates the sum of the vector elements. It's the default behavior of the `std::accumulate` function. As we mentioned previously, it is a higher-order function, which implies that a function could be passed as its argument. This will then be called for each element to produce the desired result. For example, let's find the product of the `elems` vector we declared previously:

```
auto product = std::accumulate(elems.begin(), elems.end(), 1,
  [](int prev, int cur) { return prev * cur; });
```

It takes a binary operation; that is, a function with two arguments. The first argument of the operation is the previous value that's been calculated so far, while the second argument is the current value. The result of the binary operation will be the previous value for the next step. The preceding code can be rewritten in a concise way using one of the existing operations in the STL:

```
auto product = std::accumulate(elems.begin(), elems.end(), 1,
  std::multiplies<int>());
```

A better alternative to the `std::accumulate` function is the `std::reduce` function. `reduce()` is similar to `accumulate()`, except it doesn't keep the order of the operation; that is, it doesn't necessarily process the collection elements sequentially. You can pass an execution policy to the `std::reduce` function and change its behavior, say, to processing elements in parallel. Here's how the reduce function can be applied to the `elems` vector from the previous example using the parallel execution policy:

```
std::reduce(std::execution::par, elems.begin(), elems.end(),
  1, std::multiplies<int>());
```

Though `std::reduce` seems faster compared to `std::accumulate`, you should be careful when using it with non-commutative binary operations.

Folding and recursion go hand in hand. Recursive functions also solve a problem by decomposing it into smaller tasks and solving them one by one.

Diving deeper into recursion

We've already discussed the main features of a recursive function in `Chapter 2`, *Low-level Programming with C++*. Let's take a look at the following simple example of calculating the factorial of a number recursively:

```
int factorial(int n)
{
  if (n <= 1) return 1;
  return n * factorial(n - 1);
}
```

Recursive functions provide elegant solutions compared to their iterative counterparts. However, you should carefully approach the decision to use recursion. One of the most popular issues with recursive functions is stack overflows.

Head recursion

Head recursion is the regular recursion that we are already familiar with. In the preceding example, the factorial function behaves as a head recursive function, meaning that it makes the recursive call before processing the result at the current step. Take a look at the following line from the factorial function:

```
...
return n * factorial(n - 1);
...
```

To find and return the result of the product, the function factorial is called with a reduced argument, that is, `(n - 1)`. This means that the product (the `*` operator) is kind of *on hold* and is waiting for its second argument to be returned by `factorial(n - 1)`. The stack grows in line with the number of recursive calls to the function. Let's try to compare the recursive factorial implementation with the following iterative approach:

```
int factorial(int n)
{
  int result = 1;
  for (int ix = n; ix > 1; --ix) {
    result *= ix;
  }
  return result;
}
```

One of the main differences here is the fact that we store the result of the product at each step in the same variable (named `result`). With this in mind, let's try to decompose the recursive implementation of the factorial function.

It's clear that each function call takes up a specified space on the stack. Each result at each step should be stored somewhere on the stack. Although we know that it should, and even must, be the same variable, the recursive function doesn't care; it allocates space for its variables. The counter-intuitiveness of regular recursive functions prompts us to find a solution that somehow knows that the result of each recursive call should be stored in the same place.

Tail recursion

Tail recursion is the solution to the problem of having multiple unnecessary variables that we deal with in recursive functions. The basic idea of tail-recursive functions is doing the actual processing before the recursive call. Here's how we can transform the factorial function into a tail-recursive one:

```
int tail_factorial(int n, int result)
{
  if (n <= 1) return result;
  return tail_factorial(n - 1, n * result);
}
```

Pay attention to the new argument of the function. Carefully reading the preceding code gives us a basic idea of the tail-recursion that's occurring: the processing is done before the recursive call. Before `tail_factorial` is called again in its body, the current result is calculated (`n * result`) and passed to it.

While this idea might not seem fascinating, it is really efficient if **Tail Call Optimization (TCO)** is supported by the compiler. TCO basically involves knowing that the second argument of the factorial function (the tail) can be stored at the same location for every recursive call. This allows for the stack to stay the same size, independent of the number of recursive calls.

Speaking of compiler optimizations, we can't omit template metaprogramming. We're mentioning it here alongisde compiler optimizations because we can treat metaprogramming as the biggest optimization that can be done to the program. It's always better to do calculations at compile time than at runtime.

Metaprogramming in functional C++

Metaprogramming can be treated as another programming paradigm. It's a totally different approach to coding because we are not dealing with the regular process of programming. By a regular process, we mean the three phases that a program goes through in its lifetime: coding, compiling, and running. It's obvious that a program does what it's supposed to do when it is executed. An executable is generated by the compiler through compilation and linking. Metaprogramming, on the other hand, is where the code is being *executed* during the compilation of the code. This might sound magical if you are dealing with it for the first time. How can we execute code if the program doesn't even exist yet? Recalling what we learned about templates in `Chapter 4`, *Understanding and Designing Templates*, we know that the compiler processes them with more than one pass. In the first pass, the compiler defines the necessary types and parameters that are used in the template class or function. With the next pass, the compiler starts to compile them in the way we're familiar with; that is, it generates some code that will be linked by the linker to produce the final executable file.

Since metaprogramming is something that happens during code compilation, we should already have an idea of which concepts and constructs of the language are used. Anything that can be calculated at compile-time can be used as a metaprogramming construct, such as templates.

Here's the classic mind-blowing example of metaprogramming in C++:

```
template <int N>
struct MetaFactorial
{
  enum {
    value = N * MetaFactorial<N - 1>::value
  };
};
```

```
template <>
struct MetaFactorial<0>
{
  enum {
    value = 1
  };
};

int main() {
  std::cout << MetaFactorial<5>::value; // outputs 120
  std::cout << MetaFactorial<6>::value; // outputs 720
}
```

Why would we bother to write so much code just for a factorial that we wrote in the previous section in fewer than five lines of code? The reason is due to its efficiency. While it will take a little bit more time to compile the code, it is super efficient compared to the normal factorial function (implemented either recursively or iteratively). And the reason behind this efficiency is the fact that the actual calculation of the factorial is happening at compile time. That is, when the executable is run, the results are already ready to use. We just used the calculated value when we run the program; no calculation happens at runtime. If you're seeing this code for the first time, the following explanation will make you fall in love with metaprogramming.

Let's decompose and analyze the preceding code in detail. First of all, the `MetaFactorial` template is declared with a single `enum` with a `value` property. This `enum` is chosen solely because its properties are calculated at compile time. So, whenever we access the value property of `MetaFactorial`, it is already being calculated (evaluated) at compile time. Take a look at the actual value of the enumeration. It makes a recursive dependency from the same `MetaFactorial` class:

```
template <int N>
struct MetaFactorial
{
  enum {
    value = N * MetaFactorial<N - 1>::value
  };
};
```

Some of you may have already noticed the trick here. `MetaFactorial<N - 1>` is not the same struct as `MetaFactorial<N>`. Although it has the same name, each template with a different type or value is generated as a separate new type. So, let's say we call something like the following:

```
std::cout << MetaFactorial<3>::value;
```

Here, the hard-working compiler generates three different structs for each value (the following is some pseudocode representing how we should picture the compiler working):

```
struct MetaFactorial<3>
{
  enum {
    value = 3 * MetaFactorial<2>::value
  };
};

struct MetaFactorial<2>
{
  enum {
    value = 2 * MetaFactorial<1>::value;
  };
};

struct MetaFactorial<1>
{
  enum {
    value = 1 * MetaFactorial<0>::value;
  };
};
```

In the next pass, the compiler replaces each of the generated struct's values with their respective numeric values, as shown in the following pseudocode:

```
struct MetaFactorial<3>
{
  enum {
   value = 3 * 2
  };
};

struct MetaFactorial<2>
{
  enum {
    value = 2 * 1
  };
};

struct MetaFactorial<1>
{
  enum {
    value = 1 * 1
  };
};
```

Then, the compiler removes the unused generated structs, leaving only `MetaFactorial<3>`, which is, again, only used as `MetaFactorial<3>::value`. This can also be optimized. By doing this, we get the following result:

```
std::cout << 6;
```

Compare this with the previous line we had:

```
std::cout << MetaFactorial<3>::value;
```

That's the beauty of metaprogramming F— it's done at compile time and leaves no trace, like a ninja. The compilation takes longer but the execution of the program is the fastest it can possibly be compared to regular solutions. We suggest that you try implementing meta-versions of other cost-expensive calculations, such as calculating the nth Fibonacci number. It's not as easy as coding for *runtime* rather than *compile-time*, but you already have a sense of its power.

Summary

In this chapter, we got a new perspective when it comes to using C++. As a multi-paradigm language, it can be used as a functional programming language.

We learned the main principles of functional programming, such as pure functions, higher-order functions, and folding. Pure functions are functions that do not mutate the state. One of the pros of pure functions is that they leave fewer bugs that would otherwise be introduced because of state mutations.

Higher-order functions are functions that take or return other functions. Other than in functional programming, C++ programmers use higher-order functions when dealing with the STL.

Pure functions, along with higher-order functions, allow us to decompose the whole application into a big *assembly line* of functions. Each function in this assembly line is responsible for receiving data and returning a new, modified version of the original data (without mutating the original state). When combined, these functions provide a well-coordinated line of tasks.

In the next chapter, we will dive into multithreaded programming and discuss the thread support library components that were introduced in C++.

Questions

1. List the advantages of ranges.
2. What functions are known to be pure?
3. What's the difference between a pure virtual function and a pure function in terms of functional programming?
4. What is folding?
5. What is the advantage of tail recursion over head recursion?

Further reading

For more information regarding what was covered in this chapter, please take a look at the following links:

- *Learning C++ Functional Programming* by Wisnu Anggoro: `https://www.packtpub.com/application-development/learning-c-functional-programming`
- *Functional Programming in C++: How to Improve Your C++ Programs Using Functional Techniques* by Ivan Cukic: `https://www.amazon.com/Functional-Programming-programs-functional-techniques/dp/1617293814/`

8

Concurrency and Multithreading

Concurrent programming allows the creation of more efficient programs. C++ didn't have built-in support for concurrency or multithreading for a long time. Now it has full support for concurrent programming, threads, thread synchronization objects, and other functionality that we will discuss in this chapter.

Before the language updated for thread support, programmers had to use third-party libraries. One of the most popular multithreading solutions was **POSIX** (**Portable Operating System Interface**) threads. C++ introduced thread support since C++11. It makes the language even more robust and applicable to wider areas of software development. Understanding threads is somewhat crucial for C++ programmers as they tend to squeeze every bit of the program to make it run even faster. Threads introduce us to a completely different way of making programs faster by running functions concurrently. Learning multithreading at a fundamental level is a must for every C++ programmer. There are lots of programs where you can't avoid using multithreading, such as network applications, games, and GUI applications. This chapter will introduce you to concurrency and multithreading fundamentals in C++ and best practices for concurrent code design.

The following topics will be covered in this chapter:

- Understanding concurrency and multithreading
- Working with threads
- Managing threads and sharing data
- Designing concurrent code
- Using thread pools to avoid thread creation overheads
- Getting familiar with coroutines in C++20

Technical requirements

The g++ compiler with the `-std=c++2a` option is used to compile the examples in this chapter. You can find the source files used in this chapter at `https://github.com/PacktPublishing/Expert-CPP`.

Understanding concurrency and multithreading

The simplest form of running a program involves its instructions being executed one by one by the **CPU** (**Central Processing Unit**). As you already know from previous chapters, a program consists of several sections, one of them containing the instructions of the program. Each instruction is loaded into a CPU register for the CPU to decode and execute it. It doesn't actually matter what programming paradigm you use to produce an application; the result is always the same—the executable file contains machine code.

We mentioned that programming languages such as Java and C# use support environments. However, if you cut down the support environment in the middle (usually, the virtual machine), the final instructions being executed should have a form and format familiar to that particular CPU. It's obvious to programmers that the order of statements run by the CPU is not mixed in any circumstance. For example, we are sure and can continue to be so that the following program will output `4`, `"hello"`, and `5`, respectively:

```
int a{4};
std::cout << a << std::endl;
int b{a};
++b;
std::cout << "hello" << std::endl;
b--;
std::cout << (b + 1) << std::endl;
```

We can guarantee that the value of the `a` variable will be initialized before we print it to the screen. The same way we can guarantee that the `"hello"` string will be printed before we decrement the value of `b`, and that the `(b + 1)` sum will be calculated before printing the result to the screen. The execution of each instruction might involve reading data from or writing to memory.

As introduced in `Chapter 5`, *Memory Management and Smart Pointers*, the memory hierarchy is sophisticated enough to make our understanding of program execution a little bit harder. For example, the `int b{a};` line from the previous example assumes that the value of `a` is loaded from the memory into a register in the CPU, which then will be used to write into the memory location of `b`. The keyword here is the *location* because it carries a little bit of special interpretation for us. More specifically, we speak about memory location. Concurrency support depends on the memory model of the language, that is, a set of guarantees for concurrent access to memory. Although the byte is the smallest addressable memory unit, the CPU works with words in data. That said, the word is the smallest unit the CPU reads from or writes to memory. For example, we consider the following two declarations separate variables:

```
char one;
char two;
```

If those variables are allocated in the same word (considering the word size as bigger than the size of a `char`), reading and writing any of the variables involves reading the word containing both of them. Concurrent access to the variables might lead to unexpected behavior. That's the issue requiring memory model guarantees. The C++ memory model guarantees that two threads can access and update separate memory locations without interfering with each other. A memory location is a scalar type. A scalar type is an arithmetic type, pointer, enumeration, or `nullptr_t`. The largest sequence of adjacent bit-fields of non-zero length is considered a memory location too. A classic example would be the following structure:

```
struct S
{
  char a;              // location #1
  int b: 5;            // location #2
  unsigned c: 11;
  unsigned :0;         // :0 separates bit fields
  unsigned d: 8;       // location #3
  struct {
    int ee: 8;
  } e;                 // location #4
};
```

For the preceding example, two threads accessing the same struct's separate memory locations won't interfere with each other. So, what should we consider when speaking about concurrency or multithreading?

Concurrency is usually confused with multithreading. They are similar in nature but are different concepts in detail. To make things easy, just imagine concurrency as two operations whose running times interleave together. Operation `A` runs concurrently with operation `B` if their start and end times are interleaved at any point, as shown in the following diagram:

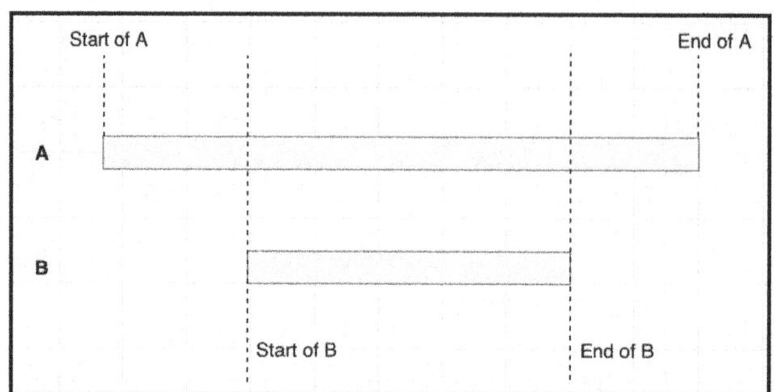

When two tasks run concurrently, they don't have to run parallel. Imagine the following situation: you are watching TV while surfing the internet. Though it's not a good practice to do so, however, let's imagine for a moment that you have a favorite TV show that you can't miss and at the same time, your friend asked you to do some research on bees. You can't actually concentrate on both tasks; at any fixed moment, your attention is grabbed by either the show you are watching or the interesting facts about bees that you are reading in an article found on the web. Your attention goes from the show to the bees from time to time.

In terms of concurrency, you are doing two tasks concurrently. Your brain gives a time portion to the show: you watch, enjoy, and then switch to the article, read a couple of sentences, and switch back to the show. This is a simple example of concurrently running tasks. Just because their start and end times interleave doesn't mean they run at the same time. On the other hand, you breathe while doing any of the tasks mentioned earlier. Breathing happens in the background; your brain doesn't switch your attention from the show or the article to your lungs to inhale or exhale. Breathing while watching the show is an example of parallel running tasks. Both examples show us the essence of concurrency.

So, what is going on when you run more than one application on your computer? Are they running in parallel? It's for sure that they run concurrently, however, the actual parallelism depends on your computer's hardware. Most mass-market computers consist of a single CPU. As we know from previous chapters, the main job of the CPU is running an application's instructions one by one. How would a single CPU handle the running of two applications at the same time? To understand that, we should learn about processes.

Processes

A process is an image of a program running in the memory. When we start a program, the OS reads the content of the program from the hard disk, copies it to the memory, and points the CPU to the starting instruction of the program. The process has its private virtual address space, stack, and heap. Two processes don't interfere with each other in any way. That's a guarantee provided by the OS. That also makes a programmer's job very difficult if they aim for **Interprocess Communication** (**IPC**). We are not discussing low-level hardware features in this book but you should have a general understanding of what is going on when we run a program. It really depends on the underlying hardware—more specifically, the kind and structure of the CPU. The number of CPUs, number of CPU cores, levels of cache memory, and shared cache memory between CPUs or their cores—all of these affect the way the OS runs and executes programs.

The number of CPUs in a computer system defines the number of processes running truly in parallel. This is shown in the following diagram:

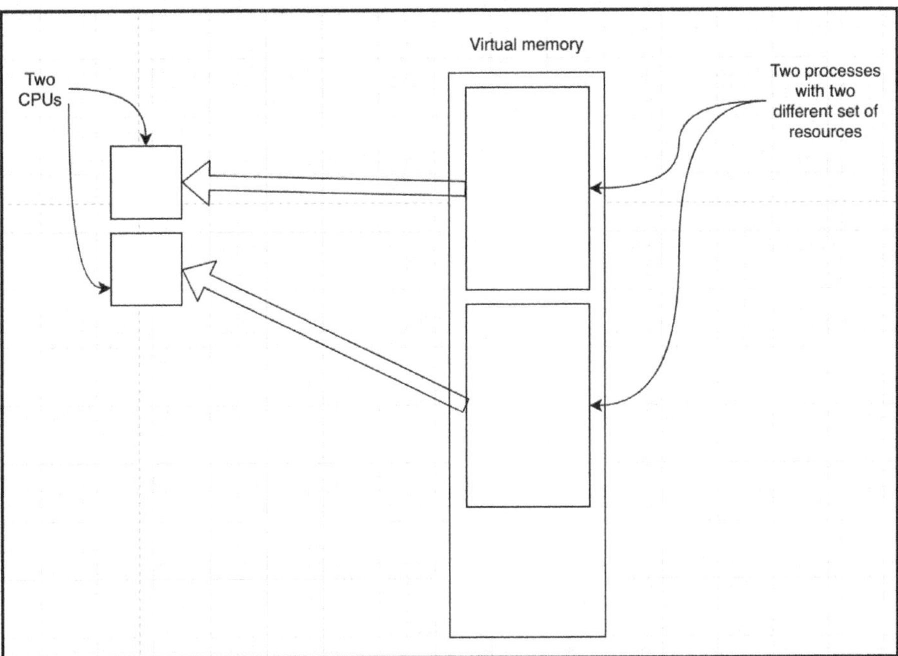

When we speak about multiprocessing, we consider an environment that allows several processes to run concurrently. And here comes the tricky part. If the processes actually run at the same time, then we say that they run in parallel. So, concurrency is not parallelism while parallelism implies concurrency.

If the system has just one CPU, processes run concurrently but not in parallel. The OS manages this with a mechanism called **context switching**. Context switching implies freezing the work of the process for a moment, copying all of the register values that the process was using at the current time, and storing all of the active resources and values of the process. When a process is stopped, another process takes on the rights to run. After the specified amount of time provided for this second process, the OS starts the context switching for it. Again, it copies all of the resources used by the process. Then, the previous process gets started. Before starting it, the OS copies back the resources and values to the corresponding slots used by the first process and then resumes the execution of this process.

The interesting thing is that the processes are not even aware of such a thing. The described process happens so fast that the user cannot actually notice that the programs running in the OS are not actually running at the same time. The following illustration depicts two processes run by a single CPU. When one of the processes is *active*, the CPU executes its instructions sequentially, storing any intermediary data in its registers (you should consider cache memory as in the game, too). The other process is *waiting* for the OS to provide its time portion to run:

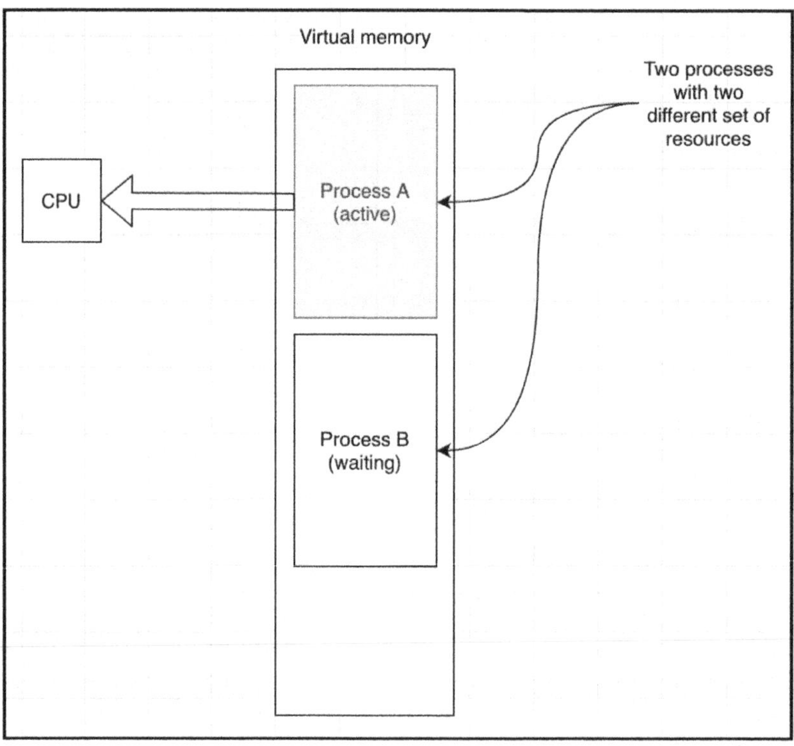

Running more than one process is a sophisticated job for the OS. It manages states of processes, defines which process should take more CPU time than others, and so on. Each process gets a fixed time to run before the OS switches to another process. This time can be longer for one process and shorter for another. Scheduling processes happens using priority tables. The OS provides more time to processes with a higher priority, for example, a system process has higher priority than user processes. Another example could be that a background task monitoring network health has a higher priority than a calculator application. When the provided time slice is up, the OS initiates a context switch, that is, it stores the state of **Process A** to resume its execution later:

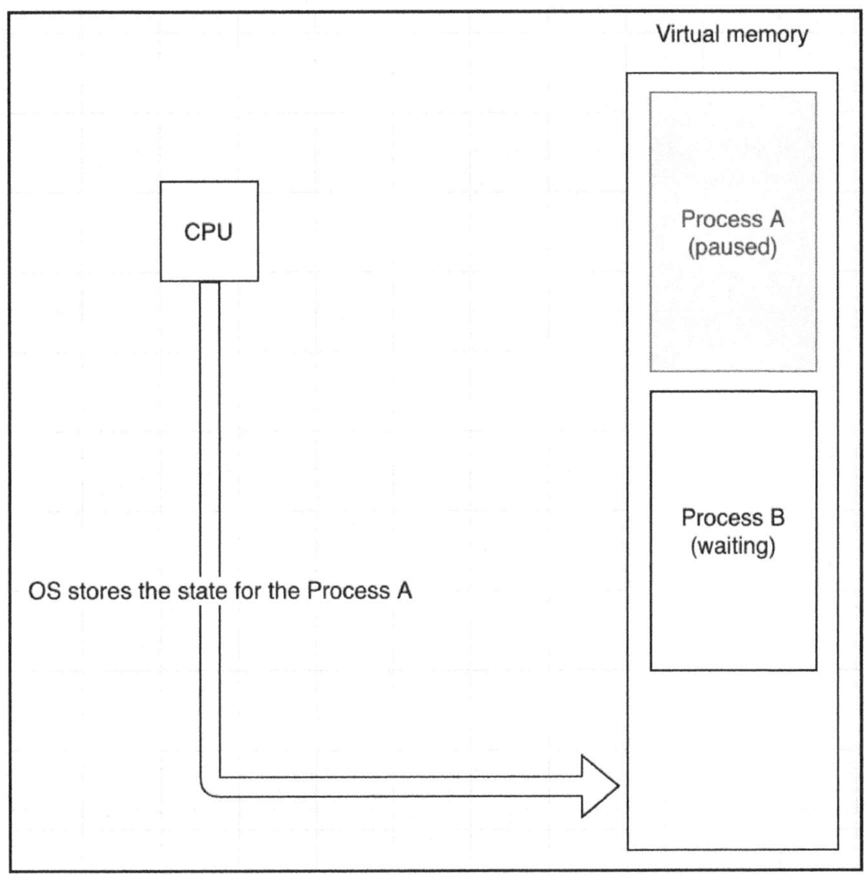

After storing the state, as showing in the following diagram, it switches to the next process to execute it:

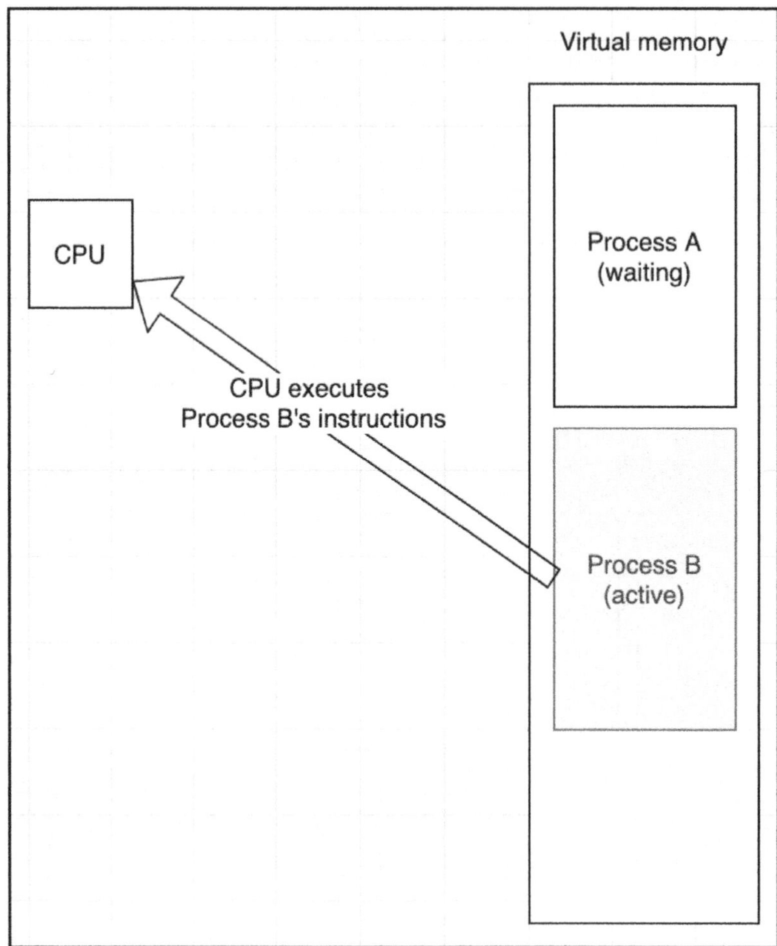

Obviously, if **Process B** was running before, its state should be loaded back to the CPU. In the same way, when the time slice (or time quantum) is up for **Process B**, the OS stores its state and loads the state of **Process A** back to the CPU (the state it had before being paused by the OS):

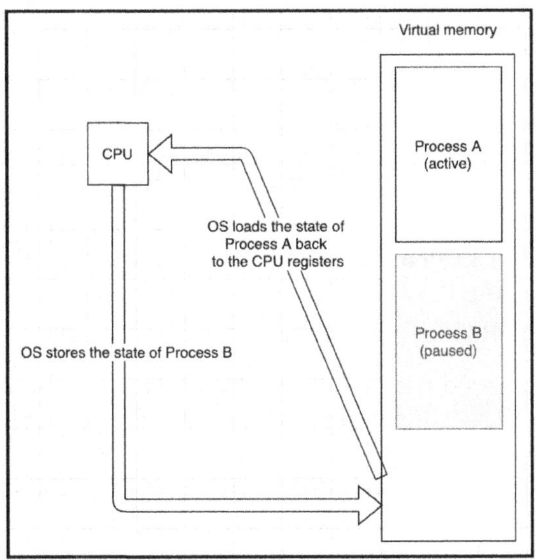

Processes do not share anything in common—or at least they think so. Each running process behaves as if it's alone in the system. It has all of the resources the OS can provide. In reality, the OS manages to keep processes unaware of each other, hence simulating freedom for each one. Finally, after loading the state of **Process A** back, the CPU continues executing its instructions like nothing happened:

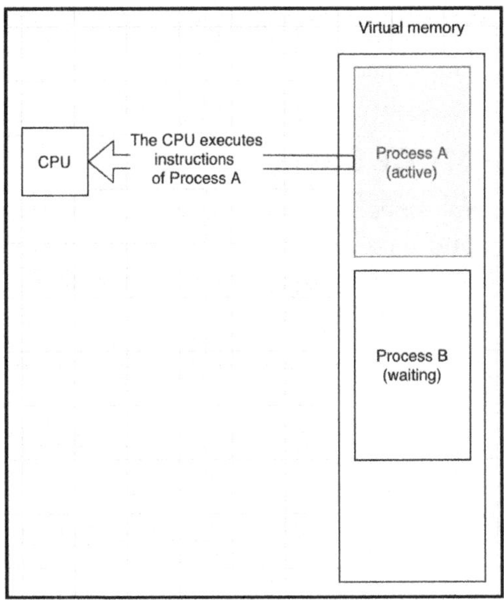

Process B is frozen until a new time slice is available for it to run.

A single CPU running more than one process is similar to a teacher checking examination papers of students. The teacher can check only one exam paper at a time, though they can introduce some concurrency by checking answers one by one for each exam test. First, they check the answer to the first question for one student, then switch to the first answer of the test of the second student, and then switches back to the first student's second answer and so on. Whenever the teacher switch from one exam paper to the other, they note down the number of the question where they left off. This way, they will know where to start when getting back to the same paper.

In the same way, the OS notes down the point of execution of a process before pausing it to resume another process. The second process can (and most probably will) use the same register set used by the paused process. This forces the OS to store register values for the first process somewhere to be recovered later. When the OS pauses the second process to resume the first one, it loads already saved register values back into corresponding registers. The resumed process won't notice any difference and will continue its work like it was never paused.

Everything described in the preceding two paragraphs relates to single-CPU systems. In the case of multi-CPU systems, each CPU in the system has its own set of registers. Also, each CPU can execute program instructions independently of the other CPUs, which allows running processes in parallel without pausing and resuming them. In the example, a teacher with a couple of assistants is similar to a system with three CPUs. Each one of them can check one exam paper; all of them are checking three different exam papers at any point in time.

Challenges with processes

Difficulties arise when processes need to contact each other in some way. Let's say a process should calculate something and pass the value to a completely different process. There are several methods to achieve IPC—one of them is using a memory segment shared between processes. The following diagram depicts two processes accessing the shared memory segment:

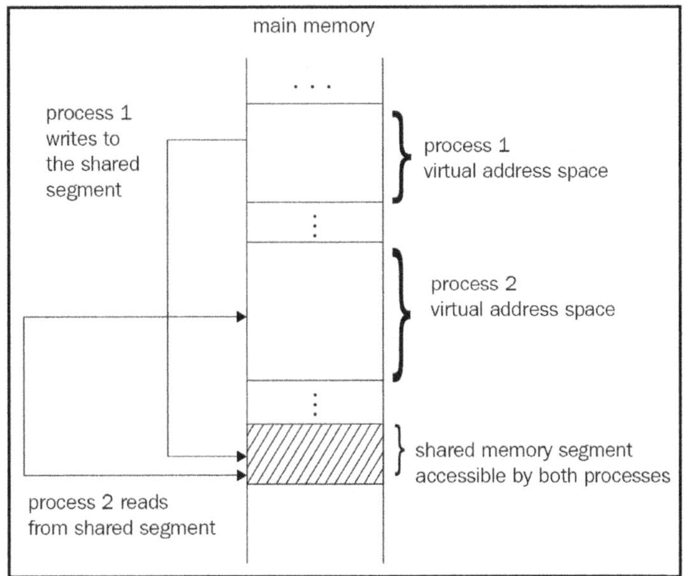

One process stores the results of the calculation to a shared segment in the memory, and the second process reads it from the segment. In the context of our previous example, the teacher and their assistants share their checking results in a shared paper. Threads, on the other hand, share address space of the process because they run in the context of the process. While a process is a program, thread is a function rather than a program. That said, a process must have at least one thread , which we call the thread of execution. A thread is the container of instructions of a program that are run in the system, while the process encapsulates the thread and provides resources for it. Most of our interest lies in threads and their orchestration mechanisms. Let's now meet them in person.

Threads

A **thread** is a section of code in the scope of a process that can be scheduled by the OS scheduler. While a process is the image of the running program, managing multi-process projects along with IPC is much harder and sometimes useless compared to projects leveraging multithreading. Programs deal with data and, usually, collections of data. Accessing, processing, and updating data is done by functions that are either the methods of objects or free functions composed together to achieve an end result. In most projects, we deal with tens of thousands of functions and objects. Each function represents a bunch of instructions wrapped under a sensible name used to invoke it by other functions. Multithreading aims to run functions concurrently to achieve better performance.

For example, a program that calculates the sum of three different vectors and prints them calls the function calculating the sum for the first vector, then for the second vector, and finally, for the last one. It all happens sequentially. If the processing of a single vector takes A amount of time, then the program will run in `3A` time. The following code demonstrates the example:

```
void process_vector(const std::vector<int>& vec)
{
 // calculate the sum and print it
}

int main()
{
 std::vector<int> vec1{1, 2, 3, 4, 5};
 std::vector<int> vec2{6, 7, 8, 9, 10};
 std::vector<int> vec3{11, 12, 13, 14, 15};
 process_vector(vec1); // takes A amount of time
 process_vector(vec2); // takes A amount of time
 process_vector(vec3); // takes A amount of time
}
```

If there was a way to run the same function for three different vectors simultaneously, it would take just A amount of time for the whole program in the preceding example. Threads of execution, or just threads, are exact ways of running tasks concurrently. By tasks, we usually mean a function, although you should remember `std::packaged_task` as well. Again, concurrency shouldn't be confused with parallelism. When we speak about threads running concurrently, you should consider the context switching discussed previously for the process. Almost the same applies to threads.

`std::packaged_task` is similar to `std::function`. It wraps a callable object—a function, lambda, function object, or bind expression. The difference with `std::packaged_task` is that it can be invoked asynchronously. There's more on that later in this chapter.

Each process has a single thread of execution, sometimes called the **main thread**. A process can have more than one thread, and that's when we call it **multithreading**. Threads run in almost the same way the processes. They also have context switching.

Threads run separately from each other, but they share most of the resources of process because all of the threads belong to the process. The process occupies hardware and software resources such as CPU registers and memory segments, including its own stack and heap. While a process doesn't share its stack or heap with other processes, its threads have to use the same resources that are occupied by the process. Everything that happens in a thread's life happens within the process.

However, threads don't share the stack. Each thread has its portion of the stack. The reason behind this segregation relies on the fact that a thread is just a function and the function itself should have access to the stack to manage the life cycle of its arguments and local variables. When we run the same function as two (or more) separately running threads, the runtime should somehow handle their boundaries. Although it's error-prone, you can pass a variable from one thread to another (either by value or by reference). Let's suppose that we started three threads running the `process_vector()` function for the three vectors in the preceding example. You should imagine that starting a thread means *copying* the underlying function somehow (its variables but not the instructions) and running it separately from any other thread. In this scenario, the same function will be copied as three different images, and each one of them will run independently of the others, hence each should have its own stack. On the other hand, the heap is shared between threads. So, basically, we arrive at the following:

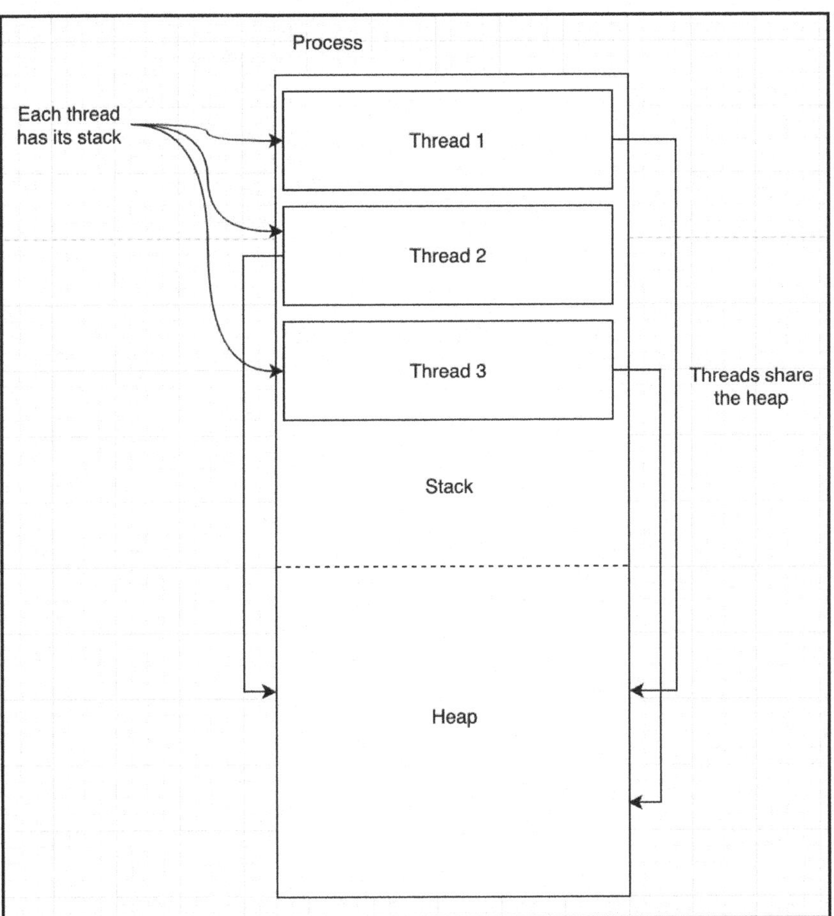

As in the case of processes, threads running concurrently are not necessarily running in parallel. Each thread gets a small portion of CPU time to be run and, again, there is an overhead regarding the switching from one thread to another. Each paused thread's state should be stored somewhere to be recovered later when resuming it. The internal structure of the CPU defines whether threads could truly run in parallel. The number of CPU cores defines the number of threads that can truly run in parallel.

The C++ thread library provides the `hardware_concurrency()` function to find out the number of threads that can truly run concurrently. You can refer to this number when designing concurrent code.

The following diagram depicts two CPUs having four cores each. Each core can run a thread independently of the other:

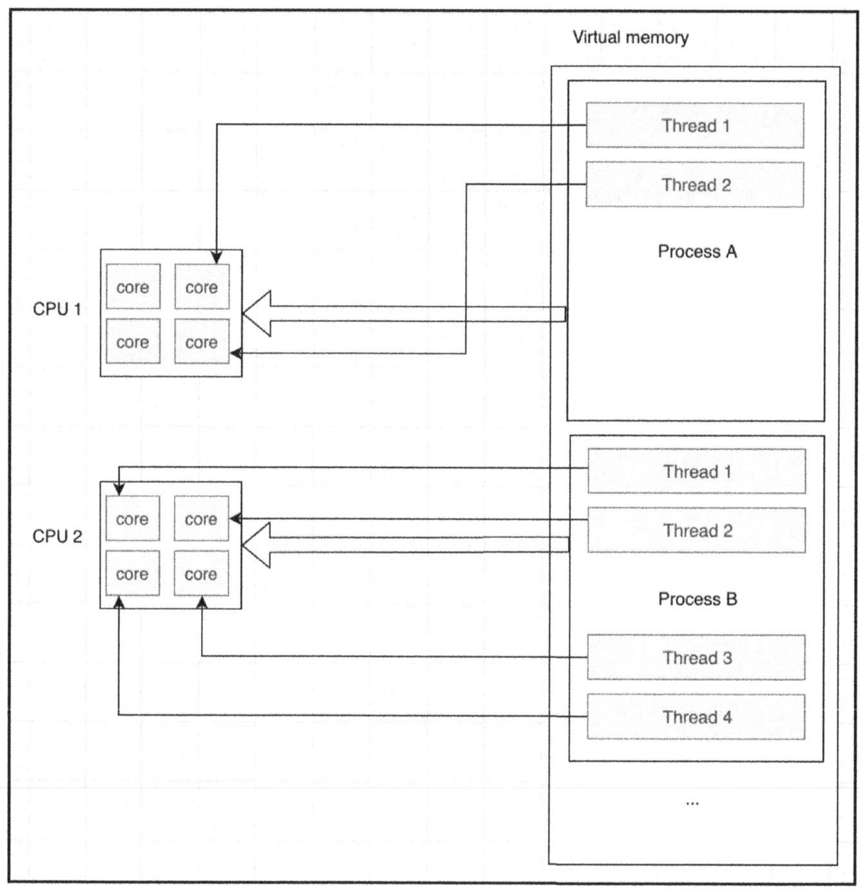

Not only do two processes run in parallel but also their threads are run in parallel using the CPU cores. Now, how will the situation change if we have several threads but one single-core CPU? Almost the same as we have illustrated earlier for processes. Look at the following diagram—it depicts how the CPU executes **Thread 1** for some time slice:

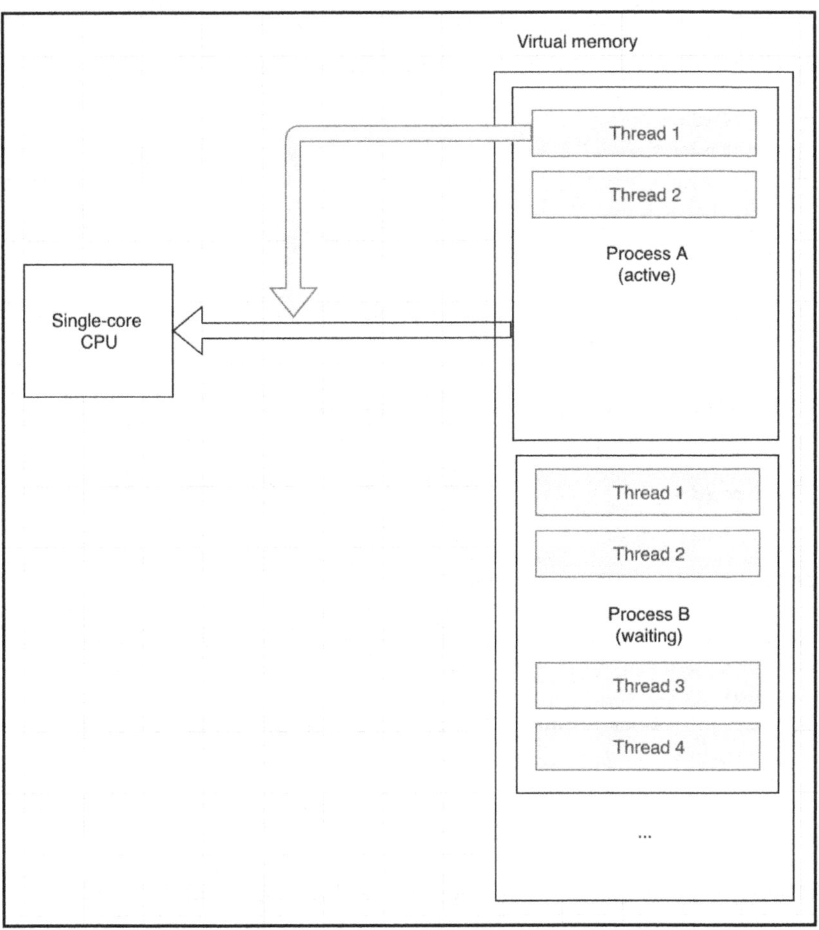

The currently active **Process A** has two threads that run concurrently. At each specified point in time, only one of the threads is executed. When the time slice is up for **Thread 1**, **Thread 2** is executed. The difference from the model we discussed for processes is that threads share the resources of the process, which leads to unnatural behavior if we aren't concerned with concurrent code design issues. Let's dive into C++ threading support and find out what issues arise when using multithreading.

Working with threads

When the C++ program starts, that is, the `main()` function starts its execution, you can create and launch new threads that will run concurrently to the main thread. To start a thread in C++, you should declare a thread object and pass it the function that you want to run concurrently to the main thread. The following code demonstrates the declaration and starting of a thread using `std::thread` defined in `<thread>`:

```
#include <thread>
#include <iostream>

void foo() { std::cout << "Testing a thread in C++" << std::endl; }

int main()
{
  std::thread test_thread{foo};
}
```

That's it. We can create a better example to show how two threads work concurrently. Let's say we print numbers in a loop concurrently to see which thread prints what:

```
#include <thread>
#include <iostream>

void print_numbers_in_background()
{
  auto ix{0};
  // Attention: an infinite loop!
  while (true) {
    std::cout << "Background: " << ix++ << std::endl;
  }
}

int main()
{
  std::thread background{print_numbers_in_background};
  auto jx{0};
  while (jx < 1000000) {
    std::cout << "Main: " << jx++ << std::endl;
  }
}
```

The preceding example will print both outputs with the `Main:` and `Background:` prefixes mixed together. An excerpt from the output might look like this:

```
...
Main: 90
Main: 91
Background: 149
Background: 150
Background: 151
Background: 152
Background: 153
Background:
Main: 92
Main: 93
...
```

Whenever the main thread finishes its work (printing to the screen one million times), the program wants to finish without waiting for the background thread to complete. It leads to program termination. Let's see how we should modify the previous example.

Waiting for threads

The `thread` class provides the `join()` function if you want to wait for it to finish. Here is a modified version of the previous example that waits for the `background` thread:

```
#include <thread>
#include <iostream>

void print_numbers_in_background()
{
  // code omitted for brevity
}

int main()
{
  std::thread background{print_numbers_in_background};
  // the while loop omitted for brevity
  background.join();
}
```

As we already discussed previously, the `thread` function is run as a separate entity independently from other threads- even the one that started it. It won't wait for the thread it has just started, and that's why you should explicitly tell the caller function to wait for it to finish. It is necessary to signal that the calling thread (the main thread) is waiting for the thread to finish before itself.

The symmetric opposite of the `join()` function is the `detach()` function. The `detach()` function indicates that the caller isn't interested in waiting for the thread to finish. In this case, the thread can have an independent life. As shown here (like it's already 18 years old):

```
std::thread t{foo};
t.detach();
```

Although detaching a thread might seem natural, there are plenty of scenarios when we need to wait for the thread to finish. For example, we might pass local to the caller variables to the running thread. In this case, we can't let the caller detach the thread as the caller might finish its work earlier than the thread started in it. Let's illustrate that for the sake of clarity. **Thread 1** declares the `loc` variable and passes it to **Thread 2**, which has been started from **Thread 1**:

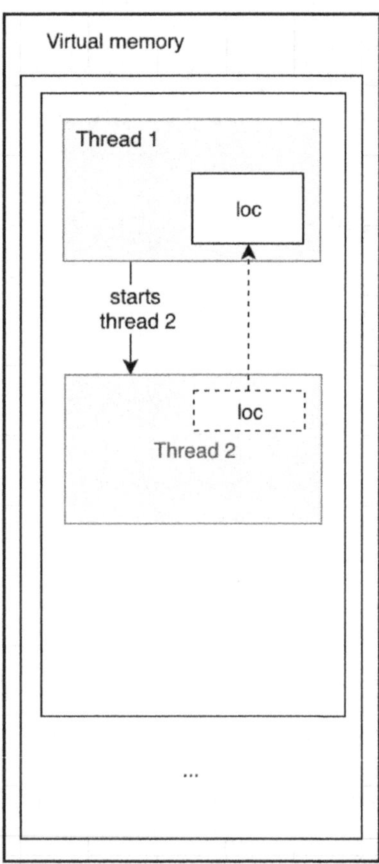

Passing the address of `loc` to **Thread 2** is error-prone if **Thread 1** doesn't join it. If **Thread 1** finishes its execution before **Thread 2**, then accessing `loc` by its address leads to an undefined behavior:

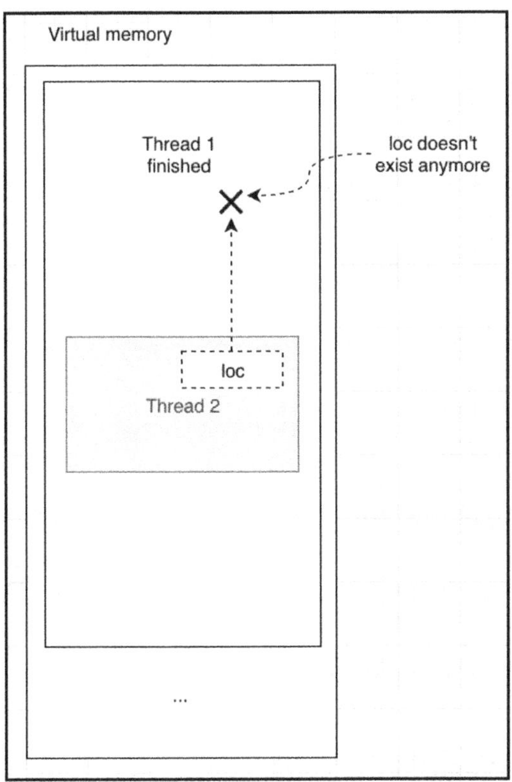

There is no such object anymore, so the best that we can hope for the program is to crash. It will lead to unexpected behavior because the running thread won't have access to the caller's local variables anymore. You should either join or detach a thread.

We can pass any callable object to `std::thread`. The following example shows passing a lambda expression to the thread:

```
#include <thread>

int main() {
  std::thread tl{[]{
    std::cout << "A lambda passed to the thread";
  }};
  tl.join();
}
```

Furthermore, we can use callable objects as thread arguments. Take a look at the following code declaring the `TestTask` class with the overridden `operator()` function:

```
#include <thread>

class TestTask
{
public:
  TestTask() = default;

  void operator()() {
    state_++;
  }
private:
  int state_ = 0;
};

int main() {
  std::thread t{TestTask()};
  t.join();
}
```

One of the advantages of a functor (the `TestTask` class with the overridden `operator()` function) is its ability to store state information. Functors are a beautiful implementation of the command design pattern that we will discuss in `Chapter 11`, *Designing a Strategy Game Using Design Patterns*. Getting back to the threads, let's move on the a new addition in the language that allows for better ways to join threads.

Using std::jthread

C++20 introduces a joinable thread, `std::jthread`. It provides the same interface `std::thread` as provides, so we can replace all threads with jthreads in the code. It actually wraps `std::thread`, so basically it delegates down to the wrapped thread.

If the version of your compiler doesn't support `std::jthread`, you are free to go with the **RAII (Resource Acquisition Is Initialization)** idiom, which is perfectly applicable to threads. Take a look at the following code:

```
class thread_raii
{
public:
  explicit thread_raii(std::thread& t)
    : thread_(std::move(t))
  {}
```

```
    ~thread_raii() {
      thread_.join();
    }

  private:
    std::thread thread_;
};

void foo() {
  std::cout << "Testing thread join";
}

int main() {
  std::thread t{foo};
  thread_raii r{t};
  // will automatically join the thread
}
```

However, the preceding code lacks an additional check because a thread passed to the RAII class might have been already detached. To see whether the thread could be joined, we use the `joinable()` function. This is how we should overwrite the `thread_raii` class:

```
class thread_raii
{
public:
  explicit thread_raii(std::thread& t)
    : thread_(std::move(t))
  {}

  ~thread_raii()
  {
    if (thread_.joinable()) {
      thread_.join();
    }
  }
private:
  std::thread thread_;
};
```

The destructor first tests whether the thread is joinable before calling the `join()` function. However, instead of dealing with idioms and being concerned about whether the thread has been joined already before joining it, we prefer using `std::jthread`. Here's how we can do that using the `TestTask` function declared previously:

```
std::jthread jt{TestTask()};
```

That's it—there's no need to call `jt.join()`, and a new cooperative interruptible feature out of the box that we use by incorporating jthread. We say that jthread is cooperative interruptible because it provides the `request_stop()` function ,which does what its name says—requests the thread to stop. Although that request fulfillment is implementation-defined, it's a nice way not to wait for the thread forever. Recall the example with the thread printing numbers in an infinite loop. We modified the main thread to wait for it, and that leads to waiting for it forever. Here's how we can modify the thread using `std::jthread` to leverage the `request_stop()` function:

```
int main()
{
  std::jthread background{print_numbers_in_background};
  auto jx{0};
  while (jx < 1000000) {
    std::cout << "Main: " << jx << std::endl;
  }
  // The main thread is about to finish, so we request the background
thread to stop
  background.request_stop();
}
```

The `print_numbers_in_background()` function now receives a request and can behave accordingly. Now, let's see how to pass arguments to the thread function.

Passing arguments to the thread function

The `std::thread` constructor takes arguments and forwards them to the underlying `thread` function. For example, to pass the arguments `4` and `2` to the `foo()` function here, we pass the arguments to the `std::thread` constructor:

```
void foo(int one, int two) {
  // do something
}

std::thread t{foo, 4, 2};
```

The arguments `4` and `2` will be passed as the first and second arguments to the `foo()` function.

The following example illustrates the passing of an argument by reference:

```
class big_object {};

void make_changes(big_object&);
```

```
void error_prone()
{
  big_object b;
  std::jthread t{make_changes, b};
  // do something else
}
```

To understand why we named the function `error_prone`, we should know that the thread constructor copies the values passed to it and then passes them to the thread function with `rvalue` references. This is done to work with move-only types. So it will try to call the `make_changes()` function with `rvalue`, which will fail to compile (you can't pass `rvalue` to a function that expects a non-constant reference). We need to wrap the arguments that need to be a reference in `std::ref`:

```
std::thread t{make_changes, std::ref(b)};
```

The preceding code emphasizes that the argument should be passed by reference. Working with threads requires being a little more attentive because there are many ways to get unexpected results or undefined behavior in the program. Let's see how we can manage threads to produce safer multithreaded applications.

Managing threads and sharing data

As discussed previously, the execution of threads involves pausing and resuming some of them if the number of threads exceeds the number of parallel running threads supported by the hardware. Besides that, the creation of a thread also has its overhead. One of the suggested practices to deal with having many threads in a project is using thread pools.

The idea of a thread pool lies in the concept of caching. We create and keep threads in some container to be used later. The container is called a pool. For example, the following vector represents a simple thread pool:

```
#include <thread>
#include <vector>

std::vector<std::thread> pool;
```

Whenever we need a new thread, instead of declaring the corresponding `std::thread` object, we use one already created in the pool. When we are done with the thread, we can push it back to the vector to use it later if necessary. This saves some time when working with 10 or more threads. A proper example would be a web server.

A web server is a program that waits for incoming client connections and creates a separate connection for each client to be processed independently from others. A typical web server usually deals with thousands of clients at the same time. Each time a new connection is initiated with some client, the web server creates a new thread and handles the client requests. The following pseudo-code demonstrates a simple implementation of a web server's incoming connection management:

```
void process_incoming_connections() {
  if (new connection from client) {
    t = create_thread(); // potential overhead
    t.handle_requests(client);
  }
}
while (true) {
  process_incoming_connections();
}
```

When using a thread pool, the preceding code will avoid the creation of a thread each time it needs to process a client request. The creation of a new thread requires additional and rather expensive work from the OS. To save that time, we use a mechanism that omits creating new threads on each request. To make the pool even better, let's replace its container with a queue. Whenever we ask for a thread, the pool will return a free thread, and whenever we are done with a thread, we push it back to the pool. A simple design of a thread pool would look like the following:

```
#include <queue>
#include <thread>

class ThreadPool
{
public:
  ThreadPool(int number_of_threads = 1000) {
    for (int ix = 0; ix < number_of_threads; ++ix) {
      pool_.push(std::thread());
    }
  }

  std::thread get_free_thread() {
    if (pool_.empty()) {
      throw std::exception("no available thread");
    }
    auto t = pool_.front();
    pool_.pop();
    return t;
  }
```

```
    void push_thread(std::thread t) {
      pool_.push(t);
    }

  private:
    std::queue<std::thread> pool_;
  };
```

The constructor creates and pushes threads to the queue. In the following pseudo-code, we replace the direct creation of a thread for client request processing with `ThreadPool` ,which we looked at previously:

```
ThreadPool pool;
void process_incoming_connections() {
  if (new connection from client) {
    auto t = pool.get_free_thread();
    t.handle_request(client);
  }
}

while (true) {
  process_incoming_connections();
}
```

Supposing that the `handle_request()` function pushes the thread back to the pool when it's done, the pool behaves as a centralized store for connection threads. Though shown in the preceding snippet is far from being ready for production, it conveys the basic idea of using thread pools in intensive applications.

Sharing data

A race condition is something that programmers using multithreading are scared of and try to avoid as much as possible. Imagine two functions that work concurrently with the same data, as shown here:

```
int global = 0;

void inc() {
  global = global + 1;
}
...
std::thread t1{inc};
std::thread t2{inc};
```

A potential race condition is happening because threads `t1` and `t2` are modifying the same variable with more than one step. Any operation that is performed in a single thread-safe step is called an **atomic operation**. In this case, incrementing the value of the variable is not an atomic operation, even if we use the increment operator.

Protecting shared data using a mutex

To protect shared data, objects called **mutexes** are used widely. A mutex is an object that controls the running of a thread. Imagine threads as humans making a deal about how to work with data one by one. When a thread locks a mutex, the other thread waits until it is done with the data and unlocks the mutex. The other thread then locks the mutex and starts working with data. The following code demonstrates how we can solve the problem of a race condition using a mutex:

```
#include <mutex>
...
std::mutex locker;
void inc() {
  locker.lock();
  global = global + 1;
  locker.unlock();
}
...
std::thread t1{inc};
std::thread t2{inc};
```

When `t1` starts executing `inc()`, it locks a mutex, which avoids any other thread to access the global variable unless the original thread doesn't unlock the next thread.

C++17 introduced a lock guard that allows guarding the mutex in order not to forget unlock it:

```
std::mutex locker;
void inc() {
  std::lock_guard g(locker);
  global = global + 1;
}
```

It's always better to use language-provided guards if possible.

Avoiding deadlocks

New problems arise with mutexes, such as **deadlocks**. A deadlock is a condition of multithreaded code when two or more threads lock a mutex and wait for the other to unlock another.

The common advice to avoid deadlock is to always lock two or more mutexes in the same order. C++ provides the `std::lock()` function, which serves the same purpose.

The following code illustrates the `swap` function, which takes two arguments of type `X`. We suppose that `X` has a member, `mt` , which is a mutex. The implementation of the `swap` function locks the mutex of the left object first, then it locks the mutex of the right object:

```
void swap(X& left, X& right)
{
  std::lock(left.mt, right.mt);
  std::lock_guard<std::mutex> lock1(left.mt, std::adopt_lock);
  std::lock_guard<std::mutex> lock2(right.mt, std::adopt_lock);
  // do the actual swapping
}
```

To avoid deadlocks in general, avoid nested locks. That said, don't acquire a lock if you are already holding one. If this is not the case, then acquire locks in a fixed order. The fixed order will allow you to avoid deadlocks.

Designing concurrent code

Project complexity rises drastically when concurrency is introduced. It's much easier to deal with sequentially executing synchronous code compared to concurrent counterparts. Many systems avoid using multithreading at all by introducing event-driven development concepts, such as the event loop. The point of using an event loop is to introduce a manageable approach to asynchronous programming. To take the concept further, imagine any application providing a **Graphical User Interface** (**GUI**). Whenever the user clicks on any GUI component, such as buttons; types in fields; or even moves the mouse, the application receives so-called events regarding the user action. Whether it's `button_press`, `button_release`, `mouse_move`, or any other event, it represents a piece of information to the application to react properly. A popular approach is to incorporate an event loop to queue any event that occurred during user interaction.

While the application is busy with its current task, the events produced by user actions are queued to be processed at some time in the future. The processing involves calling handler functions attached to each event. They are called in the order they were put into the queue.

Introducing multithreading to the project brings additional complexity with it. You should now take care of race conditions and proper thread handling, maybe even using a thread pool to reuse thread objects. In sequentially executed code, you care for the code and only the code. Using multithreading, you now care a little bit more about the ways of execution of the very same code. For example, a simple design pattern such as the singleton behaves differently in a multithreading environment. The classic implementation of a singleton looks like the following:

```
class MySingleton
{
public:
  static MySingleton* get_instance() {
    if (instance_ == nullptr) {
      instance_ = new MySingleton();
    }
    return instance_;
  }

  // code omitted for brevity
private:
  static inline MySingleton* instance_ = nullptr;
};
```

The following code starts two threads, both using the `MySingleton` class:

```
void create_something_unique()
{
  MySingleton* inst = MySingleton::get_instance();
  // do something useful
}

void create_something_useful()
{
  MySingleton* anotherInst = MySingleton::get_instance();
  // do something unique
}

std::thread t1{create_something_unique};
std::thread t2{create_something_useful};
t1.join();
t2.join();
// some other code
```

Threads `t1` and `t2` both call the `get_instance()` static member function of the `MySingleton` class. It's possible that `t1` and `t2` both pass the check for the empty instance and both execute the new operator. Clearly, we have a race condition here. The resource, in this case, the class instance, should be protected from such a scenario. Here's an obvious solution using a mutex:

```
class MySingleton
{
public:
  static MySingleton* get_instance() {
    std::lock_guard lg{mutex_};
    if (instance_ == nullptr) {
      instance_ = new MySingleton();
    }
    return instance_;
  }

  // code omitted for brevity
private:
  static std::mutex mutex_;
  static MySingleton* instance_;
}
```

Using a mutex will solve the problem, but will make the function work more slowly because each time a thread requests an instance, a mutex will be locked instead (which involves additional operations by the OS kernel). The proper solution would be using the Double-Checked Locking pattern. Its basic idea is this:

1. Lock the mutex after the `instance_` check.
2. Check the `instance_` again after the mutex has been locked because another thread might have passed the first check and wait for the mutex to unlock.

See the code for details:

```
static MySingleton* get_instance() {
  if (instance_ == nullptr) {
    std::lock_guard lg{mutex_};
    if (instance_ == nullptr) {
      instance_ = new MySingleton();
    }
  }
  return instance_;
}
```

Several threads may pass the first check and one of them will lock the mutex. Only one thread makes it to the new operator call. However, after unlocking the mutex, threads that have passed the first check will try to lock it and create the instance. The second check is there to prevent this. The preceding code allows us to reduce the performance overhead of the synchronized code. The approach we provided here is one of the ways to prepare yourself for concurrent code design.

Concurrent code design is very much based on the capabilities of the language itself. The evolution of C++ is marvelous. In its earliest versions, it didn't have built-in support for multithreading. Now, it has a solid thread library and the new C++20 standard provides us with even more powerful tools, such as coroutines.

Introducing coroutines

We discussed an example of asynchronous code execution when speaking about GUI applications. GUI components react to user actions by firing corresponding events, which are pushed in the event queue. This queue are then processed one by one by invoking attached handler functions. The described process happens in a loop; that's why we usually refer to the concept as the event loop.

Asynchronous systems are really useful in I/O operations because any input or output operation blocks the execution at the point of I/O call. For example, the following pseudo-code reads a file from a directory and then prints a welcome message to the screen:

```
auto f = read_file("filename");
cout << "Welcome to the app!";
process_file_contents(f);
```

Attached to the synchronous execution pattern, we know that the message **Welcome to the app!** will be printed only after the `read_file()` function finishes executing. `process_file_contents()` will be invoked only after `cout` completes. When dealing with asynchronous code, all we know about code execution starts to behave like something unrecognizable. The following modified version of the preceding example uses the `read_file_async()` function to read the file contents asynchronously:

```
auto p = read_file_async("filename");
cout << "Welcome to the app!";
process_file_contents(p); // we shouldn't be able to do this
```

Considering `read_file_async()` is an asynchronous function, the message **Welcome to the app!** will be printed sooner than the file contents. The very nature of asynchronous execution allows us to invoke functions to be executed in the background, which provides us with non-blocking input/output.

However, there is a slight change in the way we treat the return value of the function. If we deal with an asynchronous function, its return value is considered as something called a **promise** or a **promise object**. It's the way the system notifies us when the asynchronous function has completed. The promise object has three states:

- Pending
- Rejected
- Fulfilled

A promise object is said to be fulfilled if the function is done and the result is ready to be processed. In the event of an error, the promise object will be in the rejected state. If the promise is not rejected nor fulfilled, it is in the pending state.

C++20 introduced coroutines as an addition to the classic asynchronous functions. Coroutines move the background execution of the code to next level; they allow a function to be paused and resumed when necessary. Imagine a function that reads file contents and stops in the middle, passes the execution context to another function, and then resumes the reading of the file to its end. So, before diving deeper, consider a coroutine as a function that can be as follows:

- Started
- Paused
- Resumed
- Finished

To make a function a coroutine, you would use one of the keywords `co_await`, `co_yield`, or `co_return`. `co_await` is a construct telling the code to wait for asynchronously executing code. It means the function can be suspended at that point and resume its execution when a result is ready. For example, the following code requests an image from the network using a socket:

```
task<void> process_image()
{
  image i = co_await request_image("url");
  // do something useful with the image
}
```

As the network request operation is also considered as an **input/output** operation, it might block the execution of the code. To prevent blocking, we use asynchronous calls. The line using `co_await` in the preceding example is a point where the function execution could be suspended. In simpler words, when the execution reaches the line with `co_await`, the following happens:

1. It quits the function for a while (until there isn't ready data).
2. It continues executing from where it was before `process_image()` was called.
3. It then comes back again to continue executing `process_image()` at the point where it left it.

To achieve this, a coroutine (the `process_image()` function is a coroutine) is not handled the way regular functions are handled in C++. One of the interesting or even surprising features of coroutines is that they are **stackless.** We know that functions can't live without the stack. That's where the function pushes its arguments and local variables before even executing its instructions. Coroutines, on the other hand, instead of pushing anything to the stack, save their state in the heap and recover it when resumed.

This is tricky because there are also stackful coroutines. Stackful coroutines, also referred to as **fibers**, have a separate stack.

Coroutines are connected to callers. In the preceding example, the function that call `sprocess_image()` transfers execution to the coroutine and the pause by the coroutine (also known as **yielding**) transfers the execution back to the caller. As we stated, the heap is used to store the state of the coroutine, but the actual function-specific data (arguments, and local variables) are stored on the caller's stack. That's it—the coroutine is associated with an object that is stored on the caller function's stack. Obviously, the coroutine lives as long as its object.

Coroutines might give a wrong impression of redundant complexity added to the language, but their use cases are great in improving applications that use asynchronous I/O code (as in the preceding example) or lazy computations. That said, when we have to invent new patterns or introduce complexities into projects to handle, for instance, lazy computations, we now can improve our experience by using coroutines in C++. Please note that asynchronous I/O or lazy computations are just two examples of coroutine applications. There are more out there.

Summary

In this chapter, we've discussed the concept of concurrency and showed the difference between parallelism. We learned the difference between a process and a thread, the latter being of interest. Multithreading allows us to manage a program to be more efficient, though it also brings additional complexity with it. To handle data races, we use synchronization primitives such as a mutex. A mutex is a way to lock the data used by one thread to avoid invalid behavior produced by simultaneously accessing the same data from several threads.

We also covered the idea that an input/output operation is considered blocking and asynchronous functions are one of the ways to make it non-blocking. Coroutines as a part of the asynchronous execution of code were introduced in C++20.

We learned how to create and start a thread. More importantly, we learned how to manage data between threads. In the next chapter, we will dive into data structures that are used in concurrent environments.

Questions

1. What is concurrency?
2. What is the difference between concurrency and parallelism?
3. What is a process?
4. What's the difference between a process and a thread?
5. Write code to start a thread.
6. How could you make the singleton pattern thread-safe?
7. Rewrite the `MySingleton` class to use `std::shared_ptr` for the returned instance.
8. What are coroutines and what is the `co_await` keyword used for?

Further reading

- *Anthony Williams, C++ Concurrency in Action,* `https://www.amazon.com/C-Concurrency-Action-Anthony-Williams/dp/1617294691/`

9
Designing Concurrent Data Structures

In the previous chapter, we touched on the basics of concurrency and multithreading in C++. One of the biggest challenges in concurrent code design is properly handling data races. Thread synchronization and orchestration is not an easy topic to grasp, although we might consider it the most important one. While we can use synchronization primitives such as mutexes everywhere that we have the slightest doubt about a data race, it's not a best practice that we would advise.

A better way of designing concurrent code is to avoid locks at all costs. That would not only increase the performance of the application but also make it much safer than before. Easier said than done – lock-free programming is a challenging topic that we are introducing in this chapter. In particular, we will go further into the fundamentals of designing lock-free algorithms and data structures. This is a hard topic being continuously researched by many outstanding developers. We will touch on the basics of lock-free programming, which will give you an idea of how to construct your code in an efficient way. After reading this chapter, you will be better able to picture problems with data races and acquire the basic knowledge needed to design concurrent algorithms and data structures. It might also be helpful for your general design skills to build fault-tolerant systems.

The following topics will be covered in this chapter:

- Understanding data races and lock-based solutions
- Using atomics in C++ code
- Designing lock-free data structures

Technical requirements

The g++ compiler with the `-std=c++2a` option is used to compile the examples in this chapter. You can find the source files used in this chapter at `https://github.com/PacktPublishing/Expert-CPP` .

A closer look at data races

As already stated many times, data races are situations programmers try to avoid at all costs. In the previous chapter, we discussed a deadlock and ways to avoid it. The last example that we used in the previous chapter was making a thread-safe singleton pattern. Let's suppose we use a class for creating database connections (a classic example).

Here's a simple implementation of the pattern that tracks down the connections to the database. Keeping a separate connection each time we need access to the database is not a good practice. Instead, we reuse the existing connection for querying the database from different parts of the program:

```
namespace Db {
  class ConnectionManager
  {
  public:
    static std::shared_ptr<ConnectionManager> get_instance()
    {
      if (instance_ == nullptr) {
        instance_.reset(new ConnectionManager());
      }
      return instance_;
    }

    // Database connection related code omitted
  private:
    static std::shared_ptr<ConnectionManager> instance_{nullptr};
  };
}
```

Let's discuss that example in more detail. In the previous chapter, we incorporated locking to protect the `get_instance()` function from data races. Let's illustrate in detail why we did so. To simplify this for the example, here are the four lines of interest to us:

```
get_instance()
  if (_instance == nullptr)
    instance_.reset(new)
  return instance_;
```

Now, imagine that we run a thread that accesses the `get_instance()` function. We name it `Thread A` and the first line that it executes is the conditional statement, as shown:

```
get_instance()
  if (_instance == nullptr)     <--- Thread A
    instance_.reset(new)
  return instance_;
```

It will execute the instructions line by line. What interests us more is the second thread (marked as `Thread B`), which starts executing the function concurrent to `Thread A`. The following situation might arise during the concurrent execution of the function:

```
get_instance()
  if (_instance == nullptr)     <--- Thread B (checking)
    instance_.reset(new)        <--- Thread A (already checked)
  return instance_;
```

`Thread B` gets a positive result when it compares `instance_` against `nullptr`. `Thread A` has passed the same check and sets `instance_` to a new object. While from the perspective of `Thread A` everything looks fine, it just passed the conditional check, resets `instances`, and will move on to the next line to return `instance_`. However, `Thread B` compared `instance_` right before it had its value changed. Therefore, `Thread B` also moves on to setting the value of `instance_`:

```
get_instance()
  if (_instance == nullptr)
    instance_.reset(new)        <--- Thread B (already checked)
  return instance_;             <--- Thread A (returns)
```

The preceding issue is that `Thread B` resets `instance_` after it has already been set. Also, we view `get_instance()` as a single operation; it consists of several instructions, each of which is executed sequentially by a thread. For two threads not to interfere with each other, the operation shouldn't consist of more than one instruction.

The reason why we are concerned with data races is the gap pictured in the code block preceding. That gap between the lines is something that allows threads to interfere with each other. When you design a solution using a synchronization primitive, such as a mutex, you should picture all the gaps that you miss because the solution might not be the correct one. The following modification uses mutex and the `double-checked` locking pattern discussed in the previous chapter:

```
static std::shared_ptr<ConnectionManager> get_instance()
{
  if (instance_ == nullptr) {
    // mutex_ is declared in the private section
```

```
        std::lock_guard lg{mutex_};
        if (instance_ == nullptr) { // double-checking
          instance_.reset(new ConnectionManager());
        }
      }
      return instance_;
    }
```

Here's what happens when two threads try to access the `instance_` object:

```
get_instance()
  if (instance_ == nullptr)       <--- Thread B
    lock mutex                    <--- Thread A (locks the mutex)
    if (instance_ == nullptr)
      instance_.reset(new)
    unlock mutex
  return instance_
```

Now, even when both threads pass the first check, one of them locks the mutex. While one of the threads might try to lock the mutex, the other will reset the instance. To make sure it's not already set, we use the second check (that's why it's called **double-checked locking**):

```
get_instance()
  if (instance_ == nullptr)
    lock mutex                    <--- Thread B (tries to lock, waits)
    if (instance_ == nullptr)     <--- Thread A (double check)
      instance_.reset(new)
    unlock mutex
  return instance_
```

When `Thread A` finishes setting `instance_`, it then unlocks the mutex so `Thread B` can move on with locking and resetting `instance_`:

```
get_instance()
  if (instance_ == nullptr)
    lock mutex                    <--- Thread B (finally locks the mutex)
    if (instance_ == nullptr)     <--- Thread B (check is not passed)
      instance_.reset(new)
    unlock mutex                  <--- Thread A (unlocked the mutex)
  return instance_                <--- Thread A (returns)
```

As a rule of thumb, you should always look between the lines of the code. There is always a gap between two statements, and that gap will make two or more threads interfere with each other. The next section discusses a classic example of incrementing a number in detail.

A synchronized increment

Almost every book touching on the topic of thread synchronization uses the classic example of incrementing a number as a data racing example. This book is not an exception. The example follows:

```
#include <thread>

int counter = 0;

void foo()
{
  counter++;
}

int main()
{
  std::jthread A{foo};
  std::jthread B{foo};
  std::jthread C{[]{foo();}};
  std::jthread D{
    []{
      for (int ix = 0; ix < 10; ++ix) { foo(); }
    }
  };
}
```

We added a couple more threads to make the example more complex. The preceding code does nothing more than increment the `counter` variable using four different threads. At first glance, at any point in time, only one of the threads increments `counter`. However, as we mentioned in the previous section, we should be attentive and look for gaps in the code. The `foo()` function seems to be missing one. The increment operator behaves in the following way (as pseudocode):

```
auto res = counter;
counter = counter + 1;
return res;
```

Now, we have discovered gaps where there weren't supposed to be any. So now, at any point in time, only one thread executes one of the three preceding instructions. That is, something like the following is possible:

```
auto res = counter;     <--- thread A
counter = counter + 1;  <--- thread B
return res;             <--- thread C
```

So, for example, `thread B` might modify the value of `counter` while `thread A` reads its previous value. That means `thread A` will assign a new increment value to `counter` when it has been already done by `thread B`. The confusion introduces chaos and, sooner or later, our brains will explode trying to understand the ordering of operations. As a classic example, we'll move on to solving it by using thread-locking mechanisms. Here's a popular solution:

```
#include <thread>
#include <mutex>

int counter = 0;
std::mutex m;

void foo()
{
  std::lock_guard g{m};
  counter++;
}

int main()
{
  // code omitted for brevity
}
```

Whichever thread arrives at `lock_guard` first locks `mutex`, as shown here:

```
lock mutex;              <--- thread A, B, D wait for the locked mutex
auto res = counter;      <--- thread C has locked the mutex
counter = counter + 1;
unlock mutex;            <--- A, B, D are blocked until C reaches here
return res;
```

The problem with using locking is performance. In theory, we use threads to speed up program execution, more specifically, data processing. In the case of big collections of data, using multiple threads might increase the program's performance drastically. However, in a multithreaded environment, we take care of concurrent access first because accessing the collection with multiple threads might lead to its corruption. For example, let's look at a thread-safe stack implementation.

Implementing a thread-safe stack

Recall the stack data structure adapter from `Chapter 6`, *Digging into Data Structures and Algorithms in STL*. We are going to implement a thread-safe version of the stack using locks. The stack has two basic operations, `push` and `pop`. Both of them modify the state of the container. As you know, the stack is not a container itself; it's an adapter that wraps a container and provides an adapted interface to access. We will wrap `std::stack` in a new class by incorporating thread-safety. Besides construction and destruction functions, `std::stack` provides the following functions:

- `top()`: Accesses the top element of the stack
- `empty()`: Returns true if the stack is empty
- `size()`: Returns the current size of the stack
- `push()`: Inserts a new item into the stack (at the top)
- `emplace()`: Constructs an element in place at the top of the stack
- `pop()`: Removes the top element of the stack
- `swap()`: Swaps the contents with another stack

We will keep it simple and concentrate on the idea of thread-safety rather than making a powerful full-featured stack. The main concerns here are functions that modify the underlying data structure. Our interest lies in the `push()` and `pop()` functions. Those are functions that might corrupt the data structure if several threads interfere with each other. So, the following declaration is the class representing a thread-safe stack:

```
template <typename T>
class safe_stack
{
public:
  safe_stack();
  safe_stack(const safe_stack& other);
  void push(T value); // we will std::move it instead of copy-referencing
  void pop();
  T& top();
  bool empty() const;

private:
  std::stack<T> wrappee_;
  mutable std::mutex mutex_;
};
```

Note that we declared `mutex_` as mutable because we locked it in the `empty()` const function. It's arguably a better design choice than removing the const-ness of `empty()`. However, you should know by now that using a mutable for any of the data members suggests that we have made bad design choices. Anyway, the client code for `safe_stack` won't care much about the inner details of the realization; it doesn't even know that the stack uses a mutex to synchronize concurrent access.

Let's now look at the implementation of its member functions along with a short description. Let's start with the copy constructor:

```
safe_stack::safe_stack(const safe_stack& other)
{
  std::lock_guard<std::mutex> lock(other.mutex_);
  wrappee_ = other.wrappee_;
}
```

Note that we locked the mutex of the other stack. As unfair as it might seem, we need to make sure that the underlying data of the other stack won't get modified while we make a copy of it.

Next, let's look at the implementation of the `push()` function. It's obviously simple; we lock the mutex and push the data into the underlying stack:

```
void safe_stack::push(T value)
{
  std::lock_guard<std::mutex> lock(mutex_);
  // note how we std::move the value
  wrappee_.push(std::move(value));
}
```

Almost all functions incorporate thread synchronization in the same way: locking the mutex, doing the job, and unlocking the mutex. This ensures that only one thread is accessing the data at any one time. That said, to protect data from race conditions, we must ensure that the function invariants aren't broken.

If you are not a fan of typing long C++ type names such as `std::lock_guard<std::mutex>`, use the `using` keyword to make short aliases for types, for example, using `locker = std::guard<std::mutex>;`.

Now, moving on to the pop() function, we can modify the class declaration to make pop() directly return the value at the top of the stack. We do this mostly because we don't want someone to access the top of the stack (with a reference) and then pop that data from within another thread. So, we will modify the pop() function to make a shared object and then return the stack element:

```
std::shared_ptr<T> pop()
{
  std::lock_guard<std::mutex> lock(mutex_);
  if (wrappee_.empty()) {
    throw std::exception("The stack is empty");
  }
  std::shared_ptr<T>
top_element{std::make_shared<T>(std::move(wrappee_.top()))};
  wrappee_.pop();
  return top_element;
}
```

Note that the declaration of the safe_stack class should also change according to the pop() function modifications. Also, we don't need top() anymore.

Designing lock-free data structures

If at least one thread is guaranteed to make progress, then we say it's a lock-free function. Compared to lock-based functions, where one thread can block another and they both might wait for some condition before making progress, a lock-free state ensures progress is made by at least one of the threads. We say that algorithms and data structures using data synchronization primitives are blocking, that is, a thread is suspended until another thread performs an action. That means the thread can't make progress until the block is removed (typically, unlocking a mutex). Our interest lies in data structures and algorithms that don't use blocking functions. We call some of them lock-free, although we should make a distinction between the types of non-blocking algorithms and data structures.

Using atomic types

Earlier in the chapter, we introduced the gaps between lines of source code as the reason for data races. Whenever you have an operation that consists of more than one instruction, your brain should alert you about a possible issue. However, it doesn't matter how much you strive to make operations independent and singular; most of the time, you can't achieve anything without breaking operations into steps involving multiple instructions. C++ comes to the rescue by providing atomic types.

First, let's understand why the word atomic is used. In general, we understand atomic to mean something that can't be broken down into smaller parts. That is, an atomic operation is an operation that can't be half-done: it's done or it isn't. An example of an atomic operation might be the simple assignment of an integer:

```
num = 37;
```

If two threads access this line of code, neither of them can encounter it half-done. In other words, there are no gaps between the assignment. Of course, the same statement might have a lot of gaps if `num` represents a complex object with a user-defined assignment operator.

An atomic operation is an indivisible operation.

On the other hand, a non-atomic operation might be seen as half-done. The classic example is the increment operation that we discussed earlier. In C++, all operations on atomic types are also atomic. That means we can avoid gaps between lines by using atomic types. Before using atomics, we could create atomic operations by using mutexes. For example, we might consider the following function atomic:

```
void foo()
{
  mutex.lock();
  int a{41};
  int b{a + 1};
  mutex.unlock();
}
```

The difference between a real atomic operation and the fake one we just made is that atomic operations don't require locks. That's actually a big difference, because synchronization mechanisms such as mutexes incorporate overhead and performance penalties. To be more precise, atomic types leverage lower-level mechanisms to ensure the independent and atomic execution of instructions. The standard atomic types are defined in the `<atomic>` header. However, standard atomic types might also use internal locking. To make sure they don't use internal locking, all atomic types in the standard library expose the `is_lock_free()` function.

The only atomic type that doesn't have the `is_lock_free()` member function is `std::atomic_flag`. The operations on this type are required to be lock-free. It's a Boolean flag and most of the time it is used as a base to implement other lock-free types.

That said, obj.is_lock_free() returns true if operations on obj are done directly with atomic instructions. If it returns false, it means internal locking is used. There is more: the static constexpr function is_always_lock_free() returns true if the atomic type is lock-free for all supported hardware. As the function is constexpr, it allows us to define whether the type is lock-free at compile time. That's a big advancement and affects the organization and execution of the code in a good way. For example, std::atomic<int>::is_always_lock_free() returns true as std::atomic<int> is most probably always lock-free.

In Greek, a means not and tomo means cut. The word atom comes from the Greek atomos, which translates to uncuttable. That is, by atomic we consider indivisible smallest units. We use atomic types and operations to avoid gaps between instructions.

We use specializations for atomic types, for example, std::atomic<long>; however, you can refer to the following table for more convenient names for atomic types. The left-hand column of the table contains the atomic type and the right-hand column contains its specialization:

Atomic type	**Specialization**
atomic_bool	std::atomic<bool>
atomic_char	std::atomic<char>
atomic_schar	std::atomic<signed char>
atomic_uchar	std::atomic<unsigned char>
atomic_int	std::atomic<int>
atomic_uint	std::atomic<unsigned>
atomic_short	std::atomic<short>
atomic_ushort	std::atomic<unsigned short>
atomic_long	std::atomic<long>
atomic_ulong	std::atomic<unsigned long>
atomic_llong	std::atomic<long long>
atomic_ullong	std::atomic<unsigned long long>
atomic_char16_t	std::atomic<char16_t>
atomic_char32_t	std::atomic<char32_t>
atomic_wchar_t	std::atomic<wchar_t>

The preceding table represents basic atomic types. The fundamental difference between a regular type and, an atomic type is the kind of operations we can apply to them. Let's now discuss atomic operations in more detail.

Operations on atomic types

Recall the gaps we were discussing in the previous section. The goal of atomic types is to either eliminate gaps between instructions or provide operations that take care of combining several instructions together wrapped as a single instruction. The following are operations on atomic types:

- `load()`
- `store()`
- `exchange()`
- `compare_exchange_weak()`
- `compare_exchange_strong()`
- `wait()`
- `notify_one()`
- `notify_all()`

The `load()` operation atomically loads and returns the value of the atomic variable. `store()` atomically replaces the value of the atomic variable with the provided non-atomic argument.

Both `load()` and `store()` are similar to regular read and assign operations for non-atomic variables. Whenever we access the value of an object, we execute a read instruction. For example, the following code prints the contents of the `double` variable:

```
double d{4.2}; // "store" 4.2 into "d"
std::cout << d; // "read" the contents of "d"
```

In the case of atomic types, a similar read operation is transformed into this:

```
atomic_int m;
m.store(42);              // atomically "store" the value
std::cout << m.load();    // atomically "read" the contents
```

Although the preceding code bears no meaning, we included the example to represent the differences in treating atomic types. Accessing atomic variables should be done through atomic operations. The following code represents definitions for the `load()`, `store()`, and `exchange()` functions:

```
T load(std::memory_order order = std::memory_order_seq_cst) const noexcept;
void store(T value, std::memory_order order =
            std::memory_order_seq_cst) noexcept;
T exchange(T value, std::memory_order order =
            std::memory_order_seq_cst) noexcept;
```

As you can see, there is the additional parameter named `order` of type `std::memory_order`. We will describe it shortly. The `exchange()` function comprises the `store()` and `load()` functions in a way that atomically replaces the value with the provided argument and atomically obtains the previous value.

The `compare_exchange_weak()` and `compare_exchange_strong()` functions work similarly to each other. Here's how they are defined:

```
bool compare_exchange_weak(T& expected_value, T target_value,
                           std::memory_order order =
                            std::memory_order_seq_cst) noexcept;
bool compare_exchange_strong(T& expected_value, T target_value,
                            std::memory_order order =
                             std::memory_order_seq_cst) noexcept;
```

They compare the first argument (`expected_value`) with the atomic variable and if they are equal, replace the variable with the second argument (`target_value`). Otherwise, they atomically load the value into the first argument (that's why it is passed by reference). The difference between weak and strong exchanges is that `compare_exchange_weak()` is allowed to fail falsely (called a **spurious failure**), that is, even when `expected_value` is equal to the underlying value, the function treats them as not equal. That's done because on some platforms it leads to increased performance.

The `wait()`, `notify_one()`, and `notify_all()` functions have been added since C++20. The `wait()` function blocks the thread until the value of the atomic object modifies. It takes an argument to compare with the value of the atomic object. If the values are equal, it blocks the thread. To manually unblock the thread, we can call `notify_one()` or `notify_all()`. The difference between them is that `notify_one()` unblocks at least one blocked operation, while `notify_all()` unblocks all such operations.

Now, let's discuss the memory order that we encountered in the atomic type member functions declared previously. `std::memory_order` defines the order of memory accesses around atomic operation. When multiple threads simultaneously read and write to variables, a thread can read the changes in an order different from the order in which another thread stored them. The default order for atomic operations is sequentially consistent ordering – that's where `std::memory_order_seq_cst` comes in. There are several types of orders, including `memory_order_relaxed`, `memory_order_consume`, `memory_order_acquire`, `memory_order_release`, `memory_order_acq_rel`, and `memory_order_seq_cst`. In the next section, we'll design a lock-free stack that uses atomic types with the default memory order.

Designing a lock-free stack

One of the key things to keep in mind when designing a stack is to ensure that a pushed value is safe to return from another thread. Also important is ensuring that only one thread returns a value.

In the previous sections, we implemented a lock-based stack that wrapped `std::stack`. We know that a stack is not a real data structure but an adapter. Usually, when implementing a stack, we choose either a vector or a linked list as its underlying data structure. Let's look at an example of a lock-free stack based on a linked list. Pushing a new element into the stack involves creating a new list node, setting its `next` pointer to the current `head` node, and then setting the `head` node to point to the newly inserted node.

If you are confused by the terms head or next pointer, revisit `Chapter 6`, *Digging into Data Structures and Algorithms in STL*, where we discussed linked lists in detail.

In a single-threaded context, the steps described are fine; however, if there is more than one thread modifying the stack, we should start worrying. Let's find the pitfalls of the `push()` operation. Here are the three main steps happening when a new element is pushed into the stack:

1. `node* new_elem = new node(data);`
2. `new_elem->next = head_;`
3. `head_ = new_elem;`

In the first step, we declare the new node that will be inserted into the underlying linked list. The second step describes that we are inserting it at the front of the list – that's why the new node's `next` pointer points to `head_`. Finally, as the `head_` pointer represents the starting point of the list, we should reset its value to point to the newly added node, as done in step 3.

The node type is the internal struct that we use in the stack for representing a list node. Here's how it is defined:

```
template <typename T>
class lock_free_stack
{
private:
  struct node {
    T data;
    node* next;
```

```
    node(const T& d) : data(d) {}
  }

  node* head_;
// the rest of the body is omitted for brevity
};
```

The first thing that we suggest you do is look for gaps in the code – not in the preceding code, but in the steps we described when pushing a new element into the stack. Take a closer look at it. Imagine two threads are adding nodes at the same time. One thread at step 2 sets the next pointer of the new element to point to `head_`. The other thread makes `head_` point to the other new element. It's already obvious that this might lead to data corruption. It's crucial for a thread to have the same `head_` for both steps 2 and 3. To solve the race condition between steps 2 and 3, we should use an atomic compare/exchange operation to guarantee that `head_` wasn't modified when we read its value previously. As we need to access the head pointer atomically, here's how we modify `head_ member` in the `lock_free_stack` class:

```
template <typename T>
class lock_free_stack
{
private:
  // code omitted for brevity
  std::atomic<node*> head_;
  // code omitted for brevity
};
```

Here's how we implement a lock-free `push()` around the atomic `head_` pointer:

```
void push(const T& data)
{
  node* new_elem = new node(data);
  new_elem->next = head_.load();
  while (!head_.compare_exchange_weak(new_elem->next, new_elem));
}
```

We use `compare_exchange_weak()` to ensure that the `head_` pointer has the same value as we stored in `new_elem->next`. If it is, we set it to `new_elem`. Once `compare_exchange_weak()` succeeds, we are sure the node has been successfully inserted into the list.

See how we access nodes by using atomic operations. The atomic form of a pointer of type `T` - `std::atomic<T*>` - provides the same interface. Besides that, `std::atomic<T*>` provides pointer to the arithmetic operations `fetch_add()` and `fetch_sub()`. They do atomic addition and subtraction on the stored address. Here's an example:

```
struct some_struct {};
any arr[10];
std::atomic<some_struct*> ap(arr);
some_struct* old = ap.fetch_add(2);
// now old is equal to arr
// ap.load() is equal to &arr[2]
```

We intentionally named the pointer `old`, because `fetch_add()` adds the number to the address of the pointer and returns the `old` value. That's why `old` points to the same address that `arr` points to.

In the next section, we will introduce more operations available on atomic types. Now, let's get back to our lock-free stack. To `pop()` an element, that is, to remove a node, we need to read `head_` and set it to the next element of `head_`, as shown here:

```
void pop(T& popped_element)
{
  node* old_head = head_;
  popped_element = old_head->data;
  head_ = head_->next;
  delete old_head;
}
```

Now, take a good look at the preceding code. Imagine several threads executing it concurrently. What if two threads removing items from the stack read the same value of `head_`? This and a couple of other race conditions lead us to the following implementation:

```
void pop(T& popped_element)
{
  node* old_head = head_.load();
  while (!head_.compare_exchange_weak(old_head, old_head->next));
  popped_element = old_head->data;
}
```

We applied almost the same logic in the preceding code as we did with the `push()` function. The preceding code isn't perfect; it should be enhanced. We suggest you make the effort to modify it to eliminate memory leaks.

We have seen that lock-free implementations rely heavily on atomic types and operations. The operations we discussed in the previous section are not final. Let's now discover some more atomic operations.

More operations on atomics

In the previous section, we used `std::atomic<>` on a pointer to a user-defined type. That is, we declared the following structure for the list node:

```
// the node struct is internal to
// the lock_free_stack class defined above
struct node
{
  T data;
  node* next;
};
```

The node struct is a user-defined type. Although in the previous section we instantiated `std::atomic<node*>`, in the same way, we can instantiate `std::atomic<>` for almost any user-defined type, that is, `std::atomic<T>`. However, you should note that the interface of `std::atomic<T>` is limited to the following functions:

- `load()`
- `store()`
- `exchange()`
- `compare_exchange_weak()`
- `compare_exchange_strong()`
- `wait()`
- `notify_one()`
- `notify_all()`

Let's now look at the complete list of operations available on atomic types based on the specifics of the underlying type.

`std::atomic<>` instantiated with an integral type (such as an integer or a pointer) has the following operations along with the ones we listed previously:

- `fetch_add()`
- `fetch_sub()`
- `fetch_or()`
- `fetch_and()`
- `fetch_xor()`

Also, besides increment (`++`) and decrement (`--`), the following operators are also available: `+=`, `-=`, `|=`, `&=`, and `^=`.

Finally, there is a special atomic type called `atomic_flag` with two available operations:

- `clear()`
- `test_and_set()`

You should consider `std::atomic_flag` a bit with atomic operations. The `clear()` function clears it, while `test_and_set()` changes the value to `true` and returns the previous value.

Summary

In this chapter, we introduced a rather simple example of designing a stack. There are more complex examples to research and follow. When we discussed designing a concurrent stack, we looked at two versions, one of them representing a lock-free stack. Compared to lock-based solutions, lock-free data structures and algorithms are the ultimate goal for programmers as they provide mechanisms to avoid data races without even synchronizing the resources.

We also introduced atomic types and operations that you can use in your projects to make sure instructions are indivisible. As you already know, if an instruction is atomic, there is no need to worry about its synchronization. We strongly suggest you continue researching the topic and build more robust and complex lock-free data structures. In the next chapter, we will see how to design world-ready applications.

Questions

1. Why did we check the instance twice in the multithreaded singleton implementation?
2. In the implementation of the lock-based stack's copy constructor, we locked the mutex of the other stack. Why?
3. What are atomic types and atomic operations?
4. Why do we use `load()` and `store()` for atomic types?
5. What additional operations are supported on `std::atomic<T*>`?

Further reading

- *Concurrent Patterns and Best Practices by Atul Khot,* at https://www.packtpub.com/application-development/concurrent-patterns-and-best-practices
- *Mastering C++ Multithreading by Maya Posch,* at https://www.packtpub.com/application-development/mastering-c-multithreading

10 Designing World-Ready Applications

Using a programming language in production-ready projects is a whole new step in learning the language itself. Sometimes, the simple examples in this book may take a different approach or face many difficulties in real-world programs. When theory meets practice is when you learn the language. C++ is not an exception. It's different to learn syntax, solve some book problems, or understand somewhat simple examples in books. When creating real-world applications, we face a different range of challenges, and sometimes books lack the theory to back the practical issues on the road.

In this chapter, we will try to cover the basics of practical programming with C++ that will help you to tackle real-world applications better. Complex projects require a lot of thinking and designing. Sometimes, programmers have to completely rewrite the project and start from scratch just because they have made bad design choices at the beginning of development. This chapter tries its best to illuminate the process of designing software. You will learn the steps to better architecture for your projects.

We will cover the following topics in this chapter:

- Understanding the project development life cycle
- Design patterns and their applications
- Domain-driven design
- Designing an Amazon clone as an example of a real-world project

Technical requirements

The g++ compiler with the `-std=c++2a` option is used to compile the examples throughout this chapter. You can find the source files used in this chapter at `https://github.com/PacktPublishing/Expert-CPP`.

Project development life cycle

Whenever you approach a problem, you should carefully consider the process of the requirements analysis. One of the biggest mistakes in project development is starting coding without a thorough analysis of the problem itself.

Imagine a situation where you are tasked with creating a calculator, a simple tool that allows users to make arithmetic calculations on numbers. Let's say you have magically completed the project on time and released the program. Now, users are starting to use your calculator and sooner or later they find out that the result of their calculations doesn't exceed the maximum size of an integer. When they complain about this issue, you are ready to defend yourself (and your creation) with solid coding-backed arguments such as it's because of using the `int` data type in calculations. It's totally understandable for you and your fellow programmers, but end users just can't take your arguments. They want a tool that allows summing some big enough numbers, otherwise, they won't use your program at all. You start working on the next version of your calculator and this time, you use longs or even custom implemented big numbers. You proudly ship your program to users waiting for their applause when you suddenly realize that the same users complain of not having the functionality to find logarithms or exponents of numbers. This seems daunting because there might be more and more feature requests and more and more complaints.

Though this example is somewhat simple, it totally covers what usually happens in the real world. Even when you implement all of the features for your program and are thinking about taking a long-deserved vacation, users will start complaining about the bugs in the program. It turns out that there are several cases when your calculator behaves unexpectedly and gives no or wrong results. Sooner or later, you realize that proper testing is what you actually need before releasing the program to the masses.

We will touch on the subjects that should be considered when working on real-world projects. Whenever you are starting a new project, the following steps should be taken into account:

1. Requirements gathering and analysis
2. Specification creation

3. Design and test planning
4. Coding
5. Testing and stabilization
6. Release and maintenance

The preceding steps are not hardcoded for every project, though it might be considered as the bare minimum that every software development team should complete to achieve a successful product release. In reality, most of the steps are omitted due to the single thing everyone in the IT field lacks the most— time. However, it is strongly recommended to follow the preceding steps because, eventually, it will save more time in the long- term.

Requirements gathering and analysis

This is the most crucial step in creating a stable product. One of the most popular reasons that programmers fail to complete their tasks on time or leave a lot of bugs in code is the lack of a complete understanding of the project.

The domain knowledge is so important that it shouldn't be omitted in any circumstance. You might be lucky to develop projects that are related to something you know very well. However, you should take into account that not everyone is as lucky as you (well, you might be that unlucky, too).

Imagine that you are working on a project that automates the analysis and reporting of the stock trading in some company. Now imagine that you know nothing about stocks and the stock trading at all. You don't know about the bear or bull markets, the limitations in trading transactions, and so on. How would you complete the project successfully?

Even if you know about the stock markets and trading, you might be unaware of your next big project domain. What if you are tasked with designing and implementing (with or without a team) a project that controls the weather stations of your city? What you are going to do first when starting the project?

You should definitely start with requirements gathering and analysis. It's just a process that involves communicating with the client and asking a lot of questions about the project. If you are not dealing with any client but work in a product company, the project manager should be treated as the client. Even if the project is your idea and you are working alone, you should treat yourself as the client and, though it might sound ridiculous, ask yourself a lot of questions (about the project).

Let's suppose we are going to conquer e-commerce and want to release a product that will eventually beat the market sharks in their own business. Popular and successful e-commerce marketplaces are Amazon, eBay, Alibaba, and some others. We should state the problem as *writing our own Amazon clone*. What should we do to gather the requirements for the project?

First of all, we should list all of the features that we should implement and then we'll prioritize. For example, for the Amazon clone project, we might come up with the following list of features:

- Create a product.
- List products.
- Buy a product.
- Edit product details.
- Remove a product.
- Search for products by name, price range, and weight.
- Alert the user on product availability once in a while via email.

Features should be described in detail as much as possible; that will sort things out for the developer (you, in this case). For example, creating a product should be done either by the project administrator or any user. If a user can create a product, it should have limitations, if any. There might be cases that a user will mistakenly create hundreds of products in our system to increase the visibility of their only product.

Details should be stated, discussed, and finalized during communications with the client. If you are alone in the project and you are the client of your project, the communication is the process of *thinking for yourself* on the project requirements.

When finished getting requirements, we suggest prioritizing each feature and classifying them into one of the following categories:

- Must have
- Should have
- Nice to have

After thinking a little bit more and categorizing the preceding features, we could come up with the following list:

- Create a product [must have].
- List products [must have].
- Buy a product [must have].

- Edit product details [should have].
- Remove a product [must have].
- Search for products by name [must have].
- Search for products by price range [should have].
- Search for products by weight [nice to have].
- Alert the user on product availability once in a while via email [nice to have].

The classification will give you a basic idea of where to start first. Programmers are greedy people; they want to implement every possible feature out there for their products. It's a sure way toward failure. You should start from the most essential features first—that's why we have a couple of nice-to-have features. Some jokingly insist that nice-to-have features should be renamed to never-have features because, in practice, they never get implemented.

Specification creation

Not everyone likes creating specifications. Well, most programmers hate this step because it's not coding—it's writing.

After gathering project requirements, you should create a document that includes every detail that describes your project. There are many names and types for this specification. It might be called a **Project Requirements Document** (**PRD**), a **functional specification**, a **development specification**, and so on. Serious programmers and serious teams produce a PRD as a result of the requirements analysis. The next step of these serious guys is creating the functional specification along with the development specification and so on. We combine all of the documentation in a single step named **specification creation.**

It's up to you and your team to decide whether you need any of the sub-documents mentioned previously. It is even better to have a visual representation of the product rather than a text document. Whatever the form your document takes, it should carefully represent what you've achieved in the requirements gathering step. To have a basic understanding of this, let's try to document some of the features that we've collected earlier (we will refer to our project as *the platform)*

- Create a product. A user of the platform having administrator privileges can create a product.
- The platform must allow creating users with defined privileges. At this point, there should be two types of users, namely regular and administrator users.

- Any user using the platform must be able to see the list of available products.
- A product should have images, a price, name, weight, and description.
- To buy a product, the user provides their card details to cash out and details for the product shipment.
- Each registered user should provide a delivery address, credit card details, and an email account.

The list might go long and it actually should go long because the longer the list, the more the developers understand the project.

Design and test planning

Though we insisted on the requirement gathering step as the most crucial in software development, the designing and test planning can be considered an equally crucial step as well. If you have ever started a project without designing it first, you already have the idea of its impossibility. Though motivational quotes insist that nothing is impossible, programmers are sure that at least one thing is impossible and that is finishing a project successfully without designing it first.

The process of designing is the most interesting step; it forces us to think, draw, think again, clear everything, and start over. Many features of the project are discovered while designing it. To design a project, you should start from the top. First of all, list all of the entities and processes that are somehow involved in the project. For the Amazon clone example, we can list the following entities and processes:

- Users
- Registration and authorization
- Products
- Transactions
- Warehouses (containing products)
- Shipment

This is a high-level design—a starting point to move through the final design. In this chapter, we will mostly concentrate on the design of the project.

Decomposing entities

After listing key entities and processes, we move to decompose them into more detailed entities that will be transformed into classes later. It's even better to sketch the design of the project. Just draw rectangles containing names of entities and connect them with arrows if they are somehow connected together or are parts of the same process. You can start an arrow from entity A to entity B if there is a process that includes or is started by the entity A and is finished at or results in entity B. It doesn't matter how good the drawing is, it's a necessary step toward a better understanding of the project. For example, look at the following diagram:

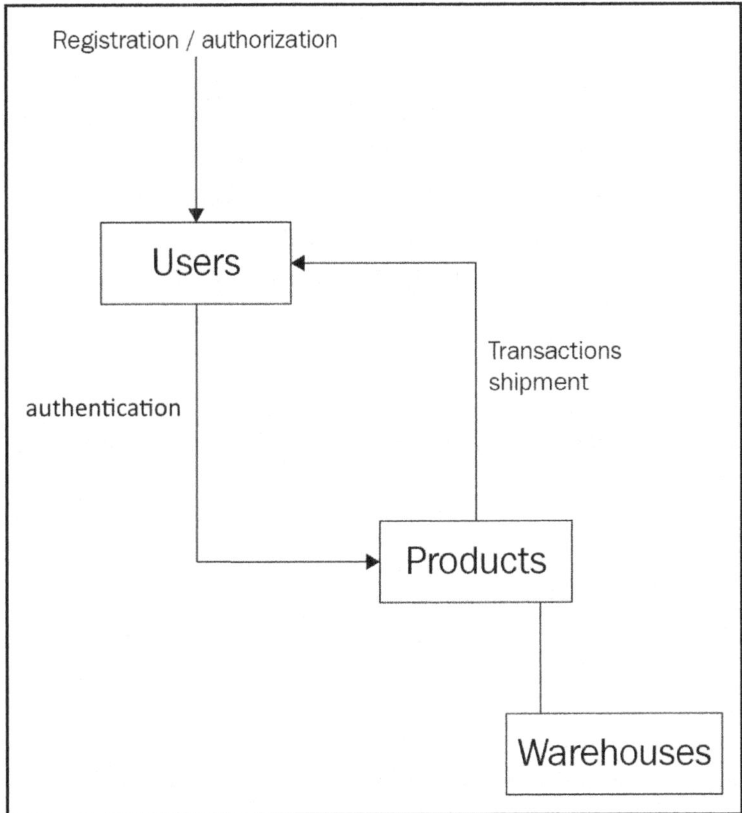

Decomposing entities and processes into classes and their intercommunication is a subtle art requiring patience and consistency. For example, let's try to add details for the **User** entity. As stated in the specification creation step, a registered user should provide a delivery address, an email address, and credit card details. Let's draw a class diagram that represents a user:

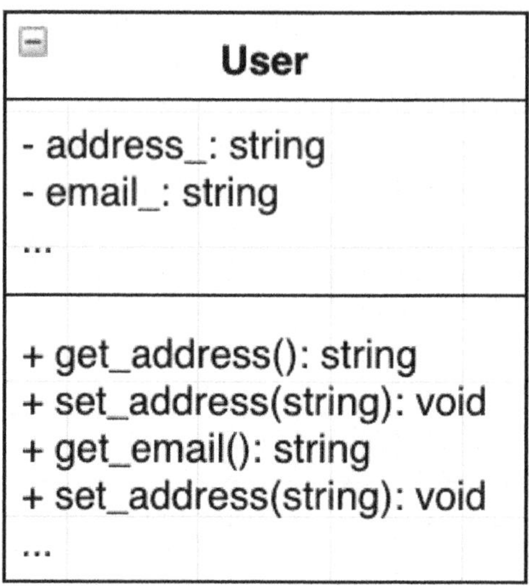

And here comes the interesting question: what should we do with complex types contained within the entity? For example, the delivery address of a user is a complex type. It couldn't be just `string`, because sooner or later we might need to sort users by their delivery addresses to make optimal shipments. For example, a shipment company might cost us (or the user) a fortune if the delivery address of the user is in a different country than the address of the warehouse that contains the purchased product. This is a great scenario because it introduces a new problem and updates our understanding of the project. It turns out that we should handle situations when a user orders a product that is assigned to a specific warehouse physically located far from the user. If we have many warehouses, we should choose the nearest one to the user that contains the required product. These are questions that couldn't be answered right away, but that is the quality result of designing the project. Otherwise, these questions would have risen during the coding and we would have been stuck at them longer than we thought we would. The initial estimation of the project wouldn't meet its completion date in any known universe.

Now, how would you store the user address in the `User` class? A simple `std::string` would be fine as shown in the following example:

```
class User
{
public:
  // code omitted for brevity
private:
  std::string address_;
  // code omitted for brevity
};
```

An address is a complex object in terms of its components. An address might consist of the country name, country code, city name, and street name, and it might even contain latitude and longitude. The latter is great if you need to find the nearest warehouse to the user. It's totally fine to make more types that would make the design more intuitive for programmers. For example, the following struct might be a good fit to express the address of a user:

```
struct Address
{
  std::string country;
  std::string city;
  std::string street;
  float latitude{};
  float longitude{};
};
```

Now, storing a user address becomes even simpler:

```
class User
{
  // code omitted for brevity
  Address address_;
};
```

We will get back to this example later in this chapter.

The process of designing the project might require to go back a couple of steps to restate project requirements. After clarifying the design step with the previous steps, we can move forward to decompose the project into smaller components. It's better to create interaction diagrams, too.

An interaction diagram like the following would depict operations such as a transaction made by a **user** to **purchase** a product:

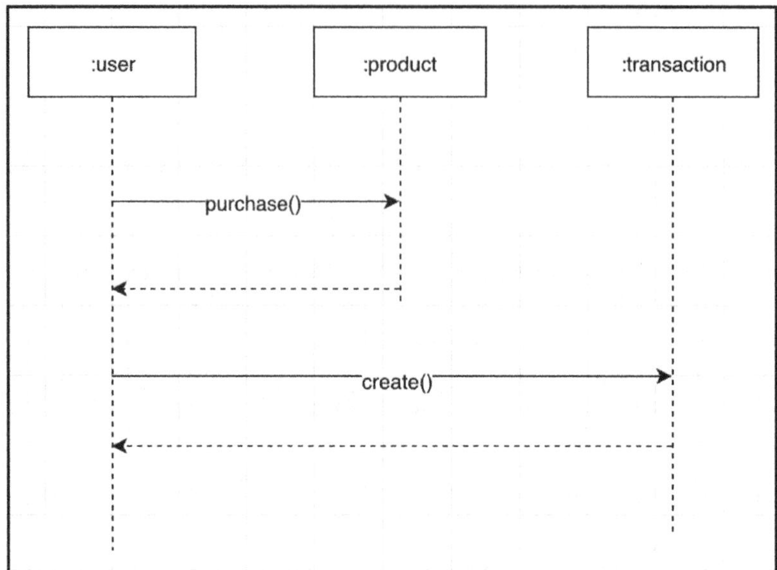

Test planning can also be considered as part of the design. It includes planning how the final application will be tested. For example, the steps before this include a concept for an address and as it turned out, the address can contain a country, city, and so on. A proper test should include checking whether a value for the country can be set successfully in the user address. Though test planning is not considered a programmer task in general, it is still a good practice to do it for your projects. A proper test plan would produce more useful information while designing the project. Most of the input data processing and security checks are discovered at test planning. For instance, setting a strict limit on the user name or email address might not be the case when doing a requirement analysis or writing a functional specification. Test planning cares for such scenarios and forces developers to take care of data checks. However, most programmers are impatient to reach the next step of project development, coding.

Coding

As already said earlier, coding is not the only part of project development. Before coding, you should carefully design your project by leveraging all of the requirements projected in the specification. Coding is a lot easier and more productive after the previous steps of project development are completed thoroughly.

Some teams practice **Test-Driven Development (TDD)**, which is a great way to produce even more stable project releases. The main concept of TDD is to write tests before the project implementation. It's a good way for programmers to define project requirements and answer further questions rising during the development.

Let's suppose we are implementing setters for the `User` class. The user object contains an email field discussed earlier, which means that we should have a `set_email()` method, as shown in the following snippet:

```
class User
{
public:
  // code omitted for brevity
  void set_email(const std::string&);

private:
  // code omitted for brevity
  std::string email_;
};
```

The TDD approach suggests writing a test function for the `set_email()` method before implementing the `set_email()` method itself. Let's say we have the following test function:

```
void test_set_email()
{
  std::string valid_email = "valid@email.com";
  std::string invalid_email = "112%$";
  User u;
  u.set_email(valid_email);
  u.set_email(invalid_email);
}
```

In the preceding code, we've declared two `string` variables, one of them containing an invalid value for an email address. Even before running the test function, we know that, in the case of invalid data input, the `set_email()` method should react somehow. One of the common approaches is throwing an exception indicating the invalid input. You could also ignore the invalid input in the `set_email` implementation and return a `boolean` value indicating the success of the operation. The error handling should be consistent in the project and agreed by all team members. Let's consider that we are going with throwing an exception, therefore, the test function should expect an exception when passing an invalid value to the method.

The preceding code is then should be rewritten as shown here:

```
void test_set_email()
{
  std::string valid_email = "valid@email.com";
  std::string invalid_email = "112%$";

  User u;
  u.set_email(valid_email);
  if (u.get_email() == valid_email) {
    std::cout << "Success: valid email has been set successfully" <<
std::endl;
  } else {
    std::cout << "Fail: valid email has not been set" << std::endl;
  }

  try {
    u.set_email(invalid_email);
    std::cerr << "Fail: invalid email has not been rejected" << std::endl;
  } catch (std::exception& e) {
    std::cout << "Success: invalid email rejected" << std::endl;
  }
}
```

The test function seems complete. Whenever we run the test function, it outputs the current state of the `set_email()` method. Even if we haven't yet implemented the `set_email()` function, the corresponding test function is a big step toward its implementation details. We now have the basic idea of how should the function react to valid and invalid data inputs. We can add more kinds of data to make sure the `set_email()` method will be thoroughly tested when its implementation is complete. For example, we can test it with empty and long strings.

Here's an initial implementation of the `set_email()` method:

```
#include <regex>
#include <stdexcept>

void User::set_email(const std::string& email)
{
  if (!std::regex_match(email,
std::regex("(\\w+)(\\.|_)?(\\w*)@(\\w+)(\\.(\\w+))+")) {
    throw std::invalid_argument("Invalid email");
  }

  this->email_ = email;
}
```

After the initial implementation of the method, we should run our test function again to make sure that the implementation conforms with the defined test cases.

Writing tests for your project is considered as a good coding practice. There are different types of tests, such as unit tests, regression tests, smoke tests, and so on. Developers should support unit test coverage for their projects.

The process of coding is one of the steps in the project development life cycle that is the most chaotic. It's hard to estimate how long will the implementation of a class or its methods will take because most of the questions and difficulties arise during coding. The previous steps of the project development life cycle described at the beginning of this chapter tend to cover most of these questions and ease the process of coding.

Testing and stabilization

After the project is done, it should be properly tested. Usually, software development companies have **Quality Assurance** (**QA**) engineers who meticulously test the project.

Issues verified during the testing phase are converted into corresponding tasks assigned to programmers to fix them. Issues might affect the release of the project or might be classified as minor issues.

The basic task of the programmer is not fixing the issue right away, but finding the root cause of the issue. For the sake of simplicity, let's take a look at the `generate_username()` function that uses random numbers combined with the email to generate a username:

```
std::string generate_username(const std::string& email)
{
  int num = get_random_number();
  std::string local_part = email.substr(0, email.find('@'));
  return local_part + std::to_string(num);
}
```

The `generate_username()` function calls `get_random_number()` to combine the returned value with the local part of the email address. The local part is the part before the `@` symbol in the email address.

QA engineers reported that the number attached to the local part of the email is always the same. For example, for the email `john@gmail.com`, the generated username is `john42`, and for `amanda@yahoo.com`, it's `amanda42`. So, the next time a user with the email `amanda@hotmail.com` tries to register in the system, the generated username, `amanda42`, conflicts with the already existing one. It's totally fine for testers not to be aware of the implementation details of the project, so they report it as an issue in the username generation functionality. While you might already guess that the real issue is hidden in the `get_random_number()` function, there can always be scenarios where the issue is fixed without finding its root cause. The wrong approach fixing the issue could mutate the implementation of the `generate_username()` function. The `generate_random_number()` function might be used in other functions as well, which in turn, will make all of the functions that call `get_random_number()` work incorrectly. Though the example is simple, it is crucial to think deeper and find the real reason behind the issue. That approach will save a lot of time in the future.

Release and maintenance

After making the project somewhat stable by fixing all of the critical and major issues, it can be released. Sometimes companies release software under the **beta** label, hence providing an excuse in case users find it buggy. It's important to note that there are rare cases of software that works flawlessly. After releasing it, more issues will arise. So, there comes the maintenance phase, when developers are working on fixes and release updates.

Programmers sometimes joke that release and maintenance are steps that are never achieved. However, if you spend enough time designing the project, releasing its first version won't take much time. As we have already introduced in the previous section, designing starts with requirements gathering. After that, we spend time on defining entities, decomposing them, breaking down into smaller components, coding, testing, and finally, releasing it. As developers, we are more interested in the designing and coding phases. As already noted, a good design choice has a great impact on further project development. Let's now have a closer look at the design process overall.

Diving into the design process

As introduced earlier, the project design starts with listing general entities, such as users, products, and warehouses when designing an e-commerce platform:

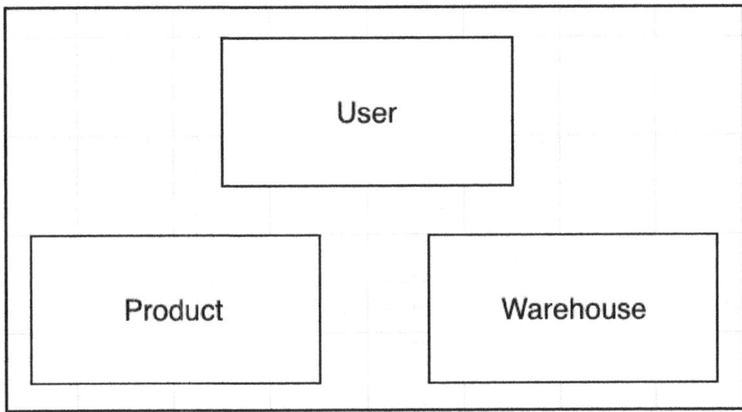

We then decompose each entity into smaller components. To make things clearer, consider each entity as a separate class. When thinking of an entity as a class, it makes more sense in terms of decomposition. For example, we express the `user` entity as a class:

```
class User
{
public:
  // constructors and assignment operators are omitted for code brevity
  void set_name(const std::string& name);
  std::string get_name() const;
  void set_email(const std::string&);
  std::string get_email() const;
  // more setters and getters are omitted for code brevity

private:
  std::string name_;
  std::string email_;
  Address address_;
  int age;
};
```

The class diagram for the `User` class is the following:

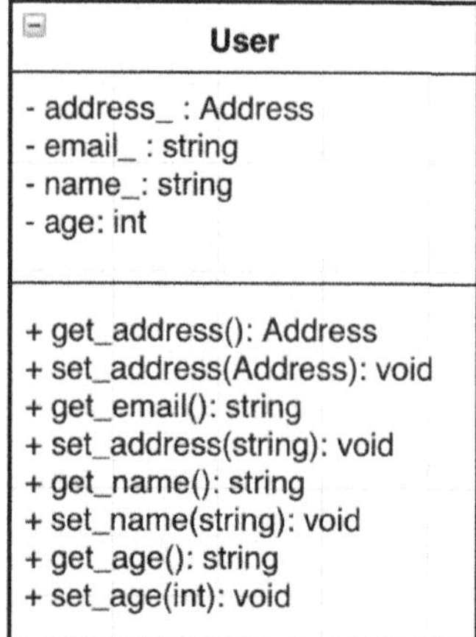

However, as we've already discussed, the address field of the `User` class might be represented as a separate type (`class` or `struct`, it doesn't matter much yet). Whether it's a data aggregate or a complex type, the class diagram takes the following changes:

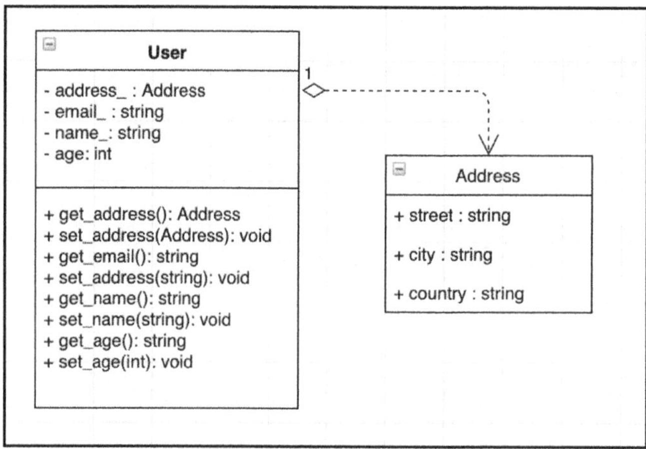

The relations between these entities will become clear during the design process. For example, the **Address** isn't an entity on its own, it's a part of the **User**, that is, it couldn't have an instance if a **User** object isn't instantiated. However, as we might want to gesture toward reusable code, the **Address** type might be used for warehouse objects as well. That is, the relation between the **User** and **Address** is a simple aggregation rather than a composition.

Moving forward, we could come up with more requirements for the **User** type when discussing the payment options. Users of the platform should be able to insert an option for paying for products. Before deciding on how will we represent payment options in the `User` class, we should find out what those options are, after all. Let's keep it simple and suppose that a payment option is one that contains a credit card number, the name of the cardholder, the expiration date, and the security code of the card. It sounds like another data aggregation, so let's collect all of that in a single struct, as shown here:

```
struct PaymentOption
{
  std::string number;
  std::string holder_name;
  std::chrono::year_month expiration_date;
  int code;
};
```

Note `std::chrono::year_month` in the preceding struct; it represents a specific month of a specific year and is introduced in C++20. Most payment cards carry only the month and year of the card expiration, so this `std::chrono::year_month` function is perfect for `PaymentOption`.

So, in the process of designing the `User` class, we came up with a new type, `PaymentOption`. A user can have more than one payment option, so the relation between `User` and `PaymentOption` is one-to-many. Let's now update our `User` class diagram with this new aggregation (though we go with composition in this case):

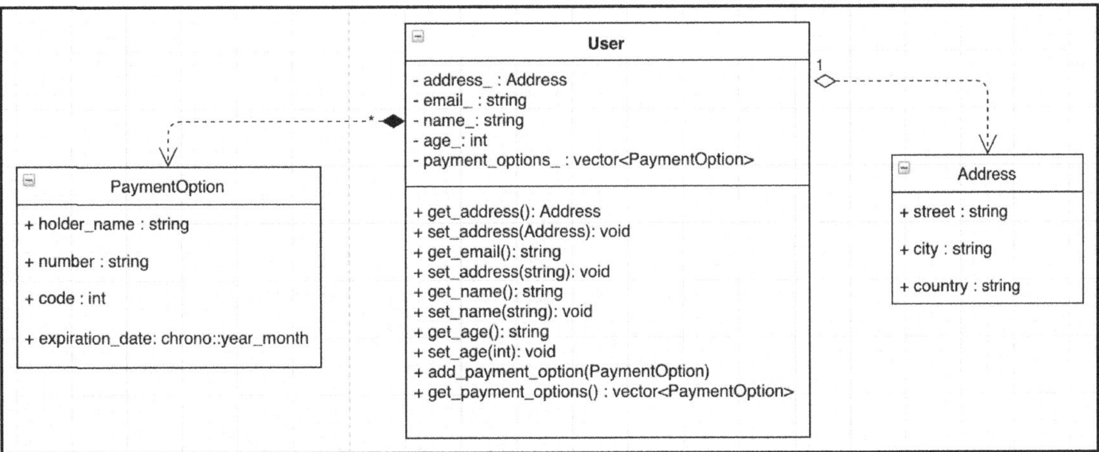

The dependency between `User` and `PaymentOption` is represented in the following code:

```
class User
{
public:
  // code omitted for brevity
  void add_payment_option(const PaymentOption& po) {
    payment_options_.push_back(op);
  }

  std::vector get_payment_options() const {
    return payment_options_;
  }
private:
  // code omitted for brevity
  std::vector<PaymentOption> payment_options_;
};
```

We should note that even though a user might have more than one payment option set up, we should mark one of them as primary. That's tricky because we could store all of the options in a vector, but now we have to make one of them the primary.

We can use a pair or `tuple` (if being fancy) to map an option in the vector with a `boolean` value, indicating whether it's primary or not. The following code depicts the usage of a tuple in the `User` class introduced earlier:

```
class User
{
public:
  // code omitted for brevity
  void add_payment_option(const PaymentOption& po, bool is_primary) {
    payment_options_.push_back(std::make_tuple(po, is_primary));
  }

  std::vector<std::tuple<PaymentOption, boolean> > get_payment_options()
const {
    return payment_options_;
  }
private:
  // code omitted for brevity
  std::vector<std::tuple<PaymentOption, boolean> > payment_options_;
};
```

We can simplify the code by leveraging type aliases in the following way:

```
class User
{
public:
```

```
  // code omitted for brevity
  using PaymentOptionList = std::vector<std::tuple<PaymentOption, boolean>
>;

  // add_payment_option is omitted for brevity
  PaymentOptionList get_payment_options() const {
    return payment_options_;
  }

private:
  // code omitted for brevity
  PaymentOptionList payment_options_;
};
```

Here's how the class user can retrieve the primary payment option for a user:

```
User john = get_current_user(); // consider the function is implemented and
works
auto payment_options = john.get_payment_options();
for (const auto& option : payment_options) {
  auto [po, is_primary] = option;
  if (is_primary) {
    // use the po payment option
  }
}
```

We used structured binding when accessing the tuple items in the `for` loop. However, after studying the chapter about data structures and algorithms, you are now aware that searching the primary payment option is a linear operation. It might be considered a bad practice to loop through the vector each time we need to retrieve the primary payment option.

You might change the underlying data structure to make things run faster. For example, `std::unordered_map` (that is, a hash table) sounds better. However, it doesn't make things faster just because it has constant-time access to its elements. In this scenario, we should map a `boolean` value to the payment option. For all of the options except one, the `boolean` value is the same falsy value. It will lead to collisions in the hash table, which will be handled by chaining values together mapped to the same hash value. The only benefit of using a hash table will be constant-time access to the primary payment option.

Finally, we come to the simplest solution to store the primary payment option separately in the class. Here's how we should rewrite the part of payment options' handling in the `User` class:

```
class User
{
public:
  // code omitted for brevity
  using PaymentOptionList = std::vector<PaymentOption>;
  PaymentOption get_primary_payment_option() const {
    return primary_payment_option_;
  }

  PaymentOptionList get_payment_options() const {
    return payment_options_;
  }

  void add_payment_option(const PaymentOption& po, bool is_primary) {
    if (is_primary) {
      // moving current primary option to non-primaries
      add_payment_option(primary_payment_option_, false);
      primary_payment_option_ = po;
      return;
    }
    payment_options_.push_back(po);
  }

private:
  // code omitted for brevity
  PaymentOption primary_payment_option_;
  PaymentOptionList payment_options_;
};
```

We took you through the process of defining the way to store payment options so far just to show the process of designing accompanied by coding. Though we've created a lot of versions for the single case of payment options, it's not final. There is always the case for handling duplicate values in the payment options vector. Whenever you add a payment option to the user as primary and then add another option as primary, the previous one goes to the non-primary list. If we change our minds and add the old payment option once again as a primary, it won't be removed from the non-primary list.

So, there are always opportunities to think deeper and avoid potential issues. Design and coding go hand in hand; however, you shouldn't forget about TDD. In most cases, writing tests before coding will help you to discover a lot of use cases.

Using SOLID principles

There are lots of principles and design methods that you can use in your project design. It's always better to keep the design simpler, however, there are principles that are useful in almost all projects in general. For example, **SOLID** comprises of five principles, all or some of which can be useful to the design.

SOLID stands for the following principles:

- Single responsibility
- Open-closed
- Liskov substitution
- Interface segregation
- Dependency inversion

Let's discuss each principle with examples.

The single responsibility principle

The single responsibility principle states the simple, that is, one object, one task. Try to reduce the functionality of your objects and their relationship complexity. Make each object have one responsibility even though it's not always easy to dissect a complex object into smaller and simpler components. Single responsibility is a context-bound concept. It's not about having just one method in a class; it's about making the class or module responsible for one thing. For example, the `User` class that we designed earlier has one responsibility: storing user information. However, we added payment options into the `User` class and forced it to have methods for adding and removing payment options. We also introduced a primary payment option, which involves additional logic in the **User** methods. We can move toward two directions.

The first one suggests decomposing the `User` class into two separate classes. Each class will have a single responsibility. The following class diagram depicts the idea:

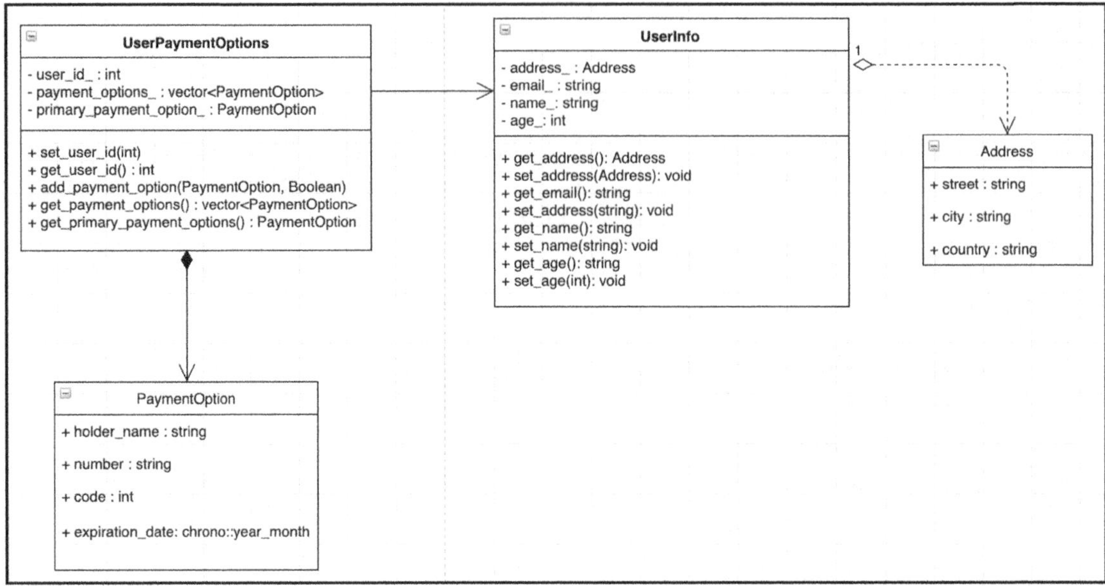

One of them will store only the user basic information, the next will store payment options for a user. We named them accordingly, `UserInfo` and `UserPaymentOptions`. Some might like this new design, but we will stick with the old one. And here's why. Though the `User` class contains both user information and payment options, the latter also represents a piece of information. We set and get payment options the same way we set and get the email of a user. So, we keep the `User` class the same because it's already satisfying the single responsibility principle. When we add the functionality to make a payment in the `User` class, that will break the peace. In that scenario, the `User` class will both store user information and make payment transactions. That's unacceptable in terms of the single responsibility principle, therefore, we won't do that.

The single responsibility principle relates to functions as well. The `add_payment_option()` method has two responsibilities. It adds a new primary payment option if the second (default) argument of the function is true. Otherwise, it adds the new payment option to the list of non-primary options. It's better to have a separate method for adding a primary payment option. That way, each of the methods will have a single responsibility.

The open-closed principle

The open-closed principle states that a class should be open for extension but closed for modification. It means that whenever you need new functionality, it's better to extend the base functionality instead of modifying it. For example, take the `Product` class of the e-commerce application that we designed. The following represents a simple diagram for the `Product` class:

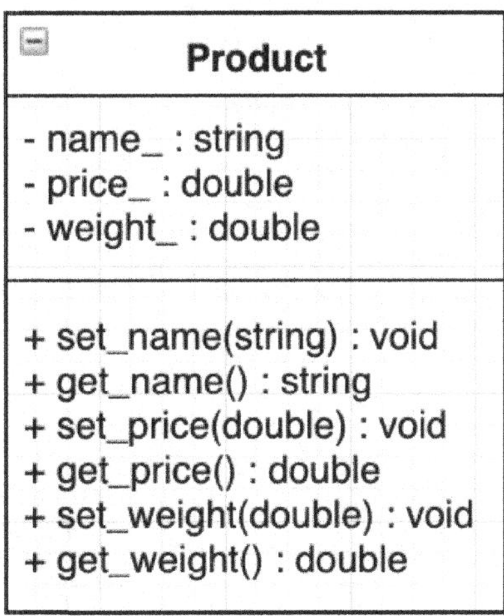

Each `Product` object has three properties: **name**, **price**, and **weight**. Now, imagine that after designing the `Product` class and the whole e-commerce platform, a new requirement comes from the clients. They now want to buy digital products, such as e-books, movies, and audio recordings. Everything is fine except for the weight of the product. Now that there might be two types of products—tangible and digital—we should rethink the logic of `Product` usage. We can incorporate a new function into `Product` as shown in the code here:

```
class Product
{
public:
  // code omitted for brevity
  bool is_digital() const {
    return weight_ == 0.0;
  }
  // code omitted for brevity
};
```

Obviously, we modified the class—contradicting the open-closed principle. The principle says that the class should be closed for modification. It should be open for extension. We can achieve that by redesigning the `Product` class and making it an abstract base class for all products. Next, we create two more classes inheriting the `Product` base class: `PhysicalProduct` and `DigitalProduct`. The following class diagram depicts the new design:

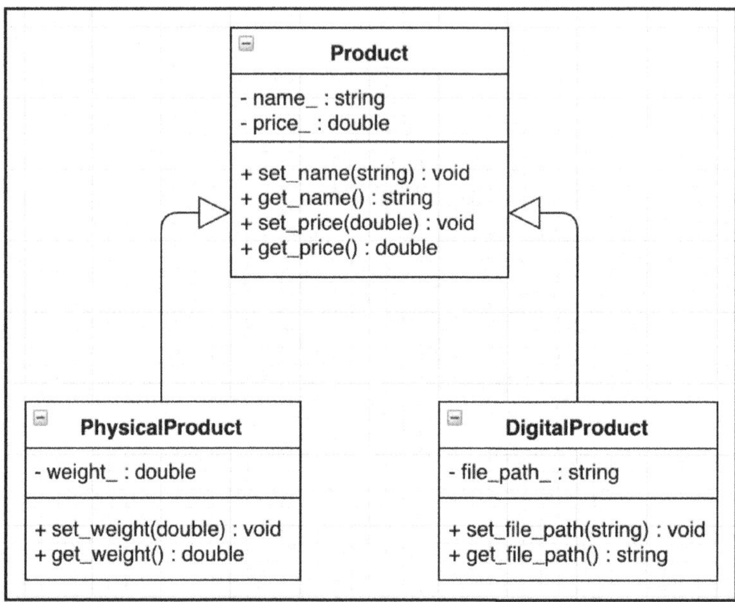

As you can see in the preceding diagram, we removed the `weight_` property from the `Product` class. Now that we have two more classes, `PhysicalProduct` has a `weight_` property and `DigitalProduct` does not have one. Instead, it has a `file_path_` property. This approach satisfies the open-closed principle because now all the classes are open for extension. We use inheritance to extend classes, and the following principle is strongly related to that.

The Liskov substitution principle

The Liskov substitution principle is about inheriting from a type the right way. In simple words, if there is a function that takes an argument of some type, then the same function should take an argument of the derived type.

The Liskov substitution principle is named after Barbara Liskov, a Turing Award winner and doctor of computer science.

Once you understand inheritance and the Liskov substitution principle, it's hard to forget it. Let's continue developing the `Product` class and add a new method that returns the price of the product based on the currency type. We can store the price in the same currency units and provide a function to convert the price for a specified currency. Here's the simple implementation of the method:

```
enum class Currency { USD, EUR, GBP }; // the list goes further

class Product
{
public:
  // code omitted for brevity
  double convert_price(Currency c) {
    // convert to proper value
  }

  // code omitted for brevity
};
```

After a while, the company decides to incorporate lifetime discounts for all digital products. Now, every digital product will have a 12% discount. Short time, we add a separate function in the `DigitalProduct` class that returns a converted price by applying the discount. Here's how it looks in `DigitalProduct`:

```
class DigitalProduct : public Product
{
public:
  // code omitted for brevity
  double convert_price_with_discount(Currency c) {
    // convert by applying a 12% discount
  }
};
```

The problem in the design is obvious. Calling `convert_price()` on the `DigitalProduct` instance will have no effect. Even worse, the client code must not call it. Instead, it should call `convert_price_with_discount()` because all digital products must sell with a 12% discount. The design contradicts the Liskov substitution principle.

Instead of damaging the class hierarchy, we should remember the beauty of polymorphism. Here's what a better version will look like:

```
class Product
{
public:
  // code omitted for brevity
  virtual double convert_price(Currency c) {
    // default implementation
  }

  // code omitted for brevity
};

class DigitalProduct : public Product
{
public:
  // code omitted for brevity
  double convert_price(Currency c) override {
    // implementation applying a 12% discount
  }

  // code omitted for brevity
};
```

As you can see, we don't need the `convert_price_with_discount()` function anymore. And the Liskov substitution principle holds. However, we should again inspect flaws in the design. Let's make it better by incorporating private virtual methods for discount calculation in the base class. The following updated version of the `Product` class contains a private virtual member function named `calculate_discount()`:

```
class Product
{
public:
  // code omitted for brevity
  virtual double convert_price(Currency c) {
    auto final_price = apply_discount();
    // convert the final_price based on the currency
  }

private:
  virtual double apply_discount() {
    return getPrice(); // no discount by default
  }

  // code omitted for brevity
};
```

The `convert_price()` function calls the private `apply_discount()` function, which returns the price as is. And here comes the trick. We override the `apply_discount()` function in derived classes as it is shown in the following `DigitalProduct` implementation:

```
class DigitalProduct : public Product
{
public:
  // code omitted for brevity

private:
  double apply_discount() override {
    return getPrice() * 0.12;
  }
  // code omitted for brevity
};
```

We can't call a private function outside the class, but we can override it in derived classes. And the preceding code shows the beauty of overriding private virtual functions. We modify the implementation leaving the interface untouched. A derived class doesn't override it if it does not need to provide custom functionality for discount calculation. On the other hand, `DigitalProduct` needs to apply a 12% discount on the price before converting it. It is not necessary to modify the public interface of the base class.

You should consider rethinking the design of the `Product` class. It seems even better to call `apply_discount()` directly in `getPrice()`, hence always returning the latest effective price. Though at some point you should force yourself to stop.

The design process is creative and sometimes unthankful. It's not uncommon to rewrite all of the code because of unexpected new requirements. We use principles and approaches to minimize the breaking changes that will follow after implementing new features. The next principle of SOLID is one of the best practices that will make your design flexible.

The interface segregation principle

The interface segregation principle suggests dividing a complex interface into simpler interfaces. This segregation allows classes to avoid implementing an interface they don't use.

In our e-commerce application, we should implement a product shipment, replacement, and expiring functionalities. The shipment of the product is moving the product item to its buyer. We don't care for the shipment details at this point. Replacement of a product considers replacing a damaged or lost product after shipping to the buyer. Finally, expiring a product means getting rid of products that did not sell by their expiry date.

We are free to implement all of the functionality in the `Product` class introduced earlier. However, eventually, we will stumble upon types of products that, for example, cannot be shipped (for example, selling a house rarely involves shipping it to the buyer). There might be products that are not replaceable. For example, an original painting is not possible to replace even if it's lost or damaged. Finally, digital products won't expire ever. Well, for most cases.

We should not force the client code to implement a behavior it doesn't need. By the client, we mean the class implementing behaviors. The following example is a bad practice, contradictory to the interface segregation principle:

```
class IShippableReplaceableExpirable
{
public:
  virtual void ship() = 0;
  virtual void replace() = 0;
  virtual void expire() = 0;
};
```

Now, the `Product` class implements the interface shown in the preceding. It has to provide an implementation for all of the methods. The interface segregation principle suggests the following model:

```
class IShippable
{
public:
  virtual void ship() = 0;
};

class IReplaceable
{
public:
  virtual void replace() = 0;
};

class IExpirable
{
public:
  virtual void expire() = 0;
};
```

Now, the `Product` class skips implementing any of the interfaces. Its derived classes derive (implement) from specific types. The following example declares several types of product classes, each of which supports a limited number of behaviors introduced earlier. Please note that we omit bodies of classes for code brevity:

```
class PhysicalProduct : public Product {};

// The book does not expire
class Book : public PhysicalProduct, public IShippable, public IReplaceable
{
};

// A house is not shipped, not replaced, but it can expire
// if the landlord decided to put it on sell till a specified date
class House : public PhysicalProduct, public IExpirable
{
};

class DigitalProduct : public Product {};

// An audio book is not shippable and it cannot expire.
// But we implement IReplaceable in case we send a wrong file to the user.
class AudioBook : public DigitalProduct, public IReplaceable
{
};
```

Consider implementing `IShippable` for `AudioBook` if you want to wrap a file downloading as shipment.

The dependency inversion principle

Finally, dependency inversion states that objects should not be strongly coupled. It allows switching to an alternate dependency easily. For example, when a user purchases a product, we send a receipt about the purchase. Technically, there are several ways to send a receipt, namely, printing and sending via mail, sending via email, or showing the receipt in the user account page on the platform. For the latter, we send a notification to the user via email or the app that the receipt is ready to be viewed. Take a look at the following interface for printing a receipt:

```
class IReceiptSender
{
public:
  virtual void send_receipt() = 0;
};
```

Let's suppose we've implemented the `purchase()` method in the `Product` class, and on its completion, we send the receipt. The following portion of code handles the sending of the receipt:

```
class Product
{
public:
  // code omitted for brevity
  void purchase(IReceiptSender* receipt_sender) {
    // purchase logic omitted
    // we send the receipt passing purchase information
    receipt_sender->send(/* purchase-information */);
  }
};
```

We can extend the application by adding as many receipt printing options as needed. The following class implements the `IReceiptSender` interface:

```
class MailReceiptSender : public IReceiptSender
{
public:
  // code omitted for brevity
  void send_receipt() override { /* ... */ }
};
```

Two more classes—`EmailReceiptSender` and `InAppReceiptSender`—both implement `IReceiptSender`. So, to use a specific receipt, we just inject the dependency to `Product` via the `purchase()` method, as shown here:

```
IReceiptSender* rs = new EmailReceiptSender();
// consider the get_purchasable_product() is implemented somewhere in the
code
auto product = get_purchasable_product();
product.purchase(rs);
```

We can move further by implementing a method in the `User` class that returns the receipt sending option desirable for the concrete user. This will make the classes even more decoupled.

All of the SOLID principles discussed in the preceding are a natural way of composing classes. It's not mandatory to stick to the principles, however, it will improve your design if you do.

Using domain-driven design

The domain is the subject area of the program. We are discussing and designing an e-commerce platform having e-commerce as the main concept with all its supplementary concepts as the domain. We rather suggest you consider domain-driven design in your projects. However, the method is not a silver bullet for program design.

It's convenient to design your projects to have the following three layers of the three-tier architecture in mind:

- Presentation
- Business logic
- Data

The three-tier architecture applies to client-server software such as the one we are designing in this chapter. The presentation layer provides users with information related to products, purchases, and shipment. It communicates with other layers by putting out the results to the client. It's a layer that clients access directly, for example, a web browser.

The business logic cares for application functionality. For example, a user browses products provided by the presentation layer and decides to purchase one of them. The processing of the request is the task of the business layer. In domain-driven design, we tend to combine domain-level entities with their attributes to tackle the application complexity. We deal with users as instances of the `User` class, with products as instances of the `Product` class, and so on. The user purchasing a product is interpreted by the business logic as a `User` object creating an `Order` object, which, in turn, is related to a `Product` object. The `Order` object is then tied to a `Transaction` object related to the purchase of the product. Corresponding results of the purchase are represented via the presentation layer.

Finally, the data layer handles storing and retrieving data. From user authentication to product purchase, each step is retrieved from or recorded in the system database (or databases).

Dividing the application into layers allows handling the complexity of it in general. It's much better to orchestrate objects having single responsibility. The domain-driven design differentiates entities from objects that don't have a conceptual identity. The latter are known as value objects. For example, users do not distinguish between each unique transaction; they are only concerned about information that a transaction represents. On the other hand, a user object has a conceptual identity in the form of a `User` class (the entity).

Operations permitted on objects using other objects(or not) are named services. A service is rather an operation that is not tied to a specific object. For example, setting the name of the user by the `set_name()` method is an operation that shouldn't be considered as a service. On the other hand, the purchase of a product by the user is an operation encapsulated by a service.

Finally, domain-driven design intensively incorporates **repository** and **factory** patterns. The repository pattern is responsible for methods for retrieving and storing domain objects. The factory pattern creates domain objects. Using these patterns allows us to interchange alternative implementations if and when needed. Let's now find out the power of design patterns in the context of the e-commerce platform.

Leveraging design patterns

Design patterns are architectural solutions to commonly occurring problems in software design. It is important to note that design patterns are not methods nor algorithms. They are architectural constructs that provide a way of organizing classes and their relationship to achieve better results in code maintainability. Even if you didn't use a design pattern before, you most probably had invented one on your own. Many problems tend to recur in software design. For example, making a better interface for an existing library is a form of a design pattern known as **facade**. Design patterns have names so that programmers use them in conversations or documentation. It should be natural for you to chit-chat with fellow programmers using facades, factories, and the like.

We've previously mentioned that domain-driven design incorporates repository and factory patterns. Let's now find out what they are and how they could be useful in our design endeavor.

The repository pattern

As Martin Fowler best describes, the repository pattern "*mediates between the domain and data mapping layers using a collection-like interface for accessing domain objects*".

The pattern provides straightforward methods for data manipulation, without the need to work with the database driver directly. Adding, updating, removing, or selecting data naturally fits with the application domain.

One of the approaches is to create a generic repository class that provides necessary functions. A simple interface is shown as follows:

```
class Entity; // new base class

template <typename T, typename = std::enable_if_t<std::is_base_of_v<Entity,
T>>>
class Repository
{
public:
 T get_by_id(int);
 void insert(const T&);
 void update(const T&);
 void remove(const T&);
 std::vector<T> get_all(std::function<bool(T)> condition);
};
```

We introduced a new class named `Entity` in the preceding. The `Repository` class works with entities and to make sure that each entity conforms to the same interface of `Entity`, it applies `std::enable_if` along with `std::is_base_of_v` to the template parameter.

`std::is_base_of_v` is a short representation for `std::is_base_of<>::value`. Also, `std::enable_if_t` replaces `std::enable_if<>::type`.

The `Entity` class is as simple as the following representation:

```
class Entity
{
public:
  int get_id() const;
  void set_id(int);
private:
  int id_;
};
```

Each business object is an `Entity`, therefore, the classes discussed earlier should be updated to inherit from `Entity`. For example, the `User` class takes the following form:

```
class User : public Entity
{
// code omitted for brevity
};
```

So, we can use the repository the following way:

```
Repository<User> user_repo;
User fetched_user = user_repo.get_by_id(111);
```

The preceding repository pattern is a simple introduction to the topic, however, you can make it even powerful. It resembles the facade pattern. Though the point of using the facade pattern is not access to the database, it is still best explained with that example. The facade pattern wraps a complex class or classes, providing the client with a simple predefined interface to work with the underlying functionality.

The factory pattern

When programmers talk about factory patterns, they might confuse the factory method and abstract factory. Both of these are creational patterns that provide various object creation mechanisms. Let's discuss the factory method. It provides an interface for creating objects in the base class and allows derived classes to modify the objects that will be created.

Now is the time to deal with logistics, and the factory method will help us in that. When you develop an e-commerce platform providing product shipments, you should consider that not all users live in the same area in which your warehouses are located. So, shipping a product from a warehouse to the buyer, you should choose the proper transportation type. A bicycle, a drone, a truck, and so on. The problem of interest is designing a flexible logistics management system.

Different means of transportation require different implementations. However, all of them conform to one interface. The following is the class diagram for the `Transport` interface and its derived specific transport implementations:

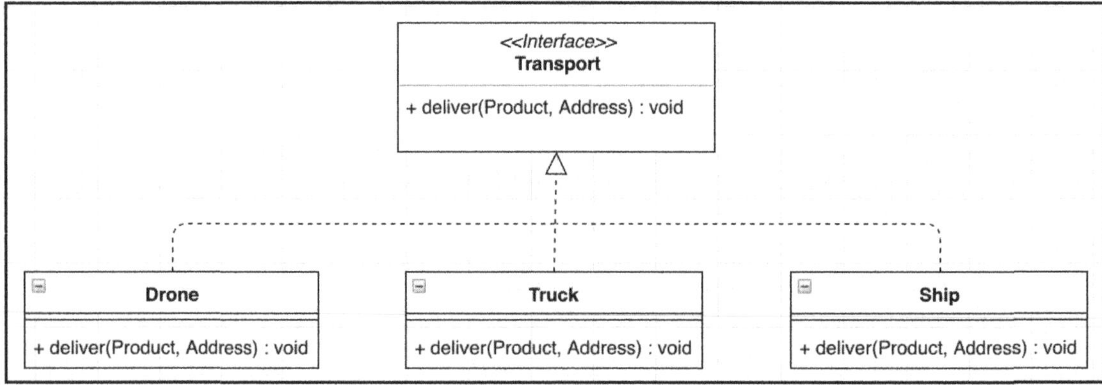

Each of the concrete classes in the preceding diagram provides specific implementation to delivery.

Let's suppose we design the following `Logistics` base class responsible for logistics-related actions, including choosing the proper transportation method as shown:

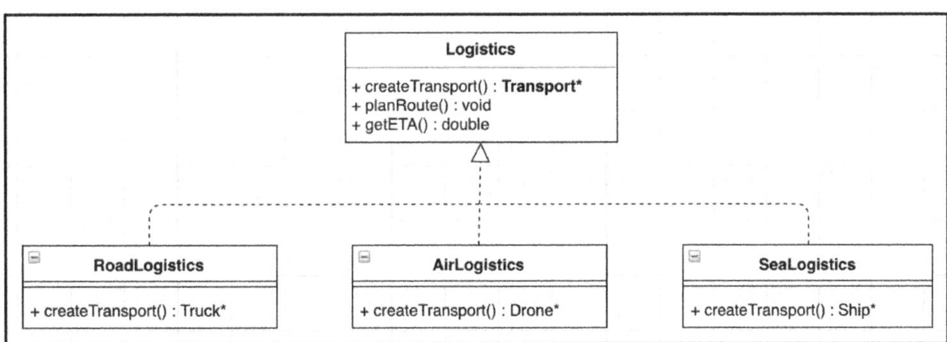

The factory method applied in the preceding allows flexibility in adding new transport types as well as new logistic methods. Pay attention to the `createTransport()` method that returns a pointer to `Transport`. Derived classes override the method, each of which returns a subclass of `Transport`, hence providing a specific mode of transport. It's possible because subclasses return a derived type, otherwise, we can't return a different type when overriding base class methods.

`createTransport()` in `Logistics` looks as shown here:

```
class Logistics
{
public:
  Transport* getLogistics() = 0;
  // other functions are omitted for brevity
};
```

The `Transport` class represents a base class for `Drone`, `Truck`, and `Ship`. That means we can create an instance of each and refer to them using a `Transport` pointer as shown:

```
Transport* ship_transport = new Ship();
```

This lays at the foundation of the factory pattern because `RoadLogistics`, for example, overrides `getLogistics()` like this:

```
class RoadLogistics : public Logistics
{
public:
```

```
    Truck* getLogistics() override {
      return new Truck();
    }
}
```

Pay attention to the return type of the function, it's `Truck` instead of `Transport`. It works because `Truck` inherits from `Transport`. Also, see how object creation is decoupled from the object itself. Creating new objects is done via factories, which keeps consistency with the SOLID principles discussed earlier.

At first glance, it might confusingly seem that leveraging a design pattern incorporates additional complexity into the design. However, you should develop a true sense of better design when practicing design patterns because they allow for flexibility and extendibility of the project overall.

Summary

Software development requires meticulous planning and design. We've learned in this chapter that project development involves the following key steps:

- Requirements gathering and analysis: This includes understanding the domain of the project, discussing and finalizing the features that should be implemented.
- Specification creation: This includes documenting requirements and project functionality.
- Design and test planning: This refers to designing the project starting from the bigger entities down to decomposing each into a separate class with regards to other classes in the project. This step also involves planning how the project will be tested.
- Coding: This step involves writing code that implements the project specified in previous steps.
- Testing and stabilization: This means checking the project against preplanned use cases and scenarios to discover issues and fix them.
- Release and maintenance: This is the final step that brings us to the project release and further maintenance.

The project design is a complex task for programmers. They should think ahead of time because part of the features is being introduced during the development of the process.

To make the design flexible and robust, we've discussed principles and patterns leading to better architecture. We have learned the process of designing a software project with all its intricacies.

One of the best ways to avoid bad design decisions is to follow already devised patterns and practices. You should consider using SOLID principles along with proven design patterns in your future projects.

In the next chapter, we will design a strategy game. We will get familiar with more design patterns and see their applications in game development.

Questions

1. What are the benefits of TDD?
2. What is the purpose of interaction diagrams in UML?
3. What's the difference between a composition and aggregation?
4. How would you describe the Liskov substitution principle?
5. Let's suppose you are given the class `Animal`, and the class `Monkey`. The latter describes a particular animal that jumps on trees. Does inheriting a `Monkey` class from an `Animal` class contradict the open-closed principle?
6. Apply the factory method on the `Product` class with its subclasses that were discussed in this chapter.

Further reading

For further information refer to :

- *Object-Oriented Analysis and Design with Applications* by Grady Booch, `https://www.amazon.com/Object-Oriented-Analysis-Design-Applications-3rd/dp/020189551X/`
- *Design Patterns: Elements of Reusable Object-Oriented Software* by Erich Gamma et al, `https://www.amazon.com/Design-Patterns-Elements-Reusable-Object-Oriented/dp/0201633612/`
- *Code Complete: A Practical Handbook of Software Construction* by Steve McConnel, `https://www.amazon.com/Code-Complete-Practical-Handbook-Construction/dp/0735619670/`
- *Domain-Driven Design: Tackling Complexity in the Heart of Software* by Eric Evans, `https://www.amazon.com/Domain-Driven-Design-Tackling-Complexity-Software/dp/0321125215/`

11
Designing a Strategy Game Using Design Patterns

Game development is one of the most interesting topics in software engineering. C++ is extensively used in game development because of its efficiency. However, since the language doesn't have GUI components, it's used on the backend. In this chapter, we will learn how to design a strategy game on the backend. We will incorporate almost everything that we've learned in previous chapters, including design patterns and multithreading.

The game that we will design is a strategy game called **Readers and Disturbers**. Here, the player creates units, known as readers, who are able to build libraries and other buildings, and soldiers, who are defending those buildings from the enemy.

In this chapter, we will cover the following topics:

- Introduction to game design
- Diving into the process of game design
- Using design patterns
- Designing the game loop

Technical requirements

The g++ compiler with the `-std=c++2a` option will be used to compile the examples throughout this chapter. You can find the source files that will be used throughout this chapter at `https://github.com/PacktPublishing/Expert-CPP` .

Introduction to game design

In this chapter, we will design the backend of a strategy game where the player can create units (workers, soldiers), build buildings, and fight the enemy. Whenever you design a game, whether it's a strategy game or a first-person shooter, there are several fundamental components that are the same, such as game physics, which are used to make the game feel more real and immersive to the player.

There are components in game design that are repeated in almost all games, such as collision detection mechanisms, the audio system, graphics rendering, and so on. When designing a game, we can either distinguish between the engine and the game or develop a strongly tied application representing both the engine and the game as a single outcome. Designing the game engine separately allows it to be extended for further releases and even used for other games. After all, games have the same mechanics and the same flow. They differ mostly by in their plotline.

When designing a game engine, you should carefully plan the types of game that will be designed using the engine. Though most fundamental features are the same. independent of the game type, there are distinctions for a 3D shooter and, for example, a strategy game. In a strategy game, the player strategically deploys units across a large playing field. The game world is displayed from a top-down viewing angle.

Introduction to the Readers and Disturbers game

The basic idea of the game is simple: the player has a limited set of resources. Those resources can be used to create buildings for game characters. We name the character units, which are divided into readers and soldiers. The Readers are smart characters who build libraries and other buildings. Each built library can host up to 10 readers. If the player moves 10 readers into the library, after a specified amount of time, the library produces one professor. A professor is a powerful unit that can destroy three enemy soldiers at once. A professor can create better weapons for the player's soldiers.

The game starts with a single house already built, two soldiers, and three readers. A house produces a new reader every 5 minutes. Readers can build new houses, which then produce more readers. They can also build barracks that produce soldiers.

The goal of the player is to build five libraries, each of which has produced at least one professor. The player has to defend his/her buildings and readers from the enemy during the game. Enemies are called **disturbers** because their goal is to disturb readers from their main goal: studying inside the libraries.

Strategy game components

As we mentioned previously, our strategy game will comprise basic components – readers and soldiers (we'll refer to them as units), buildings, and a map. The game map contains coordinates for each object in the game. We will discuss a lighter version of a game map. Now, let's leverage our project-designing skills to decompose the game itself.

The game consists of the following character units:

- A reader
- A soldier
- A professor

It also consists of the following buildings:

- A library
- A house
- A barrack

Now, let's discuss the properties for each component of the game. A game character has the following properties:

- Life points (an integer, which decreases after each attack from the enemy)
- Power (an integer, which defines the amount of damage a unit can cause to enemy units)
- Type (a reader, a soldier, or a professor)

The life property should have an initial value based on the type of the unit. For example, a reader's initial life points are 10, whereas a soldier's life points are 12. When interacting in the game, all of the units might be attacked by enemy units. Each attack is described as a decrease in life points. The amount we will decrease the life points by is based on the value of the power of the attacker. For example, the power of a soldier is set to three, which means each attack that's made by a soldier will decrease the victim's life points by three. When the victim's life points become zero, the character unit will be destroyed.

The same goes for buildings. A building has a construction duration that it will be completely built by. A complete building also has life points, and any damage caused to the building by enemy forces will decrease these life points. The following is the full list of building properties:

- Life points
- Type

- Construction duration
- Unit production duration

The unit production duration is the amount of time it takes for a new character unit to be produced. For example, a barrack produces a soldier every 3 minutes, a house produces a reader every 5 minutes, and a library produces a professor from 10 readers instantly when the last missing reader goes inside the library.

Now that we've defined the game components, let's discuss the interaction between them.

Interaction between the components

The next important thing in the design of the Readers and Disturbers game is the interaction between the characters. We already mentioned that readers can build buildings. In the game, this process should be taken care of because each type of building has its duration of construction. Therefore, if a reader is busy with the building process, we should measure the time to make sure the building will be ready after a specified time. However, to make the game even better, we should take into account that more than one reader can take part in the process of construction. This should make constructing a building faster. For example, if a barrack is built in 5 minutes by one reader, then it should be built in 2 and a half minutes by two readers, and so on. This is one example of complex interactions in the game and can be depicted with the following diagram:

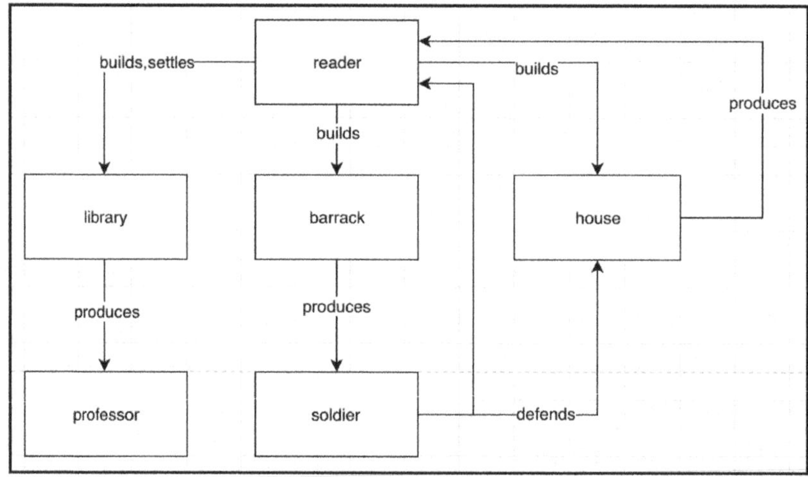

Complex interaction

Next comes the attack handling. When one unit is attacked by enemies, we should decrease the defendant's life points. The defendant itself could attack the attacker (to defend itself). Whenever there is more than one attacker or defender, we should correspondingly handle how the life points of each attacked unit decrease. We should also define the duration of each hit by the unit. A unit shouldn't hit another very fast. To make things a bit more natural, we might introduce a 1 second or 2 second pause between each hit. The following diagram depicts a simple attack interaction. This will be replaced with a class interaction diagram later in this chapter:

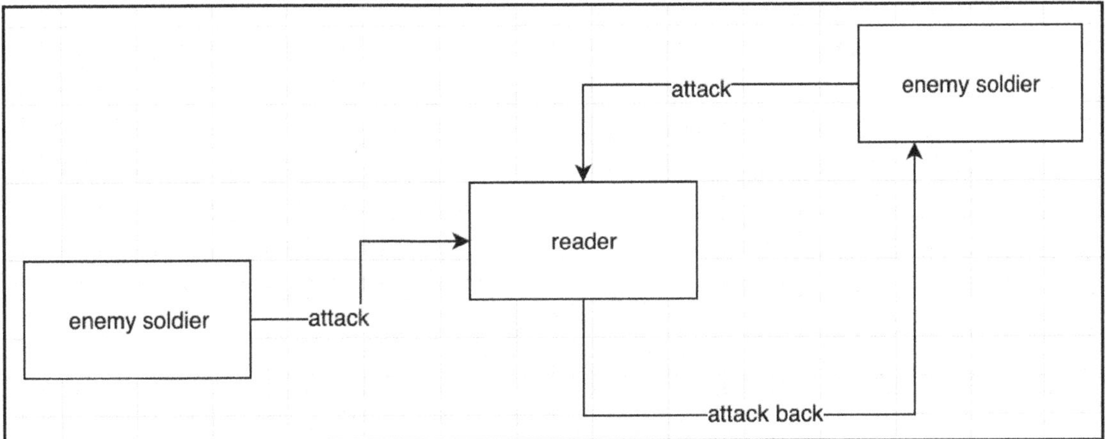

Simple attack interaction

An even bigger interaction is happening in the game in general. There are two groups in the game, one of which is controlled by the player. The other one is automatically controlled by the game itself. That means that we, as the game designers, are obliged to define the life cycle of the enemy forces. The game will automatically create readers who will be assigned the tasks of creating libraries, barracks, and houses. Each soldier should take responsibility for defending the buildings and readers (the people). And from time to time, soldiers should group together and go on an attack mission.

We will be designing a platform that lets the player create an empire; however, the game should also create the enemy to make the game complete. The player will face regular attacks from the enemy, and the enemy will evolve by constructing more buildings and producing more units. Overall, we can depict the interaction using the following diagram:

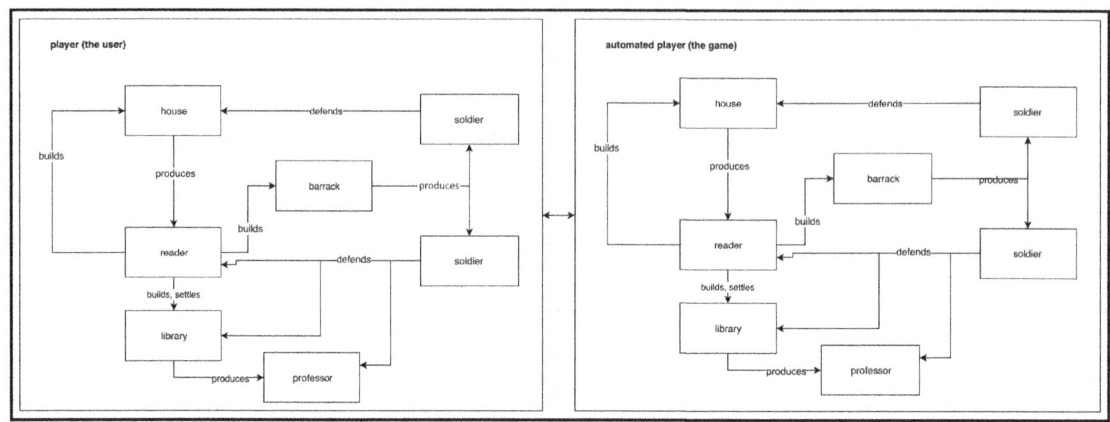

Illustration between the player and the automated player

We will refer to the preceding diagram regularly while designing the game.

Designing the game

Though a game is not a typical piece of software, its design doesn't differ much from regular application design. We will start with the main entities and decompose them further into classes and their relationships.

In the previous section, we discussed all the necessary game components and their interaction. We did a requirement analysis and gathering in terms of the project development life cycle. Now, we'll start designing the game.

Designing character units

The following class diagram represents a reader:

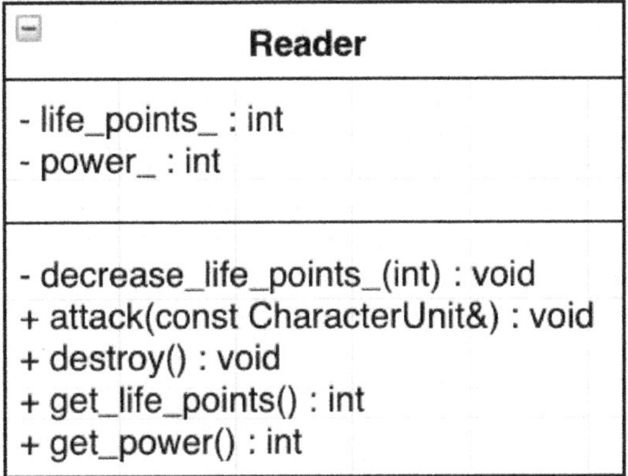

As we go through the other character units, we will come up with a base class for each character unit. Each specific unit will inherit from that base class and will add its specific properties, if any. Here's the complete class diagram for character units:

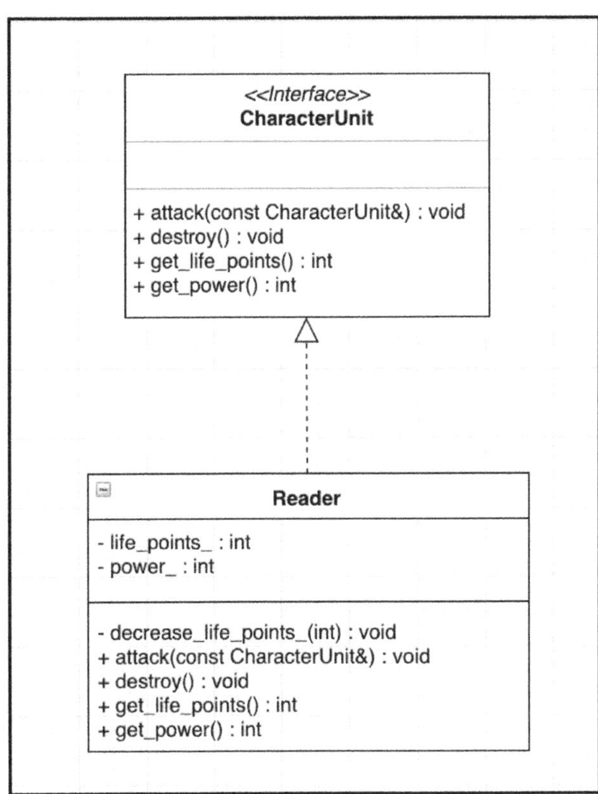

Pay attention to the base class – it's an interface rather than a regular class. It defines pure virtual functions to be implemented in derived classes. Here's what the `CharacterUnit` interface looks like in code:

```
class CharacterUnit
{
public:
  virtual void attack(const CharacterUnit&) = 0;
  virtual void destroy() = 0;
  virtual int get_power() const = 0;
  virtual int get_life_points() const = 0;
};
```

The `attack()` method decreases the life points of the character, while `destroy()` destroys the character. Destroying means not only removing the character from the scene but also stopping all the interactions that the unit has in progress (such as constructing buildings, defending itself, and so on).

The derived classes provide an implementation for the pure virtual functions of the `CharacterUnit` interface class. Let's take a look at the code for the `Reader` character unit:

```
class Reader : public CharacterUnit
{
public:
  Reader();
  Reader(const Reader&) = delete;
  Reader& operator=(const Reader&) = delete;

public:
  void attack(const CharacterUnit& attacker) override {
    decrease_life_points_by_(attacker.get_power());
  }

  void destroy() override {
    // we will leave this empty for now
  }

  int get_life_points() const override {
    return life_points_;
  }

  int get_power() const override {
    return power_;
  }

private:
  void decrease_life_points_(int num) {
```

```
      life_points_ -= num;
      if (life_points_ <= 0) {
        destroy();
      }
    }

  private:
    int life_points_;
    int power_;
  };
```

Now, we can create `Reader` units by declaring them in any of the following ways:

```
Reader reader;
Reader* pr = new Reader();
CharacterUnit* cu = new Reader();
```

We will mostly refer to character units by their base interface class.

Pay attention to the copy constructor and the assignment operators. We intentionally marked them as deleted because we don't want to create units by copying others. We will use the `Prototype` pattern for that behavior. This will be discussed later in this chapter.

Having the `CharacterUnit` interface is crucial in scenarios where we should do the same thing for different types of unit. For example, suppose that we have to calculate the complete damage that two soldiers, one reader, and a professor can cause to a building. Instead of keeping three different references to refer to three different types of unit, we are free to refer to them all as `CharacterUnits`. Here's how:

```
int calculate_damage(const std::vector<CharacterUnit*>& units)
{
  return std::reduce(units.begin(), units.end(), 0,
            [](CharacterUnit& u1, CharacterUnit& u2) {
                return u1.get_power() + u2.get_power();
            }
  );
}
```

The `calculate_damage()` function abstracts from unit types; it doesn't care about readers or soldiers. It just calls the `get_power()` method of the `CharacterUnit` interface, which is guaranteed to have an implementation for the specific object.

We will update character unit classes as we go. Now, let's move on to designing classes for buildings.

Designing buildings

Classes for buildings are similar to character units in terms of their common interface. For example, we can start by defining the class for a house as follows:

```
class House
{
public:
  House();
  // copying will be covered by a Prototype
  House(const House&) = delete;
  House& operator=(const House&) = delete;

public:
  void attack(const CharacterUnit&);
  void destroy();
  void build(const CharacterUnit&);
  // ...

private:
  int life_points_;
  int capacity_;
  std::chrono::duration<int> construction_duration_;
};
```

Here, we use `std::chrono::duration` to keep a time interval for the `House` construction duration. It is defined in the `<chrono>` header as a number of ticks and a tick period, where the tick period is the number of seconds from one tick to the next.

The `House` class needs more details, but we will soon come to the realization that we need a base interface (or even an abstract class) for all the buildings. The buildings that will be described in this chapter share certain behaviors. The interface for `Building` is as follows:

```
class IBuilding
{
public:
  virtual void attack(const CharacterUnit&) = 0;
  virtual void destroy() = 0;
  virtual void build(CharacterUnit*) = 0;
  virtual int get_life_points() const = 0;
};
```

Note the `I` prefix in front of `Building`. Many developers suggest using a prefix or postfix for interface classes for better readability. For example, `Building` might have been named `IBuilding` or `BuildingInterface`. We will use the same naming technique for the previously described `CharacterUnit`.

The House, Barrack, and Library classes implement the IBuilding interface and must provide implementations for pure virtual methods. For example, the Barrack class will look as follows:

```
class Barrack : public IBuilding
{
public:
  void attack(const ICharacterUnit& attacker) override {
    decrease_life_points_(attacker.get_power());
  }

  void destroy() override {
    // we will leave this empty for now
  }

  void build(ICharacterUnit* builder) override {
    // construction of the building
  }

  int get_life_points() const override {
    return life_points_;
  }

private:
  int life_points_;
  int capacity_;
  std::chrono::duration<int> construction_duration_;
};
```

Let's discuss the construction duration implementation in more detail, At this point, std::chrono:: duration point, kept as a reminder to us that the construction should take a specified amount of time. Also, note that the final design of classes might change over the course of this chapter. Now, let's find out how will we make the components of the game interact with each other.

Designing game controllers

Designing classes for character units and buildings is just the first step in designing the game itself. One of the most important things in the game is designing the interaction between those components. We should carefully analyze and design cases such as two or more characters constructing a building. We already introduced a construction time for a building, but we didn't take into account that a building might be constructed by more than one reader (the character unit that can build buildings).

We could say that a building built by two readers should be built twice as fast than when it's built by one reader. And if another reader joins the construction, we should recalculate the duration. However, we should limit the number of readers that can work on constructing the same building.

If any of the readers get attacked by the enemy, that should disturb the reader from building so that they can concentrate on self-defense. When a reader stops working on the building, we should recalculate the construction time again. The attack is another case that's similar to the building. When a character gets attacked, it should defend itself by fighting back. Each hit will decrease the character's life points. A character might be attacked by more than one enemy character at the same time. That will decrease their life points even faster.

A building has a timer because it produces a character periodically. The most important thing to design is the game dynamics – that is, the loop. At each specified time frame, something happens in the game. This can be enemy soldiers approaching, the character units building something, or anything else. The execution of an action is not strictly tied to the finishing of another unrelated action. This means that the construction of a building happens concurrently with the creation of a character. Unlike most applications, the game should keep moving, even if the user didn't provide any input. The game doesn't freeze if the player fails to perform an action. The character units might wait for a command, but the buildings will be continuously doing their job – producing new characters. Also, the enemy player (the automated one) strives for victory and never pauses.

Concurrent actions

Many actions in the game happen concurrently. As we've just discussed, the construction of buildings should not stop because a unit that is not involved in the construction gets attacked by the enemy. If the enemy attacks, a building should not stop producing new characters. This means we should design concurrent behavior for many of the objects in the game.

One of the best ways to achieve concurrency in C++ is using threads. We can redesign the units and buildings so that they include an overridable action in their base class that will be executed in a separate thread. Let's redesign `IBuilding` so that it's an abstract class that has an additional `run()` virtual function:

```
class Building
{
public:
  virtual void attack(const ICharacterUnit&) = 0;
  virtual void destroy() = 0;
```

```
    virtual void build(ICharacterUnit*) = 0;
    virtual int get_life_points() const = 0;

  public:
    void run() {
      std::jthread{Building::background_action_, this};
    }

  private:
    virtual void background_action_() {
      // no or default implementation in the base class
    }
  };
```

Pay attention to the `background_action_()` function; it's private, but virtual. We can override it in derived classes. The `run()` function is not virtual; it runs the private implementation in a thread. Here, the derived classes might provide an implementation for the `background_action_()`. When a unit is assigned to construct the building, the `build()` virtual function is called. The `build()` function delegates the job of calculating the construction time to the `run()` function.

The game event loop

The simplest approach to this problem is defining an event loop. An event loop looks as follows:

```
while (true)
{
  processUserActions();
  updateGame();
}
```

Even if there is no action from the user (the player), the game still goes on by calling the `updateGame()` function. Note that the preceding code is just a general introduction to the event loop. As you can see, it loops indefinitely and processes and updates the game on each iteration.

Each loop iteration advances the state of the game. If user action processing takes a long time, it might block the loop. The game will freeze for a moment. We usually measure the speed of the game in **frames per second** (**FPS**). The higher its value, the smoother the game.

We need to design the game loop that runs continuously during gameplay. It's important to design it in such a way that the user action processing won't block the loop.

The game loop takes care of everything happening in the game, including AI. By AI, we mean the automation of the enemy player we discussed previously. Other than that, the game loop handles the actions of characters, and building, and updates the state of the game accordingly.

Before diving into the game loop design, let's understand several design patterns that will help us in this complex task. After all, the game loop is another design pattern!

Using design patterns

It's natural to design a game using the **object-oriented programming (OOP)** paradigm. After all, a game represents a combination of objects that intensively interact with each other. In our strategy game, we have buildings built by units. Units defend themselves from enemy units and so on. This inter-communication leads to the growth of complexity. As the project evolves and gains more features, it will become harder to support it. It's already obvious to us that designing is one of the most important (if not the most important) part of building projects. Incorporating design patterns will drastically improve both the design process and project support.

Let's examine some design patterns that are useful in game development. We will start with classic patterns and then discuss more game-specific patterns.

The Command pattern

Developers categorize design patterns into creational, structural, and behavioral categories. The Command pattern is a behavioral design pattern. Behavioral design patterns are mainly concerned with providing flexibility in communication between objects. In this context, the Command pattern encapsulates an action in an object that contains the necessary information, along with the action itself. This way, the Command pattern behaves as a smart function. The simplest way to implement it in C++ is by overloading the `operator()` for a class, as follows:

```
class Command
{
public:
  void operator()() { std::cout << "I'm a smart function!"; }
};
```

A class with an overloaded `operator()` is sometimes referred to as a **functor**. The preceding code is almost the same as the following regular function declaration:

```
void myFunction() { std::cout << "I'm not so smart!"; }
```

Calling the regular function and the object of the `Command` class looks similar, as shown here:

```
myFunction();
Command myCommand;
myCommand();
```

The difference between these two is obvious whenever we need to use a state for the function. To store the state for a regular function, we use a static variable. To store the state in the object, we use the object itself. Here's how we can track the number of calls of the overloaded operator:

```
class Command
{
public:
  Command() : called_(0) {}

  void operator()() {
    ++called_;
    std::cout << "I'm a smart function." << std::endl;
    std::cout << "I've been called" << called_ << " times." << std::endl;
  }

private:
  int called_;
};
```

The number of calls is unique for each instance of the `Command` class. The following code declares two instances of `Command` and calls them two and three times, respectively:

```
Command c1;
Command c2;
c1();
c1();
c2();
c2();
c2();
// at this point, c1.called_ equals 2, c2.called_ equals 3
```

Now, let's try to apply this pattern to our strategy game. The final version of the game has a graphical interface that allows its users to control the game using various buttons and mouse clicks. For example, to make a character unit build a house, and not a barrack, we should choose the corresponding icon on the game panel. Let's visualize a game panel with a map of the game and a bunch of buttons to control the game dynamics.

The game provides the following commands to the player:

- Move the character unit from point A to point B
- Attack the enemy
- Construct a building
- Settle the house

The design of the game commands looks as follows:

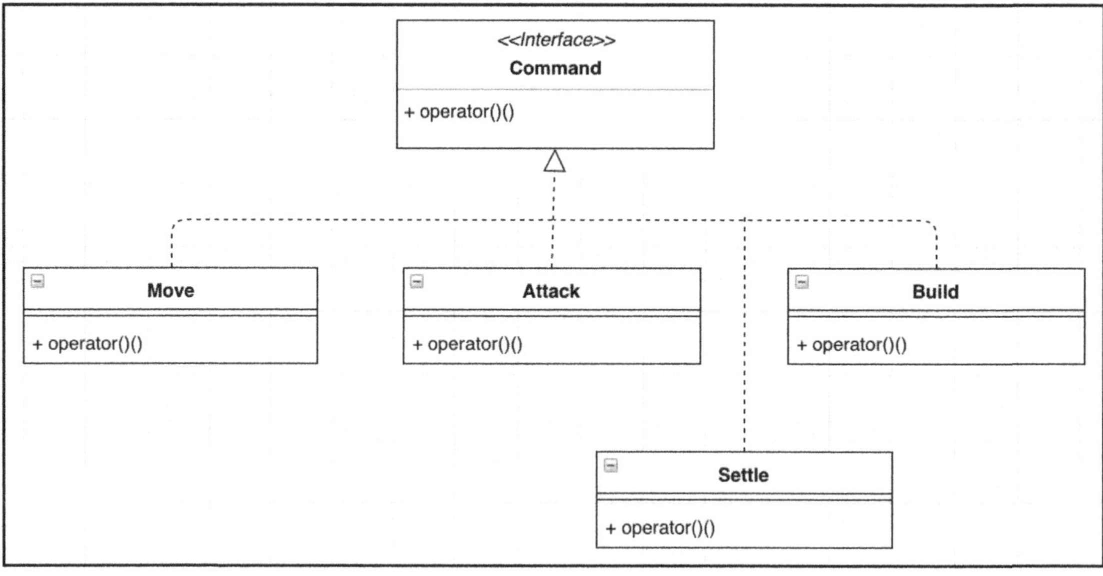

Each class encapsulates the action logic. The client code is not concerned with processing the action. It operates with command pointers, each of which will point to the concrete **Command** (as shown in the preceding image). Note that we've only depicted commands that the player will execute. The game itself communicates between modules using commands. Examples of automatic commands include **Run**, **Defend**, **Die**, and **Create**. The following is a broader diagram showing the commands in the game:

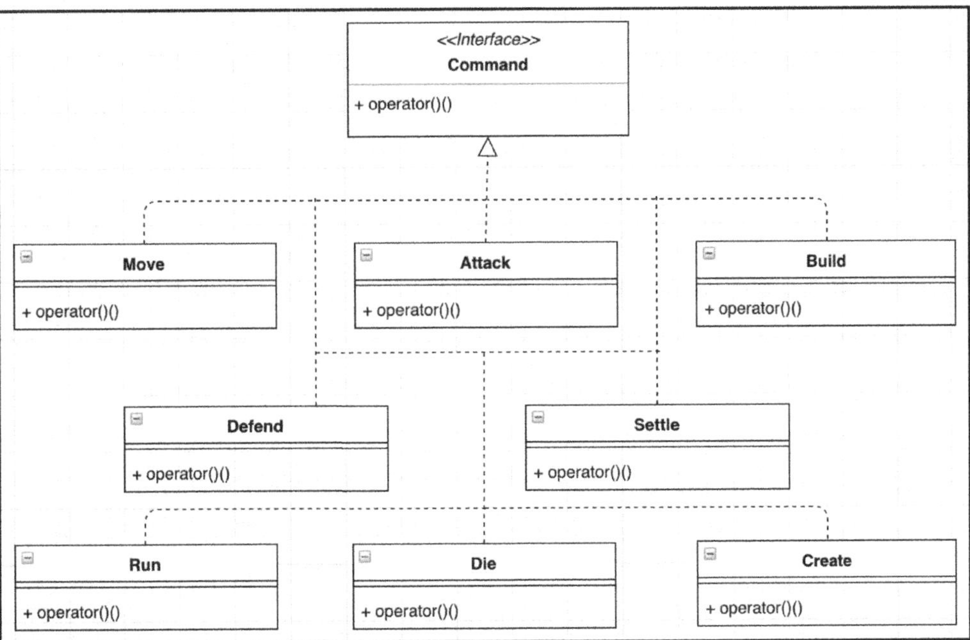

The preceding commands execute any of the aforementioned events that arise during the gameplay. To listen to those events, we should consider using the Observer pattern.

The Observer pattern

The Observer pattern is an architectural mechanism that allows us to subscribe to object state changes. We say that we observe the changes of the object. The Observer pattern is also a behavioral design pattern.

Most strategy games incorporate the concept of a resource. This might be a rock, gold, wood, and so on. For example, upon constructing a building, the player has to spend 20 units of wood, 40 units of rock, and 10 units of gold. Eventually, the player will run out of resources and has to collect them. This player creates more character units and tasks them with collecting resources – almost like what happens in real life.

Now, let's suppose we have a similar resource gathering or spending activity in our game. When the player tasks units to collect a resource, they should somehow notify us each time a fixed amount of resource is collected. The player is the subscriber to the **resource collected** event.

The same is true for buildings. A building produces a character – subscribers get a notification. A character unit finishes the building construction – subscribers get a notification. In most cases, the subscriber is the player. We update the player dashboard to keep the game state up to date for the player; that is, the player oversees how many resources, how many units, and how many buildings they have while playing the game.

The Observer involves implementing a class that stores its subscribers and calls the specified function on an event. It consists of two entities: a subscriber and a publisher. As shown in the following diagram, the number of subscribers is not limited to one:

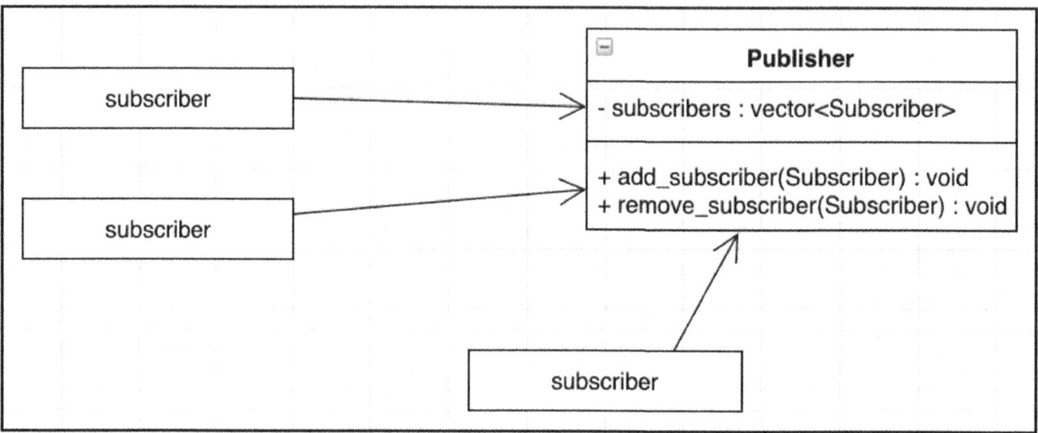

For example, when a character unit is assigned to build a building, it will continuously strive to build it unless it gets stopped. There are various reasons why this may happen:

- The player decides to cancel the process of constructing the building.
- The character unit has to defend itself from an enemy attack and pauses the construction process.
- The building has been finished, so the character unit stops working on it.

The player would also like to be notified when the building is completed because they might have plans for the character unit to perform other tasks when they're done with the building process. We can design the building process so that it notifies its listeners (subscribers) when the event is completed. The following class diagram also involves an Action interface. Consider it as an implementation of the Command pattern:

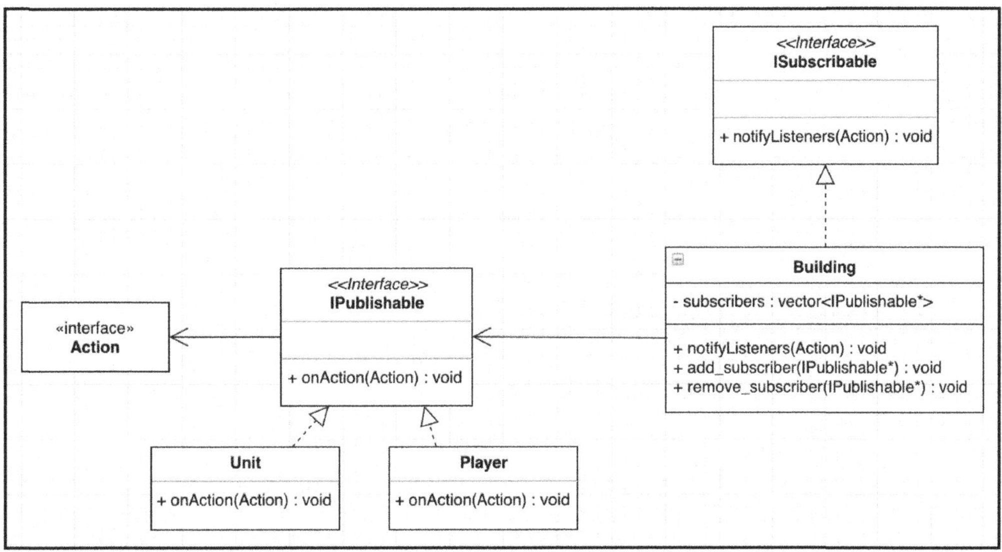

Developing classes with regards to the Observer leads us to a point where almost all the entities in the game are subscribers, publishers, or both. If you encounter a similar scenario, you might consider using the Mediator – another behavioral pattern. Objects communicate with each other via a mediator object. An object that triggers an event lets the Mediator know about it. The Mediator then passes the message to any related object that's "subscribed" to the object state. The following diagram is a simplified version of the Mediator's integration:

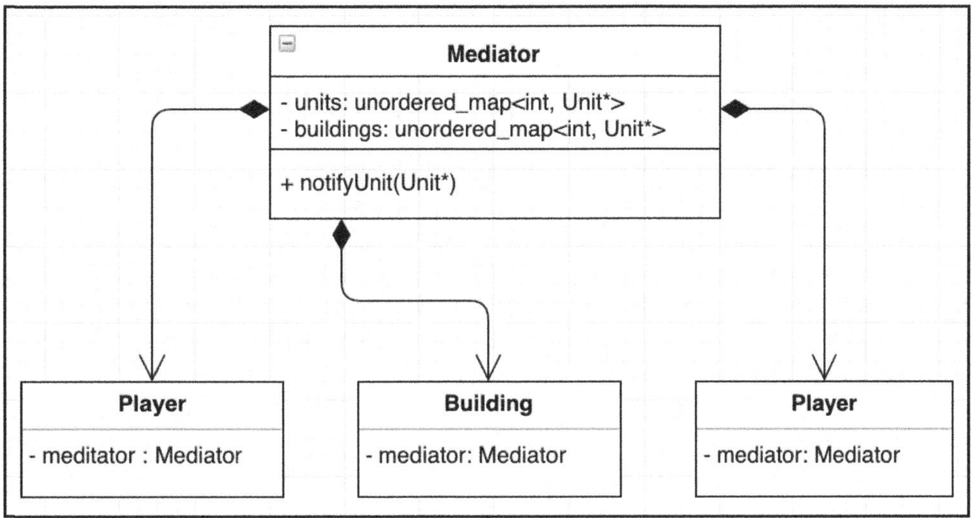

Each object contains a Mediator that's used to notify subscribers about changes. The Mediator object usually contains all the objects that communicate with each other. On an event, each object notifies the interested parties via the mediator. For example, when the building construction is done, it triggers the Mediator, which, in turn, notifies all the subscribed parties. To receive those notifications, each object should be subscribed to the Mediator beforehand.

The Flyweight pattern

Flyweight is a structural design pattern. Structural patterns take care of assembling objects and classes into larger, more flexible, structures. Flyweight allows us to cache objects by sharing their common parts.

In our strategy game, we're dealing with many objects being rendered on the screen. The number of objects increases during gameplay. The longer the player plays the game, the more character units and buildings they create (the same is true for the automated enemy). Each unit in the game represents a separate object containing data. A character unit takes at least 16 bytes of memory (for its two integer data members and the virtual table pointer).

Things get worse when we add additional fields to units in order to render them on the screen; for example, their height, width, and sprite (the image representing the unit for rendering). Besides the character units, the game should have supplementary items to make the user experience even better, for example, decorative items such as trees, rocks, and so on. At some point, we'll conclude that we have plenty of objects to render on the screen, each of which represents almost the same object, but with a small difference in their states. The Flyweight pattern comes to the rescue here. For the character unit, its height, width, and sprite store almost identical data across all units.

The Flyweight pattern suggests decomposing a heavy object into two:

- An immutable object that contains the same data for each object of the same kind
- A mutable object that uniquely identifies itself from others

For example, a moving character unit has its own height, length, and sprite, all of which are repeated for all the character units. Therefore, we can represent those properties as a single immutable object with the same values for the properties for all the objects. However, a character unit might have a different location on the screen than others, and when the player commands the unit to move somewhere else or start constructing a building, the position of the unit changes continuously until it reaches an endpoint. At each step, the unit should be redrawn on the screen. By doing this, we arrive at the following design:

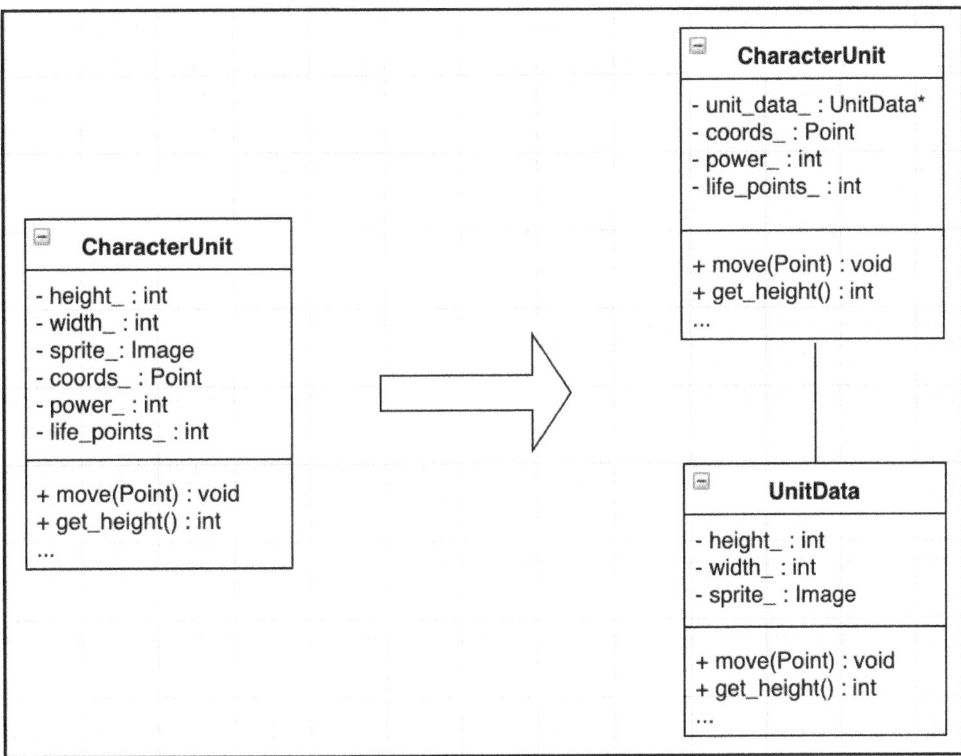

The left-hand side is the `CharacterUnit` before modifications, while the right-hand side represents recent modifications using the Flyweight pattern. The game can now deal with a bunch of `CharacterUnit` objects, while each of them will store a reference to a few `UnitData` objects. This way, we save a lot of memory. We store the values that are unique to each unit in a `CharacterUnit` object. These values change over time. The dimensions and sprite are constant, so we can keep a single object with these values. This immutable data is called the **intrinsic state**, while the mutable part of the object (the `CharacterUnit`) is called the **extrinsic state**.

We intentionally moved the data members to `CharacterUnit`, thus redesigning it from an interface into an abstract class. As we discussed in `Chapter 3`, *Details of Object-Oriented Programming*, an abstract class is almost the same as the interface that might contain an implementation. The `move()` method is an example of a default implementation for all types of units. This way, the derived classes only provide the necessary behavior because all the units share common properties, such as life points and power.

After optimizing memory usage, we should deal with copying objects. The game involves extensively creating new objects. Each building produces a specific character unit; character units construct buildings, and the game world itself renders decorative elements (trees, rocks, and so on). Now, let's try to improve `CharacterUnit` by incorporating a cloning functionality. Earlier in this chapter, we intentionally deleted the copy constructor and assignment operator. Now, it's time to provide a mechanism that will create new objects from existing ones.

The Prototype pattern

This pattern lets us create duplicates of objects independently of their type. The following code represents the final version of the `CharacterUnit` class with regard to our recent modifications. We'll also add the new `clone()` member function in order to incorporate the Prototype pattern:

```
class CharacterUnit
{
public:
  CharacterUnit() {}
  CharacterUnit& operator=(const CharacterUnit&) = delete;
  virtual ~Character() {}

  virtual CharacterUnit* clone() = 0;

public:
  void move(const Point& to) {
    // the graphics-specific implementation
  }
  virtual void attack(const CharacterUnit&) = 0;
  virtual void destroy() = 0;

  int get_power() const { return power_; }
  int get_life_points() const { return life_points_; }

private:
  CharacterUnit(const CharacterUnit& other) {
    life_points_ = other.life_points_;
    power_ = other.power_;
  }

private:
  int life_points_;
  int power_;
};
```

We deleted the assignment operator and moved the copy constructor to the private section. The derived classes override the `clone()` member function, as follows:

```
class Reader : public CharacterUnit
{
public:
 Reader* clone() override {
   return new Reader(*this);
 }

 // code omitted for brevity
};
```

The Prototype pattern delegates cloning to the objects. The common interface allows us to decouple the client code from the class of the object. Now, we can clone a character unit without knowing it's a `Reader` or a `Soldier`. Look at the following example:

```
// The unit can have any of the CharacterUnit derived types
CharacterUnit* new_unit = unit->clone();
```

A dynamic cast works fine whenever we need to convert the object into a specific type.

In this section, we've discussed many useful design patterns. This might seem a little overwhelming if you are new to these patterns; however, using them properly allows us to design flexible and maintainable projects. Let's finally get back to the game loop that we introduced earlier.

Designing the game loop

Strategy games have one of the most intensively changing gameplays. At each point in time, many actions happen simultaneously. Readers finish their building; a barrack produces a soldier; a soldier gets attacked by the enemy; the player commands units to move, build, attack, or run; and so on. The game loop handles everything. Usually, a game engine provides a well-designed game loop.

The game loop runs while we play the game. As we already mentioned, the loop handles player actions, updates the game state, and also renders the game (makes state changes visible to the player). It does so on each iteration. The loop should also control the rate of gameplay, that is, its FPS. A common term for one iteration of the game loop is a frame, which is why we emphasize the FPS as the speed of the gameplay. For example, if you design a game running at 60 FPS, this means each frame takes around 16ms.

The following code was used earlier in this chapter for a simple game loop:

```
while (true)
{
  processUserActions();
  updateGame();
}
```

The preceding code will run quickly if there are no long user actions to process. It will run even faster on fast machines. Your goal is to stick to the 16ms for a frame. This might require us to wait a bit after processing actions and updating the game state, as shown in the following diagram:

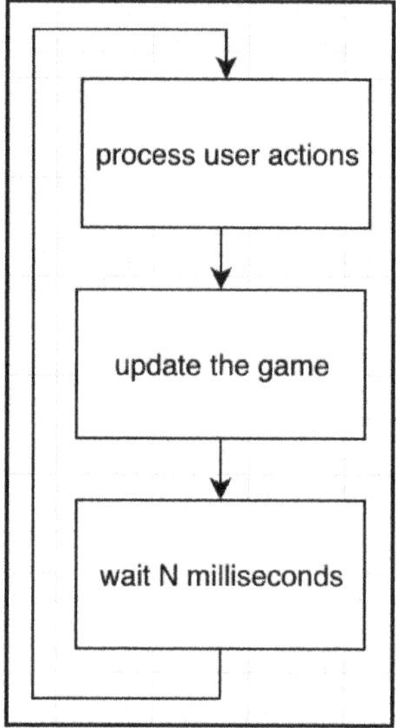

Each update advances the game time by a fixed amount, which takes a fixed amount of real-world time to process. On the other hand, the game will slow down if the processing takes longer than the specified milliseconds for a frame.

Everything that happens in the game is mostly covered in the update part of the game, as shown in the preceding diagram. Most of the time, updating might require performing several operations at a time. Also, as we mentioned earlier, we have to keep timers for some of the operations that occur in the game in the background. It mostly depends on how detailed we want to make the game. For example, constructing a building might be represented as two states: initial and final.

In terms of graphic design, those two states should represent two different images. The first image contains some fundamental part for the building and might include a couple of rocks around it as if it's just getting ready to be constructed. The next image represents the final constructed building. When a character unit just starts constructing the building, we show the player the first image (the fundament with a couple of rocks around it). When the construction is finished, we replace the first image with the image containing the final building. To make the process more natural (more real-world), we artificially make it take longer. This means we keep a timer lasting 30 seconds or more between two states of the image.

We described the simplest case with the least amount of detail. If we need to make the game more detailed, for example, by rendering every change of in the building during the construction, we should keep a lot of timers between a lot of images representing each step of the construction. Take a look at the preceding diagram once again. After updating the game, we wait for *N* milliseconds. Waiting for more milliseconds tends to make the flow of the game closer to real life. What if the update takes so long that the player experience lags behind? In that case, we need to optimize the game so that it fits the time frame that's the most optimal in terms of user experience. Now, let's say updating the game takes more than hundreds of operations to perform; the player has achieved a prosperous empire; is now constructing lots of buildings, and attacks the enemy with many soldiers.

Each action of one character unit, such as moving from one point to another one, attacking an enemy unit, constructing a building, and so on, is rendered on the screen on time. Now, what if we render states of hundreds of units on the screen at once? That's where we use a multithreaded approach. Each action involves independently modifying the state of an object (an object being any of the units in the game, including static buildings).

Summary

Designing a game is a complex task. We can consider game development as a separate programming area. Games have different genres, and one of them is strategy games. Strategy game design involves designing game components such as units and buildings. Usually, a strategy game involves collecting resources, building an empire, and fighting the enemy. The gameplay involves dynamic communication between game components, such as character units constructing buildings and collecting resources, soldiers defending the land from enemies, and so on.

To properly design a strategy game, we incorporate OOP design skills, along with design patterns. Design patterns play a huge role in designing the whole game and how its components interact. In this chapter, we discussed the Command pattern, which encapsulates actions under objects; the Observer pattern, which is used to subscribe to object events; and the Mediator pattern, which is used to advance the Observer to a level of complex interactions between components.

The most important part of the game is its loop. The game loop controls rendering, timely updates of the game state, and other subsystems. Designing it involves using event queues and timers. Modern games use networking to allow multiple players to play together via the internet.

In the next chapter, we will introduce network programming in C++ so that you will have the skills you need to incorporate networking into your games.

Questions

1. What's the purpose of overriding a private virtual function?
2. Describe the Command design pattern.
3. How does the Flyweight pattern save memory usage?
4. What's the difference between the Observer and Mediator patterns?
5. Why did we design the game loop as an infinite loop?

Further reading

- *Game Development Patterns and Best Practices: Better games, less hassle* by John P. Doran, Matt Casanova: `https://www.amazon.com/Game-Development-Patterns-Best-Practices/dp/1787127834/`.

12
Networking and Security

Network programming is becoming more and more popular. Most computers are connected to the internet, and more and more applications now rely on that. From simple program updates that might require an internet connection to applications that rely on a stable internet connection, network programming is becoming a necessary part of application development.

The C++ language did not have support for networking until recent standard updates. Networking support has been postponed later standards, most probably until C++23. However, we can prepare for that release beforehand by tackling a network application. We will also discuss the standard extension for networking and see what will it look like to have networking supported in the language. This chapter will concentrate on the main principles of networking and the protocols driving communication between devices. Designing a network application is a great addition to your skillset as a programmer.

One of the major problems developers face regularly is the security of applications. Whether it's related to the input data being processed or coding with proven patterns and practices, the security of the application must be the number-one priority. It's especially important for network applications. In this chapter, we will also delve into techniques and best practices for secure programming in C++.

We will cover the following topics in this chapter:

- Introduction to computer networks
- Sockets and socket programming in C++
- Designing a network application
- Understanding security issues in C++ programs
- Leveraging secure programming techniques in project development

Technical requirements

The g++ compiler, along with the `-std=c++2a` option, will be used to compile the examples in this chapter.

You can find the source files for this chapter at `https://github.com/PacktPublishing/Expert-CPP` .

Discovering network programming in C++

Two computers interact together using networks. Computers connect to the internet using a special hardware component called a **network adapter** or a **network interface controller**. The operating system installed on the computer provides drivers to work with the network adapter; that is, to support network communications the computer must have a network adapter installed with an OS that supports the networking stack. By stack, we mean the layers of modifications that the piece of data goes through when traveling from one computer to another. For example, opening a website on a browser renders data that's been gathered through the network. That data is received as a sequence of zeros and ones and then transformed into a form that's more intelligible to the web browser. Layering is essential in networking. Network communication as we know it today consists of several layers conforming to the OSI model we'll discuss here. The network interface controller is a hardware component that supports the physical and data link layers of the **Open System Interconnection** (**OSI**) model.

The OSI model aims to standardize communication functions between a wide range of devices. Devices differ in structure and organization. This relates to both hardware and software. For example, a smartphone using an Intel CPU running an Android OS is different from a MacBook computer running a macOS Catalina. The difference is not the names and companies behind the aforementioned products, but the structure and organization of hardware and software. To eliminate the differences in network communication, a set of standardized protocols and intercommunication functions is proposed as the OSI model. The layers that we mentioned earlier are as follows:

- Application layer
- Presentation layer
- Session layer
- Transport layer

- Network layer
- Data-link layer
- Physical layer

A more simplified model includes the following four layers:

- **Application**: This processes the details of the particular application.
- **Transport**: This provides data transmission between two hosts.
- **Network**: This handles the transferal of packets around the network.
- **Link**: This includes the device driver in the operating system, along with the network adapter inside the computer.

The link (or data-link) layer includes the device driver in the operating system, along with the network adapter in the computer.

To understand these layers, let's suppose you are using a desktop application for messaging such as *Skype* or *Telegram*. When you type in a message and hit the send button, the message goes through the network to its destination. In this scenario, let's suppose you are sending a text message to your friend who has the same application installed on their computer. This might seem simple from a high-level perspective, but the process is sophisticated and even the simplest message undergoes a lot of transformations before reaching its destination. First of all, when you hit the send button, the text message gets converted into binary form. The network adapter operates with binaries. Its basic function is to send and receive binary data through the medium. Besides the actual data that's sent over the network, the network adapter should know the destination address of the data. The destination address is one of many properties that's appended to user data. By user data, we mean the text that you typed and sent to your friend. The destination address is the unique address of your friend's computer. The typed text is packaged with the destination address and other information that's necessary for it to be sent to its target. Your friend's computer (including the network adapter, OS, and the messaging application) receives and unpackages the data. The text contained in that package is then rendered on the screen by the messaging application.

Almost every OSI layer mentioned at the beginning of this chapter adds its specific header to the data that's sent over the network. The following diagram depicts how the data from the application layer gets stacked with headers before it's moved to its destination:

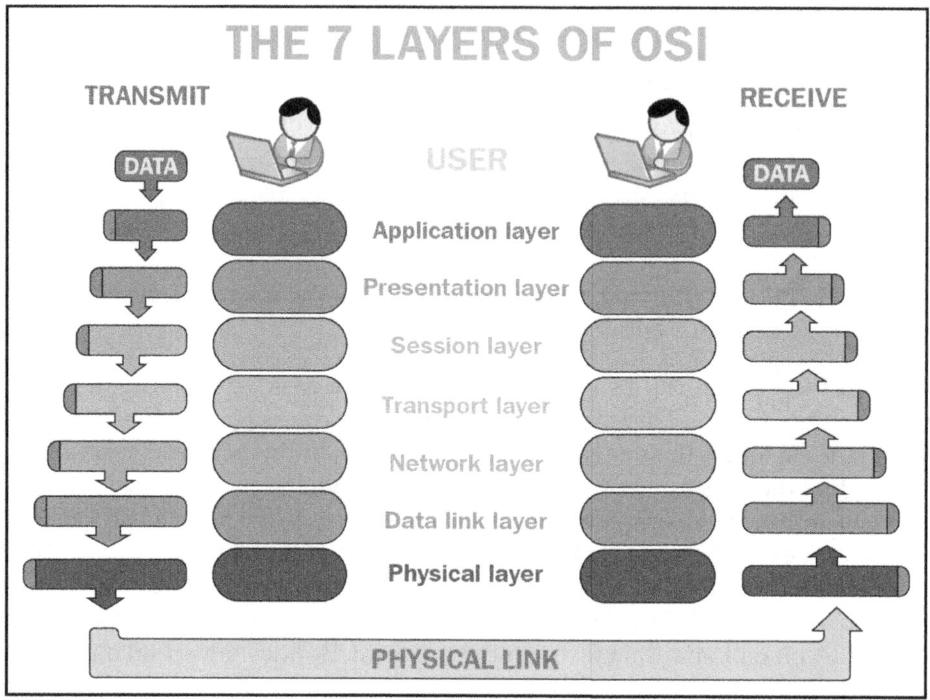

OSI model

Take a look at the first line (the **Application Layer**) in the preceding diagram. The **Data** is the text that you've typed into the messaging application in order to send it to your friend. In each layer, all the way down to the **Physical Layer**, the data is packaged with headers specific to each layer of the OSI model. The computer on the other side receives and retrieves the packaged data. In each layer, it removes the header specific to that layer and moves the rest of the package up to the next layer. Finally, the data reaches your friend's messaging application.

As programmers, we are mostly concerned with writing applications that are able to send and receive data over a network without delving into the details of the layers. However, we need a minimal understanding of how layers augment data on higher levels with headers. Let's learn how a network application works in practice.

Network applications under the hood

A network application installed on a device communicates with other applications installed on other devices through the network. In this chapter, we'll discuss applications working together through the internet. A high-level overview of this communication can be seen in the following diagram:

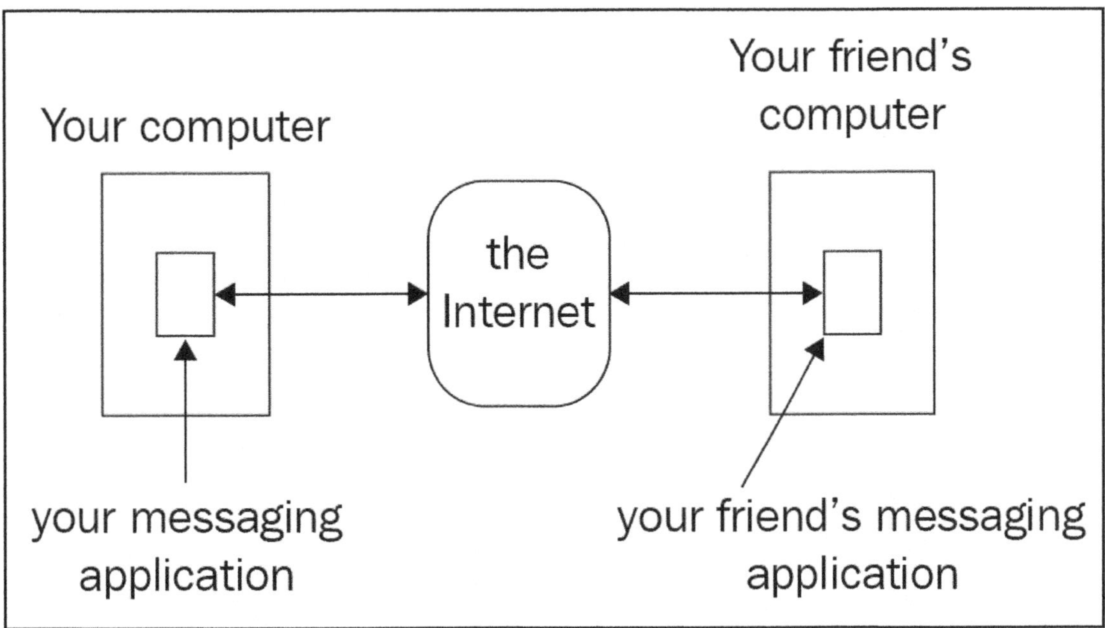

At the lowest level of communication is the physical layer, which transmits bits of data through the medium. A medium, in this case, is the network cable (consider Wi-Fi communication too). The user application abstracts from the lower levels of network communication. Everything a programmer needs is provided by the operating system. The operating system implements the low-level details of the network communication, such as the **Transmission Control Protocol/Internet Protocol** (**TCP/IP**) suite.

Whenever an application needs to access the network, whether it's a local area network or the internet, it requests the operating system to provide an access point. The OS manages to provide a gateway to the network by utilizing a network adapter and specific software that speaks to the hardware.

A more detailed illustration of this looks as follows:

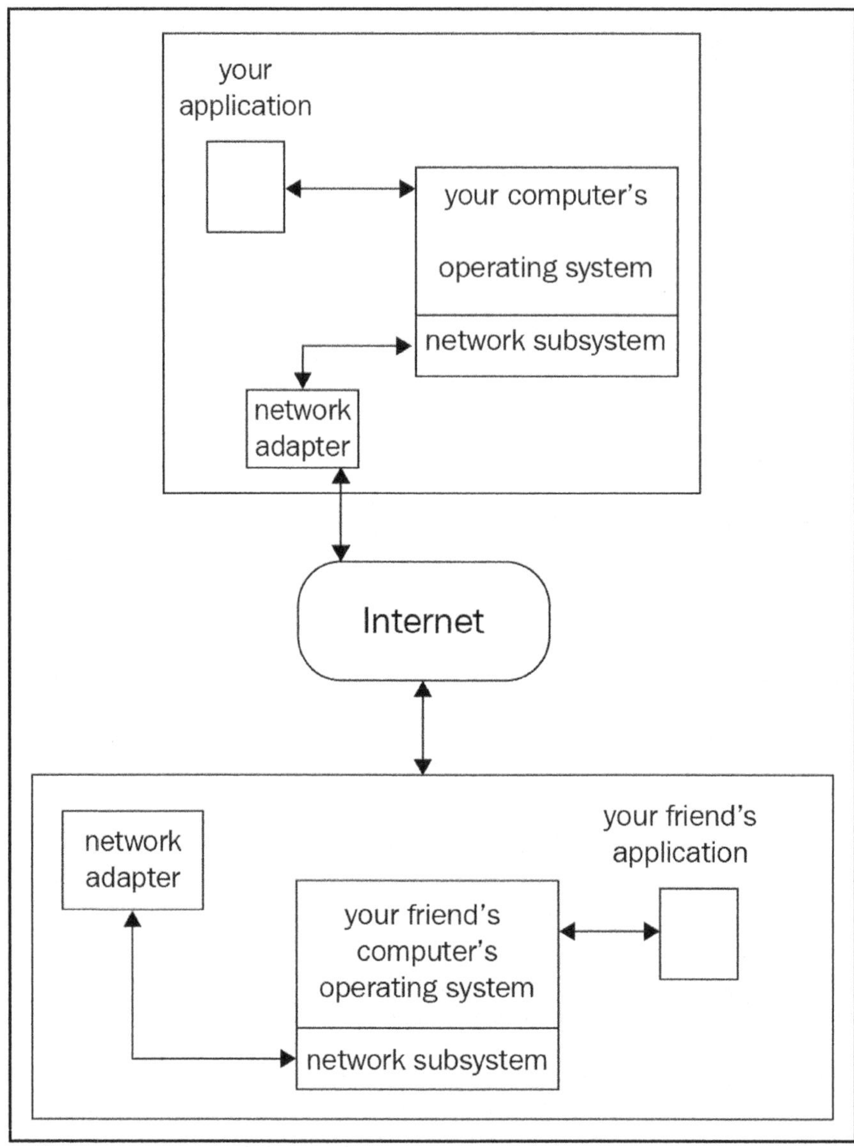

The operating system provides an API to work with its networking subsystem. The main abstraction that programmers should care about is the socket. We can treat a socket as a file that sends its contents through the network adapter. Sockets are the access points that connect two computers via the network, as depicted in the following diagram:

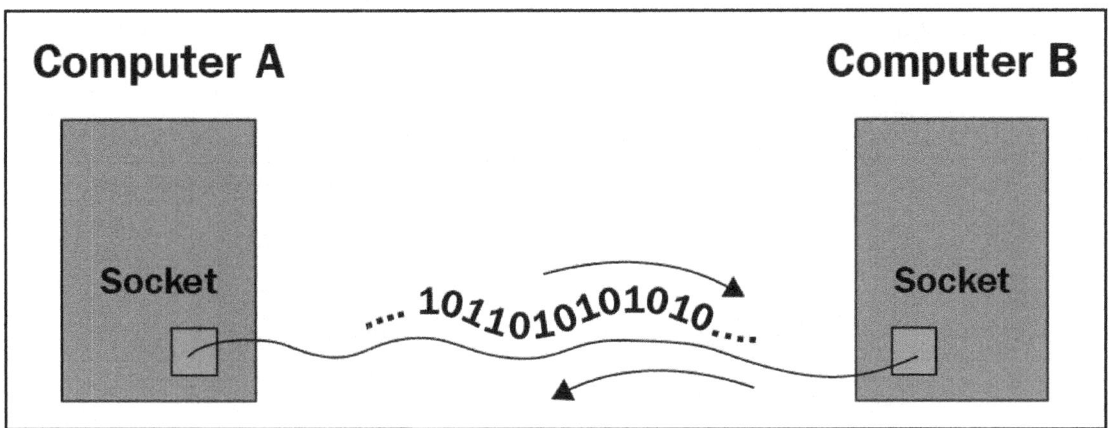

From the programmer's perspective, the socket is a structure that allows us to implement data through the network in applications. The socket is a connection point that either sends or receives data; that is, an application receives data via sockets too. The operating system provides a socket for the application upon request. An application can have more than one socket. Client applications in the client-server architecture usually operate with a single socket. Now, let's delve into socket programming in detail.

Programming network applications using sockets

As we mentioned previously, a socket is an abstraction over network communication. We treat them as regular files – everything written to a socket is sent via the network to its destination by the operating system. Everything that is received via the network is written into the socket – again, by the operating system. This way, the OS provides two-way communication for network applications.

Let's suppose that we run two different applications working with the network. For example, we open a web browser to surf the web and use a messaging application (such as Skype) to chat with friends. The web browser represents a client application in a client-server network architecture. The server, in this case, is the computer that responds with the requested data. For example, we type an address into the address bar of the web browser and see the resulting web page on the screen. Whenever we visit a website, the web browser requests a socket from the operating system. In terms of coding, the web browser creates a socket using the API provided by the OS. We can describe the socket with a more specific prefix: a client socket. For the server to process client requests, the computer running the web server must listen for incoming connections; that is, the server application creates a server socket intended to listen to connections.

Whenever a connection is established between the client and server, data communication can proceed. The following diagram depicts a web browser request to **facebook.com**:

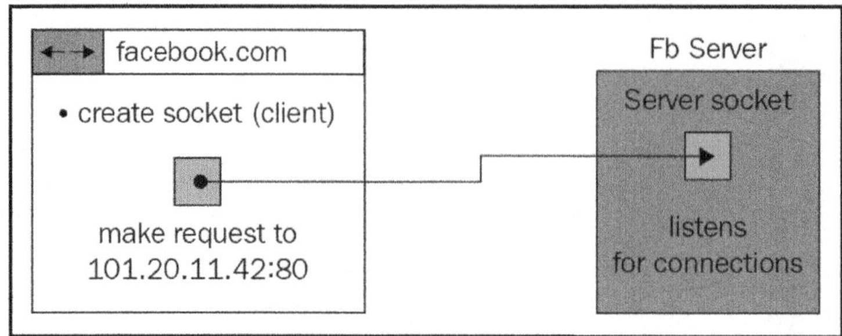

Pay attention to the group of numbers in the preceding diagram. This is called an **Internet Protocol (IP) address**. The IP address is the location that we need in order to transfer data to the device. There are billions of devices connected to the internet. To make a unique distinction between them, each device exposes a unique numeric value representing its address. A connection is established using the IP protocol, which is why we call it an IP address. An IP address consists of four groups of 1-byte length numbers. Its dotted-decimal representation is in the form X.X.X.X, where X is the 1-byte number. The values at each position range from 0 to 255. More specifically, it's a version 4 IP address. Modern systems use a version 6 address, which is a combination of numbers and letters, providing a wider range of available address values.

When creating a socket, we assign the IP address of the local computer to it; that is, we're binding the socket to the address. When using the socket to send data to another device in the network, we should set its destination address. The destination address is held by another socket on that device. To create a connection between two devices, we use two sockets. A reasonable question might arise— What if there are several applications running on the device? What if we run several applications, each of which has created a socket for itself? Which one should receive the incoming data?

To answer these questions, take a good look at the preceding diagram. You should see a number after the colon at the end of the IP address. That's called the **port number**. The port number is a 2-byte length number that's assigned to the socket by the operating system. Because of the 2-byte length limit, the OS cannot assign more than 65,536 unique port numbers to sockets; that is, you cannot have more than 65,536 simultaneous running processes or threads communicating via the network (however, there are ways to reuse sockets). Apart from that, there are port numbers that are reserved for specific applications. These ports are called well-known ports and range from 0 to 1023. They are reserved for privileged services. For example, the HTTP server's port number is 80. That doesn't mean it can't use other ports.

Let's learn how to create a socket in C++. We will design a wrapper class that encapsulates **Portable Operating System Interface (POSIX)** sockets, also known as **Berkeley** or **BSD** sockets. It has a standard set of functions for socket programming. The C++ extension for network programming will be a tremendous addition to the language. The working draft contains information on the networking interface. We will discuss this later in this chapter. Before that, let's try to create our own networking wrappers for existing and low-level libraries. When we use POSIX sockets, we depend on the operating system's API. The OS provides an API that represents the functions and objects that are used to create sockets, send and receive data, and so on.

POSIX represents a socket as a file descriptor. We use it almost as if it were a regular file. File descriptors follow the UNIX philosophy of providing a common interface to data input/output. The following code creates a socket using the `socket()` function (defined in the `<sys/socket.h>` header):

```
int s = socket(AF_INET, SOCK_STREAM, IPPROTO_TCP);
```

The declaration of the `socket()` function is as follows:

```
int socket(int domain, int type, int protocol);
```

So, `AF_INET`, `SOCK_STREAM`, and `IPPROTO_TCP` are numeric values. The domain parameter specifies the protocol family of the socket. We use `AF_INET` to specify the IPv4 protocol. For IPv6, we use `AF_INET6`. The second parameter specifies the type of the socket, that is, whether it's a stream-oriented or datagram socket. For each specific type, the last parameter should be specified accordingly. In the preceding example, we specified `SOCK_STREAM` with `IPPROTO_TCP`. The **Transmission Control Protocol (TCP)** represents a reliable stream-oriented protocol. This is why we set the type parameter to `SOCK_STREAM`. Before we implement a simple socket application, let's find out more about network protocols.

Network protocols

A network protocol is a collection of rules and data formats that define intercommunication between applications. For example, a web browser and a web server communicate via **Hyper-Text Transfer Protocol (HTTP)**. HTTP is more like a set of rules than a transport protocol. Transport protocols are at the base of every network communication. An example of a transport protocol would be TCP. When we mentioned the TCP/IP suite, we meant the implementation of TCP over IP. We can consider the **Internet Protocol (IP)** as the heart of internet communications.

It provides host-to-host routing and addressing. Everything that we send or receive via the internet is packaged as an *IP packet*. The following is what the IPv4 packet looks like:

Octet	Fields (bit positions)
0	Version (0–3) | IHL (4–7) | DSCP (8–13) | ECN (14–15) | Total Length (16–31)
4	Identification (0–15) | Flags (16–18) | Fragment Offeset (19–31)
8	Time to Live (0–7) | Protocol (8–15) | Header Checksum (16–31)
12	Source Address (0–31)
16	Destination Address (0–31)
20	Options (0–31)

[Image: IP Header]

The IP header weighs 20 bytes. It combines necessary flags and options for delivering a packet from the source address to the destination address. In the domain of the IP protocol, we usually call a packet a datagram. Each layer has its specific terms for packets. More careful specialists talk about encapsulating TCP segments into IP datagrams. It's totally fine to call them packets.

Each protocol at the higher level appends meta-information to the data that's sent and received via the network; for example, TCP data is encapsulated in an IP datagram. Besides this meta-information, the protocol also defines the underlying rules and operations that should be performed to complete a data transfer between two and more devices.

You can find more detailed information in specific documents called **Request for Comments (RFCs)**. For example, RFC 791 describes the Internet Protocol, while RFC 793 describes the Transmission Control Protocol.

Many popular applications – file transfer, email, web, and others – use TCP as their main transport protocol. For example, the HTTP protocol defines the format of the messages that are transferred from the client to the server and vice versa. The actual transfer happens using a transport protocol – in this case, TCP. However, the HTTP standard doesn't limit TCP to being the only transport protocol.

The following diagram illustrates the TCP header being appended to the data before passing it to the lower level:

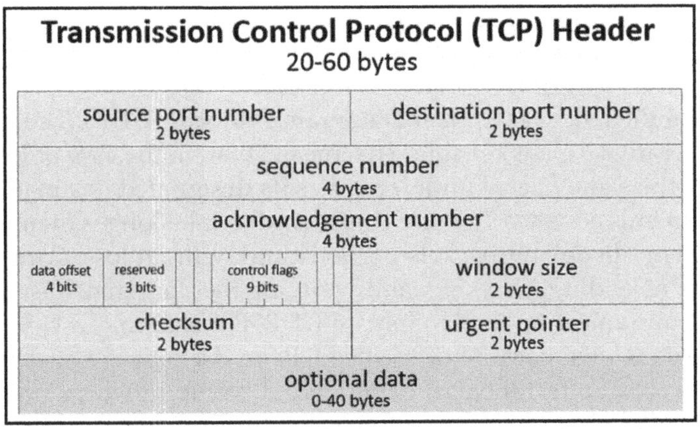

Transmission Control Protocol (TCP) Header
20-60 bytes

source port number 2 bytes		destination port number 2 bytes
sequence number 4 bytes		
acknowledgement number 4 bytes		
data offset 4 bits	reserved 3 bits	control flags 9 bits	window size 2 bytes
checksum 2 bytes		urgent pointer 2 bytes
optional data 0-40 bytes		

Pay attention to the source port number and destination port number. Those are the unique identifiers that differentiate between running processes in operating systems. Also, take a look at the sequence and acknowledgment numbers. They are TCP-specific and used for transmission reliability.

In practice, TCP is used due to its following features:

- Retransmission of lost data
- In-order delivery
- Data integrity
- Congestion control and avoidance

IP(short for Internet Protocol) is not reliable. It doesn't care for lost packets, which is why TCP handles the retransmission of lost packets. It marks each packet with a unique identifier that should be acknowledged by the other side of the transmission. If the sender does not receive an **acknowledgment code** (**ACK**) for a packet, the protocol will resend the packet (a limited number of times). It is also crucial to receive packets in the proper order. TCP reorders received packets to represent correctly ordered information. That's why, when listening to music online, we don't listen to the end of the song at its beginning.

Retransmission of packets might lead to another problem known as **network congestion**. This happens when a node doesn't manage to send packets fast enough. Packets get stuck for a while and unnecessary retransmission increases their number. Various implementations of TCP employ algorithms for congestion avoidance.

It maintains a congestion window – a factor that determines the amount of data that can be sent out. Using the slow-start mechanism, TCP slowly increases the congestion window after initializing the connection. Though the protocol is described in the corresponding **Request for Comments** (**RFC**), there are plenty of mechanisms that are implemented differently in operating systems.

On the other side of the fence is the **User Datagram Protocol** (**UDP**). The main difference between these two is that TCP is reliable. This means that, in the case of lost network packets, it resends the same packet until it reaches its designated destination. Because of its reliability, data transmissions via TCP are considered to take longer than using UDP. UDP doesn't guarantee we can deliver packets properly and without losses. Instead, developers should take care of resending, checking, and verifying the data transmission. Applications that require fast communication tend to rely on UDP. For example, a video call application or an online game uses UDP because of its speed. Even if a couple of packets get lost during the transmission, it won't affect the user experience. It's better to have small glitches while playing a game or talking to a friend in a video chat than to wait seconds for the next frame of the game or video.

One of the main reasons why TCP is slower than UDP is the bigger number of steps in the connection initiation procedure for TCP. The following diagram shows the process of connection establishment in TCP, also known as the three-way handshake:

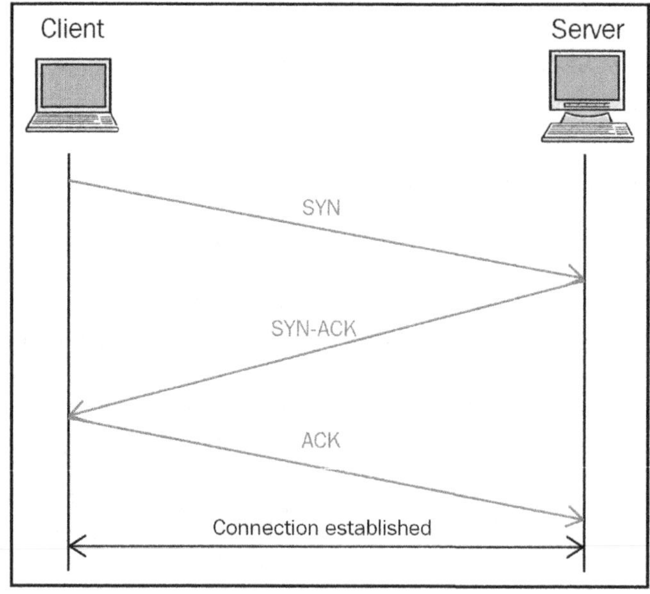

The client picks a random number when sending a SYN packet to the server. The server increments that random number by one, picks another random number, and replies with a SYN-ACK packet. The client increments both numbers received from the server by one and completes the handshake by sending the last ACK to the server. After the three-way handshake is successfully completed, the client and server can transfer packets to each other. This connection establishment process applies to every TCP connection. Details of the handshake are hidden from the developers of network applications. We create the socket and start listening to incoming connections.

Notice the difference between the two types of endpoint. One of them is the client. When implementing a network application, we should make a clear distinction between the client and the server because they have different implementations. This relates to the type of sockets as well. When creating a server socket, we are making it listen to incoming connections, while the client doesn't listen – it makes requests. The following diagram depicts certain functions and their invocation sequence for the client and server:

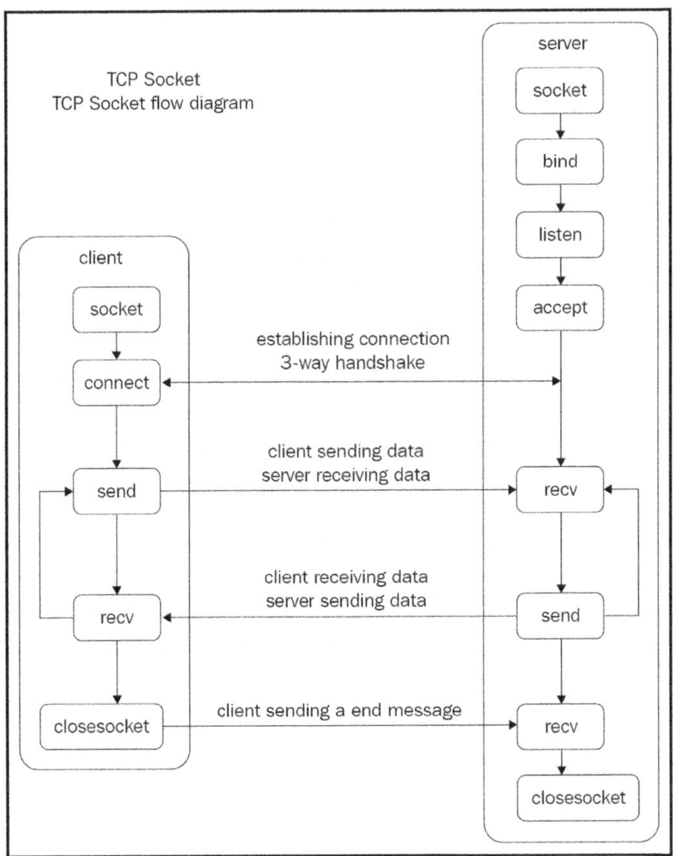

When creating a socket in code, we specify the protocol and the type of the socket. When we want a reliable connection between two endpoints, we choose TCP. The interesting thing is that we can use a transport protocol such as TCP to build our own protocol. Let's say we define a special document format to send and receive in order to treat the communication valid. For example, each document should start with the word PACKT. HTTP works the same way. It uses TCP for transport and defines a communication format over it. In the case of UDP, we should also design and implement a reliability strategy for communication. The preceding diagram shows how TCP establishes a connection between two endpoints. The client sends a `SYN` request to the server. The server answers with the `SYN-ACK` response, letting the client know that it's fine to continue the handshake. Finally, the client answers with an `ACK` to the server stating the connection is officially established. They can communicate as long as they want.

Synchronize (**SYN**) and ACK are protocol-defined terms that have become common in network programming.

UDP doesn't work this way. It sends data to the destination without worrying about an established connection. If you use UDP but need some reliability, you should implement it by yourself; for example, by checking whether a portion of data reached the destination. To check it, you can wait for the destination to answer with a custom-defined `ACK` packet. Most reliability-oriented implementations might repeat already existing protocols, such as TCP. However, there are many scenarios where you don't need them; for example, you don't need congestion avoidance because you don't need to send the same packet twice.

We designed a strategy game in the previous chapter. Suppose the game is online and you are playing with a real opponent instead of an automated enemy player. Each frame of the game is rendered based on the data that's received across the network. If we put some effort into making the data transfer reliable, increasing the data integrity, and making sure none of the packets are lost, the user experience may be hurt because of the desynchronization of players. This scenario is good for using UDP. We can implement data transfer without a retransmission strategy so that we squeeze the speed of the game. Of course, using UDP doesn't force us to avoid reliability. In the same scenario, we might need to make sure the packet is received successfully by the player. For example, when the player surrenders, we should make sure the opponent receives the message. So, we can have conditional reliability based on packet priority of. UDP provides flexibility and speed in network applications.

Let's take a look at an implementation of a TCP server application.

Designing a network application

The approach of designing an application with a small subsystem that requires a network connection is different compared to a fully network-related application. An example of the latter might be a client-server application for file storage and synchronization (such as Dropbox). It consists of a server and clients, where the client is installed as a desktop or mobile application that can also be used as a file explorer. Each update to the files in the system controlled by Dropbox will be instantly synchronized with the server. This way, you will always have your files in the cloud and can access them anywhere with an internet connection.

We will be designing a similar simplified server application for file storage and manipulation. The following are the main tasks of the server:

- Receive files from client applications
- Store files at specified locations
- Send files to clients upon request

Referring to `Chapter 10`, *Designing World-Ready Applications*, we can move forward to the following top-level design of the application:

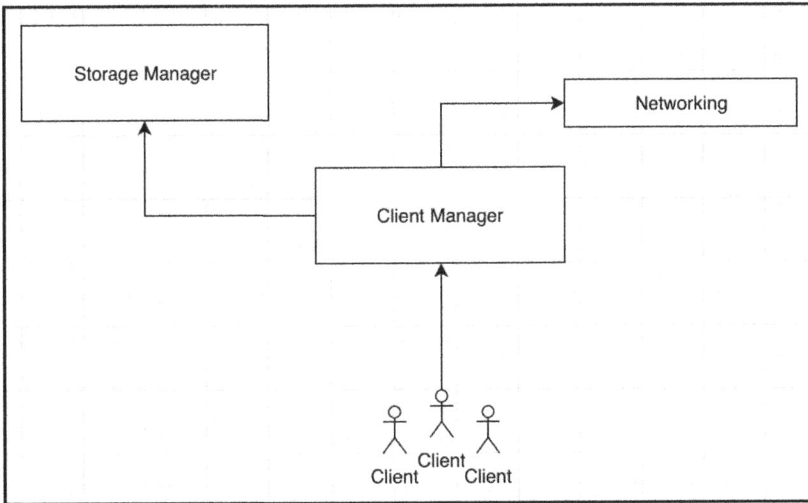

Each of the rectangles in the preceding diagram represents a class or a collection of classes concerned with specific tasks. For example, the **Storage Manager** handles everything related to storing and retrieving files. Whether it uses classes such as a file, location, database, and so on does not concern us that much at this point.

The **Client Manager** is a class or a group of classes that represent handling everything related to authenticating or authorizing clients (by client, we mean a client application), keeping steady connections with clients, receiving files from clients, sending files to clients, and so on.

We specifically emphasized **Networking** as an entity of interest in this chapter. Everything that relates to a network connection, along with data transfers from and to clients, is handled via **Networking**. Now, let's see what functionality we can use to design the Networking class (we will call it Network Manager for convenience).

Using POSIX sockets

As we mentioned previously, functions such as `socket()`, `bind()`, and `accept()` are library functions that are supported by default in most Unix systems. Previously, we included the `<sys/socket.h>` file. Besides that, we will need several other header files. Let's implement the classic TCP server example and wrap it in the Networking module for our file transfer application server.

As we mentioned previously, server-side development differs from client-side development in terms of the type of socket and its behavior. Although both sides operate with sockets, the server-side socket is continuously listening for incoming connections, while the client-side socket initiates a connection with the server. For the server socket to wait for connections, we create a socket and bind it to the server IP address and a port number that clients will try to connect to. The following C code represents the creation and binding of a TCP server socket:

```
int s = socket(AF_INET, SOCK_STREAM, 0);

struct sockaddr_in server;
server.sin_family = AF_INET;
server.sin_port = htons(port);
server.sin_addr.s_addr = INADDR_ANY;

bind(s, (struct sockaddr*)&server, sizeof(server));
```

The first call creates a socket. The third parameter is set to 0, meaning that the default protocol will be selected based on the type of the socket. The type is passed as the second parameter, `SOCK_STREAM`, which makes the protocol value equal to `IPPROTO_TCP` by default. The `bind()` function binds the socket with the specified IP address and port number. We specified them in the `sockaddr_in` structure, which combines network address-related details in it.

Although we skipped this in the preceding code, you should consider checking the calls to `socket()` and `bind()` functions (and other functions in POSIX sockets) against errors. Almost all of them return `-1` in the event of an error.

Also, note the `htons()` function. It takes care of converting its arguments into network byte order. The problem is hidden in the way computers are designed. Some machines (Intel microprocessors, for example) use **little-endian** byte ordering, while others use **big-endian** ordering. **Little-endian** ordering places the least significant byte first. **Big-endian** ordering places the most significant byte first. The following diagram shows the difference between the two:

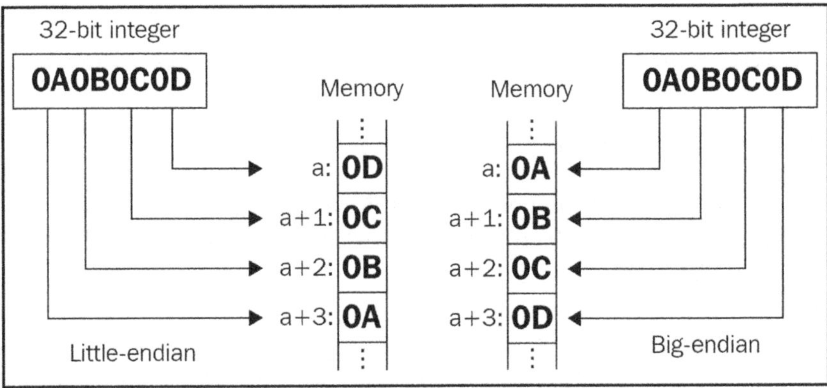

The network byte order is a convention independent of specific machine architectures. The `htons()` function converts the provided port number from host byte order (**little-** or **big-endian**) into network byte order (independent from the machine).

That's it – the socket is ready. Now, we should specify that it is ready for incoming connections. To specify that, we use the `listen()` function:

```
listen(s, 5);
```

As its name suggests, it listens for incoming connections. The second argument that's passed to the `listen()` function specifies the number of connections that the server will queue before discarding new incoming requests. In the preceding code, we specified `5` as the maximum number. In a high-load environment, we would increase this number. The maximum number is specified by the `SOMAXCONN` constant defined in the `<sys/socket.h>` header.

The choice of backlog number (the second parameter of the `listen()` function) is based on factors such as the following:

- If the rate of the connection requests is high for a short period of time, the backlog number should have a larger value.
- The duration of the server handles an incoming connection. The shorter the time, the smaller the backlog value will be.

When a connection initiation is happening, we can either to drop it or accept it and continue processing the connection. That's why we use the `accept()` function in the following snippet:

```
struct sockaddr_in client;
int addrlen;
int new_socket = accept(s, (struct sockaddr_in*)&client, &addrlen);
// use the new_socket
```

The two things to consider in the preceding code are as follows:

- First, the accepted socket connection information is written into the client's `sockaddr_in` structure. We can gather everything necessary about the client from that struct.
- Next, pay attention to the return value of the `accept()` function. It's a new socket that's created to handle requests from that particular client. The next call to the `accept()` function will return another value that will represent another client with a separate connection. We should handle this properly because the `accept()` call is blocking; that is, it waits for new connection requests. We will modify the preceding code so that it accepts multiple connections being handled in separate threads.

The last line with the comment in the preceding code states that `new_socket` can be used to receive or send data to the client. Let's see how we can achieve this and then start designing our `Networking` class. To read the data that's received by the socket, we need to use the `recv()` function, as follows:

```
char buffer[BUFFER_MAX_SIZE]; // define BUFFER_MAX_SIZE based on the
specifics of the server
recv(new_socket, buffer, sizeof(buffer), 0);
// now the buffer contains received data
```

The `recv()` function takes a `char*` buffer to write data into it. It stops writing at `sizeof(buffer)`. The last parameter of the function is the additional flag we can set for reading. You should consider calling the function several times to read bigger than the `BUFFER_MAX_SIZE` data.

Finally, to send data over the socket, we call the `send()` function, as follows:

```
char msg[] = "From server with love";
send(new_socket, msg, sizeof(msg), 0);
```

With that, we've covered almost all the functions that are required to implement a server application. Now, let's wrap them in a C++ class and incorporate multithreading so that we can process client requests concurrently.

Implementing a POSIX socket wrapper class

Let's design and implement a class that will serve as the starting point for network-based applications. The main interface of the class looks as follows:

```
class Networking
{
public:
  void start_server();

public:
  std::shared_ptr<Networking> get_instance();
  void remove_instance();

private:
  Networking();
  ~Networking();

private:
  int socket_;
  sockaddr_in server_;
  std::vector<sockaddr_in> clients_;

private:
  static std::shared_ptr<Networking> instance_ = nullptr;
  static int MAX_QUEUED_CONNECTIONS = 1;
};
```

It's natural for the `Networking` class to be a singleton because we want a single instance to listen for incoming connections. It's also important to have multiple objects, each of which represents a separate connection with a client. Let's gradually make the class design better. Earlier, we saw that each new client socket is created after the server socket listens to and then accepts a connection request.

After that, we can send or receive data through that new client socket. The server operates similarly to what can be seen in the following diagram:

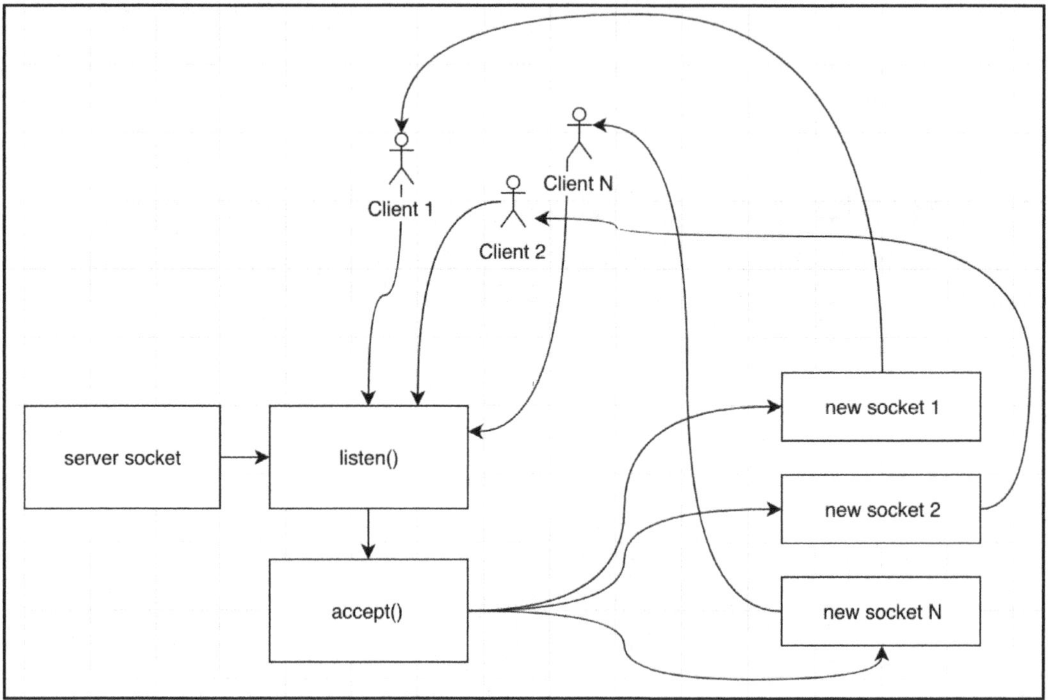

That is, after accepting each incoming connection, we will have one separate socket for a connection. We store them in the `clients_` vector in the `Networking` class. Therefore, we can write the main logic of creating a server socket, listening, and accepting new connections in a single function that can work concurrently if required. The `start_server()` function serves as the starting point for the server to listen for incoming connections. The following code block illustrates this:

```
void Networking::start_server()
{
  socket_ = socket(AF_INET, SOCK_STREAM, 0);
  // the following check is the only one in this code snippet
```

```
  // we skipped checking results of other functions for brevity,
  // you shouldn't omit them in your code
  if (socket_ < 0) {
    throw std::exception("Cannot create a socket");
  }
  struct sockaddr_in server;
  server.sin_family = AF_INET;
  server.sin_port = htons(port);
  server.sin_addr.s_addr = INADDR_ANY;

  bind(s, (struct sockaddr*)&server, sizeof(server));
  listen(s, MAX_QUEUED_CONNECTIONS);
  // the accept() should be here
}
```

Now, we've stopped at a point where we should accept incoming connections (see the comment in the preceding code snippet). We have two choices here (actually, there are more than two choices, but we will only discuss two of them). We can either place the call to `accept()` directly into the `start_server()` function or we can implement a separate function that the `Networking` class user will call whenever applicable.

It's not a bad practice to have specific exception classes for each error case that we have in the project. The preceding code might be rewritten when considering custom exceptions. You can do that as a homework project.

One of the choices has the `accept()` function in the `start_server()` function, which pushes each new connection into the `clients_` vector, as shown here:

```
void Networking::start_server()
{
  // code omitted for brevity (see in the previous snippet)
  while (true) {
    sockaddr_in client;
    int addrlen;
    int new_socket = accept(socket_, (sockaddr_in*)&client, &addrlen);
    clients_.push_back(client);
  }
}
```

Yes, we used an infinite loop. This may sound awful, but as long as the server is running, it must accept new connections. However, we all know that the infinite loop blocks the execution of code; that is, it won't ever leave the `start_server()` function. We introduced our network application as a project that has at least three components: the Client Manager, the Storage Manager, and the one we are designing right now – the `Networking` class.

The execution of one component must not affect the others in a bad way; that is, we can use threads to make some components run in the background. The `start_server()` function running in the context of a thread is a nice solution, although we should now care about the synchronization issues we covered in `Chapter 8`, *Concurrency and Multithreading*.

Also, pay attention to the incompleteness of the preceding loop. After accepting a connection, it pushes the client data into the `clients_` vector. We should consider using another structure for that as we also need to store the socket descriptor, along with the client. We can use `std::undordered_map` to map the socket descriptor to the client connection information, but a simple `std::pair` or `std::tuple` would be fine.

However, let's go even further and create a custom object representing the client connection, as shown here:

```
class Client
{
public:
  // public accessors

private:
  int socket_;
  sockaddr_in connection_info_;
};
```

We will modify the `Networking` class so that it stores a vector of `Client` objects:

```
std::vector<Client> clients_;
```

Now, we can change the design approach and make the `Client` object responsible for sending and receiving data:

```
class Client
{
public:
  void send(const std::string& data) {
    // wraps the call to POSIX send()
  }
  std::string receive() {
    // wraps the call to POSIX recv()
  }

  // code omitted for brevity
};
```

Even better, we can attach an `std::thread` object to the `Client` class so that each object handles data transfer in a separate thread. However, you should be careful not to starve the system. The number of incoming connections can increase drastically and the server application will become stuck. We will discuss this scenario in the next section when we discuss security issues. It's suggested you leverage thread pools that will both help us reuse threads and keep control over the number of threads running in the program.

The final design of the class depends on the type of data that we receive and send to the client. There are at least two different approaches. One of them is connecting to the client, receiving the necessary data, and shutting down the connection. The second approach is implementing a protocol by which the client and server will communicate. Although it sounds complex, the protocol might be simple.

It's also extensible and makes the application more robust because you can support more features as the project evolves. We will get back to designing the protocol for authenticating client requests in the next section, when we discuss how to secure the network server application.

Securing the C++ code

Compared to many languages, C++ is a little harder to master in terms of secure coding. There are plenty of guidelines that provide advice regarding how to and how not to avoid security risks in C++ programs. One of the most popular issues that we discussed in `Chapter 1`, *Building C++ Applications*, is using preprocessor macros. The example we used had the following macro:

```
#define DOUBLE_IT(arg) (arg * arg)
```

Improper use of this macro leads to logic errors that are hard to spot. In the following code, the programmer expects to get `16` printed to the screen:

```
int res = DOUBLE_IT(3 + 1);
std::cout << res << std::endl;
```

The output is `7`. The issue here is with the missing parentheses around the `arg` parameter; that is, the preceding macro should be rewritten as follows:

```
#define DOUBLE_IT(arg) ((arg) * (arg))
```

Although this example is popular, we strongly suggest avoiding macros as much as possible. C++ provides plenty of constructs that can be processed at compile time, such as `constexpr`, `consteval`, and `constinit` – even if statements have a `constexpr` alternative. Use them if you need compile-time processing in your code. And, of course, there are modules, a long-awaited addition to the language. You should prefer using modules everywhere you used an `#include` with ubiquitous include guards:

```
module my_module;
export int test;

// instead of

#ifndef MY_HEADER_H
#define MY_HEADER_H
int test
#endif
```

It's not only more secure, but also more efficient because modules are processed once (we can consider them as precompiled headers).

Although we don't want you to become paranoid about for security issues, you should be careful almost everywhere. You will avoid most of these issues by learning the language's quirks and oddities. Also, a good practice would be to use the newest features that replace or fix the disadvantages of previous versions. For example, consider the following `create_array()` function:

```
// Don't return pointers or references to local variables
double* create_array()
{
  double arr[10] = {0.0};
  return arr;
}
```

The caller of the `create_array()` function is left with a pointer to the non-existing array because `arr` has an automatic storage duration. We can replace the preceding code with a better alternative if required:

```
#include <array>

std::array<double> create_array()
{
  std::array<double> arr;
  return arr;
}
```

Strings are treated as character arrays and are the reason behind many buffer overflow issues. One of the most popular issues is writing data into a string buffer while ignoring its size. The `std::string` class is a safer alternative to C strings in that regard. However, when supporting legacy code, you should be careful when using functions such as `strcpy()`, as shown in the following example:

```
#include <cstdio>
#include <cstring>

int main()
{
  char small_buffer[4];
  const char* long_text = "This text is long enough to overflow small
buffers!";
  strcpy(small_buffer, long_text);
}
```

Given that, legally, `small_buffer` should have a null-terminator at the end of it, it will only cope with the first three characters of the `long_text` string. However, the following happens after calling `strcpy()`:

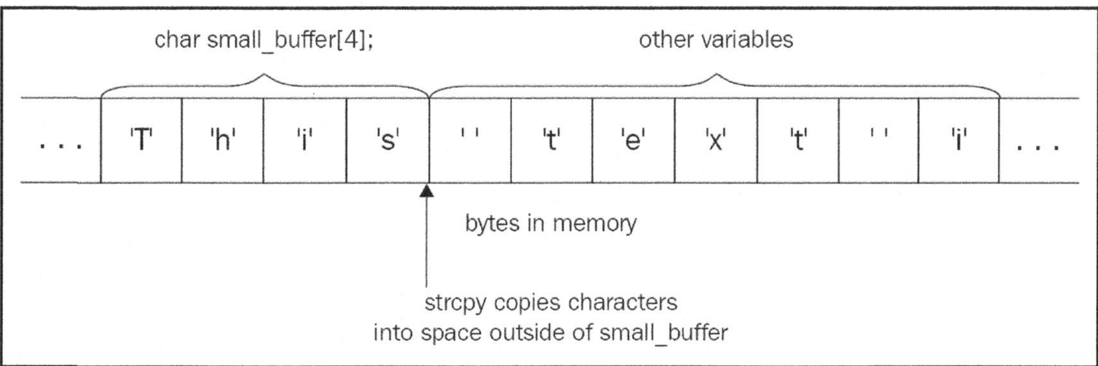

You should be even more careful when implementing network applications. Most data coming from client connections should be handled properly, and buffer overflows are not rare. Let's learn how to make network applications more secure.

Securing network applications

In the previous section of this book, we designed a network application that receives client data using socket connections. Besides the fact that most viruses that penetrate the system are from the outside world, network applications have this natural tendency to open up the computer to various threats on the internet. First of all, whenever you are running a network application, an open port exists in the system. Someone who knows the exact port that your application is listening on can intrude by faking protocol data. We will mostly discuss the server-side of network applications here; however, some of the topics here apply to client applications as well.

One of the first things you should do is incorporate client authorization and authentication. These are two terms that are easy to confuse. Be careful not to use them interchangeably; they are different:

- **Authentication** is the process of validating client access. It means that not every incoming connection request is served right away. Before transferring data to and from the client, the server application must be sure that the client is a known client. In almost the same way we access a social network platform by typing in our email and password, the authentication of a client defines whether the client has the right to access the system at all.
- **Authorization**, on the other hand, defines what exactly the client can do in the system. It's a set of permissions that are provided to specific clients. For instance, the client application we discussed in the previous section is able to upload files to the system. Sooner or later, you might want to incorporate paid subscriptions and provide paying clients with a wider range of features; for example, by allowing them to create folders to organize their files. So, when a client requests a folder's creation, we might want to authorize the request to discover if the client has the right to do so.

When the client application initiates a connection with the server, all the server gets is the connection details (IP address, port number). To let the server know who is behind the client application (the actual user), the client application sends over the user's credentials. Usually, this process involves sending the user a unique identifier (such as a username or email address) with the password to access the system. The server then checks these credentials against its database and verifies whether it should grant access to the client. This form of communication between the client and the server might be a simple text transfer or a formatted object transfer.

For example, the protocol that's defined by the server might require the client to send a **JavaScript Object Notation** (**JSON**) document in the following form:

```
{
  "email": "myemail@example.org",
  "password": "notSoSIMPLEp4s8"
}
```

The response from the server allows the client to proceed further or update its UI to let the user know the result of the operation. There are several cases that you might have encountered while using any web or network application when signing in. For example, a wrongly typed password might lead to an `Invalid username or password` error being returned by the server.

Besides this first necessary step, it is wise to validate every piece of data coming from the client application. A buffer overflow might be avoided quite easily if the email field is checked for its size. For example, the client application, when intentionally trying to break the system, might send a JSON object that has a very large value for its fields. That check is on the server's shoulders. Preventing security flaws starts with data validation.

Another form of security attack is making too many requests per second from a single or multiple clients. For example, a client application making hundreds of authentication requests in 1 second causes the server to intensively process those requests and waste its resources trying to serve them all. It would be better to check the rate of client requests, for example, limiting them to a single request per second.

These forms of attack (intentional or unintentional) are referred to as **Denial of Service** (**DOS**) attacks. The more advanced version of a DOS attack takes the form of making a huge number of requests to the server from multiple clients. This form is called a **Distributed DOS** (**DDOS**) attack. A simple approach might be to blacklist IP addresses that are trying to crash the system by making multiple requests per second. As a programmer of network applications, you should consider all the issues described here and many others outside the scope of this book when developing your applications.

Summary

In this chapter, we introduced designing network applications in C++. With effect from its first version, C++ has lacked built-in support for networking. The C++23 standard plans to finally introduce it in the language.

We started off by introducing the basics of networking. Understanding networking completely takes a lot of time, but there are several foundational concepts that every programmer must know before implementing an application in any way related to the network. Those foundational concepts include layering in the OSI model and different kinds of transport protocol, such as TCP and UDP. Having an understanding of the differences between TCP and UDP is necessary for any programmer. As we learned, TCP makes reliable connections between sockets, and sockets are the next thing that a programmer encounters when developing network applications. Those are the connection points of two instances of applications. Whenever we need to send or receive data through a network, we should define a socket and work with it almost as we would work with a regular file.

All the abstractions and concepts that we use in application development are handled by the OS and, in the end, by the network adapter. This is a device that's capable of sending data through a network medium. Receiving data from the medium doesn't guarantee safety. The network adapter receives anything coming from the medium. To make sure we are handling incoming data correctly, we should also take care of application security. The last section of this chapter was about writing secure code and validating the input to make sure no harm will be done to the program. Securing your program is a good step in making sure your programs are of high quality. One of the best approaches to developing programs is testing them thoroughly. You may recall that, in `Chapter 10`, *Designing World-Ready Applications*, we discussed software development steps and explained that one of the most important steps explained testing the program once the coding phase is complete. After testing it, you will most probably discover a lot of bugs. Some of these bugs are hard to reproduce and fix, and that's where debugging comes to the rescue.

The next chapter is all about testing and debugging your programs the right way.

Questions

1. List all seven layers of the OSI model.
2. What's the point of port numbers?
3. Why should you use sockets in network applications?
4. Describe the sequence of operations you should perform at the server-side to receive data using a TCP socket.
5. What are the differences between TCP and UDP?
6. Why shouldn't you use macro definitions in your code?
7. How would you differentiate between different client applications when implementing a server application?

Further reading

- *TCP/IP Illustrated, Volume 1: The Protocols,* by R. Stevens: `https://www.amazon.com/TCP-Illustrated-Protocols-Addison-Wesley-Professional/dp/0321336313/`
- *Networking Fundamentals,* by Gordon Davies: `https://www.packtpub.com/cloud-networking/networking-fundamentals`

13
Debugging and Testing

Debugging and testing take an extremely important role in the pipeline of the software development process. Testing helps us to find problems while debugging fixes them. However, if we follow certain rules during the implementation stage, lots of potential defects can be prevented. Additionally, since a test process is very costly, it would be great if we could automatically analyze software by using certain tools before human testing is required. Moreover, when, how, and what we should test regarding software is also important.

In this chapter, we will cover the following topics:

- Understanding the root cause of an issue
- Debugging C++ programs
- Understanding static and dynamic analysis
- Exploring unit testing, TDD, and BDD

Throughout this chapter, we will learn how to analyze a software defect, how to use a **GNU Debugger** (**GDB**) tool to debug a program, and how to use tools to automatically analyze software. We will also learn about the concepts of **unit testing**, **test-driven development** (**TDD**), and **behavior-driven development** (**BDD**), as well as how to practice using them during the software engineering development process.

Technical requirements

The code for this chapter can be found in this book's GitHub repository: `https://github.com/PacktPublishing/Expert-CPP` .

Understanding the root cause of an issue

In medicine, a good doctor needs to understand the difference between treating the symptoms and curing the condition. For example, giving painkillers to a patient with a broken arm will only take away the symptoms; surgery is probably the right way to help bones heal gradually.

Root Cause Analysis (**RCA**) is a systematic process that's used to identify the fundamental cause of a problem. With the help of associated proper tools, it tries to identify the origin of the primary cause of the problem using a specific set of steps. By doing so, we can determine the following:

- What happened?
- How did it happen?
- Why did it happen?
- What proper approach would be used to prevent or reduce it so that it never happens again?

RCA assumes that an action in one place triggers another action in another place, and so on. By tracing the action chain back to the beginning, we can discover the source of the problem and how it grows into the symptom we have. Aha! This is exactly the process we should follow to fix or reduce software defects. In the following subsections, we will learn about the basic RCA steps, how to apply the RCA process to detect software defects, and what certain rules a C++ developer should follow to prevent such defects from occurring in software.

The RCA overview

Typically, an RCA process contains the following five steps:

1. **Define the problem**: In this stage, we may find answers to the following questions: what is happening? What are the symptoms of the problem? In what environment or conditions is the problem happening in/under?
2. **Collect data**: To make a cause factor chart, we need to collect enough data. This step may be expensive and time-consuming.

3. **Make a causal factor chart**: A causal factor chart provides a visualization structure that we can use to organize and analyze the collected data. The causal factor chart is nothing but a sequence diagram with logic tests that explains the events leading up to the occurrence of a symptom. This charting process should drive the data collection process until the investigators are satisfied with the thoroughness of the chart.
4. **Identify the root causes**: By examining the causal factor chart, we can make a decision diagram known as the **root cause map** to identify the cause or causes of the root.
5. **Recommend and implement solutions**: Once a root cause or multi-causes have been identified, the answers to the following questions can help us to find a solution: What can we do to prevent the problem from happening again? How will a solution be implemented? Who will be responsible for it? What are the costs or risks of implementing the solution?

An RCA tree diagram is one of the most popular factor diagrams used in the software engineering industry. The following is an example structure of it:

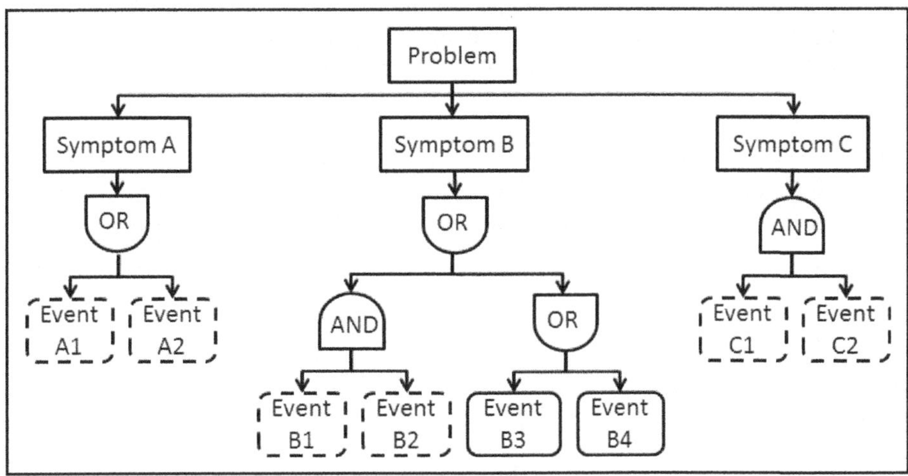

Let's assume we have a problem that has **A**, **B**, and **C** symptoms. Symptom **A** can be caused by events **A1** or **A2**, symptom **B** can be caused by either event **B1** and **B2** or **B3** and **B4**, and symptom **C** is caused by events **C1** and **C2**. After data collection, we found that symptoms **A** and **C** never appeared and that we only have symptom **B**. Further analysis shows that events **B1** and **B2** are not involved when the problem occurs, so we can identify that the root cause of this problem is happening because of events **B3** or **B4**.

If the software has a defect, instead of just fixing it at the failing point, we should apply RCA to it and investigate the original fundamental root cause(s) of the problem. Then, the root cause(s) of the problem can be traced back to the requirements, the design, the implementation, the verification, and/or the test planning and input data. When the issues at the root are found and fixed, the quality of the software can be improved and hence the maintenance expenses will be drastically reduced.

We have just learned how to find the root cause of a problem, but remember that *the best defense is a good offense*. So, instead of analyzing and fixing a problem, what if we can prevent it from happening?

Prevention is better than the cure – a good coding behavior

From a cost point of view, an IBM study has shown that assuming the overall cost of the requirements and design is 1X, then the implementation and coding process will take 5X, the unit and integration tests will take about 10X, comprehensive customer beta test costs will take about ~15X, and the costs to fix bugs in post-product release occupies about 30X! Therefore, minimizing code defects is one of the most effective ways to keep production costs down.

Although the generic methodology of finding the root causes of software defects is very important, it would be even better if we could prevent some defects at the implementation stage. To do that, we need to have good coding behavior, which means that certain rules must be followed. These rules can be classified at low and high levels. The low-level rules may include the following items:

- Uninitialized variables
- Integer divisions
- Mistakenly using `=` instead of `==`
- Potentially assign a signed variable to an unsigned variable
- Missing `break` in `switch` statements
- Side effects in compound expressions or function calls

When it comes to the high-level rules, we have topics related to the following:

- Interfaces
- Resource management

- Memory management
- Concurrency

B. Stroustrup and H. Sutter have suggested following these rules in their live document, *C++ Core Guidelines (Release 0.8)*, where static type safety and resource safety are emphasized. They also emphasize the possibilities of range checking in order to avoid dereferencing null-ptr, dangling pointers, and the systematic use of exceptions. If a developer follows such rules, it will lead to his/her code being statically type-safe without any resource leaks. Additionally, it will not only catch many more programming logic errors, but it will also run faster.

Because of page limitations, we will only look at a few examples of this in this subsection. If you want to look at more examples, please go to `https://isocpp.github.io/CppCoreGuidelines`.

Uninitialized variable problem

An uninitialized variable is one of the most common mistakes a programmer can make. When we declare a variable, a certain amount of continuous memory will be allocated to it. If it is not initialized, it still has some value, but there is no deterministic way of predicting it. Consequently, unpredictable behavior shows up when we execute the program:

```
//ch13_rca_uninit_variable.cpp
#include <iostream>
int main()
{
  int32_t x;
  // ... //do something else but not assign value to x
  if (x>0) {
    std::cout << "do A, x=" << x << std::endl;
  }
  else {
    std::cout << "do B, x=" << x << std::endl;
  }
  return 0;
}
```

In the preceding code, when `x` is declared, the OS will assign 4 bytes of unused memory to it, which means that the value of `x` is whatever value was residing in that memory. Each time we run this program, both the address and value of `x` might be different. Additionally, some compilers, such as Visual Studio, will initialize the value of `x` as `0` in the debug version but keep it uninitialized in the release version. In that case, we have a totally different output in the debug and release versions.

Side effects in compound expressions

When an operator, expression, statement, or function has finished being evaluated, it may be prolonged or may continuously exist inside its compound. This continuous existence has some side effects that may lead to some undefined behaviors. Let's have a look at the following code to understand this:

```
//ch13_rca_compound.cpp
#include <iostream>
int f(int x, int y)
{
  return x*y;
}

int main()
{
  int x = 3;
  std::cout << f(++x, x) << std::endl; //bad,f(4,4) or f(4,3)?
}
```

Because of the undefined behavior of the evaluation order of operands, the result of the preceding code could be either 16 or 12.

Mixing signed and unsigned problems

Typically, binary operators (`+`,`-`, `*`, `/`, `%`, `<`, `<=`,`>`, `>=`, `==`, `!=`, `&&`, `||`, `!`, `&`, `|`, `<<`, `>>`, `~`, `^`, `=`, `+=`, `-=`, `*=`, `/=`, and `%=`) require both side operands to be of the same type. If the two operands are of different types, one will be promoted to the same type as the other. Roughly speaking, there are three C standard conversion rules given in subclause 6.3.1.1 [ISO/IEC 9899:2011]:

- When we mix types of the same rank, the signed one will be promoted to an unsigned type.
- When we mix types of a different rank, the lower-ranked one will be promoted to the higher-ranked type if all the values of the lower-ranked side can be represented by the higher-ranked side.
- If all the values of the lower-ranked type cannot be represented by the higher-ranked type in the preceding case , then the unsigned version of the higher-ranked type will be used.

Now, let's take a look at the traditional signed integer minus unsigned integer problem:

```
//ch13_rca_mix_sign_unsigned.cpp
#include <iostream>
```

```
using namespace std;
int main()
{
 int32_t x = 10;
 uint32_t y = 20;
 uint32_t z = x - y; //z=(uint32_t)x - y
 cout << z << endl; //z=4294967286.
}
```

In the preceding example, the signed `int` will be automatically converted into an unsigned `int` and the result will be `uint32_t z = -10`. On the other hand, because `-10` cannot be represented as an unsigned `int` value, its hexadecimal value, `0xFFFFFFF6`, will be interpreted as `UINT_MAX - 9` (that is, `4294967286`) on two's complement machines.

Order of evaluation problem

The following example is concerned with the initialization order of class members in a constructor. Since the initialization order is the order the class members appear in the class definition, it's good practice to separate the declaration of each member into different lines:

```
//ch13_rca_order_of_evaluation.cpp
#include <iostream>
using namespace std;

class A {
public:
  A(int x) : v2(v1), v1(x) {
  };
  void print() {
    cout << "v1=" << v1 << ",v2=" << v2 << endl;
  };
protected:
  //bad: the order of the class member is confusing, better
  //separate it into two lines for non-ambiguity order declare
  int v1, v2;
};

class B {
public:
  //good: since the initialization order is: v1 -> v2,
  //after this we have: v1==x, v2==x.
  B(int x) : v1(x), v2(v1) {};

  //wrong: since the initialization order is: v1 -> v2,
  //after this we have: v1==uninitialized, v2==x.
  B(float x) : v2(x), v1(v2) {};
```

```
    void print() {
      cout << "v1=" << v1 << ", v2=" << v2 << endl;
    };

protected:
    int v1; //good, here the declaration order is clear
    int v2;
};

int main()
{
    A a(10);
    B b1(10), b2(3.0f);
    a.print();  //v1=10,v2=10,v3=10 for both debug and release
    b1.print(); //v1=10, v2=10 for both debug and release
    b2.print(); //v1=-858993460,v2=3 for debug; v1=0,v2=3 for release.
}
```

In class `A`, although the declaring order is `v1 -> v2`, putting them in one line confuses other developers. In the first constructor of class `B`, `v1` will be initialized as `x`, then `v2` will be initialized as `v1` because its declaration order is `v1->v2`. However, in its second constructor, `v1` will be initialized as `v2` first (at this point, `v2` is not initialized yet!), then `v2` will be initialized by `x`. This causes the different output values of `v1` in debug and release versions.

Compile-time checking versus runtime checking

The following example shows that runtime checking (number of bits for an integer type variable cloud) can be replaced by compile-time checking:

```
//check # of bits for int
//courtesy: https://isocpp.github.io/CppCoreGuidelines/CppCoreGuidelines
int nBits = 0; // don't: avoidable code
for (int i = 1; i; i <<= 1){
     ++nBits;
}
if (nBits < 32){
    cerr << "int too small\n";
}
```

Since `int` can be either 16 or 32 bits, depending on the operating system, this example fails to achieve what it is trying to achieve. We should use `int32_t` or just replace it with the following:

```
static_assert(sizeof(int) >= 4); //compile-time check
```

Another example is concerned with reading the max number of `n` integers into a one-dimensional array:

```
void read_into(int* p, int n); // a function to read max n integers into *p
...
int v[10];
read_into(v, 100); //bad, off the end, but the compile cannot catch this
error.
```

This can be fixed using `span<int>`:

```
void read_into( span<int> buf); // read into a range of integers
...
int v[10];
read_into(v); //better, the compiler will figure out the number of elements
```

The general rule here is to do the analysis at compile-time as much as possible and to not postpone it until runtime.

Avoiding memory leaks

A memory leak means that the allocated dynamic memory can never be freed. In C, we use `malloc()` and/or `calloc()` to allocate memory and `free()` to release it. In C++, the `new` operator and the `delete` or `delete []` operators are used to manage memory dynamically. Although the risks of memory leak can be reduced with the help of smart pointers and **Resource Acquisition Is Initialization** (**RAII**), there are still some rules we need to follow if we wish to build high-quality code.

First, the easiest memory management way is the memory you never allocated by your own code. For example, whenever you can write `T x;`, don't write `T* x = new T();` or `shared_ptr<T> x(new T() );`.

Next, do not manage the memory using your own code, as shown here:

```
void f_bad(){
 T* p = new T() ;
  ...                      //do something with p
 delete p ;                //leak if throw or return before reaching this line
}
```

Instead, try to use RAII, as follows:

```
void f_better()
{
 std::auto_ptr<T> p(new T()) ; //other smart pointers is ok also
```

```
  ...                                //do something with p
  //will not leak regardless whether this point is reached or not
}
```

Then, use `unique_ptr` to replace `shared_ptr` unless you need to share its ownership, as follows:

```
void f_bad()
{
  shared_ptr<Base> b = make_shared<Derived>();
  ...
} //b will be destroyed at here
```

Since `b` is locally used without copying it, its `refcount` will be always `1`. This means we can use a `unique_ptr` to replace it:

```
void f_better()
{
  unique_ptr<Base> b = make_unique<Derived>();
  ...              //use b locally
}                  //b will be destroyed at here
```

Finally, even if you really need to dynamically manage the memory by yourself, don't manually allocate the memory if there is an `std container` library class available.

In this section, we learned how to locate a problem using RCA and how to prevent a problem by coding best practices. Next, we'll learn how to use a debugger tool to control the line-by-line execution of a program and examine the values of variables and expressions during its running time.

Debugging C++ programs

Debugging is the process of finding and resolving the problems or defects of a program. This may include interactive debugging, data/control flow analysis, and unit and integration testing. In this section, we will only focus on interactive debugging, which is the process of executing your source code line-by-line with breakpoints, all while showing the values of the variables being used and their corresponding memory addresses.

Tools to debug a C/C++ program

Depending on your development environment, there are lots of tools available in the C++ community. The following list shows the most popular ones on different platforms.

- Linux/Unix:
    - **GDB**: A free open source **Command-Line Interface (CLI)** debugger.
    - **Eclipse**: A free open source **Integrated Development Environment (IDE)**. It supports not only debugging but also compiling, profiling, and smart editing.
    - **Valgrind**: Another open source dynamic analysis tool; it is good for debugging memory leaks and threading bugs.
    - **Affinic**: A commercial **Graphic User Interface** (**GUI**) tool built for the **GDB**, **LLDB**, and **LLVM debugger**.
    - **DDD** : An open source data display debugger for **GDB**, **DBX**, **JDB**, **XDB,** and **Python**, it displays data structures as graphs.
    - **GDB in Emacs mode**: An open source GUI tool that uses GNU Emacs to view and edit source code when debugging with GDB.
    - **KDevelop**: A free and open source IDE and debugger tool for programming languages such as C/C++, Objective-, and so on.
    - **Nemiver**: An open source tool that works well in the **GNOME** desktop environment.
    - **SlickEdit**: A good tool for debugging multithreaded and multiprocessor code.
- Windows:
    - **Visual Studio**: A commercial tool with GUI that's free for community versions.
    - **GDB**: This can run in Windows as well with the help of **Cygwin** or **MinGW**.
    - **Eclipse**: Its **C++ Development Tooling** (**CDT**) can be installed on Windows with the MinGW GCC compiler in the toolchains.
- macOS:
    - **LLDB**: This is the default debugger in **Xcode** on macOS and supports C/C++ and Objective-C on desktop and iOS devices and their simulators.
    - **GDB**: This CLI debugger is also used on macOS and iOS systems.
    - **Eclipse**: This free IDE using GCC works for macOS.

Since GDB can be run on all platforms, we will show you how to use GDB in the following subsections.

GDB overview

GDB stands for GNU debugger, which allows a developer to see *what is going on inside another program while it executes, or what another program was doing at the moment it crashed.* GDB can do the following four main things:

- Start a program and specify anything that might affect its behavior.
- Make a program stop on given conditions.
- Examine what happened when a program stopped.
- Change the values of variables while running a program. This means we can experiment with something to correct the effects of one bug and/or go on to learn the side effects of another.

Note that two programs or executable files are involved: one is GDB, while the other is the program to be debugged. Since these two programs can run either on the same machine or different ones, we may have three categories of debugging, as follows:

- **Native debugging**: Both programs run on the same machine.
- **Remote debugging**: GDB runs on a host machine, while the debugged program runs on a remote machine.
- **Simulator debugging**: GDB runs on a host machine, while the debugged program runs on a simulator.

Based on the latest release (GDB v8.3) at the time of writing this book, the languages supported by GDB including C, C++, Objective-C, Ada, Assembly, D, Fortran, Go, OpenCL, Modula-2, Pascal, and Rust.

Since GDB is a state-of-the-art tool in the debugging industry and is complex and has lots of functions, it won't be possible to learn about all its features in this section. Instead, we will study the most useful features by looking at examples.

Examples of GDB

Before practicing these examples, we need to check if `gdb` has been installed on our system by running the following code:

```
~wus1/chapter-13$ gdb --help
```

If the following kind of information is displayed, we will be ready to start:

```
This is the GNU debugger. Usage:
 gdb [options] [executable-file [core-file or process-id]]
 gdb [options] --args executable-file [inferior-arguments ...]

 Selection of debuggee and its files:
 --args Arguments after executable-file are passed to inferior
 --core=COREFILE Analyze the core dump COREFILE.
 --exec=EXECFILE Use EXECFILE as the executable.
 ...
```

Otherwise, we need to install it. Let's go over how we can install it on the different operating systems:

- For Debian-based Linux:

```
~wus1/chapter-13$ sudo apt-get install build-essential
```

- For Redhat-based Linux:

```
~wus1/chapter-13$sudo yum install  build-essential
```

- For macOS:

```
~wus1/chapter-13$brew install gdb
```

Windows users can install GDB through MinGW distributes. macOS will need a taskgated configuration.

Then, type `gdb --help` again to check if it was successfully installed.

Setting breakpoints and inspection variable values

In the following example, we will learn how to set breakpoints, continue, step into or step over a function, print values of variables, and how to use help in `gdb`. The source code is as follows:

```
//ch13_gdb_1.cpp
#include <iostream>
float multiple(float x, float y);
int main()
{
 float x = 10, y = 20;
 float z = multiple(x, y);
 printf("x=%f, y=%f, x*y = %f\n", x, y, z);
```

```
    return 0;
}

float multiple(float x, float y)
{
    float ret = x + y; //bug, should be: ret = x * y;
    return ret;
}
```

As we mentioned in `Chapter 3`, *Details of Object-Oriented Programming,* let's build this program in debug mode, as follows:

```
~wus1/chapter-13$ g++ -g ch13_gdb_1.cpp -o ch13_gdb_1.out
```

Note that for g++, the `-g` option means the debugging information will be included in the output binary file. If we run this program, it will show the following output:

```
x=10.000000, y=20.000000, x*y = 30.000000
```

Now, let's use `gdb` to see where the bug is. To do that, we need to execute the following command line:

```
~wus1/chapter-13$ gdb ch13_gdb_1.out
```

By doing this, we will see the following output:

```
GNU gdb (Ubuntu 8.1-0ubuntu3) 8.1.0.20180409-git
 Copyright (C) 2018 Free Software Foundation, Inc.
 License GPLv3+: GNU GPL version 3 or later
<http://gnu.org/licenses/gpl.html>
 This is free software: you are free to change and redistribute it.
 There is NO WARRANTY, to the extent permitted by law. Type "show copying"
 and "show warranty" for details.
 This GDB was configured as "aarch64-linux-gnu".
 Type "show configuration" for configuration details.
 For bug reporting instructions, please see:
 <http://www.gnu.org/software/gdb/bugs/>.
 Find the GDB manual and other documentation resources online at:
 <http://www.gnu.org/software/gdb/documentation/>.
 For help, type "help".
 Type "apropos word" to search for commands related to "word"...
 Reading symbols from a.out...done.
 (gdb)
```

Now, let's have a look at the various commands in detail:

- `break` and `run`: If we type `b main` or `break main` and press *Enter*, a `breakpoint` will be inserted at the main function. Then, we can type `run` or `r` to start debugging the program. The following information will be shown in a Terminal window. Here, we can see that our first `breakpoint` is at the sixth line in the source code and that the debugged program has been paused in order to wait for a new command:

```
(gdb) b main
Breakpoint 1 at 0x8ac: file ch13_gdb_1.cpp, line 6.
(gdb) r
Starting program: /home/nvidia/wus1/Chapter-13/a.out
[Thread debugging using libthread_db enabled]
Using host libthread_db library "/lib/aarch64-linux-
gnu/libthread_db.so.1".

Breakpoint 1, main () at ch13_gdb_1.cpp:6
6 float x = 10, y = 20;
```

- `next`, `print`, and `quit`: The `n` or `next` command will go to the next line of the code. If the line calls a subroutine, it does not enter the subroutine; instead, it steps over the call and treats it as a single source line. If we want to show the value of a variable, we can use the `p` or `print` command, followed by the variable's name. Finally, if we want to exit from `gdb`, the `q` or `quit` command can be used. Here is the output from the Terminal window after running these operations:

```
(gdb) n
 7 float z = multiple(x, y);
 (gdb) p z
 $1 = 0
 (gdb) n
 8 printf("x=%f, y=%f, x*y = %f\n", x, y, z);
 (gdb) p z
 $2 = 30
 (gdb) q
 A debugging session is active.
 Inferior 1 [process 29187] will be killed.
 Quit anyway? (y or n) y
 ~/wus1/Chapter-13$
```

- `step`: Now let's learn how to step into the `multiple()` function and find the bug. To do that, we need to start over by using the `b`, `r`, and `n` command to reach line 7 first. Then, we can use the `s` or `step` command to step into the `multiple()` function. Next, we use the `n` command to reach line 14 and `p` to print the value of the `ret` variable, which is 30. At this point, we've figured out that by using `ahha the bug is at line 14!:`, instead of `x*y`, we have a typo, that is, `x+y`. The following code block is the corresponding outputs from these commands:

```
~/wus1/Chapter-13$gdb ch13_gdb_1.out
 ...
 (gdb) b main
 Breakpoint 1 at 0x8ac: file ch13_gdb_1.cpp, line 6.
 (gdb) r
 The program being debugged has been started already.
 Start it from the beginning? (y or n) y
 Starting program: /home/nvidia/wus1/Chapter-13/a.out
 [Thread debugging using libthread_db enabled]
 Using host libthread_db library "/lib/aarch64-linux-
gnu/libthread_db.so.1".
Breakpoint 1, main () at ch13_gdb_1.cpp:6
 6 float x = 10, y = 20;
 (gdb) n
 7 float z = multiple(x, y);
 (gdb) s
 multiple (x=10, y=20) at ch13_gdb_1.cpp:14
 14 float s = x + y;
 (gdb) n
 15 return s;
 (gdb) p s
 $1 = 30
```

- `help`: Lastly, let's learn about the `help` command to end this small example. When `gdb` is launched, we can use the `help` or `h` command to get the usage information of a particular command in its command input line. For instance, the following Terminal window summarizes what have we learned so far:

```
(gdb) h b
 Set breakpoint at specified location.
 break [PROBE_MODIFIER] [LOCATION] [thread THREADNUM] [if
CONDITION]
 PROBE_MODIFIER shall be present if the command is to be placed in
a
 probe point. Accepted values are `-probe' (for a generic,
automatically
 guessed probe type), `-probe-stap' (for a SystemTap probe) or
```

```
 `-probe-dtrace' (for a DTrace probe).
 LOCATION may be a linespec, address, or explicit location as
described
 below.
  ....

 (gdb) h r
 Start debugged program.
 You may specify arguments to give it.
 Args may include "*", or "[...]"; they are expanded using the
 shell that will start the program (specified by the "$SHELL"
environment
 variable). Input and output redirection with ">", "<", or ">>"
 are also allowed.

 (gdb) h s
 Step program until it reaches a different source line.
 Usage: step [N]
 Argument N means step N times (or till program stops for another
reason).

 (gdb) h n
 Step program, proceeding through subroutine calls.
 Usage: next [N]
 Unlike "step", if the current source line calls a subroutine,
 this command does not enter the subroutine, but instead steps over
 the call, in effect treating it as a single source line.

 (gdb) h p
 Print value of expression EXP.
 Variables accessible are those of the lexical environment of the
selected
 stack frame, plus all those whose scope is global or an entire
file.

 (gdb) h h
 Print list of commands.
 (gdb) h help
 Print list of commands.
 (gdb) help h
 Print list of commands.
 (gdb) help help
 Print list of commands.
```

At this point, we have learned about a few basic commands we can use to debug a program. These commands are `break`, `run`, `next`, `print`, `quit`, `step`, and `help`. We will learn about function and conditional breakpoints, watchpoint, and the `continue` and `finish` commands in the next subsection.

Function breakpoints, conditional breakpoints, watchpoint, and the continue and finish commands

In this example, we will learn how to set function breakpoints, conditional breakpoints, and use the `continue` command. Then, we will learn how to finish a function call without the need to execute all the code lines in a step by step format. The source code is as follows:

```
//ch13_gdb_2.cpp
#include <iostream>

float dotproduct( const float *x, const float *y, const int n);
int main()
{
 float sxx,sxy;
 float x[] = {1,2,3,4,5};
 float y[] = {0,1,1,1,1};

 sxx = dotproduct( x, x, 5);
 sxy = dotproduct( x, y, 5);
 printf( "dot(x,x) = %f\n", sxx );
 printf( "dot(x,y) = %f\n", sxy );
 return 0;
}

float dotproduct( const float *x, const float *y, const int n )
{
 const float *p = x;
 const float *q = x;  //bug: replace x by y
 float s = 0;
 for(int i=0; i<n; ++i, ++p, ++q){
        s += (*p) * (*q);
 }
 return s;
}
```

Again, after building and running ch13_gdb_2.cpp, we get the following output:

```
~/wus1/Chapter-13$ g++ -g ch13_gdb_2.cpp -o ch13_gdb_2.out
~/wus1/Chapter-13$ ./ch13_gdb_2.out
dot(x,x) = 55.000000
dot(x,y) = 55.000000
```

Since both dot(x,x) and dot(x,y) give us the same results, something must be wrong here. Now, let's debug it by learning how to set a breakpoint in the dot() function:

- **Function breakpoint**: To set a breakpoint at the beginning of a function, we can use the b function_name command. As always, we can use tab completion during input. For instance, let's say we type the following:

```
(gdb) b dot<Press TAB Key>
```

The following command line will automatically pop up if we do this:

```
(gdb) b dotproduct(float const*, float const*, int)
```

If it is a member function of a class, its class name should be included, as follows:

```
(gdb) b MyClass::foo(<Press TAB key>
```

- **Conditional breakpoint**: There are several ways to set a conditional breakpoint:

```
(gdb) b f.cpp:26 if s==0 //set a breakpoint in f.cpp, line 26 if
s==0
(gdb) b f.cpp:20 if ((int)strcmp(y, "hello")) == 0
```

- **List and delete breakpoints**: Once we've set a few breakpoints, we can list or delete them, as follows:

```
(gdb) i b
(gdb) delete breakpoints 1
(gdb) delete breakpoints 2-5
```

- **Remove make a breakpoint unconditional**: Since each breakpoint has a number, we can remove a condition from a breakpoint, like so:

```
(gdb) cond 1          //break point 1 is unconditional now
```

- **Watchpoint**: A watchpoint can stop execution when the value of an expression changes, without having to predict where (in which line) it may happen. There are three kinds of watchpoints:
    - `watch`: `gdb` will break when a write occurs
    - `rwatch`: `gdb` will break when a read occurs
    - `awatch`: `gdb` will break when either a write or a read happens

  The following code shows an example of this:

```
(gdb) watch v                   //watch the value of variable v
(gdb) watch *(int*)0x12345678 //watch an int value pointed by an
address
(gdb) watch a*b + c/d           // watch an arbitrarily complex
expression
```

- **continue**: When we've finished examining the values of variables at a breakpoint, we can use the `continue` or `c` command to continue program execution until the debugger encounters a breakpoint, a signal, an error, or normal process termination.
- **finish**: Once we go inside a function, we may want to execute it continuously until it returns to its caller line. This can be done using the `finish` command.

Now, let's put these commands together to debug `ch13_gdb_2.cpp`.The following is the output from our Terminal window. For your convenience, we've separated it into three parts:

```
//gdb output of example ch13_gdb_2.out -- part 1
~/wus1/Chapter-13$ gdb ch13_gdb_2.out                          //cmd 1
 ...
 Reading symbols from ch13_gdb_2.out ... done.

 (gdb) b dotproduct(float const*, float const*, int)        //cmd 2
 Breakpoint 1 at 0xa5c: file ch13_gdb_2.cpp, line 20.
 (gdb) b ch13_gdb_2.cpp:24 if i==1                             //cmd 3
 Breakpoint 2 at 0xa84: file ch13_gdb_2.cpp, line 24.
 (gdb) i b                                                     //cmd 4
 Num Type Disp Enb Address What
 1 breakpoint keep y 0x0000000000000a5c in dotproduct(float const*, float
const*, int) at ch13_gdb_2.cpp:20
 2 breakpoint keep y 0x0000000000000a84 in dotproduct(float const*, float
const*, int) at ch13_gdb_2.cpp:24
 stop only if i==1
 (gdb) cond 2                                                 //cmd 5
 Breakpoint 2 now unconditional.
 (gdb) i b                                                    //cmd 6
```

```
Num Type Disp Enb Address What
 1 breakpoint keep y 0x0000000000000a5c in dotproduct(float const*, float
const*, int) at ch13_gdb_2.cpp:20
 2 breakpoint keep y 0x0000000000000a84 in dotproduct(float const*, float
const*, int) at ch13_gdb_2.cpp:24
```

In part one, we have the following six commands:

- `cmd 1`: We start `gdb` with the parameter of the built executable file, `ch13_gdb_2.out`. This briefly shows us its version and document and usage information, and then tells us that the reading symbols process has been completed and is waiting for the next command.
- `cmd 2`: We set a `breakpoint` function (at `dotproduct()`).
- `cmd 3`: A conditional `breakpoint` is set.
- `cmd 4`: It lists information about the breakpoints and tells us that we have two of them.
- `cmd 5`: We set `breakpoint 2` as `unconditional`.
- `cmd 6`: We list the breakpoint information again. At this point, we can see two breakpoints. These are located at lines 20 and 24 in the `ch13_gdb_2.cp` file, respectively.

Next, let's look at the `gdb` output in part two:

```
//gdb output of example ch13_gdb_2.out -- part 2
(gdb) r                                                  //cmd 7
 Starting program: /home/nvidia/wus1/Chapter-13/ch13_gdb_2.out
 [Thread debugging using libthread_db enabled]
 Using host libthread_db library "/lib/aarch64-linux-
gnu/libthread_db.so.1".

 Breakpoint 1, dotproduct (x=0x7fffffed68, y=0x7fffffed68, n=5) at
ch13_gdb_2.cpp:20
 20 const float *p = x;
 (gdb) p x                                              //cmd 8
 $1 = (const float *) 0x7fffffed68
 (gdb) c                                                //cmd 9
 Continuing.

 Breakpoint 2, dotproduct (x=0x7fffffed68, y=0x7fffffed68, n=5) at
ch13_gdb_2.cpp:24
 24 s += (*p) * (*q);
 (gdb) p i                                              //cmd 10
 $2 = 0
 (gdb) n                                                //cmd 11
 23 for(int i=0; i<n; ++i, ++p, ++q){
```

```
(gdb) n                                                    //cmd 12

Breakpoint 2, dotproduct (x=0x7fffffed68, y=0x7fffffed68, n=5) at
ch13_gdb_2.cpp:24
24 s += (*p) * (*q);
(gdb) p s                                                  //cmd 13
$4 = 1
(gdb) watch s                                              //cmd 14
Hardware watchpoint 3: s
```

Part two has the following cmds:

- `cmd 7`: By giving the `run` command, the program starts running and stops at the first breakpoint in line 20.
- `cmd 8`: We print the value of `x`, which shows its address.
- `cmd 9`: We continue the program. Once it's been continued, it stops at the second breakpoint in line 24.
- `cmd 10`: The value of `i` is printed, which is `0`.
- `cmd 11-12`: We use the `next` command twice. At this point, the `s += (*p) * (*q)` statement is executed.
- `cmd 13`: The value of `s` is printed, which is `1`.
- `cmd 14`: We print the value of `s` .

Finally, part three is as follows:

```
//gdb output of example ch13_gdb_2.out -- part 3
(gdb) n                                                    //cmd 15
 Hardware watchpoint 3: s

Old value = 1
New value = 5
dotproduct (x=0x7fffffed68, y=0x7fffffed68, n=5) at ch13_gdb_2.cpp:23
23 for(int i=0; i<n; ++i, ++p, ++q){
(gdb) finish                                               //cmd 16
Run till exit from #0 dotproduct (x=0x7fffffed68, y=0x7fffffed68, n=5) at
ch13_gdb_2.cpp:23

Breakpoint 2, dotproduct (x=0x7fffffed68, y=0x7fffffed68, n=5) at
ch13_gdb_2.cpp:24
24 s += (*p) * (*q);
(gdb) delete breakpoints 1-3                               //cmd 17
(gdb) c                                                    //cmd 18
Continuing.

dot(x,x) = 55.000000
```

```
dot(x,y) = 55.000000
[Inferior 1 (process 31901) exited normally]
[Inferior 1 (process 31901) exited normally]
(gdb) q                                         //cmd 19
~/wus1/Chapter-13$
```

In this part, we have the following commands:

- cmd 15: We use the next command to see what the value of s is if the next iteration is executed. It shows that the old value of s is 1 (s = 1*1) and that the new value is 5 (s=1*1+2*2). So far, so good!
- cmd 16: A finish command is used to continue running the program until it exits from the function.
- cmd 17: We delete breakpoints 1 to 3.
- cmd 18: A continue command is used.
- cmd 19: We quit gdb and go back to the Terminal window.

Logging gdb into a text file

When dealing with a long stack trace or multi-thread stack trace, viewing and analyzing gdb output from a Terminal window can be inconvenient. However, we can log either an entire session or specific output into a text file first, then browse it offline later using other text editor tools. To do this, we need to use the following command:

```
(gdb) set logging on
```

When we execute this command, gdb will save all the Terminal window outputs into a text file named gdb.txt in the currently running gdb folder. If we want to stop logging, we can just type the following:

```
(gdb) set logging off
```

One great thing about GDB is that we can turn set logging commands on and off as many times as we want, without worrying about the dumped file names. This is because all the outputs are concatenated into the gdb.txt file.

Here is an example of returning ch13_gdb_2.out with the gdb output being dumped:

```
~/wus1/Chapter-13$ gdb ch13_gdb_2.out           //cmd 1
 ...
Reading symbols from ch13_gdb_2.out...done.
 (gdb) set logging on                           //cmd 2
 Copying output to gdb.txt.
```

```
(gdb) b ch13_gdb_2.cpp:24 if i==1                    //cmd 3
Breakpoint 1 at 0xa84: file ch13_gdb_2.cpp, line 24.
(gdb) r                                              //cmd 4
...
Breakpoint 1, dotproduct (x=0x7ffffed68, y=0x7ffffed68, n=5) at
ch13_gdb_2.cpp:24
24 s += (*p) * (*q);
(gdb) p i                                            //cmd 5
$1 = 1
(gdb) p s                                            //cmd 6
$2 = 1
(gdb) finish                                         //cmd 7
Run till exit from #0 dotproduct (x=0x7ffffed68, y=0x7ffffed68, n=5) at
ch13_gdb_2.cpp:24
0x00000055555559e0 in main () at ch13_gdb_2.cpp:11
11 sxx = dotproduct( x, x, 5);
Value returned is $3 = 55
(gdb) delete breakpoints 1                          //cmd 8
(gdb) set logging off                               //cmd 9
Done logging to gdb.txt.
(gdb) c                                             //cmd 10
Continuing.
dot(x,x) = 55.000000
dot(x,y) = 55.000000
[Inferior 1 (process 386) exited normally]
(gdb) q                                            //cmd 11
~/wus1/Chapter-13$ cat gdb.txt                     //cmd 12
```

The commands that were used in the preceding code are as follows:

- `cmd 1`: `gdb` is launched.
- `cmd 2`: We set the logging flag to on. At this point, `gdb` says the output will be copied into the `gdb.txt` file.
- `cmd 3`: A conditional `break point` is set.
- `cmd 4`: We run the program, and it stops when it reaches the conditional `breakpoint` at line 24.
- `cmd 5`and `cmd 6`: We print the values of `i` and `s`, receptively.
- `cmd 7`: By executing the step out of the function command, it shows that `sxx` is `55` (after calling `sxx=dotproduct( x, x, 5)))`) and that the program stops at line `sxy = dotproduct( x, y, 5)`.
- `cmd 8`: We delete `breakpoint 1`.
- `cmd 9`: We set the logging flag to off.

- `cmd 10`: Once a continue instruction is given, it runs out of the `main` function and `gdb` waits for a new command.
- `cmd 11`: We input `q` to quit `gdb`.
- `cmd 12`: When it goes back to the Terminal window, we print the content of the logged `gdb.txt` file by running the `cat` command in the OS.

So far, we have learned enough GDB commands to debug a program. As you may have noticed, it's time-consuming and thus very costly. Sometimes, it becomes even worse because of debugging in the wrong places. To debug efficiently, we need to follow the right strategies. We will cover this in the following subsection.

Practical debugging strategies

Since debugging is the costliest stage in the software development life cycle, finding bugs and fixing them isn't feasible, especially for large, complex systems. However, there are certain strategies that can be used in practical processes, some of which are as follows:

- **Use printf() or std::cout**: This is the old-fashioned way of doing things. By printing some information to the Terminal, we can check the values of variables and perform where and when kinds of log profiles for further analysis.
- **Use a debugger**: Although learning to use a GDB kind of debugger tool is not an overnight thing, it can save lots of time. So, try to become familiar with it step by step and gradually.
- **Reproduce bugs**: Whenever a bug is reported in the field, make a record of the running environment and input data.
- **Dump log files**: An application program should dump log messages into a text file. When a crash happens, we should check the log files as the first step to see if an abnormal event occurred.
- **Have a guess**: Roughly guess a bug's location and then prove whether it was right or wrong.
- **Divide and conquer**: Even in the worst scenario that we do not have any idea of what bugs there are, we still can use **the binary search** strategy to set breakpoints and then narrow down and eventually locate them.
- **Simplify**: Always start from the most simplified scenario and gradually add peripherals, input modules, and so on until the bug can be reproduced.

- **Source code version controlled**: If a bug has suddenly appeared on a release but it had run fine previously, do a source code tree check first. Someone may have made a change!
- **Don't give up**: Some bugs are really hard to locate and/or fix, especially for complex and multi-team involved systems. Put them aside for a while and rethink it on your way home – the *aha moment* may reveal itself eventually.

So far, we have learned about macro-level problem localization using RCA and the good coding practices we can follow to prevent problems from occurring. Furthermore, by using a state-of-the-art debugger tool such as GDB, we can control the execution of a program line by line so that we can analyze and fix the problem at the micro level. All these activities are programmer centralized and manual. Can any automatic tools help us diagnose the potential defects of a program? We'll take a look at static and dynamic analysis in the next section.

Understanding static and dynamic analysis

In the previous sections, we learned about the root cause analysis process and how to use GDB to debug a defect. This section will discuss how to analyze a program with and without executing it. The former is called dynamic analysis, while the latter is called static analysis.

Static analysis

Static analysis evaluates the quality of a computer program without executing it. Although this can usually be done by examining source code via automatic tools and code reviews/inspections, we will only focus on automatic tools in this section.

The automatic static code analysis tools are designed to analyze a set of code against one or multiple sets of coding rules or guidelines. Normally, people use static code analysis, static analysis, or source code analysis interchangeably. By scanning the entire code base with every possible code execution path, we can find lots of potential bugs before the testing phases. However, it also has several limitations, as follows:

- It can produce false positive and false negative alarms.
- It only applies the rules that were implemented inside the scanning algorithm, and some of them may be subjectively interpreted.
- It cannot find vulnerabilities that were introduced in a runtime environment.
- It can provide a false sense of security that everything is being addressed.

There are about 30 automatic C/C++ code analysis tools [9] under both commercial and free open source categories. The names of these tools include Clang, Clion, CppCheck, Eclipse, Visual Studio, and GNU g++, just to name a few. As examples, we would like to introduce the `-Wall`, `-Weffcc++`, and `-Wextra` options, which are built into GNU compiler g++[10]:

- `-Wall`: This enables all construction warnings, which are questionable for some users. These warnings are easy to avoid or modify, even in conjunction with macros. It also enables some language-specific warnings described in C ++ Dialect Options and Objective-C/C ++ Dialect Options.
- `-Wextra`: As its name implies, it examines certain extra warning flags that are not checked by `-Wall`. Warning messages for any of the following cases will be printed:
    - A pointer is compared against integer zero with the `<`, `<=`, `>`, or `>=` operands.
    - A non-enumerator and an enumerator show up in a conditional expression.
    - Ambiguous virtual bases.
    - Subscripting a `register` type array.
    - Using the address of a `register` type variable.
    - A derived class' copy constructor does not initialize its base class. Note that (b)-(f) are C++ only.

- `-Weffc++`: It checks the violations of some guidelines suggested in *Effective and More Effective* C++, written by Scott Meyers. These guidelines include the following:
    - Define a copy constructor and an assignment operator for classes with dynamically allocated memory.
    - Prefer initialization over assignment in constructors.
    - Make destructors virtual in base classes.
    - Have the = operator return a reference to `*this`.
    - Don't try to return a reference when you must return an object.
    - Distinguish between prefix and postfix forms of increment and decrement operators.
    - Never overload `&&`, `||`, or `,`.

To explore these three options, let's look at the following example:

```
//ch13_static_analysis.cpp
#include <iostream>
int *getPointer(void)
```

```
{
    return 0;
}

int &getVal() {
    int x = 5;
    return x;
}

int main()
{
    int *x = getPointer();
    if( x> 0 ){
        *x = 5;
   }
   else{
       std::cout << "x is null" << std::endl;
   }

   int &y = getVal();
   std::cout << y << std::endl;
   return 0;
}
```

First, let's build this without any options:

```
g++ -o ch13_static.out ch13_static_analysis.cpp
```

This can be built successfully, but if we run it, as expected, it will crash with a **segmentation fault (core dumped)** message.

Next, let's add the `-Wall`, `-Weffc++`, and `-Wextra` options and rebuild it:

```
g++ -Wall -o ch13_static.out ch13_static_analysis.cpp
g++ -Weffc++ -o ch13_static.out ch13_static_analysis.cpp
g++ -Wextra -o ch13_static.out ch13_static_analysis.cpp
```

Both `-Wall` and `-Weffc++` give us the following message:

```
ch13_static_analysis.cpp: In function 'int& getVal()':
ch13_static_analysis.cpp:9:6: warning: reference to local variable 'x' returned [-Wreturn-local-addr]
int x = 5;
 ^
```

Here, it's complaining that, in the `int & getVal()` function (line 9 of the `cpp` file), a reference to a local variable is returned. This will not work because once the program goes out of the function, `x` is garbage (The lifetime of `x` is only limited in the scope of the function). It does not make any sense to reference a dead variable.

`-Wextra` gives us the following message:

```
ch13_static_analysis.cpp: In function 'int& getVal()':
ch13_static_analysis.cpp:9:6: warning: reference to local variable 'x' returned [-Wreturn-local-addr]
int x = 5;
^
ch13_static_analysis.cpp: In function 'int main()':
ch13_static_analysis.cpp:16:10: warning: ordered comparison of pointer with integer zero [-Wextra]
if( x> 0 ){
^
```

The preceding output shows that `-Wextra` not only gives us the warning from `-Wall` but also checks the six things we mentioned earlier. In this example, it warns us that there is a comparison between a pointer and integer zero in line 16 of the code.

Now that we know about how to use the static analysis options during compile time, we'll take a look at dynamic analysis by executing a program.

Dynamic analysis

Dynamic analysis is a short version of *dynamic program analysis*, which analyzes the performance of a software program by executing it either on a real or virtual processor. Similar to static analysis, dynamic analysis can also be done automatically or manually. For instance, unit tests, integration tests, system tests, and acceptance tests are typically human-involved dynamic analysis processes. On the other hand, memory debugging, memory leak detection, and profiling tools such as IBM purify, Valgrind, and Clang sanitizers are automatic dynamic analysis tools. We will focus on automatic dynamic analysis tools in this subsection.

A dynamic analysis process contains steps such as preparing the input data, launching a test program, gathering the necessary parameters, and analyzing its output. Roughly speaking, the mechanism of dynamic analysis tools is that they use code instrumentation and/or a simulation environment to perform checks on the analyzed code as it executes. We can interact with a program in the following ways:

- **Source code instrumentation**: A special code segment is inserted into the original source code before compilation.
- **Object code instrumentation**: A special binary code is added directly into the executable file.
- **Compilation stage instrumentation**: A checking code is added through special compiler switches.
- It doesn't change the source code. Instead, it uses special execution stage libraries to detect errors.

Dynamic analysis has the following pros:

- There are no false positive or false negative results because an error will be detected that isn't predicted from a model.
- It does not need source code, which means the proprietary code can be tested by a third-party organization.

The cons of dynamic analysis are as follows:

- It only detects defects on the routes related to the input data. Other defects may not be found.
- It can only check one execution path at a time. To obtain a complete picture, we need to run the test as many times as possible. This requires a significant amount of computational resources.
- It cannot check the correctness of the code. It is possible to get the correct result from the wrong operation.
- Executing incorrect code on a real processor may have unanticipated results.

Now, let's use Valgrind to find the memory leak and out-of-boundary problems given in the following example:

```
//ch13_dynamic_analysis.cpp
#include <iostream>
int main()
{
    int n=10;
    float *p = (float *)malloc(n * sizeof(float));
    for( int i=0; i<n; ++i){
```

```
        std::cout << p[i] << std::endl;
    }
    //free(p);  //leak: free() is not called
    return 0;
}
```

To use Valgrind for dynamic analysis, the following steps need to be performed:

1. First, we need to install `valgrind`. We can do this using the following command:

```
sudo apt install valgrind //for Ubuntu, Debian, etc.
```

2. Once it has been installed successfully, we can run `valgrind` by passing the executable as an argument, along with other parameters, as follows:

```
valgrind --leak-check=full --show-leak-kinds=all --track-
origins=yes \
 --verbose --log-file=valgrind-out.txt ./myExeFile myArgumentList
```

3. Next, let's build this program, as follows:

```
g++ -o ch13_dyn -std=c++11 -Wall ch13_dynamic_analysis.cpp
```

4. Then, we run `valgrind`, like so:

```
valgrind --leak-check=full --show-leak-kinds=all --track-
origins=yes \
 --verbose --log-file=log.txt ./ch13_dyn
```

Finally, we can check the contents of `log.txt`. The bold and italic lines indicate the memory leak's location and size. By checking the address (`0x4844BFC`) and its corresponding function name (`main()`), we can see that this `malloc` is in the `main()` function:

```
... //ignore many lines at begining
 by 0x108A47: main (in /home/nvidia/wus1/Chapter-13/ch13_dyn)
 ==18930== Uninitialised value was created by a heap allocation
 ==18930== at 0x4844BFC: malloc (in /usr/lib/valgrind/vgpreload_memcheck-
arm64-linux.so)
 ... //ignore many lines in middle
 ==18930== HEAP SUMMARY:
 ==18930== in use at exit: 40 bytes in 1 blocks
 ==18930== total heap usage: 3 allocs, 2 frees, 73,768 bytes allocated
 ==18930==
 ==18930== 40 bytes in 1 blocks are definitely lost in loss record 1 of 1
 ==18930== at 0x4844BFC: malloc (in /usr/lib/valgrind/vgpreload_memcheck-
arm64-linux.so)
 ==18930==
```

```
==18930== LEAK SUMMARY:
==18930== definitely lost: 40 bytes in 1 blocks
==18930== indirectly lost: 0 bytes in 0 blocks
==18930== possibly lost: 0 bytes in 0 blocks
==18930== still reachable: 0 bytes in 0 blocks
==18930== suppressed: 0 bytes in 0 blocks
```

Here, we can see that `malloc()` is called to allocate some memory at address `0x4844BFC`. The heap summary section indicates that we have 40 bytes of memory loss at `0x4844BFC`. Finally, the leak summary section shows that there is definitely one block of 40 bytes memory loss. By searching the address value of `0x4844BFC` in the `log.txt` file, we eventually figured out that there is no `free(p)` line being called in the original code. After uncommenting this line, we redo the `valgrind` analysis so that the leakage problem is now out of the report.

In conclusion, with the help of static and dynamic analysis tools, the potential defects of a program can be greatly reduced automatically. However, to ensure the quality of software, humans must be in the loop for final tests and evaluations. Now, we're going to explore the unit testing, test-driven development, and behavior-driven development concepts in software engineering.

Exploring unit testing, TDD, and BDD

We learned about automatic static and dynamic program analysis in the previous section. This section will focus on human-involved (preparing test code) tests, which are another part of dynamic analysis. These are unit testing, test-driven development, and behavior-driven development.

Unit testing assumes that if we already have a single unit of code, then we need to write a test driver and prepare input data to check if its output is correct. After that, we perform integration tests to test multiple units together, and then the acceptance tests, which test the entire application. Since the integration and acceptance tests are more difficult to maintain and more project-related than unit tests, it is very challenging to cover them in this book. Those of you who are interested can find out more by going to `https://www.iso.org/standard/45142.html`.

In contrast to unit tests, TDD believes that we should have test code and data first, develop some code and make it pass quickly, and finally refactor until the customer is happy. On the other hand, BDD has the philosophy that we should not test the implementation of a program and instead test its desired behavior. To this end, BDD emphasizes that a communication platform and language among people involved in software production should be set up as well.

We'll discuss each of these methodologies in detail in the following subsections.

Unit testing

A unit is an individual component in a larger or more complex application. Typically, a unit has its own user interface, such as a function, a class, or an entire module. Unit testing is a software testing method that's used to determine whether a unit of code behaves as expected in terms of its design requirements. The main features of unit testing are as follows:

- It is small and simple, quick to write and run, and, as a result, it finds problems in the early development cycle and hence the problems can be fixed easily.
- Since it is isolated from dependencies, each test case can be run in parallel.
- Unit test drivers help us understand the unit interface.
- It greatly helps integration and acceptance tests when tested units are integrated later.
- It is normally prepared and performed by developers.

While we can write a unit test package from scratch, there are a lot of **Unit Test Frameworks (UTFs)** already being developed in the community. Boost.Test, CppUnit, GoogleTest, Unit++, and CxxTest are the most popular ones. These UTFs typically offer the following features:

- They only require a minimal amount of work for setting up a new test.
- They depend on standard libraries and supports cross-platform, which means they are easy to port and modify.
- They support test fixtures, which allow us to reuse the same configuration for objects for several different tests.
- They handle exceptions and crashes well. This means that a UTF can report exceptions but not crashes.
- They have good assert functionalities. Whenever an assertion fails, its source code location and the values of the variables should be printed.
- They support different outputs and these outputs can be conveniently analyzed either by humans or other tools.
- They support test suites, and each suite may contain several test cases.

Now, let's take a look at an example of Boost UTF (since v1.59.0). It supports three different usage variants: the single-header only variant, the static library variant, and the shared library variant. It includes four types of test cases: test cases without parameters, data-driven test cases, template test cases, and parameterized test cases.

It also has seven types of check tools: `BOOST_TEST()`, `BOOST_CHECK()`, `BOOST_REQUIRE()`, `BOOST_ERROR()`, `BOOST_FAIL()`, `BOOST_CHECK_MESSAGE( )`, and `BOOST_CHECK_EQUAL()`. It supports fixtures and controls the test output in many ways as well. When writing a test module, we need to follow these steps:

1. Define the name of our test program. This will be used in output messages.
2. Choose a usage variant: header-only, link with a static, or as a shared library.
3. Choose and add a test case to a test suite.
4. Perform correctness checks on the tested code.
5. Initialize the code under test before each test case.
6. Customize the ways in which test failures are reported.
7. Control the runtime behavior of the built test module, which is also called runtime configuration.

For example, the following example covers *steps 1-4*. If you are interested, you can get examples of *steps 5-7* at `https://www.boost.org/doc/libs/1_70_0/libs/test/doc/html/index.html`:

```
//ch13_unit_test1.cpp
#define BOOST_TEST_MODULE my_test //item 1, "my_test" is module name
#include <boost/test/included/unit_test.hpp> //item 2, header-only

//declare we begin a test suite and name it "my_suite "
BOOST_AUTO_TEST_SUITE( my_suite )

//item 3, add a test case into test suit, here we choose
//        BOOST_AUTO_TEST_CASE and name it "test_case1"
BOOST_AUTO_TEST_CASE(test_case1) {
 char x = 'a';
 BOOST_TEST(x);         //item 4, checks if c is non-zero
 BOOST_TEST(x == 'a'); //item 4, checks if c has value 'a'
 BOOST_TEST(x == 'b'); //item 4, checks if c has value 'b'
}

//item 3, add the 2nd test case
BOOST_AUTO_TEST_CASE( test_case2 )
{
  BOOST_TEST( true );
}
```

```
//item 3, add the 3rd test case
BOOST_AUTO_TEST_CASE( test_case3 )
{
  BOOST_TEST( false );
}

BOOST_AUTO_TEST_SUITE_END() //declare we end test suite
```

To build this, we may need to install boost, as follows:

```
sudo apt-get install libboost-all-dev
```

Then, we can build and run it, as follows:

```
~/wus1/Chapter-13$ g++ -g  ch13_unit_test1.cpp
~/wus1/Chapter-13$ ./a.out
```

The preceding code results in the following output:

```
Running 3 test cases...
 ch13_unit_test1.cpp(13): error: in "my_suite/test_case1": check x == 'b'
has failed ['a' != 'b']
 ch13_unit_test1.cpp(25): error: in "my_suite/test_case3": check false has
failed

 *** 2 failures are detected in the test module "my_test"
```

Here, we can see that there are failures in `test_case1` and `test_case3`. In particular, in `test_case1`, the value of `x` is not equal to `b`, and obviously a false check cannot pass the test in `test_case3`.

TDD

As shown in the following diagram, a TDD process starts by writing failing test code and then adds/modifies the code to let the test pass. After that, we refactorize the test plan and code until all the requirements are satisfied [16,17]. Let's have a look at the following diagram:

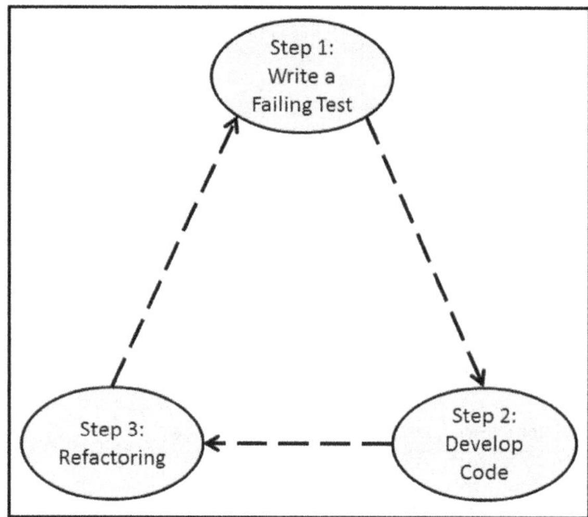

Step 1 is to write a failing test. Instead of developing code first, TDD starts to write test code initially. Because we do not have code yet, we know that, if we run the test, it will fail. During this stage, the test data format and interface is defined, and the code implementation details are imagined.

The goal of *step 2* is to make the test pass as quickly as possible with minimal development effort. We don't want to implement everything perfectly; we only want it to pass the test. Once it goes green, we will have something to show and tell to the customer, at which point the customer may refine the requirement after seeing the initial product. Then, we move on to the next phase.

The third phase is refactoring. During this stage, we may go in, look at, and see what we would like to change and how to change it.

To traditional developers, the most difficult thing about TDD is the mindset change from the coding -> testing pattern to the testing -> coding pattern. To get a vague idea of a test suite, J. Hartikainen suggested that a developer considers the following five steps[18] to start:

1. Decide the inputs and outputs first.
2. Choose class/function signatures.
3. Decide only one tiny aspect of the functionality to test.
4. Implement the test.
5. Implement the code.

Once we've finished this iteration, we can gradually refactor it until the overall comprehensive goal is achieved.

Example of TDD

Next, we will demonstrate the TDD process through the implementation of a case study. In this study, we will develop a Mat class to perform 2D matrix algebra, just like we do in the Matlab. This is a class template that can hold an m-by-n matrix for all data types. The matrix algebra includes adding, subtracting, multiplying, and dividing matrices, and it also has element operation abilities.

Let's get started.

Step 1 – writing a failing test

To begin, we will only need the following:

- Create a `Mat` object from a given a number of rows and cols (the default should be 0-by-0, which is an empty matrix).
- Print its elements row by row.
- Get the matrix size from `rows()` and `cols()`.

Based on these requirements, we can have failing unit testing code to boost UTF, as follows:

```
// ch13_tdd_boost_UTF1.cpp
#define BOOST_TEST_MODULE tdd_test
#include <boost/test/included/unit_test.hpp>
#include "ch13_tdd_v1.h"

BOOST_AUTO_TEST_SUITE(tdd_suite)  //begin a test suite: "tdd_suite"

BOOST_AUTO_TEST_CASE(test_case1) {
  Mat<int> x(2, 3);            //create a 2 x 3 int matrix
  x.print("int x=");
  BOOST_TEST(2 == x.rows());
  BOOST_TEST(3 == x.cols());

  Mat<float> y;               //create a 0 x 0 empty float matrix
  y.print("float y=");
  BOOST_TEST(0 == y.rows());
  BOOST_TEST(0 == y.cols());

  Mat<char> z(1,10);        //create a 1 x 10 char matrix
  z.print("char z=");
```

```
  BOOST_TEST(1 == z.rows());
  BOOST_TEST(10 == z.cols());
}
BOOST_AUTO_TEST_SUITE_END() //end test suite
```

Now that our testing code is ready, we are ready to develop the code.

Step 2 – developing code to let the test pass

One way to implement a minimal code segment is to pass the preceding test, as follows:

```
//file: ch13_tdd_v1.h
#ifndef __ch13_TDD_V1__
#define __ch13_TDD_V1__
#include <iostream>
#include <assert.h>
template< class T>
class Mat {
public:
  Mat(const uint32_t m=0, const uint32_t n=0);
  Mat(const Mat<T> &rhs) = delete;
  ~Mat();

  Mat<T>& operator = (const Mat<T> &x) = delete;

  uint32_t rows() { return m_rows; }
  uint32_t cols() { return m_cols; }
  void print(const char* str) const;

private:
  void creatBuf();
  void deleteBuf();
  uint32_t m_rows; //# of rows
  uint32_t m_cols; //# of cols
  T* m_buf;
};
#include "ch13_tdd_v1.cpp"
#endif
```

Once we have the preceding header file, we can develop its corresponding `cpp` file, as follows:

```
//file: ch13_tdd_v1.cpp
#include "ch13_tdd_v1.h"
using namespace std;

template< class T>
Mat<T>::Mat(const uint32_t m, const uint32_t n)
```

```
 : m_rows(m)
 , m_cols(n)
 , m_buf(NULL)
{
 creatBuf();
}

template< class T>
Mat<T> :: ~Mat()
{
 deleteBuf();
}

template< class T>
void Mat<T>::creatBuf()
{
 uint32_t sz = m_rows * m_cols;
 if (sz > 0) {
 if (m_buf) { deleteBuf();}
 m_buf = new T[sz];
 assert(m_buf);
 }
 else {
 m_buf = NULL;
 }
}

template< class T>
void Mat<T>::deleteBuf()
{
 if (m_buf) {
 delete[] m_buf;
 m_buf = NULL;
 }
}

template< class T>
void Mat<T> ::print(const char* str) const
{
 cout << str << endl;
 cout << m_rows << " x " << m_cols << "[" << endl;
 const T *p = m_buf;
 for (uint32_t i = 0; i<m_rows; i++) {
 for (uint32_t j = 0; j < m_cols; j++) {
 cout << *p++ << ", ";
 }
 cout << "\n";
 }
```

```
    cout << "]\n";
}
```

Let's say we build and execute it using g++, which supports `-std=c++11` or higher:

```
~/wus1/Chapter-13$ g++ -g ch13_tdd_boost_UTF1.cpp
~/wus1/Chapter-13$ a.out
```

This will result in the following output:

```
Running 1 test case...
 int x=2 x 3[
 1060438054, 1, 4348032,
 0, 4582960, 0,
 ]
 float y=0 x 0[
 ]
 char z=1 x 10[
 s,s,s,s,s,s,s,s,s,s,
 ]
```

In `test_case1`, we created three matrices and tested the `rows()`, `cols()`, and `print()` functions. The first one is a 2x3 `int` type matrix. Since it is not initialized, the values of its elements are unpredictable, which is why we can see these random numbers from `print()`. We also passed the `rows()` and `cols()` test at this point (no errors from the two `BOOST_TEST() calls`). The second one is an empty float type matrix; its `print()` function gives nothing, and both its `cols()` and `rows()` are zeros. Finally, the third one is a 1x10 `char` type uninitialized matrix. Again, all the outputs of the three functions are as expected.

Step 3 – refactoring

So far, so good – we passed the test! However, after showing the preceding result to our customer, he/she may ask us to add two more interfaces, such as the following:

- Create an m x n matrix with a given initial value for all elements.
- Add `numel()` to return the total number of elements of the matrix.
- Add `empty()`, which returns true if the matrix either has zero rows or zero columns and false otherwise.

Once we've added the second test case to our test suite, the overall refactorized test code will be as follows:

```
// ch13_tdd_Boost_UTF2.cpp
#define BOOST_TEST_MODULE tdd_test
```

```
#include <boost/test/included/unit_test.hpp>
#include "ch13_tdd_v2.h"

//declare we begin a test suite and name it "tdd_suite"
BOOST_AUTO_TEST_SUITE(tdd_suite)

//add the 1st test case
BOOST_AUTO_TEST_CASE(test_case1) {
  Mat<int> x(2, 3);
  x.print("int x=");
  BOOST_TEST(2 == x.rows());
  BOOST_TEST(3 == x.cols());

  Mat<float> y;
  BOOST_TEST(0 == y.rows());
  BOOST_TEST(0 == y.cols());

  Mat<char> z(1, 10);
  BOOST_TEST(1 == z.rows());
  BOOST_TEST(10 == z.cols());
}

//add the 2nd test case
BOOST_AUTO_TEST_CASE(test_case2)
{
  Mat<int> x(2, 3, 10);
  x.print("int x=");
  BOOST_TEST( 6 == x.numel() );
  BOOST_TEST( false == x.empty() );

  Mat<float> y;
  BOOST_TEST( 0 == y.numel() );
  BOOST_TEST( x.empty() ); //bug x --> y
}

BOOST_AUTO_TEST_SUITE_END() //declare we end test suite
```

The next step is to modify the code to pass this new test plan. For brevity, we won't print the `ch13_tdd_v2.h` and `ch13_tdd_v2.cpp` files here. You can download them from this book's `GitHub` repository. After building and executing `ch13_tdd_Boost_UTF2.cpp`, we get the following output:

```
Running 2 test cases...
 int x=2x3[
 1057685542, 1, 1005696,
 0, 1240624, 0,
 ]
 int x=2x3[
```

```
10, 10, 10,
10, 10, 10,
]
../Chapter-13/ch13_tdd_Boost_UTF2.cpp(34): error: in
"tdd_suite/test_case2": che
ck x.empty() has failed [(bool)0 is false]
```

In the first output, since we just defined a 2x3 integer matrix and did not initialize it in `test_case1`, the undefined behavior – that is, six random numbers – is printed out. The second output comes from `test_case2`, where all six elements of `x` are initialized to `10`. After we've done a show and tell of the preceding result, our customer may ask us to add other new features or modify the currently existing ones. But, after a few iterations, eventually, we will reach the *happy point* and stop factorizing.

Now that we've learned about TDD, we will discuss BDD.

BDD

The most difficult part of software development is communicating with business participants, developers, and the quality analysis team. A project can easily exceed its budget, miss deadlines, or fail completely because of misunderstood or vague requirements, technical arguments, and slow feedback cycles.

(BDD) [20] is an agile development process with a set of practices that aim to reduce communication gaps/barriers and other wasteful activities. It also encourages team members to continuously communicate with real-world examples during the production life cycle.

BDD contains two main parts: deliberate discovery and TDD. To let people in different organizations and teams understand the right behavior of the developed software, the deliberate discovery phase introduces an *example mapping* technique to make people in different roles have conversations through concrete examples. These examples will become automated tests and living documentation of how the system behaves later. In its TDD phase, BDD specifies that the tests for any software unit should be specified in terms of the desired behavior of the unit.

There are several BDD framework tools (JBehave, RBehave, Fitnesse, Cucumber [21], and so on) for different platforms and programming languages. Generally speaking, these frameworks perform the following steps:

1. Read a specification format document that's been prepared by a business analyst during the deliberate discovery phase.
2. Transform the document into meaningful clauses. Each individual clause is capable of being set into test cases for QA. Developers can implement source code from the clause as well.
3. Execute the test for each clause scenario automatically.

In summary, we have learned about the strategies regarding what, when, and how, and a testing process should be involved in an application development pipeline. As shown in the following diagram, the traditional V-shape[2] model emphasizes the pattern of requirement -> design -> coding -> testing. TDD believes a development process should be driven by test, while BDD adds communication between people from different backgrounds and roles into the TDD framework and focuses on behavior testing:

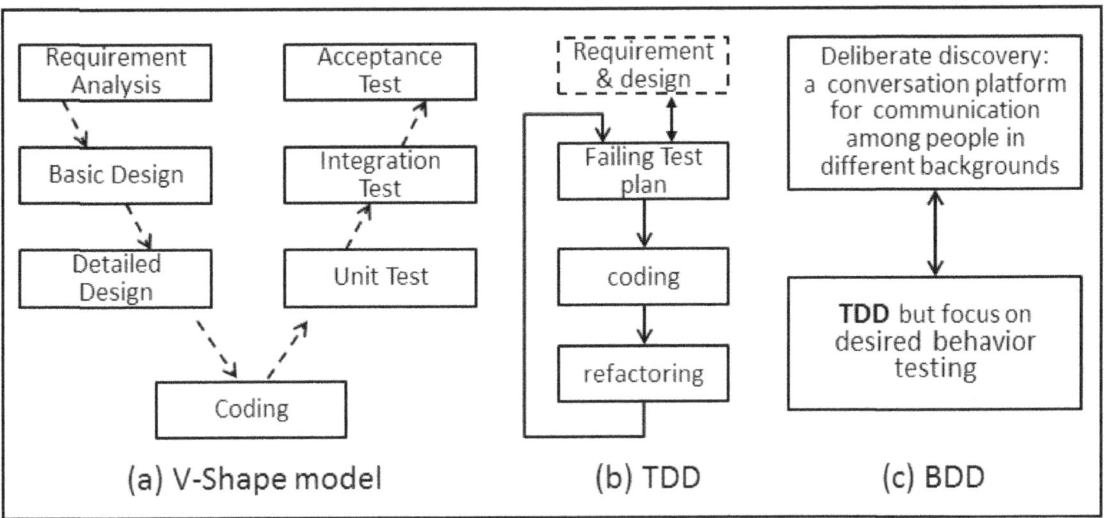

Moreover, unit testing emphasizes testing individual components when coding is complete. TDD focuses more on how to write tests before writing code, and then add/modify code through next-level test plans. BDD encourages collaborations between customers, business analysts, developers, and quality assurance analysts. Although we can use each one individually, we really should combine them for the best results in this agile software development era.

Summary

In this chapter, we briefly introduced testing and debugging-related topics in the software development process. Testing finds problems, and root cause analysis helps in locating a problem at the macro level. However, good programming practices can prevent software defects in the early stages. Additionally, the command-line interface debugging tool known as GDB can help us set breakpoints and execute a program line by line while printing the values of variables during the runtime of a program.

We also discussed the automatic analyzing tools and human-involved testing processes. Static analysis evaluates the performance of a program without executing it. On the other hand, dynamic analysis tools can find defects by executing the program. Finally, we learned about the strategies of what, when, and how, a testing process should be involved in a software development pipeline. Unit testing emphasizes testing individual components when coding is complete. TDD focuses more on how to write tests before developing code and then reiterates this process through a next-level test plan. BDD encourages collaborations between customers, business analysts, developers, and quality assurance analysts.

In the next chapter, we will learn how to use Qt to create **Graphic User Interface (GUI)** programs for cross-platform applications that run on Linux, Windows, iOS, and Android systems. First, we will dive into the fundamental concepts of cross-platform GUI programming. Then we will introduce an overview of Qt and its widgets. Finally, using a case study example, we will learn how to design and implement a network application using Qt.

Further reading

- J. Rooney and L. Vanden Heuvel, `Root Cause Analysis For Beginners`, Quality Progress, July 2004, p.45-53.
- T. Kataoka, K. Furuto and T. Matsumoto, `The Analyzing Method of Root Causes for Software Problems`, SEI Tech. Rev., no. 73, p. 81, 2011.
- K. A. Briski, et al. `Minimizing code defects to improve software quality and lower development costs`, IBM Rational Software Analyzer and IBM Rational PurifyPlus software.
- `https://www.learncpp.com/cpp-programming/eight-c-programming-mistakes-the-compiler-wont-catch`.
- B. Stroustrup and H. Sutter, *C++ Core Guidelines*: `https://isocpp.github.io/CppCoreGuidelines`.

- https://www.gnu.org/software/gdb/.
- https://www.fayewilliams.com/2014/02/21/debugging-for-beginners/.
- https://www.perforce.com/blog/qac/what-static-code-analysis.
- https://linux.die.net/man/1/g++.
- https://www.embedded.com/static-vs-dynamic-analysis-for-secure-code-development-part-2/.
- ISO/IEC/IEEE 29119-1:2013 *SOFTWARE AND SYSTEMS ENGINEERING - SOFTWARE TESTING*.
- http://gamesfromwithin.com/exploring-the-c-unit-testing-framework-jungle.
- https://www.boost.org/doc/libs/1_70_0/libs/test/doc/html/index.html.
- K. Beck, Test-Driven Development by Example, published by Addison Wesley, ISBN 978-0321146533.
- H. Erdogmus, T. Morisio, *On the Effectiveness of Test-first Approach to Programming*, Proc. of the IEEE Trans. on Software Engineering, 31(1). January 2005.
- https://codeutopia.net/blog/2015/03/01/unit-testing-tdd-and-bdd.
- https://cucumber.io/blog/intro-to-bdd-and-tdd/.
- D. North, Introducing BDD, https://dannorth.net/introducing-bdd/ (March 2006).
- D. North, E. Keogh, et. al, "jbehave.org/team-list", May 2019.

Apart from these, you can have a look at the following sources (these are not directly mentioned in this chapter):

- B. Stroustrup and H. Sutter, *C++ Core Guidelines*: https://isocpp.github.io/CppCoreGuidelines/CppCoreGuidelines.
- G. Rozental and R. Enficiaud, *Boost.Test*: https://www.boost.org/doc/libs/1_70_0/libs/test/doc/html/index.html
- D. North, *Introducing BDD*: https://dannorth.net/introducing-bdd/

Exercises and questions

1. Using `gdb` function breakpoints, conditional breakpoints and the `watchpoint`, `continue`, and `finish` commands, debug `ch13_gdb_2.cpp`.
2. Use `g++ -c -Wall -Weffc++ -Wextra  x.cpp -o x.out` to build out `cpp files ch13_rca*.cpp`. What do you see from their warning outputs?
3. Why does static analysis produce false alarms, but dynamic analysis does not?
4. Download `ch13_tdd_v2.h/.cpp` and perform next phase refactoring. In this phase, we will add a copy constructor, assignment operator, and element-wise operation operators such as `+`, `-`, `*`, `/`, and more. More specifically, we need to do the following things:
    1. Add the third test case to our test suite, that is, `ch13_tdd_Boost_UTF2.cpp`.
    2. Add the implementations of these functions to files; for example, `ch13_tdd_v2.h/.cpp`.
    3. Run the test suite to test them.

14
Graphical User Interface with Qt

C++ doesn't provide **Graphical User Interface** (**GUI**) programming out of the box. First, we should understand that a GUI is strongly tied to a specific **Operating System(OS)**. You can program GUI applications in Windows using the Windows API, or in Linux using the Linux-specific API, and so on. Each OS has its own specific forms of Windows and GUI components.

We touched on the different platforms and their differences in `Chapter 1`, *Building C++ Applications*. When discussing GUI programming, the difference between platforms is even more daunting. Cross-platform development had become a big pain in GUI developer's lives. They had to focus on a specific OS. Implementing the same application for other platforms took almost the same amount of work again. That's an unreasonably huge waste of time and resources. Languages such as *Java* provide a smart model of running applications in the virtual environment. This allows developers to focus on one language and one project since the environment takes care of running the application on different platforms. One of the main disadvantages of this approach is forcing the user to install a virtual machine and the slow execution time compared to platform-specific applications.

To solve these problems, the Qt framework was created. In this chapter, we'll find out how the Qt framework supports cross-platform GUI application development. To do this, you will need to become familiar with Qt and its key features. This will allow you to develop GUI applications using your favorite programming language – C++. We will start by understanding Qt's approach to GUI development, and then we will cover its concepts and features, such as signals and slots, and Model/View programming.

In this chapter, we will cover the following topics:

- Fundamentals of cross-platform GUI programming
- Qt core components
- Using Qt widgets
- Designing a network application using Qt Network

Technical requirements

You will need to install the latest Qt framework to run the examples in this chapter. We suggest using Qt Creator as the IDE for your projects. To download Qt, along with the corresponding tools, visit the `qt.io` website and choose the open source version of the framework. The code for this chapter could be found at: `https://github.com/PacktPublishing/Expert-CPP` .

Understanding cross-platform GUI programming

Each OS has its own API. It relates to the GUI in particular. When companies plan to design, implement, and ship desktop applications, they should decide what platform to focus on. A team of developers working on one platform will spend almost the same amount of time writing the same application for the other platform. The biggest reason for this is the different approaches and APIs provided by OS. The complexity of the API may also play a big role in implementing applications on time. For example, the following snippet from the official documentation shows how to create a button in Windows using C++:

```
HWND hwndButton = CreateWindow(
  L"BUTTON", // Predefined class; Unicode assumed
  L"OK", // Button text
  WS_TABSTOP | WS_VISIBLE | WS_CHILD | BS_DEFPUSHBUTTON, // Styles
  10, // x position
```

```
10, // y position
100, // Button width
100, // Button height
m_hwnd, // Parent window
NULL, // No menu.
(HINSTANCE)GetWindowLong(m_hwnd, GWL_HINSTANCE),
NULL); // Pointer not needed.
```

Tackling Windows GUI programming requires you to work with `HWND`, `HINSTACNCE`, and many other weirdly named and confusing components.

.NET Framework made a drastic improvement to Windows GUI programming. If you want to support OS other than Windows, you have to think twice before using .NET Framework.

However, to support multiple OS, you still have to dive into APIs to implement the same application to cover all OS users out there. The following code shows an example of creating a button in Linux using the *Gtk+* GUI toolkit:

```
GtkWidget* button = gtk_button_new_with_label("Linux button");
```

Compared to the Windows API, it seems a bit easier to understand. However, you should dive into `GtkWidgets` and other components with *Gtk* prefixes to find out more about them.

As we have already mentioned, cross-platform languages such as Java and .NET Core use virtual machines to run the code on different platforms. The Qt framework supports cross-platform GUI programming using a platform-based compilation approach. Let's discuss both approaches with regard to the C++ language.

Using C++ as Java

Languages such as Java or C# have different compilation models. The first chapter of this book introduced the C++ compilation model. First of all, we consider C++ as a fully compilable language, while Java maintains a hybrid model. It compiles the source code into a middle representation called **bytecode**, and then the virtual machine runs it by translating it into the machine code for the specific platform.

The following diagram depicts the differences between the C++ and Java compilation models:

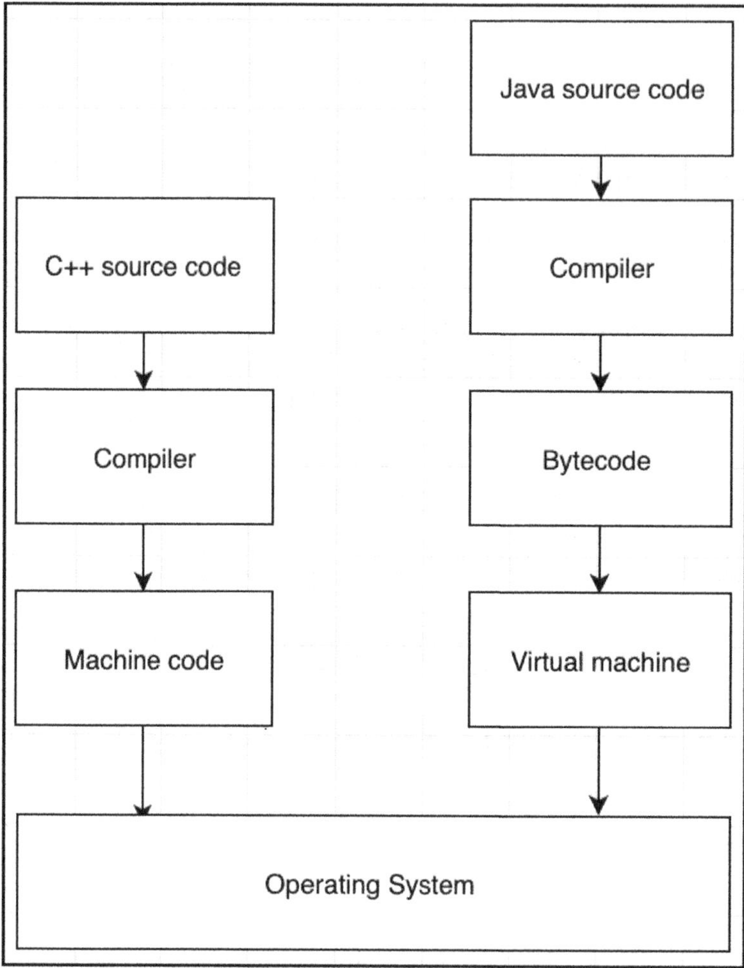

The **Java virtual machine** (**JVM**) serves as a middle tier. It has a unique implementation for each platform. Users need to install the specific implementation of the virtual machine before running Java programs. The installation process only happens once. On the other hand, C++ programs are translated into machine code, which is run without a middle-tier environment such as the JVM. That's one of the reasons why C++ applications are generally faster. When we compile C++ programs on a certain platform, the compiler outputs an executable file consisting of instructions in a format that's specific to that platform. When we move the application to another platform, it just can't run.

The other platform cannot recognize its format, nor its instructions (although they might be similar in some way). The Java approach works by presenting some bytecode that is the same for all the implementations of virtual machines. But virtual machines know exactly which instruction they should generate for the bytecode that's been provided as their input. The same bytecode can be run on many computers if they have the virtual machine installed. The following diagram demonstrates the Java application compilation model:

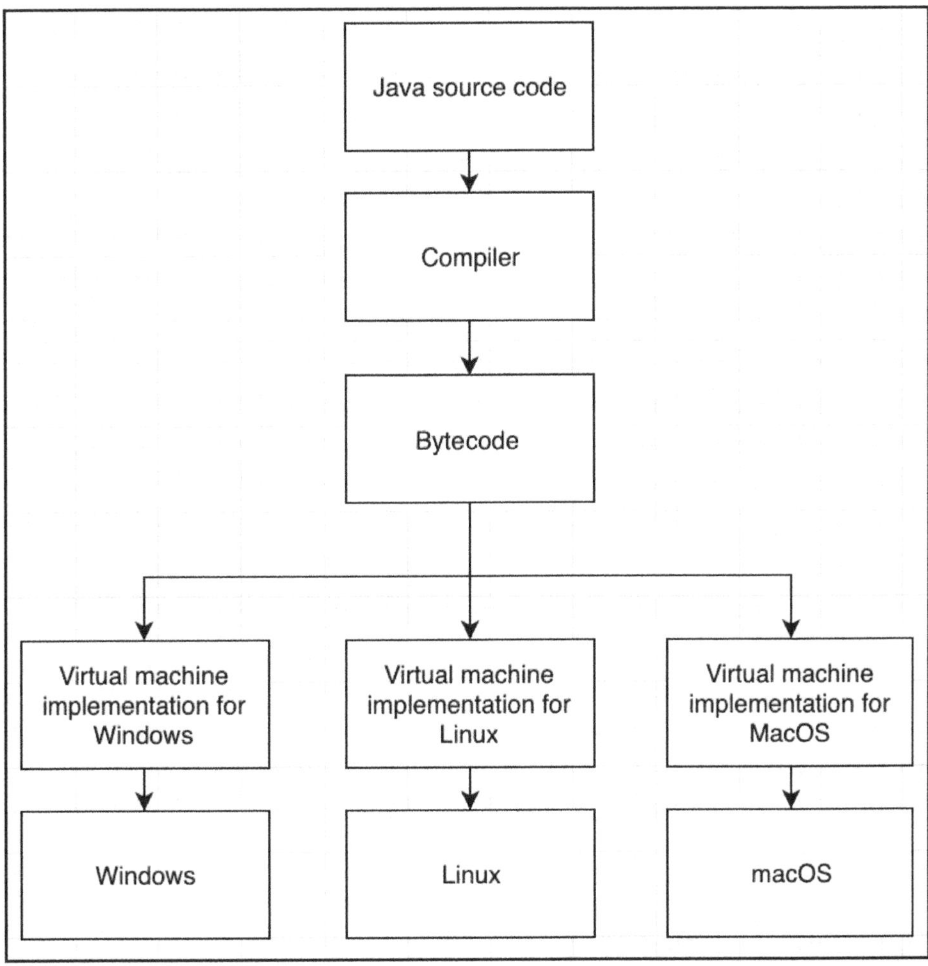

As you can see, the source code is compiled into bytecode that can be run on every OS. However, each OS must be provided with its own virtual machine implementation. This means we can run a Java application on any OS if we have installed a JVM specifically implemented for that OS.

Although C++ is a cross-platform language, meaning that we don't modify the code to compile it in other platforms, the language doesn't support GUI programming out of the box. To program GUI applications, as we mentioned previously, we need to access the OS API directly from the code. This makes C++ GUI applications platform-dependent because you need to modify the code base to compile it on the other platform. The following diagram shows how GUIs spoil the cross-platform nature of the language:

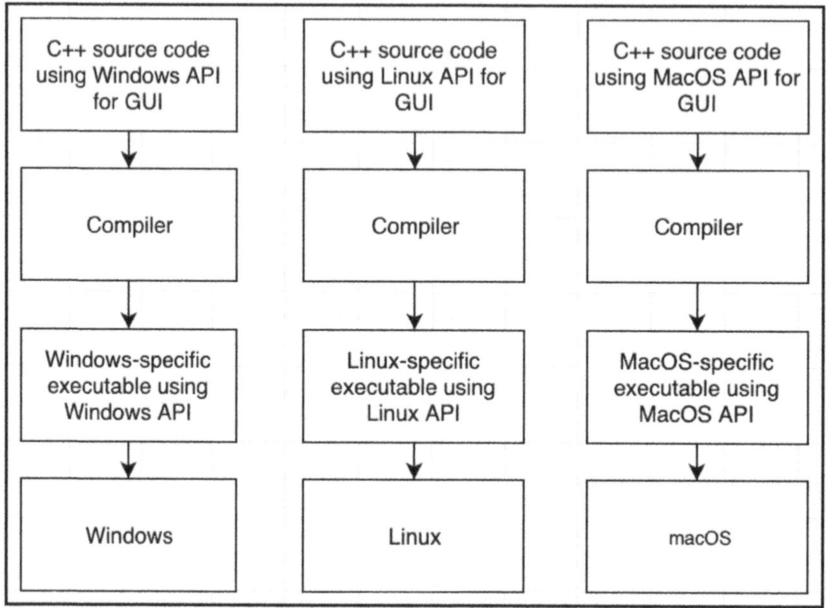

Though the application logic, name, and mission might be the same, it now has three different implementations with three different executables. To ship the application to the end user, we need to discover their OS and ship the correct executable. You might have encountered a similar scenario when downloading applications on the web. They offer download applications based on the OS. This is where Qt comes to the rescue. Let's see how.

Qt's cross-platform model

Qt is a popular widget toolkit for creating GUI applications. It also allows us to create cross-platform applications that run on various systems. Qt consists of the following modules:

- **Qt Core**: Core classes
- **Qt GUI**: Base classes for GUI components

- **Qt Widgets**: Classes to extend the Qt GUI with C++ widgets
- **Qt Multimedia**: Classes for audio, video, radio, and camera functionality
- **Qt Multimedia Widgets**: Classes for implementing multimedia functionality
- **Qt Network**: Classes for network programming (we will use them in this chapter)
- **Qt Modeling Language (QML)**: A declarative framework for building applications with custom user interfaces
- **Qt SQL**: Classes for database integration using SQL
- **Qt Quick family of modules**: A list of QML-related modules that won't be discussed in this book
- **Qt Test**: Classes for unit testing Qt applications

Every module that we use in the program is attached to the compiler via a project file that has the `.pro` extension. This file describes everything that `qmake` needs to build the application. *qmake* is a tool aimed to simplify the build process. We describe the project components (sources, Qt modules, libraries, and so on) in the `.pro` file of the project. For example, a project that uses Qt Widgets and Qt Network and consists of `main.cpp` and `test.cpp` files will have the following content for the `.pro` file:

```
QT += widgets
QT += network
SOURCES += test.cpp
SOURCES += main.cpp
```

We can specify platform-specific sources in the `.pro` file too, as follows:

```
QT += widgets
QT += network
SOURCES += test.cpp
SOURCES += main.cpp
win32 {
  SOURCES += windows_specific.cpp
}
unix {
  SOURCES += linux_world.cpp
}
```

When we build the application in a Windows environment, the `windows_specific.cpp` file will take part in the build process. Contrary to that, when building in a Unix environment, the `linux_world.cpp` file will be included while the `windows_specific.cpp` file will be ignored. With that, we've come to the compilation model of Qt applications.

The whole point of Qt's powerful abilities to provide cross-platform programming is meta-compiling the source code; that is, before the code is passed to the C++ compiler, the Qt compiler cleans it up by introducing or replacing platform-specific components. For example, when we use a button component (`QPushButton`), it will be replaced by a Windows-specific button component if compiled in a Windows environment. That's why the `.pro` file also can contain platform-specific modifications for the project. The following diagram depicts this compilation:

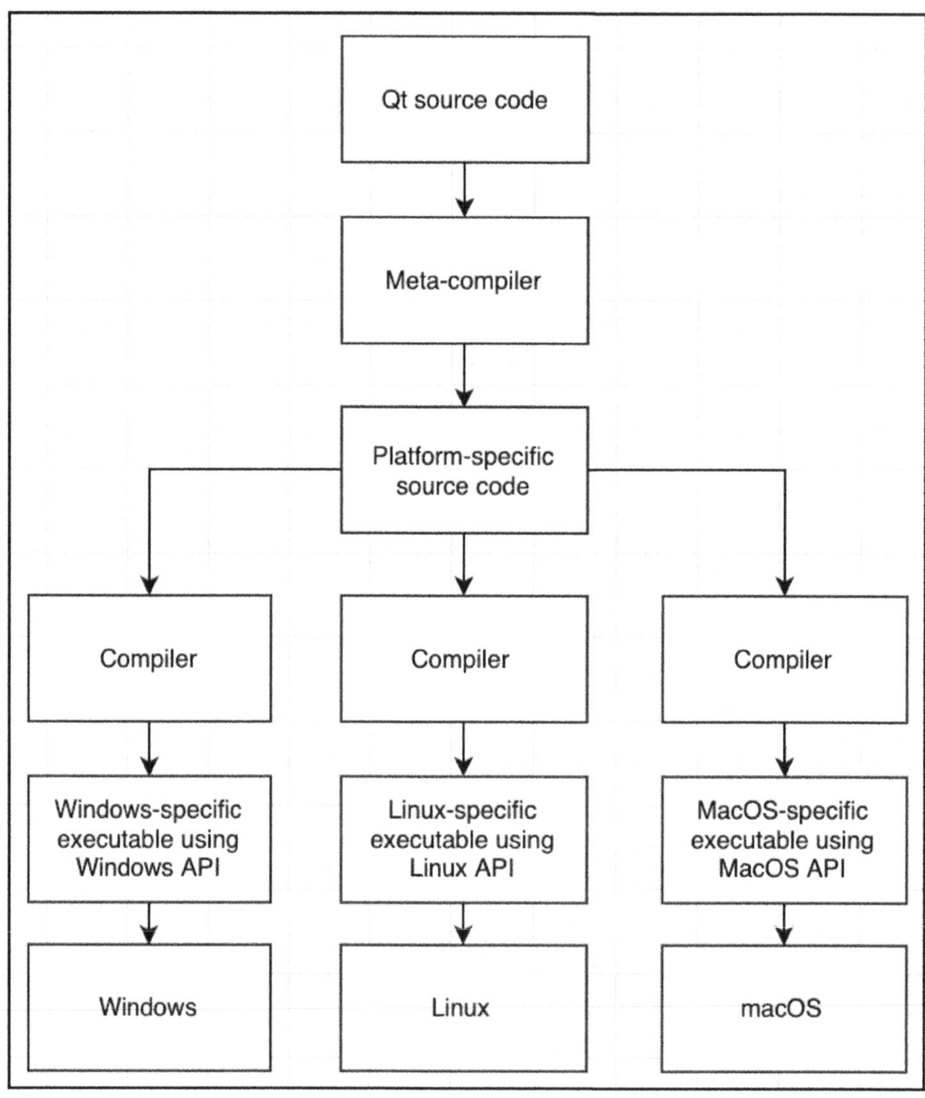

The meta-compiler is usually referred to as a **Meta-Object Compiler** (**MOC**). The beauty of this approach is that the produced output represents the same machine code that we run without a virtual machine. We can ship that executable right away. The downside of this approach is that we, again, have different executables for different platforms. However, we only write one application – there's no need to use different languages, dive into OS-specific APIs, or study OS-specific GUI component class names. As Qt says, *Write once, compile everywhere*. Now, let's move on to building a simple GUI application.

Writing a simple application

We won't discuss all the modules we mentioned previously in this book, simply because this would require a whole new book. You can refer to the books listed at the end of this chapter, in the *Further reading* section, for more information. The `main` function looks like this:

```
#include <QtWidgets>

int main(int argc, char** argv)
{
  QApplication app(argc, argv);

  QPushButton btn("Click me!");
  btn.show();
  return app.exec();
}
```

Let's take a look at the various components we used in the code. The first one is the `QtWidgets` header file. It contains widget components that we can use to build a fine-grained GUI for our application. Next, there's the `QPushButton` class, which represents a wrapper for a clickable button. We're intentionally introducing it as a wrapper here so that we can explain it when we discuss the compilation process of Qt programs later in this chapter. Here's the result of running the preceding code:

As you can see, we only declared the `QPushButton` class, but it appeared as a window with the close and minimize buttons that are standard to the OS (in the example, this is macOS). The reason for this is because `QPushButton` indirectly inherits from `QWidget`, which is a widget with a frame; that is, a window. The button took almost all the space of the window. We can resize the window and see how the button resizes along with it. We will discuss widgets in more detail later in this chapter.

The GUI builds when we run `app.exec()`. Pay attention to the type of the `app` object. It's a `QApplication` object. This is the starting point of Qt applications. When we call the `exec()` function, we start Qt's event loop. Our perception of program execution should be changed a bit to understand the GUI application life cycle. Redefining the perception of program construction and execution shouldn't be surprising for you after `Chapter 7`, *Functional Programming*. It's not that hard this time. The main thing to know here is that GUI applications have an additional entity running along with the main program. This entity is called an **event loop**.

Recall the event loop, which we discussed in `Chapter 11`, *Designing a Strategy Game Using Design Patterns*. The game represents a program with visual components that the user intensively interacts with. The same relates to regular GUI applications with buttons, labels, and other graphical components.

The user interacts with the application and each user action is interpreted as an event. Each event is then pushed to the queue. The event loop processes those events one by one. Processing an event means calling a special handler function attached to the event. For example, whenever a button is clicked, the `keyPressedEvent()` function is invoked. It's a virtual function, so we can override it when designing custom buttons, as shown in the following code:

```
class MyAwesomeButton : public QPushButton
{
  Q_OBJECT
public:
  void keyPressedEvent(QKeyEvent* e) override
  {
    // anything that we need to do when the button is pressed
  }
};
```

The only argument of the event is a pointer to `QKeyEvent`, a subtype of `QEvent`. `QEvent` is the base class of all event classes in Qt. Note the weird `Q_OBJECT` placed right after the opening block of the class. It's a Qt-specific macro that should be placed in the first line of your custom classes if you tend to make them discoverable by Qt's MOC.

In the next section, we will introduce the mechanism of signals and slots that are specific to Qt objects. To make our custom objects support that mechanism, we place the `Q_OBJECT` macro in the class definition.

Now, let's build something bigger than a simple button. The following example creates a window with the title `Mastering C++`:

```
#include <QtWidgets>

int main(int argc, char** argv)
{
  QApplication app(argc, argv);

  QWidget window;
  window.resize(120, 100);
  window.setWindowTitle("Mastering C++");
  window.show();

  return app.exec();
}
```

Here's what we get by executing the preceding program:

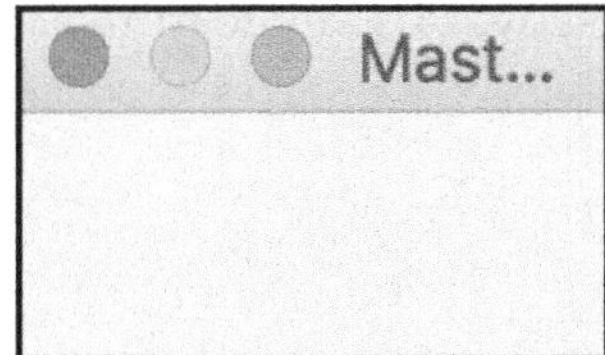

The title is cut; we can see only the **Mast...** part of **Mastering C++**. Now, if we manually resize it or change the source code so that it has a larger value for the second parameter for the `resize()` function, we get the following result:

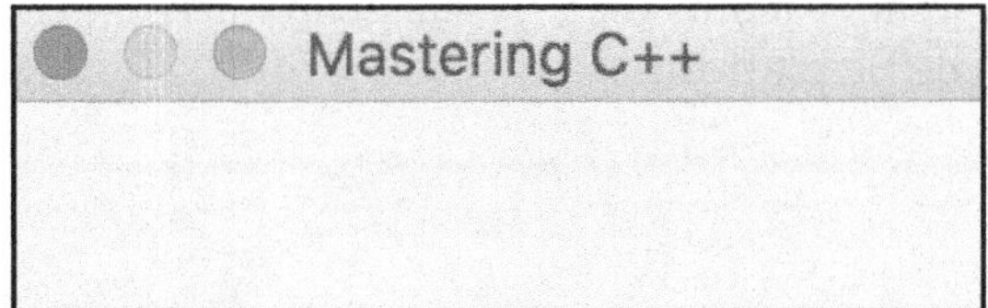

The `window` object is of the `QWidget` type. `QWidget` is the central class for all user interface objects. Whenever you want to create a custom widget or extend an existing one, you directly or indirectly inherit from `QWidget`. It has a lot of functions for every use case. You can move it through the screen using the `move()` function, you can make the window full screen by calling `showFullScreen()`, and so on. In the preceding code, we called the `resize()` function, which takes the width and height to resize the widget. Also, note the `setWindowTitle()` function, which does exactly what it says on the tin – it sets the passed string argument as the title of the window. Its good practice to use the `QApplication::translate()` function when using string values in code. It makes program localization much easier because when the language setting is changed, Qt automatically replaces the text with the right translation. Almost the same functionality is provided by `QObject::tr()`.

`QObject` is the base class of all Qt types. In languages such as Java or C#, every object is directly or indirectly inherited from a generic type, mostly named `Object`. C++ doesn't incorporate a common base class. Qt, on the other hand, introduces `QObject`, which comes with the base functionality that all objects should support.

Now that we've touched on the basics of Qt application development, let's dive a little bit deeper into the framework and discover its key features.

Discovering Qt

Qt evolved over time and at the time of writing this book, its version is 5.14. Its first public prerelease version was announced in 1995. More than two decades have passed and now Qt has a lot of powerful features that are used in almost all platforms, including mobile systems such as Android and iOS. With few exceptions, we can confidently write fully-featured GUI applications in C++ and Qt for all platforms. This is a big game-changer because companies hire smaller teams that specialize in one technology rather than having several teams for each specific platform.

If you are new to Qt, it is strongly recommended that you get familiar with it as much as you can (go to the end of this chapter for book references). Besides the regular components that GUI frameworks provide, Qt also introduces several concepts that are new or neatly implemented in the framework. One such concept is the communication between objects using signals and slots.

Grasping signals and slots

Qt introduced the concept of signals and slots as a flexible communication mechanism between objects. The concept of signals and slots and their implementation mechanism is one of the features that sets Qt aside from other GUI frameworks. In previous chapters, we discussed the Observer pattern. The main idea of this pattern is to have an object that notifies other objects (subscribers) of an event. The mechanism of signals and slots is similar to the Observer pattern's implementation. It's a way for an object to notify another object about its change. Qt provides a generic interface that can be used to connect objects together by tying a signal from one object to the slot of another. Both signals and slots are regular member functions of objects. The signal is the function that is invoked on a specified action for the object. The slot is another function that serves as the subscriber. It is invoked by the signal function.

As we mentioned previously, Qt introduced us to the base type for all objects, `QObject`. The basic functionality for supporting signals and slots is implemented in `QObject`. Any object that you declare in your code, `QWidget`, `QPushButton`, and others all inherit from `QObject`, so all of them support signals and slots. QObject provides us with two functions for managing object communication. These objects are `connect()` and `disconnect()`:

```
bool connect(const QObject* sender, const char* signal,
  const QObject* receiver, const char* method,
  Qt::ConnectionType type = Qt::AutoConnect);

bool disconnect(const QObject* sender, const char* signal,
  const QObject* receiver, const char* method);
```

As you can see, the `connect()` function takes the `receiver` and `sender` objects as arguments. Also, it takes the names of the signal and the slot. `signal` is associated with the sender, while `slot` is what the receiver provides. The following diagram shows this:

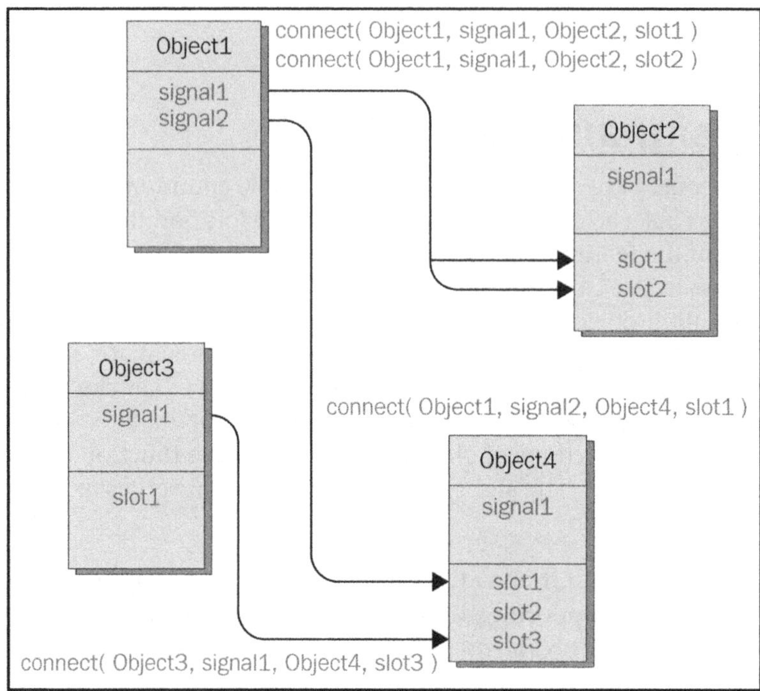

When programming Qt applications, operating with signals and slots will become natural and sooner or later, you would think that every other framework will support signals and slots because of their convenience. Also, note that the signal and the slot are processed as strings in the `connect()` and `disconnect()` functions. To specify the signal and the slot when connecting objects, we use two other macros, `SIGNAL()` and `SLOT()`, respectively. No more macros will be introduced from now on – we promise.

Here's how we connect two objects together. Let's say we want to change the text of a label (an instance of `QLabel`) so that it receives a signal when the button is clicked. To achieve this, we connect the `clicked()` signal of `QPushButton` to the slot of `QLabel`, as follows:

```
QPushButton btn("Click me!");
QLabel lbl;
lbl.setText("No signal received");
QObject::connect(&btn, SIGNAL(clicked()), &lbl, SLOT(setText(const
QString&)));
```

The preceding code might look a bit verbose, but you will get used to it. Consider it as the price for a convenient mechanism for signals and slots. However, the preceding example won't give us the required results; that is, it won't set the text of the label to state that it received a signal. We should somehow pass that string to the label's slot. The `clicked()` signal doesn't do that for us. One of the ways to achieve this is by extending `QLabel` so that it implements a custom slot that sets the text to `received a signal`. Here's how we can do that:

```
class MyLabel : public QLabel
{
Q_OBJECT
public slots:
  void setCustomText() {
    this->setText("received a signal");
  }
};
```

To declare a slot, we specify the section, just like we did in the preceding code. Signals are declared almost the same way: by specifying a section with `signals:`. The only difference is that signals cannot be private or protected. We just declare them as-is:

```
class Example
{
Q_OBJECT:
public:
  // member functions
public slots:
  // public slots
private slots:
  // private slots
signals: // no public, private, or protected
  // signals without any definition, only the prototype
};
```

Now, we should only update the preceding code in order to change the signal of the label (as well as the type of the label object):

```
QPushButton btn("Click me!");
MyLabel lbl;
lbl.setText("No signal received");
QOBject::connect(&btn, SIGNAL(clicked()), &lbl, SLOT(setCustomText()));
```

We say that the slot will be called when the signal is emitted. You can declare and emit signals from within your objects as well. An important detail related to signals and slots is that they are independent of the GUI event loop.

When a signal is emitted, the connected slot is executed immediately. However, we can specify the type of connection by passing one of `Qt::ConnectionType` as the fifth argument of the `connect()` function. It comprises the following values:

- `AutoConnection`
- `DirectConnection`
- `QueuedConnection`
- `BlockingQueuedConnection`
- `UniqueConnection`

In `DirectConnection`, the slot is invoked immediately when the signal is emitted. On the other hand, when `QueuedConnection` is used, the slot is invoked when execution returns to the event loop of the receiver object's thread. `BlockingQueuedConnection` is similar to `QueuedConnection`, except that the signaling thread is blocked until the slot returns a value. `AutoConnection` can be either `DirectConnection` or `QueuedConnection`. The type is determined when the signal is emitted. If the receiver and the emitter are in the same thread, `DirectConnection` is used; otherwise, the connection goes with `QueuedConnection`. Finally, `UniqueConnection` is used with any of the connection types described previously. It is combined with one of them using the bitwise OR. Its sole purpose is for the `connect()` function to fail if the connection has already been established between the signal and the thread.

Signals and slots form a powerful mechanism that makes Qt an outstanding framework in GUI programming. The next mechanism that we introduce is popular among frameworks and relates to the way we manipulate data in applications.

Understanding Model/View programming

Model/View programming has its roots in the **Model View Controller** (**MVC**) design pattern. The main idea behind the pattern is to decompose your problem into three loosely coupled components, as follows:

- The Model, which is responsible for storing and manipulating data
- The View, which is responsible for rendering and visualizing the data
- The Controller, which is responsible for additional business logic and providing data from the model to the view

Through its evolution, we now have a simplified and more convenient approach to programming called **Model/View programming**. It's similar to the MVC pattern, except it omits the Controller by making the View and the Model more concerned about the functionality at hand. We can say that the View and the Controller are combined together in the Model/View architecture. Take a look at the following architecture diagram:

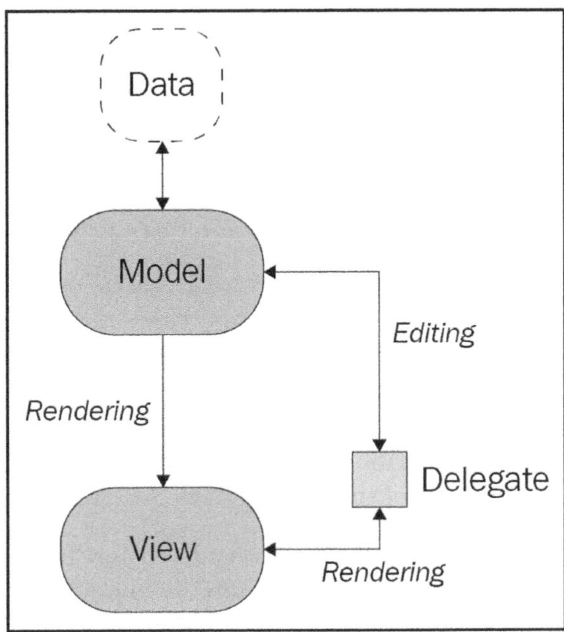

The model represents the data, which communicates with its source and provides a convenient interface for the other components in the architecture. The model's implementation and its communication with other components is based on the type of data at hand.

The view gets references to data items by obtaining so-called model indexes. The view can retrieve and supply data to the model. The point is, the data item can be edited using the view, and the delegate plays the role of communicating with the model to keep data synchronized.

Each of the introduced components – model, view, and delegate – are defined by abstract classes that provide common interfaces. In some cases, classes also provide default implementations of features. To write specialized components, we subclass from abstract classes. And of course, models, views, and delegates communicate using signals and slots, which we introduced in the previous section.

When the model encounters changes in the data, it informs the view. On the other hand, user interactions with rendered data items are informed by signals from the view. Finally, signals from the delegate inform the model and view about the state of data editing.

Models are based on the `QAbstractItemModel` class, which defines an interface that's used by views and delegates. Qt provides a set of existing model classes that we can use without modifications; however, if you need to create new models, you should inherit your class from `QAbstractItemModel`. For example, the `QStringListModel`, `QStandardItemModel`, and `QFileSystemModel` classes are ready-made to handle data items. `QStringListModel` is used to store a list of string items (represented as `QString` objects). Also, there are convenient model classes for working with SQL databases. `QSqlQueryModel`, `QSqlTableModel`, and `QSqlRelationalTableModel` allow us to access relational databases in the context of model/view conventions.

Views and delegates also have corresponding abstract classes, that is, `QAbstractItemView` and `QAbstractItemDelegate`. Qt provides existing views that can be used right away, such as `QListView`, `QTableView`, and `QTreeView`. These are the basic types of views that most applications deal with. `QListView` displays a list of items, `QTableView` displays data in a table, and `QTreeView` displays data in a hierarchical list. If you want to work with those view classes, Qt suggests inheriting your custom models from `QAbstractListModel` or `QAbstractTableModel` instead of subclassing `QAbstractItemModel`.

`QListView`, `QTreeView`, and `QTableView` are considered core and low-level classes. There are more convenient classes that provide better usability to novice Qt programmers – `QListWidget`, `QTreeWidget`, and `QTableWidget`. We will look at examples of using widgets in the next section of this chapter. Before that, let's look at a simple example of a `QListWidget` in action:

```
#include <QListWidget>

int main(int argc, char** argv)
{
  QApplication app(argc, argv);
  QListWidget* listWgt{new QListWidget};
  return app.exec();
}
```

One of the ways to add items to the list widget is by creating them, which we can do by setting the list widget as its owner. In the following code, we're declaring three `QListWidgetItem` objects, each holding a name and associated with the list widget we declared preceding:

```
new QListWidgetItem("Amat", listWgt);
new QListWidgetItem("Samvel", listWgt);
new QListWidgetItem("Leia", listWgt);
```

Alternatively, we can declare an item and then insert it into the list widget:

```
QListWidgetItem* newName{new QListWidgetItem};
newName->setText("Sveta");
listWgt->insertItem(0, newName);
```

The first parameter of the `insertItem()` member function is the number of `row` to insert the item in. We placed the `Sveta` item in the first position of the list.

Now that we've touched on the concept of the row, we should get back to models and their indexes. The model encapsulates the data as a collection of data items. Each item in the model has a unique index specified by a `QModelIndex` class. This means that every item in the model can be accessed by the associated model index. To obtain the model index, we need to use the `index()` function. The following diagram depicts a model that organizes its data in a table-like structure:

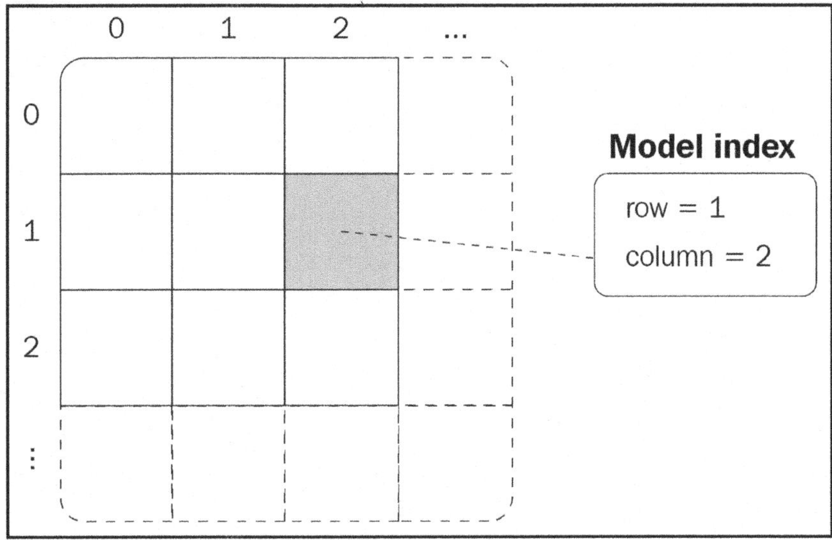

Views use this convention to access data items in the model. However, note that views are not restricted in terms of how they present the data to the user. It's up to the view implementation to render and present the data in a way that's convenient to the user. The following diagram shows how the data is organized within a model:

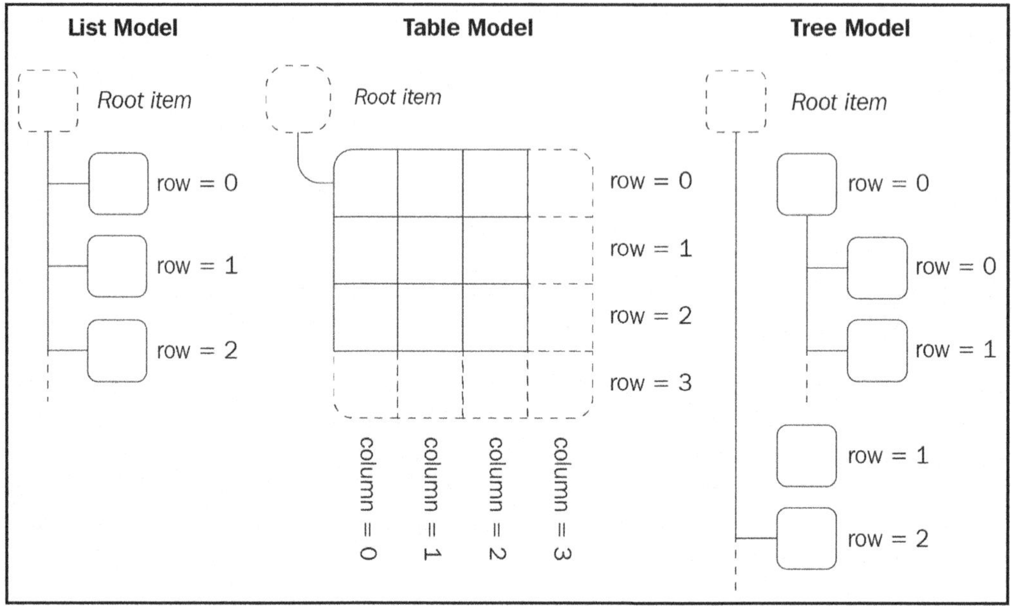

Here's how we can access a specific data item at row 1, column 2 using the model index:

```
QModelIndex itemAtRow1Col2 = model->index(1, 2);
```

Finally, let's declare a view and set a model to it to see model/view programming in action:

```
QStringList lst;
lst << "item 1" << "item 2" << "item 3";

QStringListModel model;
model.setStringList(lst);

QListView lview;
lview.setModel(model);
```

We will continue this example in the next section, once we become familiar with the various widgets provided by Qt.

Using Qt widgets

Widgets are visual GUI components. If a widget doesn't have a parent, it is treated as a window, otherwise known as a **top-level widget**. Earlier in this chapter, we created the simplest possible window in Qt, as shown in the following code:

```
#include <QtWidgets>

int main(int argc, char** argv)
{
  QApplication app(argc, argv);

  QWidget window;
  window.resize(120, 100);
  window.setWindowTitle("Mastering C++");
  window.show();

  return app.exec();
}
```

As you can see, the `window` object doesn't have a parent. The thing is, the constructor of `QWidget` takes another `QWidget` as the parent of the current one. So, when we declare a button and want it to be a child of our `window` object, we do so in the following way:

```
#include <QtWidgets>

int main(int argc, char** argv)
{
  QApplication app(argc, argv);

  QWidget window;
  window.resize(120, 100);
  window.setWindowTitle("Mastering C++");
  window.show();

  QPushButton* btn = new QPushButton("Click me!", &window);
  return app.exec();
}
```

Observe the second argument of the `QPushButton` constructor. We passed a reference to the `window` object as its parent. When a parent object is destroyed, its children are automatically destroyed. There are many other widgets supported by Qt; let's have a look at some of them.

Common Qt widgets

In the previous section, we introduced the `QPushButton` class and stated that it indirectly inherits the `QWidget` class. To create a window, we used the `QWidget` class. As it turns out, QWidget represents the capability to render to the screen, and it's the basic class that all widgets inherit from. It has a lot of properties and functions, such as `enabled`, a boolean property that's true if the widget is enabled. To access it, we use the `isEnabled()` and `setEnabled()` functions. To control the size of the widget, we use its `height` and `width`, which represent the height and width of the widget. To get their values, we call `height()` and `width()`, respectively. To set a new height and width, we should use the `resize()` function, which takes two arguments – the width and the height. You can also control the minimum and maximum size of the widget using the `setMinimumWidth()`, `setMinimumHeight()`, `setMaximumWidth()`, and `setMaximumHeight()` functions. This might come in useful when you set up widgets in layouts (see the next section). Besides properties and functions, we are mainly interested in the public slots of QWidget, which are as follows:

- `close()`: Closes the widget.
- `hide()`: Equivalent to `setVisible(false)`, this function hides the widget.
- `lower()` and `raise()`: Move the widget through the parent widget's stack (to the bottom or to the top). Each widget can have a parent widget. A widget without a parent widget becomes an independent window. We can set a title and an icon for this window using the `setWindowTitle()` and `setWindowIcon()` functions.
- `style`: The property holds the style of the widget. To modify it, we use the `setStyleSheet()` function by passing a string describing the style of the widget. Another way to do this is by calling the `setStyle()` function and passing an object of the `QStyle` type that encapsulates style-related properties.

Qt widgets have almost all the necessary properties out there to use out of the box. You rarely encounter situations where you have to build your own widget. However, some teams create an entire set of custom widgets for their software. That's fine if you are planning to have a custom look and feel for your programs. For example, you can incorporate flat-styled widgets, which means you have to modify the style of the default widgets provided by the framework. Custom widgets should inherit from `QWidget` (or any of its descendants), as shown here:

```
class MyWidget : public QWidget
{};
```

If you want the widget to expose signals and slots, you need to use the Q_OBJECT macro at the beginning of the class declaration. The definition of the updated MyWidget class will look as follows:

```
class MyWidget : public QWidget
{
Q_OBJECT
public:
  // public section

signals:
  // list of signals

public slots:
  // list of public slots
};
```

As you have probably already guessed, signals don't have an access modifier, while slots can be separated into public, private, and protected sections. As we mentioned previously, Qt provides enough widgets out of the box. To go over the set of widgets, Qt provides a set of examples that compose widgets together. If you have installed Qt Creator (the IDE for developing Qt applications), you should be able to go over the examples in a single click. Here's what it looks like in the Qt Creator:

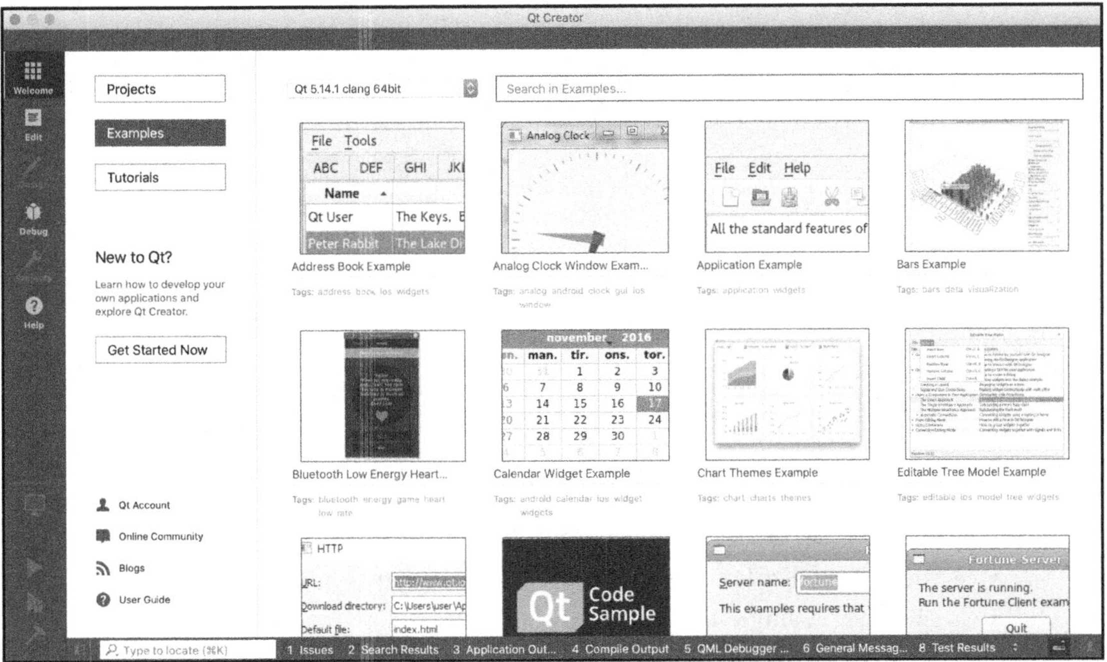

Configuring and running the **Address Book** example will give us the following interface:

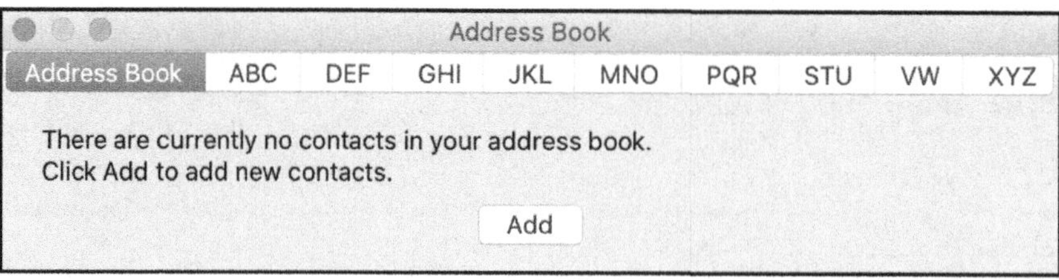

Clicking the **Add** button will open a dialog so that we can add a new entry to the address book, as shown here:

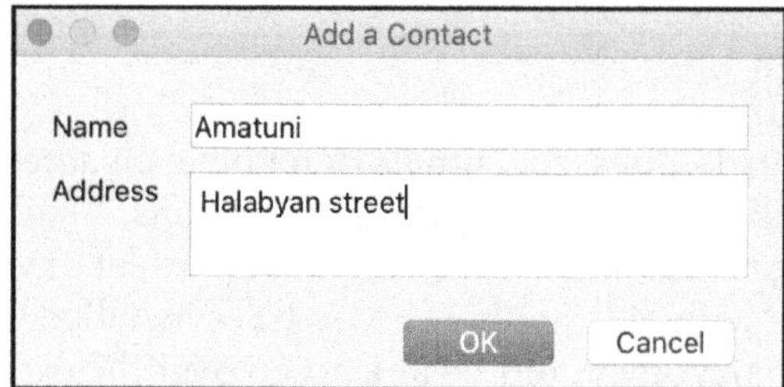

After adding a couple of entries, the main window shows the entries in a table, as shown here:

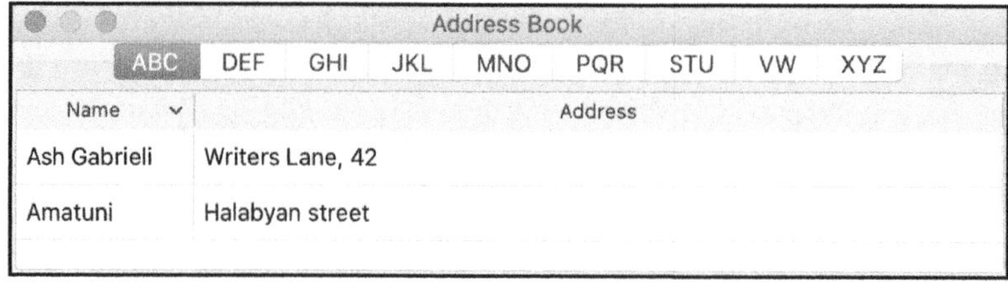

The preceding screenshots show a wide range of widgets composed together in one application. Here are some of the most common widgets that we regularly use in GUI application development:

- `QCheckBox`: Represents a checkbox with a text label.
- `QDateEdit`: Represents a widget that you can use to input the date. You can also use `QDateTimeEdit` if want to input the time as well.
- `QLabel` : Text display. Also used to display images.
- `QLineEdit`: A single-line edit box.

- `QProgressBar`: Renders a vertical or horizontal progress bar.
- `QTabWidget`: As stack of tabbed widgets. This is one of the many organizer widgets. Some of the other organizers are `QButtonGroup`, `QGroupBox`, and `QStackedWidget`.

The preceding list is not final, but it gives a basic idea of Qt's capabilities. The address book example we used here uses many of these widgets. `QTabWidget` represents an organizing widget. It groups several widgets together. Another way to organize widgets is using layouts. In the next section, we will introduce you to how to organize widgets together.

Composing widgets using layouts

Qt provides us with a flexible and simple platform where we can use the widgets arrangement mechanism in the form of layouts. This helps us ensure the space inside the widget is used both efficiently and provides a friendly user experience.

Lets look at the basic usage of layout management classes. The advantage of using layout management classes is that they automatically resize and position widgets when the container widget changes its size. Another advantage of Qt's layout classes is that they allow us to arrange the widgets by writing code rather than using a UI composer. While Qt Creator provides a great way of composing widgets by hand (dragging and dropping widgets on the screen), most programmers feel more comfortable when they actually write code that arranges the look and feel of their widgets. Assuming you like the latter approach as well, we are going to introduce the following layout classes:

- `QHBoxLayout`
- `QVBoxLayout`
- `QGridLayout`
- `QFormLayout`

All of these classes inherit from `QLayout`, the base class for geometry management. `QLayout` is an abstract base class that inherits from `QObject`. It doesn't inherit from `QWidget` because it doesn't have anything to do with rendering; instead, it takes care of organizing widgets that should be rendered on the screen. You probably won't need to implement your own layout manager, but if you do, you should inherit your class from `QLayout` and provide implementations for the following functions:

- `addItem()`
- `sizeHint()`
- `setGeometry()`

- `itemAt()`
- `takeAt()`
- `minimumSize()`

The classes listed here are more than enough to compose widgets of almost any complexity. And what's more important is that we can place one layout into another, resulting in a more flexible organization of widgets. Using `QHBoxLayout`, we can organize widgets horizontally from left to right, as shown in the following screenshot:

To achieve the preceding organization, we need to use the following code:

```
QWidget *window = new QWidget;
QPushButton *btn1 = new QPushButton("Leia");
QPushButton *btn2 = new QPushButton("Patrick");
QPushButton *btn3 = new QPushButton("Samo");
QPushButton *btn4 = new QPushButton("Amat");

QHBoxLayout *layout = new QHBoxLayout;
layout->addWidget(btn1);
layout->addWidget(btn2);
layout->addWidget(btn3);
layout->addWidget(btn4);

window->setLayout(layout);
window->show();
```

Take a look at the line where we call the `setLayout()` function on the widget. Each widget can be assigned a layout. A layout itself doesn't do much without a container, so we need to set it to a widget that serves as a container for organized widgets (buttons, in our case). `QHBoxLayout` inherits from `QBoxLayout`, which has another descendant that we listed previously – `QVBoxLayout`. It's similar to `QHBoxLayout` but organizes widgets vertically, as shown in the following screenshot:

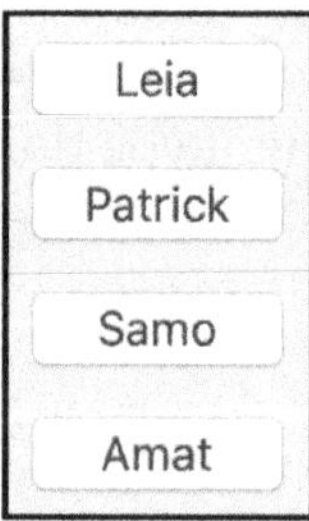

The only thing that we need to do in the preceding code is replace `QHBoxLayout` with `QVBoxLayout`, as shown here:

```
QVBoxLayout* layout = new QVBoxLayout;
```

`GridLayout` allows us to organize widgets into a grid, as shown in the following screenshot:

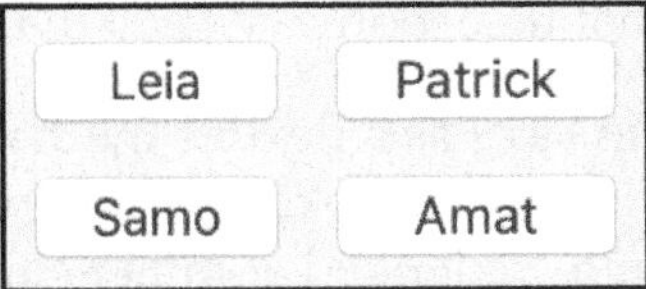

And here's the corresponding code block:

```
QGridLayout *layout = new QGridLayout;
layout->addWidget(btn1, 0, 0);
layout->addWidget(btn2, 0, 1);
layout->addWidget(btn3, 1, 0);
layout->addWidget(btn4, 1, 1);
```

Finally, similar to `QGridLayout`, `QFormLayout` is more helpful when it comes to designing input forms because it lays out widgets in a two-column descriptive style.

As we mentioned previously, we can compose a layout into another one. To do so, we need to use the `addItem()` function, as shown here:

```
QVBoxLayout *vertical = new QVBoxLayout;
vertical->addWidget(btn1);
vertical->addWidget(btn2);

QHBoxLayout *horizontal = new QHBoxLayout;
horizontal->addWidget(btn3);
horizontal->addWidget(btn4);

vertical->addItem(horizontal);
```

Layout managers are flexible enough to build complex user interfaces.

Summary

If you are new to Qt, this chapter will have served as a general introduction to the framework. We touched on the basics of GUI application development and compared the Java approach with Qt's approach. One of the biggest pros of using Qt is its support for cross-platform development. While Java does the same, Qt goes beyond that by producing executables that are native to the platform. This makes applications written in Qt much faster compared to alternatives that incorporate virtual machines.

We also discussed Qt's signals and slots as a flexible mechanism for inter-object communication. By using this, you are able to design complex communication mechanisms in your GUI applications. Although we looked at rather simple examples in this chapter, you are free to experiment with various ways of using signals and slots. We also became familiar with common Qt widgets and the mechanism of layout management. You now have a fundamental understanding that allows you to design even the most complex GUI layouts. This means you're free to implement a complex Qt application by applying the techniques and widgets that were introduced in this chapter. In the next chapter, we are going to discuss a popular topic nowadays – artificial intelligence and machine learning.

Questions

1. Why doesn't Qt need a virtual machine?
2. What does the `QApplication::exec()` function do?
3. How would you change the title of a top-level widget?
4. Given the `m` model, how would you access an item at row 2 and column 3?
5. Given the `wgt` widget, how would you change its width to 400 and height to 450?
6. Which functions should you implement when inheriting from `QLayout` to create your own layout manager class?
7. How can you connect a signal to a slot?

Further reading

- *Qt5 C++ GUI Programming Cookbook* by Lee Zhi Eng: `https://www.packtpub.com/application-development/qt5-c-gui-programming-cookbook-second-edition`
- *Mastering Qt5* by Guillaume Lazar, Robin Penea: `https://www.packtpub.com/web-development/mastering-qt-5-second-edition`

3
Section 3: C++ in the AI World

This section is an overview of recent advances in AI and machine learning. We will be tackling machine learning tasks using C++ and designing a dialog-based search engine.

This section comprises the following chapters:

- `Chapter 15`, *Using C++ in Machine Learning Tasks*
- `Chapter 16`, *Implementing a Dialog-Based Search Engine*

15
Using C++ in Machine Learning Tasks

Artificial intelligence (**AI**) and **machine learning** (**ML**) have become more and more popular recently. From a simple food delivery website to complex industrial robots, AI has been declared as one of the main features powering software and hardware. While, most of the time, the terms are used to make the product look more serious, some companies are intensively researching and incorporating AI into their systems.

Before we go further, take into account the fact that this chapter is a gentle introduction to ML from a C++ programmer's perspective. For more comprehensive literature, refer to the list of books at the end of the chapter. In this chapter, we will introduce the concepts of AI and ML. While it is preferred to have a mathematical background, we almost don't use any math in this chapter. If you are planning to enlarge your skillset and dive into ML, you must consider studying mathematics first.

Besides introducing the concepts, the chapter also provides examples of tasks in ML. We are going to implement them and give you a basic idea of how you should research and move forward with solving more complex tasks.

We will cover the following topics in the chapter:

- Introduction to AI and ML in general
- Categories and applications of ML
- Designing a C++ class for calculations
- Neural network structure and implementation
- Regression analysis and clustering

Technical requirements

The g++ compiler with the `-std=c++2a` option is used to compile the examples throughout the chapter. You can find the source files used in this chapter at `https://github.com/PacktPublishing/Expert-CPP`.

Introduction to AI

The simplest definition of AI is robots acting like humans. It is the intelligence demonstrated by machines. And here goes the discussion around the definition of intelligence. How can we define it for machines, and at what level should we shout out loud that we are dealing with an intelligent machine?

If you are not familiar with the different tests to verify the intelligence of a machine, one of the popular ways to do so is the Turing test. The idea is to have an interrogator asking questions to two people, one of them being a machine and the other a human. If the interrogator can't make a clear distinction between those two, the machine should be considered intelligent.

The Turing test is named after Alan Turing. The test was introduced in his paper *Computing Machinery and Intelligence* in 1950. He proposed using the imitation game to determine whether a machine thinks like a human.

The people being interrogated are behind a wall so that the interrogator can't see them. The interrogator then asks several questions to both the participants. The following diagram demonstrates how the interrogator communicates with the human and the machine, but can't physically see them:

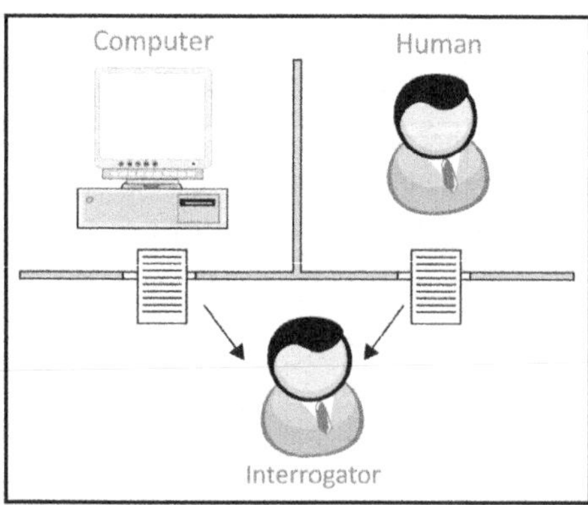

When you start diving into the field of AI, the definition of intelligence gets more and more vague. Questions can be asked to a machine in any form: in text, in audio, in visual form, and so on. There are numerous things that might never be available in machines, such as the look on their face. Sometimes people understand each other's mood by the look on their faces. You can't be sure whether a robot will understand or will even be able to imitate the mood on its face. No one taught us to look angry when we are angry. No one taught us to have emotions. They are just there. It's hard to tell whether some day, something similar might be achieved for machines.

When speaking about AI, most of the time we presume it's about a robot that talks and behaves similar to humans. But when you try to dissect it as a programmer, you meet a lot of sub-fields, each of which takes a lot of time to understand. Many of the fields have a lot of tasks in progress or are in the early research phase. Here are some of the sub-fields in AI that you might be interested in focusing on in your career:

- **Computer vision**: Designing algorithms for visual object recognition and understanding objects by analyzing their visual representation. It's easy for humans to spot a familiar face in the crowd, but implementing a similar functionality for machines might take a lot of time to gain accuracy equal to humans.
- **Natural language processing** (**NLP**): A linguistic analysis of text by machines. It has applications in various segments, such as machine translation. Imagine the computer completely understands human written text so that we can tell it what to do instead of spending months learning a programming language.
- **Knowledge reasoning**: This might seem the obvious goal for machines to behave intelligently. Knowledge reasoning is concerned with making machines reason and provide solutions based on the information they have; for example, provide a diagnosis by examining medical conditions.
- **ML**: A field of study of algorithms and statistical models used by machines to perform tasks without explicit instructions. Instead of direct instructions, ML algorithms rely on patterns and inference. That said, ML allows machines to do the job on their own, without human involvement.

Let's discuss the preceding sub-fields separately and then concentrate on ML.

Computer vision

Computer vision is a comprehensive field of study and has a lot of ongoing research projects. It is concerned with almost everything related to visual data processing. It has wide applications in various areas; for example, face recognition software processing data from various cameras spread over the city to find and determine criminal suspects, or optical character recognition software that produces text from images containing it. Combined with some **augmented reality** (**AR**) technologies, the software is able to translate text in images to language familiar to the user.

Study in this field is making progress by the day. Combined with AI systems, computer vision is the field that makes machines perceive the world as we do. A simple task for us, however, is challenging to implement in terms of computer vision. For example, when we see an object in an image, we easily spot its dimensions. For example, the following image represents the front view of a bicycle:

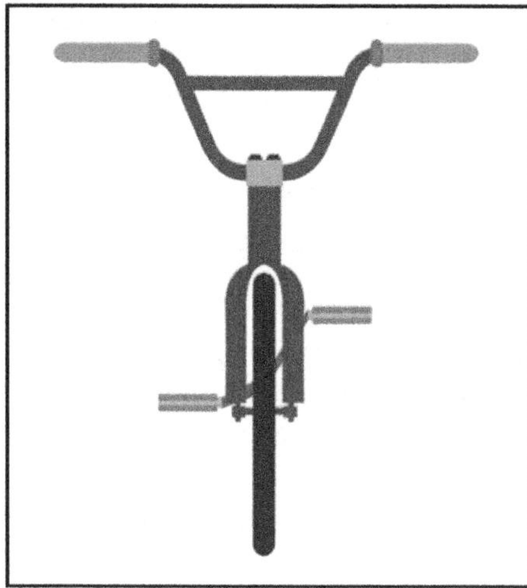

Even if we don't mention that it's a bicycle, it's not so hard for a human to determine it. It's obvious for us that the black bold line at bottom center is the front wheel of the bicycle. It's hard to tell the computer to understand that it is a wheel. All the computer sees is a collection of pixels, some of which have the same color:

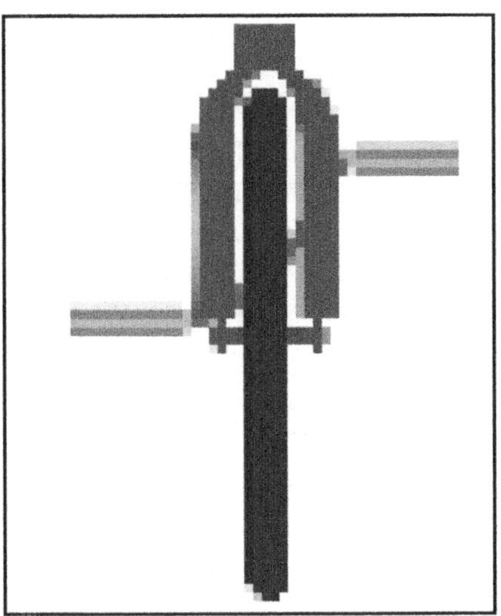

Besides understanding the wheel of the bicycle, it also should deduce that this bicycle must have another wheel that is not visible in the image. And again, we might have a guess for the approximate size of the bicycle, while it's a comprehensive task for the computer to determine it from the image. That said, the simple thing in our perspective might become a real challenge in computer vision.

We suggest using the OpenCV library for computer vision tasks. It is a cross-platform library written in C and C++. OpenCV represents a set of functions aimed at real-time computer vision, including ,but not limited to, facial recognition, gesture recognition, motion understanding, motion tracking, and other features.

Typical tasks in computer vision include object recognition, identification, and detection. Object recognition is the understanding that the object is a vehicle from the preceding image. Identification is the recognizing of an individual instance of an object, for example, the wheel of the bicycle in the preceding image. Object detection tasks might include finding corrupted areas of a bicycle from its image. All of these tasks combined with ML algorithms might comprise a comprehensive software that understands its surroundings close to the way humans do.

NLP

Another interesting field of study is NLP. NLP makes efforts to make computers understand human languages. A more generalized approach is automatic speech recognition and natural language understanding; a key feature of virtual assistants. Today, it's not magic anymore to talk with your phone and ask it to search for something on the web, for example. All of the process is powered by complex algorithms in speech and text analysis. The following diagram shows the high-level view of the process happening behind the conversational agents:

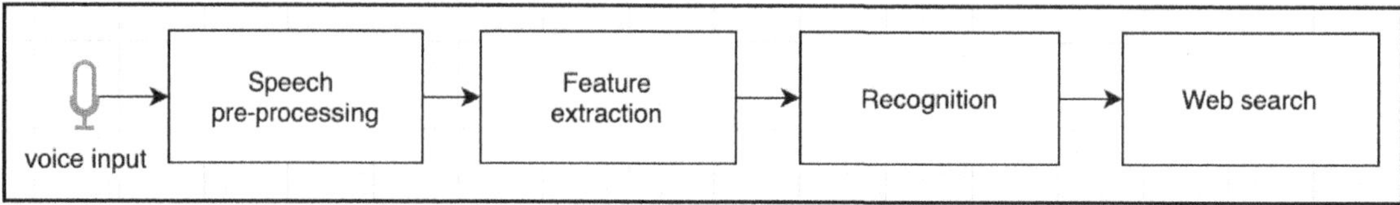

Many language processing tasks are related to the web. A search engine processing the user input to search among millions of documents on the web is one of the top applications of NLP. In the next chapter, we are diving a lot deeper into search engine design and implementation. One of the main concerns in search engine design is processing the text data. The search engine cannot just store all the websites and respond to the user for the first match for the query. There are numerous tasks in NLP that have complex implementations. Suppose that we are designing a program that is fed with a text document and we should output sentences within the document. Recognizing the beginning and the end of a sentence is one of the complex tasks. The following sentence is a simple example:

```
I love studying C++. It's hard, but interesting.
```

The program will output two sentences:

```
I love studying C++.
It's hard, but interesting.
```

In terms of a coding task, we just search for the . (dot) character at the end and make sure the first word started with the capital letter. How would the program behave if one of the sentences had the following form?

```
I love studying C++!
```

As there is an exclamation point at the end of the sentence, we should revisit our program to add another rule for recognizing the ending of a sentence. What if a sentence ends like this?

```
It's hard, but interesting...
```

One by one, more and more rules and definitions are introduced to have a fully functional sentence extractor. Leveraging ML moves us to a smarter direction when solving NLP tasks.

Another language-related task is machine translation that, which automatically translates a document from one language to another. Also, note that building a comprehensive NLP system will benefit other fields of study, such as knowledge reasoning.

Knowledge reasoning

Knowledge reasoning is making computers think and reason in a similar way to humans. Imagine having a conversation with a machine, starting like this:

```
[Human] Hello
[Machine] Hello
```

We can program the machine to answer specific questions or understand complex text input by user, but it's a lot harder to make the machine reason based on previous experience. For example, the following reasoning is one of the goals of the study:

```
[Human] I was walking yesterday and it was raining.
[Machine] Nice.
[Human] I should dress warmer next time.
[Machine] OK.
[Human] I think I have a temperature.
[Machine] Did you caught a cold yesterday?
[Human] I guess so.
```

While it might seem easy to spot the connection between catching a cold and the rain, it takes a lot of effort for the program to deduce it. It must associate the rain with cold and having a temperature with catching a cold. It also should remember the previous input to use it for intelligently keeping the dialog.

All of the preceding mentioned fields of study are exciting areas for a programmer to dive deeper. Finally, ML in general is something that sits at the fundament for all other fields in terms of designing algorithms and models for each specific application.

ML

ML takes us to a whole new level of making machines execute tasks the way humans do, maybe even better. Compared to the fields we introduced previously, the goal of ML is to build systems that are able to do things without specific instructions. In the journey of inventing artificially intelligent machines, we should take a closer look at human intelligence. When it is born, a child doesn't express intelligent behavior but starts to slowly become familiar with the surrounding world. There is no recorded evidence of any 1-month-old child solving differential equations or composing music. In the same way a child learns and discovers the world, ML is concerned with building the foundational models that directly perform the tasks, but rather are able to learn how to do it. That's the fundamental difference between setting the system to carry out predefined instructions and letting it figure it out on its own.

When a child starts walking, taking things, talking, and asking questions, they are gaining knowledge about the world step by step. She or he takes a book, tries its flavor, and sooner or later stops chewing books as something edible. Years pass and the child now opens the pages of the book and looks for images in it and the little figures comprising the text. A few more years pass and, the child starts to read them. Over the years, the brain gets more and more complicated and creates more and more connections between its neurons. The child becomes an intelligent human being.

Imagine a system that has some magical algorithms and models in it. After feeding it with a bunch of data, it will be able to understand more and more, the same way the child gets to know the world by processing the input data in the form of visual data (looking through their eyes), or smell, or flavor. Later on, by developing a way to ask questions, the child gets to understand words and associates those words with objects in the real world, and even intangible concepts. ML systems act almost in the same way. They process the input data and produce some output that conforms to the results expected by us. The following diagram illustrates the idea:

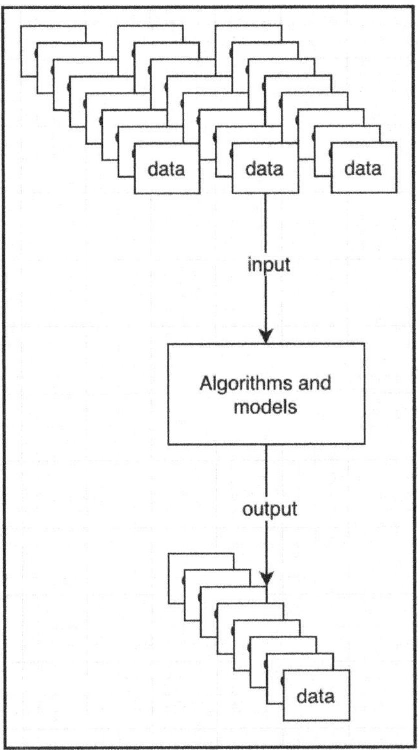

Let's now dive deeper into ML. As always, the best way to understand something new is to try to implement it first.

Understanding ML

ML is a big field of study with a lot of research in progress and is expanding rapidly. To understand ML, we should first understand the nature of learning. Thinking and reasoning are the key concepts that make us – humans – special. The core of ML is to make the system learn and use the knowledge to act upon tasks. You might recall your first steps in studying programming. We are sure it wasn't easy. You had to learn new concepts, build abstractions, and make your brain understand what's going on under the hood of program execution. After that, you were supposed to build complex systems using those small building blocks described in primers as keywords, instructions, conditional statements, functions, classes, and so on.

However, an ML program differs from the programs we usually create. Take a look at the following code:

```
int calculate()
{
  int a{14};
  int b{27};
  int c{a + b};
  return c;
}
```

The simple precedent program does what we instructed it to do. It contains several simple instructions that lead to the variable `c` representing the sum of `a` and `b`. We can modify the function to take user input as follows:

```
int calculate(int a, int b)
{
  int c{a + b};
  return c;
}
```

The preceding function will never gain any intelligence. It doesn't matter how many times we call the `calculate()` function. It also doesn't matter what numbers we provide as its input. The function represents a collection of instructions. We might say even a collection of hardcoded instructions. That is, the function will never modify its own instructions to behave differently based on the input. However, we can introduce some logic; let's say we make it return 0 each time it receives negative numbers:

```
int calculate(int a, int b)
{
  if (a < 0 && b < 0) {
    return 0;
  }
  int c{a + b};
  return c;
}
```

The conditional statement introduced the simplest form of a decision that the function makes based on its input. We can add more and more conditionals so that the function will grow and have a complex implementation. However, no number of conditional statements will make it smarter because it is not something that the code comes up with its own. And here comes the limit that we face when dealing with programs. They don't think; they act as we programmed them to act. We are the ones who decide how they must behave. And they always obey. Well, as long as we didn't introduce bugs.

Now, imagine an ML algorithm in action. Suppose the `calculate()` function has some magic in it, so that it returns a value based on the input. Let's say it has the following form:

```
int calculate(int a, int b)
{
  // some magic
  // return value
}
```

Now, suppose that we are calling `calculate()` and passing `2` and `4` as its arguments, hoping that it will calculate their sum and return `6`. Also, imagine that we can somehow tell it whether the result is what we expected. After a while, the function behaves in a way that it understands how to use those input values and return their sum. The following class that we are building represents our first steps toward understanding ML.

Designing an algorithm that learns

The following class represents a calculation machine. It comprises four arithmetic operations and expects that we provide examples of how it should calculate the input values:

```
struct Example
{
  int input1;
  int input 2;
  int output;
};

class CalculationMachine
{
public:
  using Examples = std::vector<Example>;
  // pass calculation examples through the setExamples()
  void setExamples(const Examples& examples);

  // the main function of interest
  // returns the result of the calculation
  int calculate(int a, int b);

private:
  // this function pointer will point to
  // one of the arithmetic functions below
  int (*fptr_)(int, int) = nullptr;

private:
```

```
  // set of arithmetic functions
  static int sum(int, int);
  static int subtract(int, int);
  static int multiply(int, int);
  static int divide(int, int);
};
```

Before using the `calculate()` function, we should provide a list of examples for the `setExamples()` function. Here's a sample of the examples that we provide to `CalculationMachine`:

```
3 4 7
2 2 4
5 5 10
4 5 9
```

The first two numbers in each line represent the input arguments; the third number is the result of the operation. The `setExamples()` function is how the `CalculationMachine` learns to use the correct arithmetic function. The same way we can guess what's going on from the preceding examples, the same way `CalculationMachine` tries to find the best fit for its operations. It goes through examples and defines which of the functions it should use when `calculate()` is called. The implementation is similar to the following:

```
void CalculationMachine::setExamples(const Examples& examples)
{
  int sum_count{0};
  int sub_count{0};
  int mul_count{0};
  int div_count{0};
  for (const auto& example : Examples) {
    if (CalculationMachine.sum(example.input1, example.input2) ==
example.output) {
      ++sum_count;
    }
    if (CalculationMachine.subtract(example.input1, example.input2) ==
example.output) {
      ++sub_count;
    }
    // the same for multiply() and divide()
  }

  // the function that has the maximum number of correct output results
  // becomes the main function for called by calculate()
  // fptr_ is assigned the winner arithmetic function
}
```

As you can see from the preceding example, the function calls all the arithmetic functions and compares their return value with the example output. Each time the result is correct, it increases the count of correct answers for the specific function. Finally, the function having the maximum number of correct answers is assigned to `fptr_` that is used by the `calculate()` function as follows:

```
int CalculationMachine::calculate(int a, int b)
{
  // fptr_ points to the sum() function
  return fptr_(a, b);
}
```

We have devised a simple learning algorithm. The `setExamples()` function might be renamed `setDataSet()` or `trainWithExamples()` or something similar. The point of the example with `CalculationMachine` is that we define a model and algorithm working with it and we can call it ML. It learns from data. Or, even better, it learns from experiences. Each record in the vector of examples that we provided to `CalculationMachine` can be regarded as an experience. We say that the performance of the calculation improves with experience. That is, the more we provide examples, the more it becomes confident in choosing the right function to perform the task. And the task is calculating the value based on two input arguments. The process of learning itself is not the task. Learning is what leads to performing the task. Tasks are usually described as how the system should process an example, where an example is a collection of features. Although, in ML terms, an example is represented as a vector (mathematical) where each entry is another feature, the choice of the vector data structure is just a coincidence. As one of the fundamental principles is the training of the system, ML algorithms can be categorized as supervised or unsupervised. Let's examine their differences and then establish various applications of ML systems.

Categories of ML

The following diagram illustrates the categorization of ML:

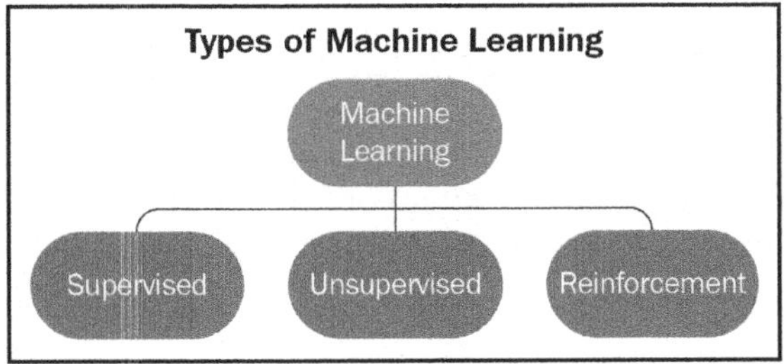

Categorization of ML algorithms depends on the kind of experience they have during the learning process. We usually call the collection of examples a *dataset*. Some books also use the term *data points*. A dataset is basically a collection of data representing anything useful to the target system. It might include measurements of weather for periods of time, a list of prices for the stock of some company or companies, or any other set of data. While the dataset might be unprocessed or so-called raw, there are also datasets having additional information for each contained experience. In the `CalculationMachine` example, we used a raw dataset, although we already programmed the system to recognize that the first two values are the operands of the operation and the third value is its result. As already mentioned, we categorize ML algorithms into supervised and unsupervised.

Supervised learning algorithms learn from labeled datasets; that is, each record contains additional information describing the data. `CalulcationMachine` is an example of a supervised learning algorithm. Supervised learning is also known as **training with an instructor**. The instructor teaches the system using the dataset.

The supervised learning algorithm will be able to label new unknown data after learning from experiences provided. The following diagram describes it best:

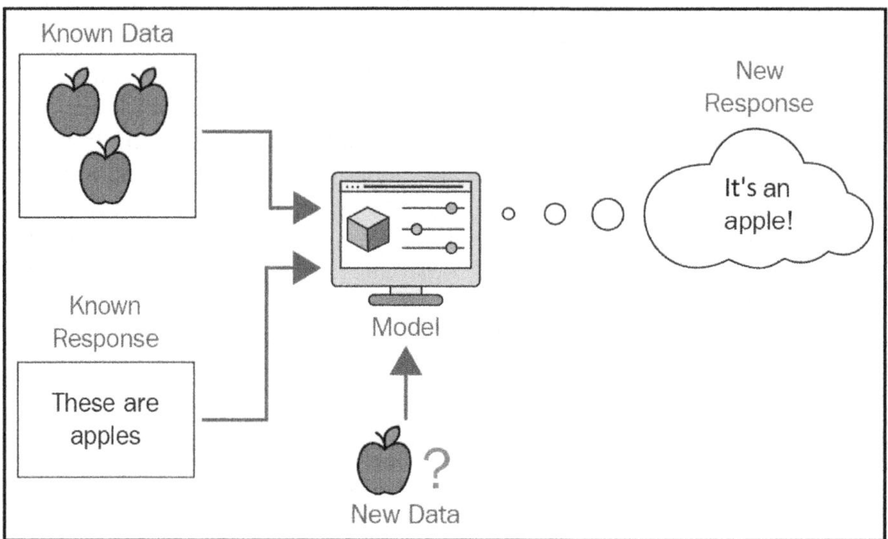

A good example of an application of supervised learning algorithms is the spam filter in email applications. Users label emails as spam or not and the system then tries to find patterns in new incoming emails to detect potential spam emails.

The example with `CalculationMachine` is another case for supervised learning. We fed it with the following dataset:

```
3 4 7
2 2 4
5 5 10
4 5 9
```

We programmed `CalculationMachine` to read the first two numbers as input arguments, and the third number as the output produced by a function applied to the input. This way, we provided necessary information on what exactly the system should get as a result.

Unsupervised learning algorithms are even more complex— they process the dataset containing a bunch of features and then try to find useful properties of the features. Unsupervised learning algorithms are mostly left alone to define what's in the dataset on their own. In terms of intelligence, an unsupervised learning approach meets the description of an intelligent creature more than supervised learning algorithms. In contrast, supervised learning algorithms are trying to predict which input values map to the output values, while unsupervised algorithms perform several operations to discover patterns in a dataset. Following the same association in the preceding diagram, the following diagram describes an unsupervised learning algorithm:

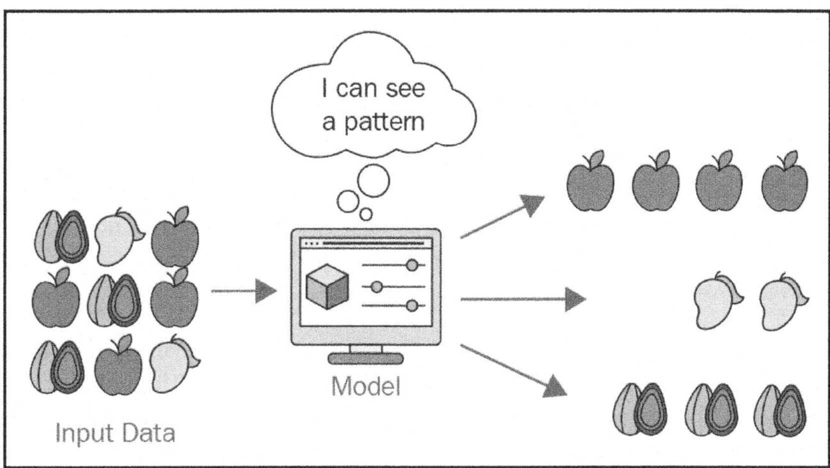

Examples of applications of unsupervised learning algorithms are recommendation systems. We will be discussing one in the next chapter, where we design a web search engine. Recommendation systems analyze user activity to recommend similar data, for example, movie recommendations.

As you can see from the preceding illustration, there is also *reinforcement learning*. This is the category of algorithms that learns from mistakes. There is a feedback loop between the learning system and its experiences so that reinforcement learning algorithms interact with an environment. It might make a lot of mistakes in the beginning and, after processing the feedback, correct itself to improve the algorithm. The learning process becomes part of task execution. Imagine that `CalculationMachine` receives only input numbers but not the result of the calculation. For each experience, it will produce a result by applying one of the arithmetic operations and then receive a feedback. Let's say it subtracts the numbers and then modifies itself to calculate the sum based on the feedback.

Applications of ML

Understanding the categorization of ML helps apply it better to various kinds of tasks. There is a wide range of tasks that can be solved with ML. We have already mentioned *classification* as one of the tasks solved with ML algorithms. Basically, classification is the process of filtering and ordering the input to specify the categories the input belongs to. Solving classification with ML usually means that it produces a function that maps input to specific output. Outputting a probability distribution over classes is also a type of classification task. One of the best examples of a classification task is object recognition. The input is a set of pixel values (in other words, an image) and the output is a value identifying the object in the image. Imagine a robot that can recognize different kinds of tools and deliver them to workers on command.;that is, a mechanic working in garage has an assistant robot that is able to recognize a screwdriver and bring it on command.

More challenging is classification with missing inputs. In the preceding example, it's similar to asking the robot to bring something to screw the bolts. When some of the input is missing, the learning algorithm must operate with more than one function to achieve a successful result. For example, the assistant robot might bring pliers first and then come up with a screwdriver as the correct solution.

Similar to classification is *regression*, where the system is asked to predict a numerical value given some input that is provided. The difference is the format of the output. An example of a regression task is prediction of future prices of stocks. These and other applications of ML are making it rapidly grow as a field of study. Learning algorithms are not just a list of conditional statements as they might feel at first. They are based on more comprehensive constructs modeled after human brain neurons and their connections. This leads us to the next section, the study of **artificial neural networks** (**ANNs**).

Neural networks

Neural networks are designed to recognize patterns. They are modeled after the human brain; more specifically, we speak about neurons of the brain and their artificial counterparts – artificial neurons. A neuron in the human brain is illustrated in the following diagram:

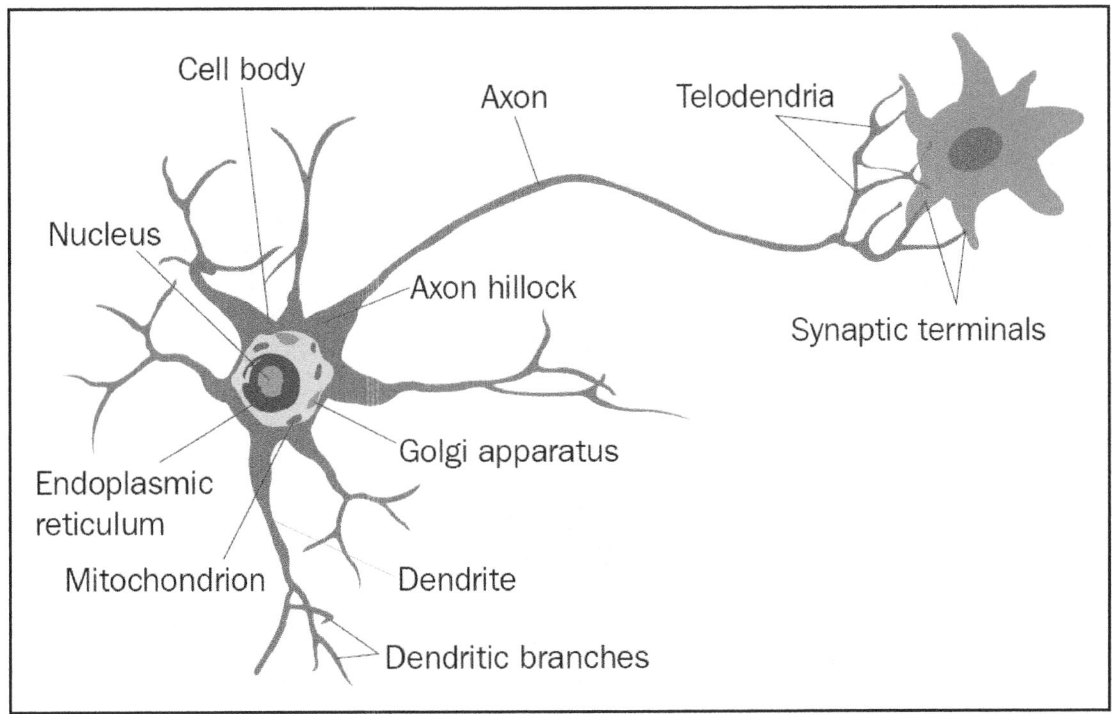

A neuron communicates with other neurons via *synapses*. The basic functionality of a neuron is processing a portion of data and producing signals based on that data. In programming terms, a neuron takes a set of inputs and produces an output.

That's why the following diagram makes it clear why an artificial neuron is similar to the human brain neuron structure:

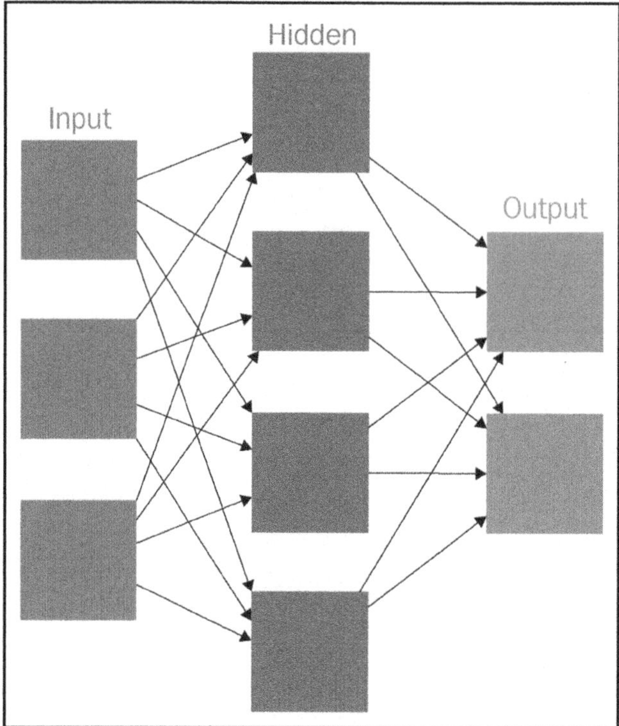

An ANN is a much simplified model of a natural neural network. It represents a group of interconnected nodes, each node representing a model after a neuron. Each node connection can transmit signals similar to synapses in biological brain neurons. Neural networks are a set of algorithms that help to cluster and classify. As you can see from the preceding diagram, the neural network consists of three layers:

- Input layer
- Hidden layer
- Output layer

The input and output layers speak for themselves; the initial inputs are external data, for example, images, audio, or text files. The output is the accomplishment of the task, such as classification of the text content or the recognized objects in images. The hidden layer is what makes the network produce reasonable results. The transition of input to output goes through the hidden layer, which does the heavy analyzing, processing, and modifications necessary to produce the output.

Consider the preceding diagram; it shows that a neuron can have multiple input and output connections. Usually, each connection has a weight that specifies the importance of the connection. The layering in the preceding diagram tells us that neurons in each layer are connected to neurons of the immediately preceding and immediately following layers. You should note that there might be several hidden layers between the input and output layers. While the primary purpose of input and output layers is reading external data and returning calculated (or deduced) output, the purpose of hidden layers is to adapt by learning. Learning also involves adjusting connections and weights aiming to improve the output accuracy. This is the part where ML comes to play. So, if we create a complex neural network with several hidden layers ready to learn and improve, we get an AI system. For example, let's examine the clustering problem and then move on to regression analysis.

Clustering

Clustering is concerned with grouping a set of objects to distribute them in groups of similar objects. Also known as **cluster analysis**, it is a set of techniques and algorithms intended to group similar objects together, producing clusters. The simplest illustrative introduction would be grouping a set of colored objects into different groups consisting of objects of the same color, as follows:

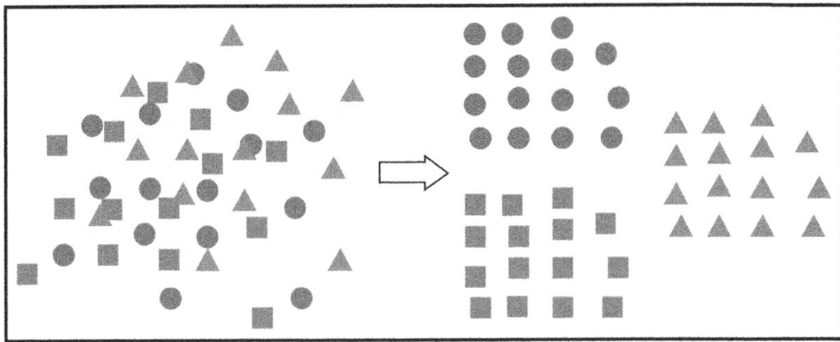

Although we are discussing AI tasks in this chapter, we suggest you first try to solve problems with the knowledge base that you have so far. That is, let's think about how we would categorize objects by similarity. First of all, we should have a basic idea of what the object will look like. In the preceding example, an object `shape`, `color`, dimensions (`width` and `height` for a 2D object), and so on. Without going much deeper, a basic object representation might look like this:

```
struct Object
{
  int color;
  int shape;
```

```
    int width;
    int height;
};
```

Let's consider the fact that values for color and shapes are in a some range of predefined values. We could use enumerations for better readability. Clustering analysis involves analyzing objects to categorize them somehow. The first thing that comes to mind is having a function that accepts a list of objects. Let's try to define one:

```
using objects_list = std::vector<Object>;
using categorized_table = std::unordered_map<int, objects_list>;
categorized_table clusterize(const objects_list& objects)
{
  // categorization logic
}
```

Think for a moment about the implementation details. We need to define the clustering points. It might be the color, or the type of the shape. The challenging thing is that it might be unknown. That said, to cover everything just in case, we categorize objects for every property as follows:

```
categorized_table clusterize(const objects_list& objects)
{
  categorized_table result;
  for (const auto& obj : objects) {
    result[obj.color].push_back(obj);
    result[obj.shape].push_back(obj);
  }
  return result;
}
```

Objects with a similar color or shape are grouped together in a hash table. While the preceding code is rather simple, it bears the basic idea for grouping objects by some similarity criterion. What we did in the previous example is more likely to be described as hard clustering. An object either belongs to a cluster or it doesn't. On the contrary, soft clustering (also known as **fuzzy clustering**) describes an object's belonging to a cluster to a certain degree.

For example, the similarity of objects for the shape property could be defined by the result of a function applied to the objects. That is, the function defines whether object A and object B have a similar shape if, let's say, object A's shape is a square and object B's shape is a rhombus. That means we should update the logic in the previous example to compare objects against several values and define their shape as a group. By developing this idea further, we will sooner or later arrive at different strategies and algorithms of clustering, such as K-means clustering.

Regression analysis

Regression analysis is concerned with finding the deviations for one value from another. The simplest way of understanding regression analysis is through the graphs for functions in mathematics. You might recall the graph for the function f(x) = y:

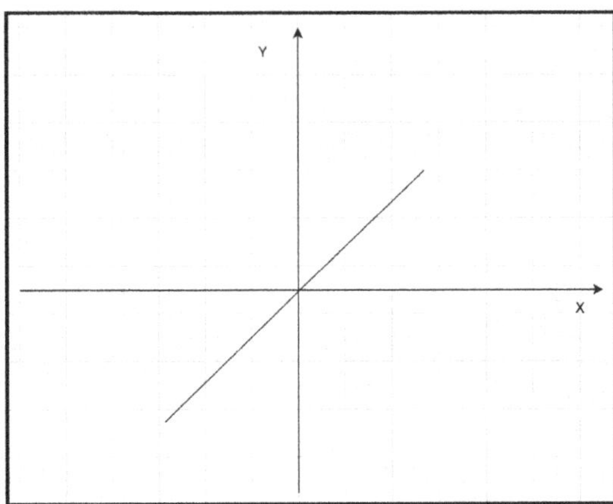

For every value of x, the function results in a fixed value for y. Regression analysis is somewhat similar to the preceding graph as it is concerned with finding a relationship between variables. More specifically, it estimates relationships between a dependent variable and several independent variables. The dependent variable is also know as an **outcome**, while the independent variables are also referred to as **features**. The number of features might be one.

The most common form of regression analysis is linear regression. It looks similar to the preceding graph. Here's an example representing the relationship between hours spent on testing programs and the number of bugs discovered in the release version:

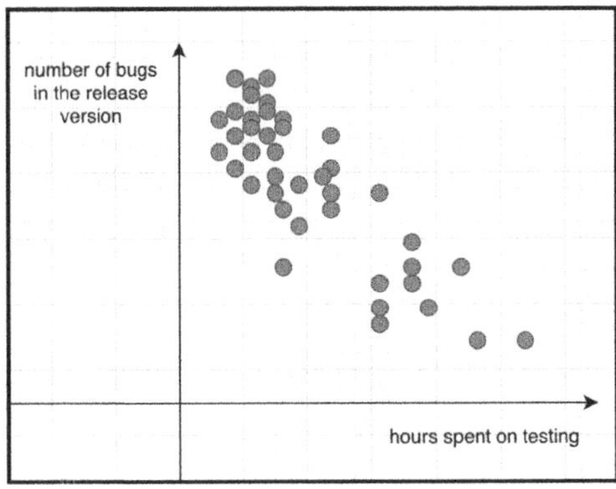

There are two types of regression: a negative regression is the one shown in the preceding diagram, as the independent values decrease while the dependent variable increases. Positive regressions, on the contrary other hand, have increasing values for independent variables.

Regression analysis in ML is used as a way of forecasting. You might develop a program to predict an outcome based on the values for dependent variables. As you have already guessed so far, ML is a big field with a wide range of topics. Although programmers tend to use math as little as possible, ML makes it impossible. You still need to grasp some of the math subjects to get the most out of ML. Regression analysis strongly depends on math statistics.

C++ and ML

It's now no longer a secret that ML is more about math than programming. Computer science has its roots in mathematics and, in the early years, computer scientists were mathematicians first. You might be familiar with several eminent scientists, including Alan Turing, John von Neuman, Claude Shannon, Norbert Wiener, Niklaus Wirth, Donald Knuth, and many others. All of them are mathematicians with a special love for technology. During its development, computer programming became a more friendly field to newcomers. In the last two or three decades, a computer programmer stopped being forced to learn math before developing useful programs. Languages evolved into more and more high-level tools that allow almost everyone to code.

There are plenty of frameworks that make the job easier for programmers. It now takes a matter of weeks to grasp some framework or a high-level programming language and create a new program. Programs, however, tend to repeat themselves. It's not so hard to build something nowadays because there are a lot of patterns and best practices that help us along the way. The role of mathematics has been pushed back and more and more people become programmers without even the slightest need to use math. That's not actually an issue; it's more like a natural flow for the technology to evolve. In the end, the aim for technology is to make the human living more comfortable. The same relates to engineers. While, back in the 1960s, engineers at NASA made calculations using computers, they were not computers as we know them today. Those were real human beings with this special specialty called being a *computer*, although being a computer meant being great in mathematics and solving equations much faster than others.

Now we are part of the new age in computer science where mathematics is back again. ML engineers are now using mathematics the same way mathematicians used programming languages in the 1970s or 1980s. It's now not enough to know a programming language or a framework to devise a new algorithm or incorporate ML into your applications. You should also be good at least in some sub-fields of mathematics, such as linear algebra, statistics, and probability theory.

Almost the same logic applies to C++. Modern languages provide a wide range of functionality out of the box, while C++ developers are still striving to design flawless programs with manual memory management. If you do some quick research into the field of ML, you will find that most of the libraries or examples out there are using Python. At first, this might be seen as the default language to use in ML tasks. However, ML engineers are starting to touch a new threshold in evolution – performance. This threshold is not new; lots of tools out there are still using C++ in parts where they need performance. Game development, operating systems, mission-critical systems, and many other fundamental areas are using C++ (and C) as the *de facto* standard. It's now time for C++ to conquer a new area. Our best advice to the reader would be to study both ML and C++ because it is slowly becoming critical for ML engineers to incorporate C++ to get the best performance out there.

Summary

We have introduced ML with its categories and applications. It is a rapidly growing field of study having numerous applications in building intelligent systems. We have categorized ML into supervised, unsupervised, and reinforcement learning algorithms. Each of the categories have their applications in solving tasks such as classification, clustering, regression, and machine translation.

We have implemented a simple learning algorithm that defines a calculation function based on experiences provided as an input. We called it a dataset that we used to train the system. Training with datasets (called **experiences**) is one of the key properties in ML systems.

Finally, we introduced and discussed ANNs applied to recognize patterns. ML and neural networks go hand in hand in solving tasks. The chapter provides you with the necessary introduction to the field along with several examples of tasks so that you can spend some time diving into the topic. This will help you to have a general idea of AI and ML as it's becoming increasingly necessary for engineers in real-world application development. In the next chapter, we will learn how to implement a dialog-based search engine.

Questions

1. What is ML?
2. What are the differences between supervised and unsupervised learning algorithms?
3. Give some examples of ML applications.
4. How would you modify the `CalculationMachine` class to change its behavior after training it with a different set of experiences?
5. What is the purpose of neural networks?

Further reading

- *Artificial Intelligence and Machine Learning Fundamentals,* at `https://www.packtpub.com/big-data-and-business-intelligence/artificial-intelligence-and-machine-learning-fundamentals`
- *Machine Learning Fundamentals,* at `https://www.packtpub.com/big-data-and-business-intelligence/machine-learning-fundamentals`
- *Hands-On Machine Learning for Algorithmic Trading,* at `https://www.packtpub.com/big-data-and-business-intelligence/hands-machine-learning-algorithmic-trading`

16
Implementing a Dialog-Based Search Engine

We have come so far in this book! We have learned the fundamentals of C++ application development and discussed architecting and designing world-ready applications. We also dove into data structures and algorithms, which are at the heart of efficient programming. It's now time to leverage all of these skills to design complex software, such as a search engine.

With the popularity of the internet, search engines have become the most in-demand products out there. Most users start their journey through the web from a search engine. Various web search services, such as Google, Baidu, Yandex, and so on, receive huge amounts of traffic, serving trillions of requests daily. Search engines process each request in less than a second. Although they maintain thousands of servers to tackle the load, at the heart of their efficient processing are data structures and algorithms, data architecture strategies, and caching.

The problem of designing an efficient searching system doesn't just appear in web search engines. Local databases, **Customer Relationship Management** (**CRM**) systems, accounting software, and others need robust searching functionality. In this chapter, we will discover the fundamentals of search engines and discuss the algorithms and data structures used to build fast search engines. You will learn how web search engines generally work and meet the new data structures used in projects requiring high processing capabilities. You will also build the confidence to go out there and build your own search engine that will compete with existing ones.

In this chapter, we will cover the following topics:

- Understanding the structure of a search engine
- Understanding and designing an inverted index used to map keywords to documents in the search engine

- Designing and building a recommendation engine for users of a search platform
- Using knowledge graphs to design a dialog-based search engine

Technical requirements

A `g++` compiler with a `-std=c++2a` option is used to compile the examples throughout this chapter. You can find the source files used in this chapter at `https://github.com/PacktPublishing/Expert-CPP`.

Understanding the structure of a search engine

Imagine the billions of web pages in the world. Typing a word or phrase into a search engine interface returns us a long list of results in less than a second. The speed at which a search engine processes so many web pages is miraculous. How does it find the correct document so quickly? To answer this question, we will do the wisest thing a programmer can do design an engine of our own.

The following diagram shows the basic idea behind a search engine:

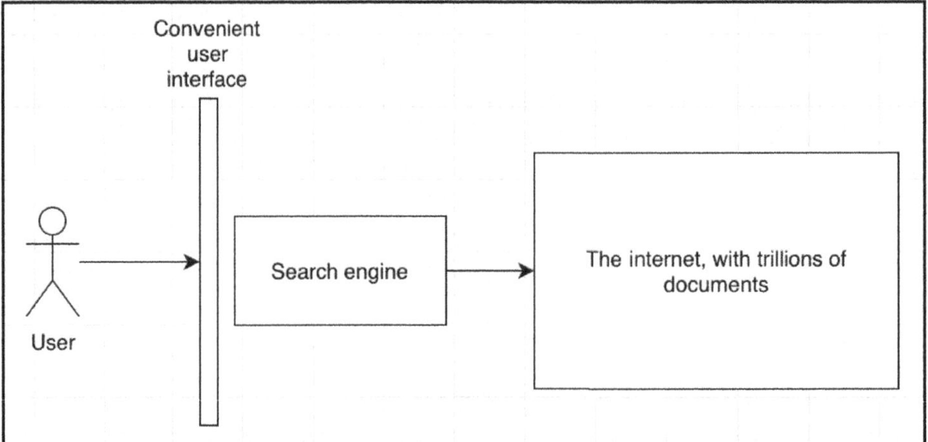

The **User** types in words using the search engine's **user interface**. The **Search engine** scans all the documents, filters them, sorts them by relevance, and responds to the user as fast as it can. Our main interest lies in the web search engine's implementation. Looking for something will require searching for it among billions of documents.

Let's try to devise an approach to find the phrase *Hello, world!* from among billions of documents (we will refer to web pages as documents for the sake of brevity). Scanning each document for the phrase would take a huge amount of time. If we consider each document to have at least 500 words, searching for a specific word or a combination of words would take a lot of time. It would be more practical to scan all the documents beforehand. This scanning process includes building an index of each occurrence of words in the documents and storing the information in a database, which is also known as **indexing documents**. When the user types in a phrase, the search engine will look up the words in its database and respond with links to documents that satisfy the query.

Before searching the documents, it wouldn't hurt for the engine to validate the user's input. It's not uncommon for users to have typos in phrases. Aside from typos, the user experience would be a lot better if the engine autocompleted words and phrases. For example, while the user is typing *hello*, the engine might suggest searching for the phrase *Hello, world!*. Some search engines keep track of users, storing information about their recent searches, details of the device they're using to make the request, and so on. For example, a user searching *how to restart the computer* will get an even better result if the search engine knows the operating system of the user. If it's a Linux distribution, the search engine will sort the search results so that documents describing the restarting of a Linux-based computer appear first.

We should also be careful of new documents appearing on the web regularly. A background job might analyze the web continuously to find new content. We call this job a **crawler**, as it crawls the web and indexes documents. The crawler downloads documents in order to parse their contents and build an index. Already-indexed documents might get updated, or worse, removed. So, another background job should take care of updating existing documents regularly. You might encounter the term **spider** for tasks that crawl the web to parse documents.

The following updated diagram illustrates the structure of a search engine in a bit more detail:

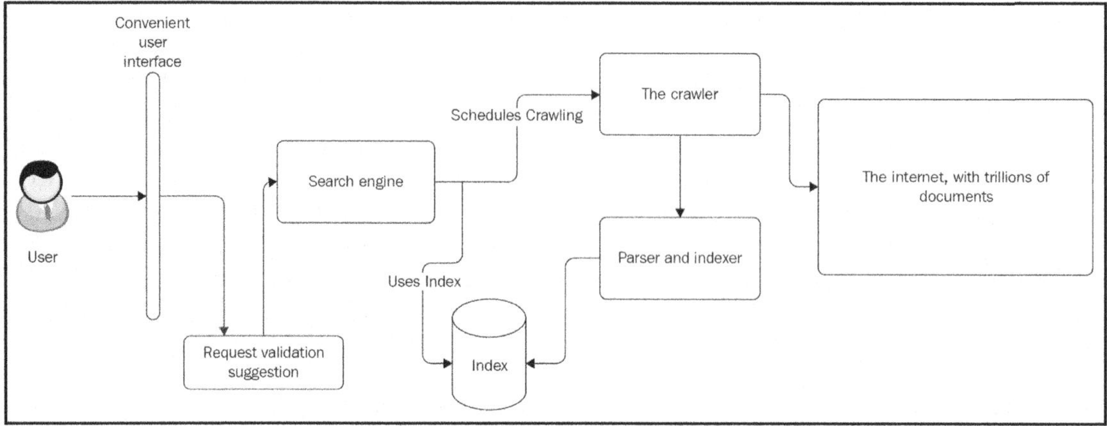

Searching has a wide range of applications. Imagine the simplest form of searching—finding a word in an array:

```
using words = std::vector<std::string>;
words list = get_list_of_words(); // suppose the function is implemented

auto find_in_words(const std::string& term)
{
  return std::find(list.begin(), list.end(), term);
}
```

Although the previous example applies to the simplest search engine, the real deal is designing a search engine that scales. You don't want to serve user requests by searching through an array of strings. Instead, you should strive to implement a scalable search engine that is able to search through millions of documents. This requires a lot of thinking and designing because everything matters, from the right choice of data structure to efficient algorithms for data processing. Let's now discuss the components of a search engine in more detail. We will incorporate all of the skills learned from previous chapters to design a good search engine.

Providing a convenient user interface

It's crucial to invest time and resources in building a fine-grained user interface that will provide an astonishing user experience. The key here is simplicity. The simpler the interface, the better its usage. We will use the market-dominant Google as an example. It has a simple input field at the center of the page. The user types their request in the field and the engine suggests a number of phrases:

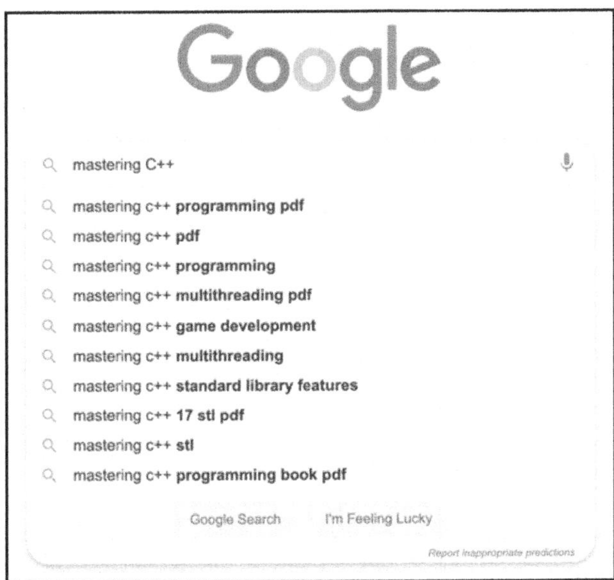

We don't think of users as lazy people, but providing a list of suggestions is helpful because sometimes users don't know the exact term they are looking for. Let's concentrate on the structure and implementation of the suggestions list. After all, we are interested in solving problems rather than designing nice user interfaces. We will not discuss user interface design in this chapter; it would be better to concentrate on the backend of the search engine. However, there is just one thing that we should consider before moving on. The search engine that we are implementing here is dialog-based. The user queries the engine and can choose from several answers to narrow down the list of results. For example, suppose the user queries *a computer* and the search engine asks *a desktop or a laptop?*. That cuts down the search results drastically and provides a better result for the user. We will use a decision tree to achieve this. But, before that, let's understand the complexity of search engines.

First of all, there is the problem of **input tokenization**. This relates to both document parsing and search-phrase analysis. You might build a great query parser that breaks just because the user made a mistake in their query. Let's take a look at a couple of approaches to dealing with vague queries.

Dealing with typos in queries

It's not uncommon for users to make typos while typing. While it might seem like a simple thing, it can be a real problem for search engine designers. Searching through millions of documents might give unexpectedly wrong results if the user typed **helo worl** instead of **hello world**. You may be familiar with autosuggestions provided by a search engine. For example, here's how the Google Search interface looks when we type with mistakes:

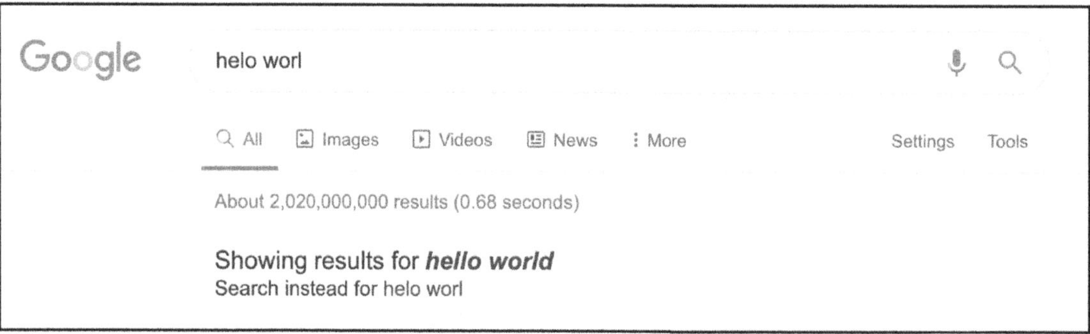

Pay attention to the two lines at the bottom of the screenshot. One of them says **Showing results for hello world**, which suggests that the search engine has assumed that the user typed the query with typos and has taken the initiative of showing results for the correct query. However, there is still a possibility that the user did want to search for the exact words they typed. So, the user experience provides the next line as **Search instead for helo worl**.

So, when building search engines, we have several problems to solve, starting with user requests. First of all, we need to provide a convenient interface for users to type in their text. The interface should also interact with them to provide better results. This includes providing suggestions based on partially typed words, as discussed earlier. Making the search engine interact with the user is another improvement in the user interface that we are going to discuss in this chapter.

Next comes a check for typos or incomplete words, which is not an easy task. Keeping a list of all the words in a dictionary and comparing the words typed by the user might take a while. To solve this problem, using specific data structures and algorithms is a must. For example, finding the **Levenshtein distance** between words might be helpful when checking for typos in user queries. The Levenshtein distance is the number of characters that should be added, removed, or substituted in a word for it to be equal to another one. For example, the Levenshtein distance between the words *world* and *worl* is 1 because removing the letter *d* from *world* or adding *d* to *worl* makes these words equal. The distance between the words *coding* and *sitting* is 4 since the following four edits change one word into the other:

1. coding -> cod**t**ing (insertion of **t** in the middle)
2. co**d**ting -> co**t**ting (substitution of **t** for **d**)
3. c**o**tting -> c**i**tting (substitution of **i** for **o**)
4. **c**itting -> **s**itting (substitution of **s** for **c**)

Now, imagine how long processing would take if we were to compare each user input with tens of thousands of words to find the closest ones. Another approach would be to use a big **trie** (data structure) to discover possible typos beforehand. A trie is an ordered search tree where keys are strings. Take a look at the following diagram representing a trie:

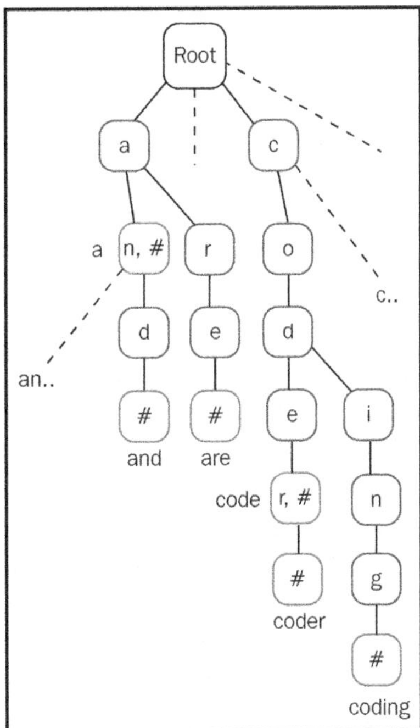

Each path represents a valid word. For example, the **a** node points to the **n** and **r** nodes. Pay attention to the # after **n.** It tells us that the path up to this node represents a word, **an**. However, it continues to point to **d**, which is then followed by another #, meaning that the path up to this node represents another word, **and**. The same logic applies to the rest of the trie. For example, imagine the portion of the trie for the word *world*:

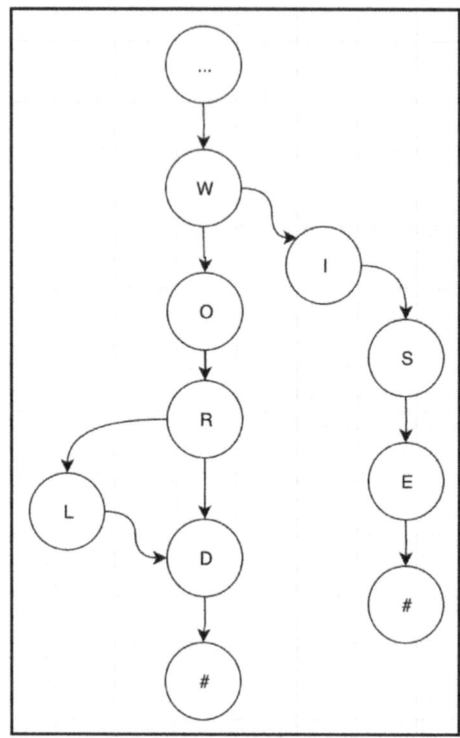

When the engine encounters *worl*, it goes through the preceding trie. **w** is fine, as is **o**, and everything else is fine up until the second-to-last character in the word, **l**. In the preceding diagram, there is no terminal node after **l**, only **d**. That means we are sure that there is no such word as *worl;* so it might be *world*. To provide good suggestions and check for typos, we should have a complete dictionary of words in the user's language. It gets even harder when you plan to support multiple languages. However, while collecting and storing the dictionary is arguably an easy task, the harder task is collecting all the documents on the web and storing them accordingly to perform a fast search. The tool, program, or module of the search engine that collects and parses websites to build the search engine database (as discussed previously) is called a crawler. Before looking in more depth into the way we will store these website pages, let's take a quick look at the functionality of a crawler.

Crawling websites

Searching through millions of documents each time the user types a query is not realistic. Imagine a search engine that parses websites to search for a user query right after the user hits the search button on the UI of a system. That would take forever to complete. Each request to the website from the search engine takes some time. Even if it is less than a millisecond (0.001 seconds), it will take a long time to analyze and parse all of the websites while the user waits for their query to complete. To make things clearer, let's suppose accessing and searching one website takes about 0.5 milliseconds (even then, that's unreasonably fast). That means searching through 1 million websites will take around 8 minutes. Now imagine you open a Google search and make a query—would you wait for 8 minutes?

The correct approach is to store all the information in the database efficiently accessible by the search engine. The crawler downloads website pages and stores them as temporary documents until parsing and indexing take place. A complex crawler might also parse documents to keep them in a format more convenient for the indexer. The important point here is that downloading a web page is not an action that happens just once. The contents of a web page might get updated. Also, new pages might appear during this time. So, the search engine has to keep its database up to date. To achieve this, it schedules the crawler to download pages regularly. A smart crawler might compare the differences in the content before passing it on to the indexer.

Usually, the crawler works as a multithreaded application. Developers should take care to make crawling as fast as possible because keeping billions of documents up to date is not an easy task. As we have already mentioned, the search engine doesn't search through documents directly. It performs searches in the so-called index file. Although crawling is an interesting coding task, we will mostly concentrate on indexing in this chapter. The next section introduces indexing in the search engine.

Indexing documents

The key functionality of search engines is indexing. The following diagram shows how documents downloaded by the crawler are processed to build the index file:

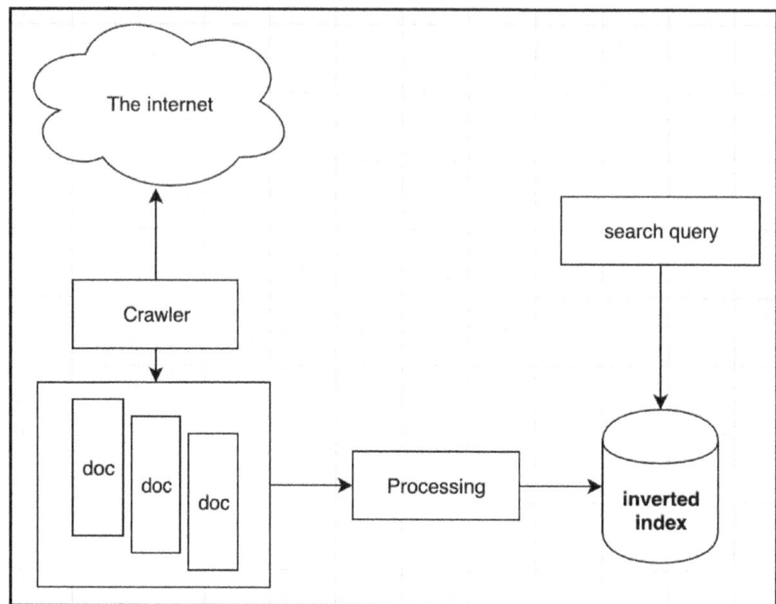

The index is shown as an **inverted index** in the preceding diagram. As you can see, the user queries are directed to the inverted index. Although we use the terms **index** and **inverted index** interchangeably in this chapter, **inverted index** is a more accurate name for it. First, let's see what the index for the search engine is. The whole reason for indexing documents is to provide a fast searching functionality. The idea is simple: each time the crawler downloads documents, the search engine processes its contents to divide it into words that refer to that document. This process is called **tokenization**. Let's say we have a document downloaded from Wikipedia containing the following text (for brevity, we will only a part of a paragraph as an example):

```
In 1979, Bjarne Stroustrup, a Danish computer scientist, began work on "C
with Classes", the predecessor to C++. The motivation for creating a new
language originated from Stroustrup's experience in programming for his PhD
thesis. Stroustrup found that Simula had features that were very helpful
for large software development...
```

The search engine divides the preceding document into separate words, as follows (only the first few words are shown here for brevity):

```
In
1979
Bjarne
Stroustrup
a
Danish
computer
scientist
began
work
...
```

After dividing the document into words, the engine assigns an **identifier** (**ID**) to each word in the document. Assuming the ID of the preceding document is 1, the following table shows that words refer to (occur in) the document with ID 1 :

In	1
1979	1
Bjarne	1
Stroustrup	1
a	1
Danish	1
computer	1
scientist	1
...	

There might be several documents that contain the same words, so the preceding table might actually look more like the following one:

In	1, 4, 14, 22
1979	1, 99, 455
Bjarne	1, 202, 1314
Stroustrup	1, 1314
a	1, 2, 3, 4, 5, 6, 7, 8, 9, 10, 11, ...
Danish	1, 99, 102, 103
computer	1, 4, 5, 6, 24, 38, ...
scientist	1, 38, 101, 3958, ...

The following table represents the inverted index. It maps words with the IDs of the documents downloaded by the crawler. It now becomes much faster to find documents that contain words typed by the user as a query. Now, when the user queries the engine by typing *computer*, the result is generated based on the ID retrieved from the index, that is, **1, 4, 5, 6, 24, 38, ...** in the preceding example. Indexing also helps to find results for more complex queries. For example, *computer scientist* matches the following documents:

computer	**1**, 4, 5, 6, 24, **38**, ...
scientist	**1**, **38**, 101, 3958, ...

To respond to the user with the documents that contain both terms, we should find the intersection of the referenced documents (see the bold numbers in the preceding table), for example, **1** and **38**.

Note that the user query is also tokenized before matching it with the index. Tokenization usually involves word normalization. If it is not normalized, a *Computer Scientist* query wouldn't give any results (note the capital letters in the query). Let's learn a bit more about this.

Tokenizing documents

You might remember the concept of tokenization from `Chapter 1`, *Building C++ Applications*, where we discussed how a compiler parses the source files by tokenizing them into smaller, indivisible units called tokens. A search engine parses and tokenizes documents in a similar way.

We won't go into too much detail about this but you should consider that the document is processed in a way that means tokens (the indivisible terms bearing meaning in terms of search engine context) are normalized. For example, all of the words we are looking at are lowercase. So, the index table should look like the following:

in	1, 4, 14, 22
1979	1, 99, 455
bjarne	1, 202, 1314
stroustrup	1, 1314
a	1, 2, 3, 4, 5, 6, 7, 8, 9, 10, 11, ...
danish	1, 99, 102, 103
computer	1, 4, 5, 6, 24, 38, ...
scientist	1, 38, 101, 3958, ...

As C++ programmers, you might feel uncomfortable with seeing **bjarne** or **stroustrup** in lowercase. However, as we are matching the user input with the inverted index keys, we should consider that the user input might not have the form that we expect it to have. So, we need to apply the same rules to the user input so that it matches that of the inverted index.

Next, pay attention to **a**. Without exaggeration, that's a word that appears in every document. Other examples of this are the words *the, an, in,* and so on. We refer to them as **stop words**; they are filtered out before the actual processing. Usually, search engines ignore them, so the inverted index updates to the following form:

1979	1, 99, 455
bjarne	1, 202, 1314
stroustrup	1, 1314
danish	1, 99, 102, 103
computer	1, 4, 5, 6, 24, 38, ...
scientist	1, 38, 101, 3958, ...

You should note that normalization is not just making words lowercase. It also involves changing words to their normal forms.

Normalizing a word to its root form (or to its word stem) is also called **stemming**.

Take a look at the following sentence from the document we used as an example at the beginning of the section:

```
The motivation for creating a new language originated from Stroustrup's
experience in programming for his PhD thesis.
```

creating, **originated**, and **Stroustrup's** are normalized, so the inverted index will have the following form:

motivation	1
create	1
new	1
language	1
originate	1
stroustrup	1
experience	1
programming	1
phd	1
thesis	1

Also, note that we have ignored the stop words and didn't include *the* in the preceding table.

Tokenization is the first step in index creation. Besides that, we are free to process the input in any way that makes searching better, as shown in the next section.

Sorting the results

Relevance is one of the most important features of search engines. Responding with documents that match the user input is not enough. We should rank them in a way that means the most relevant documents appear first.

One strategy is recording the number of occurrences of each word in a document. For example, a document describing a computer might contain several occurrences of the word *computer*, and if the user searches for *a computer*, the results will display the document that contains the most occurrences of *computer* first. Here's an example index table:

computer	1{18}, 4{13}, 899{3}
map	4{9}, 1342{4}, 1343{2}
world	12{1}

The values in curly braces define the number of occurrences of each word in the document.

There are numerous factors that we can consider when presenting search results to a user. Some search engines store user-related information in order to respond with personalized results. Even the program that the user uses to access the search engine (usually a web browser) might change the results of search platforms. For example, a user searching for *reinstalling the operating system* on a Linux OS gets results that contain *reinstalling Ubuntu* at the top of the list because the browser provided the search engine with the OS type and version information. However, taking into account privacy concerns, there are search engines that completely eliminate the use of personalized user data.

Another property of a document is the date it was updated. Fresh content always has a higher priority. So, when returning a list of documents to the user, we might also reorder them in the order that their content was updated. Concern about the relevant ranking of documents brings us to the next section, where we will discuss recommendation engines.

Building a recommendation engine

We introduced **Artificial Intelligence** (**AI**) along with **machine learning** (**ML**) in the previous chapter. A recommendation engine could be treated as an AI-driven solution or a simple collection of conditional statements. Building a system that takes in user data and returns the options that best satisfy that input is a complex task. Incorporating ML into such a task might sound quite reasonable.

However, you should take into account the fact that a recommendation engine might comprise a list of rules by which data is processed before being output to the end user. Recommendation engines can run in both expected and unexpected places. For example, when browsing products on Amazon, a recommendation engine suggests products to us based on the product that we are currently viewing. Movie databases suggest new movies based on the movies we have previously watched or rated. It might seem unexpected to many but a recommendation engine also runs behind search engines.

You may be familiar with the way some e-commerce platforms suggest products. Most of the time, the suggestions pane is titled something similar to *Customers who bought this, also bought....* Recall cluster analysis, which we introduced in the previous chapter. Now, if we try to understand how these suggestions work under the hood, we will likely discover some clustering algorithms.

Let's take a simpler look at and try to devise some recommendation mechanisms. Let's take, for example, a bookstore website. John buys a book titled *Mastering Qt5*, so let's put that information in the table as follows:

	Mastering Qt5
John	yes

Next, John decides to buy a C++ book, *Mastering C++ Programming*. Leia buys a book called *Design Patterns*. Karl buys three books, called *Learning Python, Mastering Machine Learning*, and *Machine Learning with Python*. The table is updated and now looks like this:

	Mastering Qt5	Mastering C++ Programming	Design Patterns	Learning Python	Mastering Machine Learning	Machine Learning with Python
John	yes	yes	no	no	no	no
Leia	no	no	yes	no	no	no
Karl	no	no	no	yes	yes	yes

So, now let's imagine Harut visits the website and buys two of the books listed earlier, *Learning Python* and *Machine Learning with Python*. Would it be reasonable to recommend the book *Mastering Qt5* to him? We don't think so. But we are aware of the books that he bought and we are also aware that one of the other users, Karl, bought three books, two of which are the same as the books that Harut bought. So, it might be reasonable to recommend *Mastering Machine Learning* to Harut by telling him that customers who bought those other two books also bought this one. That's a simple example of how a recommendation engine works from a high-level perspective.

Using a knowledge graph

Now, let's get back to our search engine. A user is searching for an eminent computer scientist— say, **Donald Knuth**. They type the name in the search field and get results from all over the web that are sorted to provide the best results. Let's, once again, take a look at Google Search. To make the most of the user interface, Google shows us some brief information about the search topic. In this case, it shows several pictures of the great scientist and some information about him to the right side of the web page with the results. Here's what that section looks like:

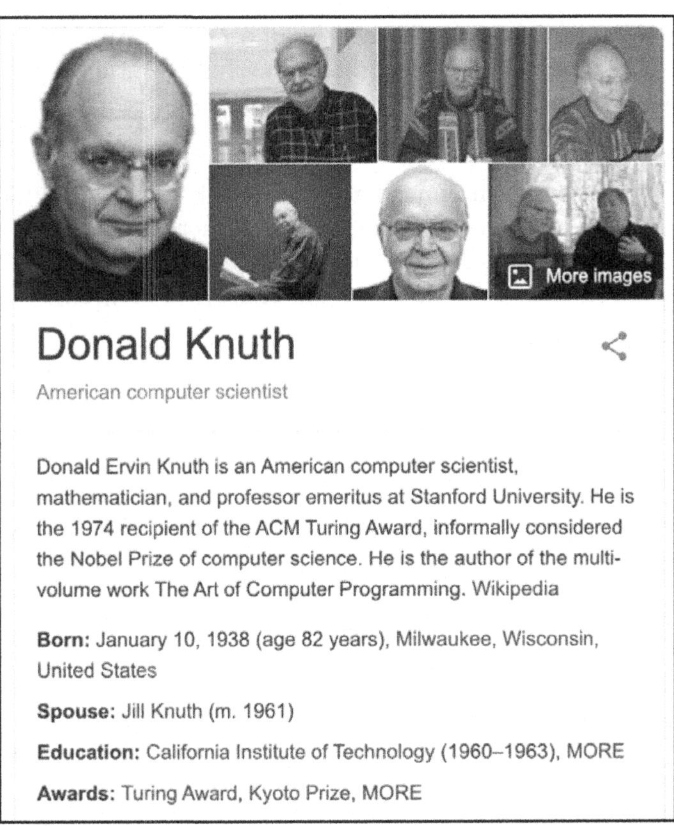

This way, the search engine tries to cover the user's basic needs to allow them to find the information faster without even having to visit any websites. What interests us most, in this case, is the suggestion box placed under the preceding information box. It is titled **People also search for** and here's how it looks:

These are recommendations based on the activity of users who searched for, let's say, **Alan Turing**, right after they searched for **Donald Knuth**. This prompted the recommendation engine to come up with the suggestion that if someone new is searching for **Donald Knuth**, they might also be interested in **Alan Turing**.

We can organize a similar suggestion mechanism through something that Google calls a **knowledge graph**. This is a graph consisting of nodes, each of which represents some topic, person, movie, or anything else that is searchable. A graph data structure is a collection of nodes and edges connecting these nodes, as in the following diagram:

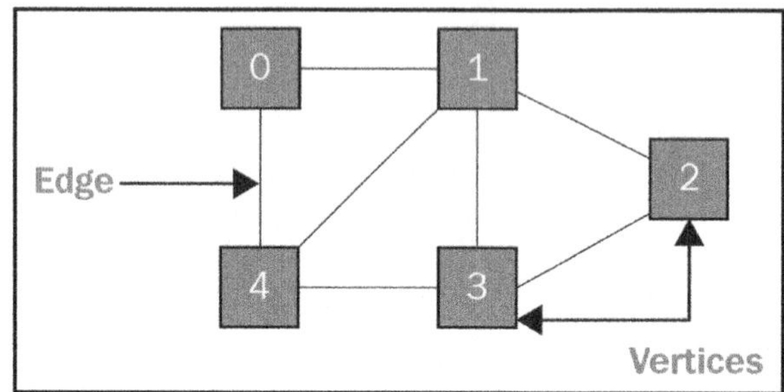

In a knowledge graph, each node represents a single entity. By entity, we mean a city, a person, a pet, a book, or almost anything else that you can imagine. Now, edges in that graph represent the connections between entities. Each node can be connected to another by more than one node. For example, take a look at these two nodes:

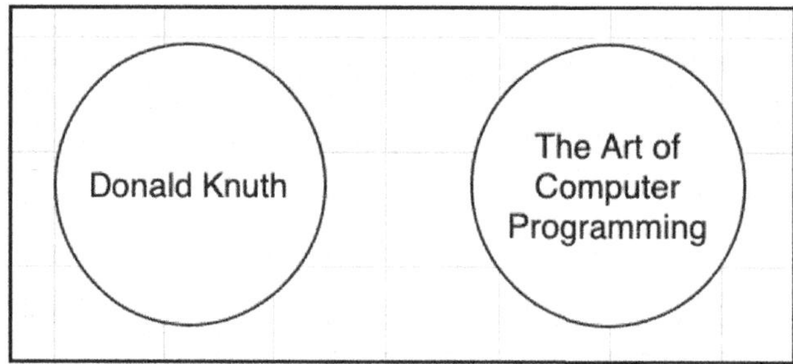

These two nodes only contain text. We might guess that **Donald Knuth** is a name and **The Art of Computer Programming** is some sort of art. The essence of building a knowledge graph is that we can relate each node to another node that represents its type. The following diagram expands on the previous graph:

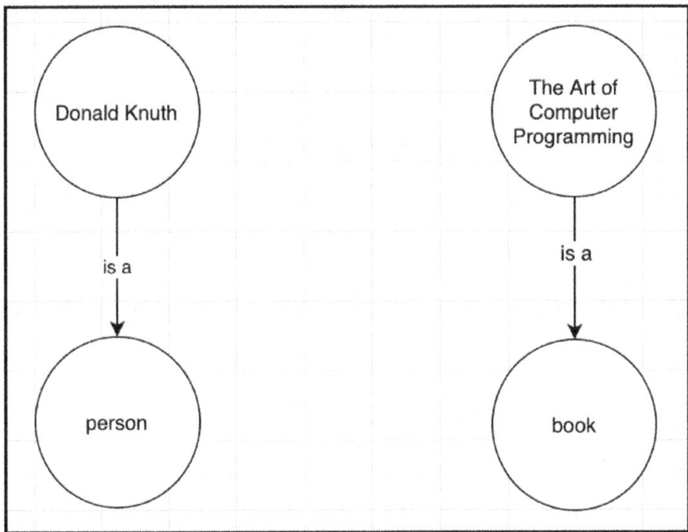

Take a look at the two new nodes that we have added. One of them represents a **person**, while the other one a **book**. And what is even more exciting is that we connected the **Donald Knuth** node with an edge to the **person** node and labeled it as an **is a** relationship. In the same way, we have connected the **The Art of Computer Programming** node to the **book** node and so we can say that **The Art of Computer Programming** is a book. Let's now connect **Donald Knuth** to the book he wrote:

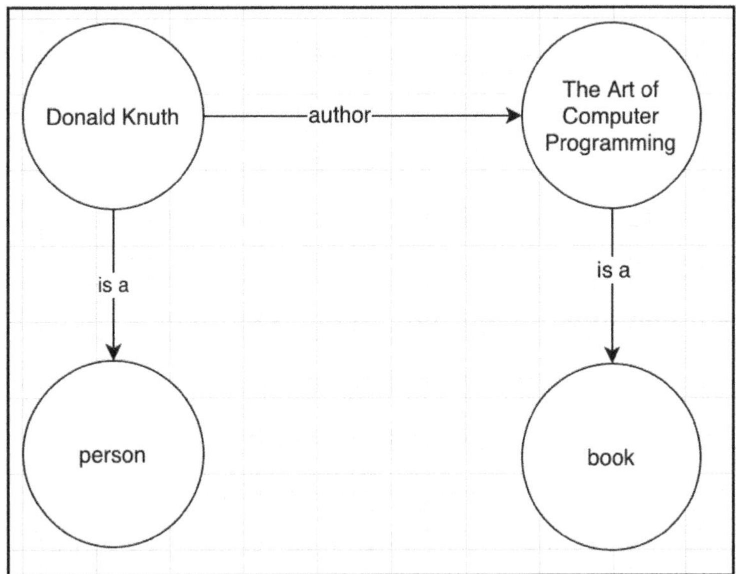

So, now we have a complete relationship because we know that **Donald Knuth** is a person who is the author of **The Art of Computer Programming**, which in turn represents a book.

Let's add a couple more nodes that represent people. The following graph shows how we've added the **Alan Turing** and **Peter Weyland** nodes:

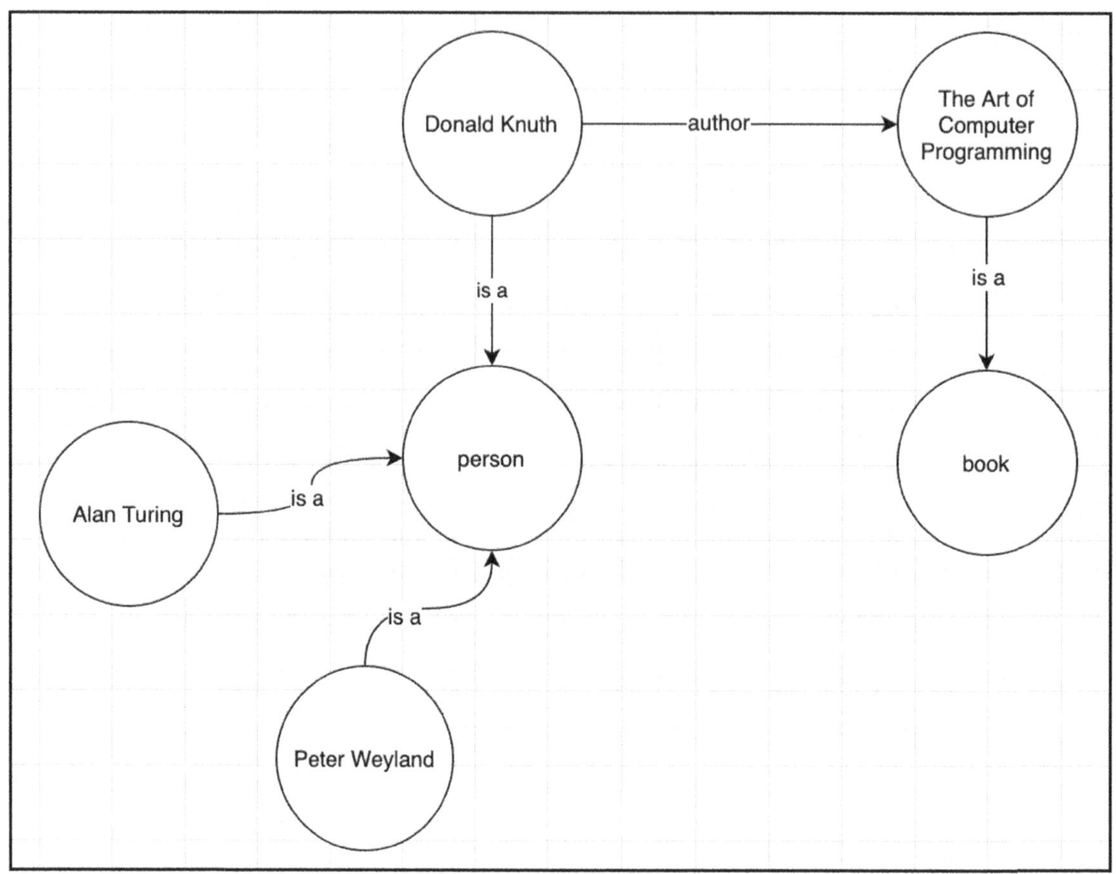

So, both **Alan Turing** and **Peter Weyland** are people. Now, if this is a part of the search engine knowledge base, then it gives us a good insight into the search intent of the user. When we hit the result for **Donald Knuth**, we know that it is about a person. If necessary, we can recommend that the user takes a look at the other people that we have accumulated knowledge of in our knowledge graph. Would it be reasonable to recommend that the user searching for **Donald Knuth** also takes a look at the **Alan Turing** and **Peter Weyland** pages? Well, here comes the tricky part: although both are people, they are not strongly connected. So, we need something extra to define the relevancy of the connection between two different people. Take a look at the following additions to the graph:

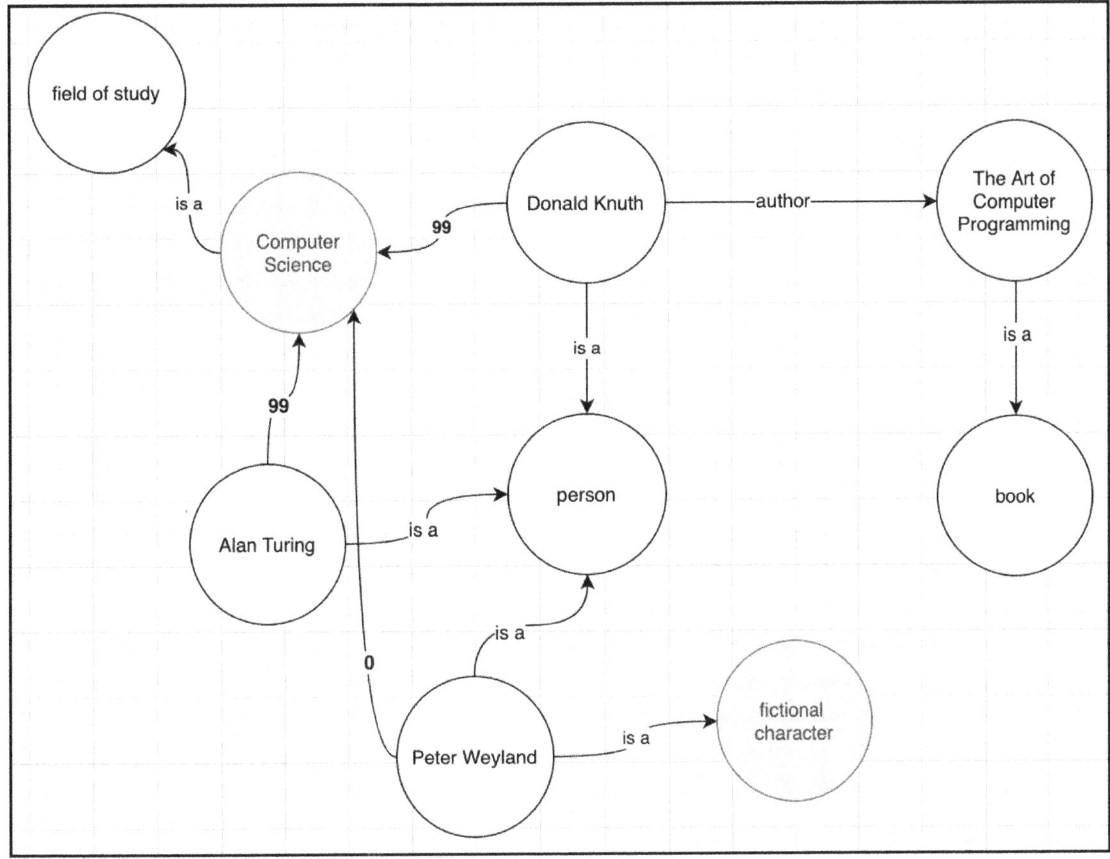

It is now clear that **Donald Knuth** and **Alan Turing** share the same activity, presented as the **Computer Science** node, which represents a **field of study**, while **Peter Weyland** turns out to be a **fictional character.** So, the only thing that makes **Peter Weyland** and **Donald Knuth** related is that they are both people. Take a look at the numbers that we put on the edges leading from the **person** node to the **Computer Science** node. Let's say we rate the relationship from **0** to **100**, with the latter meaning the relationship is the strongest. So, we put **99** for both **Alan Turing** and **Donald Knuth**. We should have omitted the edge from **Peter Weyland** to **Computer Science** instead of putting **0**, but we have done this on purpose to show the contrast. Those numbers are weights. We add weights to the edges to emphasize the connectivity factor; that is, **Alan Turing** and **Donald Knuth** share the same thing and are strongly related to each other. If we add **Steve Jobs** as a new person in the knowledge graph, the graph will look like this:

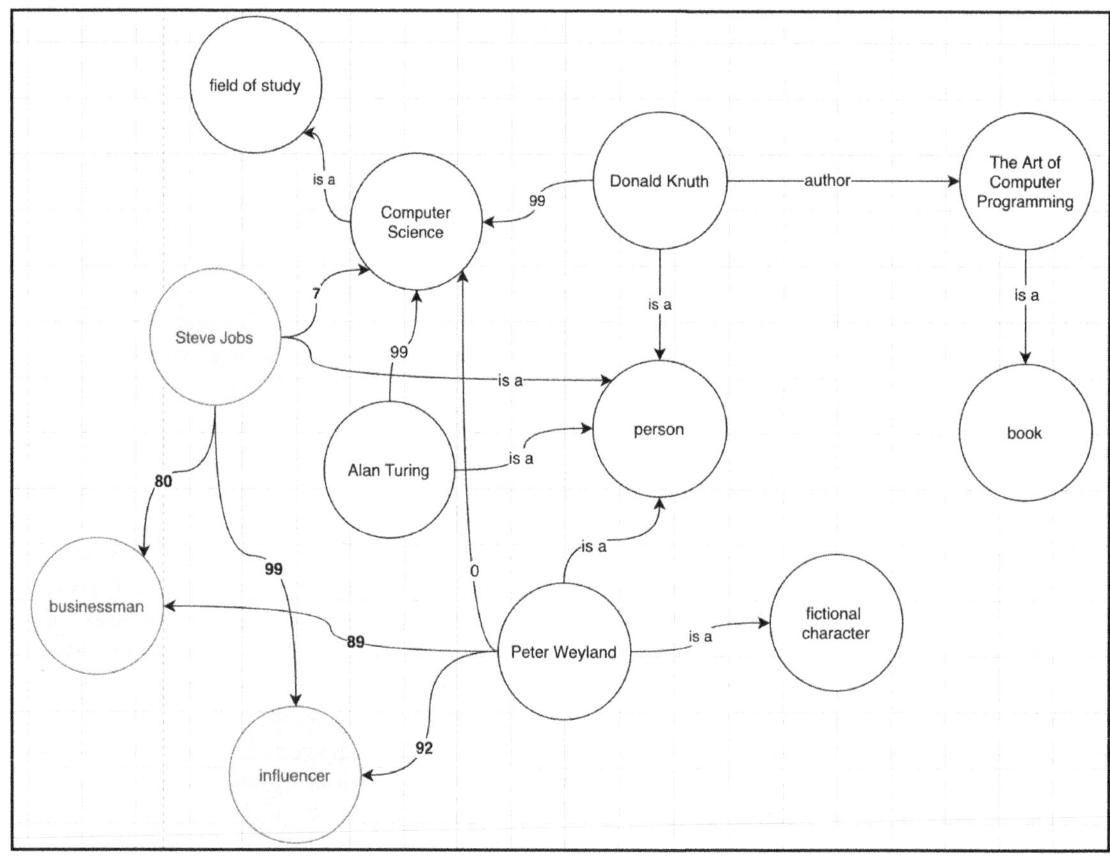

Take a look at the weights for the edges. **Steve Jobs** is somehow related to **Computer Science**, but he is mostly related to the **businessman** and **influencer** nodes. In the same way, we can now see that **Peter Weyland** shares more with **Steve Jobs** than with **Donald Knuth**. Now, it's more informative for a recommendation engine to suggest that the user searching for **Donald Knuth** should also take a look at **Alan Turing** because they are both people and connected to **Computer Science** with equal or near-to-equal weights. That was a great example of incorporating such a graph in a search engine. The next thing that we are going to do is introduce you to using a similar knowledge graph to build an even smarter framework to provide relevant search results. We call this dialog-based searching.

Implementing a dialog-based search engine

Finally, let's tackle designing the part of our search engine that will give us our fine-grained user interface. As we mentioned at the beginning of the chapter, a dialog-based search engine involves building a user interface that asks the user questions related to their query. This approach is most applicable in situations where we have ambiguous results. For example, a user searching for **Donald** might have in mind one of the following:

- *Donald Knuth*, the great computer scientist
- *Donald Duck*, the cartoon character
- *Donald Dunn*, the real name of Jared Dunn, the fictional character
- *Donald Trump*, the businessman and 45th US president

The preceding list is just a small example of potential results for the **Donald** search term. Now, what do search engines lacking a dialog-based approach do? They provide a list of relevant results for the best match for the user input. For example, at the time of writing this book, searching for **Donald** resulted in a list of websites all related to Donald Trump, even though I had Donald Knuth in mind. Here, we can see the thin line between the best match and the best match for the user.

Search engines collect a lot of data to use for personalized search results. If the user works in the field of website development, most of their search requests will somehow be related to that particular field. This is quite helpful in providing a user with better search results. For example, a user that has a big search history, consisting mostly of requests related to website development, will get better, more focused results when searching for **zepelin**. The ideal search engine will provide websites linking to the Zeplin application for building a web UI, while for other users, the engine will provide results with information on the rock band named Led Zeppelin.

Designing a dialog-based search engine is the next step in providing the user with a better interface. Now, it's simple enough to build if we already have a strong knowledge base. We are going to use the concept of the knowledge graph described in the previous section. Let's suppose when the user types a search word we fetch all the matched topics from the knowledge graph and have a list of potential hits for the user, as in the following diagram:

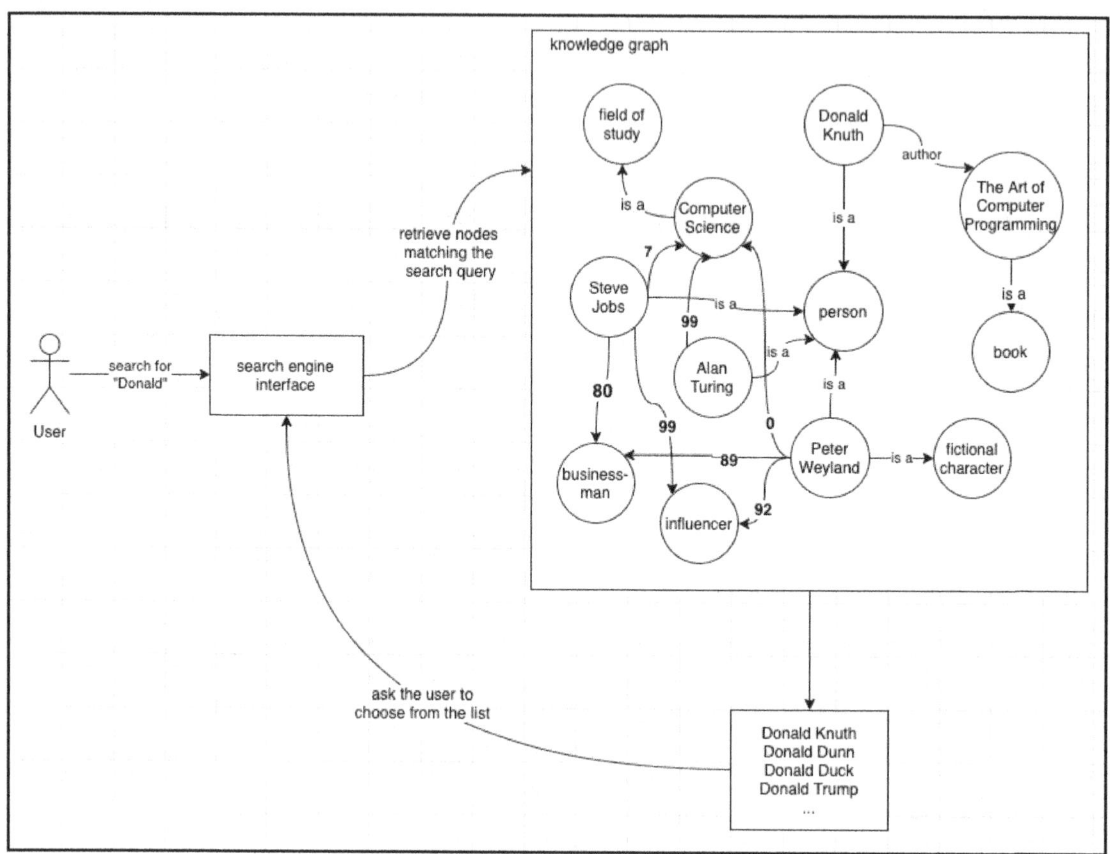

So, it's now much easier for the user to choose a topic and save time on recalling the full name. The information from the knowledge graph can be (and for some search engines it is) incorporated in automatic suggestions when the user is typing the query. Further, we are going to tackle the major components of the search engine. Obviously, this chapter cannot cover every aspect of the implementation, but the fundamental components we will discuss are enough for you to jump into the design and implementation of your own search engine.

We won't bother with the UI part of the search engine. What concerns us most is the backend. When talking about the backend of an application, we usually mean the part that is invisible to the user. To be more specific, let's take a look at the following diagram:

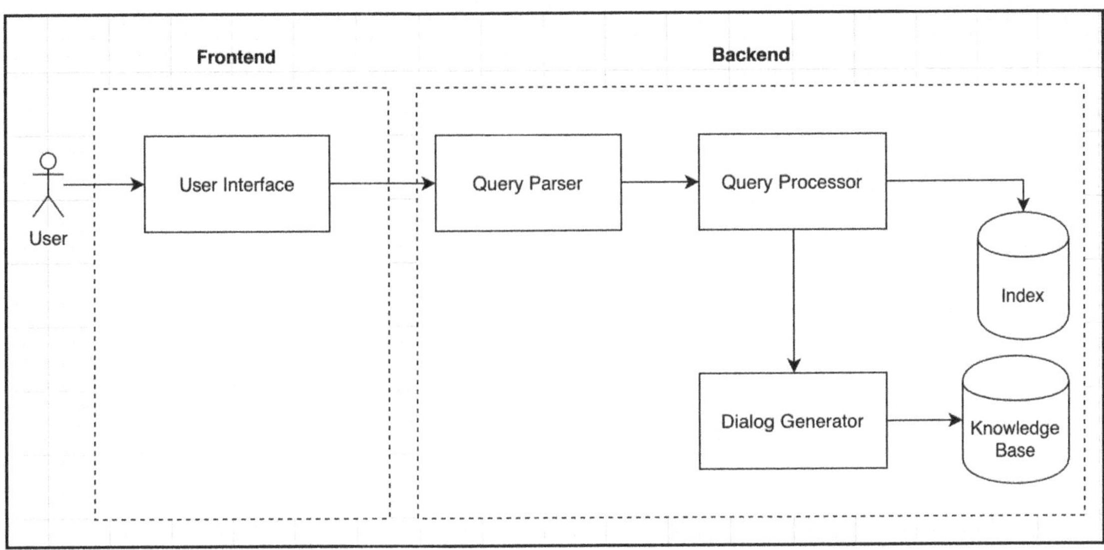

As you can see, most of the engine lies at the backend. While the UI might feel simple, it is an important part of the search system overall. That's where the user starts their journey and the more the UI is designed to offer the best possible experience, the less discomfort the user experiences when searching for something. We will concentrate on the backend; the following are several major modules that we are going to discuss:

- **The query parser**: Analyzes the user query, normalizes words, and gathers information for each term in the query to later pass on to the query processor.
- **The query processor**: Retrieves data associated with the query using the index and supplementary databases and constructs the response.
- **The dialog generator**: Provides more options for the user to choose from while searching for something. The dialog generator is a supplementary module. The user making requests can omit the dialog or use it to further narrow down the search results.

We have skipped some of the components that are common in search engines (such as the crawler) and instead we will concentrate on those components that are strongly related to the dialog-based search engine. Let's now start with the query parser.

Implementing the query parser

The query parser does what its name suggests: *parses* the query. As a base task for the query parser, we should divide the words by space. For example, the user query *zeplin best album* is divided into the following terms: `zeplin`, `best`, and `album`. The following class represents the basic query parser:

```
// The Query and Token will be defined in the next snippet
class QueryParser
{
public:
  static Query parse(const std::string& query_string) {
    auto tokens = QueryParser::tokenize(query_string);
    // construct the Query object and return
    // see next snippet for details
  }

private:
  static std::vector<Token> tokenize(const std::string& raw_query) {
    // return tokenized query string
  }
};
```

Take a look at the preceding `parse()` function. It's the only public function in the class. We will add more private functions that are called from the `parse()` function to completely parse the query and get results as a `Query` object. `Query` represents a simple struct containing information on the query, as follows:

```
struct Query
{
  std::string raw_query;
  std::string normalized_query;
  std::vector<Token> tokens;
  std::string dialog_id; // we will use this in Dialog Generator
};
```

`raw_query` is the textual representation of the query that the user typed, while `normalized_query` is the same query after normalization. For example, if the user types *good books, a programmer should read.*, `raw_query` is that exact text and `normalized_query` is *good books programmer should read*. In the following snippets, we don't use `normalized_query`, but you will need it later when you complete the implementation. We also store tokens in the `Token` vector, where `Token` is a struct, as follows:

```
struct Token
{
  using Word = std::string;
  using Weight = int;
  Word value;
  std::unordered_map<Word, Weight> related;
};
```

The `related` property represents a list of words that are **semantically related** to the token. We call two words **semantically related** if they express similar meanings conceptually. For example, the words *best* and *good*, or *album* and *collection*, can be considered semantically related. You may have guessed the purpose of the weight in the hash table value. We use it to store the `Weight` of similarity.

The range for the **weight** is something that should be configured during the exploitation of the search engine. Let's suppose we chose the range to be between 0 to 99. The weight of the similarity of the words *best* and *good* could be expressed as a number near to 90, while the weight of the similarity of the words *album* and *collection* could deviate from 40 to 70. Choosing these numbers is tricky and they should be tuned in the course of the development and exploitation of the engine.

Finally, `dialog_id` of the `Query` struct represents the ID of the generated dialog if the user chose a path suggested by the generator. We will come to this soon. Let's now move on to finalizing the `parse()` function.

Take a look at the following additions to the `QueryParser` class:

```
class QueryParser
{
public:
  static Query parse(const std::string& query_string,
                     const std::string& dialog_id = "")
  {
    Query qr;
    qr.raw_query = query_string;
    qr.dialog_id = dialog_id;
```

```
    qr.tokens = QueryParser::tokenize(query_string);
    QueryParser::retrieve_word_relations(qr.tokens);
    return qr;
  }

private:
  static std::vector<Token> tokenize(const std::string& raw_string) {
    // 1. split raw_string by space
    // 2. construct for each word a Token
    // 3. return the list of tokens
  }

  static void retrieve_word_relations(std::vector<Token>& tokens) {
    // for each token, request the Knowledge Base
    // to retrieve relations and update tokens list
  }
};
```

Although the two private functions (`tokenize` and `retrieve_word_relations`) are not implemented in the preceding snippet, the basic idea is that they normalize and collect information on the search query. Take a look at the preceding code before we continue on to implementing the query processor.

Implementing the query processor

The query processor carries out the main job of the search engine; that is, it retrieves the results from the search index and responds with a relevant list of documents according to the search query. In this section, we will also cover dialog generation.

As you have seen in the previous section, the query parser constructs a `Query` object that contains tokens and `dialog_id`. We will use both here in the query processor.

It is recommended to have a separate component for the dialog generator due to scalability concerns. For educational purposes, we will keep the implementation succinct, but you are free to redesign the dialog-based search engine and complete the implementation along with the crawler and other supplementary modules.

The tokens in the `Query` object are used to make a request to the search index in order to retrieve the set of documents associated with each word. Here's how the corresponding `QueryProcessor` class looks:

```
struct Document {
  // consider this
```

```
};

class QueryProcessor
{
public:
  using Documents = std::vector<Document>;
  static Documents process_query(const Query& query) {
    if (!query.dialog_id.empty()) {
      // request the knowledge graph for new terms
    }
    // retrieve documents from the index
    // sort and return documents
  }
};
```

Consider the preceding code snippet as an introduction to the implementation. We want to express the fundamental idea of the `QueryProcessor` class. It has the `process_query()` function that retrieves documents from the index based on the tokens inside the query argument. The crucial role here is played by the search index. The way we define its construction and the way it stores documents is essential in terms of making fast queries. In the meantime, the dialog ID, provided as an additional argument, allows the `process_query()` function to request the knowledge base (or the knowledge graph) to retrieve more relevant tokens related to the query.

It's also essential to consider that `QueryProcessor` is also responsible for producing dialogs (that is, defining a set of paths to offer the user possible scenarios for the query). The produced dialogs are sent to the user and, when the user makes another query, the used dialog is associated with that query by the dialog ID that we have seen already.

Although the preceding implementation is mostly introductory (because the real size of the code is too big to fit into the chapter), it's a great fundament for you to move further in designing and implementing the engine.

Summary

Building a search engine from scratch is a task for seasoned programmers. We have touched on many topics in this book and combined most of them in this chapter by designing a search engine.

We have learned that web search engines are complex systems consisting of several components, such as the crawler, the indexer, and user interface. The crawler is responsible for regularly checking the web to download web pages for the search engine to index. Indexing results in the production of a big data structure called an inverted index. An inverted index, or just an index, is a data structure that maps words with the documents in which they have occurred.

Next, we defined what a recommendation engine is and tried to design a simple one for our search engine. The recommendation engine was connected to the dialog-based features of the search engine discussed in this chapter. A dialog-based search engine aims to provide targeted questions to the user to find out more about what the user actually intended to search for.

We reached the end of the book by discussing various subjects in computer science from a C++ perspective. We started with the details of C++ programs and then briefly went through efficient problem-solving using data structures and algorithms. Knowing a programming language is not enough to succeed in programming. You need to tackle coding problems requiring intensive skills in data structures, algorithms, multithreading, and so on. Also, tackling different programming paradigms may greatly enhance your view of computer science and allow you to take a fresh look at problem-solving. In this book, we have touched on several programming paradigms, such as functional programming.

Finally, as you know by now, software development is not limited to coding only. Architecting and designing a project is one of the crucial steps toward successful application development. Chapters `10`, *Designing World-Ready Applications,* to `16`, *Implementing a Dialog-Based Search,* are mostly related to the approaches to and strategies of designing real-world applications. Let this book be your introductory guide to the world of programming from a C++ developer's perspective. Develop your skills by developing more complex applications and share your knowledge with colleagues and those who are just starting their careers. One of the best ways to learn something new is by teaching it.

Questions

1. What is the role of the crawler in a search engine?
2. Why do we call the search index an inverted index?
3. What are the main rules for tokenizing words before indexing them?
4. What is the role of recommendation engines?
5. What is a knowledge graph?

Further reading

For more information, refer to the following book:

Introduction to Information Retrieval, Christopher Manning, et al., `https://www.amazon.com/Introduction-Information-Retrieval-Christopher-Manning/dp/0521865719/`

Assessments

Chapter 1

1. The process of making an executable from the source code is called compilation. Compiling a C++ program is a sequence of complex tasks that results in machine code generation. Typically, a C++ compiler parses and analyzes the source code, generates intermediate code, optimizes it, and finally, generates machine code in a file called an object file. An interpreter, on the other hand, doesn't produce machine code. Instead, it executes instructions in the source code line by line.
2. First, pre-processing, and then the compiler compiles the code by parsing it, performing syntax and semantic analysis, after which an intermediate code is generated. After optimizing the generated intermediate code, the compiler generates the final object file (containing machine code), which can then be linked with other object files.
3. A pre-processor is intended to process source files to make them ready for compilation. A pre-processor works with pre-processor directives, such as `#define` and `#include`. Directives don't represent program statements, but they are commands for the pre-processor, telling it what to do with the text of the source file. The compiler cannot recognize those directives, so whenever you use pre-processor directives in your code, the pre-processor resolves them accordingly before the actual compilation of the code begins.
4. The compiler outputs an object file for each compilation unit. The task of the linker is to combine these object files into a single object file.
5. Libraries can be linked with the executable file either as static or dynamic libraries. When you link them as a static library, they become a part of the final executable file. A dynamically linked library should also be loaded into memory by the operating system to provide your program with the ability to call its functions.

Chapter 2

1. Typically, the `main()` function has two parameters, `argc` and `argv`, where `argc` is the number of input arguments to the program and `argv` constitutes those input arguments. Very occasionally, you can see a widely supported, but not standardized, third argument, most commonly named `envp`. The type of `envp` is an array of char pointers and it holds the environment variables of the system.
2. The `constexpr` specifier declares that the value of the function can be evaluated at compile time. The same definition applies to variables as well. The name consists of `const` and expressions.
3. Recursion leads to the allocation of additional space for function invocations. It is expensive to allocate space for the function and call compared to an iterative solution.
4. The stack holds objects with automatic storage duration; that is, programmers do not concern themselves with the construction and destruction of those objects in memory. Typically, a stack is used for function arguments and local variables. The heap, on the other hand, allows new memory to be allocated during the program execution. However, proper deallocation of memory space is now the responsibility of the programmer.
5. The size of the pointer doesn't depend on the type of the pointer because a pointer is a value that represents an address in memory. The size of the address depends on the system. Usually, it's either 32 or 64 bits. Therefore, we say that the size of the pointer is 4 or 8 byte.
6. An array has a unique structure in terms of item locations. They are placed contiguously in memory; the second item is placed right after the first item, the third right after the second, and so on. Considering this feature, and also the fact that the array consists of elements of the same type, accessing an item at any position takes a constant amount of time.
7. If we forget the `break` keyword in the `case` statement, the execution will pass to the next `case` statement without checking for its condition.
8. For example, `operations['+'] = [](int a, int b) { return a + b; }`

Chapter 3

1. Identity, state, and behavior.
2. When moving objects instead of copying, we omit the creation of temporary variables.
3. There aren't any differences between a struct and a class in C++ except the default access modifier. This is public for the struct, and private for the class.
4. In the case of aggregation, the class that contains an instance or instances of other classes could be instantiated without the aggregate. The composition, on the other hand, expresses strong containment.
5. Private inheritance hides the inherited members from the client code of the derived class. Protected inheritance does the same, but allows the derived classes in the chain to have access to those members.
6. Typically, an introduction of a virtual function leads to augmenting the class with addition data members pointing to the table of virtual functions. Usually, that adds up to 4 or 8 bytes of space (based on the size of the pointer) to the class object.
7. The Singleton design pattern allows the construction of a single instance of the class. This is helpful in a lot of projects where we need to ensure that the number of instances of the classes is limited to one. For example, a database connection class works best if implemented as a Singleton.

Chapter 4

1. Macros are powerful tools if used in the right way. However, the following aspects limit the usage of macros. (1) You cannot debug macros; (2) Macro expansion can lead to strange side effects; (3) Macros have no namespace, so if you have a macro that clashes with a name used elsewhere, you get macro replacements where you didn't want them, and this usually leads to strange error messages; and (4) Macros may affect things you are not aware of. For further details, please go to `https://stackoverflow.com/questions/14041453`.
2. A class/function template refers to a kind of template used to generate template classes/functions. It's just a template but not a class/function, and hence the compiler does not generate any object code for it. A template class/function is an instance of a class/function template. Since it is a class/function, the corresponding object code is generated by the compiler.

3. When we define a class/function template, there is a <> symbol after the `template` keyword, in which one or more type parameters must be given. The type parameter(s) inside <> is known as the template parameter list. When we instantiate a class/function template, all the template parameters must be replaced with their corresponding template arguments, which is known as a template argument list.

   Implicit instantiation happens on demand. However, when providing library files (`.lib`), you have no idea what type of argument list will be used by users in the future, hence, you need to explicitly instantiate all potential types.

4. *Polymorphism* means that something exists in different forms. Specifically, in programming languages, polymorphism means that some functions, operations, or objects have several different behaviors in different contexts. In C++, there are two kinds of polymorphism: dynamic polymorphism and static polymorphism. Dynamic polymorphism allows users to determine the actual function method to be executed at runtime, while static polymorphism means that the actual function to call (or, in general, the actual code to run) is known at compile time.

   Function overloading means that functions are defined with the same name but a different set of parameters (different signatures).

   Function overriding is the ability of the child class rewriting the virtual methods defined in the parent classes.

5. A type trait is a technique that is used to collect information regarding types. With its help, we can make more intelligent decisions to develop high-quality optimized algorithms in generic programming. Type traits can be implemented by partial or full template specialization.
6. We can write an error statement in `g()`, and build the code. If an unused function is instantiated, the compiler will report errors, otherwise it will be built successfully. You can find the example code in the following files, `ch4_5_class_template_implicit_inst_v2.h` and `ch4_5_class_template_implicit_inst_B_v2.cpp`, at `https://github.com/PacktPublishing/Mastering-Cpp-Programming./tree/master/Chapter-4`.
7. Refer to `ch4_q7.cpp` at `https://github.com/PacktPublishing/Mastering-Cpp-Programming./tree/master/Chapter-4`.
8. This is a laboratory exercise; no answer is required.

Chapter 5

1. Computer memory can be described as a single concept – the **Dynamic RAM (DRAM)**, or as a combination of all the memory units that the computer contains, starting with the registers and cache memory, and ending with the hard drive. From the programmers' perspective, DRAM is of the most interest because it holds the instructions and data of the program running in the computer.
2. Virtual memory is an approach to efficiently manage the physical memory of the computer. Typically, the operating system incorporates virtual memory to handle memory accesses from programs and to efficiently allocate chunks of memory to particular programs.
3. In C++, we use the `new` and `delete` operators to allocate and deallocate memory space.
4. `delete` deallocates the space allocated for a single object, while `delete[]` is used for dynamic arrays and frees all the elements of the array on the heap.
5. A garbage collector is a tool or a set of tools and mechanisms that provide automatic resource deallocation on the heap. For a garbage collector, a support environment is required, such as a virtual machine. C++ directly compiles into machine code that can be run without a support environment.

Chapter 6

1. When inserting a new element into the vector, it is placed at the already allocated free slot of the vector. If the size of the vector and its capacity are equal, this means that the vector has no free slot for the new element. In these (rare) cases, the vector automatically resizes itself, which involves allocating new memory space and copying the existing elements to that new bigger space.
2. When inserting an element at the front of the linked list, we only create the new element and update the list pointers to effectively place the new element in the list. Inserting a new element at the front of the vector requires all of the vector elements to be shifted right to free up a slot for that element.
3. Refer to the chapter source code in GitHub.
4. It will look like a linked list.
5. Selection sort searches for the maximum (or minimum) element and replaces the current one with that maximum (or minimum). Insertion sort divides the collection into two sections and walks through the unsorted section and places each of its elements in the proper slot of the sorted section.
6. Refer to the chapter source code in GitHub.

Chapter 7

1. The ranges library in C++ allows ranges of elements to be handled, manipulating them using view adapters, which are far more efficient because they don't store the entire collection as an adapter result.
2. A function is pure if it doesn't modify the state, and produces the same result for the same input.
3. A pure virtual function is a characteristic of a function without an implementation. Pure virtual functions are used to describe interface functions for derived classes. Pure functions in functional programming are those functions that do not modify the state.
4. Folding (or reduction) is the process of combining a collection of values together to generate a reduced number of results.
5. Tail recursion allows compilers to optimize the recursive calls by omitting the allocation of new memory space for each recursive call.

Chapter 8

1. Two operations run concurrently if their start and end times are interleaved at any point.
2. Parallelism means that tasks run simultaneously, while concurrency does not force the tasks to run at the same time.
3. A process is the image of the program. It's a combination of program instructions and data loaded into the computer memory.
4. A thread is a section of code in the scope of a process that can be scheduled by the operating system scheduler, while a process is the image of the running program.
5. Refer to any example in the chapter.
6. By using double-checked locking.
7. Refer to the source code for the chapter in GitHub.
8. C++20 introduced coroutines as an addition to the classic asynchronous functions. Coroutines move the background execution of the code to the next level. They allow a function to be paused and resumed when necessary. `co_await` is a construct telling the code to wait for asynchronously executing code. This means the function can be suspended at that point and resume its execution when a result is ready.

Chapter 9

1. Double-checked locking is a way to make the Singleton pattern work flawlessly in a multithreaded environment.
2. That's a way to make sure that the underlying data of the other stack won't get modified while we make a copy of it.
3. An atomic operation is an indivisible operation, and atomic types leverage lower-level mechanisms to ensure the independent and atomic execution of instructions.
4. `load()` and `store()` leverage low-level mechanisms to ensure that the write and read operations are done atomically.
5. Besides `load()` and `store()`, there are operations such as `exchange()`, `wait()`, and `notify_one()`.

Chapter 10

1. TDD stands for test-driven development, and the aim is to write tests before the actual implementation of the project. This helps to define project requirements more clearly and avoid most of the bugs in the code beforehand.
2. Interaction diagrams picture the exact process of communication of the objects. This allows developers to have a high-level view of the actual program execution for any given moment.
3. In the case of aggregation, the class that contains an instance or instances of other classes could be instantiated without the aggregate. The composition, on the other hand, expresses the strong containment.
4. In simple terms, the Liskov substitution principle ensures that any function taking an object of some type T as an argument will also take an object of type K if K extends T.
5. The open-closed principle states that the class should be open for extension and closed for modification. In the stated example, `Animal` is open for extension, so it doesn't contradict the principle to inherit the `monkey` class from `Animal`.
6. Refer to the chapter source code in GitHub.

Chapter 11

1. Overriding a private virtual function allows modification of the behavior of the class by keeping its public interface untouched.
2. It's a behavioral design pattern in which an object encapsulates an action and all the information required to perform the action.
3. By sharing data with other objects as much as possible. When we have a lot of objects with a similar structure, sharing repeated data across objects minimizes the use of memory.
4. The observer notifies subscriber objects regarding an event, while the mediator plays the role of a connection hub between intercommunicating objects.
5. Designing the game loop as an infinite loop is reasonable because, theoretically, the game might never end and only end when the player commands it to.

Chapter 12

1. Physical, Data-Link, Network, Transport, Session, Presentation, and Application.
2. Port numbers provide a way to differentiate between several network applications running in the same environment.
3. Sockets are abstractions providing programmers with a means to send and receive data over a network.
4. First, we need to create and bind the socket with an IP address. Next, we should listen for incoming connections and, if there is one, we should accept the connection to further process the data communication.
5. The TCP is a reliable protocol. It handles a strong connection between endpoints and also handles packet loss by resending packets not received by the receiver. UDP, on the other hand, is not reliable. Almost every aspect of handling rests on programmers' shoulders. The advantage of UDP is its speed given that it omits handshakes, checks, and packet loss handling.
6. Macro definitions lead to logic bugs in the code that are hard to spot. It's always better to use `const` expressions rather than macros.
7. Client applications must have unique identifiers as well as tokens (or passwords) used to authorize and/or authenticate them.

Chapter 13

1. This is a laboratory exercise; no answer is required.
2. The following output is from Ubuntu 18.04 on NVIDIA Jetson Nano:

```
swu@swu-desktop:~/ch13$ g++ -c -Wall -Weffc++ -Wextra
ch13_rca_compound.cpp
 ch13_rca_compound.cpp: In function 'int main()':
 ch13_rca_compound.cpp:11:17: warning: operation on 'x' may be
undefined [-Wsequence-point]
 std::cout << f(++x, x) << std::endl; //bad,f(4,4) or f(4,3)?
 ^~~

swu@swu-desktop:~/ch13$ g++ -c -Wall -Weffc++ -Wextra
ch13_rca_mix_sign_unsigned.cpp
nothing is detected

swu@swu-desktop:~/ch13$ g++ -c -Wall -Weffc++ -Wextra
ch13_rca_order_of_evaluation.cpp
 ch13_rca_order_of_evaluation.cpp: In constructor 'A::A(int)':
 ch13_rca_order_of_evaluation.cpp:14:14: warning: 'A::v3' will be
initialized after [-Wreorder]
 int v1, v2, v3;
 ^~
 ch13_rca_order_of_evaluation.cpp:14:6: warning: 'int A::v1' [-
Wreorder]
 int v1, v2, v3;
 ^~
 ch13_rca_order_of_evaluation.cpp:7:2: warning: when initialized
here [-Wreorder]
 A(int x) : v2(v1), v3(v2), v1(x) {
 ^
 ch13_rca_order_of_evaluation.cpp: In constructor 'B::B(float)':
 ch13_rca_order_of_evaluation.cpp:32:6: warning: 'B::v2' will be
initialized after [-Wreorder]
 int v2;
 ^~
 ch13_rca_order_of_evaluation.cpp:31:6: warning: 'int B::v1' [-
Wreorder]
 int v1; //good, here the declaration order is clear
 ^~
 ch13_rca_order_of_evaluation.cpp:25:2: warning: when initialized
here [-Wreorder]
 B(float x) : v2(x), v1(v2) {};
 ^
 swu@swu-desktop:~/ch13$ g++ -c -Wall -Weffc++ -Wextra
ch13_rca_uninit_variable.cpp
```

```
ch13_rca_uninit_variable.cpp: In function 'int main()':
ch13_rca_uninit_variable.cpp:7:2: warning: 'x' is used
uninitialized in this function [-Wuninitialized]
if (x) {
^~
```

3. Because static analysis tools predict the errors from their models, and dynamic analysis tools detect errors via the execution of a program.
4. Please refer to the sample code, `ch13_tdd_v3.h`, `ch13_tdd_v3.cpp`, and `ch13_tdd_Boost_UTF3.cpp`, at `https://github.com/PacktPublishing/Mastering-Cpp-Programming./tree/master/Chapter-13`.

Chapter 14

1. Qt's compilation model allows the omission of a virtual machine. It uses a **meta-object compiler** (**MOC**) to translate into C++, which is then compiled into the machine code of the specific platform.
2. `QApplication::exec()` is the starting point of the application. It starts Qt's event loop.
3. By calling `setWindowTitle()`.
4. `m->index (2, 3)`.
5. `wgt->resize (400, 450)`.
6. When inheriting from `QLayout`, you should provide implementation for the `addItem()`, `sizeHint()`, `setGeometry()`, `itemAt()`, `takeAt()`, and `minimumSize()` functions.
7. By using the `connect()` function that takes the source and target objects and names of signals and slots as arguments.

Chapter 15

1. **ML** stands for **machine learning** and is a field of study of algorithms and statistical models that computer systems use to perform a specific task without using explicit instructions, relying on patterns and inference instead.
2. Supervised learning algorithms (also known as training with an instructor) learn from labeled datasets; that is, each record contains additional information describing the data. Unsupervised learning algorithms are even more complex—they process the dataset containing a bunch of features and then try to find useful properties of the features.
3. ML applications include machine translation, natural language processing, computer vision, and email spam detection.
4. One of the ways is to add a weight for each outcome, if the weight for the subtract operation overweighs others, it will become the dominant operation.
5. The purpose of neural networks is to recognize patterns.

Chapter 16

1. The crawler downloads web pages and stores their content for the search engine to index it.
2. We call it an inverted index because it maps words back to their locations in documents.
3. Before indexing, tokenization normalizes words.
4. Recommendation engines verify and recommend the best outcomes fitting to the particular request.
5. A knowledge graph is a graph where nodes are topics (the knowledge) and edges are connections between topics.

Other Books You May Enjoy

If you enjoyed this book, you may be interested in these other books by Packt:

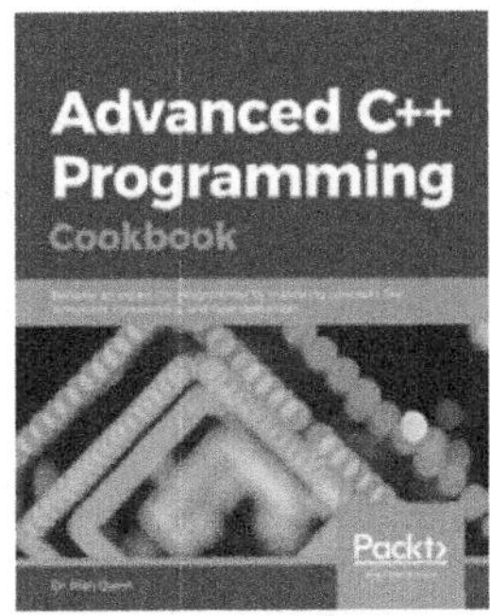

Advanced C++ Programming Cookbook
Dr. Rian Quinn

ISBN: 978-1-83855-991-5

- Solve common C++ development problems by implementing solutions in a more generic and reusable way
- Achieve different levels of exception safety guarantees by introducing precise declarations
- Write library-quality code that meets professional standards
- Practice writing reliable, performant code that exposes consistent behavior in programs
- Understand why you need to implement design patterns and how it's done
- Work with complex examples to understand various aspects of good library design

C++ System Programming Cookbook
Onorato Vaticone

ISBN: 978-1-83864-655-4

- Get up to speed with the fundamentals including makefile, man pages, compilation, and linking and debugging
- Understand how to deal with time interfaces, signals, and CPU scheduling
- Develop your knowledge of memory management
- Use processes and threads for advanced synchronizations (mutexes and condition variables)
- Understand interprocess communications (IPC): pipes, FIFOs, message queues, shared memory, and TCP and UDP
- Discover how to interact with the console (console I/O)

Leave a review - let other readers know what you think

Please share your thoughts on this book with others by leaving a review on the site that you bought it from. If you purchased the book from Amazon, please leave us an honest review on this book's Amazon page. This is vital so that other potential readers can see and use your unbiased opinion to make purchasing decisions, we can understand what our customers think about our products, and our authors can see your feedback on the title that they have worked with Packt to create. It will only take a few minutes of your time, but is valuable to other potential customers, our authors, and Packt. Thank you!

Index

A

B

C

D

E

F

G

H

I

J

K

L

P

Q

R

S

T

U

V

W

X

Made in the USA
Coppell, TX
10 October 2020

39517766R00332